The Humanities

VOLUME II

Mary Ann Frese Witt

North Carolina State University at Raleigh

Charlotte Vestal Brown

Duke University

Roberta Ann Dunbar

University of North Carolina at Chapel Hill

Frank Tirro

Yale University

Ronald G. Witt

Duke University

With the collaboration of
Ernest D. Mason

North Carolina Central University

The

HUMANITIES

CULTURAL ROOTS AND CONTINUITIES

Volume II—The Humanities and the Modern World

D. C. HEATH AND COMPANY   Lexington, Massachusetts   •   Toronto

COVER ILLUSTRATION: *The Dancers*, by Edgar Degas.
The Toledo Museum of Art, Toledo, Ohio. Gift of Edward Drummond Libbey.

Drawings by Eugene Brown.

Published simultaneously in Canada.

Printed in the United States of America.

International Standard Book Number: 0-669-01451-6

Library of Congress Catalog Card Number: 78-78360

CREDITS

CONTENTS

COLOR ILLUSTRATIONS

MAPS

PREFACE

This book is designed to introduce students to the humanities in an interdisciplinary context. We feel that in an introductory humanities course the student's personal growth should take place on three levels: 1) historical, 2) aesthetic, and 3) philosophical. The overall purpose of the two volumes can best be described by breaking it down into these three categories.

The Historical Level

We stress the concept of "cultural roots" because one cannot understand the culture in which one lives without some notion of what went into its making. Therefore, we have made every effort here to link the "roots" discussed to aspects of the contemporary American cultural environment. This can be a knotty problem because such links can sometimes be too facile, and we would also like students to discover that cultures remote in time or space can be worth studying simply for themselves. This, too, is part of a growth process in historical depth. Volume I treats three cultural roots: Greco-Roman, Judeo-Christian, and West African. This choice needs some justification, since many Americans have other cultural roots as well: oriental, Middle Eastern, north European, Latin American, American Indian, to name a few. Still, the Greco-Roman and the

Judeo-Christian traditions undoubtedly constitute the bases of the Western humanities. African culture, a long neglected field of study, has contributed significantly to modern Afro-American art and thought and in many ways to Western culture in general. In addition, African culture offers the opportunity to study some fundamental aspects of the humanities in a truly interdisciplinary context.

In the discussion of each of these "roots," we adopted the policy of focusing on one period and/or place. The focus for the Greco-Roman root is on fifth-century B.C. Athens, that for the Judeo-Christian on medieval Europe, that for Africa on the Yoruba people. This means, for example, that some significant monuments of classical Greek drama, sculpture, and architecture can be examined rather extensively, while early Greece and Rome receive a briefer treatment. In our discussion of the Renaissance and Reformation periods we emphasize the fusion of the Greco-Roman and Judeo-Christian roots and focus on the development of humanism in fifteenth-century Italy and its diffusion in the north.

If we pursued the same metaphor, Volume II might be called "stems, leaves, and flowers." Here, too, an attempt is made to focus and spread out, more than to survey and to spread thin. The court of Louis XIV in the seventeenth century, the Enlightenment in France and America, the romantic movement, the Industrial Revolution, the modernist movement and Black culture in the United States all provide centers around which interrelated humanities can be discussed.

The Aesthetic Level

On the whole, we follow the same "focal" principle in the aesthetic domain. In presenting music, we operate on the assumption that a student will retain more from listening to and analyzing an entire work than from reading music history and theory and hearing snippets. In dealing with art and literature, it is sometimes possible to make an important point with a photograph and a caption or with a close analysis of a brief literary passage. Nevertheless, in the presentation of major works in the focal periods, we assume that it is more useful for a student to look at the whole of Chartres cathedral than to skim the history of medie-

val art, and to read all of *Oedipus Rex* rather than bits and summaries from several Greek tragedies. With lengthy works such as epics and novels this is, of course, not possible. The analyses of extremely short passages such as those from the *Iliad* and the *Aeneid* are intended to serve as introductions to the works. A teacher may well wish to assign one or more epics or novels as supplementary reading.

Dance, an often neglected art form, is given more extensive treatment here than in other humanities texts. Entire dance compositions can, of course, be appreciated only in live performance or film, and we will list resources for the latter in the Instructor's Guide. Also in the guide will be some suggestions for "sensitivity exercises" designed to involve students actively in the aesthetic process and in interrelating the arts. These may be used as warm-ups during the first few days of class or introduced at any point. It has been our experience that a long introductory chapter on how to look, listen, and read is largely wasted; therefore, we treat such matters in the introductions to individual works. Questions on the nature of genre are treated in the cultural context in which they originate, notably in ancient Greece. We place much importance on study questions that require the student to read, look, and listen carefully.

While we try to avoid jargon, we feel that some knowledge of the technical vocabulary of criticism in the arts is essential for literate discussion. Difficult or unfamiliar terms appear in italics the first time they are used in any given chapter, indicating that they are defined in the Glossary.

The Philosophical Level

It may well be objected that we compromise the focal method in our presentation of philosophy since no entire philosophical works appear in the book. This is largely due to considerations of space; but it is also true that, when dealing with a work in terms of certain fundamental ideas rather than in terms of aesthetic wholeness, the "snippet" method is not so objectionable. Beginning humanities students are probably not ready to read Aristotle's *Ethics* in its entirety, yet they should be able to see how Aristotle's ideas are essential to the cultural roots of the modern world.

The student's personal growth in the philosophical area means, however, something much broader than his or her contact with formal philosophy. The (ideal) student whose historical awareness is increased by an understanding of cultural roots and whose aesthetic sensitivity is heightened by personal confrontation with a variety of works of art should also be able to expand his or her mind through contact with diverse ideas. A humanities course should enable students to refine their thinking on the basic questions that affect all mankind, to formulate more clearly their personal values, and to discuss these with intellectual rigor rather than in vaporous bull sessions. Teachers should welcome debates that might arise from a comparison between Genesis and African mythology, the "woman"

question in *Lysistrata* and in John Stuart Mill, and the relative merits of realistic and abstract art or tonal and atonal music. We offer some topics for controversial discussion in the guide, but teachers and students will find many more.

Individual teachers will decide which aspects of the humanities and which cultural roots they wish to emphasize. We hope that this book will offer enough flexibility to be useful for a variety of approaches.

MARY ANN FRESE WITT
CHARLOTTE VESTAL BROWN
ROBERTA ANN DUNBAR
FRANK TIRRO
RONALD G. WITT

ACKNOWLEDGMENTS

Many people have contributed time, work, ideas, and encouragement to the creation of this book. Gratitude is due first of all to those who provided their own research and writing: Professor Edmund Reiss of Duke University wrote the section on courtly love in Volume I, translated *Equitan* and *The Miller's Tale*, and provided introductions to those selections, as well as to the two anonymous medieval English poems; Professor Alan Gonzalez of North Carolina State University wrote the sections on literature and social commitment and on writers and the Spanish Civil War in Volume II and translated *El Cojo*; Professor Ernest Mason of North Carolina Central University wrote the introduction to Freud as well as the unit on Afro-American culture in Volume II; D. D. Williams of Raleigh, North Carolina wrote the film section in Volume II.

The plan for this textbook grew out of the four years I spent initiating and directing an interdisciplinary humanities program at North Carolina Central University in Durham. It would not have been possible without the stimulation and aid of my students and colleagues there. Professor Charles Ray and Dean Cecil Patterson, who provided me with the time, encouragement, and wherewithal to create the program, deserve a special word of thanks. The professors who worked closely with me, Elizabeth Lee, Phyllis Lotchin, Ernest Mason, Norman Pendergraft, Earl Sanders, Winifred Stoelting, and Randolph Umberger, have all left their mark on this book. The generous support of the Kenan Foundation, which provided the humanities program with a four-year grant, enabled me to research and compile much of the material here. The Kenan Foundation also provided me with the opportunity to attend numerous conferences on the humanities. The stimulating workshops given at North Carolina Central University by Clifford Johnson, of the Institute for Services to Education, also provided inspiration for this book.

The preparation of the manuscript, often a difficult and time-consuming task, has also been the work of several people. I would especially like to thank Jane Birken, Deborah Crowder, Anita Hix, Lorraine Hollis, Jan Krob, and Dorothy Sapp.

Others helped to improve the quality of the manuscript by their reading and suggestions. Professor Christina Sorum of North Carolina State University gave a critical reading of the Greek and Roman material; Professor Peter Wood of Duke University was of great assistance in the material dealing with American history and culture; Paul Clifford of the Duke Art Museum offered many valuable suggestions for the African art section. The analysis and suggestions of Professor J. Lee Greene of the University of North Carolina at Chapel Hill informed the discussion of Afro-American literature in the section on African continuities. Professors Brian Lindsay, University of South Carolina at Spartanburg; Walter Klarner, Johnson County Community College; Aurelia N. Young, Jackson State University; Michael Geis, Western Michigan University; Dorothy J. Corsberg, Northeastern Junior College; Judith Krabbe, Jackson State University; and Brother Paul French, Lewis University, read versions of the manuscript and made many helpful comments.

I have been fortunate to work with co-authors who combine intelligence and sensitivity with a spirit of cooperation. We have all been most fortunate to have been guided by the interest and the diligence of assistant editor Jessie Solodar and the tact, patience, enthusiasm and sound judgments of editor Holt Johnson, both of D. C. Heath and Company.

MARY ANN FRESE WITT

Chronicle of Events

Chronicle of Events

	AFRICA	MESOPOTAMIA-SYRIA-PALESTINE	GREECE
3000 B.C.	Lower and Upper Egypt unite First to Second Dynasty (3110–2615)	Sumerian city-states Successive waves of Semites occupy Palestine	
2900			
2800			
2700			
2600	Age of Pyramids (c. 2650–2150)		
2500			
2400			
2300			
2200			
2100			Minoan palace construction begins on island of Crete
2000		Phoenician (Canaanite) city culture	
1900			
1800		Babylonian Dynasty established	
1700			
1600	Hyksos invasions (1678–1570)		High point of Minoan civilization (1600–1400)
1500	Eighteenth Dynasty and Imperial Age (1525–1075)		
1400		Phoenicians develop alphabet	
1300	Akhenaten introduces monotheism (1370–1353)		Destruction of Minoan palace Mycenaean expansion
1200		Hebrews enter Palestine Phoenicians flourish (1200–900)	Traditional date for sack of Troy (c. 1184)

Timeline chart (read vertically by date).

Date	AFRICA	MESOPOTAMIA-SYRIA-PALESTINE	ROME	GREEK POLITICAL EVENTS	GREEK CULTURAL EVENTS
(c. 1100–1025)		Early Assyrian Empire; Early Biblical books written; Saul made King of Hebrews (c. 1025)			Greek cities on Aegean coast and Greek colonies in Asia Minor established
1000 B.C.		David King of Hebrews (1000–961)			
		Solomon (961–922)			
900		Hebrew kingdom divides into Israel and Judah (922)			
		Assyria conquers Phoenicians and Israel (876–605)			
800	Phoenicians found Carthage (814)				
			Traditional date for founding of Rome (753)	Beginning of *polis*	Homer?
700	Iron age begins at Meroe				
		Nineveh falls (612); Neo-Babylonian Empire of Nebuchadrezzar			
600					Sappho (c. 600)
		Jews taken captive to Babylon (586)			Beginning of Drama and Panathenian Festivals
		Persians take Babylon (539)			
		Jews return home (538); Darius of Persia (521–486)			Aeschylus (525–456)
525	Persia conquers Egypt (525)				
			Kings expelled and Republic created (509)		
500				Persian Wars (499–479); Pericles (498–427)	Euripides (480–406); Thucydides (470–400); Socrates (470–399); Building of Parthenon (447–432)
				Peloponnesian War (431–404)	Plato (427–347); Aristophanes' *Lysistrata* (411); Sophocles' *Oedipus* (406)
400				Philip of Macedon (382–336)	Aristotle (384–322)

Archaic Age (750–480)

Classical Age (480–350)

Timeline (400 B.C. – A.D. 100)

	AFRICA	MESOPOTAMIA-SYRIA-PALESTINE	ROME	GREEK POLITICAL EVENTS	GREEK CULTURAL EVENTS
400 B.C.	Alexander conquers Egypt (332) Greek dynasty rules (331–304)		Vigorous program of Roman conquest of Italy begins (343)	Alexander of Macedon (the Great) (356–323)	Epicurus (342–270) Zeno (336–264) and founding of Stoic school
300			I Punic War (264–241) Sardinia and Corsica annexed (238) II Punic War (218–201)		*Hellenistic Age (350–150)*
200	Nok civilization at its height (200 B.C.– 200 A.D.) Carthage sacked (146) Rome conquers North Africa		Terence (195–159) III Punic War (149–146) Cicero (106–43) Caesar (100–44) Lucretius (99–55)	Rome begins conquest of Greece	
100		Occupation of Israel by Romans (63) Reign of Herod the Great in Palestine (37 B.C.– 4 A.D.)	Horace's *Satires* (35–29) Virgil's *Aeneid* (29–19) Augustus begins reign (27)		

Timeline (A.D. – 200)

	AFRICA	ROME AND EUROPE	PAGAN AND CHRISTIAN CULTURE
A.D.			Birth of Jesus Christ
		Death of Augustus (14) Conquest of Britain (43–51) Sack of Jerusalem (70)	Persecution of Christians by Nero (64)
100			Juvenal's *Satires* (c. 100) Roman Pantheon built (118–125)
200		Period of disorder (235–284)	Plotinus (205–270) and Neo-Platonism

EUROPEAN CULTURE

Building of St. Sernin—Romanesque (11th and 12th centuries)

Romanesque Style (11th and 12th centuries)

St. Bernard (1090–1153)

Play of Daniel (12th century)
Rebuilding of St. Denis on new lines—early Gothic

Bernart de Ventadorn (late 12th century)
Marie de France (late 12th century)
Chartres Cathedral begun (1194)

Aquinas (1225–1274)

EUROPE

Norman invasion of England (1066)

First Crusade (1095)

Mongol invasion of Russia

European embassy sent to China

AFRICA

Revolt of Mande peoples against Ghana (c. 1200) and rise of Mali Empire

---

Edict of Toleration by Constantine (313)
Building of Old St. Peter's (330–340)

Alaric sacks Rome (410)

Vandals sack Rome (455)
Traditional date for end of Western Roman Empire (476)

Justinian (483–565) extends Roman Empire in East and temporarily conquers parts of Italy, Africa, and Spain—Codifies Roman Law

First systematic teaching of Aristotle's Logic (975)

Reforms of Diocletian (285–305)

Moslem conquest of Spain (711)
Defeat of Moslems at Poitiers (732)

Charlemagne (768–814)
Second period of invasions (c. 800–950): Northmen, Hungarians, and Saracens

Northmen establish Normandy (911)
Otto I founds German Empire (962)
Hugh Capet King of France (987)

Moslem conquest of Africa
Empire of Ghana (700–1230)

Beginnings of Benin

300
400
500
600
700
800
900

1000
1050
1100
1150
1200

Timeline: 1250–1450

Year	AFRICA	EUROPE	EUROPEAN CULTURE
1250		St. Louis (1214–1270)	Giotto (1276–1337)
1300			Dante's *Divine Comedy* (1300–1321)
	Mansa Musa pilgrimage to Mecca (1324)	Hundred Years War begins (1337)	Petrarch (1304–1374)
	Exploration of Canaries (1330's and 1340's)	First appearance of Black Death (1348–1350)	Boccaccio (1310–1375)
1350			Bruni (1370–1444)
			Brunelleschi (1377–1446)
			Chaucer's *Canterbury Tales* (1390–1400)
1400			Masaccio (1401–1428)
			Henry the Navigator founds navigation school at Sagres (1419)
		Jeanne d'Arc burned (1431)	Piero della Francesca (1420–1492)
			Medici dominate Florence (1434)
			Alberti's *On Painting* (1435)
			Leonardo da Vinci (1442–1519)
			Botticelli (1444–1510)
			Lorenzo il Magnifico (1449–1492)
1450	John Affonso d'Aveiro visits Benin (1485–1486)	Spanish Inquisition established (1478)	Pico della Mirandola (1463–1494)
		Columbus discovers America (1492)	Isaac's *On the Death of Lorenzo*
		DaGama sails for India (1497)	

Gothic Style (12th–15th centuries)

Renaissance Style (15th and 16th centuries)

Timeline: 1500–1550

Year	AFRICA	EUROPE	EUROPEAN CULTURE	NEW WORLD
1500	Duarte Pacheco Pereira's *Esmeraldo de situ orbis* (1507)		Michelangelo's *David* (1504)	First black slaves in New World (1505)
	Benin at the height of its power (16th and 17th centuries)		Raphael's *School of Athens* (1510–1511)	
			Machiavelli's *Prince* (1513)	
			First edition of Erasmus' *Colloquies* (1516)	Magellan circumnavigates the globe (1519)
			Luther publishes German New Testament (1521)	Cortez in Mexico (1519–1521)
				Verrazano establishes French claims in North America (1524)
1525		Peasants' Revolt in Germany (1525)		
		Henry VIII declares himself head of Church of England (1534)	First edition of Calvin's *Institutes* (1536)	
		Jesuit Order founded (1540)	Copernicus' *Revolution of Heavenly Bodies* (1543)	
		Council of Trent (1545–1563)	Titian (1477–1576)	
1550		Peace of Augsburg legalizes Lutheranism in Germany (1555)	Bruegel (1520–1569)	

Renaissance Style (15th and 16th centuries)

1575   1600   1625   1650   1700

Building of St. Augustine in Florida (1565)

Settlement at Jamestown (1607)
Founding of Quebec (1608)

First slaves in Virginia (1619)
Plymouth colony established (1620)

New York City taken by English from Dutch (1664)

Salem Witch Trials (1692)

First edition of Montaigne's *Essays* (1580–1588)

Shakespeare (1564–1616)
Kepler (1571–1630)
Caravaggio's *Calling of St. Matthew* (1599–1600)
Rubens' *Raising of the Cross* (1609–1610)

Giambattista Marino (1569–1625)
John Donne (1572–1631)
Descartes (1596–1650)
Corneille (1606–1684)

Harvey demonstrates circulation of blood (1628)
French Academy founded (1635)
Galileo's *Discourse on Two New Sciences* (1638)
Richard Crashaw (1612–1649)

Rome's Cornaro Chapel (1645–1652)
Rembrandt (1606–1669)
Milton (1609–1674)
Lully (1632–1687)
Royal Society of London created (1662)
Construction of Versailles begins (1669)
Molière's *Le Bourgeois Gentilhomme* (1670)
Robert Boyle (1627–1691)

Newton publishes *Mathematical Principles* (1687)
Locke's *An Essay Concerning Human Understanding* (1690)

Darby cokes coal (1709)

Johann Sebastian Bach (1685–1750)

Reign of Queen Elizabeth I of England (1558–1603)
Wars of Religion begin in France (1561)
Massacre of French Protestants (1572)

Defeat of Spanish Armada (1588)
Edict of Nantes (1598)

Thirty Years War begins (1618)

Civil War in England begins (1643)
Peace of Westphalia in Germany (1648)

Restoration of English Monarchy (1660)
Louis XIV (1638–1715)
Louis revokes Edict of Nantes (1685)

Union of Scotland and England (1707)
War of Spanish Succession (1701–1713)
Hanover (Windsor) dynasty begins in England (1714)

Foundation of Ashanti Confederacy (1701)

Timeline 1725–1848

Year	AFRICA	EUROPE	EUROPEAN CULTURE	NEW WORLD
1725			Building of Hotel Soubise (1732); Kay's Flying Shuttle (1733); English repeal laws against witchcraft (1736); Voltaire's *Micromegas* (1739); Handel's *Messiah* (1742); Montesquieu's *Spirit of the Laws* (1748)	Georgia, last of original thirteen colonies, founded (1733)
		War of Austrian Succession (1740–1748)		
1750			Volume I of the *Encyclopédie* (1751); Mozart (1756–1791); Rousseau's *On the Origins of Inequality* (1755); First blast furnace (1761); Rousseau's *Social Contract* (1762); Watt patents steam engine (1769); Schiller (1759–1805)	French and Indian War (1754–1763); English take Quebec (1759); English acquire Canada by Treaty of Paris (1763); Boston Massacre (1770); Revolutionary War begins (1775)
		Death of George II (1760)		
1775		Accession of Louis XVI (1774); Meeting of Estates General (May, 1789); Taking of Bastille (July, 1789); Fall of Robespierre (1794); Napoleon's coup d'état (1799)	Goethe's *Werther* (1787); Wollstonecraft's *Vindication of Rights of Women* (1792)	Treaty of Paris ends war (1783); Constitution goes into effect (1789); Washington dies (1799)

Year	AFRICA	EUROPE	EUROPEAN CULTURE	AMERICA
1800	Rise of Fulani Empire (19th century); Britain abolishes slave trade (1807)	Napoleon Consul for life (1802); Napoleon crowned Emperor (1804); End of Holy Roman Empire (1806)	David (1748–1825); Madame de Staël (1766–1817); Wordsworth (1770–1850); Constable (1776–1837)	Jefferson elected President (1801)
1810	France abolishes slave trade (1815)	Defeat of Napoleon and Congress of Vienna (1815); Industrialization of England (1815–1850)	Stephenson's locomotive (1814); Byron (1788–1824); Goya *Executions of the 3rd of May* (1814); Blake (1757–1827)	War of 1812 (1812–1814); Founding of *North American Review* (1815)
1820	Liberia established (1822)	Greek War of Independence (1821–1829)	Beethoven's *Ninth Symphony* (1824)	
1830	France annexes Algeria (1830)	Revolutions in France, Germany, Italy, Belgium, and Poland (1830); Industrialization of France and Belgium (1830–1860); Industrialization of Germany (1840–1870)	Heine (1797–1856)	Emerson (1803–1882); Poe (1809–1849)
1840		Revolutions in France, Italy, Germany, and Austria (1848)	Delacroix (1799–1863); Dickens' *Old Curiosity Shop* (1840); *Giselle* (1841); Chopin (1810–1849); Turner's *Rain, Steam, and Speed* (1845); *Communist Manifesto* (1848)	Mexican War (1846–1848); Gold discovered in California (1848)

1850–1889

Year	AFRICA	INTERNATIONAL POLITICS	EUROPEAN CULTURE	AMERICAN CULTURE
1850	Livingstone at Victoria Falls (1853–1856)	Second Empire founded in France (1852); Crimean War (1855)	Crystal Palace (1851); Millet (1814–1875); Courbet's *Manifesto* (1855); Baudelaire (1821–1867); Darwin's *Origin of Species* (1859)	Walt Whitman (1819–1892)
1860	Opening of Suez Canal (1869)	Foundation of Kingdom of Italy (1860); Emancipation of serfs in Russia (1861); Creation of Dual Monarchy Austria-Hungary (1867)	Mill's *On Subjection of Women* (1861); Ford Maddox Brown's *Work* (1862–1863); van Gogh (1853–1890)	Civil War (1861–1865); Emily Dickinson (1830–1886); Period of Reconstruction (1867–1877)
1870	Brazza explores Lower Congo (1875)	Franco-Prussian War (1870–1871); German Empire and Third French Republic created (1871)	Nietzsche (1844–1900); Monet's *Impressions: Sunrise* (1873); Gauguin (1848–1903)	Stephen Crane (1871–1900)
1880	France occupies Tunisia (1881); Britain occupies Egypt (1882); Germans in Togo and Cameroon (1886); Gold found in South Africa (1886); Rhodes establishes Rhodesia (1889–1891)	Dual Alliance: Germany and Austria-Hungary (1879); Triple Alliance: Germany, Austria-Hungary, and Italy (1882); German-Russian Reinsurance Treaty (1887)	Dostoevsky's *Brothers Karamazov* (1880); Mallarmé (1842–1898); Verlaine (1844–1896); Rimbaud (1854–1891)	William Dean Howells (1837–1920); Henry James (1843–1916)

1890–1929

Year	AFRICA	INTERNATIONAL POLITICS	EUROPEAN CULTURE	AMERICAN CULTURE
1890	French annex Guinea and Ivory Coast (1893)	Industrialization of Russia (1890–1914); Franco-Russian Alliance (1894)	Cézanne (1839–1906)	Reliance Building (1891); Spanish-American War (1898); Chesnutt's *The Conjure Woman* (1899)
1900	British conquest of N. Nigeria (1900–1903); Senghor born (1903)	Entente Cordiale: France and Great Britain (1902); First Russian Revolution (1905)	Matisse (1869–1954); Apollinaire (1880–1918); Picasso's *Les demoiselles d'Avignon* (1907)	Louis H. Sullivan (1856–1924)
1910	Morocco becomes French protectorate (1912); Conquest of German colonies (1914–1915)	Balkan Wars (1912–1913); First World War (1914–1918); Russian Revolution (1917); Treaty of Versailles (1919); German Weimar Republic created (1919)	Duchamp's *Nude Descending a Staircase* (1912); Mondrian (1872–1944); Kandinsky's *On the Spiritual in Art* (1912); *Rite of Spring* (1913); Kirchner's *Street* (1914); Bauhaus founded (1919)	U.S. declares war on Germany and Austria-Hungary (1917); Harlem Renaissance (1919–1932)
1920		Irish Free State (1922); Mussolini establishes Fascism in Italy (1922); Great Depression begins (1929)	Kafka (1883–1924); Niinsky (1890–1950); Lipchitz' *Figure* (1926–1928); Brancusi's *Bird in Space* (1928)	W.E.B. Dubois (1868–1963); Davis' *Egg Beater No. 1* (1927); Stock Market Crash (1929)

Year	AFRICA	INTERNATIONAL POLITICS	EUROPEAN CULTURE	AMERICAN CULTURE
1930	Nigerian youth movement begins (early 1930's) Italy conquers Ethiopia (1936)	Hitler rises to power (1933) Official rearmament of Germany (1935) Spanish Civil War (1936–1939) Second World War begins (1939)	Freud's *Civilization and Its Discontents* (1930) Le Corbusier's *Villa Savoye* (1929–1930) James Joyce (1882–1941) Picasso's *Guernica* (1937)	Shahn's *Passion of Sacco and Vanzetti* (1930) New Deal begins (1933) Louis Armstrong (1900–1971)
1940	Ethiopia liberated (1941)	Formation of United Nations (1945) Fourth French Republic established (1945) Communist takeover in E. Europe (1946–1948) China becomes communist (1949) Korean War (1950–1953)	Einstein (1879–1955)	T. S. Eliot (1888–1965) Jackson Pollock (1912–1956) Japanese attack Pearl Harbor (1941) Richard Wright (1908–1960) E. E. Cummings (1894–1962)
1950	Algerian War begins (1954) Morocco and Tunisia freed (1955) Ghana first colony to gain independence (1957) Guinea independent (1958)	Russian Sputnik (1957) Common Market (1957) de Gaulle's Fifth Republic (1958)	Sartre (1905–) Camus (1913–1960) Charlie Chaplin (1889–1977) Arrabal's *Picnic on the Battlefield* (1952) Beckett's *Endgame* (1957)	Langston Hughes (1902–1967) Ezra Pound (1885–1972) Duke Ellington (1899–1974) Martha Graham (1895–)
1960	Nigeria and most French colonies independent (1960) Algeria and Tanganyika freed (1962)	Berlin Wall (1961) Beginning of Russia-China split (1962) Great Cultural Revolution in China (1966)		Ralph Ellison (1914–) Katherine Dunham (1919–) Kurt Vonnegut, Jr. (1922–) James Baldwin (1924–) Miles Davis (1926–)
1970	Amin gains power in Uganda (1971) Breakdown of Portuguese African Empire (1974)	Withdrawal of U.S. from Vietnam (1972)		Adrienne Rich (1929–) Alvin Ailey (1931–) LeRoi Jones (1938–) Nikki Giovanni (1943–)
1980				

The Humanities

VOLUME II

INTRODUCTION

The Humanities and the Modern World

The three cultural roots that formed the nucleus of our introduction to the humanities in Volume I—the Greco-Roman, Judeo-Christian, and West African—have all in some way contributed to the development of the cultural environment we live in today. Obviously, these are not the only cultural roots of North Americans. The Greco-Roman and Judeo-Christian cultural traditions, however, as we emphasized in Volume I, gave birth to the Humanities as a mode of education. At the same time that humanistic learning was flourishing in Europe, the African cultural tradition became linked to the West through European travelers, as well as through acts of brutality and violence. Because of the long oppression of Africans by Europeans, the cultural traditions of West Africa do not have a real impact on the Western humanities until the twentieth century.

The seventeenth, eighteenth, and nineteenth centuries were for good or ill the age of Europe. The scientific developments, the technology, the artistic expression, and the philosophical attitudes that created the way of life we call "modern" came into being there in those years. Yet if Europe dominated the rest of the world, her culture was also vastly enriched because of her contacts with Africa, Asia, and the Americas. It is, then, to Western Europe that we must look if we are to understand the formation of the modern world.

PART FIVE

SCIENCE AND SPLENDOR: THE SEVENTEENTH CENTURY

19

THE BEGINNINGS OF MODERNITY

There are a number of reasons for designating the seventeenth century as the beginning of a new era for the Western world. By 1650 religious issues had ceased to be matters of life and death, religion had become detached from politics, and life was secular six days a week. Literature, painting, and sculpture increasingly depicted secular subjects by this time; the palace and the theater exerted immense influence on the architectural, artistic, and ceremonial forms of the churches.

The centralized state resting on a bureaucracy, a standing army, and a system of taxation developed into the dominant form of European government in the seventeenth century. These relatively stronger governments (which had their roots in the Middle Ages) endeavored to control and expand the economic life of their respective countries, fostering in the process the conception of a national economy in competition with other national economies for the world's riches. While importation of gold and spices from other continents had been important for European commerce before 1600, the development of the plantation system in the Americas (tied to the African slave trade and the establishment of elaborate networks of trading posts on the coasts of Africa and Asia) reflects the existence of a worldwide market by the late seventeenth century. To meet the demands of such expanded economic horizons, Europeans devised such financial and business institutions as the joint-stock company and the national bank that characterize modern commercial life. At the same time that Europe set out to dominate the rest of the world through its stronger political and economic structures, its scientists turned their attention as never before to mastering nature for man's use. This attitude, born in the so-called Scientific Revolution, has eventually made possible immense material improvements in the human condition and has become the dominant goal—for good or ill—not only of Europeans but of the rest of the world as well.

Reform and Counter Reform

By 1550 an objective observer of the European scene would perhaps have predicted the ultimate triumph of Protestantism over the old religion. England, which had broken with the Roman church in 1534 primarily for political motives, was by this time a Protestant power. The Lutherans had gained half of Germany and were advancing; theirs had become the dominant religion in the Scandinavian peninsula. Calvinism was spreading rapidly in areas like France, the Low Countries, and Poland.

The Catholics, however, made a counteroffensive beginning at the Council of Trent, the great church council that met at Trent in northern Italy at various times between 1545 and 1563. The basic results of the Council of Trent were to define clearly what Catholics should believe, to make some crucial administrative reforms, and to provide for the creation of seminaries for the education of the clergy. Henceforth Catholics could no longer fall into heresy because they were not aware of the orthodox doctrines. The administrative reforms made the Church less vulnerable to criticism, and the steps to raise the educational level of the clergy

resulted after decades in a new respect by laymen for their priests. Therefore, while establishing a platform on which to base an attack on the Protestants, Trent also provided a program of reforms that would attract individual Christians back to the faith.

The new agencies of the Church (the Jesuit order founded in 1540 and the Holy Office of the Roman Inquisition established in 1542) played an extremely important part in seconding these efforts. Heresy or false belief had always been regarded as a disease that not only destroyed the soul of the heretic but also, if diffused, could corrupt the immortal souls of others. Once identified by a commission of experts, the *inquisition*, the heretic was expected to abjure the errors for the good of the immortal soul. If he or she did not, or first abjured and then returned to the errors, the duty of the inquisition was to have the person executed to prevent further infecting the community of believers.

The Inquisition   There had been various forms of inquisitions established over the centuries, mostly at the level of the bishopric or archbishopric. The most famous of all, however, was the Spanish Inquisition. It was set up in 1478 by Ferdinand and Isabella of Spain as a department of their government to ferret out Moors who, while professing Christianity, remained faithful to Islam. Independent of the papacy, this inquisition was introduced into North America along with the Spanish conquistadors. By contrast, the Holy Office of the Roman Inquisition represented an effort of the papacy to concentrate investigation of heresy throughout the Catholic world at Rome. From that vantage point heresy could be pursued even among the princes of Europe and the Church. In the decades after its foundation more than one cardinal, for example, was forced to renounce a heretical or dangerous belief under threat of death or imprisonment. The efficiency of the new organization had the desired effect of preventing the diffusion of Protestantism as well as of more exotic beliefs among Catholic populations.

The Jesuits   Recognized as an order by the papacy in 1540, the Jesuits, founded by the Spanish knight Ignatius Loyola, were to become the right arm of the pope in the Counter Reformation. Like previous religious orders the Jesuits took a vow of poverty, chastity, and obedience, but in their case the last vow included a promise of complete obedience to the papacy at all times. As Loyola wrote: "If we wish to proceed securely in all things, we must hold fast to the following principle: What seems to be white, I will believe black if the hierarchical Church so defines."

The Jesuits formed an elitist body, composed of men admitted because of their intelligence, finesse, physical stamina, and deep commitment. Given a superb university education, they were capable of holding their own in any situation or discussion. They actively promoted papal policies on the international level as diplomats. More humbly, but perhaps more importantly in the long run, they became the prime educators of the middle and upper classes of Catholic Europe through the hundreds of schools that they established over the next century. Everywhere they diffused the brand of spirituality developed by their founder. In his effort to bring the believer to a higher state of religious awareness, Loyola focused on training and disciplining the will. All sorts of appeals were made, at least in the initial stages of development, to the senses, emotions, and imagination. As we will see, this type of spirituality was intimately related to the evolution of the artistic styles called *baroque* in Catholic countries.

Having in a sense experienced a revival of heart and conviction through the Council of Trent, resting on two powerful instruments for orthodoxy, the Inquisition and the Jesuits, the Church in the last forty years of the sixteenth century set off on its campaign to drive the Protestant menace back and eventually to destroy its heresies. By 1600 Poland had all but completely returned to the Catholic camp; in France the French Calvinists, the Huguenots, had already reached their maximum membership and their power was on the wane. In Germany as well, the Protestant advance was by this date turning into a retreat. The Catholic reform, relying there on two powerful German states, Austria and Bavaria, was meeting success in converting one city after another back to the old faith. Everywhere the Jesuits were leaders in the campaign.

Religious Wars This German Catholic campaign, however, was to precipitate one of the bloodiest wars in modern times. We have already discussed in the Reformation section of Volume I the thirty-year period of French religious wars that ended in 1594. In terms of the extent of destruction and the numbers of people killed, the German Thirty Years' War between 1618 and 1648 dwarfed its earlier French counterpart. This war began directly as a response of Bohemian Protestants to the efforts of their Catholic king (who was also the ruler of Austria) to suppress the Protestant faith in their country. After the Bohemians revolted, the war gradually spread to the whole empire; no one could safely remain neutral. The war was fought on both sides by large mercenary armies over which the German princes had little control. These armies had no interest in peace; wherever they went they brought death and devastation. Moreover, after the first few years the war in Germany became the focus for international rivalries, and the provinces of the empire served as a battlefield for invading armies of Denmark, Sweden, Spain, and France.

By 1648, when peace was finally signed at Westphalia, Germany was ruined from one end to the other. In effect the peace treaty reestablished the religious policy that had dominated Germany in the seventy years prior to the war: each German prince had the right to determine the religion of his state. The advance of the Counter Reformation was, for all practical purposes, stopped. The Thirty Years' War, at least in the beginning a religious struggle, constitutes the last major European war fought for motives of religion. Europe had had its orgy of religious passion; now both sides sensibly recognized the sphere of influence held by the other. The lines separating Catholics in southern Europe from Protestants in the northern areas have remained fairly stable from that time to this. While religious persecution of minorities might continue within individual countries, even at this level a new sense of toleration was developing. King Louis XIV's revocation of the Protestant rights to worship in 1685 and his expulsion of Protestants from France were perhaps the last grand gestures of the Counter Reformation.

By the end of the Thirty Years' War Europeans generally realized the senselessness of such struggles and the misery that they produced. But beneath the apparent tolerance of religious dissent also lay a growing religious indifference. Europeans on the whole no longer felt the need to judge their experience and to set their goals within a Christian frame of reference. Well might

EUROPE in 1648

- Austrian Habsburgs
- Spanish Monarchy
- Swedish Dominions
- Brandenburg-Prussia
- Church Lands
- —— Boundary of the Holy Roman Empire

the student of European culture after 1650 ask: "What happened to God?"

The Scientific Revolution

So enormous and dazzling was the progress made in the course of the seventeenth century toward the understanding of the human body, the earth, and the heavens, that it is not too much to say that by 1700 a radical change was taking place in the attitude of Europeans toward the interrelationship between man, God, and nature. At least in its initial stages this progress consisted in a rejection of the "commonsense" approach of ancient and medieval science. The European view of the universe in 1500 was substantially the same as that of Dante in 1300. The earth was at rest in the center, just as it appears, and the heavens rotated around it. These heavens—beginning with the moon, the sun, the planets out to the fixed stars—were either nine or ten in number. Beyond the outermost heaven, or the "first mover" that gave motion to everything in the universe, lay the region of God and the blessed. This universe was finite. God made the earth of heavy inferior substance, placing the finer heavenly bodies above the earth in ascending order of perfection. Since ancient times, however, astronomers had recognized a good deal of irregularity in the movement of the heavens. In order to make this conception fit the appearances, the astronomers had to add a whole series of special movements for individual bodies.

While medieval and early Renaissance scholars were often very dedicated to the investigation of nature, they worked within the shadow of the ancients. The diffusion of knowledge of Greek in the fifteenth century, moreover, made available to Europeans a great number of ancient scientific writings not hitherto known, and this new scientific literature had to be absorbed. By the beginning of the sixteenth century, however, that process was completed. The translated works of Plato and his followers provided Europeans with the idea that all physical objects could be reduced to numbers and that mathematics was the key to understanding nature. This approach differed considerably from the medieval conception of science that investigated nature in terms of qualities: heavy or light, colored or transparent, voluntary or natural in movement, and the like. The increased cooperation during the Renaissance between workmen skilled with their hands and scholars laid the basis for a joint effort in making new instruments for observing and calculating nature's operations. While the methodology of ancient philosophers could be useful, their authority now had to be tested against experience.

Copernicus and Kepler   The first fruit of the new concern with mathematics and experimentation was the work of the Polish priest and astronomer Nicholas Copernicus (1473–1543), who in fact had no intention of making an aggressive attack on received ideas of his day. In his *On the Revolution of the Heavenly Bodies*, published in 1543 and dedicated to the pope, Copernicus generally accepted the traditional concep-

tion of a finite universe characterized by a series of heavens, the moon, the planets, and the fixed stars. Copernicus' innovation was to substitute the sun for the earth at the center of the universe. For him the earth became one of the planets and, like other bodies, circulated around the center.

Copernicus' primary reason for switching the position of the sun and earth was that this conception furnished a better explanation of the observed motions of the heavens, reducing the need to ascribe exceptional movements to individual bodies as in the earth-centered theory. According to the deeply religious Copernicus, the ability of his sun-centered theory to explain the appearances and to show heavenly motion to be simple and regular magnified the perfection of the divine creator.

Copernicus presented his ideas as an hypothesis; but, over succeeding decades as new observations were recorded and found to support it, some thinkers came to insist that the theory was proved. The ancient picture of the universe gradually disintegrated. Although embracing the finitude of the universe, Copernicus' theory laid the foundation for the idea of the infinite nature of God's creation. Whereas the earth-centered view of the universe maintained an absolute up and down, potentially Copernicus' theory suggested that space was relative. Even though the Copernican earth circulated around the sun, heavy bodies still fell to the earth. If the sun, which all agreed was a nobler body than the earth, was at the center of the universe, then the old view (that, beginning with the earth, other heavenly bodies increased in perfection as they came nearer to the outermost sphere) made no sense at all. Finally, the fact that mathematics played such a primary role in Copernicus' original analysis and in subsequent efforts to test it made mathematics appear as a key to scientific truth.

It fell to the mathematician-astronomer Johann Kepler (1571–1630) to discover that the orbit of the planets around the sun, including that of the earth, took the form of an ellipse. Kepler worked out a single set of mathematical formulas that could be applied to every planet. While he could not say why the planets moved in this way, he was finally able to make sense of the appearance of planetary motion with his simple equations.

Galileo An aggressive publicist of the Scientific Revolution and one of its greatest contributors was a Florentine, Galileo Galilei (1564–1642). Both Copernicus and Kepler had worked with the naked eye. Galileo, informed of a new optical instrument developed in the Netherlands, the telescope, constructed one for himself and turned it on the heavens. Through the lens of the fantastic instrument he was the first human being to see that Jupiter had moons like the earth and that the earth's own moon was made of material similar to that found on earth. The momentous conclusion was that heavenly bodies were not made of more perfect material. Rather they resembled the earth and were governed by the same laws.

Galileo's conclusions were equally revolutionary when he turned to consider the behavior of bodies in motion. Traditional theories of dynamics, geared to the assumption that the natural state of a body was at rest, attempted to explain what caused motion to occur. For Galileo there was no "natural" motion of the body; rather, if a body was in motion, it would continue in a straight line at the same speed forever unless deflected, quickened, or retarded by another force—the principle of inertia. Thus, what concerned Galileo was not why things move but why changes in motion occur and how one describes these changes mathematically. His formula for the acceleration of a freely falling body in terms of time and space represents the kind of solutions he had in mind.

A magnificent stylist, courageous to the point of rashness, Galileo trumpeted his discoveries in a series of eloquent works that brought him to the attention of the Inquisition. The Inquisition found his teachings dangerous in that they not only reduced the eternal heavens to the level of the earth but specifically contradicted passages of Scripture. After a period of imprisonment Galileo was forced to live under house arrest in Florence until his death. Although he was forbidden to work on astronomy, he was allowed to continue his researches on motion. In 1638 his *Discourse on Two New Sciences*, which provided the foundation for modern physics, was published in the Dutch republic.

Newton The achievement of the Englishman Isaac Newton (1642–1727) was to bring together Galileo's laws of inertia and falling bodies, Kepler's laws of celestial mechanics, and his own theory of gravitational force into a monumental system of physical principles and mathematical formulas by which every physical movement in the universe could potentially be described. Newton came to see that every body in the universe attracted every other body with a force proportional to the product of the two masses and inversely proportional to the square of the distance between them. Galileo's law that a moving body would fly off in a straight line unless affected by an external force held true for the heavens as for the earth. A planet moved in an elliptical motion around the sun and the moon in similar fashion around the earth because the mutual attraction of the two bodies drew the smaller in toward the larger and deflected the motion of the smaller into an orbit. The shape of the orbit and its velocity could be described by Galileo's formula for falling bodies.

Other Scientific Discoveries and Their Effects Newton's findings, published in his *Mathematical Principles of Natural Philosophy* in 1687, marked the high point of the scientific revolution of the seventeenth century. But, if less spectacular, the discoveries in other areas of science were nonetheless important. In 1628 William Harvey (1578–1657) demonstrated the circulation of the blood, and at mid-century Anton Leeuwenhoek (1632–1723) had developed the microscope, thus revealing a whole world hidden from the naked eye. Scientists like Robert Boyle (1627–1691) were in subsequent decades involved in investigation of the action of gases.

No longer working in isolation, the scientists of this "revolution" developed communities. Societies like the Royal Society of London, founded in 1662, not only helped the diffusion of information among scientists but also brought their work to the attention of an educated public. For many, there were great expectations of a new era when, through the use of reason and new instruments, the human race would gradually eliminate the area of the unknown. But if the new discoveries brought confidence to some, others felt uncertain and confused. The Inquisition had justifiably regarded Galileo's doctrines as dangerous: men had now to deal with an order of truth appearing to contradict the Bible at several points. More than this, whereas the God of the Christians had been a God intimately connected with man's life and world, scientists like Galileo and Newton approached the universe as if, after creating it, God had stepped aside and let nature run itself. The French philosopher Blaise Pascal phrased it: "The eternal silence of infinite spaces terrifies me."

Economic Life

Historians tend to date the birth of modern capitalism in the late sixteenth and early seventeenth centuries, but to understand what actually occurred an important distinction must be made. There are basically two types of capitalism: commercial and industrial. In commercial capitalism the capitalist is usually a merchant who invests his money both in buying the raw material and in marketing the finished product once produced. In the case of wool cloth, for example, the merchant buys the raw wool; then either he or an agent carries the wool to artisans who spin, weave, and dye it in their shops or homes. They usually work by the piece and own or rent their equipment. When the cloth is finished, the merchant then sells the product; his profit lies in the difference between what the cloth cost him to produce and market and the purchase price of the finished goods.

This form of capitalism, with the merchant as the capitalist, began in the Middle Ages and remained the dominant form for the production of industrial goods down to the eighteenth century. The economic boom of the sixteenth century did not significantly affect the way that goods were produced; what did change was the number of people engaged in producing. The production of industrial goods significantly increased in the sixteenth century because the merchant had so many more independent producers working for him.

Industrial capitalism, on the other hand, refers to investment in the modes or means of production. In this case the capitalist is not the merchant but the factory or mine owner. Investment in machines means more productivity per worker or more variety in products. In order to print books at all, for example, a significant investment must be made in a printing press. In the sixteenth century a rapid surge in the amount of investment in machinery occurred in areas like metal, glass, paper, coal mining, and firearms. While the output of goods provided by industrial capitalism climbed significantly after 1550, still down to the end of the eighteenth century commercial capitalism was responsible for most of the industrial production of Europe.

The seventeenth century witnessed the definitive movement of the economic center of Europe from Italy to the North Atlantic countries: France, England, and Holland. The two latter countries, both dominated by Protestants, were the leading seapowers of Europe. Both were also advanced in developing organizational forms of business capable of collecting large amounts of capital. While the rest of Europe was characterized by family businesses until the nineteenth century, these two countries utilized the means of the joint-stock company in order to attract money into business ventures. Amsterdam was the center of a thriving stock exchange. In England and especially in Holland banking arrangements so developed that business and private individuals were able to borrow large sums of money on credit.

These relatively enormous financial assets available for commercial investment meant that the Dutch and English would play a preponderant role in business ventures overseas. The plantation economy of the New World was in large part a product of this flow of capital that brought the slaves from Africa, purchased the sugar, rice, coffee, tobacco, and other commodities that the slaves produced, and marketed the goods in Europe. Even French, Spanish, and Portuguese planters depended for their survival on Dutch willingness to extend credit on purchases from harvest to harvest, a convenience that their own countrymen could not provide.

The Age of Absolutism

The last half of the seventeenth century and most of the eighteenth has come to be recognized as the age of "absolute" monarchs. While the king or queen had all sorts of practical limitations on what could be done without provoking a rebellion, he or she was absolute in the sense that there were no legal restraints or alternative constitutional institutions that could block the monarch's will. Of course, even in France, the ideal absolute monarchy, there were law courts and some provincial assemblies that could lawfully impede the royal decrees for a time; but eventually, if the king was willing to pay the price for publicizing the opposition, he could have his way.

By 1650 such investment of power in the royal office appeared to most observers the only way that the centralized state could advance against forces of decentralization such as the great nobility, the provincial government, and the autonomous cities. The two notable exceptions to this situation were the Dutch and the English. The fact that the Dutch had a small country, densely populated, with good communications and a weak nobility made its republican government feasible. The development of constitutional monarchy in England must be explained in the light of its small size and its early centralization and development of Parliament.

Whereas the English Parliament had established a tradition of consultation with the monarch, assemblies in France, Spain, Germany, and elsewhere brought together forces of localism opposed to concentration of power. Since the Middle Ages these were the elements that, in moments when the monarchy was weak, seized the opportunity to destroy the carefully accumulated powers of the state over its territories. The religious wars of the sixteenth and early seventeenth centuries had created an ideal situation for subjects of one religion to revolt against their king who had another. For instance, the revolt of some of the highest French nobility in the sixteenth century, while done in the name of the Protestant faith, was unquestionably also motivated by political ambitions. Consequently, monarchs and their advisers came to believe that only by taking legal authority out of the hands of cities, provinces, and the nobility—instead centering it in the monarch's hands—could their countries ever experience domestic peace. In large part this policy was also supported by intellectuals and by the common people who had to choose between this or institutionalized anarchy.

Yet the monarch could not make a frontal attack on political privileges without provoking massive revolt. Basically the European social structure was divided into three general classes: the nobility, the peasants (both in the countryside), and the bourgeois in the towns and cities. The latter class included groups as far apart as humble shoemakers and wealthy bankers. Consequently, we must distinguish the upper bourgeoisie, who controlled the cities, from the lower bourgeoisie, who often were economically not superior to the peasants.

From the sixteenth century in Spain and France and a century later in other parts of the continent, the monarchy developed a policy of compromise with the privileged middle classes in the cities and with the nobility. In return for sanctioning the political domination of the monarch and accepting the extension of his authority, the powerful interest groups were promised exemption from many of the burdens entailed. The king guaranteed the nobility and the upper bourgeoisie that they would not have to pay many of the new taxes and that the heaviest impositions would fall on the poor. Besides, the king acknowledged the monopoly of the nobility over the officer corps in the army and over the great ceremonial posts at court. By dazzling the bourgeoisie with the prospect of offices in his expanded central bureaucracy, the absolute monarch of the seventeenth century had the means to incorporate families of new wealth into the establishment and thus to render them supporters of the system; otherwise they would have constituted a disgruntled and potentially subversive bourgeois leadership.

Farther to the east, in countries like Brandenburg-Prussia and Austria, the monarchies had emerged from the Middle Ages much weaker and more unstable than those in the west; as a result, eastern rulers were forced to go even further in order to obtain absolute political power. They granted the nobility (the middle class was really insignificant in numbers) the right to reduce the local rural populations to the status of serfs. In Brandenburg-Prussia, moreover, the *Junkers*, or nobility, were made the only class capable of owning land.

As a result of this compromise, the class structure of these various countries became more clearly defined: each had a legal relationship with the central government. At the same time the king became the sole judge of who would be admitted to the privileged classes, especially to the nobility. This right proved a great financial asset to the royal treasury, as most offices in the government were sold at a fixed price. The buyer earned only a small yearly salary from the government but was expected to make his profits from those who needed his services in that position. Some of the higher government offices—and naturally the most expensive—carried with them a patent of nobility, ennobling forever the buyer and his descendants. This system permitted humble men who had made money to put their families into the upper class. If an unlikely way to staff a bureaucracy, the method proved a good means of permitting social mobility.

But the concentration of power in the hands of kings, while affording domestic peace, had a different effect on international relations. More powerful monarchs with money to spend presided over larger armies and more far-ranging wars. In the Middle Ages and Renaissance, war was fought with troops raised for short periods of time; even a war like the Hundred Years' War between France and England primarily consisted of a long series of summer campaigns spread out over more than a century. With the greater taxing power of seventeenth-century monarchies, however, kings could afford to keep an army in the field for years at a time and to do so at a distance from the sources of supply. Consequently, there was a danger that one country might try to take over the whole of Europe, and kings felt it vital to their interests to know what their colleagues were about. This led to the increasing importance of diplomacy and to wars fought on the basis of international alliances.

Furthermore, as Europe became a political system based on a balance-of-power concept, in this century Europeans spread their rivalries to the rest of the world: to the Americas, Africa, and Asia. An important consequence of the increase in royal power was that the central government assumed the responsibility of regulating the economic life of the country and a commitment to fostering its development. Thus, more than ever before, hostilities between European powers appeared to be dictated by economic concerns: having influence in other areas of the world was regarded as significant for prosperity at home.

20

THE BAROQUE STYLE
IN THE ARTS

pagan - an irreligious person

The social, religious, intellectual, and economic upheavals that characterized the late sixteenth and early seventeenth centuries were accompanied
by a new style in the arts. The High Renaissance conventions of human
beauty expressed in ideal proportions seemed to lead to a dead end. Luther
and Calvin took to task the whole Catholic tradition of visual art in the
service of religion, and they found Italian religious painting of the sixteenth century completely pagan. In literature and in music, too, Protestant doctrine demanded an art form less tied to classical antiquity and formal standards and more suitable to individualistic piety. Some of the best
poetry and music of seventeenth-century Protestant Europe took the form
of hymns. Catholics, zealous to defend their faith after the Council of
Trent, found High Renaissance art inadequate for other reasons. In contrast to the Protestants, they vigorously reaffirmed the importance of rich

visual and auditory imagery in churches and worship rituals. The intellectual and classical qualities of Renaissance art were found wanting in emotional appeal. They wanted art that could enrapture the viewer, listener, or reader, appealing to the spirit through the senses and serving as an instrument of conversion.

Political and economic changes also had their effect on the development of new artistic forms. If the Protestant capitalists discouraged the decoration of churches, they encouraged paintings of themselves and the material objects surrounding them. Absolutist monarchy created a style of its own. Catholic monarchs liked to be shown in opulence and splendor, thus also encouraging a sensuous exploration of reality. One of the persistent characteristics of the new style in visual arts, literature, and music was a heightened sensuality combined with spirituality. Perhaps the long-lived disasters of the religious wars gave human beings zest for a life that seemed precarious and, at the same time, fervor for the life to come. Expanded trade and colonization in Africa and the New World gave artists wealth, more exotic themes, and an enlarged sense of space. The scientific and philosophical revolutions inevitably influenced artists' portrayals of reality. The shift from a metaphysical and authoritarian view of nature to an experimental one also encouraged the artist to portray what he actually saw.

On the other hand, the new knowledge that the earth was no longer the center of the universe led artists to seek a depiction of enlarged space in contrast to the ordered, limited space suggested by Renaissance conventions. Seventeenth-century church architects and painters loved to give illusions of infinite space; poets and playwrights became preoccupied with the idea that life on earth is not what it seems to be, that "reality" may be an illusion; musicians enlarged their tonal space to echo an illusion of infinity. An English poet of the new age, John Donne, captured something of the effect of the scientific revolution on men's minds and spirits in a poem called "An Anatomie of the World."

And new Philosophy calls all in doubt,
The element of fire is quite put out;
The Sun is lost, and th'earth, and no man's wit
Can well direct him where to looke for it.
And freely men confess that this world's spent,

When in the Planets, and the Firmament
They seeke so many new; they see that this
Is crumbled out againe to his Atomies.
'Tis all in peeces, all coherence gone;
All just supply, and all Relation.

The sense of being on a little planet in space rather than on firm earth is accompanied by a kind of breathless vertigo that is characteristic of much of seventeenth-century art. Yet the sense of earthly life as an illusion often appears along with a realistic depiction of it. This is one of the many contradictions of the period.

Historians of Spanish, Dutch, French, and sometimes English culture call the seventeenth century the "great century" or the "golden century." The power attained by these countries was accompanied by a great cultural outpouring in all fields. Italy, though waning in prominence, took an early lead in architecture, painting, music, and poetry, while Germany, toward the end of the century, produced the period's greatest musicians. Yet this period of rich productivity in the arts shows a diversity of style that makes it hard to classify. The stylistic terms most often used now to describe all of the arts in this century are taken from the vocabulary of visual arts: *baroque* and *neoclassical*.

Some cultural historians, particularly the French, like to divide the century into two neat parts: the first half, still politically and religiously chaotic is baroque, and the second half, characterized by relative stability, is neoclassical. This may work to a certain extent for literature and for art, yet everyone agrees that the great period of baroque music does not end until the middle of the eighteenth century. It is also possible to argue, as we will do here, that the concept "baroque" can be applied to the art of the entire century, even though much of it is widely dissimilar.

Baroque in the Visual Arts

The rather strange word *baroque* originally meant (from Italian *baroco*) a logical process that was contorted or involuted. In Portuguese, *perola barroca* was a term used by jewelers to designate a rough or irregularly shaped pearl. The French, by the eighteenth century, used the word *baroque* to mean "a painting . . . in which the rules of proportion are not observed and everything is represented according to the artist's whim."

All of these meanings were, like "Gothic," originally pejorative. What these definitions share in common is the sense of divergence from an established, accepted ideal. As art history and criticism evolved and the seventeenth century was revalued, *baroque* appeared to be the opposite of *classical*, either in reference to antiquity or to the High Renaissance. In this sense the term suggested art that was naturalistic rather than ideal, and emotional rather than rational. Translated visually, this would produce an art of movement, vitality, and brilliant color, with interest in the realistic rendering of the world and with a powerful emotional impact. The following comparison demonstrates the contrast between classical and baroque aesthetics.

Baroque and Classical Compared Raphael's fresco *The School of Athens* (1510–1511), which decorates a wall in the Vatican, exemplifies the painting of the High Renaissance (Fig. 20-1). With Michelangelo and Leonardo, Raphael was responsible for those masterpieces that provided the standard for Renaissance painting. The painting represents an imaginary discussion between the chief philosophers of antiquity. The architectural setting is a series of lofty vaulted and domed spaces reproduced with fidelity to Roman and Albertian architecture. The light of the blue, cloud-filled sky falls evenly into the space to illuminate the crowd whose central focus is a circle of auditors gathered around Plato and Aristotle who stand, center, at the top of a low flight of steps. On the steps and left and right in the foreground, groups of contemplative discussants ask questions among themselves. Two isolated figures, left and right of center, carry the eye into the painting and to the central pair, reinforcing the effect of the architectural arrangement and the figures surrounding Plato and Aristotle.

Figures at the top of the steps, left and right of the great arched opening, provide more *balance* and reinforce a feeling of *symmetry* and order. All the figures are clothed in drapery whose chief feature is the way that it enhances the body. The faces of the figures show us men of all ages, but all are marked with calm contemplation or query. Powerful emotions, colors, or gestures are limited by the vital harmony and order. The *fresco* itself, contained within a real arch on a wall, creates a limited, definitive stage space for this scene. The observer would stand the same distance from the fresco as the figures seem to stand from the viewer.

20–1 Raphael, "The School of Athens," Vatican. (Vatican Museums, Rome— Alinari/Editorial Photocolor Archives)

The Calling of Saint Matthew (1599–1600), one of three scenes from the life of Saint Matthew painted by Michelangelo Merisi (1573–1610), called Caravaggio after his native town in Lombardy, represents one type of baroque style (Color Plate I). The event takes place in a bare Roman tavern; some light comes directly from the upper right, slashing across the top third of the canvas. This light reveals the face and uplifted hand of Jesus who, with Peter, steps into the room. Matthew himself, the publican, is seated at a table with two somewhat tacky youths, another who seems to study the coins scattered on the table, and an older man who leans over Matthew. That Christ was unexpected we are told by poses, by gestures, and by Matthew, who looks surprised, bewildered, and a little sheepish. Many elements of Raphael's painting are present, but what is different?

First, Caravaggio has located this event in a specific, nonideal setting. Second, the arrangement of figures is asymmetrical, almost casual; in fact, the main figures themselves seem hardly emphasized but are part of a total ensemble whose mood contrasts sharply with event. Third, the figures themselves are not idealized; Christ and Peter are rough-haired; Matthew looks like the minor bureaucrat that he was. They act and react in an awkward, very human way. Fourth, the dramatic spotlighting of the chief actors creates a feeling of uneasy ambiguity, for, combined with Christ's presence and gesture, the light could be heavenly or earthly—we just do not know. Fifth, we are placed very close to the scene itself—everything happens in a space that makes us one with it. Finally, Caravaggio has rendered his figures and setting with hard, firm edges; with substantial, varied *textures* and surfaces that provide another contrast to the intervention of the spiritual in everyday life. It seems so real that it could hardly be happening—but it does. Using the accomplishments and conventions of High Renaissance painting, Caravaggio has altered them by means of a naturalism that strives for a personal, emotional response. Both its rendering of everyday reality and its suggestion of a supernatural event would seem to be the opposite of the classical aesthetic, of the ordered, harmonious, universal art of the Renaissance. Yet aspects of the baroque style grow out of tendencies found in Raphael as well as in Caravaggio.

Baroque Architecture and Sculpture in Rome

It was in a Rome dominated by the papacy and the militant Counter Reformation that the baroque style began. In the late sixteenth century the popes began to transform the city. A system of wide thoroughfares and squares united the major churches and sites of the pilgrim processional. There was innovative accommodation for wheeled and pedestrian traffic. There was also a sense of order to the city, recalling that produced by the ancient Forum. The pope's cathedral, Saint Peter's, was begun in the early sixteenth century (Fig. 20-2); the dome and east end, carried forth under Michelangelo, was brought to completion and aggrandized by a succession of powerful popes. Gian Lorenzo Bernini, the greatest sculptor of the seventeenth century, was commissioned to finish the interior. He designed the great canopy that stands over the high altar; the enormous elevated throne, the Chair of Saint Peter, in the east end (Fig. 20-3); and the magnificent staircase that connects the papal apartments with the west front of the church.

All these features seem like sets for a grand spectacle but none more so than the great plaza and colonnade set before the church to provide the necessary vista for a view of the great hovering dome of Saint Peter's. The arms of the Tuscan Doric colonnade reach down from the ends of the church façade, compress slightly, and then swell into the curved arms of the oval that welcomes the pilgrim to Saint Peter's (Fig. 20-4). The architectural vocabulary is that of Rome and the Renaissance but employed on a massive, monumental scale. The colonnade, for example, is four columns deep. Decorated with fountains and an Egyptian obelisk, this piazza—and others like it, opened in Rome and decorated by Bernini and his peers—became important in the development of urban planning. Rome itself was adorned with new churches and palaces. In their interiors are still found painting and sculptures that represent persuasive, powerful propaganda for the faith.

In contrast to the vast adornments of Saint Peter's, Bernini planned other, more intimate decorative schemes that were focused on his magnificent sculptures. Such a scheme is the Cornaro Chapel at Santa Maria della Vittoria in Rome (1645–1652) (Fig. 20-5). An anonymous eighteenth-century painting of the chapel gives us the best idea of the ensemble, whose

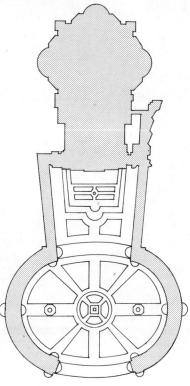

20–2 Above left. Saint Peter's, Rome, aerial view. (Alinari/Editorial Photocolor Archives)

20–3 Above right. Bernini, Chair of Saint Peter. (St. Peter's, Rome—Alinari/Editorial Photocolor Archives)

20–4 Left. Groundplan. Saint Peter's Square.

multaneously felt such infinite sweetness that I wished the pain to last eternally. It was the sweetest caressing of the soul by God." The saint's mouth is open, as if to cry out, but the movement of her complex drapery contrasts with her thrown-back head and arm so that she seems to move both away from and toward this awesome divine love (Fig. 20-6). There is a distinctly erotic tone to pose and gesture, which is enhanced by the realistic rendition of hands, feet, and face of the saint and the angel's soft feathered wings and curls. The bronze rays falling behind the group reinforce the real light, and the marble paneling of the wall is continuous with that in the rest of the chapel. We observe from the ground, but members of the Cornaro family are in boxes on either side—these are also part of the total ensemble of sculpted and painted decoration, for the figures are marble reliefs. It is significant that many Cath-

20–5 Cornaro Chapel, Santa Maria della Vittoria, Rome. Anonymous 18th-century painting. (Staatliches Museum Schwerin, German Democratic Republic)

20–6 Bernini, "The Ecstacy of Saint Theresa," (S. Maria della Vittoria, Rome—Alinari/Editorial Photocolor Archives)

subject is *The Ecstasy of Saint Theresa*. Theresa of Avila was a sixteenth-century Spanish nun whose writings on her ecstatic vision particularly appealed to the sensibility of the seventeenth century. The ceiling of the vaulted chapel seems to disappear as angels greet the dove of the Holy Spirit in a burst of divine, heavenly light. The architectural frame swells out to create a stage for the cloud with its burden of a limp, sagging Saint Theresa and a beautiful, smiling angel who holds an arrow in his upraised hand and with the other gently raises her habit to reveal her heart. In her autobiography Saint Theresa had described this vision in which an angel with a flaming golden arrow pierced her heart. "The pain was so great that I screamed aloud, but si-

olics, including Bernini, practiced exercises of prayer and self-denial that were designed to induce suffering and delight comparable to that of Christ and the saints.

It was in Rome, then, that some of the greatest monuments of the seventeenth century were produced. It was from Rome also that the baroque was carried to other artistic centers. Such a courier and another great seventeenth-century artist was the Flemish painter Peter Paul Rubens.

Baroque Painting: Rubens Rubens, an older contemporary of Bernini, was born in 1577, the son of a wealthy Antwerp Protestant who fled to Germany to avoid persecution by the Catholics seeking control of the Netherlands. The family returned to Antwerp after the father's death, and Rubens grew up as a Catholic. Amiable, handsome, and energetic, he was already a master when he journeyed to Italy in 1600. He remained there until 1608, assimilating the art of the High Renaissance, as well as that of ancient Rome, from which he created his own distinctive vision of the world.

When Rubens returned to Flanders, he was made court painter to the Spanish regent, and commissions began to flow into his workshop. He married well and lived in a magnificent townhouse in Antwerp that housed his collections of sculptures, paintings, antique coins and gems, and his personal library. His studio was soon filled with assistants who transferred his sketches onto large canvases. Even when he was absent on diplomatic and professional visits to France, England, or Spain, work was still produced to await his final approval and finishing touches.

The Raising of the Cross (Fig. 20-7), painted in 1609–1610, is the central panel of a *triptych*, a three-part altarpiece executed for the cathedral in Antwerp. It is a splendid example of the new style that emerged from his Italian sojourn. The athletic, muscular figure of Christ on the cross is placed on a diagonal away from the front plane established by the surface of the canvas. Massive, muscular figures struggle to raise the cross. The background is a dark one, where leaves are silhouetted against a stormy sky. The light, falling from right to left, is a dramatic stage light that picks out faces and limbs. The physical stress and earthly faces of the soldiers contrast with Christ's upward-turned eyes

20–7 Rubens, "The Raising of the Cross," Antwerp Cathedral. (Copyright A.C.L. Bruxelles)

and sagging body. The body types owe much to Michelangelo, and the essentially triangular *composition* is based on a similar Renaissance device. But the energy and vitality of the figures, the movement back into deep space, and the dramatic lighting contrast with the order and symmetry of Renaissance painting. There is a loving attention to the color and textures of flesh, armor, and other objects—such as the curly, soft coat of the agitated dog in the lower foreground—that heightens our awareness of this event. *Colors* themselves are strong, and the paint surface is a smooth, rich one, which enables paint to be seen as paint as well as the delineator of form and surface. Compare your reaction to this work with that of Bernini's *Saint Theresa* and to Caravaggio's *Saint Matthew*. What specifically engenders your emotional response?

Rubens received many important commissions, but surely one of the most important was for a series of twenty-one canvases to celebrate the career of Marie de' Medici, widow of Henry IV and regent of France during the minority of her son, Louis XIII. These canvases transform an inglorious, occasionally unscrupulous, and not too beautiful woman into an object of splendor through the unity of myth, fact, history, and allegory. For example, Marie's arrival at Marseilles (Fig. 20-8) shows her greeted by helmeted France, attended by Fame and Neptune, whose court rises from the water to celebrate her safe voyage. Marie, at the center right, is only a part of the rather glorious assemblage, which is beautiful for its rich colors, textures, and vitality of light and movement. We realize that the paintings for Marie were commissioned not only for self-glorification but also for the glorification of the French monarchy and its increasing power. Baroque art could serve to glorify the absolute monarchy as well as the Church Militant.

Rubens was adept at this kind of commission; indeed his portraits of kings and queens, prelates and courtiers depict the brilliant world of the first half of the seventeenth century. But it is important to remember that this great master could render not only memorable scenes of both spiritual and temporal power but also those of his own life and of the world of persons and objects that he loved.

The Garden of Love, painted in 1638 and inspired by Rubens' second marriage, demonstrates the earthly love whose divine counterpart was the impetus for his great paintings of Christian subjects (Color Plate II). Rubens and his young wife, Helene, the couple at the far left, are shown in a garden, about to join a group of obviously loving couples—husbands and wives or friends and lovers, it is hardly important. The fantastic fountain house from the artist's garden in Antwerp provides background. A statue of Venus and mischievous cupids complete this vision. The colors are soft and warm, light, gay, ripe, and sensuous. The figures—who stand, sit, lean, talk, and gaze—melt into each other in a soft, flowing rhythm. Velvet and satin, soft skin and hair, sparkling eyes, and rosy lips seduce us with a vision of the joy of life and love that is suspended in this spring garden. The courtly man in the broad-brimmed

20–8   Rubens, "Arrival of Marie de' Medici at Marseilles." (Louvre, Paris/photo © ARCH. PHOT. PARIS—S.P.A.D.E.M., 1980)

hat introduces us to a world that will be, more and more, the subject of art—a golden time without pain or anxiety.

Rembrandt   Rubens' was a world of brilliant successes. His life, though not without real difficulties and grief, exemplifies the artist who is accepted, adored, and lives to enjoy his fame. His optimism, energy, and success permit us one view of life in the first half of the seventeenth century. Rembrandt van Rijn (1606–1669), younger than Rubens by almost thirty years, shows us another equally important aspect of that society.

Rembrandt's patrons were not the Catholic monarchy, church, and court but the powerful, successful Lutherans and Calvinists of Holland. The wealthy, individualistic burghers did not decorate their churches nor did they glorify the state, but they memorialized themselves and the infinite variety of objects and experiences that made up their lives.

Seated around a table covered with a magnificent red oriental rug, attended by a servant, the black-coated *Syndics of the Drapers' Guild* discuss the affairs of the guild (Fig. 20-9). Yet the moment is not altogether public, for they seem to have been caught in a quiet conversation. One man rises from his seat to greet someone who has come into the room, and all eyes focus on that person. The intruder is, of course, the viewer, and this is one of the qualities that gives the picture its life. The men, who seem completely unposed, become the focus of our attention through their glances, their alert faces, the direction of light, and the white collars and broad-brimmed hats. Each is an individual; each face exhibits age, experience, and reserve. The surface textures, contours of form, and the features of faces and hair are all rendered with soft, easily flowing brushstrokes. The firm clarity that is present in much of Rubens' work is absent here, but the painting exhibits a softness derived from suffused light more comparable to that in *The Garden of Love.*

Rembrandt's sympathy with his patrons and their view of life grew from his own experience. One can follow his transformation from a pugnacious and witty young man to a mature, introspective adult in his many self-portraits. He was never a social success like Rubens, but, like Rubens, he was deeply reliant on his art as the source of meaning in his life, and, like Rubens, he transformed his technique and skills to accommodate his vision of faith and the meaning of love.

Rembrandt's genius, like Rubens', lay in the unity of composition achieved by light and by the revelation of surface features, textures, and colors in light. Renaissance painting developed conventions in which light was generally clear, even, and uniformly revealing. Masaccio, Piero, Botticelli, Raphael, and Leonardo all employed a representation of light that is not intrusive. It is a steady light that has been studied in nature but controlled in the studio. It may be slightly *warm*—that is, tending to emphasize the warm reds, yellows, and oranges of the spectrum—or it may be *cool*—emphasizing the cool blues, greens, and purples of the spectrum—but, above all, it is consistent. Along with this convention of uniform light, the Renaissance painters used another by designating *shade* or *shadow* with gray, brown, or black layers of paint. This is not the way that shades and shadows are colored in nature, but

20–9 Rembrandt, "Syndics of the Drapers Guild." (Rijksmuseum, Amsterdam)

it is the way that they were conventionally depicted. Without shade and shadow there is little or no sense of volume and space. Showing shade and shadow as an absence of color gives a great sense of uniformity to a picture, particularly uniformity of light.

Both Rubens and Rembrandt experimented with, and elaborated on, these conventions. Rubens used light dramatically to reveal and focus on objects and to enliven and enhance the colors of things. Rembrandt used light to create much sharper contrasts between figures and objects in space. In deep shadows and shadowed faces we find that same mystery of life and death, pain and joy. Though these themes were present in Rubens' work, Rembrandt portrays them without explosive theatricality. The drama becomes more personal and introspective; it is not something that we witness; it is something that we experience. The contrast is indicative of the difference in emphasis between the theatricality of Counter Reformation Catholicism and the individual piety of the Protestant north.

The Return of the Prodigal Son (ca. 1669) (Color Plate III) is such a shadowed, almost soundless picture. The warm light falling on figures and faces reinforces the general warmth of the picture that is derived from gesture as well as from color scheme. The faces that witness this reunion seem observed in light reflected from the two major figures. There is no boisterous welcome but, instead, tender, loving forgiveness. This is earthly love raised to a divine power by the simplicity of composition. The paint itself seems thin except in the figures of father and son, where heavy *impastoed* layers, creating form and shadow, allude to textures. Unlike the uniformly smooth surface of Renaissance pictures, these contrasting layers of paint tell, as they do in Rubens' work, of the expansion of another Renaissance convention.

Vermeer   The ability to make paint give us an illusion of what we see has almost no limits. The degree of expansion of that ability was also tested by the third great northern painter, Vermeer of Delft, Holland. The relativity of experience, the limits of reality, and the fragmented perception of the world are denied and confirmed in the ordered visions of Vermeer. The apparently simple subjects—city views and figures in interiors (Color Plate IV)—are chosen in transient mo-

ments and rendered permanent. These pictures, all small, are deceptively simple. A maidservant stands before a window pouring milk from a pitcher into a basin. The light from the window is cool and subdued; the colors of her sleeves, apron, and tablecloth are all cool. The pottery, the bread, and the gold of her bodice and red of her skirt challenge the quiet coolness. The gesture endures forever.

What is so remarkable about this painting? The original, more than a reproduction, emits an incredible transparency and glow. It is possible to imagine that, should the light be gone from the room, the painting itself would provide light—so natural and convincing is its revelation of every surface, fold, and wrinkle. The colors themselves vibrate; shadows and folds are not rendered in gray, brown, or black but in thin layers of color itself—deeper blue in her apron, deeper golden red on the basin.

Light, of course, is the most essential and most recalcitrant element in all painting that seeks to render an account of nature as we perceive it. Artists have captured it by conventionalizing its representation. Raphael's even harmonious light, Rubens' dramatic spotlight effects, or Rembrandt's reflected light are some examples of the different ways to render light convincingly without absolute fidelity to light as it is experienced naturally. Vermeer, however, by confining his subjects almost exclusively to figures before windows, proclaims his interest in the transient, cool light that comes from outside and is therefore subject to immediate change. Yet change never occurs, and that is what delights: it is "real" and it is not! We know that *The School of Athens* or *Primavera* are rendered through knowledge of the behavior of light, but there is no attempt to cajole us into thinking that it is "real" or experienced light—not so with Vermeer. Moreover, a woman weighing gold, a girl reading a letter, or a geographer in his study are all intimate revelations of transience where light reveals and suggests the brevity of life and the ephemeral pleasure of things.

As we experience these pictures by Vermeer, we add another layer to our perception of the seventeenth century. Here is a vision very different from that of a Rubens or a Rembrandt. In its realism it is more like Caravaggio, but its order recalls Piero and Raphael. Above all, however, Vermeer's study of light and delineation of space is uniquely his own, as individual and personally centered as he could make it. Baroque in the visual arts thus includes a rich diversity of styles and cultural patterns from the Catholic south to the Protestant north, with the work of Rubens as a bridge between the two. Yet another aspect of its diversity will be seen in the architecture, painting, and sculpture created for the absolute monarch Louis XIV. Let us now turn to a few examples of seventeenth-century poetry to determine if the baroque style as we have seen it in the visual arts can be applied to literature.

Literary Baroque

Marino   The term *baroque* has been borrowed from art history to describe similar characteristics in literature. The beginnings of the baroque style in literature can be found in some of the late sixteenth-century mystic writers in Spain and, in a different vein, in the influential Italian poet Giambattista Marino (1569–1625). Both display one of the most salient characteristics of baroque literature: the mingling of the sensuous with the spiritual. The mystics, as one can tell from Bernini's statue of Saint Theresa, used an erotic vocabulary to describe spiritual experiences. Marino wrote with equal facility devotional poetry and love poetry, some of it very sensual. Like baroque painters he loved rich colors, contrasts of light and dark, and intricate language. He gives us another example of white Europe's view of "exotic" black Africa in one of his best-known poems, "The Beautiful Slave" (translated by Mary Ann Witt).

GIAMBATTISTA MARINO

The Beautiful Slave

You are black, but beautiful, or
A graceful wonder of Nature amongst love's beauties.
Near you, the dawn is dark, beside your ebony
Ivory and the pearl fade away.
   Now where or when did the ancient world or ours
See such living light, feel such purity
To be born from shady ink,
Or fire to spring from burnt coal?
   Servant of my servant, see, I bear

Around my heart a dark noose,
Which will never be loosed by white hand.
   There where you burn the brightest, Sun, a Sun
Is born for your sole shaming, a Sun whose lovely face
Wears the night, whose eyes contain the day.

COMMENTS AND QUESTIONS

1. The conventional Renaissance love poem praised the beauty of the poet's beloved in terms of her snow-white skin, rosy lips, and golden hair. Her eyes were often compared to the light of the sun. The poet would often declare himself her slave or prisoner. How does Marino play with this convention here?
2. How do the images in this poem achieve a dramatic contrast between light and dark? Can you compare this to techniques in any of the baroque painting that we have seen?
3. Note Marino's intricate play of language, particularly in the last three lines. What are the different meanings here assigned to the word "Sun"? In Italian, the word for "alone" (*sole*) and the word for "sun" (*sole*) are the same.

English Baroque Poetry   In order not to be limited by translation, we will take the rest of the examples of baroque poetry from England, where a rich poetic school (until recently called "metaphysical" more often than "baroque") flourished in the early seventeenth century. Primarily Protestant, though a few were Catholic, these poets wrote both religious and amatory verse, often combining the spiritual with the sensual in rather surprising ways.

Crashaw   Perhaps the most baroque of all the seventeenth-century English poets was Richard Crashaw (1612–1649). Crashaw was raised in the Puritan tradition—his father was a preacher—but he converted to Roman Catholicism and spent the last years of his life in Rome. He was greatly attracted to mysticism and especially to female saints; three of his best-known poems are on Saint Theresa of Avila. Although it is unlikely that Crashaw saw Bernini's famous statue before writing the poems, they share its spirit. Below is the last part of the third poem in the series, entitled "The Flaming Heart." In the first part of the poem, Crashaw criticizes conventional pictorial representations of the saint (where she usually appears as a rather placid nun). He then describes how she should be represented. First, he says that she, not the seraphim beside her, should hold the dart. He then concedes to the angel "the bravery of all those Bright things," including "the radiant dart," and asks that Theresa be left only "the flaming heart." (The spelling has been modernized in all of the following poems.)

RICHARD CRASHAW

from *The Flaming Heart*

Leave Her alone The Flaming Heart.
   Leave her that; and thou shalt leave her
Not one loose shaft but love's whole quiver.
For in love's field was never found
A nobler weapon than a Wound.
Love's passives are his activ'st part.
The wounded is the wounding heart.
O Heart! the equal poise of love's both parts
Big alike with wounds and darts.
Live in these conquering leaves; live all the same;
And walk through all tongues one triumphant Flame.
Live here, great Heart; and love and die and kill;
And bleed and wound; and yield and conquer still.
Let this immortal life where'er it comes
Walk in a crowd of loves and Martyrdoms.
Let mystic Deaths wait on it; and wise souls be
The love-slain witnesses of this life of thee.
O sweet incendiary! show here thy art,
Upon this carcass of a hard, cold hart,
Let all thy scatter'd shafts of light, that play
Among the leaves of thy large books of day,
Combin'd against this Breast at once break in
And take away from me my self and sin,
This gracious Robbery shall thy bounty be;
And my best fortunes such fair spoils of me.
O thou undaunted daughter of desires!
By all thy dower of Lights and Fires;
By all the eagle in thee, all the dove;
By all thy lives and deaths of love;
By thy large draughts of intellectual day,
And by thy thirsts of love more large than they;

By all thy brim-fill'd Bowls of fierce desire
By thy last Morning's draught of liquid fire;
By the full kingdom of that final kiss
That seiz'd thy parting Soul, and seal'd thee his;
By all the heav'ns thou hast in him
(Fair sister of the Seraphim!)
By all of Him we have in Thee;
Leave nothing of my Self in me.
Let me so read thy life, that I
Unto all life of mine may die.

COMMENTS AND QUESTIONS

1. Many of the characteristics of baroque literature are here. Baroque poets, like baroque artists, loved extreme contrasts; they expressed these with the rhetorical figures known as *oxymoron* (the juxtaposition of words with opposing meanings) and *antithesis* (the balance of parallel word groups conveying opposing ideas). An example of oxymoron here is the phrase "sweet incendiary." An example of antithesis is: "Love's passives are his activ'st part./The wounded is the wounding heart." What other examples of these figures can you find? How do they serve the poet's purpose here?

2. Another characteristic of baroque poetry is the extended use of *metaphor*. Renaissance poets tended to make more use of the *simile*, which makes a comparison between two things on an intellectual level; but the baroque sensibility preferred the more emotional fusion and identification that the metaphor provided. In this poem the poet does not compare himself to a deer but suddenly *becomes* "this carcass of a hard, cold hart." (Plays on words like *heart/hart* were also dear to baroque poets.) What other metaphors does Crashaw use here?

3. Baroque poems often tend to have a cumulative effect, comparable to the rich profusion of matter in baroque art. One way of achieving this is through the rhetorical device of *anaphora* (the repetition of the same word to introduce two or more clauses or lines). Notice here the number of lines that begin with "By all." What is the effect of this device?

4. How would you describe Crashaw's interpretation of the mystic experience of Theresa? Compare it with Bernini's in the statue.

5. Do this style and sensibility appeal to you? What in your own personality makes you answer negatively or positively?

Donne The next three poems are by John Donne (1572–1631), whose lines on the new science we quoted earlier. In contrast to Crashaw, Donne was brought up as a Catholic but became an Anglican. He became, in fact, one of the most successful preachers of his age, and his sermons are still read for their force and brilliant style. At the same time, Donne was a worldly man, fond of women and involved in several passionate love affairs. He was thus suited to the baroque combination of the ardently religious and the ardently erotic; his best poems successfully combine the two. The first poem here is a kind of prayer, quite comparable to Bernini's and to Crashaw's Saint Theresa in its use of erotic and violent imagery to describe mystic experience. The second is frankly erotic, but in it the poet speaks of the bed as "love's hallowed temple" and of women as angels and "mystic books." The third poem is set up as an argument for seduction. Centered around a tiny, apparently insignificant object (a flea), it makes use of extreme detail to portray matters of larger significance; in this sense it is more comparable to the Dutch than to the Italian baroque style in art.

JOHN DONNE

from *Holy Sonnets*

SONNET 14

Batter my heart, three-personed God; for you
As yet but knock, breathe, shine, and seek to mend;
That I may rise, and stand, o'erthrow me, and bend
Your force, to break, blow, burn, and make me new.
I, like an usurped [1] town, to another due,
Labor to admit you, but Oh, to no end,
Reason your viceroy[2] in me, me should defend,
But is captived, and proves weak or untrue.
Yet dearly I love you, and would be loved fain,[3]
But am betrothed unto your enemy:

----

[1] Captured.
[2] Representative.
[3] Gladly.

Divorce me, untie, or break that knot again,
Take me to you, imprison me, for I
Except you enthral me, never shall be free,
Nor ever chaste, except you ravish me.

QUESTIONS

1. How do the baroque characteristics of contrast and repetition appear in this poem?
2. Are there extreme contrasts in the rhythm of the lines as well? How is this achieved?
3. How are the war metaphor and the sexual metaphor worked in together?
4. How does the use of this kind of language to describe religious experience affect you?

Elegy XIX

TO HIS MISTRESS GOING TO BED

Come, madam, come, all rest my powers defy,
Until I labor, I in labor lie.
The foe oft-times having the foe in sight,
Is tired with standing though he never fight.
Off with that girdle,[1] like heaven's zone glistering,
But a far fairer world encompassing.
Unpin that spangled breastplate which you wear,
That th' eyes of busy fools may be stopped there.
Unlace yourself, for that harmonious chime
Tells me from you that now it is bed time.
Off with that happy busk,[2] which I envy,
That still can be, and still can stand so nigh.
Your gown, going off, such beauteous state reveals,
As when from flowry meads th' hill's shadow steals.
Off with that wiry coronet and show
The hairy diadem which on you doth grow:
Now off with those shoes, and then safely tread
In this love's hallowed temple, this soft bed.
In such white robes, heaven's angels used to be
Received by men; thou, Angel, bring'st with thee
A heaven like Mahomet's Paradise;[3] and though
Ill spirits walk in white, we easily know

----

[1] Belt.
[2] Undergarment worn over the breast.
[3] The Muslim idea of paradise includes beautiful women.

By this these angels from an evil sprite:
Those set our hairs, but these our flesh upright.
    License my roving hands, and let them go
Before, behind, between, above, below.
O my America! my new-found-land,
My kingdom, safeliest when with one man manned,
My mine of precious stones, my empery,
How blest am I in this discovering thee!
To enter in these bonds is to be free;
Then where my hand is set, my seal shall be.
    Full nakedness! All joys are due to thee,
As souls unbodied, bodies unclothed must be
To taste whole joys. Gems which you women use
Are like Atalanta's balls,[4] cast in men's views,
That when a fool's eye lighteth on a gem,
His earthly soul may covet theirs, not them.
Like pictures, or like books' gay coverings made
For lay-men, are all women thus arrayed;
Themselves are mystic books, which only we
(Whom their imputed grace will dignify)
Must see revealed. Then, since that I may know,
As liberally as to a midwife, show
Thyself: cast all, yea, this white linen hence,
There is no penance due to innocence.
    To teach thee, I am naked first; why then,
What needst thou have more covering than a man?

QUESTIONS

1. Why does Donne spend so much time describing each article of clothing that he wants the woman to take off? What is the effect of this "slow motion"?
2. Could you compare the enumeration here to the numbers of sensuously depicted objects in baroque painting?
3. What use does Donne make here of the "new world" discoveries? What is the effect of this metaphor?

---

[4] Atalanta agreed to marry Hippomenes if he could defeat her in a foot race. As she was about to overtake him, he cast in her path three golden apples given to him by Venus. Distracted by their beauty, Atalanta stopped to retrieve them, and Hippomenes won the race.

THE FLEA

Mark but this flea, and mark in this,
How little that which thou deny'st me is;
It sucked me first, and now sucks thee,
And in this flea our two bloods mingled be;[1]
Thou know'st that this cannot be said
A sin, nor shame, nor loss of maidenhead;
    Yet this enjoys before it woo,
    And pampered swells with one blood made of two,
    And this, alas, is more than we would do.

O stay, three lives in one flea spare,
Where we almost, yea, more than married are.
This flea is you and I, and this
Our marriage bed and marriage temple is;
Though parents grudge, and you, we are met
And cloistered in these living walls of jet.
    Though use[2] make you apt to kill me,
    Let not to that, self-murder added be,
    And sacrilege, three sins in killing three.

Cruel and sudden, hast thou since
Purpled thy nail in blood of innocence?
Wherein could this flea guilty be,
Except in that drop which it sucked from thee?
Yet thou triumph'st and say'st that thou
Find'st not thyself nor me the weaker now;
    'Tis true, then learn how false fears be:
    Just so much honor, when thou yield'st to me,
    Will waste, as this flea's death took life from thee.

COMMENTS AND QUESTIONS

1. Donne begins this poem almost as if he were beginning a sermon, using the flea as an object-lesson. He then begins a series of arguments on the *carpe diem* ("seize the day," or "let's make love now before it's too late") theme. What arguments does he use? Are they meant to be logical?
2. Notice that the poem is set up like a three-act drama. What is supposed to have happened after stanza 1 and after stanza 2?

---

[1] It was believed at this time that conception occurred through the mixing of the man's blood with the woman's.
[2] Habit, custom.

3. What is the effect of externalizing the lover's desire in the flea?

Baroque Music

The baroque style in music, like that in the visual arts and in literature, had its origins in late Renaissance Italy. Humanism, the same cultural and intellectual movement that used the ideas and ideals of Greece and Rome as models for contemporary artistic creation (and to a large degree, gave rise to the Renaissance itself), was also largely responsible for creating a new or "second practice" at the height of the Renaissance period.

Well before the end of the sixteenth century, musicians in Italy tried to resurrect the affective power of Greek drama: they began to experiment with *dramma per musica*, theatrical genres that developed and were later named opera and oratorio. A whole theory of *affects* became a doctrine of the baroque, a method whereby a composer could invoke specific emotional responses in an audience by employing specific musical devices. As Plato's Dorian mode stirred manly feelings in the youth of Greece, Bach's and Handel's D-major trumpet parts evoked victorious martial responses in the listeners of the eighteenth, nineteenth, and twentieth centuries.

As in the other arts, baroque music had both a Catholic and Protestant form. The Church of Rome partook in the new musical developments during the late Renaissance, since the Reformation of Luther was evidently successful in winning converts through music that was particularly attractive and meaningful to laymen—vernacular texts, simple settings, and short, "catchy" melodies. The Catholic church's Counter Reformation thus experimented with similarly appealing music. One discovers that Saint Philip Neri's congregation of secular priests sang *laude spirituali* (spiritual songs of praise) in the oratory (a large room for public discussions) of his church in Rome. His group of followers was named after the room (*Congregazione del'Oratorio*), and the baroque musical form (oratorio) was likewise named after this place of origin. A loosely connected historical line binds together a development or metamorphosis from the *laude spirituali* to spiritual dialogues and early oratorios with biblical characters to the mature oratorio of the late baroque.

Attractive dramatic music became fairly common throughout Italy toward the end of the sixteenth century, and we see that Andrea Gabrieli composed choruses for a presentation of a revived Greek drama, *Oedipus Rex*, at Vicenza in 1585; Orazio Vecchi presented his madrigal comedy *L'Amfiparnaso* in Modena in 1594; and the Florentines Jacopo Corsi, Ottavio Rinuccini, and Jacopo Peri produced an entire dramatic pastoral in a representational style inspired by antique models, *Dafne*, in Corsi's palace in 1598.

By this time musicians were calling Renaissance music old, and this music of the "second practice" new or modern. The key stylistic feature of the best music of the High Renaissance was its marvelous *counterpoint*, the smooth and complex interweaving of several melodies into a unified, organic whole. In contrast, the most distinctive feature of the new music of the early baroque was the declamatory style, a technique that might use chordal declamation by several singers or a sung recitation by a soloist to a harmonic accompaniment, a device named recitativo or *recitative*. (See examples on following page.)

Although a straightforward declamation of text is the most obvious feature of these works to the musical layman, most musicians identify the new baroque style by its harmonic characteristics. The counterpoint of Renaissance music was clothed by *modal* sonorities—the distinctive scales or *modes* of the melodies and the coincidental blending of the various musical parts sounding simultaneously. Baroque music was produced within a new system of tonal harmonies, music that was composed with chords and chord relationships in mind. Regardless of what individual lines in a baroque composition might do, a progression of chord changes leads the ear from beginning to end, from level to level, forming the basic framework of the piece. *Harmonic* organization forms the basis of music from this period and, in fact, of all European music from the seventeenth through the twentieth centuries. The seventeenth-century composer writing in the new dramatic style notated a melodic line and a bass line, the upper and lower limits of sound for the piece; and he filled in the middle by composing or improvising chords that he indicated with figures over the bass notes. Although this generalization oversimplifies a bit, it serves to illus-

ORAZIO VECCHI

L'Amfiparnaso

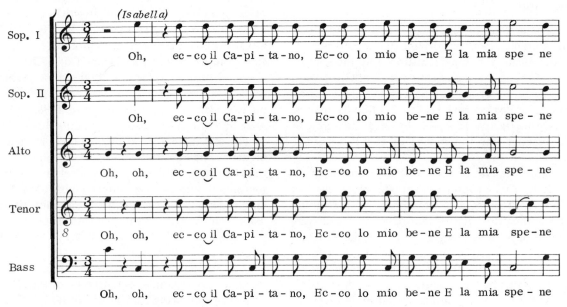

(Trans: *Oh, oh! Here is the captain. Here is my loved one and my hope.*)

Chordal declamation.

JACOPO PERI

Euridice

(Trans: *I do not cry, nor do I sigh. O my dear Eurydice.*)

Recitative.

trate an essential element of baroque musical style. This bass part with numbers and signs over the notes was called *continuo, through bass,* or *figured bass.* Since this musical and notation feature was pervasive in baroque music, several music historians have suggested that the period ought to be called after the musical device. Be that as it may, the important fact for our understanding of the music of this period is its shift from melodic to harmonic thinking and its new approach to text setting that signaled a change from one musical style to the next.

The artistic skies of the seventeenth and eighteenth centuries were spangled with musical lights of great magnitude: Monteverdi, Corelli, Alessandro Scarlatti, and Vivaldi in Italy; Domenico Scarlatti in Spain; Rameau, Lully, and Couperin in France; Purcell in England; Schütz, Buxtehude, and (perhaps greatest of all) Johann Sebastian Bach in Germany; and a figure of international fame and travels, George Frideric Handel. He began his career in Germany, traveled and worked in Italy, and eventually emigrated to London. Although this German musician first established his reputation in England as a composer of Italian operas, the masterwork from his pen that has endeared him to the hearts of all English-speaking Christians is his sacred oratorio *Messiah,* a work we will examine later as an example of the culmination of baroque music (containing at the same time new sounds of the classical era).

Baroque and Neoclassical Styles at the Court of Louis XIV

The baroque, as we have seen, was a phenomenon that spread from Italy throughout Europe and manifested itself in diverse ways. No other artistic style is so hard to "pin down"; for in no other style or period is there such disagreement as to definitions and limits. Some would limit the concept *baroque* to the exuberant phase of the arts in the early seventeenth century, maintaining that styles after 1650 are primarily *neoclassical,* that is, espousing the virtues of reason, order, and clarity as found in classical (Greco-Roman) art.

There is no doubt that neoclassical *theories* of art and literature grew to prominence in the mid-seventeenth century, primarily in France. Doctrines advocating the primacy of reason and order over passion and

fantasy had their influence on the production of buildings, paintings, poetry, drama, and music. And yet the very order and symmetry of French art in the late seventeenth century are used in such a way as to give it a kind of grandeur and showiness, at times a dazzling illusion that can only be called baroque.

It was France that created the models for most aspects of Western culture in the late seventeenth century and throughout a good part of the eighteenth. Louis XIV, the most powerful monarch in Europe, unified France not only politically but culturally as well. France under Louis produced a culture with a narrow base, created by and for the aristocracy and upper bourgeoisie, always with a view toward the king (contrast the cultures of ancient Athens, the Middle Ages, and Africa), but one that impressed people from all social classes. This culture was born out of the lifestyle created by the king at his court.

Louis XIV and Absolutism *Absolutism* as a form of government began to take shape under Louis' predecessors, Henry IV and Louis XIII, but Louis XIV made it an unchangeable fact. He managed to transform France's traditionally restless, independent nobles into fawning courtiers eager to catch the smile of their king. As a child, Louis had witnessed the evils that seditious upper classes could inflict on society; now the central aim of his life was to transform these elements into loyal servants of the crown. A master showman, he created around him such an aura of grandeur that he became known as the Great Monarch. The upper nobility were expected to live at court, rather than in their own castles on their own lands. Louis moved his court from the palace of the Louvre in Paris to Versailles, twelve miles outside. There he built up a somewhat insulated world where he could entertain the nobles and keep an eye on them. The bourgeois, eager to buy their way into the nobility and to be presented at court, were not likely to cause any trouble; and the peasants and lower classes were so heavily taxed that they remained in an almost feudal stage of dependence. Louis saw to it that the monarchy became the primary source of privilege and honor in the society so that men would look to him as to the light. The "Sun King" was extolled as the center and source of all power, just as the sun was the center of the universe.

A noble from a once powerful family—not at all pleased with the new absolutism—has left us a sometimes scathing, but nonetheless vivid and penetrating, portrayal of Louis and his court. The memoirs of the duke of Saint-Simon, although written in the last years of the Sun King's reign, are the best record that we have of what went on throughout. Here, for example, is Saint-Simon's account of why Louis built his palace at Versailles and how he lived there. The translation is by Bayle St. John.

LOUIS DE ROUVROY, DUC DE SAINT-SIMON

Versailles

He early showed a disinclination for Paris. The troubles that had taken place there during the minority[1] made him regard the place as dangerous; he wished, too, to render himself venerable by hiding himself from the eyes of the multitude; all these considerations fixed him at St. Germains[2] soon after the death of the Queen, his mother. It was to that place he began to attract the world by fêtes and gallantries, and by making it felt that he wished to be often seen.

His love for Madame de la Vallière,[3] which was at first kept secret, occasioned frequent excursions to Versailles, then a little card castle, which had been built by Louis XIII . . . the King, his son, slept there, so that he might be more in private with his mistress, pleasures unknown to the hero and just man, worthy son of Saint Louis, who built the little château.

These excursions of Louis XIV by degrees gave birth to those immense buildings he erected at Versailles; and their convenience for a numerous court, so different from the apartments at St. Germains, led him to take up his abode there entirely shortly after the death of the Queen. He built an infinite number of apartments, which were asked for by those who wished to pay their court to him; whereas at St. Germains nearly everybody was obliged to lodge in the town, and the few who found accommodation at the château were strangely inconvenienced.

The frequent fêtes, the private promenades at Versailles, the journeys, were means on which the King seized in order to distinguish or mortify the courtiers, and thus render them more assiduous in pleasing him. He felt that of real favours he had not enough to bestow; in order to keep up the spirit of devotion, he therefore unceasingly invented all sorts of ideal ones, little preferences and petty distinctions, which answered his purpose as well.

He was exceedingly jealous of the attention paid him. Not only did he notice the presence of the most distinguished courtiers, but those of inferior degree also. He looked to the right and to the left, not only upon rising but upon going to bed, at his meals, in passing through his apartments, or his gardens of Versailles, where alone the courtiers were allowed to follow him; he saw and noticed everybody; not one escaped him, not even those who hoped to remain unnoticed. He marked well all absentees from the court, found out the reason of their absence, and never lost an opportunity of acting towards them as the occasion might seem to justify. With some of the courtiers (the most distinguished), it was a demerit not to make the court their ordinary abode; with others 'twas a fault to come but rarely; for those who never or scarcely ever came it was certain disgrace. When their names were in any way mentioned, "I do not know them," the King would reply haughtily. Those who presented themselves but seldom were thus characterised: "They are people I never see;" these decrees were irrevocable. He could not bear people who liked Paris.

Every action of the day at court was performed with such ceremony and ritual that life must have seemed like a continuous formal ballet. Courtiers were present and assisted at *le lever du roi* and *le coucher du roi*, the king's getting up in the morning and going to bed at night. (The same words in French are used for the rising and setting of the sun.) Here is Saint-Simon's description of the king's rising:

Le Lever du Roi

At eight o'clock the chief valet de chambre on duty, who alone had slept in the royal chamber, and who had dressed himself, awoke the King. The chief physician,

---

[1] The "Fronde," a revolt of nobles against the power of the king.
[2] Another palace outside of Paris.
[3] Louis XIV's first mistress.

the chief surgeon, and the nurse (as long as she lived), entered at the same time. The latter kissed the King; the others rubbed and often changed his shirt, because he was in the habit of sweating a great deal. At the quarter, the grand chamberlain was called (or, in his absence, the first gentleman of the chamber), and those who had, what was called the *grandes entrées*. The chamberlain (or chief gentleman) drew back the curtains which had been closed again, and presented the holy water from the vase, at the head of the bed. These gentlemen stayed but a moment, and that was the time to speak to the King, if any one had anything to ask of him; in which case the rest stood aside. When, contrary to custom, nobody had aught to say, they were there but for a few moments. He who had opened the curtains and presented the holy water, presented also a prayer-book. Then all passed into the cabinet of the council. A very short religious service being over, the King called, they re-entered. The same officer gave him his dressing-gown; immediately after, other privileged courtiers entered, and then everybody, in time to find the King putting on his shoes and stockings, for he did almost everything himself and with address and grace. Every other day we saw him shave himself; and he had a little short wig in which he always appeared, even in bed, and on medicine days. He often spoke of the chase, and sometimes said a word to somebody. No toilette table was near him; he had simply a mirror held before him.

As soon as he was dressed, he prayed to God, at the side of his bed, where all the clergy present knelt, the cardinals without cushions, all the laity remaining standing; and the captain of the guards came to the balustrade during the prayer, after which the King passed into his cabinet.

It may well be argued that the court of Louis XIV represents an overcivilized society. Form often took precedence over content: it was extremely important to know, for example, when to tip your hat (and to whom) and what kind of bow or curtsey to make (and when). Rarely did a courtier say what he or she really thought; yet external forms, like dancing, could sometimes reveal the inner person. It was absolutely essential to know how to dance well—the king himself was an excellent dancer. Dancing could conceal a great deal, but it could also expose a character. In this pas-

sage the high value that the courtiers place on dancing succeeds in exposing pretentiousness in one of them.

On Dancing

On Mardi Gras, there was a grand toilette of the Duchesse de Chartres, to which the King and all the Court came; and in the evening a grand ball, similar to that which had just taken place, except that the new Duchesse de Chartres was led out by the Duc de Bourgogne. Every one wore the same dress, and had the same partner as before.

I cannot pass over in silence a very ridiculous adventure which occurred at both of these balls. A son of Montbron, no more made to dance at Court than his father was to be chevalier of the order (to which, however, he was promoted in 1688), was among the company. He had been asked if he danced well; and he had replied with a confidence which made every one hope that the contrary was the case. Every one was satisfied. From the very first bow, he became confused, and he lost step at once. He tried to divert attention from his mistake by affected attitudes, and carrying his arms high; but this made him only more ridiculous, and excited bursts of laughter, which, in despite of the respect due to the person of the King (who likewise had great difficulty to hinder himself from laughing), degenerated at length into regular hooting. On the morrow, instead of flying the Court or holding his tongue, he excused himself by saying that the presence of the King had disconcerted him, and promised marvels for the ball which was to follow. He was one of my friends, and I felt for him. I should even have warned him against a second attempt, if the very different success I had met with had not made me fear that my advice would be taken in ill part. As soon as he began to dance at the second ball, those who were near stood up, those who were far off climbed wherever they could to get a sight; and the shouts of laughter were mingled with clapping of hands. Every one, even the King himself, laughed heartily, and most of us quite loud, so that I do not think any one was ever treated so before. Montbron disappeared immediately afterwards, and did not show himself again for a long time. It was a pity he exposed himself to this defeat, for he was an honourable and brave man.

Dancing became both a prime social pastime and a high art form under Louis XIV, and we will return to it. Let us examine now the framework in which this lifestyle was created: the palace at Versailles.

Versailles

The art and architecture of Versailles provided the setting for the spectacle of the monarchy of Louis XIV. It remains as the example of a place designed and refined to enhance the ideal of kingship and power.

The transformation of the medieval castle, secure from attack with its high walls and battlements, into an open palace tells the story of the transformation from a feudal way of life to the ascendancy of one ruler. When the court had an urban location, the rich and powerful built in the city. By the sixteenth century, however, in both Italy and France wealthy nobility and gentry had begun to build splendid country houses. In Italy the Venetian architect Palladio was the greatest designer of this type of residence (Fig. 20-10). In France sixteenth-century palatial architecture tended to grow from the local traditions with some influence from Renaissance Italy.

By the early seventeenth century the great country house, the château, had become a magnificent retreat for the summer; for hunting, games, and entertainments; and for escape from life at the royal court. Louis XIII and his ministers had established a pattern that Louis XIV accepted and transformed. Vaux-le-Vicomte (1657–1661), built by Le Vau for one of Louis' ministers, was the most splendid and sumptuous of these residences (Fig. 20-11). With this (and the beautiful Louise de la Vallière) in mind, Louis XIV decided to enlarge the small hunting lodge at Versailles that had served Louis XIII. This extravaganza is based on the adaptation of the architectural language of Rome and the Renaissance.

The palace of Versailles was begun in 1669 by Le Vau, who incorporated the old brick and stone lodge

20–10 Above. Palladio, Villa Rotunda, Vicenza. (Alinari/Editorial Photocolor Archives)

20–11 Right. Villa Vaux-le-Vicomte, Le Vau. (Giraudon, Paris)

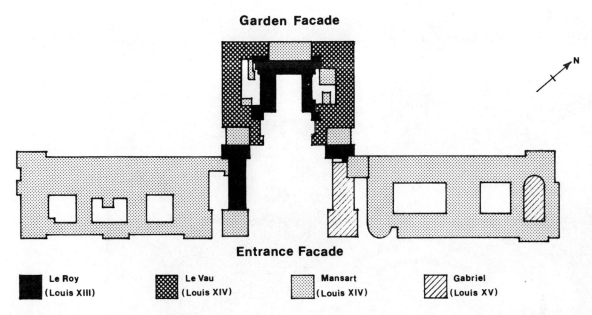

Garden Facade

Entrance Facade

| Le Roy (Louis XIII) | Le Vau (Louis XIV) | Mansart (Louis XIV) | Gabriel (Louis XV) |

20–12 Versailles (plan)

into the new designs. Originally the building was a three-sided rectangle with the chief entrance on the east and the garden façade on the west with its courtyard (Fig. 20-12). Le Vau extended the wings east to create a courtyard on the entrance side; on the west garden façade he encased the building in the same pale, warm marble of the other sides, centering the courtyard with a six-columned portico and the ends of the flanking wings with smaller porticoes with paired columns. When Le Vau died in 1670, he was replaced by Jules Hardouin Mansart. It was Mansart who gave the palace its present scale.

On the east side Mansart focused attention on the entrance by the convergence of three great avenues (Fig. 20-13). In the angles were the horseshoe-shaped stables. He also added the long flanking wings that run north and south. On the garden façade (Fig. 20-14) Mansart joined the wings with the Hall of Mirrors, and the façade became an unbroken expanse, punctuated by a central portico, like the original one.

As the garden façade was meant as the principal view, it is appropriate to examine it more closely. The ground floor has a deep substantial base and round arches for the windows. The masonry is fairly smooth, but deep grooves run parallel to the ground and break to create the *voussoirs*. The only other decoration is on the *keystones* of the arches; each has the relief of a head; the sequence depicts the ages of man. On the next level, which is slightly taller than the first, the arched windows are repeated and are separated by Ionic *pilasters* on bases that support the *entablature*. Each window is also framed by other pilasters and a profiled molding with decorative keystone. The central portico and those on either side have Ionic columns and free-standing sculpture above the entablature. The masonry is smooth, the joints filled even with the surface. The third, attic story is lower in height; its rectangular windows with simple molding, pilaster, and balustrade with urns and sculpture act as a *cornice*, weighing down the whole flat-roofed block. All the details are familiar from the Greek, Roman, and Renaissance vocabularies. Their elaborate combination gives

20–13   Versailles, aerial view. (French Government Tourist Office)

the wall rhythm and interest but only begins to suggest the complexity of weight, load, and plan that lies behind. In its strict continuity and order it also disguises scale. It is difficult to know how big it is, how tall, wide, or long. One cannot easily relate to the building, which is even more impressive as one walks around the palace. The exterior detailing is essentially continuous, and if one walks from long end to end, the distance is some six hundred yards or six football fields. From his bedroom on the east, facing the rising sun, the Sun King had an unimpeded view of three miles.

Begun with the work on the palace, the gardens were designed as its setting. André Le Notre, their designer, combined plantings, ponds, canals, fountains, and falls to enhance and repeat the symmetry and order of the palace. The long tree-lined or hedged walks and the intricately planted beds of brilliantly colored flowers provided the vistas, reflections, and light of outdoor rooms. Everywhere the court's formality was recalled in the total subjugation of nature to order and design, a formality that showed absolute control. Everywhere the Sun King's magnificence was proclaimed. The garden

façade faced two great fountains: one featured the ancestors of Apollo; the other, on axis with the Hall of Mirrors and the long canal, was dedicated to Apollo himself, the god of light and sun (Fig. 20-15).

The Hall of Mirrors, which fills the central block of the west side, was the gathering place for the court and the site for balls and other performances (Fig. 20-16). Its great windows drew light from the expansive open vistas, and its mirrors reflected that light. At night, filled with candles, it glittered icily. On either end of this opulent vast room are the Salons of War and Peace. The ceilings and walls are decorated with allegorical paintings celebrating the deeds of Louis XIV. Le Brun, chief painter to the king, was responsible for this and for all the interior decoration. The paintings themselves, executed by swarms of assistants, are a bit mechanical and cold. Rather the rich marble paneled walls, inlaid floors, and gilded pilasters and moldings attract our attention.

The Royal Chapel, added by Hardouin-Mansart between 1689 and 1710, gives us another experience of the palace (Fig. 20-17). Already the Sun King's power

20–14   Above. Versailles, garden façade. (Lauros-Giraudon, Paris)

20–15   Below. Versailles, Fountain of Apollo. (Giraudon, Paris)

20–16   Right. Versailles, Hall of Mirrors. (Giraudon, Paris)

20–17 Versailles, Royal Chapel. (Lauros-Giraudon, Paris)

blue, gold, and ermine robes of state almost obscure the Sun King.

The overwhelming feeling at Versailles is domination: domination by order, symmetry, balance, and repetition; domination achieved by forcing grass, flowers, hedges, and trees into intricate patterns and by channeling water into pools, fountains, and falls, subduing nature itself to Louis' ego. This architectural complex created by the classical vocabulary contradicts the intent of the vocabulary by its vast scale and its disregard for restraint and simplicity. In a similar way there is a conflict in our response to Versailles. It vacillates between respect for, and delight in, the intricate workmanship and a kind of horrified awe at the vast scale and richness, at this complex produced at great expense to the people of France. We sense that the glittering spectacle could not endure or be endured. Art and architecture had to become more and more accessible and essential to the rising bourgeoisie.

was waning; battles were lost, treasure spent. In his old age, when religion became more important, Louis abandoned all building, except for this light, very beautiful chapel. Its great height (lower floor for the court, gallery level for royalty) recalls the Gothic style, though the architectural members and details have their origin in antiquity and the Renaissance. Compare this with Brunelleschi's interior at San Lorenzo. (See Chapter 10 in Volume I.) What are the most significant departures from his ideals? Compare this with the Cornaro chapel.

The marble, gilded, painted, and paneled rooms of Versailles echoed with the feet of courtiers, ambassadors, and kings of France until the French revolution, but no one was truly accommodated except Louis XIV. This portrait bust by Bernini shows him shortly after his ascension (Fig. 20-18). The sensuous hair and mouth, the sharp-eyed gravity, the swirling drapery reveal the youthful, virile Sun King. The later portrait by Hyacinthe Rigaud gives us a better idea of the pomp and ceremony that defined the formal court (Fig. 20-19). The face is older, strong but sagging. The sweeping

20–18 Bernini, "Louis XIV." (Versailles—Alinari/Editorial Photocolor Archives)

French Court Ballet and the Origins of Modern Theatrical Dancing

The showy, dramatic qualities of the palace at Versailles were appropriate to the highly theatrical rituals constituting life at court. Central to this life were the great festivals given in the gardens and halls at Versailles, where the nobles staged their own shows. It is then hardly surprising that in this world theatrical spectacles were the favorite form of entertainment and that the arts of ballet, opera, tragedy, and comedy reached new heights in France under the reign of Louis XIV.

Around the same time that baroque opera was developing in Italy, another new baroque art form was taking shape in France. The *ballet de cour* (court ballet) developed at the French court in the early seventeenth century but had its most splendid age under Louis XIV, who was himself an excellent dancer and took the starring role in a number of performances. The court ballet, though a short-lived art form, is nonetheless a crucial one because it is one of the important roots of both our social and our theatrical dancing. It demonstrates not only another facet of seventeenth-century art but also of something of the nature of dance itself.

Why do people dance? The urge springs from the same desire to express that motivates the other arts, but the medium is the most accessible—the human body. Dancing is in a sense "body language." We have all felt the need to express fear, sorrow, anger, love, and joy with gesture and with movement. This kind of expression is both preverbal and postverbal—one can express an emotion in movement before it can be put into words and also gesture feelings beyond the limits of words. Yet no real dancing is simply an acting out of feelings. It is related to body language as poetry is to conversation; that is, it is more concentrated and more stylized.

We have seen something of the function of dance and its relation to the other arts in the cultures studied in Volume I. Dancing in ancient Greece served a ceremonial or religious function that was incorporated into tragedy and comedy at the festival of Dionysus. King David, according to the Bible, "danced before the Lord," and dance enhanced medieval Christianity in religious dramas such as *The Play of Daniel*. It is certain, too, that medieval Europeans had secular folk

20–19 Rigaud, "Portrait of Louis XIV." (Louvre, Paris—Alinari/Editorial Photocolor Archives)

dances to celebrate festivities such as harvest time. During the Renaissance, dance became less religious in function but remained linked with ceremony and festival, as Lorenzo de' Medici's carnivals show. Nearly all African cultures place great value on dance, which remains a highly developed art form in modern Africa. We saw in the African section of Volume I how dance in Africa influences all the arts and how dance expresses dramatic and religious feeling in ceremonies such as the Gelede. While all of these cultures have had a direct or indirect impact on the way that we dance today, it is in seventeenth-century Europe that we find the origins of stage dancing as we know it.

Court ballet, the first theatrical dancing, evolved from court dances, many of which were themselves influenced by folk dances. Court dancing as a form of entertainment probably began in Italy. Manuals by dancing masters published in the fifteenth and sixteenth centuries make it clear that dancing was considered an essential social grace for courtiers. Since the young nobles spent so much of their time learning to dance well, there was little need to hire professional dancers for entertainment. Nobles entertained each other with "dinner ballets"—great feasts of several courses with a dance between each course. Balls became popular in all the courts of Europe, and nobles raged to learn the latest dances from Italy. A few, like "La Volta," scandalous to many because the gentleman lifted his lady in the air (but nonetheless danced by Queen Elizabeth), were couple dances (Fig. 20-20). Most, however, were dances for couples in large groups, intended to be danced as processions or in circles, lines, or other formations.

When Catherine de' Medici, great-granddaughter of Lorenzo, became queen of France through her marriage to Henry II, she brought many aspects of Italian culture to her new country. She was especially fond of dancing and feasts. Dancing masters at Catherine's court discovered that they could make dancers move in geometric patterns; they also experimented with imitative dances that mimed dramatic actions. As musicians, poets, and stage designers worked with dancing masters, the lavish spectacles known as court ballets were born.

Histories of theatrical dancing often open with *The Comic Ballet of the Queen*, a spectacle staged by Catherine's dancing master, Balthasar de Beaujoyeulx, at the Salle Bourbon in the Louvre palace in 1581. Like an all-star gala, it lasted from ten in the evening until three in the morning. It included drama, music, poetry, extravagant costumes, and an elaborate baroque stage set, as well as dance. The ballet had a mythological subject but a political purpose: it was intended to impress upon the French people the triumph of reason and order (in the person of the king) over chaos and disorder. This and most of the court ballets following it were,

20–20 Lord de l'Isle, "Queen Elizabeth I Dancing 'La Volta'." (By permission of Viscount De L'Isle, VC, KG, from his collection at Penhurst Place, Kent, England)

like the palace at Versailles, excellent examples of the adoption of the French baroque style to the ideal of absolutism.

The theme of order and harmony that appears in many of the ballets was not, however, a mere political expedient. Dancing masters (or *choreographers*, as they came to be called) made high theoretical claims for their art, as Leonardo had done for painting. Dance, which united all the arts in the court ballet, was said to establish harmony among them. It reflected not only the unity of the arts but the grand design of nature as well. One choreographer concluded: "The Author of the Universe is the greatest Master of ballet."

The court ballet continued to grow in appeal throughout the seventeenth century. The prime minister under Louis XIII and XIV, Cardinal Mazarin, used this popularity for political purposes by impressing on the court the royal authority of the young Louis XIV through his performances. At the age of fifteen, Louis made his most celebrated appearance in the role of Apollo, the sun god, in *The Royal Ballet of Night* (1653). This is a typical piece of baroque theater in its mixtures of tones and genres, its extravagant scenery and costumes, its use of machines and surprises, and its ballet within a ballet, similar to a play within a play. The *entrées* (the term comes from the dinner ballet) included serious mythology, magical allegory, court dances, and comic and burlesque characters. A loose plot concerned with the events of a night holds it together. In the end the political purpose is manifest, for Louis appears to dance as the rising sun while the cast sings the glories of his realm. His title of Sun King derived from this role and the splendid costume that he wore (Fig. 20-21) while playing it.

As he grew to maturity, Louis continued both to dance himself and to encourage the production of more ballets. He was also an accomplished guitar player and fond of poetry and drama, but dance was his favorite of the arts. His dancing master was Pierre Beauchamps; his court musician the former Florentine, Jean-Baptiste Lully. They collaborated on some opera-ballets, but eventually these two arts separated. In 1661 Louis founded the Royal Academy of Dance and in 1669 the Royal Academy of Music, which became the Paris Opera. The dance academy was primarily for noble amateurs, but in 1672 Louis founded a school to

20–21   Louis XIV as the Sun King in the "Ballet de la Nuit." (Bibliothèque Nationale, Paris)

train professional dancers; this date marks the beginning of stage dancing as we know it today. Beauchamps codified the five positions and other steps still taught in ballet classes. Dance in the ballroom and dance in the theater from then on went their separate ways.

Beauchamps and Lully did collaborate with the actor-director-playwright Molière in another type of production that flourished at the end of the century. The "comedy-ballet," of which we will read an example, *The Would-Be Gentleman*, represented a more impressive unity of the arts than did the court ballet. Molière, as we will see, is justly considered the father of modern comedy. To understand this art form, we must know something about drama in seventeenth-century France.

21

FRENCH THEATER UNDER THE REIGN OF THE SUN KING: MOLIÈRE AND LULLY

The late seventeenth century is generally considered the great age of French drama, termed by French historians *classical* or *neoclassical* as opposed to the *baroque* plays of the early part of the century. Certainly the earlier plays, which resemble court ballets in their mixture of genres (tragedy, comedy, pastoral, and so on), their extravagant and complicated plots, and their sheer length, have little to do with the aesthetic we call classical. Yet we have seen in examples from painting and architecture how aspects of neoclassicism may be incorporated into the concept baroque; the same case may be made for drama. Classical standards of clarity, order, and harmony can be used to accentuate baroque qualities such as extremes of emotion, extravagance, *grandeur*, and high-flown rhetoric.

Classical Tragedy   Classicism as an aesthetic first appeared in tragedy and in theories of tragedy. Basing their ideas on the Italian humanists' revival and imitations of Greek and Roman tragedy (see Chapter 9 in Volume I), French writers found rules that they believed must be followed in order to produce good tragedy. The rules that they set down became a kind of standard doctrine after they were accepted by the French Academy, founded in 1635. The academy, still in operation today, was charged with putting together theoretical works of importance to the French language: dictionaries, grammars, and treatises on rhetoric and poetics. It became in fact a kind of watchdog over matters of style and usage. Its members standardized the rules for tragedy when they pronounced judgment on the first important tragedy by Pierre Corneille, based on a Spanish work, entitled *The Cid* (1637). The members of the academy found the tragedy basically a good one but lacking in certain points. What were the standards by which they judged?

Most important to the "classical" ideal of tragedy were the so-called three unities: unity of time, place, and action. The tragedy was to take place in no more than twenty-four hours, in the same setting, and was to have only one plot. Related to these three basic unities was unity of tone—tragedy and comedy were not to appear in the same play. The characters of tragedy were to be nobles, kings and queens, who would speak in a dignified manner. No vulgar realism and no violent action could appear on the stage: such events necessary to the plot could be related by a messenger. Also, the events and characters could not be contemporary: they had to be far away either in time or space. In fact, most of the French classical tragedies were based on Greek or Roman history or mythology. And yet, the plots were to follow the rule of *verisimilitude*. They were not to be fantasies but to seem as if they could actually happen.

One can see how these rules might be applied to a Greek tragedy such as *Oedipus Rex*, but the French were in fact stricter than the Athenians; many Greek tragedies do not fit these standards. Certainly every play by Shakespeare would fail the French Academy's test. It is hard for us to understand now how such strict rules could be effectively applied to art; but French classicism did produce two great tragedians: Pierre Corneille (1606–1684), who admittedly did have some trouble with the rules; and Jean Racine (1639–1699), whose pure, compressed works seem to have benefited by the limits imposed on them. The grandeur and magnificence characteristic of all the art in the era of Louis XIV is evident in the tragedies of these two writers.

Corneille and Racine were (and are) considered by many to be the glories of their age; but when the influential literary critic Boileau was asked by Louis XIV to name the greatest contemporary writer, he replied, "Molière, Sire." Most people today would concur with that judgment, for while the two tragedians seem particularly French, the comedy writer Molière is universal. Yet Molière, too, was obliged to write in conformity with the standards of his day and, especially, for the pleasure of the king.

Molière

Jean-Baptiste Poquelin, who later assumed the stage name of Molière, was born to a solidly bourgeois Parisian family in 1622. After receiving a good education, he abandoned a possible career in law to pursue two passions—the theater and the actress Madeleine Béjart. Molière and Mlle. Béjart together founded a company of actors, the *Illustre Théâtre*, in 1643. During the years in which the company toured France, Molière gained valuable experience as an actor, director, and manager. He also wrote and produced two of his own comedies, heavily influenced by the Italian *commedia dell'arte*, with its improvisations on stock characters, which he often saw during his travels. Like Shakespeare, Molière was not just a writer but a complete man of the theater.

The great breakthrough for the *Illustre Théâtre* came when the company pleased the king, performing before him at the Louvre. Louis then offered them a theater to play in, the Petit Bourbon, which they were to share with an Italian company. From then on, Molière turned more seriously to writing, though he continued to act in his own comedies throughout his lifetime (in fact, he died during a performance). Continuing to enjoy the protection and interest of the king, Molière staged his comedies not only at the Louvre but also at the palace at Versailles and at other castles. He thus became intimately involved in the atmosphere of festiv-

ity surrounding the court of Louis XIV, but his comedies reached a much wider audience. Common people,
as well as bourgeois and nobles, attended them with
great enthusiasm when they played in Paris. Molière
was accused by certain purists of catering to the vulgar
element of the audience, but it is exactly his wide human experience and his refusal to become too refined
that helped to make him a great writer of comedy.

Molière's comedies range from rather gross farces,
based on the stock character of the ridiculous dupe and
almost slapstick effects, to subtle analyses of human
character that are close to serious drama. Although he
was indirectly rather than directly influenced by the
Greeks, one can find elements of both "old comedy"
and "new comedy" in his works. His greatest originality lay in his ability to observe keenly the society and
the people around him and to create from them characters both of their time and for all times and places. On
the whole, his comedies observe the classical three
unities originally laid down for tragedy, as well as other
classical canons such as simplicity and verisimilitude,
yet Molière did not hesitate to deviate from the rules
when it suited his purposes. The only really important
rule, he maintained, was to *please*. The audience, not
the theoreticians, were the best judges. It was necessary, too, to please the king. Luckily, Louis was not a
man of narrow tastes.

One of Molière's greatest comedies was written for a
great festival at Versailles called "The Pleasures of the
Enchanted Island" (Fig. 21-1) in 1664. The title character of the play, *Tartuffe*, is a religious hypocrite, and its
proposed moral clearly favors good common sense
against fanaticism. The play so shocked the religious
elements of the court that the archbishop used his influence to persuade Louis to ban it; not until five years
later was Molière free to produce it. Another of his
most admired plays, *The Misanthrope*, is about a man
who hates the pretensions and superficiality of upper-
class society but is in love with a girl who accepts them
fully. Both of these plays are centered around a complex character and are satirical studies of human life in
society.

21-1 Staging for an outdoor
ballet at Versailles, "Alcina's
Island." (Crown copyright.
Victoria and Albert
Museum, London)

Le Bourgeois Gentilhomme, translated here as *The Would-Be Gentleman*, is not Molière's most complex or most literary play, but it remains a favorite on stage. The king himself suggested part of the subject of this spectacle, created for festivities at the royal hunting castle at Chambord in 1670. The preceding year Louis had established diplomatic relations with the Ottoman empire, receiving an ambassador from the Grand Turk Suleiman. This exotic embassy had so impressed the French court that Louis wanted a spectacle with a Turkish ceremony in it. He left the assignment and the actual planning to the musician Lully, the dancing master Beauchamps, and the comedian Molière.

The three had collaborated before on "comedy-ballets," but this was their most successful production. At first glance it seems an unlikely combination: what has the gross realism of comedy to do with the courtly and imaginary world of ballet? And yet it is just this contrast between solid reality and make-believe that is the subject of the comedy-ballet. As usual, Molière's comedy is centered around a character through whom he depicts a whole society. Monsieur Jourdain, the main figure here, comes from the most everyday "prosaic" milieu possible, the Parisian bourgeoisie. He is the very type of the self-made man—obviously shrewd and practical enough to have made himself a great deal of money. And yet this solid merchant is a man with a dream: he senses that there is a world of ideas, art, culture, and refinement out beyond his experience, and he longs to enter into it. For him, the dream world is summed up by one word, *gentleman*, which at that time meant a member of a particular social class, the nobility. The gentlemen are those with titles, taste, fine clothes, fine educations, and exquisite ladies—and Monsieur Jourdain feels that he now has the money to buy all these things. But Jourdain is also a man with very common human defects: pretentiousness, vanity, and egotism. These qualities receive the full force of Molière's satire; yet many readers and spectators feel a great deal of sympathy for this man with a dream. The dream world itself (as seen by Molière and the spectator, not by Jourdain) is hardly admirable: Molière's satiric comedy hits the cynicism and complacency of the petty nobility and the foppery of the artists and teachers as hard as it hits the bourgeois. (Naturally the king and the powerful nobles around him, Molière's pa-trons, are not attacked!) The only people with good sense, bourgeois and servants, are rather limited as characters.

The comedy-ballet combination admirably demonstrates the two realms of real world/dream world. At the end of the first act the music master and dance master put on a show that represents the world of culture to which Jourdain aspires. At the end of the second act the tailors who have brought the bourgeois "dream" clothes perform a dance. Song and dance accompany the dinner that Jourdain gives for his dream lady, the marquise, at the end of Act III. The "Turkish" ceremony at the end of Act IV brings Jourdain, now a complete dupe, into a fantasy world, and the entire play dissolves into fantasy with the long ballet at the end. It may be argued that the solid, clear, "real-seeming" prose comedy constitutes the classical element of the play and the fantasy-ballets its baroque element. This version is from the English translation published by John Watts, London, in 1739.

MOLIÈRE

The Would-Be Gentleman

CHARACTERS

M. JOURDAIN, *a self-made man*
MME JOURDAIN, *his wife*
LUCILE, *their daughter*
NICOLE, *their maid*
CLÉONTE, *a suitor to Lucile*
COVIELLE, *his valet, suitor to Nicole*
DORANTE, *a courtier*
DORIMÈNE, *a marchioness, widowed*
MUSIC MASTER AND PUPIL
DANCING MASTER
FENCING MASTER
PHILOSOPHY MASTER
MASTER TAILOR
JOURNEYMAN TAILORS
SINGERS AND MUSICIANS
PAGES AND LACKEYS

ACT I

THE SCENE. *Music Master, a Pupil of the Music Master (composing at a table in the middle of the stage), a Woman Singer, and two Men Singers; a Dancing Master and Dancers*

MUSIC MASTER (*to the musicians*)   Here, step into this hall, and sit there till he comes.

DANCING MASTER (*to the dancers*)   And you too, on this side.

MUSIC MASTER (*to his pupil*)   Is it done?

PUPIL   Yes.

MUSIC MASTER   Let's see. . . . 'Tis mighty well.

DANCING MASTER   Is it anything new?

MUSIC MASTER   Yes, 'tis an air for a serenade, which I set him to compose here while we wait till our gentleman's awake.

DANCING MASTER   May one see what it is?

MUSIC MASTER   You will hear it, with the dialogue, when he comes. He won't be long.

DANCING MASTER   We have no want of business, either of us, at present.

MUSIC MASTER   'Tis true. We have found a man here, just such a one as we both of us want. This same Monsieur Jourdain is a sweet income, with his visions of nobility and gallantry which he has got into his noddle, and it would be well for your capers and my crotchets, were all the world like him.

DANCING MASTER   Not altogether so well; I wish, for his sake, that he were better skilled than he is in the things we give him.

MUSIC MASTER   It is true he understands 'em ill, but he pays for 'em well. And that's what our art has more need of at present than of anything else.

DANCING MASTER   For my part, I own it to you, I regale a little upon glory. I am sensible of applause, and think it a very grievous punishment in the liberal arts to display one's self to fools and to expose our compositions to the barbarous judgment of the stupid. Talk no more of it, there is a pleasure in working for persons who are capable of relishing the delicacies of an art, who know how to give a kind reception to the beauties of a work, and, by titillating approbation, regale you for your labour. Yes, the most agreeable recompense one can receive for the things one does is to see them understood, to see 'em caressed with an applause that does you honour. There's nothing, in my opinion, which pays us better than this for all our fatigues. And the praises of connoisseurs give an exquisite delight.

MUSIC MASTER   I grant it, and I relish them as well as you. There is nothing certainly that tickles more than the applause you speak of, but one cannot live upon this incense. Sheer praises won't make a man easy. There must be something solid mixed withal, and the best method of praising is to praise with the open hand. This indeed is one whose understanding is very shallow, who speaks of everything awry, and cross of the grain, and never applauds but in contradiction to sense. But his money sets his judgment right. He has discernment in his purse. His praises are current coin; and this ignorant commoner is more worth to us, as you see, than that grand witty lord who introduced us here.

DANCING MASTER   There's something of truth in what you say; but I find you lean a little too much towards the pelf. And mere interest is something so base that an honest man should never discover an attachment to it.

MUSIC MASTER   For all that, you decently receive the money our spark gives you.

DANCING MASTER   Certainly; but I don't place all my happiness in that: and I wish that, with his fortune, he had also some good taste of things.

MUSIC MASTER   I wish the same; 'tis what we both labour at as much as we can. But, however, he gives us the opportunity of making ourselves known in the world; and he'll pay for others what others praise for him.

DANCING MASTER   Here he comes.

(*Enter* M. JOURDAIN *in a nightgown and cap, and two* LACKEYS)

M. JOURDAIN   Well, gentlemen? What have you there? Will you let me see your little drollery?

DANCING MASTER   How? What little drollery?

M. JOURDAIN   Why the—how do you call that thing? your prologue, or dialogue of songs and dancing.

DANCING MASTER   Ha, ha!

MUSIC MASTER   You see we are ready.

M. JOURDAIN   I have made you wait a little, but 'tis because I am to be dressed out to-day like your people of quality;[1] and my hosier has sent me a pair

---

[1] Jourdain's concern with dress is representative of the importance that he now gives to *appearance*. He judges something to be good or bad according to whether "people of quality" (the nobility) appear to have it or not.

of silk stockings which I thought I should never have got on.

MUSIC MASTER   We are here only to wait your leisure.

M. JOURDAIN   I desire you'll both stay till they have brought me my clothes, that you may see me.

DANCING MASTER   As you please.

M. JOURDAIN   You shall see me most exactly equipped from head to foot.

MUSIC MASTER   We don't doubt it.

M. JOURDAIN   I have had this Indian thing made up for me.

DANCING MASTER   'Tis very handsome.

M. JOURDAIN   My tailor tells me that people of quality go thus in a morning.

MUSIC MASTER   It fits you to a miracle.

M. JOURDAIN   Why, ho! Fellow there! both my fellows!

FIRST LACKEY   Your pleasure, sir?

M. JOURDAIN   Nothing! 'Tis only to try whether you hear me readily. (to the MUSIC and DANCING MASTERS) What say you of my liveries?

DANCING MASTER   They are magnificent.

M. JOURDAIN (half-opens his gown and reveals a tight pair of breeches of scarlet velvet, and a green velvet jacket)   Here again is a kind of dishabille to perform my exercises in a morning.

MUSIC MASTER   'Tis gallant.

M. JOURDAIN   Lackey!

FIRST LACKEY   Sir?

M. JOURDAIN   T'other lackey!

SECOND LACKEY   Sir?

M. JOURDAIN (taking off his gown)   Hold my gown. (to the MUSIC and DANCING MASTERS) Do you like me so?

DANCING MASTER   Mighty well; nothing can be better.

M. JOURDAIN   Now for your affair a little.

MUSIC MASTER   I should be glad first to let you hear an air (pointing to his pupil) he has just composed for the serenade which you gave me orders about. He is one of my pupils, who has an admirable talent for these sort of things.

M. JOURDAIN   Yes, but that should not have been put to a pupil to do; you were not too good for that business yourself.

MUSIC MASTER   You must not let the name of pupil impose upon you, sir. These sort of pupils know as much as the greatest masters, and the air is as good as

can be made. Hear it only.

M. JOURDAIN (to his servants)   Give me my gown that I may hear the better.—Stay, I believe I shall be better without the gown.—No, give it me again, it will do better.

MUSICIAN
I languish night and day, nor sleeps my pain,
Since those fair eyes imposed the rigorous chain;
But tell me, Iris, what dire fate attends
Your enemies, if thus you treat your friends?

M. JOURDAIN   This song seems to me a little upon the dismal; it inclines one to sleep; I should be glad you could enliven it a little here and there.

MUSIC MASTER   'Tis necessary, sir, that the air should be suited to the words.

M. JOURDAIN   I was taught one perfectly pretty some time ago. Stay—um—how is it?

DANCING MASTER   In good troth, I don't know.

M. JOURDAIN   There's lamb in it.

DANCING MASTER   Lamb?

M. JOURDAIN   Yes—Ho!
I thought my dear Namby
  As gentle as fair-o:
I thought my dear Namby
  As mild as a lamb-y:
Oh dear, oh dear, oh dear-o!
For now the sad scold is a thousand times told,
More fierce than a tiger or bear-o.
Isn't it pretty?

MUSIC MASTER   The prettiest in the world.

DANCING MASTER   And you sing it well.

M. JOURDAIN   Yet I never learnt music.

MUSIC MASTER   You ought to learn it, sir, as you do dancing. They are two arts which have a strict connection one with the other.

DANCING MASTER   And which open the human mind to see the beauty of things.

M. JOURDAIN   What, do people of quality learn music too?

MUSIC MASTER   Yes, sir.

M. JOURDAIN   I'll learn it then. But I don't know how I shall find time. For, besides the fencing master who teaches me, I have also got me a philosophy master, who is to begin this morning.

MUSIC MASTER   Philosophy is something; but music, sir, music—

DANCING MASTER   Music and dancing—music and

dancing, that is all that's necessary.

MUSIC MASTER   There's nothing so profitable in a state as music.

DANCING MASTER   There's nothing so necessary for men as dancing.

MUSIC MASTER   A state cannot subsist without music.

DANCING MASTER   Without dancing, a man can do nothing.

MUSIC MASTER   All the disorders, all the wars one sees in the world, happen only from not learning music.

DANCING MASTER   All the disasters of mankind, all the fatal misfortunes that histories are replete with, the blunders of politicians, the miscarriages of great commanders, all this comes from want of skill in dancing.

M. JOURDAIN   How so?

MUSIC MASTER   Does not war proceed from want of concord amongst men?

M. JOURDAIN   That's true.

MUSIC MASTER   And if all men learnt music, would not that be a means of keeping them better in tune, and of seeing universal peace in the world?

M. JOURDAIN   You're in the right.

DANCING MASTER   When a man has been guilty of a defect in his conduct—be it in the affairs of his family, or in the government of the state, or in the command of an army—don't we always say, such a one has made a false step in such an affair?

M. JOURDAIN   Yes, we say so.

DANCING MASTER   And can making a false step proceed from anything but not knowing how to dance?

M. JOURDAIN   'Tis true, and you are both in the right.[2]

DANCING MASTER   This is to let you see the excellence and advantage of dancing and music.

M. JOURDAIN   I now comprehend it.

MUSIC MASTER   Will you see each of our compositions?

M. JOURDAIN   Yes.

MUSIC MASTER   I have told you already that this is a slight essay which I formerly made upon the

different passions that may be expressed by music.

M. JOURDAIN   Very well.

MUSIC MASTER (to the musicians)   Here, come forward. (to M. JOURDAIN) You are to imagine with yourself that they are dressed like shepherds.

M. JOURDAIN   Why always shepherds? One sees nothing but such stuff everywhere.

MUSIC MASTER   When we are to introduce persons as speaking in music, 'tis necessary to probability that we give in to the pastoral way. Singing has always been appropriated to shepherds; and it is by no means natural in dialogue that princes or citizens should sing their passions.

M. JOURDAIN   Be it so, be it so. Let's see.

(Dialogue in music between a Woman and two Men)

WOMAN   *The heart that must tyrannic love obey,*
A thousand fears and cares oppress.
Sweet are those sighs and languishments,
* they say;*
Say what they will for me,
Nought is so sweet as liberty.

FIRST MAN   *Nothing so sweet as love's soft fire,*
Which can two glowing hearts inspire
With the same life, the same desire.
The loveless swain no happiness can
* prove.*
From life take soothing love,
All pleasure you remove.

SECOND MAN   *Sweet were the wanton archer's sway,*
Would all with constancy obey;
But, cruel fate!
No nymph is true:
The faithless sex more worthy of our
* hate,*
To love should bid eternally adieu.

FIRST MAN   *Pleasing heat!*

WOMAN   *Freedom blest!*

SECOND MAN   *Fair deceit!*

FIRST MAN   *O how I love thee!*

WOMAN   *How I approve thee!*

SECOND MAN   *I detest!*

FIRST MAN   *Against love's ardour quit this mortal*
* hate.*

WOMAN   *Shepherd, myself I bind here,*
To show a faithful mate.

SECOND MAN   *Alas! but where to find her?*

---

[2] Molière mocks the pretentiousness of the two teachers here, but beneath the comedy is some serious contemporary thought on the benefits of the arts, with which Molière probably agreed. Jourdain, however, must be convinced by a strictly utilitarian argument that distorts the theory.

WOMAN   *Our glory to retrieve,*
         My heart I here bestow.
SECOND MAN   *But, nymph, can I believe*
              That heart no change will know?
WOMAN   *Let experience decide,*
         Who loves best of the two.
SECOND MAN   *And the perjured side*
              May vengeance pursue.
ALL THREE   *Then let us kindle soft desire,*
             Let us fan the amorous fire.
             Ah! how sweet it is to love,
             When hearts united constant prove!
M. JOURDAIN   Is this all?
MUSIC MASTER   Yes.
M. JOURDAIN   I find 'tis very concise, and there are some little sayings in it pretty enough.
DANCING MASTER   You have here, for my composition, a little essay of the finest movements, and the most beautiful attitudes with which a dance can possibly be varied.
M. JOURDAIN   Are they shepherds too?
DANCING MASTER   They're what you please. *(to the dancers)* Hola!

(Four dancers execute all the different movements and steps that the dancing master commands. This dance constitutes the first "intermission.")

ACT II

THE SCENE.   *Monsieur Jourdain, Music Master, Dancing Master*

M. JOURDAIN   This is none of your stupid things, and these same fellows flutter it away bravely.
MUSIC MASTER   When the dance is mixed with the music, it will have a greater effect still, and you will see something gallant in the little entertainment we have prepared for you.
M. JOURDAIN   That's however for by and by; and the person for whom I have ordered all this, is to do me the honour of dining with me here.
DANCING MASTER   Everything's ready.
MUSIC MASTER   But in short, sir, this is not enough, 'tis necessary such a person as you, who live great and have an inclination to things that are handsome, should have a concert of music at your house every Wednesday, or every Thursday.
M. JOURDAIN   Why so? Have people of quality?
MUSIC MASTER   Yes, sir.
M. JOURDAIN   I'll have one then. Will it be fine?
MUSIC MASTER   Certainly. You must have three voices, a treble, a counter-tenor, and bass, which must be accompanied with a bass-viol, a theorbo-lute, and a harpsichord for the thorough-bass, with two violins to play the symphonies.
M. JOURDAIN   You must add also a trumpet-marine. The trumpet-marine is an instrument that pleases me, and is very harmonious.
MUSIC MASTER   Leave us to manage matters.
M. JOURDAIN   However, don't forget by and by to send the musicians to sing at table.
MUSIC MASTER   You shall have everything you should have.
M. JOURDAIN   But above all, let the entertainment be fine.
MUSIC MASTER   You will be pleased with it, and, amongst other things, with certain minuets you will find in it.
M. JOURDAIN   Ay, the minuets are my dance; and I have a mind you should see me dance 'em. Come, master.
DANCING MASTER   Your hat, sir, if you please.

(M. JOURDAIN takes off his foot-boy's hat, and puts it on over his own nightcap; upon which his master takes him by the hand and makes him dance to a minuet-air which he sings)

Tol, lol, lol, lol, lol, lol,
Tol, lol, lol,
    twice;
Tol, lol, lol; tol, lol.
    In time, if you please,
Tol, lol,
    the right leg.
Tol, lol, lol.
    Don't shake your shoulders so much.
Tol, lol, lol, lol, lol.
    Why, your arms are out of joint.
Tol, lol, lol, lol, lol.
    Hold up your head. Turn out your toes.
Tol, lol, lol.

Your body erect.[1]

M. JOURDAIN   Heh?

MUSIC MASTER   Admirably well performed.

M. JOURDAIN   Now I think of it, teach me how I must bow to salute a marchioness; I shall have occasion for it by and by.

DANCING MASTER   How you must bow to salute a marchioness?

M. JOURDAIN   Yes, a marchioness whose name is Dorimène.

DANCING MASTER   Give me your hand.

M. JOURDAIN   No. You need only to do it, I shall remember it easily.

DANCING MASTER   If you would salute her with a great deal of respect, you must first of all make a bow and fall back, then advancing towards her, bow thrice, and at the last bow down to her very knees.

M. JOURDAIN   Do it a little. *(after the* DANCING MASTER *has made three bows)* Right.

(Enter a LACKEY *holding two foils)*

LACKEY   Sir, your fencing master is here.

M. JOURDAIN   Bid him come in that he may give me a lesson. *(to the* MUSIC *and* DANCING MASTERS*)* I'd have you stay and see me perform.

(Enter a FENCING MASTER*)*

FENCING MASTER *(taking the two foils out of the* LACKEY'S *hand, and giving one to* M. JOURDAIN*)* Come, sir, your salute. Your body straight. A little bearing upon the left thigh. Your legs not so much a-straddle. Your feet both on a line. Your wrist opposite to your hip. The point of your sword over-against your shoulder. Your arm not quite so much extended. Your left hand on a level with your eye. Your left shoulder more square. Hold up your head. Your look bold. Advance. Your body steady. Beat carte, and push carte. One, two. Recover. Again with it, your foot firm. One, two. Leap back. When you make a pass, sir, 'tis necessary your sword should

21–2   Scene from Act I of "Le Bourgeois Gentilhomme" (1951 Comédie Française production) with Louis Seigneur and Jacques Charon. (Photo Lipnitzki-Viollet, Paris)

disengage first, and your body make as small a mark as possible. One, two. Come, beat tierce, and push the same. Advance. Your body firm. Advance. Quit after that manner. One, two. Recover. Repeat the same. One, two. Leap back. Parry, sir, parry.

(The FENCING MASTER *gives him two or three home-thrusts, crying, "Parry")*

M. JOURDAIN   Ugh!

MUSIC MASTER   You do wonders.

FENCING MASTER   I have told you already—the whole secret of arms consists but in two things, in giving and not receiving. And as I showed you t'other day by demonstrative reason, it is impossible you should receive if you know how to turn your adversary's sword from the line of your body; which depends only upon a small motion of your wrist, either inward, or outward.

M. JOURDAIN   At that rate therefore, a man without any courage is sure to kill his man and not to be killed.

FENCING MASTER   Certainly. Don't you see the demonstration of it?

M. JOURDAIN   Yes.

---

[1] The minuet was the favorite social dance at court at this time, and continued to be so throughout the eighteenth century (both George Washington and Thomas Jefferson were very good at it). It is usually done in couples, with a bit of flirtation, and requires a good deal of precision and balance.

FENCING MASTER   By this one may see of what consideration such persons as we should be esteemed in a state, and how highly the science of arms excels all the other useless sciences, such as dancing, music, and—

DANCING MASTER   Soft and fair, Monsieur *Sa, sa.* Don't speak of dancing but with respect.

MUSIC MASTER   Pray learn to treat the excellence of music in a handsomer manner.

FENCING MASTER   You're merry fellows, to pretend to compare your sciences with mine.

MUSIC MASTER   Do but see the importance of the creature!

DANCING MASTER   The droll animal there, with his leathern stomacher!

FENCING MASTER   My little master skipper, I shall make you skip as you should do. And you, my little master scraper, I shall make you sing to some tune.

DANCING MASTER   Monsieur Tick-tack, I shall teach you your trade.

M. JOURDAIN (*to the* DANCING MASTER)   Are you bewitched to quarrel with him, who understands tierce and carte, who knows how to kill a man by demonstrative reason?

DANCING MASTER   I laugh at his demonstrative reason, and his tierce and his carte.

M. JOURDAIN (*to the* DANCING MASTER)   Softly, I say.

FENCING MASTER (*to the* DANCING MASTER)   How? Master Impertinence!

M. JOURDAIN   Nay, my dear fencing master!

DANCING MASTER (*to the* FENCING MASTER)   How? You great dray-horse!

M. JOURDAIN   Nay, my dancing master.

FENCING MASTER   If I lay my—

M. JOURDAIN (*to the* FENCING MASTER)   Gently.

DANCING MASTER   If I lay my clutches on you—

M. JOURDAIN   Easily.

FENCING MASTER   I shall curry you with such an air—

M. JOURDAIN (*to the* FENCING MASTER)   For goodness' sake.

DANCING MASTER   I shall drub you after such a manner—

M. JOURDAIN (*to the* DANCING MASTER)   I beseech you.

MUSIC MASTER   Let us teach him a little how to speak.

M. JOURDAIN (*to the* MUSIC MASTER)   Lack-a-day, be quiet.

(*Enter a* PHILOSOPHY MASTER)

Hola, Monsieur Philosopher, you are come in the nick of time with your philosophy. Come, and make peace a little amongst these people here.

PHILOSOPHY MASTER   What's to do? What's the matter, gentlemen?

M. JOURDAIN   They have put themselves into such a passion about the preference of their professions as to call names, and would come to blows.

PHILOSOPHY MASTER   O fie, gentlemen, what need was there of all this fury? Have you not read the learned treatise upon anger, composed by Seneca? Is there anything more base and shameful than this passion, which makes a savage beast of a man? And should not reason be master of all our commotions?

DANCING MASTER   How, sir? Why he has just now been abusing us both, in despising dancing which is my employment, and music which is his profession.

PHILOSOPHY MASTER   A wise man is above all foul language that can be given him, and the grand answer one should make to all affronts is moderation and patience.

FENCING MASTER   They had both the assurance to compare their professions to mine.

PHILOSOPHY MASTER   Should this disturb you? Men should not dispute about vainglory and rank; that which perfectly distinguishes one from another is wisdom and virtue.

DANCING MASTER   I maintained to him that dancing was a science to which one cannot do sufficient honour.

MUSIC MASTER   And I, that music is one of those that all ages have revered.

FENCING MASTER   And I maintained against 'em both that the science of defence is the finest and most necessary of all sciences.

PHILOSOPHY MASTER   And what becomes of philosophy, then? You are all three very impertinent fellows, methinks, to speak with this arrogance before me; and impudently to give the name of science to things that one ought not to honour even with the name of art, that can't be comprised but under the name of a pitiful trade of gladiator, ballad-singer, and morris-dancer.

FENCING MASTER   Out, ye dog of a philosopher.

MUSIC MASTER   Hence, ye scoundrel of a pedant.

DANCING MASTER   Begone, ye arrant pedagogue.

(The PHILOSOPHER falls upon them, they all three lay him on)

PHILOSOPHY MASTER   How? Varlets as you are—

M. JOURDAIN   Monsieur Philosopher!

PHILOSOPHY MASTER   Infamous dogs! Rogues! Insolent curs!

M. JOURDAIN   Monsieur Philosopher!

FENCING MASTER   Plague on the animal!

M. JOURDAIN   Gentlemen!

PHILOSOPHY MASTER   Impudent villains!

M. JOURDAIN   Monsieur Philosopher!

DANCING MASTER   Deuce take the pack-saddled ass!

M. JOURDAIN   Gentlemen!

PHILOSOPHY MASTER   Profligate vermin!

M. JOURDAIN   Monsieur Philosopher!

MUSIC MASTER   The devil take the impertinent puppy!

M. JOURDAIN   Gentlemen!

PHILOSOPHY MASTER   Knaves! Ragamuffins! Traitors! Impostors!

M. JOURDAIN   Monsieur Philosopher! Gentlemen! Monsieur Philosopher! Gentlemen! Monsieur Philosopher!

(The four MASTERS beat each other out)

Nay, beat your hearts out if you will, I shall neither meddle nor make with you, I shan't spoil my gown to part you. I should be a great fool to thrust myself among them, and receive some blow that might do me a mischief.[2]

(Enter the PHILOSOPHY MASTER)

PHILOSOPHY MASTER (setting his band right)   Now to our lesson.

M. JOURDAIN   Ah! Sir, I'm sorry for the blows they have given you.

PHILOSOPHY MASTER   'Tis nothing at all. A philosopher knows how to receive things in a proper manner; and I'll compose a satire against 'em, in the manner of Juvenal, that shall cut 'em most gloriously. Let that pass. What have you a mind to learn?

M. JOURDAIN   Everything I can, for I have all the desire in the world to be a scholar, and it vexes me that my father and mother had not made me study all the sciences when I was young.

PHILOSOPHY MASTER   'Tis a very reasonable sentiment. Nam, sine doctrinâ vita est quasi mortis imago. You understand that, and are acquainted with Latin, without doubt?

M. JOURDAIN   Yes; but act as if I were not acquainted with it. Explain me the meaning of that.

PHILOSOPHY MASTER   The meaning of it is, that without learning, life is as it were an image of death.[3]

M. JOURDAIN   That same Latin's in the right.

PHILOSOPHY MASTER   Have you not some principles, some rudiments of science?

M. JOURDAIN   Oh! yes, I can read and write.

PHILOSOPHY MASTER   Where would you please to have us begin? Would you have me teach you logic?

M. JOURDAIN   What may that same logic be?

PHILOSOPHY MASTER   It's that which teaches us the three operations of the mind.

M. JOURDAIN   What are those three operations of the mind?

PHILOSOPHY MASTER   The first, the second, and the third. The first is to conceive well, by means of universals. The second, to judge well, by means of categories. The third, to draw the conclusion right, by means of figures: Barbara, Celarent, Darii, Ferio, Baralipton, etc.

M. JOURDAIN   These words are too crabbed. This logic does not suit me by any means. Let's learn something else that's prettier.

PHILOSOPHY MASTER   Will you learn morality?

M. JOURDAIN   Morality?

PHILOSOPHY MASTER   Yes.

M. JOURDAIN   What means morality?

PHILOSOPHY MASTER   It treats of happiness, teaches men to moderate their passions, and—

---

[2] Jourdain here shows solid middle-class sense, opposed to his "masters." How does each defend his art? Is there anything serious beneath their foolishness? Can you think of any modern equivalents to this squabble (college departments?)?

[3] How has this philosopher contradicted the image of the philosopher that he expounds? Here, again, Molière quotes something that he believes in while ridiculing the person who says it. What do you think of the philosophy master's teaching methods? Why is Jourdain so intimidated that he pretends to know Latin? How could you use this scene to illustrate the difference between a humanist and a pedant?

M. JOURDAIN   No, no more of that. I'm as choleric as the devil, and there's no morality holds me; I will have my belly full of passion whenever I have a mind to it.

PHILOSOPHY MASTER   Would you learn physics?

M. JOURDAIN   What is it that physics treat of?

PHILOSOPHY MASTER   Physics are what explain the principles of things natural and the properties of bodies; which discourse of the nature of elements, of metals, of minerals, of stones, of plants, and animals, and teach us the cause of all the meteors; the rainbow, *ignes fatui*, comets, lightnings, thunder, thunder-bolts, rain, snow, hail, winds, and whirlwinds.

M. JOURDAIN   There's too much hurly-burly in this, too much confusion.

PHILOSOPHY MASTER   What would you have me teach you then?

M. JOURDAIN   Teach me orthography.

PHILOSOPHY MASTER   With all my heart.

M. JOURDAIN   Afterwards you may teach me the almanack, to know when there's a moon, and when not.

PHILOSOPHY MASTER   Be it so. To pursue this thought of yours right and treat this matter like a philosopher, we must begin, according to the order of things, with an exact knowledge of the nature of letters and the different manner of pronouncing them. And on this head I am to tell you that letters are divided into vowels, called vowels because they express the voice: and into consonants, so called because they sound with the vowels and only mark the different articulations of the voice. There are five vowels or voices, A, E, I, O, U.

M. JOURDAIN   I understand all that.

PHILOSOPHY MASTER   The vowel A is formed by opening the mouth very wide, A.

M. JOURDAIN   A, A. Yes.

PHILOSOPHY MASTER   The vowel E is formed by drawing the under-jaw a little nearer to the upper, A, E.

M. JOURDAIN   A, E. A, E. In troth it is. How pretty that is!

PHILOSOPHY MASTER   And the vowel I, by bringing the jaws still nearer one to the other, and stretching the two corners of the mouth towards the ears, A, E, I.

M. JOURDAIN   A, E, I, I, I, I. 'Tis true. Long live learning!

PHILOSOPHY MASTER   The vowel O is formed by re-opening the jaws and drawing the lips near at the two corners, the upper and the under, O.

M. JOURDAIN   O, O. There's nothing more just, A, E, I, O, I, O. 'Tis admirable! I, O, I, O.

PHILOSOPHY MASTER   The opening of the mouth makes exactly a little ring, which resembles an O.

M. JOURDAIN   O, O, O. You're right, O. How fine a thing it is but to know something!

PHILOSOPHY MASTER   The vowel U is formed by bringing the teeth near together without entirely joining them, and pouting out both your lips, bringing them also near together without absolutely joining 'em, U.

M. JOURDAIN   U, U. There's nothing more true, U.

PHILOSOPHY MASTER   Your two lips pout out, as if you were making faces. Whence it comes that if you would do that to anybody and make a jest of him, you need say nothing to him but U.

M. JOURDAIN   U, U. It's true. Ah! why did not I study sooner, that I might have known all this!

PHILOSOPHY MASTER   To-morrow we shall take a view of the other letters, which are the consonants.

M. JOURDAIN   Is there anything as curious in them, as in these?

PHILOSOPHY MASTER   Doubtless. The consonant D, for example, is pronounced by clapping the tip of your tongue above the upper teeth, DE.

M. JOURDAIN   DE, DE. 'Tis so. Oh! charming things! charming things!

PHILOSOPHY MASTER   The F, in leaning the upper teeth upon the lower lip, EF.

M. JOURDAIN   EF, EF. 'Tis truth. Ah! father and mother o' mine, how do I owe you a grudge!

PHILOSOPHY MASTER   And the R, in carrying the tip of the tongue up to the roof of your mouth; so that being grazed upon by the air which bursts out with a force, it yields to it, and returns always to the same part, making a kind of trill, R, ra.

M. JOURDAIN   R, r, ra. R, r, r, r, r, ra. That's true. What a clever man are you! And how have I lost time! R, r, r, ra.

PHILOSOPHY MASTER   I will explain to you all these curiosities to the bottom.

M. JOURDAIN   Pray do. But now, I must commit a secret to you. I'm in love with a person of great quality, and I should be glad you would help me to write something to her in a short *billet-doux,* which I'll drop at her feet.

PHILOSOPHY MASTER   Very well.

M. JOURDAIN   That will be very gallant, won't it?

PHILOSOPHY MASTER   Without doubt. Is it verse that you would write to her?

M. JOURDAIN   No, no, none of your verse.

PHILOSOPHY MASTER   You would only have prose?

M. JOURDAIN   No, I would neither have verse nor prose.

PHILOSOPHY MASTER   It must be one or t'other.

M. JOURDAIN   Why so?

PHILOSOPHY MASTER   Because, sir, there's nothing to express one's self by, but prose, or verse.

M. JOURDAIN   Is there nothing then but prose, or verse?

PHILOSOPHY MASTER   No, sir, whatever is not prose, is verse; and whatever is not verse, is prose.

M. JOURDAIN   And when one talks, what may that be then?

PHILOSOPHY MASTER   Prose.

M. JOURDAIN   How? When I say, Nicole, bring me my slippers, and give me my nightcap, is that prose?

PHILOSOPHY MASTER   Yes, sir.

M. JOURDAIN   On my conscience, I have spoken prose above these forty years without knowing anything of the matter;[4] and I have all the obligations in the world to you for informing me of this. I would therefore put into a letter to her: Beautiful marchioness, your fair eyes make me die with love; but I would have this placed in a gallant manner; and have a gentle turn.

PHILOSOPHY MASTER   Why, add that the fire of her eyes has reduced your heart to ashes: that you suffer for her night and day all the torments—

M. JOURDAIN   No, no, no, I won't have all that—I'll have nothing but what I told you. Beautiful marchioness, your fair eyes make me die with love.

PHILOSOPHY MASTER   You must by all means lengthen the thing out a little.

M. JOURDAIN   No, I tell you, I'll have none but those very words in the letter: but turned in a modish way, ranged handsomely as they should be. I desire you'd show me a little, that I may see the different manners in which one may place them.

PHILOSOPHY MASTER   One may place them first of all as you said: Beautiful marchioness, your fair eyes make me die for love. Or suppose: For love die me make, beautiful marchioness, your fair eyes. Or perhaps: Your eyes fair, for love me make, beautiful marchioness, die. Or suppose: Die your fair eyes, beautiful marchioness, for love me make. Or however: Me make your eyes fair die, beautiful marchioness, for love.

M. JOURDAIN   But of all these ways, which is the best?

PHILOSOPHY MASTER   That which you said: Beautiful marchioness, your fair eyes make me die for love.

M. JOURDAIN   Yet at the same time, I never studied it, and I made the whole of it at the first touch. I thank you with all my heart, and desire you would come in good time to-morrow.

PHILOSOPHY MASTER   I shall not fail.

(*Exit* PHILOSOPHY MASTER)

M. JOURDAIN (*to his* LACKEY)   What? Are my clothes not come yet?

LACKEY   No, sir.

M. JOURDAIN   This cursed tailor makes me wait unreasonably, considering it's a day I have so much business in. I shall go mad. A quartan ague wring this villain of a tailor. D—l take the tailor. A plague choke the tailor. If I had him but here now, this detestable tailor, this dog of a tailor, this traitor of a tailor, I—

(*Enter a* MASTER TAILOR *and a* JOURNEYMAN TAILOR *bringing a suit of clothes for* M. JOURDAIN)

Oh! You're there. I was going to be in a passion with you.

MASTER TAILOR   I could not possibly come sooner, and I set twenty fellows to work at your clothes.

M. JOURDAIN   You have sent me a pair of silk hose so tight that I had all the difficulty in the world to get 'em on, and there are two stitches broke in 'em.

MASTER TAILOR   They'll grow rather too large:

---

[4] M. Jourdain's realization that he has been speaking prose all his life is cited in various contexts more often than anything else in the play. Why do you think this is so?

M. JOURDAIN   Yes, if I break every day a loop or two. You have made me a pair of shoes too, that pinch me execrably.

MASTER TAILOR   Not at all, sir.

M. JOURDAIN   How, not at all?

MASTER TAILOR   No, they don't pinch you at all.

M. JOURDAIN   I tell you they do hurt me.

MASTER TAILOR   You fancy so.

M. JOURDAIN   I fancy so because I feel it. There's a fine reason indeed.

MASTER TAILOR   Hold, stay, here's one of the handsomest suits at court, and the best-matched. 'Tis a masterly work to invent a grave suit of clothes that should not be black, and I'll give the cleverest tailor in town six trials to equal it.

M. JOURDAIN   What a deuce have we here? You have put the flowers downwards.

MASTER TAILOR   Why, you did not tell me you would have 'em upwards.

M. JOURDAIN   Was there any need to tell you of that?

MASTER TAILOR   Yes, certainly. All the people of quality wear 'em in that way.

M. JOURDAIN   Do people of quality wear the flowers downwards?

MASTER TAILOR   Yes, sir.

M. JOURDAIN   Oh, 'tis very well, then.

MASTER TAILOR   If you please I'll put 'em upwards.

M. JOURDAIN   No, no.

MASTER TAILOR   You need only say the word.

M. JOURDAIN   No, I tell you, you have done right. Do you think my clothes will fit me?

MASTER TAILOR   A pretty question! I defy a painter with his pencil to draw you anything that shall fit more exact. I have a fellow at home who, for fitting a pair of breeches, is the greatest genius in the world; another who, for the cut of a doublet, is the hero of the age.

M. JOURDAIN   Are the peruke[5] and feather as they should be?

MASTER TAILOR   Everything's well.

M. JOURDAIN   (looking earnestly at the tailor's clothes)   Ah, hah! Monsieur Tailor, here's my stuff of the last suit you made for me. I know it very well.

MASTER TAILOR   The stuff appeared to me so handsome, that I had a mind to cut a coat out of it for myself.

M. JOURDAIN   Yes, but you should not have cabbaged it out of mine.

MASTER TAILOR   Will you put on your clothes?

M. JOURDAIN   Yes, give 'em me.

MASTER TAILOR   Stay; the matter must not go so. I have brought men along with me to dress you to music; these sort of suits are put on with ceremony. Soho? come in there, you.

(Enter four JOURNEYMEN TAILORS, dancing)

Put on this suit of the gentleman's, in the manner you do to people of quality.

(Two of the tailors pull off his straight breeches made for his exercises, and two others his waistcoat; then they put on his new suit to music, and M. JOURDAIN walks amongst them to show them his clothes to see whether they fit or no)

JOURNEYMAN TAILOR   My dear gentleman, please to give the tailor's men something to drink.

M. JOURDAIN   How do you call me?

JOURNEYMAN TAILOR   My dear gentleman.

M. JOURDAIN   "My dear gentleman!" See what it is to dress like people of quality. You may go clothed like a commoner all your days, and they'll never call you "my dear gentleman." (gives them something) Stay, there's for "my dear gentleman."

JOURNEYMAN TAILOR   My lord, we are infinitely obliged to you.

M. JOURDAIN   My lord! Oh, ho! My lord! Stay, friend; "my lord" deserves something, "my lord" is none o' your petty words. Hold, there, "my lord" gives you that.

JOURNEYMAN TAILOR   My lord, we shall go drink your grace's health.

M. JOURDAIN   Your grace! oh, oh, oh! stay, don't go. Your grace, to me! (aside) I'faith if he goes as far as highness, he'll empty my purse. (aloud) Hold, there's for "my grace."

JOURNEYMAN TAILOR   My lord, we most humbly thank your grace for your liberality.

M. JOURDAIN   He did very well; I was going to give him all.

---

[5] Wig.

(The four JOURNEYMAN TAILORS *perform a dance that constitutes the second intermission.)*

ACT III

THE SCENE.   *Monsieur Jourdain and his two Lackeys*

M. JOURDAIN   Follow me, that I may go and show my clothes a little through the town; and especially take care, both of you, to walk immediately at my heels, that people may plainly see you belong to me.

LACKEYS   Yes, sir.

M. JOURDAIN   Call me Nicole, that I may give her some directions. You need not go—here she comes.

(Enter NICOLE*)*

Nicole?

NICOLE   Your pleasure, sir?

M. JOURDAIN   Harkee.

NICOLE *(laughing)*   Ha, ha, ha, ha, ha.

M. JOURDAIN   Who do ye laugh at?

NICOLE   Ha, ha, ha, ha, ha, ha.

M. JOURDAIN   What does this slut mean?

NICOLE   Ha, ha, ha. How you are bedizened! Ha, ha, ha.

M. JOURDAIN   How's that?

NICOLE   Oh! oh! my stars! ha, ha, ha, ha, ha.

M. JOURDAIN   What a jade is here! What! do ye make a jest of me?

NICOLE   No, no, sir, I should be very sorry to do so. Ha, ha, ha, ha, ha, ha.

M. JOURDAIN   I shall give ye a slap o' the chops, if you laugh any more.

NICOLE   Sir, I cannot help it. Ha, ha, ha, ha, ha, ha.

M. JOURDAIN   Won't ye have done?

NICOLE   Sir, I ask your pardon; but you are so comical, that I cannot hold from laughing. Ha, ha, ha.

M. JOURDAIN   Do but see the insolence!

NICOLE   You are so thoroughly droll there! Ha, ha.

M. JOURDAIN   I shall—

NICOLE   I beg you would excuse me. Ha, ha, ha, ha.

M. JOURDAIN   Hold, if you laugh again the least in the world, I protest and swear I'll give ye such a box o' the ear as ye never had in your life.

NICOLE   Well, sir, I have done; I won't laugh any more.

M. JOURDAIN   Take care you don't. You must clean out against by and by—

NICOLE   Ha, ha.

M. JOURDAIN   You must clean out as it should be—

NICOLE   Ha, ha.

M. JOURDAIN   I say, you must go clean out the hall, and—

NICOLE   Ha, ha.

M. JOURDAIN   Again?

NICOLE *(tumbles down with laughing)*   Hold, sir, beat me rather, and let me laugh my belly-full, that will do me more good. Ha, ha, ha, ha.[1]

M. JOURDAIN   I shall run mad!

NICOLE   For goodness' sake, sir, I beseech you let me laugh. Ha, ha, ha.

M. JOURDAIN   If I take you in hand—

NICOLE   Si-ir, I shall bu-urst, if I do—not laugh. Ha, ha, ha.

M. JOURDAIN   But did ever anybody see such a jade as that, who insolently laughs in my face, instead of receiving my orders!

NICOLE   What would you have me do, sir?

M. JOURDAIN   Why, take care to get ready my house for the company that's to come by and by.

NICOLE *(getting up)*   Ay, i'fakins, I've no more inclination to laugh; all your company makes such a litter here that the very word's enough to put one in an ill humour.

M. JOURDAIN   What! I ought to shut my doors against all the world for your sake?

NICOLE   You ought at least to shut it against certain people.

(Enter MME JOURDAIN*)*

MME JOURDAIN   Ah, hah! Here's some new story. What means this, husband, this same equipage? D'ye despise the world, that you harness yourself out in this manner? Have you a mind to make yourself a laughing-stock wherever ye go?

M. JOURDAIN   None but fools, wife, will laugh at me.

MME JOURDAIN   In truth, people have not stayed thus long to laugh; 'tis a good while ago that your ways have furnished all the world with a laugh.

---

[1] Here is a comic portrayal of Molière's deep belief in the therapeutic value of laughter for all human beings.

M. JOURDAIN   Who is that "all the world," pray?

MME JOURDAIN   That "all the world" is a world perfectly in the right, and much wiser than yourself. For my part, I am shocked at the life you lead. I don't know what to call our house. One would swear 'twere carnival here all the year round; and from break o' day, for fear there should be any respite, there's nothing to be heard here but an uproar of fiddles and songsters which disturb the whole neighbourhood.

NICOLE   Madame says right. I shall never see my things set to rights again for that gang of folks that you bring to the house. They ransack every quarter of the town with their feet for dirt to bring here; and poor Frances is e'en almost slaved off her legs with scrubbing of the floors, which your pretty masters come to daub as regularly as the day comes.

M. JOURDAIN   Hey-day! our maid Nicole! you have a pretty nimble tongue of your own for a country-wench.

MME JOURDAIN   Nicole's in the right, and she has more sense than you have. I should be glad to know what you think to do with a dancing master, at your age?

NICOLE   And with a lubberly fencing master, that comes here with his stamping to shake the whole house, and tear up all the pavement of the hall.

M. JOURDAIN   Peace, our maid, and our wife.

MME JOURDAIN   What! will you learn to dance against the time you'll have no legs?

NICOLE   What! have you a mind to murder somebody?

M. JOURDAIN   Hold your prate; I tell you you are ignorant creatures, both of you, and don't know the advantage of all this.

MME JOURDAIN   You ought much rather to think of marrying your daughter, who is of age to be provided for.

M. JOURDAIN   I shall think of marrying my daughter when a suitable match presents itself; but I shall think too of learning the *belles sciences*.

NICOLE   I've heard say further, madame, that to pin the basket, he has got him a philosophy master to-day.

M. JOURDAIN   Very well. I've a mind to have wit, and to know how to reason upon things with your genteel people.

MME JOURDAIN   Won't you go to school one of these days, and be whipped at your age?

M. JOURDAIN   Why not? Would I were whipped this very instant before all the world, so I did but know what they learn at school!

NICOLE   Yes, forsooth, that would be a mighty advantage t'ye.

M. JOURDAIN   Without doubt.

MME JOURDAIN   This is all very necessary to the management of your house.[2]

M. JOURDAIN   Certainly. You talk, both of you, like asses, and I'm ashamed of your ignorance. (*to* MME JOURDAIN) For example, do you know, you, what it is you now speak?

MME JOURDAIN   Yes, I know that what I speak is very right, and that you ought to think of living in another manner.

M. JOURDAIN   I don't talk of that. I ask you what the words are that you now speak?

MME JOURDAIN   They are words that have a good deal of sense in them, and your conduct is by no means such.

M. JOURDAIN   I don't talk of that, I tell you. I ask you, what is that I now speak to you, which I say this very moment?

MME JOURDAIN   Mere stuff.

M. JOURDAIN   Pshaw, no, 'tis not that. That which we both of us say, the language we speak this instant?

MME JOURDAIN   Well?

M. JOURDAIN   How is it called?

MME JOURDAIN   'Tis called just what you please to call it.

M. JOURDAIN   'Tis prose, you ignorant creature.

MME JOURDAIN   Prose?

M. JOURDAIN   Yes, prose. Whatever is prose, is not verse; and whatever is not verse, is prose. Now, see what it is to study. And you, (*to* NICOLE) do you know very well how you must do to say U?

NICOLE   How?

M. JOURDAIN   Yes. What is it you do when you say U?

---

[2] Madame Jourdain, the voice of the middle class and Nicole, the voice of the lower class, represent good sense and honesty as opposed to Monsieur Jourdain's pretentiousness and the nobles' dishonesty. And yet, are they entirely in the right? Typically, Madame Jourdain can see no benefit in the arts unless they are directly *useful*.

NICOLE   What?

M. JOURDAIN   Say U a little, to try.

NICOLE   Well, U.

M. JOURDAIN   What is it you do?

NICOLE   I say U.

M. JOURDAIN   Yes, but when you say U, what is it you do?

NICOLE   I do as you bid me.

M. JOURDAIN   O! what a strange thing it is to have to do with brutes! You pout out your lips, and bring your under-jaw to your upper, U, d'ye see? I make a mouth, U.

NICOLE   Yes, that's fine.

MME JOURDAIN   'Tis admirable!

M. JOURDAIN   'Tis quite another thing, had but you seen O, and DE, DE, and EF, EF.

MME JOURDAIN   What is all this ridiculous stuff?

NICOLE   What are we the better for all this?

M. JOURDAIN   It makes one mad, to see these ignorant women.

MME JOURDAIN   Go, go, you should send all these folks apacking with their silly stuff.

NICOLE   And especially that great lubberly fencing master, who fills all my house with dust.

M. JOURDAIN   Hey-day! This fencing master sticks strangely in thy stomach. I'll let thee see thy impertinence presently.

(*He orders the foils to be brought, and gives one to* NI-COLE)

Stay, reason demonstrative, the line of the body. When they push in carte one need only do so; and when they push in tierce one need only do so. This is the way never to be killed; and is not that clever to be upon sure grounds, when one has an encounter with anybody? There, push at me a little, to try.

NICOLE   Well, how?

(NICOLE *gives him several thrusts*)

M. JOURDAIN   Gently! Hold! Oh! Softly; deuce take the hussy.

NICOLE   You bid me push.

M. JOURDAIN   Yes, but you push me in tierce before you push in carte, and you have not patience while I parry.

MME JOURDAIN   You are a fool, husband, with all these whims, and this is come to you since you have taken upon you to keep company with quality.

M. JOURDAIN   When I keep company with quality, I show my judgment; and that's much better than herding with your bourgeoisie.

MME JOURDAIN   Yes, truly, there's a great deal to be got by frequenting your nobility; and you have made fine work with that count you are so bewitched with.

M. JOURDAIN   Peace, take care what you say. Do you well know, wife, that you don't know whom you speak of when you speak of him? He's a man of more importance than you think of; a nobleman of consideration at court, who speaks to the king just for all the world as I speak to you. Is it not a thing that does me great honour, that you see a person of that quality come so often to my house, who calls me his dear friend and treats me as if I were his equal? He has more kindness for me than one would ever imagine, and he caresses me in such a manner before all the world that I myself am perfectly confounded at it.

MME JOURDAIN   Yes, he has a great kindness for you, and caresses you; but he borrows your money of you.

M. JOURDAIN   Well, and is it not a great honour to me to lend money to a man of that condition? And can I do less for a lord who calls me his dear friend?

MME JOURDAIN   And what is it this lord does for you?

M. JOURDAIN   Things that would astonish you if you did but know 'em.

MME JOURDAIN   And what may they be?

M. JOURDAIN   Peace, I can't explain myself. 'Tis sufficient that if I have lent him money, he'll pay it me honestly, and that before 'tis long.

MME JOURDAIN   Yes, stay you for that.

M. JOURDAIN   Certainly. Did he not tell me so?

MME JOURDAIN   Yes, yes, and he won't fail to disappoint you.

M. JOURDAIN   He swore to me on the faith of a gentleman.

MME JOURDAIN   A mere song.

M. JOURDAIN   Hey! You are mighty obstinate, wife of mine; I tell you he will keep his word with me, I am sure of it.

MME JOURDAIN   And I am sure that he will not, and all the court he makes to you is only to cajole you.

M. JOURDAIN   Hold your tongue. Here he comes.

MME JOURDAIN   That's all we shall have of him. He comes perhaps to borrow something more of you; the very sight of him gives me my dinner.

M. JOURDAIN   Hold your tongue, I say.

(*Enter* DORANTE)

DORANTE   My dear friend, Monsieur Jourdain, how do you do?

M. JOURDAIN   Very well, sir, to do you what little service I can.

DORANTE   And Madame Jourdain there, how does she do?

MME JOURDAIN   Madame Jourdain does as well as she can.

DORANTE   Hah! Monsieur Jourdain, you're dressed the most genteelly in the world!

M. JOURDAIN   As you see.

DORANTE   You have a very fine air with that dress, and we have ne'er a young fellow at court that's better made than you.

M. JOURDAIN   He, he.

MME JOURDAIN   (*aside*)   He scratches him where it itches.

DORANTE   Turn about. 'Tis most gallant.

MME JOURDAIN   (*aside*)   Yes, as much of the fool behind as before.

DORANTE   'Faith, Monsieur Jourdain, I was strangely impatient to see you. You're the man in the world I most esteem, and I was talking of you again this morning at the king's levee.[3]

M. JOURDAIN   You do me a great deal of honour, sir. (*to* MME JOURDAIN) At the king's levee!

DORANTE   Come, be covered.[4]

M. JOURDAIN   Sir, I know the respect I owe you.

DORANTE   Lack-a-day, be covered; no ceremony, pray, between us two.

M. JOURDAIN   Sir—

DORANTE   Put on your hat, I tell you, Monsieur Jourdain; you are my friend.

M. JOURDAIN   Sir, I am your humble servant.

DORANTE   I won't be covered, if you won't.

M. JOURDAIN (*puts on his hat*)   I choose rather to be unmannerly than troublesome.

DORANTE   I am your debtor, you know.

MME JOURDAIN (*aside*)   Yes, we know it but too well.

DORANTE   You have generously lent me money upon several occasions; and have obliged me, most certainly, with the best grace in the world.

M. JOURDAIN   You jest, sir.

DORANTE   But I know how to repay what is lent me, and to be grateful for the favours done me.

M. JOURDAIN   I don't doubt it, sir.

DORANTE   I'm willing to get out of your books, and came hither to make up our accounts together.

M. JOURDAIN (*aside to* MME JOURDAIN)   Well, you see your impertinence, wife.

DORANTE   I'm one who loves to be out of debt as soon as possible.

M. JOURDAIN (*aside to* MME JOURDAIN)   I told you so.

DORANTE   Let's see a little what 'tis I owe you.

M. JOURDAIN (*aside to* MME JOURDAIN)   You there, with your ridiculous suspicions.

DORANTE   Do you remember right all the money you have lent me?

M. JOURDAIN   I believe so. I made a little memorandum of it. Here it is. Let you have at one time two hundred louis d'or.

DORANTE   'Tis true.

M. JOURDAIN   Another time, six-score.

DORANTE   Yes.

M. JOURDAIN   And another time a hundred and forty.

DORANTE   You are right.

M. JOURDAIN   These three articles make four hundred and sixty louis d'or, which come to five thousand and sixty livres.

DORANTE   The account is very right. Five thousand and sixty livres.

M. JOURDAIN   One thousand eight hundred and thirty-two livres to your plume-maker.

DORANTE   Just.

M. JOURDAIN   Two thousand seven hundred and four-score livres to your tailor.

DORANTE   'Tis true.

M. JOURDAIN   Four thousand three hundred and seventy-nine livres, twelve sols, and eight deniers to your tradesman.

DORANTE   Very well. Twelve sols, eight deniers. The

---

[3] The king's levee—the ceremony of the king's morning rising, which courtiers attended (see Saint-Simon in Chapter 20).

[4] Put your hat back on.

account is just.

M. JOURDAIN   And a thousand seven hundred and forty-eight livres, seven sols, four deniers to your saddler.

DORANTE   'Tis all true. What does that come to?

M. JOURDAIN   Sum total, fifteen thousand eight hundred livres.

DORANTE   The sum total, and just. Fifteen thousand and eight hundred livres. To which add two hundred pistoles, which you are going to lend me, that will make exactly eighteen thousand francs, which I shall pay you the first opportunity.

MME JOURDAIN (*aside to* M. JOURDAIN)   Well, did I not guess how 'twould be!

M. JOURDAIN (*aside to* MME JOURDAIN)   Peace.

DORANTE   Will it incommode you to lend me what I tell you?

M. JOURDAIN   Oh! no.

MME JOURDAIN (*aside to* M. JOURDAIN)   This man makes a mere milch cow of you.

M. JOURDAIN (*aside to* MME JOURDAIN)   Hold your tongue.

DORANTE   If this will incommode you, I'll seek it elsewhere.

M. JOURDAIN   No, sir.

MME JOURDAIN (*aside to* M. JOURDAIN)   He'll ne'er be satisfied till he has ruined you.

M. JOURDAIN (*aside to* MME JOURDAIN)   Hold your tongue, I tell you.

DORANTE   You need only tell me if this puts you to any straits.

M. JOURDAIN   Not at all, sir.

MME JOURDAIN (*aside to* M. JOURDAIN)   'Tis a true wheedler.

M. JOURDAIN (*aside to* MME JOURDAIN)   Hold your tongue then.

MME JOURDAIN (*aside to* M. JOURDAIN)   He'll drain you to the last farthing.

M. JOURDAIN (*aside to* MME JOURDAIN)   Will you hold your tongue?

DORANTE   I've a good many people would be glad to lend it me, but as you are my very good friend, I thought I should wrong you if I asked it of anybody else.

M. JOURDAIN   'Tis too much honour, sir, you do me. I'll go fetch what you want.

MME JOURDAIN (*aside to* M. JOURDAIN)   What! going to lend him still more?

M. JOURDAIN (*aside to* MME JOURDAIN)   What can I do? Would you have me refuse a man of that rank, who spoke of me this morning at the king's levee?

MME JOURDAIN (*aside to* M. JOURDAIN)   Go, you're a downright dupe.

(*Exit* M. JOURDAIN)

DORANTE   You seem to me very melancholy. What ails you, Madame Jourdain?

MME JOURDAIN   My head's bigger than my fist, even if it is not swelled.

DORANTE   Where is Mademoiselle your daughter that I don't see her?

MME JOURDAIN   Mademoiselle my daughter is pretty well where she is.

DORANTE   How does she go on?

MME JOURDAIN   She goes on her two legs.

DORANTE   Won't you come with her, one of these days, and see the ball, and the play that's acted at court?

MME JOURDAIN   Yes, truly, we've a great inclination to laugh, a great inclination to laugh have we.

DORANTE   I fancy, Madame Jourdain, you had a great many sparks in your younger years, being so handsome and good-humoured as you were.

MME JOURDAIN   Tredame, sir! what, is Madame Jourdain grown decrepit, and does her head totter already with a palsy?

DORANTE   Odso, Madame Jourdain, I ask your pardon. I was not thinking that you are young. I'm very often absent. Pray excuse my impertinence.

(*Enter* M. JOURDAIN)

M. JOURDAIN (*to* DORANTE)   Here's two hundred pieces for you, hard money.

DORANTE   I do assure you, Monsieur Jourdain, I am absolutely yours; and I long to do you service at court.

M. JOURDAIN   I'm infinitely obliged to you.

DORANTE   If Madame Jourdain inclines to see the royal diversion, I'll get her the best places in the ballroom.

MME JOURDAIN   Madame Jourdain kisses your hand.

DORANTE (*aside to* M. JOURDAIN)   Our pretty

marchioness, as I informed you in my letter, will be here by and by to partake of your ball and collation; I brought her, at last, to consent to the entertainment you design to give her.

M. JOURDAIN   Let us draw to a distance a little, for a certain reason.

DORANTE   'Tis eight days since I saw you, and I gave you no tidings of the diamond you put into my hands to make her a present of, as from you; but the reason was, I had all the difficulty in the world to conquer her scruples, and 'twas no longer ago than to-day, that she resolved to accept of it.

M. JOURDAIN   How did she like it?

DORANTE   Marvellously; and I am much deceived if the beauty of this diamond has not an admirable effect upon her.

M. JOURDAIN   Grant it, kind Heaven!

MME JOURDAIN (to NICOLE)   When he's once with him, he can never get rid of him.

DORANTE   I made her sensible in a proper manner of the richness of the present and the strength of your passion.

M. JOURDAIN   These kindnesses perfectly overwhelm me; I am in the greatest confusion in the world to see a person of your quality demean himself on my account as you do.

DORANTE   You jest sure. Does one ever stop at such sort of scruples among friends? And would not you do the same thing for me, if occasion offered?

M. JOURDAIN   Oh! certainly, and with all my soul.

MME JOURDAIN (aside to NICOLE)   How the sight of him torments me!

DORANTE   For my part, I never mind anything when a friend is to be served; and when you imparted to me the ardent passion you had entertained for the agreeable marchioness, with whom I was acquainted, you see that I made an immediate offer of my service.

M. JOURDAIN   'Tis true, these favours are what confound me.

MME JOURDAIN (to NICOLE)   What! will he never be gone?

NICOLE   They are mighty great together.

DORANTE   You've taken the right way to smite her. Women, above all things, love the expense we are at on their account; and your frequent serenades, your continual entertainments, that sumptuous firework she saw on the water, the diamond she received by way of present from you, and the regale you are now preparing—all this speaks much better in favour of your passion than all the things you yourself could possibly have said to her.

M. JOURDAIN   There's no expense I would not be at, if I could by that means find the way to her heart. A woman of quality has powerful charms for me, and 'tis an honour I would purchase at any rate.

MME JOURDAIN (aside to NICOLE)   What can they have to talk of so long together? Go softly, and listen a little.

DORANTE   By and by you will enjoy the pleasure of seeing her at your ease; your eyes will have full time to be satisfied.

M. JOURDAIN   To be at full liberty, I have ordered matters so that my wife shall dine with my sister, where she'll pass the whole afternoon.

DORANTE   You have done wisely, for your wife might have perplexed us a little. I have given the proper orders for you to the cook, and for everything necessary for the ball. 'Tis of my own invention; and provided the execution answers the plan, I am sure 'twill be—

M. JOURDAIN (perceives that NICOLE listens, and gives her a box on the ear)   Hey, you're very impertinent. (to DORANTE) Let us go if you please.

(Exeunt M. JOURDAIN and DORANTE)

NICOLE   I'faith, curiosity has cost me something; but I believe there's a snake in the grass, for they were talking of some affair which they were not willing you should be present at.

MME JOURDAIN   This is not the first time, Nicole, that I have had suspicions of my husband. I am the most deceived person in the world, or there is some amour in agitation, and I am labouring to discover what it should be. But let's think of my daughter. You know the love Cléonte has for her. He is a man who hits my fancy, and I have a mind to favour his addresses and help him to Lucile, if I can.

NICOLE   In truth, madame, I am the most ravished [5]

---

[5] Delighted. Nicole wishes to marry Cléonte's servant.

creature in the world, to find you in these sentiments; for if the master hits your taste, the man hits mine no less; and I could wish our marriage might be concluded under favour of theirs.

MME JOURDAIN   Go, and talk with him about it, as from me, and tell him to come to me presently, that we may join in demanding my daughter of my husband.

NICOLE   I fly, madame, with joy, and I could not have received a more agreeable commission.

(*Exit* MME JOURDAIN)

I believe I shall very much rejoice their hearts.

(*Enter* CLÉONTE *and* COVIELLE)

Hah, most luckily met. I'm an ambassadress of joy, and I come—

CLÉONTE   Be gone, ye perfidious slut, and don't come to amuse me with thy traitorous speeches.

NICOLE   Is it thus you receive—

CLÉONTE   Be gone, I tell thee, and go directly and inform thy false mistress, that she never more, while she lives, shall impose upon the too simple Cléonte.

NICOLE   What whim is this? My dear Covielle, tell me a little what does this mean.

COVIELLE   Thy dear Covielle, wicked minx? Away quickly out of my sight, hussy, and leave me at quiet.

NICOLE   What! dost thou, too—

COVIELLE   Out o' my sight, I tell thee, and talk not to me, for thy life.

NICOLE (*aside*)   Hey-day! What gadfly has stung 'em both? Well, I must march and inform my mistress of this pretty piece of history.

(*Exit* NICOLE)

CLÉONTE   What! treat a lover in this manner; and a lover the most constant, the most passionate of all lovers!

COVIELLE   'Tis a horrible trick they have served us both.

CLÉONTE   I discover all the ardour for her, all the tenderness one can imagine. I love nothing in the world but her, have nothing in my thoughts besides her. She is all my care, all my desire, all my joy. I speak of nought but her, think of nought but her, dream of nought but her, I breathe only for her, my heart lives wholly in her; and this is the worthy recompense of such a love! I am two days without seeing her, which are to me two horrible ages; I meet her accidentally, my heart feels all transported at the sight; joy sparkles in my face; I fly to her with ecstasy, and the faithless creature turns away her eyes, and brushes hastily by me, as if she had never seen me in her life!

COVIELLE   I say the same as you do.

CLÉONTE   Is it possible to see anything, Covielle, equal to this perfidy of the ungrateful Lucile?

COVIELLE   Or to that, sir, of the villainous jade Nicole?

CLÉONTE   After so many ardent sacrifices of sighs and vows that I have made to her charms!

COVIELLE   After so much assiduous sneaking, cares, and services that I have paid her in the kitchen!

CLÉONTE   So many tears that I have shed at her feet!

COVIELLE   So many buckets of water that I have drawn for her!

CLÉONTE   Such ardour as I have shown, in loving her more than myself!

COVIELLE   So much heat as I have endured, in turning the spit in her place!

CLÉONTE   She flies me with disdain!

COVIELLE   She turns her back upon me with impudence!

CLÉONTE   This is a perfidy worthy the greatest punishment.

COVIELLE   This a treachery that deserves a thousand boxes o' the ear.[6]

CLÉONTE   Prithee, never think to speak once more to me in her favour.

COVIELLE   I, sir? Marry, Heaven forbid.

CLÉONTE   Never come to excuse the action of this perfidious woman.

COVIELLE   Fear it not.

CLÉONTE   No, d'ye see, all discourses in her defence will signify nothing.

COVIELLE   Who dreams of such a thing?

CLÉONTE   I'm determined to continue my resentment against her, and break off all correspondence.

COVIELLE   I give my consent.

---

[6] This scene has an operatic quality, as if the master and valet are singing a duet. How does each one reflect his social class?

CLÉONTE   This same count that visits her, pleases perhaps her eye; and her fancy, I see plainly, is dazzled with quality. But I must, for my own honour, prevent the triumph of her inconstancy. I'll make as much haste as she can do towards the change which I see she's running into, and won't leave her all the glory of quitting me.

COVIELLE   'Tis very well said, and for my share, I enter into all your sentiments.

CLÉONTE   Second my resentments, and support my resolutions against all the remains of love that may yet plead for her. I conjure thee, say all the ill things of her thou canst. Paint me her person so as to make her despicable; and, in order to disgust me, mark me out well all the faults thou canst find in her.

COVIELLE   She, sir? A pretty mawkin, a fine piece to be so much enamoured with. I see nothing in her but what's very indifferent, and you might find a hundred persons more deserving of you. First of all she has little eyes.

CLÉONTE   That's true, she has little eyes; but they are full of fire, the most sparkling, the most piercing in the world, the most striking that one shall see.

COVIELLE   She has a wide mouth.

CLÉONTE   Yes; but one sees such graces in it, as one does not see in other mouths, and the sight of that mouth inspires desire: 'tis the most attractive, the most amorous in the world.

COVIELLE   As to her height, she's not tall.

CLÉONTE   No; but she's easy, and well-shaped.

COVIELLE   She affects a negligence in speaking and acting.

CLÉONTE   'Tis true; but all this has a gracefulness in her, and her ways are engaging; they have I don't know what charms that insinuate into our hearts.

COVIELLE   As to her wit—

CLÉONTE   Ah! Covielle, she has the most refined, the most delicate turn of wit.

COVIELLE   Her conversation—

CLÉONTE   Her conversation is charming.

COVIELLE   She's always grave.

CLÉONTE   Would you have flaunting pleasantry, a perpetual profuse mirth? And d'ye see anything more impertinent than those women who are always upon the giggle?

COVIELLE   But in short, she is the most capricious creature in the world.

CLÉONTE   Yes, she is capricious, I grant ye, but everything sits well upon fine women; we bear with everything from the fair.

COVIELLE   Since that's the case, I see plainly you desire always to love her.

CLÉONTE   I! I should love death sooner; and I am now going to hate her as much as ever I loved her.

COVIELLE   But how, if you think her so perfect?

CLÉONTE   Therein shall my vengeance be more glaring; therein shall I better display the force of my resolution in hating her, quitting her, most beautiful as she is; most charming, most amiable, as I think her. Here she is.

(*Enter* LUCILE *and* NICOLE)

NICOLE (*to* LUCILE)   For my part, I was perfectly shocked at it.

LUCILE   It can be nothing else, Nicole, but what I said. But there he comes.

CLÉONTE (*to* COVIELLE)   I won't so much as speak to her.

COVIELLE   I'll follow your example.

LUCILE   What means this, Cléonte, what's the matter with you?

NICOLE   What ails thee, Covielle?

LUCILE   What trouble has seized you?

NICOLE   What cross humour possesses thee?

LUCILE   Are you dumb, Cléonte?

NICOLE   Hast thou lost thy speech, Covielle?

CLÉONTE   The abandoned creature!

COVIELLE   Oh! the Judas!

LUCILE   I see very well that the late meeting has disordered your mind.

CLÉONTE (*to* COVIELLE)   O, ho! She sees what she has done.

NICOLE   The reception of this morning has made thee take snuff.

COVIELLE (*to* CLÉONTE)   She has guessed where the shoe pinches.

LUCILE   Is it not true, Cléonte, that this is the reason of your being out of humour?

CLÉONTE   Yes, perfidious maid, that is it, since I must speak; and I can tell you that you shall not triumph, as you imagine, by your unfaithfulness, that I shall be beforehand in breaking with you, and you won't have the credit of discarding me. I shall, doubtless, have some difficulty in conquering the passion I have for you: 'twill cause me uneasiness; I shall suffer for a while; but I shall compass my point, and I would sooner stab myself to the heart than have the weakness of returning to you.

COVIELLE (*to* NICOLE)   As says the master, so says the man.

LUCILE   Here's a noise indeed about nothing. I'll tell you, Cléonte, the reason that made me avoid joining you this morning.

CLÉONTE (*endeavouring to go to avoid* LUCILE)   No, I'll hear nothing.

NICOLE (*to* COVIELLE)   I'll let thee into the cause that made us pass you so quick.

COVIELLE (*endeavouring to go to avoid* NICOLE)   I will hear nothing.

LUCILE (*following* CLÉONTE)   Know that this morning—

CLÉONTE (*walks about without regarding* LUCILE)   No, I tell you.

NICOLE (*following* COVIELLE)   Learn that—

COVIELLE (*walks about likewise without regarding* NICOLE)   No, traitress.

LUCILE   Hear me.

CLÉONTE   Not a bit.

NICOLE   Let me speak.

COVIELLE   I'm deaf.

LUCILE   Cléonte!

CLÉONTE   No.

NICOLE   Covielle!

COVIELLE   No.

LUCILE   Stay.

CLÉONTE   Idle stuff.

NICOLE   Hear me.

COVIELLE   No such thing.

LUCILE   One moment.

CLÉONTE   Not at all.

NICOLE   A little patience.

COVIELLE   A fiddle-stick.

LUCILE   Two words.

CLÉONTE   No, 'tis over.

NICOLE   One word.

COVIELLE   No more dealings.

LUCILE (*stopping*)   Well, since you won't hear me, keep your opinion, and do what you please.

NICOLE (*stopping likewise*)   Since that's thy way, e'en take it all just as it pleases thee.

CLÉONTE   Let's know the subject then of this fine reception.

LUCILE (*going in her turn to avoid* CLÉONTE)   I've no longer an inclination to tell it.

COVIELLE   Let us a little into this history.

NICOLE (*going likewise in her turn to avoid* COVIELLE)   I won't inform thee now, not I.

CLÉONTE (*following* LUCILE)   Tell me—

LUCILE   No, I'll tell you nothing.

COVIELLE (*following* NICOLE)   Say—

NICOLE   No, I say nothing.

CLÉONTE   For goodness' sake.

LUCILE   No, I tell you.

COVIELLE   Of all charity.

NICOLE   Not a bit.

CLÉONTE   I beseech you.

LUCILE   Let me alone.

COVIELLE   I conjure thee.

NICOLE   Away with thee.

CLÉONTE   Lucile!

LUCILE   No.

COVIELLE   Nicole!

NICOLE   Not at all.

CLÉONTE   For Heaven's sake.

LUCILE   I will not.

COVIELLE   Speak to me.

NICOLE   Not a word.

CLÉONTE   Clear up my doubts.

LUCILE   No, I'll do nothing towards it.

COVIELLE   Cure my mind.

NICOLE   No, 'tis not my pleasure.

CLÉONTE   Well, since you are so little concerned to ease me of my pain, and to justify yourself as to the unworthy treatment my passion has received from you, ungrateful creature, 'tis the last time you shall see me, and I am going far from you to die of grief and love.

COVIELLE (*to* NICOLE)   And I'll follow his steps.

LUCILE (*to* CLÉONTE, *who is going*)   Cléonte!

NICOLE (*to* COVIELLE, *who follows his master*)   Covielle!

CLÉONTE (*stopping*)   Hey?

COVIELLE (*likewise stopping*)   Your pleasure?

LUCILE   Whither do you go?

CLÉONTE   Where I told you.

COVIELLE   We go to die.

LUCILE   Do you go to die, Cléonte?

CLÉONTE   Yes, cruel, since you will have it so.

LUCILE   I? I have you die?

CLÉONTE   Yes, you would.

LUCILE   Who told you so?

CLÉONTE (*going up to* LUCILE)   Would you not have it so, since you would not clear up my suspicions?

LUCILE   Is that my fault? Would you but have given me the hearing, should I not have told you that the adventure you make such complaints about was occasioned this morning by the presence of an old aunt who will absolutely have it that the mere approach of a man is a dishonour to a girl, who is perpetually lecturing us upon this head, and represents to us all mankind as so many devils, whom one ought to avoid.

NICOLE (*to* COVIELLE)   There's the whole secret of the affair.

CLÉONTE   Don't you deceive me, Lucile?

COVIELLE (*to* NICOLE)   Dost thou not put a trick upon me?

LUCILE (*to* CLÉONTE)   There's nothing more true.

NICOLE (*to* COVIELLE)   'Tis the very thing, as it is.

COVIELLE (*to* CLÉONTE)   Shall we surrender upon this?

CLÉONTE   Ah, Lucile, what art have you to calm my passions with a single word! How easily do we suffer ourselves to be persuaded by those we love!

COVIELLE   How easily is one wheedled by these plaguy animals! [7]

(*Enter* MME JOURDAIN)

MME JOURDAIN   I am very glad to see you, Cléonte, and you are here apropos. My husband's acoming; catch your opportunity quick, and demand Lucile in marriage.

CLÉONTE   Ah, madame, how sweet is that word, how it flatters my wishes! Could I receive an order more charming? a favour more precious?

(*Enter* M. JOURDAIN)

Sir, I was not willing to employ any other person to make a certain demand of you which I have long intended. It concerns me sufficiently to undertake it in my own person; and, without further circumlocution, I shall inform you that the honour of being your son-in-law is an illustrious favour which I beseech you to grant me.

M. JOURDAIN   Before I give you an answer, sir, I desire you would tell me whether you are a gentleman.

CLÉONTE   Sir, the generality of people don't hesitate much on this question. People speak out bluff, and with ease. They make no scruple of taking this title upon 'em, and custom now-a-days seems to authorise the theft. For my part, I confess to you, my sentiments in this matter are somewhat more delicate. I look upon all imposture as unworthy an honest man, and that there is cowardice in denying what Heaven has made us; in tricking ourselves out, to the eyes of the world, in a stolen title; in desiring to put ourselves off for what we are not. I am undoubtedly born of parents who have held honourable employments. I have had the honour of six years' service in the army; and I find myself of consequence enough to hold a tolerable rank in the world; but for all this I won't give myself a name, which others in my place would think they might pretend to, and I'll tell you frankly that I am no gentleman. [8]

M. JOURDAIN   Your hand, sir; my daughter is no wife for you.

CLÉONTE   How?

M. JOURDAIN   You are no gentleman, you shan't have my daughter.

MME JOURDAIN   What would you be at then with your gentlemen? D'ye think we sort of people are of the line of St. Louis? [9]

M. JOURDAIN   Hold your tongue, wife, I see you're acoming.

MME JOURDAIN   Are we either of us otherwise descended than of plain citizens?

M. JOURDAIN   There's a scandalous reflection for you!

---

[7] This scene between the four lovers has been compared to a ballet because of its schematic, patterned quality. Can you imagine it danced or mimed?

[8] Cléonte, as opposed to Jourdain, accepts his station in life with neither pretense nor shame. It is a fact that many bourgeois were literally buying their way into the nobility at this time.

[9] Louis IX, King of France 1226–1270.

MME JOURDAIN   And was not your father a tradesman as well as mine?

M. JOURDAIN   Plague take the woman! She never has done with this. If your father was a tradesman, so much was the worse for him; but as for mine, they are numskulls that say he was. All that I have to say to you is that I will have a gentleman for my son-in-law.

MME JOURDAIN   Your daughter should have a husband that's proper for her, and an honest man who is rich and well made would be much better for her than a gentleman who is deformed and a beggar.

NICOLE   That's very true. We have a young squire in our town who is the most awkward looby, the veriest driveller that I ever set eyes on.

M. JOURDAIN   Hold your prate, Madame Impertinence. You are always thrusting yourself into conversation. I've means sufficient for my daughter, and want nothing but honour, and I will have her a marchioness.

MME JOURDAIN   A marchioness!

M. JOURDAIN   Yes, a marchioness.

MME JOURDAIN   Marry, Heaven preserve me from it!

M. JOURDAIN   'Tis a determined thing.

MME JOURDAIN   'Tis what I shall never consent to. Matches with people above one are always subject to grievous inconveniences. I don't like that a son-in-law should have it in his power to reproach my daughter with her parents, or that she should have children who should be ashamed to call me grandmother. Should she come and visit me with the equipage of a grand lady and, through inadvertency, miss curtsying to some of the neighbourhood, they would not fail, presently, saying a hundred idle things. Do but see, would they say, this lady marchioness, what haughty airs she gives herself! She's the daughter of Monsieur Jourdain, who was over and above happy, when she was a little one, to play children's play with us. She was not always so lofty as she is now; and her two grandfathers sold cloth near St. Innocent's Gate. They amassed great means for their children, which they are paying for now, perhaps very dear, in the other world. People don't generally grow so rich by being honest. I won't have all these tittle-tattle stories; in one word, I'll have a man who shall be beholden to me for my daughter, and to whom I can say, Sit you down there,

son-in-law, and dine with me.

M. JOURDAIN   See there the sentiments of a little soul, to desire always to continue in a mean condition. Let me have no more replies; my daughter shall be a marchioness in spite of the world; and if you put me in a passion, I'll make her a duchess.

(*Exit* M. JOURDAIN)

MME JOURDAIN   Cléonte, don't be discouraged by all this. (*to* LUCILE) Follow me, daughter, and come tell your father resolutely that if you have not him, you won't marry anybody at all.

(*Exeunt* MME JOURDAIN, LUCILE, *and* NICOLE)

COVIELLE   You have made a pretty piece of work of it with your fine sentiments.

CLÉONTE   What wouldst thou have me do? I have a scrupulousness in this case that no precedents can conquer.

COVIELLE   You're in the wrong to be serious with such a man as that. Don't you see that he's a fool? And would it cost you anything to accommodate yourself to his chimeras?

CLÉONTE   You're in the right; but I did not dream it was necessary to bring your proofs of nobility, to be son-in-law to Monsieur Jourdain.

COVIELLE (*laughing*)   Ha, ha, ha.

CLÉONTE   What d'ye laugh at?

COVIELLE   At a thought that's come into my head to play our spark off and help you to obtain what you desire.

CLÉONTE   How?

COVIELLE   The thought is absolutely droll.

CLÉONTE   What is it?

COVIELLE   There was a certain masquerade performed a little while ago, which comes in here the best in the world; and which I intend to insert into a piece of roguery I design to make for our coxcomb. This whole affair looks a little like making a joke of him; but with him we may hazard everything. There's no need here to study finesse so much—he's a man who will play his part to a wonder, and will easily give in to all the sham tales we shall take in our heads to tell him. I have actors, I have habits all ready, only let me alone.

CLÉONTE   But inform me of it.

COVIELLE   I am going to let you into the whole of it. Let's retire; there he comes.

(*Exeunt* COVIELLE *and* CLÉONTE. *Enter* M. JOURDAIN)

M. JOURDAIN   What a deuce can this mean? They have nothing but great lords to reproach me with; and I for my part see nothing so fine as keeping company with your great lords; there's nothing but honour and civility among 'em, and I would it had cost me two fingers of a hand to have been born a count or a marquis.

(*Enter a* LACKEY)

LACKEY   Sir, here's the count, and a lady whom he's handing in.

M. JOURDAIN   Good lack-a-day, I have some orders to give. Tell 'em that I'm acoming in a minute.

(*Exit* M. JOURDAIN. *Enter* DORANTE *and* DORIMÈNE)

LACKEY   My master says that he's acoming in a minute.

(*Exit* LACKEY)

DORANTE   'Tis very well.

DORIMÈNE   I don't know, Dorante; I take a strange step here in suffering you to bring me to a house where I know nobody.

DORANTE   What place then, madame, would you have a lover choose to entertain you in, since, to avoid clamour, you neither allow of your own house nor mine?

DORIMÈNE   But you don't mention that I am every day insensibly engaged to receive too great proofs of your passion. In vain do I refuse things, you weary me out of resistance, and you have a civil kind of obstinacy which makes me come gently into whatsoever you please. Frequent visits commenced, declarations came next, which drew after them serenades and entertainments, which were followed by presents. I opposed all these things, but you are not disheartened, and you become master of my resolutions step by step. For my part, I can answer for nothing hereafter, and I believe in the end you will bring me to matrimony, from which I stood so far aloof.

DORANTE   Faith, madame, you ought to have been there already. You are a widow, and depend upon nobody but yourself. I am my own master, and love you more than my life. What does it stick at, then, that you should not, from this day forward, complete my happiness?

DORIMÈNE   Lack-a-day, Dorante, there must go a great many qualities on both sides, to make people live happily together; and two of the most reasonable persons in the world have often much ado to compose a union to both their satisfactions.

DORANTE   You're in the wrong, madame, to represent to yourself so many difficulties in this affair; and the experience you have had concludes nothing for the rest of the world.

DORIMÈNE   In short, I always abide by this. The expenses you put yourself to for me disturb me for two reasons; one is, they engage me more than I could wish; and the other is, I'm sure (no offence to you!) that you can't do this but you must incommode yourself, and I would not have you do that.

DORANTE   Fie, madame, these are trifles, and 'tis not by that—

DORIMÈNE   I know what I say; and, amongst other things, the diamond you forced me to take, is of value—

DORANTE   Nay, madame, pray don't enhance the value of a thing my love thinks unworthy of you: and permit—Here's the master of the house.

(*Enter* M. JOURDAIN)

M. JOURDAIN (*after having made two bows, finding himself too near* DORIMÈNE)   A little farther, madame.

DORIMÈNE   How?

M. JOURDAIN   One step, if you please.

DORIMÈNE   What then?

M. JOURDAIN   Fall back a little for the third.

DORANTE   Monsieur Jourdain, madame, knows the world.

M. JOURDAIN   Madame, 'tis a very great honour that I am fortunate enough to be so happy, but to have the felicity that you should have the goodness to grant me the favour, to do me the honour, to honour me with the favour of your presence; and had I also the merit to merit a merit like yours, and that Heaven—envious of my good—had granted me—the advantage of being worthy—of—

DORANTE   Monsieur Jourdain, enough of this; my lady does not love great compliments, and she knows you are a man of wit. (*aside to* DORIMÈNE) 'Tis a downright bourgeois, ridiculous enough, as you see, in his whole behaviour.

DORIMÈNE (*aside to* DORANTE)   It is not very difficult to perceive it.

DORANTE   Madame, this is a very good friend of mine.

M. JOURDAIN   'Tis too much honour you do me.

DORANTE   A very polite man.

DORIMÈNE   I have a great esteem for him.

M. JOURDAIN   I have done nothing yet, madame, to merit this favour.

DORANTE (*aside to* M. JOURDAIN)   Take good care however not to speak to her of the diamond you gave her.

M. JOURDAIN (*aside to* DORANTE)   Mayn't I ask her only how she likes it?

DORANTE (*aside to* M. JOURDAIN)   How! Take special care you don't. 'Twould be villainous of you; and to act like a man of gallantry, you should make as if it were not you who made the present. (*aloud*) Monsieur Jourdain, madame, says that he's in raptures to see you at his house.

DORIMÈNE   He does me a great deal of honour.

M. JOURDAIN (*aside to* DORANTE)   How am I obliged to you, sir, for speaking to her in that manner on my account!

DORANTE (*aside to* M. JOURDAIN)   I have had a most terrible difficulty to get her to come hither.

M. JOURDAIN (*aside to* DORANTE)   I don't know how to thank you enough for it.

DORANTE   He says, madame, that he thinks you the most charming person in the world.

DORIMÈNE   'Tis a great favour he does me.

M. JOURDAIN   Madame, it's you who do the favours, and—

DORANTE   Let's think of eating.

(*Enter a* LACKEY)

LACKEY (*to* M. JOURDAIN)   Everything is ready, sir.

DORANTE   Come, then, let us sit down to table; and fetch the musicians.[10]

(*Six cooks, who have prepared the feast, dance together for the third intermission. After this, they carry on a table covered with several dishes.*)

ACT IV

THE SCENE.   *Dorimène, Monsieur Jourdain, Dorante, three Musicians, Lackeys*

DORIMÈNE   How, Dorante? Why here's a most magnificent repast!

M. JOURDAIN   You are pleased to banter, madame; I would it were more worthy of your acceptance.

(DORIMÈNE, M. JOURDAIN, DORANTE *and three* MUSICIANS *sit down at the table*)

DORANTE   Monsieur Jourdain, madame, is in the right in what he says, and he obliges me in paying you, after so handsome a manner, the honours of his house. I agree with him that the repast is not worthy of you. As it was myself who ordered it, and I am not so clearly sighted in these affairs as certain of our friends, you have here no very learned feast; and you will find incongruities of good cheer in it, some barbarisms of good taste. Had our friend Damis had a hand here, everything had been done by rule; elegance and erudition would have run through the whole, and he would not have failed exaggerating all the regular pieces of the repast he gave you, and force you to own his great capacity in the science of good eating; he would have told you of bread *de rive*, with the golden kissing-crust, raised too all round with a crust that crumples tenderly in your teeth; of wine with a velvet sap, heightened with a smartness not too overpowering; of a breast of mutton stuffed with parsley; of a loin of veal *de rivière*, thus long, white, delicate, and which is a true almond paste between the teeth; of your partridges heightened with a surprising *goût*; and then by way of farce or entertainment, of a soup with jelly broth, fortified with a young plump turkey-pout, cantoned with pigeons, and garnished with white onions married to succory. But, for my part, I confess to you my ignorance; and, as Monsieur Jourdain has very well said, I wish the repast were more worthy of your acceptance.[1]

---

[10] This is a key scene of the play, prepared for in the first scene of Act I. What do we learn about the characters of Dorante and Dorimène here?

[1] This speech gives us a good idea of what a seventeenth-century court meal was like. The French were already famous for their cuisine.

DORIMÈNE   I make no other answer to this compliment than eating as I do.

M. JOURDAIN   Ah! what pretty hands are there!

DORIMÈNE   The hands are so so, Monsieur Jourdain; but you mean to speak of the diamond, which is very pretty.

M. JOURDAIN   I, madame? Marry, Heaven forbid I should speak of it; I should not act like a gentleman of gallantry, and the diamond is a very trifle.

DORIMÈNE   You are wondrous nice.

M. JOURDAIN   You have too much goodness—

DORANTE (*having made signs to* M. JOURDAIN)
    Come, give some wine to Monsieur Jourdain, and to those gentlemen who will do us the favour to sing us a catch.

DORIMÈNE   You give a wondrous relish to the good cheer by mixing music with it; I am admirably well regaled here.

M. JOURDAIN   Madame, it is not—

DORANTE   Monsieur Jourdain, let us listen to these gentlemen, they'll entertain us with something better than all we can possibly say.

FIRST AND SECOND MUSICIANS (*together, each with a glass in his hand*)
Put it round, my dear Phyllis, invert the bright glass;
    Oh what charms to the crystal those fingers impart!
You and Bacchus combined, all resistance surpass,
    And with passion redoubled have ravished my heart.
        'Twixt him, you, and me, my charmer, my fair,
        Eternal affection let's swear.

At the touch of those lips how he sparkles more bright!
    And his touch, in return, those lips does embellish:
I could quaff 'em all day, and drink bumpers all night.
    What longing each gives me, what gusto, what relish!
        'Twixt him, you, and me, my charmer, my fair,
        Eternal affection let's swear.

SECOND AND THIRD MUSICIANS (*together*)
Since time flies so nimbly away,
    Come drink, my dear boys, drink about;
Let's husband him well while we may,
    For life may be gone before the mug's out.
When Charon has got us aboard,
    Our drinking and wooing are past;
We ne'er to lose time can afford,
    For drinking's a trade not always to last.

Let your puzzling rogues in the schools,
    Dispute of the bonum *of man;*
Philosophers dry are but fools—
    The secret is this: drink, drink off your can.
When Charon has got us aboard,
    Our drinking and wooing are past;
We ne'er to lose time can afford,
    For drinking's a trade not always to last.

ALL THREE (*together*)
Why bob there! some wine, boys! come fill the glass, fill,
Round and round let it go, till we bid it stand still.

DORIMÈNE   I don't think anything can be better sung; and 'tis extremely fine.

M. JOURDAIN   I see something here though, madame, much finer.

DORIMÈNE   Hey! Monsieur Jourdain is more gallant than I thought he was.

DORANTE   How, madame! who do you take Monsieur Jourdain for?

M. JOURDAIN   I wish she would take me for what I could name.

DORIMÈNE   Again?

DORANTE (*to* DORIMÈNE)   You don't know him.

M. JOURDAIN   She shall know me whenever she pleases.

DORIMÈNE   Oh! Too much.

DORANTE   He's one who has a repartee always at hand. But you don't see, madame, that Monsieur Jourdain eats all the pieces you have touched.

DORIMÈNE   Monsieur Jourdain is a man that I am charmed with.

M. JOURDAIN   If I could charm your heart, I should be—

(*Enter* MME JOURDAIN)

MME JOURDAIN   Hey-day! why here's a jolly company of you, and I see very well you did not expect me. It was for this pretty affair, then, Monsieur Husband o' mine, that you were in such a violent hurry to pack me off to dine with my sister; I just now found a play-house below, and here I find a dinner fit for a wedding. Thus it is you spend your money, and thus it is you feast the ladies in my absence, and present 'em with music and a play, whilst I'm sent abroad in the meantime.

DORANTE   What do you mean, Madame Jourdain? and what's your fancy to take it into your head that your husband spends his money, and that 'tis he who entertains my lady? Know, pray, that 'tis I do it, that he only lends me his house, and that you ought to consider a little better what you say.

M. JOURDAIN   Yes, Madame Impertinence, 'tis the count that presents the lady with all this, who is a person of quality. He does me the honour to borrow my house, and is pleased to let me be with him.

MME JOURDAIN   'Tis all stuff, this. I know what I know.

DORANTE   Madame Jourdain, take your best spectacles, take 'em.

MME JOURDAIN   I've no need of spectacles, sir, I see clear enough; I've smelt things out a great while ago, I am no ass. 'Tis base in you, who are a great lord, to lend a helping hand, as you do, to the follies of my husband. And you, madame, who are a great lady, 'tis neither handsome nor honest in you to sow dissension in a family, and to suffer my husband to be in love with you.

DORIMÈNE   What can be the meaning of all this? Go, Dorante, 'tis wrong in you to expose me to the silly visions of this raving woman.

DORANTE (following DORIMÈNE, who goes out)   Madame, why madame, where are you running?

M. JOURDAIN   Madame—My lord, make my excuses to her and endeavour to bring her back.

(Exit DORANTE)

(To MME JOURDAIN) Ah! impertinent creature as you are, these are your fine doings; you come and affront me in the face of all the world, and drive people of quality away from my house.

MME JOURDAIN   I value not their quality.

(LACKEYS take away the table)

M. JOURDAIN   I don't know what hinders me, you plaguy hussy, from splitting your skull with the

fragments of the feast you came here to disturb.

MME JOURDAIN (going)   I despise all this. I defend my own rights, and I shall have all the wives on my side.

M. JOURDAIN   You do well to get out of the way of my fury.

(Exit MME JOURDAIN)

She came here at a most unlucky time. I was in the humour of saying fine things, and never did I find myself so witty. What have we got here?

(Enter COVIELLE, disguised)

COVIELLE   Sir, I don't know whether I have the honour to be known to you.

M. JOURDAIN   No, sir.

COVIELLE   I have seen you when you were not above thus tall.

M. JOURDAIN   Me?

COVIELLE   Yes. You were one of the prettiest children in the world; and all the ladies used to take you in their arms to kiss you.

M. JOURDAIN   To kiss me?

COVIELLE   Yes, I was an intimate friend of the late gentleman your father.

M. JOURDAIN   Of the late gentleman my father!

COVIELLE   Yes. He was a very honest gentleman.

M. JOURDAIN   What is't you say?

COVIELLE   I say that he was a very honest gentleman.

M. JOURDAIN   My father?

COVIELLE   Yes.

M. JOURDAIN   Did you know him very well?

COVIELLE   Certainly.

M. JOURDAIN   And did you know him for a gentleman?

COVIELLE   Without doubt.

M. JOURDAIN   I don't know then what the world means.

COVIELLE   How?

M. JOURDAIN   There is a stupid sort of people who would face me down that he was a tradesman.

COVIELLE   He a tradesman? 'Tis mere scandal; he never was one. All that he did was, that he was very obliging, very officious, and as he was a great connoisseur in stuffs, he used to pick them up everywhere, have 'em carried to his house, and gave 'em to his friends for money.

M. JOURDAIN   I'm very glad of your acquaintance, that

you may bear witness that my father was a gentleman.

COVIELLE   I'll maintain it in the face of all the world.

M. JOURDAIN   You will oblige me. What business brings you here?

COVIELLE   Since my acquaintance with the late gentleman your father, honest gentleman, as I was telling you, I have travelled round the world.

M. JOURDAIN   Round the world?

COVIELLE   Yes.

M. JOURDAIN   I fancy 'tis a huge way off, that same country.

COVIELLE   Most certainly. I have not been returned from these tedious travels of mine but four days. And because I have an interest in everything that concerns you, I come to tell you the best news in the world.

M. JOURDAIN   What?

COVIELLE   You know that the son of the Great Turk is here.

M. JOURDAIN   I? No.

COVIELLE   How? He has a most magnificent train. All the world goes to see him, and he has been received in this country as a person of importance.

M. JOURDAIN   In troth, I did not know that.

COVIELLE   What is of advantage to you in this affair is that he is in love with your daughter.

M. JOURDAIN   The son of the Great Turk?

COVIELLE   Yes, and wants to be your son-in-law.

M. JOURDAIN   My son-in-law, the son of the Great Turk?

COVIELLE   The son of the Great Turk your son-in-law. As I have been to see him, and perfectly understand his language, he held a conversation with me; and after some other discourse, says he to me: "Acciam croc soler, onch alla moustaph gidelum amanahem varahini oussere carbulath." That is to say, "Have you not seen a young handsome person, who is the daughter of Monsieur Jourdain, a gentleman of Paris?"

M. JOURDAIN   The son of the Great Turk said that of me?

COVIELLE   Yes, as I made answer to him that I knew you particularly well, and that I had seen your daughter. Ah, says he to me, "Marababa sahem"; that is to say, "Ah! how am I enamoured with her!"

M. JOURDAIN   "Marababa sahem" means: "Ah! how am I enamoured with her"?

COVIELLE   Yes.

M. JOURDAIN   Marry, you did well to tell me so, for as for my part, I should never have believed that "Marababa sahem" had meant, "Ah! how am I enamoured with her!" 'Tis an admirable language, this same Turkish!

COVIELLE   More admirable than one can believe. Do you know very well what is the meaning of "Cacaramouchen"?

M. JOURDAIN   "Cacaramouchen"? No.

COVIELLE   'Tis as if you should say, "My dear soul."

M. JOURDAIN   "Cacaramouchen" means, "My dear soul"?

COVIELLE   Yes.

M. JOURDAIN   Why, 'tis very wonderful! "Cacaramouchen—my dear soul." Would one ever have thought it? I am perfectly confounded at it.

COVIELLE   In short, to finish my embassy, he comes to demand your daughter in marriage; and to have a father-in-law who should be suitable to him, he designs to make you a Mamamouchi, which is a certain grand dignity of his country.

M. JOURDAIN   Mamamouchi?

COVIELLE   Yes, Mamamouchi; that is to say, in our language, a Paladin. Paladin is your ancient—Paladin, in short—there's nothing in the world more noble than this; and you will rank with the grandest lord upon earth.

M. JOURDAIN   The son of the Great Turk does me a great deal of honour, and I desire you would carry me to him, to return him my thanks.

COVIELLE   How? Why he's just acoming hither.

M. JOURDAIN   Is he acoming hither?

COVIELLE   Yes. And he brings all things along with him for the ceremony of your dignity.

M. JOURDAIN   He's main hasty.

COVIELLE   His love will suffer no delay.

M. JOURDAIN   All that perplexes me, in this case, is that my daughter is an obstinate hussy who has took into her head one Cléonte, and vows she'll marry no person besides him.

COVIELLE   She'll change her opinion when she sees the son of the Grand Turk; and then there happens here a very marvellous adventure, that is, that the son of the Grand Turk resembles this Cléonte, with a trifling difference. I just now came from him, they showed him me; and the love she bears for one may easily pass to the other, and—I hear him coming; there he is.

(Enter CLÉONTE, *like a Turk, and three* PAGES *holding up his gown)*

CLÉONTE   Ambousahim oqui boraf, Iordina, salamalequi.[2]

COVIELLE *(to* M. JOURDAIN*)*   That is to say, Monsieur Jourdain, "May your heart be all the year like a rose-tree in flower!" These are obliging ways of speaking in that country.

M. JOURDAIN   I am His Turkish Highness's most humble servant.

COVIELLE   Carigar camboto oustin moraf.

CLÉONTE   Oustin yoc catamalequi basum base alla moran.

COVIELLE   He says, "Heaven give you the strength of lions and the prudence of serpents!"

M. JOURDAIN   His Turkish Highness does me too much honour; and I wish him all manner of prosperity.

COVIELLE   Ossa binamin sadoc babally oracaf ouram.

CLÉONTE   Bel-men.

COVIELLE   He says that you should go quickly with him to prepare yourself for the ceremony, in order afterwards to see your daughter and to conclude the marriage.

M. JOURDAIN   So many things in two words?

COVIELLE   Yes, the Turkish language is much in that way; it says a great deal in a few words. Go quickly where he desires you.

(Exeunt M. JOURDAIN, CLÉONTE, *and* PAGES*)*

Ha, ha, ha. I'faith, this is all absolutely droll. What a dupe! Had he had his part by heart, he could not have played it better. O, ho!

(Enter DORANTE*)*

I beseech you, sir, lend us a helping hand here, in a certain affair which is in agitation.

DORANTE   Ah! ah! Covielle, who could have known thee? How art thou trimmed out there!

COVIELLE   You see, ha, ha!

DORANTE   What do ye laugh at?

COVIELLE   At a thing, sir, that well deserves it.

DORANTE   What?

COVIELLE   I could give you a good many times, sir, to guess the stratagem we are making use of with Monsieur Jourdain, to bring him over to give his daughter to my master.

DORANTE   I don't at all guess the stratagem, but I guess it will not fail of its effect, since you undertake it.

COVIELLE   I know, sir, you are not unacquainted with the animal.

DORANTE   Tell me what it is.

COVIELLE   Be at the trouble of withdrawing a little farther off, to make room for what I see acoming. You will see one part of the story whilst I give you a narration of the rest.

THE TURKISH CEREMONY

The Mufti, Dervishes, Turks (assisting the Mufti), Singers and Dancers

THE SCENE.   *Six Turks enter gravely, two and two, to the sound of instruments. They bear three carpets, with which they dance in several figures, and then lift them up very high. The Turks, singing, pass under the carpets and range themselves on each side of the stage. The Mufti, accompanied by Dervishes, closes the march.*

Then the Turks spread the carpets on the ground and kneel down upon them, the Mufti and the Dervishes standing in the middle of them; while the Mufti invokes Mahomet in dumb contortions and grimaces, the Turks prostrate themselves to the ground, singing Allah, raising their hands to heaven, singing Allah, and so continuing alternately to the end of the invocation, when they all rise up, singing Allahekber.

Then two Dervishes bring Monsieur Jourdain, clothed like a Turk, his head shaved, without a turban or sabre.

MUFTI *(to* M. JOURDAIN*)*
    If thou understandest,
        Answer;
    If thou dost not understand,
        Hold thy peace, hold thy peace.

    I am Mufti,
        Thou! who thou art
    I don't know:
        Hold thy peace, hold thy peace.

(Two DERVISHES *retire with* M. JOURDAIN*)*

---

[2] This is, of course, an invented language, but Molière has made it sound somewhat like Arabic.

Say, Turk, who is this, An Anabaptist, an Anabaptist?
THE TURKS   No.
MUFTI   A Zwinglian?
THE TURKS   No.
MUFTI   A Coffite?
THE TURKS   No.
MUFTI   A Hussite? A Morist? A Fronist?
THE TURKS   No, no, no.
MUFTI   No, no, no. Is he a Pagan?
THE TURKS   No.
MUFTI   A Lutheran?
THE TURKS   No.
MUFTI   A Puritan?
THE TURKS   No.
MUFTI   A Brahmin? A Moffian? A Zurian?
THE TURKS   No, no, no.
MUFTI   No, no, no. A Mahometan, a Mahometan?
THE TURKS   There you have it, there you have it.
MUFTI   How is he called? How is he called?
THE TURKS   Jourdain, Jourdain.
MUFTI (dancing)   Jourdain! Jourdain!
THE TURKS   Jourdain, Jourdain.
MUFTI
  To Mahomet for Jourdain
  I pray night and day,
  That he would make a Paladin
  Of Jourdain, of Jourdain.
  Give him a turban, and give a sabre,
  With a galley and a brigantine,
  To defend Palestine.
  To Mahomet for Jourdain
  I pray night and day.[3]
  (to the Turks) Is Jourdain a good Turk?
THE TURKS   That he is, that he is.
MUFTI (singing and dancing)   Ha, la ba, ba la chou,
  ba la ba, ba la da.

  (Exit MUFTI)

THE TURKS   Ha, la ba, ba la chou, ba la ba, ba la da.

THE SCENE.   The Mufti returns with the State Turban,
which is of an immeasurable largeness, garnished with
lighted wax candles, four or five rows deep, accompanied by
two Dervishes, bearing the Alcoran, with comic caps garnished also with lighted candles.

---

[3] The resemblance of Monsieur Jourdain's name to the Jordan river is
  used to make him "defender of Palestine."

The two other Dervishes lead up Monsieur Jourdain and
place him on his knees with his hands to the ground so that
his back, on which the Alcoran is placed, may serve for a
desk to the Mufti, who makes a second burlesque invocation, knitting his eyebrows, striking his hands sometimes
upon the Alcoran, and tossing over the leaves with precipi-
tation, after which, lifting up his hands, and crying with a
loud voice, Hoo.
  During this second invocation the assistant Turks, bowing down and raising themselves alternately, sing likewise,
HOO, HOO, HOO.

M. JOURDAIN (after they have taken the Alcoran off
  his back)   Ouf!
MUFTI (to M. JOURDAIN)   Thou wilt not be a knave?
THE TURKS   No, no, no.
MUFTI   Not be a thief?
THE TURKS   No, no, no.
MUFTI (to the TURKS)   Give the turban.
THE TURKS
  Thou wilt not be a knave?
    No, no, no.
  Not be a thief?
    No, no, no.
  Give the turban.

  (The TURKS, dancing, put the turban on M. JOURDAIN's
  head at the sound of the instruments)

MUFTI (giving the sabre to M. JOURDAIN)
  Be brave, be no scoundrel,
  Take the sabre.
THE TURKS (drawing their sabres)
  Be brave, be no scoundrel,
  Take the sabre.

  (The TURKS, dancing, strike M. JOURDAIN several times
  with their sabres, to music)

MUFTI
  Give, give
  The bastonade.
THE TURKS
  Give, give
  The bastonade.

  (The TURKS, dancing, give M. JOURDAIN several strokes
  with a cudgel, to music)

MUFTI
  Don't think it a shame,
  This is the last affront.

THE TURKS
> *Don't think it a shame,*
> *This is the last affront.*

(*The* MUFTI *begins a third invocation. The* DERVISHES *support him with great respect, after which the* TURKS, *singing and dancing round the* MUFTI, *retire with him and lead off* MONSIEUR JOURDAIN.)

ACT V

THE SCENE.   *Madame Jourdain, Monsieur Jourdain*

MME JOURDAIN   Bless us all! Mercy upon us! What have we got here? What a figure! What! dressed to go a-mumming, and is this a time to go masked? Speak therefore, what does this mean? Who has trussed you up in this manner?

M. JOURDAIN   Do but see the impertinent slut, to speak after this manner to a Mamamouchi.

MME JOURDAIN   How's that?

M. JOURDAIN   Yes, you must show me respect now I am just made a Mamamouchi.

MME JOURDAIN   What d'ye mean with your Mamamouchi?

M. JOURDAIN   Mamamouchi, I tell you. I am a Mamamouchi.

MME JOURDAIN   What beast is that?

M. JOURDAIN   Mamamouchi, that is to say, in our language, a Paladin.

MME JOURDAIN   A Paladin? Are you of an age to be a morris-dancer? [1]

M. JOURDAIN   What an ignoramus! I say, Paladin. 'Tis a dignity of which I have just now gone through the ceremony.

MME JOURDAIN   What ceremony then?

M. JOURDAIN   Mahameta per Jordina.

MME JOURDAIN   What does that mean?

M. JOURDAIN   Jordina, that is to say, Jourdain.

MME JOURDAIN   Well, how Jourdain?

M. JOURDAIN   Voler far un Paladina de Jordina. [2]

MME JOURDAIN   What?

M. JOURDAIN   Dar turbanta con galera.

MME JOURDAIN   What's the meaning of that?

M. JOURDAIN   Per deffender Palestina.

MME JOURDAIN   What is it you would say?

M. JOURDAIN   Dara, dara, bastonnara.

MME JOURDAIN   What is this same jargon?

M. JOURDAIN   Non tener honta, questa star l'ultima affronta.

MME JOURDAIN   What in the name of wonder can all this be?

M. JOURDAIN (*singing and dancing*)   Hou la ba, ba la chou, ba la ba, ba la da. (*falls down to the ground*)

MME JOURDAIN   Alas and well-a-day! My husband is turned fool.

M. JOURDAIN (*getting up and walking off*)   Peace! insolence, show respect to Monsieur Mamamouchi.

MME JOURDAIN (*alone*)   How could he lose his senses? I must run and prevent his going out. (*seeing* DORIMÈNE *and* DORANTE) So, so, here come the rest of our gang. I see nothing but vexation on all sides.

(*Exit* MME JOURDAIN. *Enter* DORANTE *and* DORIMÈNE)

DORANTE   Yes, madame, you'll see the merriest thing that can be seen; and I don't believe it's possible, in the whole world, to find another man so much a fool as this here. And besides, madame, we must endeavour to promote Cléonte's amour and to countenance his masquerade. He's a very pretty gentleman and deserves that one should interest one's self in his favour.

DORIMÈNE   I've a very great value for him, and he deserves good fortune.

DORANTE   Besides, we have here, madame, an entertainment that will suit us, and which we ought not to suffer to be lost; and I must by all means see whether my fancy will succeed.

DORIMÈNE   I saw there magnificent preparations, and these are things, Dorante, I can no longer suffer. Yes, I'm resolved to put a stop, at last, to your profusions; and to break off all the expenses you are at on my account, I have determined to marry you out of hand. This is the real secret of the affair, and all these things end, as you know, with marriage.

DORANTE   Ah! madame, is it possible you should form so kind a resolution in my favour?

DORIMÈNE   I only do it to prevent you from ruining yourself; and without this, I see plainly that before 'tis long you won't be worth a groat.

---

[1] In the original, "a ballet dancer." Morris dances were (and are) done in the English countryside, in costume.

[2] This "language," which resembles Italian, is used in the ceremony in the original.

DORANTE   How am I obliged to you, madame, for the care you take to preserve my estate! 'Tis entirely at your service, as well as my heart, and you may use both of 'em just in the manner you please.

DORIMÈNE   I shall make a proper use of them both. But here comes your man; an admirable figure.

(Enter M. JOURDAIN)

DORANTE   Sir, my lady and I are come to pay our homage to your new dignity, and to rejoice with you at the marriage you are concluding betwixt your daughter and the son of the Grand Turk.

M. JOURDAIN (bowing first in the Turkish manner) Sir, I wish you the force of serpents and the wisdom of lions.

DORIMÈNE   I was exceeding glad to be one of the first, sir, who should come and congratulate you upon the high degree of glory to which you are raised.

M. JOURDAIN   Madame, I wish your rose-tree may flower all the year round; I am infinitely obliged to you for interesting yourselves in the honour that's paid me; and I am greatly rejoiced to see you returned hither, that I may make my most humble excuses for the impertinence of my wife.

DORIMÈNE   That's nothing at all, I can excuse a commotion of this kind in her; your heart ought to be precious to her, and 'tis not at all strange the possession of such a man as you are should give her some alarms.

M. JOURDAIN   The possession of my heart is a thing you have entirely gained.

DORANTE   You see, madame, that Monsieur Jourdain is none of those people whom prosperity blinds, and that he knows, in all his grandeur, how to own his friends.

DORIMÈNE   'Tis the mark of a truly generous soul.

DORANTE   Where is His Turkish Highness? We should be glad, as your friends, to pay our devoirs to him.

M. JOURDAIN   There he comes, and I have sent to bring my daughter to join hands with him.

(Enter CLÉONTE, in a Turkish habit)

DORANTE (to CLÉONTE)   Sir, we come to compliment Your Highness, as friends of the gentleman your father-in-law, and to assure you, with respect, of our most humble services.

M. JOURDAIN   Where's the dragoman, to tell him who you are and make him understand what you say? You shall see that he'll answer you, and he speaks Turkish marvellously. Hola! there; where the deuce is he gone? (to CLÉONTE)

Stref,

strif,

strof,

straf.

The gentleman is a

> grande segnore, grande segnore,
> grande segnore;

and madame is a

> granda dama, granda dama.

(Seeing he cannot make himself be understood)

Lack-a-day!

(to CLÉONTE) Sir, he be a French Mamamouchi, and madame a French Mamamouchess. I can't speak plainer. Good, here's the dragoman.

(Enter COVIELLE, disguised)

Where do you run? We can say nothing without you. (pointing to CLÉONTE) Inform him a little that the gentleman and lady are persons of great quality who come to pay their compliments to him, as friends of mine, and to assure him of their services. (to DORIMÈNE and DORANTE) You shall see how he will answer.

COVIELLE   Alabala crociam, acci boram alabamen.

CLÉONTE   Catalequi tubal ourin soter amalouchan.

M. JOURDAIN (to DORIMÈNE and DORANTE)   Do ye see?

COVIELLE   He says that the rain of prosperity waters, at all seasons, the garden of your family.

M. JOURDAIN   I told you that he speaks Turkish.

DORANTE   This is admirable.

(Enter LUCILE)

M. JOURDAIN   Come, daughter, come nearer, and give the gentleman your hand who does you the honour of demanding you in marriage.

LUCILE   What's the matter, father, how are you dressed here? What! are you playing a comedy?

M. JOURDAIN   No, no, 'tis no comedy, 'tis a very serious affair; and the most honourable for you that possibly can be wished. (pointing to CLÉONTE) This is the husband I bestow upon you.

LUCILE   Upon me, father?

M. JOURDAIN   Yes, upon you. Come, take him by the hand, and thank Heaven for your good fortune.

LUCILE   I won't marry.

M. JOURDAIN   I'll make you; am I not your father?

LUCILE   I won't do it.

M. JOURDAIN   Here's a noise indeed! Come, I tell you. Your hand here.

LUCILE   No, father, I've told you before that there's no power can oblige me to take any other husband than Cléonte; and I am determined upon all extremities rather than—(discovering CLÉONTE) 'Tis true that you are my father; I owe you absolute obedience; and you may dispose of me according to your pleasure.

M. JOURDAIN   Hah, I am charmed to see you return so readily to your duty; and it is a pleasure to me to have my daughter obedient.

(Enter MME JOURDAIN)

MME JOURDAIN   How, how, what does this mean? They tell me you design to marry your daughter to a mummer.[3]

M. JOURDAIN   Will you hold your tongue, impertinence? You're always coming to mix your extravagances with everything; there's no possibility of teaching you common sense.

MME JOURDAIN   'Tis you whom there's no teaching to be wise, and you go from folly to folly. What's your design, what would you do with this flock of people?

M. JOURDAIN   I design to marry my daughter to the son of the Grand Turk.

MME JOURDAIN   To the son of the Grand Turk?

M. JOURDAIN   Yes. (pointing to COVIELLE) Make your compliments to him by the dragoman there.

MME JOURDAIN   I have nothing to do with the dragoman, and I shall tell him plainly to his face that he shall have none of my daughter.

M. JOURDAIN   Will you hold your tongue once more?

DORANTE   What, Madame Jourdain, do you oppose such an honour as this? Do you refuse His Turkish Highness for a son-in-law?

MME JOURDAIN   Lack-a-day, sir, meddle you with your own affairs.

---

[3] An actor.

DORIMÈNE   'Tis a great honour, 'tis by no means to be rejected.

MME JOURDAIN   Madame, I desire you too not to give yourself any trouble about what no ways concerns you.

DORANTE   'Tis the friendship we have for you that makes us interest ourselves in what is of advantage to you.

MME JOURDAIN   I shall easily excuse your friendship.

DORANTE   There's your daughter consents to her father's pleasure.

MME JOURDAIN   My daughter consent to marry a Turk?

DORANTE   Certainly.

MME JOURDAIN   Can she forget Cléonte?

DORANTE   What would one not do to be a great lady?

MME JOURDAIN   I would strangle her with my own hands, had she done such a thing as this.

M. JOURDAIN   Here's tittle-tattle in abundance. I tell you this marriage shall be consummated.

MME JOURDAIN   And I tell you that it shall not be consummated.

M. JOURDAIN   What a noise is here?

LUCILE   Mother!

MME JOURDAIN   Go, you are a pitiful hussy.

M. JOURDAIN (to MME JOURDAIN)   What! do you scold her for being obedient to me?

MME JOURDAIN   Yes, she belongs to me as well as you.

COVIELLE (to MME JOURDAIN)   Madame.

MME JOURDAIN   What would you say to me, you?

COVIELLE   One word.

MME JOURDAIN   I've nothing to do with your word.

COVIELLE (to M. JOURDAIN)   Sir, would she hear me but one word in private, I'll promise you to make her consent to what you have a mind.

MME JOURDAIN   I won't consent to it.

COVIELLE   Only hear me.

MME JOURDAIN   No.

M. JOURDAIN (to MME JOURDAIN)   Give him the hearing.

MME JOURDAIN   No, I won't hear him.

M. JOURDAIN   He'll tell you—

MME JOURDAIN   He shall tell me nothing.

M. JOURDAIN   Do but see the great obstinacy of the woman! Will it do you any harm to hear him?

COVIELLE   Only hear me; you may do what you please afterwards.

MME JOURDAIN   Well, what?

COVIELLE (*aside to* MME JOURDAIN)   We have made signs to you, madame, this hour. Don't you see plainly that all is done purely to accommodate ourselves to the visions of your husband; that we are imposing upon him under this disguise, and that it is Cléonte himself who is the son of the Great Turk?

MME JOURDAIN (*aside to* COVIELLE)   Oh, oh?

COVIELLE (*aside to* MME JOURDAIN)   And that 'tis me, Covielle, who am the dragoman?

MME JOURDAIN (*aside to* COVIELLE)   Oh! in that case, I give up.

COVIELLE (*aside to* MME JOURDAIN)   Don't seem to know anything of the matter.

MME JOURDAIN (*aloud*)   Yes, 'tis all done, I consent to the marriage.

M. JOURDAIN   Ay, all the world submits to reason. (*to* MME JOURDAIN) You would not hear him. I knew he would explain to you what the son of the Great Turk is.

MME JOURDAIN   He has explained it to me sufficiently, and I'm satisfied with it. Let us send for a notary.

DORANTE   'Tis well said. And, Madame Jourdain, that you may set your mind perfectly at rest, and that you should this day quit all jealousy which you may have entertained of the gentleman your husband, my lady and I shall make use of the same notary to marry us.

MME JOURDAIN   I consent to that too.

M. JOURDAIN (*aside to* DORANTE)   'Tis to make her believe.

DORANTE (*aside to* M. JOURDAIN)   We must by all means amuse her a little with this pretence.

M. JOURDAIN   Good, good. (*aloud*) Let somebody go for the notary.

DORANTE   In the meantime, till he comes and has drawn up the contracts, let us see our entertainment, and give His Turkish Highness the diversion of it.

M. JOURDAIN   Well advised; come let us take our places.

MME JOURDAIN   And Nicole?

M. JOURDAIN   I give her to the dragoman; and my wife, to whosoever pleases to take her.

COVIELLE   Sir, I thank you. (*aside*) If it's possible to find a greater fool than this, I'll go and publish it in Rome.

(The play ends with the "ballet des nations," a spectacle of music, singing, and dancing in which various nationalities are impersonated.)

COMMENTS AND QUESTIONS

1. Outline the plot of this comedy. Notice its simplicity. Some elements—the young lovers who wish to marry against the father's wishes, the marriages at the end—are stock features of comedy. How does Molière maintain interest?

2. Is anything really resolved in the end? Do you wonder about M. Jourdain's future? Could Molière have ended the comedy differently? More satisfactorily?

3. Do you feel that it is appropriate for each of the acts, and the whole show, to end with ballets? Why or why not?

4. What is Molière really ridiculing here, in your opinion? The bourgeoisie? The nobility? A particular type of character or character defect? The defects of an overcivilized society? Support your answer.

5. For which character do you feel the most sympathy? The least? There has always been considerable disagreement on this point—why?

6. How does a playwright succeed in portraying a character? What makes M. Jourdain memorable?

7. How does this play differ from and resemble other examples of comedy that we read in Volume I both as drama (*Lysistrata*) and as narrative ("The Miller's Tale")?

8. Could *The Would-Be Gentleman* be rewritten as a sentimental drama or as a tragedy? How and why does it make human weakness funny?

Lully's Music from *The Would-Be Gentleman*

Modern audiences view Molière's text as the most important element of this comedy-ballet, but the seventeenth-century audience thought of it as "a ballet composed of six *entrées* accompanied by comedy."[1] The music and dance were thus highly significant elements. The composer Lully enjoyed at the time a greater prestige than did Molière. He dominated French music

---

[1] The music and the entire play in French can be heard on London Records, LL 1447.

from the time of his appointment as superintendent of Music of the Chamber in 1661 until his death in 1687, and his taste for magnificence is reflected in his compositions for the king: theater pieces with acting, dance, orchestra, costumes, and elaborate scenery. He directed two string orchestras—the *Grande Bande* or "The King's 24 Violins" and the *Petite Bande.* Of course he wrote other music, but his operas and ballets stand out as the most characteristic of the types of music enjoyed at court at this time. In his comedy-ballets, Lully perfected all the elements of his mature style: appro-

priately pompous overtures for string orchestra; massive and spectacular choruses; rhythmically attractive dances that reflect the tastes of the French court; and musical recitatives suited to the French language.

Le Bourgeois Gentilhomme begins with a "French Overture," an instrumental form established by Lully for the introduction of large works—operas and ballets. It was also used as an independent composition and as an opening movement of an instrumental *suite, sonata,* or *concerto.* These compositions for the *24 Violons du Roi* are composed in two parts: the first section in duple *meter,* jagged *rhythm, homophonic* or *chordal texture,* and slow, majestic movement; the second section in triple meter, sprightly rhythm, and *fugal* or *contrapuntal texture.*

JEAN-BAPTISTE LULLY

Le Bourgeois Gentilhomme

(Beginning of the Overture)

A reduction demonstrating homophonic character and jagged rhythm

(Beginning of the second section of the Overture)

In listening to the opening section, one hears not only the jagged or dotted rhythm of the melodies but also an underlying pulse or beat of steady eighth notes, a stylistic feature of the period that some have referred to as the "baroque motor rhythm." This new sense of beat, like the jazz drummer's sense of time, pervades the music and infuses it with life and motion.

A clever baroque device occurs immediately after the conclusion of the overture. The play opens with a play within the play. We discover the composer at work at his harpsichord preparing music for the *comédie-ballet* to follow.

We see and hear him trying phrases, accepting and rejecting passages, humming and strumming, and otherwise reworking a number heard later in its polished form, *Je languis nuit et jour* ("I pine night and day.").

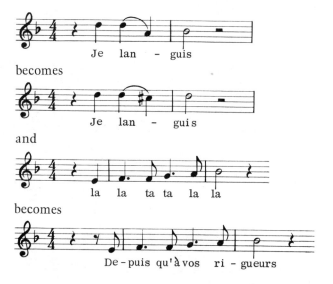

Actually, Lully is not giving us a true glimpse into the composer's workshop, for the unfinished version is as complete, correct, and baroque as the shorter final song; but he gives the impression of something not real, and that is very characteristic of French baroque theater. It delighted Louis XIV and is capable of delighting audiences today.

Molière's story line, of course, outlines the formal structure of the entire comedy-ballet, but, according to taste, Lully inserts favorite court dances throughout.

Both Lully and Louis took music seriously. For political reasons, the court composer had to do his best to please his sovereign, as inferior performance was rewarded harshly. On the other hand, for political reasons, too, Louis XIV took his court entertainments most seriously. Besides satisfying his vanity and love of pleasure, they helped to perpetuate the mystique of absolutist monarchy. Keeping the nobles and even the bourgeoisie pleasantly entertained was another way of keeping them in their place.

Sarabande

Bourrée

Gavotte

Turkish March

22

A MASTERPIECE OF BAROQUE MUSIC: HANDEL'S *MESSIAH*

No matter how fine the compositions of Lully, the centuries have taught us that two baroque composers rise above all others—Johann Sebastian Bach and George Frideric Handel. Each has left us a vast store of musical riches that span the compass from small to large, easy to difficult, sacred to secular, instrumental to vocal, incidental to monumental. No single work selected for analysis can represent an entire age, and no single work will ever be universally judged the finest product of a period; but in the case of baroque music, one single work has more performances in our day than any other, more people are personally involved in its preparation and presentation than any other, and it shows every sign of remaining on top of the classical hit parade for decades to come: Handel's English masterpiece, *Messiah*. For these reasons it becomes important to step out of seventeenth-century France and into the bustle of eighteenth-century England to investigate in some depth a work that, like Molière's comedies, was in part created for the pleasure of a monarch (George II) but became popular with people from all walks of life. Although written over two hundred years ago, the *Messiah* will be available to most Americans through live performance or live broadcast at least twice a year, at Christmas and Easter. Universal recognition is not the only criterion for greatness in music, but it is clear that no other musical composition has captured the sincere affection of the English-speaking world more completely. In every aspect of its existence—concept, design, scale, quality—it is a monumental work, a superb pinnacle of artistic creation, a masterpiece that brought tears to the eyes of the composer himself and caused him to say, "I did think I did see all Heaven before me and the great God Himself." In spite of all the technical accounts of how this grand work was organized and composed with borrowed material and practical concerns for particular singers' voice ranges and abilities, nothing can detract from the fact that it was an inspired work completed in feverish haste by a musical genius of the first rank.

Messiah speaks to modern ears with the same honesty of religious expression that has stirred fervent emotions in listeners for over two hundred years. It is one of the greatest expressions of the Protestant baroque. It is not enough to deal with this *oratorio* as a musical composition only, for it is first and foremost a religious piece, a remarkable setting of biblical texts dealing with the redemption of man from sin through the intervention of the Messiah. The *libretto* is a compilation of verses from the Bible, a selection that draws from both the Old and the New Testaments. The organization and unity of the work is primarily text-centered, for, like three acts of an opera, the three large divisions of the oratorio reveal the following plan: PART I. A messianic prophecy, the coming and birth of Christ. The revelation of God's plan to save mankind by the coming of the Messiah. PART II. The suffering and death of Christ, the defeat of man who rejects God's offer, and the spread of His doctrine. PART III. The redemption of man through faith, the final overthrow of death, and a hymn of thanksgiving.

With this large framework in mind, Handel fleshed out a massive construct for soloists, chorus, and orchestra by using standard forms that were second nature to him and were a regular part of the fully developed operatic style of the baroque era. He sets the spell for the entire work by opening with an orchestral overture with the same characteristics as the French overture developed by Lully decades before: a slow, majestic first movement in jagged *rhythms*, duple *meter*, and *chordal texture*; a lively, *fugal* second movement with an impressive *contrapuntal* display.[1]

Messiah.   OVERTURE   *(1st Movement)*

Oboes, Strings, and Continuo

---

[1] Any number of excellent recordings of *Messiah* complete are available, but the reader is advised to find a recent recording that seeks to approximate Handel's original scoring for small orchestra and modest chorus. The loss in dramatic power supplied by a romantic orchestra and gigantic chorus is amply compensated for by the increased clarity of line and decreased ponderosity.

Messiah.   OVERTURE   *(2nd Movement)*

The *fugue* impresses the listener because the composer successfully takes a melody and uses it against itself, or in conjunction with itself, to create logical and beautiful harmonies. Exquisite fugues are a hallmark of the baroque masters, who displayed their melodic inventiveness through this process of imitating short and distinctive melodies in succession. We can see three successive entrances of the same tune (very slightly altered) in measures 1, 5, and 9 of the fugue, and we might compare their identity by playing them simultaneously:

The fugal process was one of the most compelling in the repertoire of the baroque composers, for although its texture is "lighter in weight" than most *chordal*, or *homophonic*, compositions, it has a forward-driving rhythm and additive-layer-of-melody effect that propels the listener to the final release of the closing chords. Handel was a master of this mature form of the late baroque, and we can see its dramatic effect in the vocal fugues that he favors for climactic moments.

The overall design of the first part of *Messiah* can be seen in the chart at the top of the following page. The regularity or symmetry and the simplicity of the design are in fact *classical*, and we must keep in mind that Handel was working at the culmination of an age, a period in which the influence of new ideas in opposition to the norms of the baroque are beginning to make themselves felt. Simplicity of design is of great advantage in the function of a work that depends heavily upon text, for unnecessary complexity detracts by drawing attention to itself. No one was more aware of this than Handel himself, for he understood better than any other composer of his time how to employ the operatic forms of recitative and *aria* to communicate the inner message of the text.

A *recitative* is a musical form that has almost no melodic interest; consequently, a great store of informa-

Subject	Sinfonia	God's Promise			Distance between God and Man			Message of Joy			Fulfillment through Christ's Birth		
Selection Number	1	2	3	4	5	6	7	7a	8	8a	9	10	11
Form	O	R	A	C	R	A	C	R	A	C	R	A	C

Subject	Pifa	Christmas Story					Rapture at the Lord's Coming			
Selection Number	12	12a	13	13a	14	15	16	16a	17	18
Form	O	R	A	R	R	C	A	R	AA	C

O = Orchestra; R = Recitative; A = Air; AA = Air (Duet); C = Chorus

Messiah. PART I. Overall design.

tion can be related to the listener in a short time. Those points in the narrative where several ideas await telling, where persons need adequate introduction, where details of plot need be unfolded quickly, and in general where there are a great many words to be dealt with are the proper domain of the recitative. Still, within that general plan, certain points need emphasis; there Handel uses chord change and chord selection as well as slight *melodic elaboration* to achieve these ends.

Other devices are available to him too, such as *orchestration*, but the essential concept that the recitative should be used to carry a high volume of words per unit of time is not disturbed. In the last example (c) we see a typical Handelian affective device. On the statement of the word "shake," Handel literally shakes the music. He takes the notes and rapidly wiggles them back and forth, a visual effect for the performer and an aural effect for the listener. As the chorus sings "All we like sheep have gone astray" the melodic lines diverge; with "we have turned," a quickly twisting and turning figure is introduced, and with "every one to his own way" a single note is stubbornly repeated.

The *aria* or "air" has a purpose almost diametrically opposed to that of the recitative. An aria usually contains two ideas often expressed in two sentences. It is an opportunity for the soloist (or composer) to wax eloquent, to spin out gradually a thought that grows fuller in meaning as the music progresses. It is usually some-

what introspective, personal to the character of the person portrayed by the soloist. The second idea is related to the first, but it casts a slightly different light on the subject or adds to it in some contrasting way. Most Handelian airs are cast in the mold of the *da capo aria*, the *ABA* form that returns to the beginning to reiterate the message of the first idea in the new light of the second statement. The bass aria "But who may abide" is a demonstration of this principle. The soloist asks the questions, "But who may abide the day of His coming, and who shall stand when He appeareth?" In response, the listener might ask, "Why does he ask, for would we not all stand to greet the Lord?" In the B section of the aria, the soloist states the difficulty, "For He is like a refiner's fire." God is judge and he will separate the righteous from the sinful. He is like the refiner who smelts metal from ore and separates the gold or silver from the rock. When the bass returns to his initial question of who shall stand, the listener might reconsider whether he dares be among those who rise to meet God eyeball to eyeball. And the mighty chorus, like impartial observers from another world, responds in frightening tone, "And He shall purify the sons of Levi, that they may offer unto the Lord an offering in righteousness." Thus, the plan of the specific recitative-aria-chorus combination serves as the model for all the subsections of the entire work: develop an idea rapidly (recitative), elaborate a single aspect (aria), and hammer the message home (chorus). After four exact repetitions of the

a. Straightforward recitative - simple statement

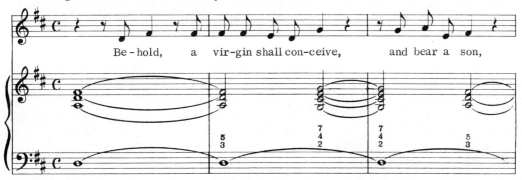

Be - hold,   a   vir-gin shall con-ceive,   and bear a son,

b. Recitative heightened by chordal activity.

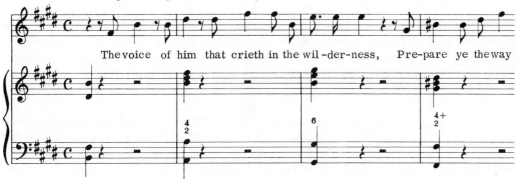

The voice of him that crieth in the wil-der-ness,   Pre-pare ye the way

c. Recitative heightened by melodic embellishment.

Yet once a lit-tle while   and I will shake

plan, Handel, of course, varies the scheme by omitting, inverting, or repeating the three basic elements—recitative, aria, and chorus—but the affective function of each always remains the same. Thus the listener gears his expectations to the type of music offered.

The second and third parts of the *oratorio* are naturally similar in format to that of the first. The tone of the second part is sorrowful, for it accompanies the music of the Passion and, only toward the end, Easter. The libretto tells vividly how Christ was despised: "He hid not His face from shame and spitting," "He was bruised for our iniquities," "All they that see Him laugh Him to scorn," and "He was cut off out of the land of the living." This intense, doleful atmosphere is relieved briefly with words and music promising the Resurrection: "But Thou didst not leave His soul in hell" and "Lift up your heads...the King of Glory shall come in"; but it quickly returns to a drama of death and fear when the people are reminded of their shortcomings: "Why do the nations so furiously rage together?" and "He that dwelleth in heaven shall laugh them to scorn." In other words, a religious drama is taking place; the listeners are no longer observers but participants. They do not have to identify with characters on stage as they would at the theater or opera house; they are being explicitly identified themselves as the words of the Bible preach to them. And when the words are completely damning and reduce the attentive listener to dust—"Thou shalt break them with a rod of iron, Thou shalt dash them in pieces like a potter's vessel"—then Handel steps in and saves the victory with one of the most exultant choruses of all time: "Hallelujah! for the Lord God Omnipotent reigneth." The Hallelujah Chorus alone would have brought fame to George Frideric Handel, for it is one of those resounding strokes of genius that is able in itself to embody the concept of a victorious Lord.

Hal -le- lu -jah,   Hal -le- lu -jah,   Hal-le -
lu-jah, Hal -le- lu-jah,   Hal - le - lu -jah

The Hallelujah Chorus creates a problem for the composer. In it he achieves an artistic peak making material that follows necessarily anticlimactic. But, the oratorio is not yet over. In this hurried world of the twentieth century, one still finds *Messiah* concerts that cut off the work at this point. Musically, one comes to a satisfactory conclusion at the end of the Hallelujah Chorus, but spiritually one has missed the message of the text if the portion dealing with individual redemption through faith is left out. The only possible, or impossible, solution, of course, was to write an even more stirring and more climactic chorus for the final portion; unbelievably, Handel was able to do this. The Amen Chorus which acts as finale to the third part and the work as a whole, is one of the most awesome choral fugues conceived by man. It grows and swells, piling layer upon layer in a surprisingly brief sprint to the finish. An alternation of slow and fast chordal passages sets the stage: "Worthy is the Lamb...to receive power...worthy is the Lamb...to receive power...." This introduction is followed by a fugue whose vocal entrances rise successively from the low range of the men's voices to the upper register of the sopranos': "Blessing and honour, glory and pow'r be unto Him that sitteth on the throne." A fugal device called *stretto* collapses the interval of time between successive entrances so that the music, which seemed to work only at greater length and expansiveness, suddenly feels to be moving faster—to be propelling forward with less caution but no greater recklessness. The voices begin to pair and rise together; suddenly they join in a unison line that reduces the texture to a penetrating knife edge. Expanding again, the voices move into a series of high, sustained chords that virtually teeter on the brink of a musical chasm. Then, at last, the voices begin to move and gain momentum in the final *fugue* to the single word "Amen." The sense of completion is achieved; the restoration of balance is accomplished; the work is consummated.

Strangely enough, *Messiah* was not composed for a church service. Handel was a bankrupt impresario-composer who was currently out of favor as a local opera composer. He seized an opportunity to perform "some of his choicest Musick" for the benefit of Mercer's Hospital in Dublin, Ireland. On the 12th of April, 1742, he performed his new oratorio in public for the first time. With its baroque harmonies and standard-ized forms, it reflected ideas seen emerging out of the past with a steady linkage back to the Renaissance through the operas of Lully to the congregational sacred music of Saint Philip Neri in Rome. In its expansive-ness and classical balance, in its communication with a growing middle class, and in its seeming power to at-tract listeners from all walks of life in the modern world, it is a searching tendril that stretches upward to the future. Many works of art seem to be understood fully only within the context of the age in which they were created. Handel's *Messiah* is an exception to this rule, for it seems to have had an immediacy and direct impact on musicians and laymen alike from its origin in 1742 to the present day. It is perhaps the most sub-stantial monument of Western musical art of all time.

THE SEVENTEENTH CENTURY: CONTINUITIES

No historical period is more complex and contradictory than the one we have just studied. Every general statement made about seventeenth-century culture almost seems to generate an equally valid opposite. Perhaps this is because the first half of the century, at least, was a time of tremendous change, of birth and growth. By the second half of the century, Europe was established as a world power and had become more stable at home, culturally as well as politically. Let us review briefly some of the often conflicting aspects of the seventeenth century and their significance.

Religion   In the area of religion, Europe by 1650 was divided into Catholic and Protestant territories, which have more or less survived as such into the present. Protestantism evolved from a revolutionary movement into an establishment or series of establishments, each with its own set of orthodox beliefs. With the subsidence of religious warfare came a growing indifference to religion and a secular view of the world. Attempts by new reform movements among Catholics and Protestants could not halt the trend.

Science   The rapid developments in science were in part responsible for this increasing nonreligious view of the world. First the revolutionary Copernican theory and then experiments conducted by men such as Newton and Galileo taught people to trust their own minds or senses rather than the decrees of authority. Scientific discoveries led generally to great confidence in the powers of human beings, for it seemed that man would eventually be able to understand and control nature. Nature itself appeared to be a self-regulating, autonomous machine: God was needed only to explain how the world came into being in the first place. But some felt uneasy about living in such a world. A few experienced a kind of terror. If earth was no longer perceived as the center of the universe, the position of man also had to be rethought.

Economics   The seventeenth century witnessed a new stage in the development of a highly important modern economic institution: industrial capitalism. The desire for world markets and wealth led to the exploitation of African and American cultures by Europeans. Whereas in the sixteenth century, America had furnished Europe with precious metals primarily, in the seventeenth the American colonies supplied important agricultural products and raw materials. The colonies became an important outlet for European investment. Slaves were a significant cost factor here. In turn, trade with the New World and Africa stimulated intracontinental trade in Europe as well. The new economic interests were another influence in the growth of secularism.

Politics   The rapid accumulation of wealth allowed many middle-class people, "would-be gentlemen," literally to buy their way into the nobility. After very unsettled political conditions in the first half of the century, after 1650 the European monarchs (most strikingly Louis XIV) learned how to keep the upper classes politically subservient; royal absolutism became the political order of the day. Absolutism was the means by which strong central government was established in most of Europe. Accordingly, the modern state owes more to absolutism than to republican or constitutional monarchical forms.

The Baroque Style   The baroque style in the arts in many ways reflects the turmoil, contradictions, and dynamism of the age in which it flourished. Exuberance is perhaps its most overriding quality. We have seen in many instances that baroque art is characterized by intense sensuality combined with intense spirituality, by a realistic depiction of everyday life along with a love of fantasy and illusion, by a delight in the material aspects of life with a sense of the impermanence of life in this world. Aesthetically, we have seen that the concept *baroque* may include the neoclassical

—a classicism expanded to create a sense of magnificence and grandeur. This classicism fitted well with the increase in political stability in the last half of the century.

Performing Arts   Theatricality is characteristic of much of seventeenth-century culture. The Catholic mass became more like a show as churches came to resemble theaters; Bernini transformed Rome into something like a huge theater. Louis XIV, the master showman, built a showplace and ran his court ritual like a ballet. It is not surprising that the theatrical arts rose to great importance during this period. The first theaters that we can call modern were built in Italy and influenced those in other parts of Europe. Two forms of modern stage entertainment, the opera and the ballet, came into being in the seventeenth century; Handel developed the *oratorio* into a form that could be used for a popular show. Greek and Roman tragedies were reborn in neoclassical form with the dramas of Corneille and Racine. Molière, with his ability to depict characters both everyday and universal, created the first truly modern comedies. The combined arts of dance, drama, and music make Molière's comedy-ballets enchanting spectacles as well as incisive commentaries on human nature. A stage piece like *The Would-Be Gentleman*, with its play between reality and fantasy, is another illustration of the diverse richness of seventeenth-century art.

The grandeur, magnificence, and exuberance that characterize the baroque style are nowhere more apparent than in Handel's *Messiah*. Musically speaking, we have extended the limit of the seventeenth century into the mid-eighteenth because of the longer duration of musical baroque. The early eighteenth century, which saw a flowering of great religious music, was on the whole for the other humanities a most nonreligious time. We will see the secular spirit that developed in the seventeenth century take a more profound hold on Western culture in the eighteenth as the larger-than-life dimensions of baroque art become scaled down to a more "reasonable" level.

PART SIX

REASON, REVOLUTION, ROMANTICISM: THE EIGHTEENTH AND EARLY NINETEENTH CENTURIES

23

THE EUROPEAN ENLIGHTENMENT

A Pre-revolutionary Movement   If the modern world was initiated in the seventeenth century, it was brought into being in the eighteenth. The thinkers formed by the Scientific Revolution taught reliance on individual experience or reason rather than on authority and tradition. Within the age of absolutism, seeds were being planted for a cultural, and eventually political, revolution that would destroy everything the age stood for. France, which dominated Europe culturally and politically throughout the eighteenth century, began the period with Louis XIV, king by the grace of God, and ended it with General Napoleon, sovereign by popular support. In the interim Louis' royal line, the Bourbon family, was swept away by the earthshaking revolution of 1789, which toppled in its turn one European crowned head after the other. The ideas originating in France also had a profound impact on the formation of a new republic across the Atlantic.

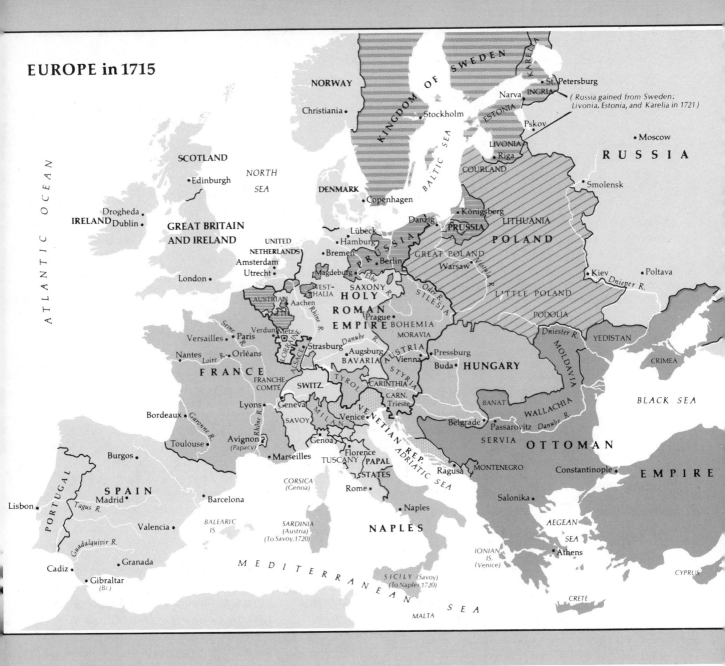

EUROPE in 1715

ATLANTIC OCEAN

NORWAY

KINGDOM OF SWEDEN

Christiania

Stockholm

NORTH SEA

SCOTLAND

Edinburgh

DENMARK

Copenhagen

St. Petersburg

Narva INGRIA

Pskov

ESTONIA

LIVONIA

Riga

COURLAND

(Russia gained from Sweden:
Livonia, Estonia, and Karelia in 1721)

Moscow

RUSSIA

Smolensk

KARELIA

BALTIC SEA

Drogheda

IRELAND Dublin

GREAT BRITAIN
AND IRELAND

UNITED
NETHERLANDS

Amsterdam

Utrecht

London

Königsberg

Danzig

PRUSSIA

LITHUANIA

POLAND

Lübeck

Hamburg

Bremen

Berlin

GREAT POLAND

Warsaw

RUSSIA

Magdeburg

SAXONY

Elbe

WEST-
PHALIA

HOLY
ROMAN
EMPIRE

SILESIA

Oder R.

LITTLE POLAND

Kiev

Poltava

Dnieper R.

AUSTRIAN

Aachen

Rhine R.

Prague

BOHEMIA

MORAVIA

PODOLIA

Versailles Paris

Seine R.

Verdun Metz

LORRAINE

ALSACE

Strasburg

Danube R.

Augsburg

AUSTRIA

STYRIA

Vienna

Pressburg

Buda

HUNGARY

Dniester R.

MOLDAVIA

YEDISTAN

CRIMEA

Nantes

Orléans

Loire R.

FRANCE

FRANCHE
COMTÉ

SWITZ.

BAVARIA

TYROL

CARINTHIA

CARN.

Trieste

BANAT

WALLACHIA

BLACK SEA

Bordeaux

Garonne R.

Lyons

Geneva

SAVOY

Rhône R.

MILAN

VENETIAN REP.

Venice

ADRIATIC SEA

Belgrade

Passarovitz Danube R.

SERVIA

OTTOMAN

Constantinople

EMPIRE

Toulouse

Avignon
(Papacy)

Genoa

Florence

TUSCANY

PAPAL
STATES

Rome

Ragusa

MONTENEGRO

Salonika

Burgos

Marseilles

CORSICA
(Genoa)

Lisbon

PORTUGAL

SPAIN

Madrid

Barcelona

Tagus R.

Valencia

BALEARIC
IS.

SARDINIA
(Austria)
(To Savoy, 1720)

NAPLES

Naples

AEGEAN
SEA

Athens

IONIAN
IS.
(Venice)

Guadalquivir R.

Cadiz

Granada

Gibraltar
(Br.)

MEDITERRANEAN

SEA

SICILY (Savoy)
(To Naples, 1720)

MALTA

CRETE

CYPRUS

The Philosophes

The intellectual movement that came to be known as the Enlightenment was led by a group of diverse, individualistic Frenchmen who are usually labeled together as the *philosophes*. Although the word literally means "philosopher," these men were not on the whole creators of new philosophical systems. Rather, they were propagandists for a general set of ideas that they believed would bring "light" to their generation and so improve the life of the human race as a whole. Primarily middle-class, skilled and prolific writers, the philosophes reached their public through the burgeoning printed media—not only books and pamphlets but also the newly introduced weekly newspaper and monthly journal. Their mission would have been impossible in prior centuries when the level of literacy was low even in the upper class. The philosophes were able to reach a wide, literate upper- and middle-class public, but not the poor. The lower classes throughout the eighteenth century remained, in general, as oppressed as before, though they joined the bourgeoisie at the end to overthrow the monarchy and to enthrone the goddess of reason. The philosophes had a rather abstract, if genuine, concern for the poor, but they associated primarily with the polished, witty, urbane men and women who frequented the Parisian *salons*. Paris was now replacing Versailles as the center of cultural life.

The SALON The Hôtel de Soubise, designed by Germain Boffrand and begun in 1732, is an example of the smaller and more intimate quarters fashioned for the nobility in Paris (Fig. 23-1). Located on small and sometimes awkwardly shaped urban sites, these buildings had a fairly simple exterior; the architects and clients concentrated on the interiors, where the salon was used for small gatherings that replaced the great festivities of the court. The salons were run primarily by women—Madame du Deffand and Madame Geoffrin were two of the most celebrated—and the sexes conversed and exchanged ideas on an equal footing. These conversations were also means for spreading ideas. As the century progressed, educated men and women everywhere strove to be recognized as "enlightened"; even the sovereigns of Europe sought to win the title of "enlightened monarch."

Foundations of the Enlightenment: John Locke How did the Enlightenment develop, and what were its common tenets? Essentially the French philosophes' conceptions of the sources of knowledge were confused. They claimed to be *empiricists*, deriving their ideas from experience, but they also espoused a belief in natural rights determined by examination of the human conscience. In *rationalist* fashion they used these natural rights as criteria for judging both the society and government of their time. The confusions in their thought, however, were in a sense inherited from the late seventeenth-century English philosopher Locke, from whom they took much of the methodological approach.

23–1 Hôtel de Soubise, Paris. (Giraudon, Paris)

John Locke (1632–1704) was the author of two fundamental tracts, *Essay on Human Understanding* and *Essay Concerning the True Original Extent and End of Civil Government*. In the tradition of Bacon, Locke held in his *Essay on Human Understanding* that all knowledge comes from sense perception. The mind begins as a blank slate, a *tabula rasa*, and what the mind comes to know is a product of combining perceptions and reflection on those combinations. What this in effect meant was that man was a product of his environment: change the environment and the man is changed. Inspired in his turn by the scientific discoveries taking place in his time, Locke attempted to establish laws of human behavior by *inductive* means.

The *Essay Concerning Civil Government* begins by assuming that originally men lived in a state of nature before the existence of government—much as Locke imagined the Indians in the New World living. In that state men possessed by nature certain rights to life, liberty and property. The natural rights of all men, of course, could not be proven by experience, but were deduced by an examination of the conscience. Because without government individuals could not adequately protect all their rights, they created the state to guarantee them. The original state had very limited power and an executive closely watched by a legislature. If, however, the state ceased to perform the express functions for which it was created and began to rob and oppress its citizens, then Locke advocated revolution and the creation of a new government.

The PHILOSOPHES' Political and Religious Doctrines

Empiricism and a rationalistic doctrine of natural rights formed the core of the Enlightenment. With a few exceptions the philosophes believed that all men were essentially equal—in that they all possessed reason. As a creature of reason and equal to every other man by nature, every individual had the right to life, liberty, and a happy life. Associated with these natural rights were others like the right to freedom of speech and to religious liberty. The philosophes deplored the intolerance to Protestants still practiced by the Catholic church in France; in fact they viewed the Church itself as a source of superstition, ignorance, and subservience. Priests and others in the hierarchy served to benight, rather than to enlighten the multitudes. A philosophe motto, "Crush the infamous!" *(Écrasez l'infâme)* referred to all irrational and superstitious forces but was directed primarily against the Church.

Although the philosophes supported tolerance for Protestants, they had little respect for any Christian doctrines. They called their own form of religion *deism.* Drawing heavily on the conception of God fostered by Descartes and the Scientific Revolution, they held that God has created the world and set it running on its own, as a watchmaker makes a watch. Heaven and hell were not to be found in the hereafter but on this earth. If human beings would follow their God-given reason rather than their momentary passions, they could create a world in which everyone would enjoy felicity and peace.

Although their ideas were to influence the revolution, the majority of the philosophes were politically proponents of *despotism,* or rule by one enlightened man, harking back to Plato's notion of the philosopher-king. Turgot, a philosophe and one of Louis XV's ministers, declared: "Give me five years of despotism and I

will make France free." Given the situation in France, the greatest concern was to establish a basic equality among the classes and to eliminate privilege; the only way to do this practically was to give the central government absolute control of reform. In England where, despite the existence of classes, there was a basic equality before the law, Locke stressed constitutional monarchy; in France the worst source of oppression came from the privileged classes and groups. If there was to be toleration and freedom of the press in France, it would have to come from the king: the Church and other interest groups were violently opposed to such freedoms.

The reason that Frenchmen did not enjoy natural rights in the present was the fault of evil institutions. Men are good, but corrupted institutions have damaged them. Reform the institutions and men will improve. Indeed they believed that if the proper institutions could be designed, men might eventually perfect themselves. Thus, the philosophes introduced a doctrine of progress. They placed great hope in the reform of the state because they saw it as a central means for reforming all the other institutions of society.

Diderot and the Encyclopedia

The philosophes were the first to broadcast an idea both widely accepted and under attack today: progress through education. If human beings are to be enlightened, to be able to use their reason to unmask lies and superstitions, then they must *know.* To this end, one of the most intelligent and versatile of their number, Denis Diderot (1713–1784), conceived and directed the compiling of a vast encyclopedia called *Dictionnaire Raisonné des Sciences, des Arts et des Métiers.* French authorities saw the whole idea as dangerous—twice they suppressed the Encyclopedia. It contained articles, written by philosophes and others, on everything from how to make wallpaper to the definition of God. It was full of information on science and technology. Eighteenth-century socialites, as well as the philosophes, were passionate amateur scientists, often performing experiments for company after dinner in their elegant salons.

Voltaire

A contributor to the Encyclopedia and the giant of the French Enlightenment, whose life spanned most of the eighteenth century, was François Arouet, better known under his pen name Voltaire

23–2   Marianne Loir, "Portrait de la Marquise de Châtelet." (Musée et Galerie des Beaux-Arts, Bordeaux/photo © Alain Danvers)

(1694–1778). Probably no other writer was so adored and so hated during his lifetime. Not a profoundly original thinker, he was endowed with an ability to see through hypocrisy and delusion and a witty, satiric style that he used mercilessly against his enemies and anti-Enlightenment forces.

Son of a bourgeois lawyer, the young Voltaire wanted nothing so much as to ingratiate himself with the court nobility; with his wit, intelligence, and good education, he accomplished this. Becoming well known as a writer of neoclassical tragedies, he discovered that in spite of his talents he was not socially equal to aristocrats when one of them had him publicly beaten and then thrown into the infamous French prison, the Bastille. He also suffered from an inefficient censorship law, which arbitrarily swooped down on a victim and punished him with imprisonment or exile. After his release from the Bastille, Voltaire chose exile in England, where he found a constitutional government, an enlightened noble class that obeyed the law, a tolerant spirit, and the works of John Locke. It was Voltaire who introduced Locke's ideas into France. He also brought

back to France the idea that its government and society could, indeed should, be changed. But Voltaire's *Philosophical Letters* (1734) on his impressions of England were seized by the French censors; the philosophe then sought a safe haven in northeastern France at Cirey, with his friend and mistress for the next ten years, Emilie du Châtelet.

Madame du Châtelet herself deserves attention as one of the liberated women of eighteenth-century France. Her portrait (Fig. 23-2), by a woman, Marianne Loir, reveals a subtle intelligence and love of learning coupled with a smile—typical features of the Enlightenment. Forced into an early marriage with an unintellectual nobleman, she astonished Parisian society by exiling herself to a small town to devote herself to intellectual pursuits. She was a mathematician who wrote several treatises on natural philosophy as well as mathematics. While Voltaire lived with her, they observed a rigid schedule filled with scientific experiments, studies, and theatrical performances put on by themselves and their visitors. The short story by Voltaire printed here, *Micromegas*, may have been originally planned as a magic lantern show at Cirey.

Voltaire called his short stories and novels "philosophical tales." The fact that he turned to this genre as a means of expression is characteristic of new trends in eighteenth-century art. If the baroque was an age of the grandiose, the mid-eighteenth century (as we saw, for example, in the Hôtel de Soubise) changed in taste to the petite and the well ordered. Voltaire's tragedies observe the three unities and the rules of taste with such precision that they now seem somewhat mechanical and dry. His talents were best suited to forms in which he could exercise his quick, sharp style and especially his gift for satire. Voltaire was not lacking in imagination, as *Micromegas* shows, and eighteenth-century readers were in fact fond of fantastic tales. But the fantastic (Swift's *Gulliver's Travels* is a good example) usually had a very definite bearing on reality. Voltaire's philosophical tale *Micromegas*, written in 1739, might be considered an early work of science fiction. If it is fiction, however, it is also very much concerned with contemporary developments in science—and with contemporary ignorance. Written with satiric verve, it is a tale of the Enlightenment, influenced by the Scientific Revolution and the ideas of Locke. This translation is by William Fleming.

VOLTAIRE

Micromegas

I

A Voyage to the Planet Saturn by a Native of Sirius

In one of the planets that revolve round the star known by the name of Sirius, was a certain young gentleman of promising parts, whom I had the honor to be acquainted with in his last voyage to this our little ant-hill. His name was Micromegas,[1] an appellation admirably suited to all great men, and his stature amounted to eight leagues in height, that is, twenty-four thousand geometrical paces of five feet each.[2]

Some of your mathematicians, a set of people always useful to the public, will, perhaps, instantly seize the pen, and calculate that Mr. Micromegas, inhabitant of the country of Sirius, being from head to foot four and twenty thousand paces in length, making one hundred and twenty thousand royal feet, that we, denizens of this earth, being at a medium little more than five feet high, and our globe nine thousand leagues in circumference: these things being premised, they will then conclude that the periphery of the globe which produced him must be exactly one and twenty millions six hundred thousand times greater than that of this our tiny ball. Nothing in nature is more simple and common. The dominions of some sovereigns of Germany or Italy, which may be compassed in half an hour, when compared with the empires of Ottoman, Russia, or China, are no other than faint instances of the prodigious difference that nature hath made in the scale of beings. The stature of his excellency being of these extraordinary dimensions, all our artists will agree that the measure around his body might amount to fifty thousand royal feet,—a very agreeable and just proportion.

His nose being equal in length to one-third of his face, and his jolly countenance engrossing one-seventh part of his height, it must be owned that the nose of this same Sirian was six thousand three hundred and thirty-three royal feet to a hair, which was to be demonstrated. With regard to his understanding, it is one of the best cultivated I have known. He is perfectly well acquainted with abundance of things, some of which are of his own invention; for, when his age did not exceed two hundred and fifty years, he studied, according to the custom of the country, at the most celebrated university of the whole planet, and by the force of his genius discovered upwards of fifty propositions of Euclid, having the advantage by more than eighteen of Blaise Pascal,[3] who, (as we are told by his own sister,) demonstrated two and thirty for his amusement and then left off, choosing rather to be an indifferent philosopher than a great mathematician.

About the four hundred and fiftieth year of his age, or latter end of his childhood, he dissected a great number of small insects not more than one hundred feet in diameter, which are not perceivable by ordinary microscopes, of which he composed a very curious treatise, which involved him in some trouble. The mufti[4] of the nation, though very old and very ignorant, made shift to discover in his book certain lemmas that were suspicious, unseemly, rash, heretic, and unsound, and prosecuted him with great animosity; for the subject of the author's inquiry was whether, in the world of Sirius, there was any difference between the substantial forms of a flea and a snail.

Micromegas defended his philosophy with such spirit as made all the female sex his proselytes; and the process lasted two hundred and twenty years; at the end of which time, in consequence of the mufti's interest, the book was condemned by judges who had never read it, and the author expelled from court for the term of eight hundred years.

Not much affected at his banishment from a court that teemed with nothing but turmoils and trifles, he made a very humorous song upon the mufti, who gave himself no trouble about the matter, and set out on his travels from planet to planet, in order (as the saying is) to improve his mind and finish his education. Those who never travel but in a postchaise or berlin, will, doubtless, be astonished at the equipages used above; for we that strut upon this little mole-hill are at a loss

---

[1] Two Greek words meaning "little-great."
[2] That is, 38.880 km.

[3] French philosopher and scientist (1623–1662). Voltaire deplored his religious philosophy.
[4] Member of the Muslim clergy charged with enforcing the religious laws. Voltaire has in mind his own difficulties with censorship.

to conceive anything that surpasses our own customs. But our traveler was a wonderful adept in the laws of gravitation, together with the whole force of attraction and repulsion, and made such seasonable use of his knowledge, that sometimes by the help of a sunbeam, and sometimes by the convenience of a comet, he and his retinue glided from sphere to sphere, as the bird hops from one bough to another.[5] He in a very little time posted through the milky way, and I am obliged to own he saw not a twinkle of those stars supposed to adorn that fair empyrean, which the illustrious Dr. Derham brags to have observed through his telescope. Not that I pretend to say the doctor was mistaken. God forbid! But Micromegas was upon the spot, an exceeding good observer, and I have no mind to contradict any man. Be that as it may, after many windings and turnings, he arrived at the planet Saturn; and, accustomed as he was to the sight of novelties, he could not for his life repress a supercilious and conceited smile, which often escapes the wisest philosopher, when he perceived the smallness of that globe, and the diminutive size of its inhabitants; for really Saturn is but about nine hundred times larger than this our earth, and the people of that country mere dwarfs, about a thousand fathoms high. In short, he at first derided those poor pigmies, just as an Italian fiddler laughs at the music of Lully,[6] at his first arrival in Paris: but as this Sirian was a person of good sense, he soon perceived that a thinking being may not be altogether ridiculous, even though he is not quite six thousand feet high; and therefore he became familiar with them, after they had ceased to wonder at his extraordinary appearance. In particular, he contracted an intimate friendship with the secretary of the Academy of Saturn, a man of good understanding, who, though in truth he had invented nothing of his own, gave a very good account of the inventions of others, and enjoyed in peace the reputation of a little poet and great calculator. And here, for the edification of the reader, I will repeat a very singular conversation that one day passed between Mr. Secretary and Micromegas.

---

[5] Voltaire makes an imaginative, poetic use of the recently discovered law of gravity.

[6] Lully was by this time considered the chief of the "French style" in music.

II

The Conversation Between Micromegas and the Inhabitant of Saturn

His excellency having laid himself down, and the secretary approached his nose:

"It must be confessed," said Micromegas, "that nature is full of variety."

"Yes," replied the Saturnian, "nature is like a bed, whose flowers—"

"Pshaw!" cried the other, "a truce with your flower beds."

"It is," resumed the secretary, "like an assembly of fair and brown women, whose dresses—"

"What a plague have I to do with your brunettes?" said our traveler.

"Then it is like a gallery of pictures, the strokes of which—"

"Not at all," answered Micromegas, "I tell you once for all, nature is like nature, and comparisons are odious." [7]

"Well, to please you," said the secretary—

"I won't be pleased," replied the Sirian, "I want to be instructed; begin, therefore, without further preamble, and tell me how many senses the people of this world enjoy."

"We have seventy and two," said the academician, "but we are daily complaining of the small number, as our imagination transcends our wants, for, with the seventy-two senses, our five moons and ring, we find ourselves very much restricted; and notwithstanding our curiosity, and the no small number of those passions that result from these few senses, we have still time enough to be tired of idleness."

"I sincerely believe what you say," cried Micromegas "for, though we Sirians have near a thousand different senses, there still remains a certain vague desire, an unaccountable inquietude incessantly admonishing us of our own unimportance, and giving us to understand that there are other beings who are much our superiors in point of perfection. I have traveled a little, and seen mortals both above and below myself in the scale of being, but I have met with none who had not more desire

---

[7] What sort of style is Voltaire mocking here? What does this tell us about his own beliefs in matters of style?

than necessity, and more want than gratification. Perhaps I shall one day arrive in some country where nought is wanting, but hitherto I have had no certain information of such a happy land."

The Saturnian and his guest exhausted themselves in conjectures upon this subject, and after abundance of argumentation equally ingenious and uncertain, were fain to return to matter of fact.

"To what age do you commonly live?" said the Sirian.

"Lack-a-day! a mere trifle," replied the little gentleman.

"It is the very same case with us," resumed the other, "the shortness of life is our daily complaint, so that this must be an universal law in nature."

"Alas!" cried the Saturnian, "few, very few on this globe outlive five hundred great revolutions of the sun; (these, according to our way of reckoning, amount to about fifteen thousand years). So, you see, we in a manner begin to die the very moment we are born: our existence is no more than a point, our duration an instant, and our globe an atom. Scarce do we begin to learn a little, when death intervenes before we can profit by experience. For my own part, I am deterred from laying schemes when I consider myself as a single drop in the midst of an immense ocean. I am particularly ashamed, in your presence, of the ridiculous figure I make among my fellow-creatures."

To this declaration, Micromegas replied:

"If you were not a philosopher, I should be afraid of mortifying your pride by telling you that the term of our lives is seven hundred times longer than the date of your existence: but you are very sensible that when the texture of the body is resolved, in order to reanimate nature in another form, which is the consequence of what we call death—when that moment of change arrives, there is not the least difference betwixt having lived a whole eternity, or a single day. I have been in some countries where the people live a thousand times longer than with us, and yet they murmured at the shortness of their time. But one will find everywhere some few persons of good sense, who know how to make the best of their portion, and thank the author of nature for his bounty.[8] There is a profusion of variety scattered through the universe, and yet there is an admirable vein of uniformity that runs through the whole: for example, all thinking beings are different among themselves, though at bottom they resemble one another in the powers and passions of the soul. Matter, though interminable, hath different properties in every sphere. How many principal attributes do you reckon in the matter of this world?"

"If you mean those properties," said the Saturnian, "without which we believe this our globe could not subsist, we reckon in all three hundred, such as extent, impenetrability, motion, gravitation, divisibility, et caetera."

"That small number," replied the traveler, "probably answers the views of the creator on this your narrow sphere. I adore his wisdom in all his works. I see infinite variety, but everywhere proportion. Your globe is small: so are the inhabitants. You have few sensations; because your matter is endued with few properties. These are the works of unerring providence. Of what color does your sun appear when accurately examined?"

"Of a yellowish white," answered the Saturnian, "and in separating one of his rays we find it contains seven colors."

"Our sun," said the Sirian, "is of a reddish hue, and we have no less than thirty-nine original colors. Among all the suns I have seen there is no sort of resemblance, and in this sphere of yours there is not one face like another."

After divers questions of this nature, he asked how many substances, essentially different, they counted in the world of Saturn; and understood that they numbered but thirty: such as God; space; matter; beings endowed with sense and extension; beings that have extension, sense, and reflection; thinking beings who have no extension; those that are penetrable; those that are impenetrable, and also all others. But this Saturnian philosopher was prodigiously astonished when the Sirian told him they had no less than three hundred, and that he himself had discovered three thousand more in the course of his travels. In short, after having communicated to each other what they knew, and even what they did not know, and argued during a complete revolution of the sun, they resolved to set out together on a small philosophical tour.

---

[8] Here Voltaire gets in some jibes at the whole Christian tradition that views heaven as the proper end of man after death.

III

The Voyage of These Inhabitants of Other Worlds

Our two philosophers were just ready to embark for the atmosphere of Saturn, with a large provision of mathematical instruments, when the Saturnian's mistress, having got an inkling of their design, came all in tears to make her protests. She was a handsome brunette, though not above six hundred and threescore fathoms high; but her agreeable attractions made amends for the smallness of her stature.

"Ah! cruel man," cried she, "after a courtship of fifteen hundred years, when at length I surrendered, and became your wife, and scarce have passed two hundred more in thy embraces, to leave me thus, before the honeymoon is over, and go a rambling with a giant of another world! Go, go, thou art a mere virtuoso, devoid of tenderness and love! If thou wert a true Saturnian, thou wouldst be faithful and invariable. Ah! whither art thou going? what is thy design? Our five moons are not so inconstant, nor our ring so changeable as thee! But take this along with thee, henceforth I ne'er shall love another man."

The little gentleman embraced and wept over her, notwithstanding his philosophy; and the lady, after having swooned with great decency, went to console herself with more agreeable company.

Meanwhile our two virtuosi set out, and at one jump leaped upon the ring, which they found pretty flat, according to the ingenious guess of an illustrious inhabitant of this our little earth. From thence they easily slipped from moon to moon; and a comet chancing to pass, they sprang upon it with all their servants and apparatus. Thus carried about one hundred and fifty million of leagues, they met with the satellites of Jupiter, and arrived upon the body of the planet itself, where they continued a whole year; during which they learned some very curious secrets, which would actually be sent to the press, were it not for fear of the gentlemen inquisitors, who have found among them some corollaries very hard of digestion.

But to return to our travelers. When they took leave of Jupiter, they traversed a space of about one hundred millions of leagues, and coasting along the planet Mars, which is well known to be five times smaller than our little earth, they descried two moons subservient to that orb, which have escaped the observation of all our astronomers.... Be that as it may, our gentlemen found the planet so small, that they were afraid they should not find room to take a little repose; so that they pursued their journey like two travelers who despise the paltry accommodation of a village, and push forward to the next market town. But the Sirian and his companion soon repented of their delicacy; for they journeyed a long time without finding a resting place, till at length they discerned a small speck, which was the Earth. Coming from Jupiter, they could not but be moved with compassion at the sight of this miserable spot, upon which, however, they resolved to land, lest they should be a second time disappointed. They accordingly moved toward the tail of the comet, where, finding an Aurora Borealis ready to set sail, they embarked, and arrived on the northern coast of the Baltic on the fifth day of July, new style, in the year 1737.

IV

What Befell Them Upon This Our Globe

Having taken some repose, and being desirous of reconnoitering the narrow field in which they were, they traversed it at once from north to south. Every step of the Sirian and his attendants measured about thirty thousand royal feet: whereas, the dwarf of Saturn, whose stature did not exceed a thousand fathoms, followed at a distance quite out of breath; because, for every single stride of his companion, he was obliged to make twelve good steps at least. The reader may figure to himself, (if we are allowed to make such comparisons,) a very little rough spaniel dodging after a captain of the Prussian grenadiers.

As those strangers walked at a good pace, they compassed the globe in six and thirty hours; the sun, it is true, or rather the earth, describes the same space in the course of one day; but it must be observed that it is much easier to turn upon an axis than to walk a-foot. Behold them then returned to the spot from whence they had set out, after having discovered that almost imperceptible sea, which is called the Mediterranean; and the other narrow pond that surrounds this mole-hill, under the denomination of the great ocean; in wading through which the dwarf had never wet his mid-leg, while the other scarce moistened his heel.[9] In going and coming through both hemispheres, they did

---

[9] Voltaire had no idea of the depth of the Atlantic Ocean.

all that lay in their power to discover whether or not the globe was inhabited. They stooped, they lay down, they groped in every corner; but their eyes and hands were not at all proportioned to the small beings that crawl upon this earth; and, therefore, they could not find the smallest reason to suspect that we and our fellow-citizens of this globe had the honor to exist.

The dwarf, who sometimes judged too hastily, concluded at once that there was no living creatures upon earth; and his chief reason was, that he had seen nobody. But Micromegas, in a polite manner, made him sensible of the unjust conclusion:

"For," said he, "with your diminutive eyes you cannot see certain stars of the fiftieth magnitude, which I easily perceive; and do you take it for granted that no such stars exist?"

"But I have groped with great care," replied the dwarf.

"Then your sense of feeling must be bad," said the other.

"But this globe," said the dwarf, "is ill contrived; and so irregular in its form as to be quite ridiculous. The whole together looks like a chaos. Do but observe these little rivulets; not one of them runs in a straight line: and these ponds which are neither round, square, nor oval, nor indeed of any regular figure; together with these little sharp pebbles, (meaning the mountains,) that roughen the whole surface of the globe, and have torn all the skin from my feet. Besides, pray take notice of the shape of the whole, how it flattens at the poles, and turns round the sun in an awkward oblique manner, so as that the polar circles cannot possibly be cultivated. Truly, what makes me believe there is no inhabitant on this sphere, is a full persuasion that no sensible being would live in such a disagreeable place."

"What then?" said Micromegas, "perhaps the beings that inhabit it come not under that denomination; but, to all appearance, it was not made for nothing. Everything here seems to you irregular; because you fetch all your comparisons from Jupiter or Saturn. Perhaps this is the very reason of the seeming confusion which you condemn; have I not told you, that in the course of my travels I have always met with variety?"

The Saturnian replied to all these arguments; and perhaps the dispute would have known no end, if Micromegas, in the heat of the contest, had not luckily broken the string of his diamond necklace, so that the jewels fell to the ground; they consisted of pretty small unequal karats, the largest of which weighed four hundred pounds, and the smallest fifty. The dwarf, in helping to pick them up, perceived, as they approached his eye, that every single diamond was cut in such a manner as to answer the purpose of an excellent microscope. He therefore took up a small one, about one hundred and sixty feet in diameter, and applied it to his eye, while Micromegas chose another of two thousand five hundred feet. Though they were of excellent powers, the observers could perceive nothing by their assistance, so they were altered and adjusted. At length, the inhabitant of Saturn discerned something almost imperceptible moving between two waves in the Baltic. This was no other than a whale, which, in a dexterous manner, he caught with his little finger, and, placing it on the nail of his thumb, showed it to the Sirian, who laughed heartily at the excessive smallness peculiar to the inhabitants of this our globe. The Saturnian, by this time convinced that our world was inhabited, began to imagine we had no other animals than whales; and being a mighty debater, he forthwith set about investigating the origin and motion of this small atom, curious to know whether or not it was furnished with ideas, judgment, and free will. Micromegas was very much perplexed upon this subject. He examined the animal with the most patient attention, and the result of his inquiry was, that he could see no reason to believe a soul was lodged in such a body. The two travelers were actually inclined to think there was no such thing as mind in this our habitation, when, by the help of their microscope, they perceived something as large as a whale floating upon the surface of the sea. It is well known that, at this period, a flight of philosophers were upon their return from the polar circle,[10] where they had been making observations, for which nobody has hitherto been the wiser. The gazettes record, that their vessel ran ashore on the coast of Bothnia and that they with great difficulty saved their lives; but in this world one can never dive to the bottom of things. For my own part, I will ingenuously recount the transaction just as it happened, without any addition of my own; and this is no small effort in a modern historian.

---

[10] Expedition to the North Pole organized by Maupertius in 1736. The ship was wrecked during its return in 1737.

V

The Travelers Capture a Vessel

Micromegas stretched out his hand gently toward the place where the object appeared, and advanced two fingers, which he instantly pulled back, for fear of being disappointed, then opening softly and shutting them all at once, he very dexterously seized the ship that contained those gentlemen, and placed it on his nail, avoiding too much pressure, which might have crushed the whole in pieces.

"This," said the Saturnian dwarf, "is a creature very different from the former."

Upon which the Sirian placing the supposed animal in the hollow of his hand, the passengers and crew, who believed themselves thrown by a hurricane upon some rock, began to put themselves in motion. The sailors having hoisted out some casks of wine, jumped after them into the hand of Micromegas: the mathematicians having secured their quadrants, sectors, and Lapland servants, went overboard at a different place, and made such a bustle in their descent, that the Sirian at length felt his fingers tickled by something that seemed to move. An iron bar chanced to penetrate about a foot deep into his forefinger; and from this prick he concluded that something had issued from the little animal he held in his hand; but at first he suspected nothing more: for the microscope, that scarce rendered a whale and a ship visible, had no effect upon an object so imperceptible as man.

I do not intend to shock the vanity of any person whatever; but here I am obliged to beg your people of importance to consider that, supposing the stature of a man to be about five feet, we mortals make just such a figure upon the earth, as an animal the sixty thousandth part of a foot in height, would exhibit upon a bowl ten feet in circumference. When you reflect upon a being who could hold this whole earth in the palm of his hand, and is provided with organs proportioned to those we possess, you will easily conceive that there must be a great variety of created substances;—and pray, what must such beings think of those battles by which a conqueror gains a small village, to lose it again in the sequel?

I do not at all doubt, but if some captain of grenadiers should chance to read this work, he would add two large feet at least to the caps of his company; but I assure him his labor will be in vain; for, do what he will, he and his soldiers will never be other than infinitely diminutive and inconsiderable.

What wonderful address must have been inherent in our Sirian philosopher, that enabled him to perceive those atoms of which we have been speaking. When Leeuwenhoek and Hartsoecker[11] observed the first rudiments of which we are formed, they did not make such an astonishing discovery. What pleasure, therefore, was the portion of Micromegas, in observing the motion of those little machines, in examining all their pranks, and following them in all their operations! With what joy did he put his microscope into his companion's hand; and with what transport did they both at once exclaim:

"I see them distinctly,—don't you see them carrying burdens, lying down and rising up again?"

So saying, their hands shook with eagerness to see, and apprehension to lose such uncommon objects. The Saturnian, making a sudden transition from the most cautious distrust to the most excessive credulity, imagined he saw them engaged in their devotions and cried aloud in astonishment.

Nevertheless, he was deceived by appearances: a case too common, whether we do or do not make use of microscopes.

VI

What Happened in Their Intercourse With Men

Micromegas being a much better observer than the dwarf, perceived distinctly that those atoms spoke; and made the remark to his companion, who was so much ashamed of being mistaken in his first suggestion, that he would not believe such a puny species could possibly communicate their ideas: for, though he had the gift of tongues, as well as his companion, he could not hear those particles speak; and therefore supposed they had no language.

"Besides, how should such imperceptible beings have the organs of speech? and what in the name of Jove can they say to one another? In order to speak, they must have something like thought, and if they think, they must surely have something equivalent to a soul. Now, to attribute anything like a soul to such an insect species appears a mere absurdity."

---

[11] Dutch scientists. Leeuwenhoek (see Chapter 19) invented the microscope.

"But just now," replied the Sirian, "you believed they were engaged in devotional exercises; and do you think this could be done without thinking, without using some sort of language, or at least some way of making themselves understood? Or do you suppose it is more difficult to advance an argument than to engage in physical exercise? For my own part, I look upon all faculties as alike mysterious."

"I will no longer venture to believe or deny," answered the dwarf: "in short I have no opinion at all. Let us endeavor to examine these insects, and we will reason upon them afterward." [12]

"With all my heart," said Micromegas, "who, taking out a pair of scissors which he kept for paring his nails, cut off a paring from his thumb nail, of which he immediately formed a large kind of speaking trumpet, like a vast tunnel, and clapped the pipe to his ear: as the circumference of this machine included the ship and all the crew, the most feeble voice was conveyed along the circular fibres of the nail; so that, thanks to his industry, the philosopher could distinctly hear the buzzing of our insects that were below. In a few hours he distinguished articulate sounds, and at last plainly understood the French language. The dwarf heard the same, though with more difficulty."

The astonishment of our travelers increased every instant. They heard a nest of mites talk in a very sensible strain: and that *Lusus Naturae* seemed to them inexplicable. You need not doubt but the Sirian and his dwarf glowed with impatience to enter into conversation with such atoms. Micromegas being afraid that his voice, like thunder, would deafen and confound the mites, without being understood by them, saw the necessity of diminishing the sound; each, therefore, put into his mouth a sort of small toothpick, the slender end of which reached to the vessel. The Sirian setting the dwarf upon his knees, and the ship and crew upon his nail, held down his head and spoke softly. In fine, having taken these and a great many more precautions, he addressed himself to them in these words:

"O ye invisible insects, whom the hand of the Creator hath deigned to produce in the abyss of infinite littleness! I give praise to his goodness, in that he hath

been pleased to disclose unto me those secrets that seemed to be impenetrable."

If ever there was such a thing as astonishment, it seized upon the people who heard this address, and who could not conceive from whence it proceeded. The chaplain of the ship repeated exorcisms, the sailors swore, and the philosophers formed a system: but, notwithstanding all their systems, they could not divine who the person was that spoke to them. Then the dwarf of Saturn, whose voice was softer than that of Micromegas, gave them briefly to understand what species of beings they had to do with. He related the particulars of their voyage from Saturn, made them acquainted with the rank and quality of Monsieur Micromegas; and, after having pitied their smallness, asked if they had always been in that miserable state so near akin to annihilation; and what their business was upon that globe which seemed to be the property of whales. He also desired to know if they were happy in their situation? if they were inspired with souls? and put a hundred questions of the like nature.

A certain mathematician on board, braver than the rest, and shocked to hear his soul called in question, planted his quadrant,[13] and having taken two observations of this interlocutor, said: "You believe then, Mr. what's your name, that because you measure from head to foot a thousand fathoms——"

"A thousand fathoms!" cried the dwarf, "good heavens! How should he know the height of my stature? A thousand fathoms! My very dimensions to a hair. What, measured by a mite! This atom, forsooth, is a geometrician, and knows exactly how tall I am: while I, who can scarce perceive him through a microscope, am utterly ignorant of his extent!"

"Yes, I have taken your measure," answer the philosopher, "and I will now do the same by your tall companion."

The proposal was embraced: his excellency reclined upon his side; for, had he stood upright, his head would have reached too far above the clouds. Our mathematicians planted a tall tree near him, and then, by a series of triangles joined together, they discovered that the object of their observation was a strapping

---

[12] The "scientific method."

[13] Instrument for measuring distant objects.

youth, exactly one hundred and twenty thousand royal feet in length. In consequence of this calculation, Micromegas uttered these words:

"I am now more than ever convinced that we ought to judge of nothing by its external magnitude. O God! who hast bestowed understanding upon such seemingly contemptible substances, thou canst with equal ease produce that which is infinitely small, as that which is incredibly great: and if it be possible, that among thy works there are beings still more diminutive than these, they may nevertheless be endued with understanding superior to the intelligence of those stupendous animals I have seen in heaven, a single foot of whom is larger than this whole globe on which I have alighted."

One of the philosophers assured him that there were intelligent beings much smaller than men, and recounted not only Virgil's whole fable of the bees; but also described all that Swammerdam hath discovered, and Reaumur dissected. In a word, he informed him that there are animals which bear the same proportion to bees, that bees bear to man; the same as the Sirian himself compared to those vast beings whom he had mentioned; and as those huge animals as to other substances, before whom they would appear like so many particles of dust. Here the conversation became very interesting, and Micromegas proceeded in these words:

"O ye intelligent atoms, in whom the Supreme Being hath been pleased to manifest his omniscience and power, without all doubt your joys on this earth must be pure and exquisite: for, being unincumbered with matter, and, to all appearance, little else than soul, you must spend your lives in the delights of pleasure and reflection, which are the true enjoyments of a perfect spirit. True happiness I have no where found; but certainly here it dwells."

At this harangue all the philosophers shook their heads, and one among them, more candid than his brethren, frankly owned, that excepting a very small number of inhabitants who were very little esteemed by their fellows, all the rest were a parcel of knaves, fools, and miserable wretches.

"We have matter enough," said he, "to do abundance of mischief, if mischief comes from matter; and too much understanding, if evil flows from understanding. You must know, for example, that at this very moment, while I am speaking, there are one hundred thousand animals of our own species, covered with hats, slaying an equal number of their fellow-creatures, who wear turbans; at least they are either slaying or being slain; and this hath usually been the case all over the earth from time immemorial." [14]

The Sirian, shuddering at this information, begged to know the cause of those horrible quarrels among such a puny race; and was given to understand that the subject of the dispute was a pitiful mole-hill no larger than his heel. Not that any one of those millions who cut one another's throats pretends to have the least claim to the smallest particle of that clod. The question is, whether it shall belong to a certain person who is known by the name of Sultan, or to another whom (for what reason I know not) they dignify with the appellation of Tsar. Neither the one nor the other has seen or ever will see the pitiful corner in question; and probably none of these wretches, who so madly destroy each other, ever beheld the ruler on whose account they are so mercilessly sacrificed!

"Ah, miscreants!" cried the indignant Sirian, "such excess of desperate rage is beyond conception. I have a good mind to take two or three steps, and trample the whole nest of such ridiculous assassins under my feet."

"Don't give yourself the trouble," replied the philosopher, "they are industrious enough in procuring their own destruction. At the end of ten years the hundredth part of those wretches will not survive; for you must know that, though they should not draw a sword in the cause they have espoused, famine, fatigue, and intemperance, would sweep almost all of them from the face of the earth. Besides, the punishment should not be inflicted upon them, but upon those sedentary and slothful barbarians, who, from their palaces, give orders for murdering a million of men and then solemnly thank God for their success."

Our traveler was moved with compassion for the entire human race, in which he discovered such astonishing contrast. "Since you are of the small number of the wise," said he, "and in all likelihood do not engage yourselves in the trade of murder for hire, be so good as to tell me your occupation."

---

[14] Reference to the war between the Russians and the Turks over Crimea.

"We anatomize flies," replied the philosopher, "we measure lines, we make calculations, we agree upon two or three points which we understand, and dispute upon two or three thousand that are beyond our comprehension."

"How far," said the Sirian, "do you reckon the distance between the great star of the constellation Gemini and that called Caniculae?"

To this question all of them answered with one voice: "Thirty-two degrees and a half."

"And what is the distance from hence to the moon?"

"Sixty semi-diameters of the earth."

He then thought to puzzle them by asking the weight of the air; but they answered distinctly, that common air is about nine hundred times specifically lighter than an equal column of the lightest water, and nineteen hundred times lighter than current gold. The little dwarf of Saturn, astonished at their answers, was now tempted to believe those people sorcerers, who, but a quarter of an hour before, he would not allow were inspired with souls.

"Well," said Micromegas, "since you know so well what is without you, doubtless you are still more perfectly acquainted with that which is within. Tell me what is the soul, and how do your ideas originate?"

Here the philosophers spoke altogether as before; but each was of a different opinion. The eldest quoted Aristotle; another pronounced the name of Descartes; a third mentioned Malebranche; a fourth Leibnitz; and a fifth Locke. An old peripatecian lifting up his voice, exclaimed with an air of confidence. "The soul is perfection and reason, having power to be such as it is, as Aristotle expressly declares, page 633, of the Louvre edition:

"Εντελεχεια τις εςι, και λογος τ8 δυναμιν εχοντθς τοι8δι ειται."

"I am not very well versed in Greek," said the giant.

"Nor I either," replied the philosophical mite.

"Why then do you quote that same Aristotle in Greek?" resumed the Sirian.

"Because," answered the other, "it is but reasonable we should quote what we do not comprehend in a language we do not understand."

Here the Cartesian interposing: "The soul," said he, "is a pure spirit or intelligence, which hath received before birth all the metaphysical ideas; but after that

event it is obliged to go to school and learn anew the knowledge which it hath lost." [15]

"So it was necessary," replied the animal of eight leagues, "that thy soul should be learned before birth, in order to be so ignorant when thou hast got a beard upon thy chin. But what dost thou understand by spirit?"

"I have no idea of it," said the philosopher, "indeed it is supposed to be immaterial."

"At least, thou knowest what matter is?" resumed the Sirian.

"Perfectly well," answered the other. "For example: that stone is gray, is of a certain figure, has three dimensions, specific weight, and divisibility."

"I want to know," said the giant, "what that object is, which, according to thy observation, hath a gray color, weight, and divisibility. Thou seest a few qualities, but dost thou know the nature of the thing itself?"

"Not I, truly," answered the Cartesian.

Upon which the Sirian admitted that he also was ignorant in regard to this subject. Then addressing himself to another sage, who stood upon his thumb, he asked "what is the soul? and what are her functions?"

"Nothing at all," replied this disciple of Malebranche; "God hath made everything for my convenience. In him I see everything, by him I act; he is the universal agent, and I never meddle in his work."

"That is being a nonentity indeed," said the Sirian sage; and then, turning to a follower of Leibnitz, he exclaimed: "Hark ye, friend, what is thy opinion of the soul?"

"In my opinion," answered this metaphysician, "the soul is the hand that points at the hour, while my body does the office of the clock; or, if you please, the soul is the clock, and the body is the pointer; or again, my soul is the mirror of the universe, and my body the frame. All this is clear and uncontrovertible."

A little partisan of Locke who chanced to be present, being asked his opinion on the same subject, said: "I do not know by what power I think; but well I know that I should never have thought without the assistance of my senses. That there are immaterial and intelligent substances I do not at all doubt; but that it is impos-

---

[15] Descartes believed in innate ideas.

sible for God to communicate the faculty of thinking to matter, I doubt very much. I revere the eternal power, to which it would ill become me to prescribe bounds. I affirm nothing, and am contented to believe that many more things are possible than are usually thought so."

The Sirian smiled at this declaration, and did not look upon the author as the least sagacious of the company: and as for the dwarf of Saturn, he would have embraced this adherent of Locke, had it not been for the extreme disproportion in their respective sizes. But unluckily there was another animalcule in a square cap,[16] who, taking the word from all his philosophical brethren, affirmed that he knew the whole secret. He surveyed the two celestial strangers from top to toe, and maintained to their faces that their persons, their fashions, their suns and their stars, were created solely for the use of man. At this wild assertion our two travelers were seized with a fit of that uncontrollable laughter, which (according to Homer) is the portion of the immortal gods: their bellies quivered, their shoulders rose and fell, and, during these convulsions, the vessel fell from the Sirian's nail into the Saturnian's pocket, where these worthy people searched for it a long time with great diligence. At length, having found the ship and set everything to rights again, the Sirian resumed the discourse with those diminutive mites, and promised to compose for them a choice book of philosophy which would demonstrate the very essence of things. Accordingly, before his departure, he made them a present of the book, which was brought to the Academy of Sciences at Paris, but when the old secretary came to open it he saw nothing but blank paper.

"Ay, ay," said he, "this is just what I suspected."

COMMENTS AND QUESTIONS

1. Voltaire's tale is a good example of the "philosophical" combination of critical reason, admiration for science, and fantasy. Find instances of Voltaire's use of all of these.
2. Where, specifically, does Voltaire say what he does not mean so that the reader will infer the opposite (irony)?
3. Against what ideas and what people is his satire directed?
4. Blaise Pascal concluded from the new scientific discoveries that man's place between the infinitely large and the infinitely small is a terrifying one, and that man can be saved only by God's grace. What is Voltaire's opinion of this view?
5. How does Voltaire attack the traditional Christian position that God created the universe with man at its center as the master of creation? What scientific discoveries made this position seem ridiculous?
6. What is Voltaire's own view of mankind? Would you call it "humanistic"? (Compare that of Pico della Mirandola in Chapter 9 of Volume I.) Is it optimistic? Pessimistic?
7. Do you as a modern reader find it easy to enter into the spirit of this tale of giants? Is the story still lively, amusing, and relevant?
8. What similarities and differences exist between Micromegas and twentieth-century works of science fiction?

Voltaire returned to Paris after his sojourn in Cirey but continued to have trouble with the authorities all his life. He spent much time in the company of Frederick of Prussia, whom he saw as a kind of ideal "enlightened despot." In his later life, he abandoned the relative optimism and faith in the progress of civilization that characterize his early writings. His most famous work, the short novel Candide, is an attack on the current philosophical doctrine that "everything is for the best in this best of all possible worlds." One of Voltaire's appealing characteristics was his willingness to use his pen in the service of social causes, particularly for victims of intolerance. He was successful in vindicating the memory of the French Protestant Jean Calas, accused of murdering his son and tortured on the rack. The Church claimed that the father murdered the son because he had converted to Catholicism, but the boy had in fact killed himself. Voltaire exposed the facts in his Treatise on Toleration and at the end appended a prayer to his deistic God. This prayer, below (translated by William Fleming) is a classic statement on the virtues of tolerance.

---

[16] A theologian.

VOLTAIRE

An Address to the Deity

No longer then do I address myself to men, but to Thee, God of all beings, of all worlds, and of all ages; if it may be permitted weak creatures lost in immensity and imperceptible to the rest of the universe, to presume to petition Thee for aught, who hast given plenty of all things, and whose decrees are immutable as eternal. Deign to look with an eye of pity on the errors annexed to our natures! let not these errors prove the sources of misery to us! Thou hast not given us hearts to hate, nor hands to kill one another; grant then that we may mutually aid and assist each other to support the burden of this painful and transitory life! May the trifling differences in the garments that cover our frail bodies, in the mode of expressing our insignificant thoughts, in our ridiculous customs and our imperfect laws, in our idle opinions, and in our several conditions and situations, that appear so disproportionate in our eyes, and all are equal in Thine; in a word, may the slight variations that are found amongst the atoms called men not be made use of by us as signals of mutual hatred and persecution! May those who worship Thee by the light of tapers at noonday bear charitably with those who content themselves with the light of that glorious planet Thou hast placed in the midst of the heavens! May those who dress themselves in a robe of white linen to teach their hearers that Thou art to be loved and feared, not detest or revile those who teach the same doctrine in long cloaks of black wool! May it be accounted the same to adore Thee in a dialect formed from an ancient or a modern language! May those who, clothed in vestments of crimson or violet color, rule over a little parcel of that heap of dirt called the world, and are possessed of a few round fragments of a certain metal, enjoy without pride or insolence what they call grandeur and riches, and may others look on them without envy; for Thou knowest, O God, that there is nothing in all these vanities proper to inspire envy or pride.

May all men remember that they are brethren! May they alike abhor that tyranny which seeks to subject the freedom of the will, as they do the rapine which tears from the arms of industry the fruits of its peaceful labors! And if the scourge of war is not to be avoided,

23-3 Houdon, "Bust of Voltaire." (Louvre, Paris)

let us not mutually hate and destroy each other in the midst of peace; but rather make use of the few moments of our existence to join in praising, in a thousand different languages, from one extremity of the world to the other, Thy goodness, O all-merciful Creator, to whom we are indebted for that existence!

COMMENTS AND QUESTIONS

1. Tolerance of different beliefs and customs is more or less accepted—ideally if not in practice—in our society today, but it was quite a new idea in the eighteenth century. Could this have been written in the Middle Ages? The Reformation? The seventeenth century? Why not?
2. Is Voltaire himself really tolerant of all views and practices?
3. Define for yourself what, exactly, tolerance means and how far its limits extend.
4. What do different people who claim to practice toleration term intolerable?

The old Voltaire, admirably portrayed in a statue by the sculptor Houdon (Fig. 23-3) was confident that he had witnessed the triumph of reason in his lifetime. "It is certain," he wrote, "that the knowledge of nature, the skeptical attitude toward old fables dignified by the name of history, a healthy metaphysic freed from the absurdities of the schools, are the fruits of that century when reason was perfected." Skeptical and civilized as he was, he undoubtedly would not have approved of the revolution that came a decade after his death. Yet the crowds that gathered to honor him by placing his body in the Pantheon in Paris in 1790 inscribed on the tomb: "He taught us to be free."

Montesquieu

One of the greatest objections leveled agains the philosophes by later generations is that they had no appreciation for the effect of history on man. Too analytical, they saw man in the abstract and were therefore unable to effect reform within a historical context. One perceptive critic of the eighteenth century, the Baron de Montesquieu (1689–1755), attacked this neglect of history on the very same grounds. His belief was that men are basically a product of history and that constitutions must be tailored to meet the conditions and historical traditions of the particular society.

Yet Montesquieu himself is usually regarded as a philosophe on the grounds that despite his historical interests he, like most of the others in the movement, was a deist, a believer in natural rights, and a reformer, especially of the penal code. Though he was also an empiricist, he included history as a vital part of the human experience; his insistence on history as an important factor when considering reforms of society and government led him to be politically conservative. A member of the privileged provincial nobility, he was both by self-interest and conviction antagonistic to political reforms predicated on the belief that the past could simply be wiped away. Frankly fearing for personal liberty in a state ruled by a despot no matter how enlightened, he found Locke's theory of an executive checked by a legislature very appealing. Admiring English government but basically misunderstanding its constitutional machinery, Montesquieu developed a theory of separation of powers among legislative, judicial, and executive agencies; he insisted that the individual could be free only where the power of one of these branches of government was checked by the

other two. Of almost no importance in France, the theory had tremendous influence in the conception of the United States Constitution.

An issue dealt with by Montesquieu in *The Spirit of the Laws*, which did not take effect in America until much later, was the question of slavery. Seventeenth-century absolutists and capitalists had accepted slavery in the course of their trade; Montesquieu and other philosophes, scrutinizing the institution under the light of reason, found it unnatural and evil. It is clear that slavery would be abhorrent to those who believe in the natural rights of human beings. (We will examine the paradox of its continuation in the new, "enlightened" United States in the next chapter.) The translation is by Thomas Nugent.

MONTESQUIEU

from *The Spirit of the Laws*

OF CIVIL SLAVERY

Slavery, properly so called, is the establishment of a right which gives to one man such a power over another as renders him absolute master of his life and fortune. The state of slavery is in its own nature bad. It is neither useful to the master nor to the slave; not to the slave, because he can do nothing through a motive of virtue; nor to the master, because by having an unlimited authority over his slaves he insensibly accustoms himself to the want of all moral virtues, and thence becomes fierce, hasty, severe, choleric, voluptuous, and cruel.

In despotic countries, where they are already in a state of political servitude, civil slavery is more tolerable than in other governments. Every one ought to be satisfied in those countries with necessaries and life. Hence the condition of a slave is hardly more burdensome than that of a subject.

But in a monarchical government, where it is of the utmost importance that human nature should not be debased or dispirited, there ought to be no slavery. In democracies, where they are all upon equality; and in aristocracies, where the laws ought to use their utmost endeavors to procure as great an equality as the nature of the government will permit, slavery is contrary to the spirit of the constitution: it only contributes to give a power and luxury to the citizens which they ought not to have. . . .

Knowledge humanizes mankind, and reason inclines to mildness; but prejudices eradicate every tender disposition.

ANOTHER ORIGIN OF THE RIGHT OF SLAVERY

I would as soon say that religion gives its professors a right to enslave those who dissent from it, in order to render its propagation more easy.

This was the notion that encouraged the ravagers of America in their iniquity. Under the influence of this idea they founded their right of enslaving so many nations; for these robbers, who would absolutely be both robbers and Christians, were superlatively devout.

Louis XIII was extremely uneasy at a law by which all the negroes of his colonies were to be made slaves; but it being strongly urged to him as the readiest means for their conversion, he acquiesced without further scruple.

OF THE SLAVERY OF THE NEGROES

Were I to vindicate our right to make slaves of the negroes, these should be my arguments:—

The Europeans, having extirpated the Americans, were obliged to make slaves of the Africans, for clearing such vast tracts of land.

Sugar would be too dear if the plants which produce it were cultivated by any other than slaves.

These creatures are all over black, and with such a flat nose that they can scarcely be pitied.

It is hardly to be believed that God, who is a wise Being, should place a soul, especially a good soul, in such a black, ugly body.

It is so natural to look upon color as the criterion of human nature, that the Asiatics, among whom eunuchs are employed, always deprive the blacks of their resemblance to us by a more opprobrious distinction.

The color of the skin may be determined by that of the hair, which, among the Egyptians, the best philosophers in the world, was of such importance that they put to death all the red-haired men who fell into their hands.

The negroes prefer a glass necklace to that gold which polite nations so highly value. Can there be a greater proof of their wanting common sense?

It is impossible for us to suppose these creatures to be men, because, allowing them to be men, a suspicion would follow that we ourselves are not Christians.

Weak minds exaggerate too much the wrong done to the Africans. For were the case as they state it, would the European powers, who make so many needless conventions among themselves, have failed to enter into a general one, in behalf of humanity and compassion?

QUESTIONS

1. How do you think Montesquieu's arguments would strike an eighteenth-century public?
2. Is the irony in the last section effective?
3. How does Montesquieu turn to ridicule statements that were undoubtedly believed by many?

Rousseau

Jean-Jacques Rousseau (1712–1778) is a paradoxical figure who in some ways belongs with the philosophes and in others may be seen as a precursor of romanticism. Of humble origins, Rousseau was born in the city-state of Geneva, in Switzerland; he came to Paris at the age of thirty after fifteen years of living a vagabond existence. An insecure, unhappy man, suffering from a sense of persecution and an embarrassing urinary problem, Rousseau found the source of his problems in the artificiality of society. Among the many contradictions of his life was his writing in praise of the simple, virtuous life in Geneva while he continued to live in Paris.

In two essays that brought him his first literary honors, *The Discourse on the Arts and Sciences* (1749) and *On the Origins of Inequality among Men* (1755), he attacked the corruptions of society and characterized the progress that men had made in the arts and sciences as contributing to this degeneration. Accordingly, he idealized the state of nature, the time when men were originally free. Although he did not deny the rational capacity of men, Rousseau believed that the deepest part of the human being was at the level of the instincts and that by nature men are loving, sympathetic, and kind. When Voltaire finished reading *On the Origins*, he commented that Rousseau's work made him feel like getting down on four legs.

In the society of his own time Rousseau idealized the lower classes, who seemed to him to be living closest to the natural life. In works like *Émile*, a treatise on "natural" education, and his novel, *The New Heloise*, he depicted the beauties of the simple life led amid nature. So popular were these works by the last quarter of the century that all over France the upper classes, including the queen herself, entertained themselves by dressing as shepherds and peasants, picnicking and playing in the woods and fields. It became fashionable to speak of one's feelings in public, to act "naturally," and to idealize the poor.

Rousseau's most important work on political theory, *The Social Contract* (1762) reflects the contradictions found in this paradoxical figure, whose tortured genius endeavored to reconcile into a system his philosophe inheritance with his own intense experience of life. Terminology like "contract" and "state of nature" is that of Locke and Voltaire. On man's emerging from the state of nature to set up a government, the philosophes commonly spoke of a contract being made among the members of the society and the government that they created. This contract was to stipulate the duties and limitations of the government and to afford a legal basis for destroying the government if it violated the terms.

In Rousseau's hands the language of the Enlightenment remains, but the meanings are very different. Whereas previously he had seen man as good in the state of nature and subsequently corrupted by evil institutions, in this work man in nature is depicted as a brute driven by his impulses and appetite. He becomes truly human only when living in a civil state: "By dint of being exercised, his sentiments become ennobled and his whole soul becomes so elevated that, but for the fact that misuse of the new conditions still, at times, degrades him to a point below that from which he has emerged, he would unceasingly bless the day which freed him for ever from his ancient state, and turned him from a limited and stupid animal into an intelligent being and a man." Against his own earlier view and that of earlier philosophes, Rousseau maintains that the state is not a creation of fully formed men, but rather that men become men only by living in a community. There is no interest in returning to a state of nature; man's task is to create a better society where one's humanity can be fully realized.

Moreover, for Rousseau the contract is not an agreement between a society and its government but between the various free individuals in the state of nature to create the society itself. Driven by the desire for self-preservation, brutish and lonely men unite themselves out of fear and voluntarily surrender their natural freedom in exchange for the benefits of social life. Merging their individual wills into a "general will," they agree to obey everything that "will" decrees. Rousseau's ideal society is small enough so that the collective body of the citizens can assemble to express the general will, which rules that state. The actual government consists just of administrators who carry out its orders. Rousseau probably had in mind a society like the city-state of Geneva where he grew up. But whereas Geneva was governed by an *aristocracy*, Rousseau's ideal state was a *democracy*. The translations are by Henry J. Tozer.

JEAN-JACQUES ROUSSEAU

from *The Social Contract*

THE SOCIAL PACT

I assume that men have reached a point at which the obstacles that endanger their preservation in the state of nature overcome by their resistance the forces which each individual can exert with a view to maintaining himself in that state. Then this primitive condition can no longer subsist, and the human race would perish unless it changed its mode of existence.

Now, as men cannot create any new forces, but only combine and direct those that exist, they have no other means of self-preservation than to form by aggregation a sum of forces which may overcome the resistance, to put them in action by a single motive power, and to make them work in concert.

This sum of forces can be produced only by the combination of many; but the strength and freedom of each man being the chief instruments of his preservation, how can he pledge them without injuring himself, and without neglecting the cares which he owes to himself? This difficulty, applied to my subject, may be expressed in these terms:

"To find a form of association which may defend and protect with the whole force of the community the person and property of every associate, and by means of which each, coalescing with all, may nevertheless obey only himself, and remain as free as before." Such is the fundamental problem of which the social contract furnishes the solution.

The clauses of this contract are so determined by the nature of the act that the slightest modification would render them vain and ineffectual; so that, although they have never perhaps been formally enunciated, they are everywhere the same, everywhere tacitly admitted and recognised, until, the social pact being violated, each man regains his original rights and recovers his natural liberty, whilst losing the conventional liberty for which he renounced it.

These clauses, rightly understood, are reducible to one only, viz. the total alienation to the whole community of each associate with all rights; for, in the first place, since each gives himself up entirely, the conditions are equal for all; and, the conditions being equal for all, no one has any interest in making them burdensome to others.

Further, the alienation being made without reserve, the union is as perfect as it can be, and an individual associate can no longer claim anything; for, if any rights were left to individuals, since there would be no common superior who could judge between them and the public, each being on some point his own judge, would soon claim to be so on all; the state of nature would still subsist, and the association would necessarily become tyrannical or useless.

In short, each giving himself to all, gives himself to nobody; and as there is not one associate over whom we do not acquire the same rights which we concede to him over ourselves, we gain the equivalent of all that we lose, and more power to preserve what we have.

If, then, we set aside what is not of the essence of the social contract, we shall find that it is reducible to the following terms: "Each of us puts in common his person and his whole power under the supreme direction of the general will; and in return we receive every member as an indivisible part of the whole."

Forthwith, instead of the individual personalities of all the contracting parties, this act of association produces a moral and collective body, which is composed of as many members as the assembly has voices, and which receives from this same act its unity, its common self, its life, and its will. This public person, which is thus formed by the union of all the individual members, formerly took the name of "city" and now takes that of "republic" or "body politic," which is called by its members "State" when it is passive, "sovereign" when it is active, "power" when it is compared to similar bodies. With regard to the associates, they take collectively the name of "people," and are called individually "citizens," as participating in the sovereign power, and "subjects," as subjected to the laws of the State. But these terms are often confused and are mistaken one for another; it is sufficient to know how to distinguish them when they are used with complete precision.

QUESTIONS

1. What societies do not have a social contract? Why?
2. Why must the individual give up all his rights on entering the contract?
3. Why, after the creation of the social contract, does each individual remain as free as before?
4. What limitations are there on the actions of the community in regard to the individual? What kind of laws can the community not make?

What is the general will? One thing is clear: for Rousseau it is not the will of the majority. Often the vote of the multitude reflects only the combined self-interest of every individual and not the public interest. For Rousseau the general will is mysteriously found in each citizen below the level of his individual selfish will. It is the common will that seeks the good of the whole community; when it speaks, it reflects the true interests even of those who violently opposed its decision. In the case of citizens who differ with the general will, they are literally forced to be free, that is, to accept what the deepest part of their being really wants.

WHETHER THE GENERAL WILL CAN ERR

It follows from what precedes that the general will is always right and always tends to the public advantage; but it does not follow that the resolutions of the people have always the same rectitude. Men always desire their own good, but do not always discern it; the people are never corrupted, though often deceived, and it is only then that they seem to will what is evil.

There is often a great deal of difference between the will of all and the general will; the latter regards only

23-4 Joseph Wright, "Experiment with the Air-Pump." (The Tate Gallery, London)

the common interest, while the former has regard to private interests, and is merely a sum of particular wills; but take away from these same wills the pluses and minuses which cancel one another, and the general will remains as the sum of the differences.

If the people came to a resolution when adequately informed and without any communication among the citizens, the general will would always result from the great number of slight differences, and the resolution would always be good. But when factions, partial associations, are formed to the detriment of the whole society, the will of each of these associations becomes general with reference to its members, and particular with reference to the State; it may then be said that there are no longer as many voters as there are men, but only as many voters as there are associations. The differences become less numerous and yield a less general result. Lastly, when one of these associations becomes so great that it predominates over all the rest, you no longer have as the result a sum of small differences, but a single difference; there is then no longer a general will, and the opinion which prevails is only a particular opinion.

It is important, then, in order to have a clear declaration of the general will, that there should be no partial association in the State, and that every citizen should express only his own opinion.

QUESTIONS

1. Why does Rousseau feel as he does about political parties?
2. How did most philosophes regard such organizations? Why?

3. What does Rousseau mean by natural rights? Who determines the limits of these rights in society?

Voltaire and other philosophes envisaged men as atoms of rationality alike all over the earth. Rousseau saw man rather as essentially a bundle of feelings and instincts determined to a large extent by the society in which he lives. For Rousseau an individual's community was not simply a convenience; rather, it provided the framework in which the individual realized himself. But for full personal development to occur, every member of the community had to participate in deliberations. Only in this way could the collective, or general, will be expressed and the good of all best be served. Of course, by maintaining that even the will of the majority does not necessarily express that will, he left the door open for the rise of a demagogue who knew better what the people needed than they did themselves. At various times, and with valid reasons, Rousseau has been called the father of democracy, socialism, communism, nationalism, and fascism.

Aspects of Painting in the Enlightenment

Many of the tendencies found in the philosophes—the movement from the nobility to the bourgeois, from the grandiose to the petite, from tragedy to satire, as well as the interests in science and in society—are reflected in the art of the early eighteenth century. An example of the new middle class passion for science and homemade experiments may be seen in the painting *Experiment with the Air-Pump* (1768) by an Englishman, Joseph Wright (Fig. 23-4). Exhibited in London, it would have appealed to Diderot and Voltaire,

23–5   Boucher, "Diana after the Hunt," (Musée Cognacq-Jay/Photographie Bulloz, Paris)

for it records a scientific experiment in explicit detail. The air pump, on the table in the center of the composition, has been purchased by a prosperous bourgeois to entertain and to educate. The glass globe contains a dove that will die when the air is pumped from the globe to create a vacuum. The two young girls are sad, but the others, youths and elders, watch with interest. The surfaces and textures of objects are rendered with extreme *verisimilitude*—the painter is as observant as the scientist.

Paintings such as this indicate one characteristic of eighteenth-century art: the decline in importance of the art of the court. Another type, a more intimate and sensual art, replaced the neoclassicism of Le Brun and his school. Watteau's *Pilgrimage to Cythera* (Color Plate V) is thematically the progeny of Rubens' *Garden of Love* (Color Plate II). Yet these couples who move

through the forest of the enchanted island of Venus are not arriving, but leaving, to return to the real world. Watteau has given a sense of melancholy to the beautiful but shallow world of entertainments and parties that seemed more and more to occupy the life of the nobility.

Boucher, who followed Watteau, continued the decorative and intimate character of his art while adding a more sexual, sensuous content (Fig. 23-5). The golden colors, the flesh tones and textures, and the delightful abandon of these figures are the subject. Mythological or other themes are only an excuse for these handsome paintings that celebrate the life of the senses.

The *philosophe* Diderot, who also wrote essays on contemporary art, was not impressed by these frivolous objects. Diderot's taste ran rather toward *genre* painting—scenes from everyday life among the peasants and the lower classes. In particular he praised Chardin and Greuze, two painters whose work have only the most superficial elements in common. Chardin imparts to his subjects, whether a maid, a mother and child, or a still life, a monumental and quiet objectivity that recalls Vermeer (Color Plate IV). His pictures of still-life subjects seem constructed from a careful, loving observation of nature that renders textures, surfaces, and light with verisimilitude (Color Plate VI). Order and harmony are extracted from the simple events and objects of the middle classes. We know that Chardin meant his pictures to educate and to instruct in virtue, but the depiction of objects seems to mean as much to him as the portrayal of a moral. It was Chardin's naturalism that so appealed to Diderot; yet, in contrast to Vermeer, Chardin's paint has a creamy sensual surface that is as covertly appealing as his objects.

Greuze's work appealed to Diderot because his scenes suggested narratives that praised virtue or had a didactic moral. Too frequently these scenes also had a marked sentimentalizing attitude toward the event. *The Village Bride*, shown in the Salon of 1761, is a sample of his work. A youthful bride watches while the dowry is negotiated, the grandfather admonishes, the mother is pensive, the hen in the foreground protects her chicks (Fig. 23-6). These sweet, clean, honest, virtuous, natural peasants provide a vivid contrast to what we know of life. But these pictures appealed to the upper bourgeoisie of the mid-eighteenth century, who saw in these peasants natural virtue.

23–6   Greuze, "The Village Bride." (Louvre, Paris)

In the works of the English artist William Hogarth, people hardly seem virtuous, but they do seem more human. Hogarth produced visual equivalents to satire, a favorite literary mode in eighteenth-century Europe (as it had been in ancient Rome). Interested in art theory as well as practice, Hogarth wrote about 1730 that he wanted to depict "modern moral subjects; . . . a field not broken up in any country or any age." He seems to have believed that people might be reformed from their excesses by the examples of these paintings. This may have been rather ambitious, but his paintings still give delight with their portrayal of the awful glamour of hu-

man folly, of the dangers of greed, pride, and conceit within the context of conventional morality. A serial narrative painting called *The Rake's Progress* ends with the rake alcoholic and incarcerated in an insane asylum. Another, *The Election*, satirizes the corruption of that institution (Fig. 23-7). Hogarth gives an account of excessive behavior that could be prevented by rational thought. But this answer, like Greuze's natural virtue, is, to us, too easy, and inadequate to the troubles of people. Although rationalism characterizes the early Enlightenment, it becomes insufficient by the end of the century when reason seems to sleep (Fig. 25-3).

23–7   Hogarth, "Canvassing for Votes," (Courtesy of the Trustees of Sir John Soane's Museum, London)

24

THE ENLIGHTENMENT IN THE UNITED STATES

Political events in North America in the last four decades of the eighteenth century fascinated European observers. While the French philosophes were forced to adapt their goals for improving the human condition to the circumstances of a very traditional social and political structure, English-speaking North America presented the situation of a new people in an underdeveloped land largely untrammeled by the weight of past institutions. Once the colonists had thrown off the control imposed on their society by the imperial system of the mother country, the possibilities for political creativity and experimentation seemed limitless. As the new nation emerged from the endless deliberations of the political leadership, European intellectuals watched intently for signs to determine whether the American republic, the most populous and geographically extensive republican government in the history of the world, would succeed or fail.

The history of the creation of the United States, following more than a century of colonial development, can be divided into three basic phases. The first phase began with the defeat of French armies in the New World by combined British and colonial forces, part of a worldwide struggle between rival European powers. When British officials then tried to impose increased taxes upon the growing colonies to help cover the rising military and administrative costs of the empire, the colonists resisted in increasing numbers and finally declared themselves politically independent in 1776. The second phase comprises the period from the first years of the war until the creation of the Constitution in 1787, when the dominant minds in America attempted to devise some sort of lasting union among the thirteen loosely confederated states. The final period is that of the first decades after ratification of the Constitution (which went into effect in 1789) as Americans endeavored to make the new government work in the face of forces for decentralization that threatened at times to pull the new federal structure apart.

European Influences   From the early eighteenth century the dominant stream of ideas shaping politics in America was English. The *empiricism* of English thinkers like Bacon and Newton made a strong impact on Americans, and theory was reinforced by a pioneer culture that respected labor and practical know-how. Products of a highly mobile society with a flexible social structure, the colonists worked well together at the local level in meeting their common needs. The validity of Locke's doctrine of natural rights of man seemed borne out by their experience. Beginning as they did in a new environment, the colonists tended to view critically any limitation on their freedom of action unless it could be justified in terms of personal advantage. With the executive power firmly in the hands of British governors, they also found Locke's emphasis on the duty of legislative assemblies to supervise the executive authority to their liking. Characteristically, the Declaration of Independence, which claimed rights to life, liberty, and the pursuit of happiness to be self-evident, justified severance with England on the grounds of George III's tyranny, not because of oppression by Parliament. Furthermore, the Declaration of Independence and the Constitution echo Locke in their state-

ments that governments derive their just powers from the consent of the governed and that when governments exceed their power, the people have the right to institute new governments.

French philosophes were, on the whole, ardent supporters of the American revolution. They admired versatile diplomats like Benjamin Franklin and Thomas Jefferson, both of whom lived for long periods in France, as the kind of "enlightened" men that the New World could produce. Men like Turgot used their influence at court to bring the French government into the war on the rebels' side in 1778, and the French intervention was decisive. On the intellectual level, Montesquieu doubtless had the most significant influence on American political thought in the revolutionary period. His conception of a balance of power among the legislative, executive, and judicial branches of government suited the American distrust of the executive and made the Constitution more attractive to many who looked on a strong executive as a potential threat to individual freedom. In the 1780s and 1790s, however, Rousseau's democratic theories provided ammunition against elitist conceptions of political authority held by most American thinkers. For example, property qualifications for voting rights were reduced at this time. By 1800 the American republic was becoming more democratic.

American Federalism   Federalism, perhaps the United States' most original contribution to the theory and practice of republican government, owed little to either the French or the English; it was born of necessity. Under no circumstances able to induce strong, independent state governments to become mere agencies of the central government, the writers of the Constitution established a principle of separation of powers between the central government and the states. Such a system of power division was to have a great future because it permitted unification of large areas of land and supported regional diversity while still limiting the power of local opposition.

The Heritage of Ancient Rome   No account of the ideology of the American revolutionary epoch would be complete without acknowledging the extent to which these patriots thought of themselves and were considered by their European sympathizers as the heirs to the republican tradition of ancient Rome. Since the Renaissance the educated class of the Western world had been deeply imbued with classical culture; one aspect of that culture, clearly defined since the early fifteenth century (see Volume I) was its *republican* tradition. The leaders of the revolution appeared to contemporaries as the simple, honest descendants of Roman statesmen like Cato, or the general, Cincinnatus, who left his own plow to lead an army against the enemies of the Roman republic. Americans often signed their letters of protest against English tyranny with Roman names, and Washington and other officers of the revolutionary army took part in a controversial Society of Cincinnatus. In their struggle for liberty, these patriots (from Latin *patria*—homeland) seemed the modern counterparts of Roman heroes like Horatio and Brutus. The architects of the Constitution drew on words of Latin derivation like *president* and *senate*, and the Great Seal of the new nation and its coinage were marked with Latin phrases and classical emblems (Fig. 24-1). Houdon's statue of Washington in the capital at Richmond dramatically illustrates these associations of the new republic with the old. In 1786 the French sculptor represented the future president of the United States in modern dress; but he stands beside the Roman *fasces*, a bundle of rods symbolic of power and union, in a pose based on that of a classical statue (Fig. 24-2).

Thomas Jefferson The figure who best represents the American Enlightenment is Thomas Jefferson (1743–1826). Jefferson combined the Old World's tradition of scholarship and philosophy with the New World's practicality and readiness to experiment. Both philosopher and plantation manager, he was at home in the salons of Paris and the still untamed parts of Virginia. Like the French philosophes, he combined wide learning in the classical humanities with a lively interest in recent scientific developments. He regarded the republic of letters and ideas as an international one.

In addition to his career as a politician, Jefferson was an excellent writer, an educator, a farmer, and an architect. One of his masterpieces is his home near Charlottesville, Virginia, which he called Monticello ("the little mountain"). The house itself is symbolic of the

24–1 "Great Seal of the United States." (Bureau of Engraving and Printing, U.S. Department of the Treasury)

24–2 Houdon, "George Washington." (Virginia State Library)

nature of the American Enlightenment. Jefferson used the *Palladian* Villa Rotunda as his model (Fig. 20-10), but the plan of the interior exhibits a functional adaptation of the symmetrical plan to his own particular needs (Fig. 24-3). Similarly, the building originally designed for stone execution is rendered in red brick with white wooden trim—an elegant, rich contrast to the building's general simplicity of shape. These adaptations to use and surroundings do not, however, detract from the *portico* and *dome*, the two forms that link it with Greek democracy and the Roman republic. Facing westward, to the wilderness, dominating but sympathetic to the landscape, the house is almost a metaphor for the man—aristocratic, cosmopolitan, inventive, practical—a farmer and a philosopher.

Designing his own tomb for the grounds at Monticello, Jefferson composed the following inscription: "Here was buried Thomas Jefferson, author of the Declaration of American Independence, of the Statute of Virginia for Religious Freedom, and Father of the University of Virginia." He apparently did not consider that being the third president of the United States was among his most significant accomplishments. Those that he lists are excellent examples of the application of the principles of the Enlightenment to the American experience.

The Declaration of Independence The Declaration, written largely by Jefferson and approved by the Continental Congress on July 4, 1776, is a statement of political philosophy as well as an act of rebellion. It is in fact typical of the American Enlightenment that theory and its practical application are combined in the same document. The Declaration may be divided into two distinct parts: the first sets forth principles of democratic government and proves, in the abstract, philosophical terms of the Enlightenment, the right of the colonies to rebel. The second part is a specific list of grievances against the king of Great Britain, George III.

Because of its ready availability, we will not print the entire Declaration here. A close reading of the first two paragraphs, however, reveals the purpose of the document and a theoretical basis for rebellion.

24–3 Jefferson, Monticello, west front. (Thomas Jefferson Memorial Foundation)

When, in the course of human events, it becomes necessary for one people to dissolve the political bands which have connected them with another, and to assume, among the powers of the earth, the separate and equal station to which the laws of nature and of nature's God entitle them, a decent respect to the Opinions of mankind requires that they should declare the causes which impel them to the separation.

We hold these truths to be self-evident: That all men are created equal; that they are endowed by their Creator with certain unalienable rights; that among these are life, liberty & the pursuit of happiness; that to secure these rights governments are instituted among men, deriving their just powers from the consent of the governed; that whenever any form of government becomes destructive of these ends, it is the right of the people to alter or to abolish it, and to institute new government, laying its foundation on such principles and organizing its powers in such form, as to them shall seem most likely to effect their safety and happiness.

COMMENTS AND QUESTIONS

1. Is there any religious basis for the rebellion? Does it seem to be Christian?
2. How do the expressions "laws of nature," "nature's God," and "truths" that are "self-evident" reflect values of the Enlightenment?
3. Did the American political system in fact guarantee the "unalienable rights" that Jefferson lists? What do you think that he meant by "the pursuit of happiness"? By "all men are created equal"?
4. How do Jefferson's political ideals differ from, or resemble, those of Thucydides or Bruni? (See Vol. I.)
5. Do the principles of the Enlightenment found here (such as self-evident truths) seem a valid basis from which to argue legal and moral questions today?

The questions raised here may be applied to the entire Declaration. The second part of the document purports to show, by the list of grievances, that George III deliberately and malevolently attempted to establish an "absolute tyranny" over the colonies. It is consistent with Jefferson's idea of a government that derives its powers from the "consent of the governed" that he blames all sorts of evils on the tyrannical will of the king. The last of Jefferson's charges, omitted by the Congress in the final draft of the Declaration, was an indictment against the enslavement of Africans.

He has waged cruel war against human nature itself, violating its most sacred rights of life and liberty in the persons of a distant people who never offended him, captivating and carrying them into slavery in another hemisphere, or to incur miserable death in their transportation thither. This piratical warfare, the opprobrium of *infidel* powers, is the warfare of the *Christian* king of Great Britain. Determined to keep open a market where MEN should be bought and sold, he has prostituted his negative for suppressing every legislative attempt to prohibit or to restrain this execrable commerce; and that this assemblage of horrors might want no fact of distinguished die, he is now exciting these very people to rise in arms among us, and to purchase that liberty of which *he* deprived them, by murdering the people upon whom *he* also obtruded them; thus paying off former crimes committed against the *liberties* of one people, with crimes which he urges them to commit against the *lives* of another.

QUESTIONS

1. How does Jefferson's application of the principles of the Enlightenment to the question of slavery differ from and/or resemble that of Montesquieu?
2. Does it make good historical sense to blame the existence of slavery and the slave trade on George III?
3. What important factors does Jefferson omit?

Jefferson's own position on slavery was fraught with ambiguity. He owned many slaves on his plantation at Monticello. After the death of his wife he probably lived with a mulatto woman, one of his slaves, who bore him several children. He seems to have been tormented by his contradictory feelings that slavery was a moral wrong and would eventually be abolished, but that the time was not yet ripe for black Americans to be free. Recent biographies of Jefferson wrestle with this and other contradictions in this multifaceted man.

The Virginia Statute The second accomplishment on which Jefferson prided himself, the *Virginia Statute of Religious Liberty* (October 1785), is in the spirit of Voltaire's *Treatise on Toleration*. The statute was part of the constitution of the state of Virginia, which served as a model for other state constitutions.

THOMAS JEFFERSON

The Virginia Statute of Religious Liberty

AN ACT FOR ESTABLISHING RELIGIOUS
FREEDOM

I. Whereas Almighty God hath created the mind free; that all attempts to influence it by temporal punishments or burthens, or by civil incapacitations, tend only to beget habits of hypocrisy and meanness, and are a departure from the plan of the Holy author of our religion, who being Lord both of body and mind, yet chose not to propagate it by coercions on either, as was in his Almighty power to do; that the impious presumption of legislators and rulers, civil as well as ecclesiastical, who being themselves but fallible and uninspired men, have assumed dominion over the faith of others, setting up their own opinions and modes of thinking as the only true and infallible, and as such endeavouring to impose them on others, hath established and maintained false religions over the greatest part of the world, and through all time; that to compel a man to furnish contributions of money for the propagation of opinions which he disbelieves, is sinful and tyrannical; that even the forcing him to support this or that teacher of his own religious persuasion, is depriving him of the comfortable liberty of giving his contributions to the particular pastor whose morals he would make his pattern, and whose powers he feels most persuasive to righteousness, and is withdrawing from the ministry those temporary rewards, which proceeding from an approbation of their personal conduct, are an additional incitement to earnest and unremitting labours for the instruction of mankind; that our civil rights have no dependence on our religious opinions, any more than our opinions in physics or geometry; that therefore the proscribing any citizen as unworthy the public confidence by laying upon him an incapacity of being called to offices of trust and emolument, unless he profess or renounce this or that religious opinion, is depriving him injuriously of those privileges and advantages to which in common with his fellow-citizens he has a natural right; that it tends only to corrupt the principles of that religion it is meant to encourage, by bribing with a monopoly of worldly honours and emoluments, those who will externally profess and conform to it; that though indeed these are

criminal who do not withstand such temptation, yet neither are those innocent who lay the bait in their way; that to suffer the civil magistrate to intrude his powers into the field of opinion, and to restrain the profession or propagation of principles on supposition of their ill tendency, is a dangerous fallacy, which at once destroys all religious liberty, because he being of course judge of that tendency will make his opinions the rule of judgment, and approve or condemn the sentiments of others only as they shall square with or differ from his own; that it is time enough for the rightful purposes of civil government, for its officers to interfere when principles break out into overt acts against peace and good order; and finally, that truth is great and will prevail if left to herself, that she is the proper and sufficient antagonist to error, and has nothing to fear from the conflict, unless by human interposition disarmed of her natural weapons, free argument and debate, errors ceasing to be dangerous when it is permitted freely to contradict them.

II. Be it enacted by the General Assembly, that no man shall be compelled to frequent or support any religious worship, place or ministry whatsoever, nor shall be enforced, restrained, molested, or burthened in his body or goods, nor shall otherwise suffer on account of his religious opinions or belief; but that all men shall be free to profess, and by argument to maintain their opinion in matters of religion, and that the same shall in no wise diminish, enlarge or affect their civil capacities.

III. And though we well know that this Assembly, elected by the people for the ordinary purposes of legislation only, have no power to restrain the acts of succeeding Assemblies, constituted with powers equal to our own, and that therefore to declare this Act to be irrevocable would be of no effect in law; yet as we are free to declare, and do declare, that the rights hereby asserted are of the natural rights of mankind, and that if any Act shall hereafter be passed to repeal the present, or to narrow its operation, such Act will be an infringement of natural right.

QUESTIONS

1. On what basis does Jefferson seek to establish religious tolerance?

2. Is he critical of Christianity? How?
3. What does Jefferson mean by *truth*, and what are his criteria for determining what is true?
4. Does his optimistic belief that truth will inevitably triumph over error strike you as typical of the Enlightenment? As typically American?
5. What specific human rights does Jefferson consider "natural"?

Jefferson remained a nominal Anglican until the end of his life but continued to combat what he considered to be superstitions and unnecessary dogmas in Christianity. He respected Jesus as a great moral teacher but did not necessarily believe him to be divine. He did his own edition of the Bible, cutting out references to miracles. Unitarians today consider Jefferson one of their forefathers. In an "unenlightened" age a century or two earlier, he would have been arrested as a heretic.

The University of Virginia   In keeping with Jefferson's beliefs, his third monumental project, the University of Virginia, was the only early university not to be associated with a church. Jefferson viewed this "academical village" as an opportunity not only to create an ideal educational environment but also to improve the tastes of the Americans who would be educated there (Fig. 24-4).

Jefferson had always scorned the architecture of Williamsburg, where he was educated, and had tried to mold taste with his designs for the capitol of Virginia at Richmond (Fig. 24-5). He used no Renaissance models, for he now felt it appropriate to turn only to classical

24-4 Jefferson, University of Virginia. 1856 engraving by C. Bohn. (University of Virginia Library)

24–5   Jefferson, Capitol, Richmond. (Virginia State Library)

sources. Having seen engravings of the Maison Carrée in Nîmes, he adopted it for the new capitol.

That the pure temple form was not immediately adopted nationally can be seen by comparing it with the State House in Boston, designed by Charles Bulfinch in 1795 (Fig. 24-6). The sources of the State House are from the English Renaissance as well as from Rome. Both buildings, however, provided strong images of the state.

This belief, that art and architecture reinforce and perpetuate strong, appropriate images for ideals was much in Jefferson's mind when the university was laid out. The heart of the university is a rectangular quadrangle bounded on each of its long sides by a one-story covered colonnade broken at intervals by the two-story houses of the professors. Students lived in rooms off the colonnades; professors held classes downstairs in their living quarters (Fig. 24-7). The east end of the quad is closed by the domed, porticoed rotunda—the library (Fig. 24-8). Suggested by Benjamin Latrobe, another important architect, the rotunda acted as the focus and capstone, while the west end of the campus

24–6   Bulfinch, Boston State House. (Courtesy of the Boston Public Library, Print Department)

was open to the mountains. This very regular pattern for the central campus was relieved by the dining rooms, kitchens, and other service facilities located behind the two parallel rows of colonnades. There were found gardens (which students were expected to help work), pathways, and private walks for the students, who would participate in the educative life in the main quad but still have time for meditation, contemplation and studies, close to nature.

The rotunda and professors' houses were carefully detailed with what Jefferson considered the best forms of the classical *orders;* the Corinthian was reserved for the interior of the rotunda. All are used in correct proportion and with their correct *entablatures* and *moldings.* Jefferson drew on ancient and Renaissance treatises in his planning.

The architecture of the campus reflects the two areas in which students were supposed to grow to become successful men—the active and the contemplative lives. Conspicuously absent is a chapel or church—re-

24–7   Jefferson, University of Virginia, Pavilion and Colonnade. (University of Virginia Library)

24–8   Jefferson, University of Virginia, Rotunda. (University of Virginia Library)

ligion was to be a personal, private affair. Unlike Harvard, Yale, or Princeton, this early university of the new republic was a monument to free thought.

The ideal behind the University of Virginia was, in typical Enlightenment fashion, universal. "Enlighten the people generally," Jefferson wrote, "and oppressions of body and mind will vanish like evil spirits at the dawn of day." Practically, however, because of the nature of the education planned, it could accommodate only an elite few. Women of all races, blacks, and white males from poor familes were excluded. Jefferson, though he educated his daughters, held in fact very conventional ideas regarding women: they should not mix in politics or public meetings or be outspoken in any way; their proper place was in the domestic sphere. The educated elite, who alone were fit to rule the American nation in Jefferson's view, would have been limited to white men of some means if his plan had remained the pattern. Fortunately, as is the case with most important thinkers, Jefferson's ideas outgrew his era's limitations and eventually served the causes of the struggles in which we are still involved.

The University of Virginia is one of the latest manifestations of the style and ideals of the Enlightenment. The product of Jefferson's old age and retirement years, it opened its doors in 1824 when he was eighty-one. It was perhaps natural that the revolutionary, politician, and diplomat should retire into creating an ideal world on a reduced scale. Like many of his time, Jefferson saw in the excesses of the French revolution at the end of the eighteenth century a lesson in debasement through politics. Earlier he had been not only an ardent francophile (he spent several years as a diplomat in France) but also an enthusiastic supporter of the early stages of the French revolution, which he saw as a triumph of the Enlightenment and in some ways an extension of the American revolution that he had helped to prepare. In this enthusiasm he differed profoundly from John Adams and other more conservative American leaders. On the bloody storming of the Bastille he wrote: "the tree of liberty must be refreshed from time to time with the blood of patriots and tyrants." Many intellectuals as well as common people on both sides of the Atlantic shared his fervent hope that "so beautiful a revolution" should "spread throughout the whole world," and, like him, many were disillusioned when the revolution seemed to be devouring its own children. One of the most momentous political events in modern Western history, the French revolution is also of great significance to the humanities as a catalyst in transforming the culture of the Enlightenment into that of romanticism.

25
REVOLUTION AND ROMANTICISM

The American experiment demonstrated to Europeans that Enlightenment ideas could be realized in practice. The Declaration of Independence and the Virginia Statute of Religious Liberty were not abstract treatises but statements by a government of its official beliefs and policies. Heretofore, the principles of limited government and a system of checks endorsed by the American Constitution had been considered by most Europeans to be connected with feudal privilege and aristocratic domination. This is why many of the philosophes had espoused absolute monarchy. America seemed to prove that this kind of constitutional structure could in fact foster the freedom and equality sought by Enlightenment thinkers.

The French Revolution

Causes of the Revolution   The American example was particularly important for France. The most populous country in Europe and among the most prosperous, France in the last half of the eighteenth century was a troubled society. All phases of French life were dominated by an outmoded social structure that endured primarily because it was legally defined and protected. All Frenchmen except the royal family were divided into three classes: the clergy, the nobility, and the third estate, by far the largest of the three, comprising the peasants, the artisans of the towns, and the middle class or *bourgeois*. Of France's 24,000,000 people, only about 2 percent belonged to the clergy and nobility. Yet in a society where land remained the greatest form of wealth, the other 98 percent owned only 60 percent of the landed property. This was the social group from which the revolution came.

But there was a greater source of discontent among the third estate. The clergy and nobility paid almost no taxes. Moreover, while giving little or nothing to support it, the nobility enjoyed all the highest offices in the government; they also constituted the officer corps of the army. As for the clergy, this class had the right to levy a tax, for its maintenance, on all agricultural goods produced by the third estate.

What made the situation volatile was that for most of the eighteenth century the economy was expanding. Bankers, merchants, and other members of the middle class had accumulated great wealth, and many of the peasants were prosperous. Traditionally there had been various avenues by which successful members of the third estate could work their way into the nobility, but in the course of the eighteenth century these avenues had gradually been shut off by an aristocracy resolved not to dilute its membership further. The upper bourgeois, therefore, felt cheated of the social and financial privileges to which their success entitled them.

Economic prosperity also entailed rising prices and higher living costs. The nobility and clergy, barred by law from entering commerce or industry to reap the profits of the boom, increasingly came to insist on their economic rights over the third estate. Indeed, this was the heyday of lawyers employed by the upper classes to dredge up old, long-neglected rights over the peasantry.

Moreover, while the bourgeois and the upper peasantry were profiting in these decades, the lower classes saw their wages rise more slowly than prices and their standard of living fall.

The most immediate cause of the revolution, which began in the summer of 1789, was the government's financial crisis. Because some of the wealthiest elements in the country were exempt from taxation, the state could not balance its budget. An important element in the French public debt was the expense incurred by helping the Americans in their revolt against England. For years the enlightened advisers of the French king had endeavored to abolish the tax privileges of the clergy and the nobility, but these two orders had solidly resisted the effort. The king could proclaim the necessary laws, but the courts, completely controlled by the nobility, would never enforce them. Finally, in 1788, the royal government simply abolished the old court system and created a new one.

The result was an aristocratic revolt: the army officers and the king's officials at Paris and in the provinces refused to serve, and the whole state was brought to a halt. Unable to persevere in the attempt at reform, the king (Louis XVI) acceded to noble demands that, for the first time since 1614, a National Assembly be called to settle the nation's problems. The nobility clearly intended to gain a larger control over the king's government through an assembly that, by tradition, gave them and the clergy (dominated by the aristocracy) two votes against one for the third estate.

Beginning of the Revolution   The Assembly met in May 1789 at Versailles, but in the months preceding the meeting, the third estate, growing conscious of its massive power, resolved to use the Assembly as a means of abolishing legal classes. Refusing their places in the Royal Assembly, where they were given one of the three votes, the delegates of the third estate declared themselves to be the Assembly of the Nation and defied the monarchy. Though Louis XVI called troops to Versailles at the end of June, he hesitated to arrest the disobedient delegates. In the atmosphere of tension prevailing over the next weeks, the common people of Paris rose on July 14, 1789, stormed and captured the Bastille (the king's prison in the city), and the revolution was on. The terrified king ordered the nobility and clergy to join with the third estate; those who had not already joined out of sympathy or gone home did so.

One of the first steps of the new one-house National Assembly was the publication of a Declaration of the Rights of Man and the Citizen on August 26, 1789. Like the American Bill of Rights, its provisions emphasized the freedom and equality of every man. Subsequently, all privilege was abolished and the church's property confiscated; henceforth, the clergy was to receive salaries from the state. The leaders of the Assembly at this stage were determined to make France a constitutional monarchy like that of England. Before the new constitution could be approved, however, the would-be constitutional monarch, Louis XVI, fled in July 1791. Despite his capture, the position of the leadership was undercut, and the Jacobins or republicans seized power in the National Assembly in September 1791.

The Jacobins The Jacobins were interested in more than establishing liberty and equality in France; they were also the party of international revolution. Their control naturally brought on conflict with the rest of Europe, and from the spring of 1792 France was at war. When the war began badly and the politicians blamed the defeat of the army on treachery behind the lines, the pursuit of traitors was underway. Starting in May 1793, when the radical Jacobins displaced the more moderate leadership, a reign of terror lasting over a year ensued. A new device, the guillotine, was introduced to expedite the execution of traitors to the revolution.

Robespierre Whereas the moderate Jacobins had aimed at establishing a republic governed by an electorate with modest property qualifications, the radical Jacobins wanted an eventual democratic republic. Their leader Robespierre believed that, before this could be brought about, a dictatorship representing Rousseau's general will must destroy all the reactionaries. His dictatorship took the form of an executive committee of twelve men called the Committee of Public Safety. Nevertheless, by July 1794, France was tired of blood, and the assembly, now called the National Convention, had Robespierre arrested and guillotined.

The government emerging from the reaction was dominated by large property owners. The fragility of its control, with radicals to the left and royalists on the right, was to an extent balanced by the success that French armies were having on the battlefield. Actually, after a bad start, the French by the fall of 1792 were having one success after another. By mid-1794 they had occupied what is now Belgium, the Netherlands, and Germany up to the Rhine as well as parts of northern Italy. In large part their success derived from the fact that the volunteer armies were enormous as opposed to the small professional armies of their opponents. Under the command of officers who held their commissions because of merit rather than family position, highly motivated by intense patriotic zeal, the French soldiers were irresistible. Everywhere they went they were welcomed by revolutionaries opposed to the local regime of despotism and privilege. French conquest meant the abolition of a legal class system and the establishment of a more equitable law code and social system.

Napoleon Bonaparte By 1796 one of the revolutionary generals, Napoleon Bonaparte, had distinguished himself above the others by a brilliant invasion of Italy and a swift capture of most of the northern part of the peninsula. Born in 1769 of minor Corsican nobility, Napoleon would probably never have risen above the rank of captain in the old aristocratic French army. But, as it was in the new army, he was a general by the age of twenty-five. Not only a military genius but a brilliant statesman as well, Napoleon in 1797 purged the leadership of the conservative government that had come in after the Reign of Terror. In 1799, after an invasion of Egypt that stirred the imagination of all Europe, Napoleon abolished the whole government and declared himself the First Consul of France.

Napoleon had been deeply influenced by the Enlightenment. He has been referred to as "the last of the Enlightened despots," and he once said of himself: "I am the revolution." Napoleon believed that the real concern of the French was not so much political liberty as social equality. Political participation was for them secondary to their desire for a society where all men were equal before the law and where advancement derived from merit. While Napoleon's constitution provided for a parliamentary government with universal male suffrage, there could be no question that Napoleon governed France.

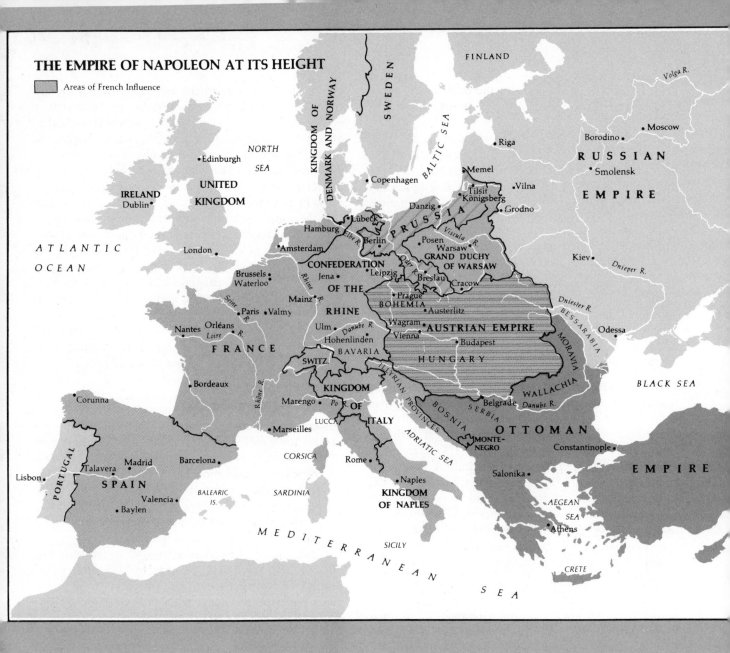

THE EMPIRE OF NAPOLEON AT ITS HEIGHT

Areas of French Influence

Napoleon established a meritocracy in the bureaucracy and army, and he reformed laws to enable more equality. His fiscal system was run by professionals, and there were no tax exemptions. On the whole, it is fair to say that Napoleon realized in his government most of the goals of the Enlightenment: those dealing with political freedom had always been secondary in any case.

Between 1799 and 1814 Napoleon, who took the title of emperor of the French in 1802, almost succeeded in conquering all of continental Europe. But when he penetrated Russia as far as Moscow in 1812, this invasion cost him dearly; 500,000 men never returned, and from this point on, his fortune waned.

With the heavy loss in troops and resistance growing among subject peoples to French war taxation, Napoleon decided to surrender to an allied coalition of England, Austria, Russia, and Prussia. He abdicated and was sent in exile to Elba off the Italian coast in 1814. With hopes of turning the tables, he appeared again in France early in 1815. The French rallied, his old soldiers gathered again, and in the spring of 1815 he fought and lost the great battle of Waterloo. Defeated, he was exiled this time to Saint Helena in the Atlantic Ocean, and a brother of Louis XVI was made king of France by the allies.

Effects of the Revolution The French revolution and its aftermath, however, left a lasting mark on Western Europe. No longer could rulers fight with the small professional armies of the past: the levy *en masse* was an absolute necessity in a new age of war. Rulers had to put arms in the hands of their subjects. Despite their conservative temper and fear of reform, kings, including the new French monarch, could not reimpose the old legal class structure where it had been abolished. The law codes destroying legal privilege in these areas were permanent. Moreover, French nationalism had proven infectious. At first welcomed as liberators by many in the conquered countries, the French ended by creating a national feeling directed against them in Germany, Italy, Spain, and elsewhere. Until later in the nineteenth century, however, nationalism would be considered the property of liberals wishing to imitate the French. After that time monarchs would learn how to use it for their own purposes. Although the allies reduced France to her boundaries before 1789, the French were considered as the most dangerous people of Europe until 1870. The figure of Napoleon, the keen rationalist, became a symbol of the creative, mysterious, and at times demonic personality that fascinated the first generation of the nineteenth century.

The Art of the French Revolution

Just as the leaders of the American revolution instigated the search for a new visual and architectural language for the new republic, so the French revolution and its aftermath profoundly affected art in France and England. The citizens of France, like those of the United States, first adopted the severe classical style of republican Rome; Napoleon, however, preferred to imitate the empire. The foremost painter of the revolutionary and Napoleonic eras was Jacques Louis David.

David David revolted against the sensual elegance of the court style as exemplified by the paintings of Boucher (Fig. 23-5) and Fragonard. He sought to renew art by contact with the art of Rome and the Italian High Renaissance. While in Italy he painted his first important picture in this fresh style. Displayed in his Roman studio, *The Oath of the Horatii* (1784–85) combined qualities from the 16th and 17th centuries to convey what some saw as revolutionary sentiments. Based on a story from Livy, *The Oath* places loyalty to the state above all other concerns, even those of family. The painting shows heroic male figures in a stark architectural setting. Like the *Marat* (below) the figures are somewhat idealized but retain a degree of intense realism through an almost photographic rendering of flesh and muscle. Such detail makes them highly convincing. Colors are cool; the harsh light isolates form and gesture. Crisp and clear, the figures seem like a sculpted bas relief.

Returning to Paris where his style was immediately recognized as revolutionary, though not necessarily politically so, David nevertheless moved away from the sentiments of the Royal Academy that had sent him to Rome. In *The Death of Socrates* (1787) he explored the theme of injustice by a government fearing the truth. This picture and others like it were celebrated as manifestos of those virtues most lacking in monarchial France and their artist became a leading revolutionary painter.

David was commissioned by the Committee of Public Safety to make three paintings of revolutionary heroes; only one of them was finished, *The Death of Marat* (Fig. 25-1). It portrays the murder of the Jacobin Marat by Charlotte Corday, from a rival revolutionary group. Sending a note to Marat, she gained access to him while, seated in a medicinal bath, he received petitioners. She stabbed him when he could offer no resistance. An almost ludicrous scene is transformed by David into the final act of a great tragedy. The dead revolutionary still lies in his draped tub, the focus of a cold, dramatic light. His wound gapes, blood stains his drapery and the water, and his limp arm and hand fall to the floor, his pen permanently stilled. The figure is

25–1　David, "The Death of Marat." (Musées Royaux des Beaux-Arts © A.C.L. Bruxelles)

The revolution in style begun by David would take on new forms with the birth of the sensibility called *romantic*.

Romanticism: A Revolutionary Movement

The two great revolutions of the eighteenth century, the American and the French, were followed not only by upheavals altering the course of European politics but also by rapid changes in other spheres of life: taste, feeling, thought, behavior, social and domestic relations. The varied, often contradictory cultural movement that swept over Europe and America and became known as romanticism had profound effects on the humanities—effects still very much felt in the contemporary world. The individualism, sense of isolation, and alienation of which we are now so aware have their roots in the Renaissance and Reformation period, but they were cultivated and brought to flower by the romantics.

rendered with sculptural intensity. Though there is a pervasive sense of reality, the body bears no marks of the skin disease that forced him to sit in the tub. His face shows little age, no anguish. In the contrast between reality and abstraction, David creates a magnificent tension—a tension like that between reason and intuition, calculation and passion.

Recognizing this formidable talent, Napoleon made David the pageant master of the consular government and then of the empire. In his *Napoleon Crossing the Alps* (Fig. 25-2) David's abstract clarity has given way to an ideal image. The youthful general, astride a rearing horse, his cloak blowing in the wind as he gestures forward, has become a romantic hero comparable to Hannibal and Charlemagne, whose names are carved in the rocks. This is not a real general; it is how all generals might see themselves—indeed how men might envision a hero—commanding, youthful, virile, clean, shiny, and dry, in spite of cold, snow, and the hell of war.

25–2　David, "Napoleon Crossing the Alps," Versailles Museum. (Cliché des Musées Nationaux France © S.P.A.D.E.M., 1980)

Plate I Caravaggio, "The Calling of Saint Matthew." (S. Luigi dei Francesi, Rome—Scala/Editorial Photocolor Archives)

Plate II Rubens, "The Garden of Love." (Copyright © Museo del Prado, Madrid. All rights reserved)

Plate V Watteau, "Pilgrimage to Cythera." (Clichés Musées Nationaux, Paris)

Plate III Rembrandt, "The Return of the Prodigal Son." (The Hermitage Museum, Leningrad)

Plate VI Jean-Baptiste-Siméon Chardin, "The Morning Toilet." (The National Museum, Stockholm, Sweden)

Plate IV Vermeer, "The Kitchen-Maid." (Rijksmuseum, Amsterdam)

Plate VII Constable, "Dedham Vale with the house called 'Dedham Valley'." (The Tate Gallery, London)

Plate VIII Turner, "Rain, Steam and Speed, The Great Western Railway." (Reproduced by courtesy of the Trustees, The National Gallery, London)

Romanticism as a movement may be said to have originated in Germany, but the word *romantic* first appeared in England in the mid-eighteenth century. It originated from an association with medieval "romances," the (predominately French) stories of knights and ladies. As the word became coined in all European languages, it took on connotations of fanciful, picturesque, rugged, spontaneous, natural, and sentimental. During the early nineteenth century it was applied to groups of rebellious young artists promoting creativity, individualism, and free expression of emotion in opposition to classical canons and the regulations and standards based on "enlightened" reason that their parents' generation had espoused. For the romantics, life and art were one: as they threw out the old standards for art, so they lived their lives with bohemian freedom, following their passions or imagination rather than their reason or the "artificial" rules of society. Artistic and political ideals also intertwined: the French writer Victor Hugo called romanticism "liberalism in literature" and proclaimed that words, like postrevolutionary human beings, were now free from tyranny. By the middle of the century, however, many romantics had grown conservative, Catholic, or nationalistic, or they had retreated into an asocial dream world. This was partly because of the political scene in Europe: many who had first adored Napoleon as the bearer of the revolution became disillusioned with Napoleon the emperor. Yet some romantics were intensely conservative from the beginning, looking back toward the Middle Ages as an ideal period of order and spirituality. (The liberals, too, liked medieval themes but for other reasons.) It is impossible to attribute an exact beginning and end to this complex, varied, pan-European and American movement; but the French revolution gave impetus to its latent beginnings, and it died out in most places before 1850. In Slavic countries, however, the romantic movement in literature (and in nationalistic politics) continued longer, and romantic music flourished in Germany, France, and Italy throughout the nineteenth century. It is hardly possible to attempt a global history or definition of romanticism here. We will instead isolate some of the major themes with which the movement was concerned and observe their expression in the arts, bearing in mind their profound impact on modern culture.

Enlightened Ideas, Romantic Style

The American and French revolutions, in many ways the political culminations of the ideals of the Enlightenment, fired the imaginations of the romantics as they had seemed to confirm the reasonableness of the philosophes. Jean-Jacques Rousseau is the single most important figure for understanding the transition between the Enlightenment and romanticism. Revered as a forefather of the revolution because of his analyses of social injustice and his "enlightened" beliefs in the dignity and freedom of man, Rousseau was the first in French letters to promote feeling above reason and nature above institutions. Above all, he raised the unique, individual self to a position of prime importance. The individualism propounded by Rousseau seemed to be the philosophical foundation of the new American republic, the largest territory ever ruled by a government proclaiming men to be free and equal.

Unspoiled Nature and Natural Man   Also dear to the hearts of the romantics was the fact that America was a land still unspoiled by too much civilization or urbanity. In its wildernesses the rugged individual could commune with nature. Romantics eulogized the American Indian as a "noble savage" with a free spirit superior to that of civilized man, though few seemed to understand the social and economic threat that the new republic posed to him. The social ideals promoted by the revolutions *were* used by romantics, first British and later American, in the service of the antislavery cause that culminated in the abolitionist movement. In the romantic view the black African was a proud, noble individual who had suffered the oppression and tyranny of the old order of Europe, an order that was now to be overthrown on all levels. The romantic liberals championed the cause of the peasant, the worker, the poor, and the oppressed; they looked with contempt on the rich bourgeois, smug and materialistic. Naturally the champions of the oppressed tended to, as we would say, "romanticize" those that they perceived as victims, sometimes endowing them with sublime, superhuman characters. They were, in fact, more interested in lofty ideals than in everyday reality. Out of the revolution, they believed, a new order would be born that would bring with it the creative freedom of the individual and the brotherhood of all mankind.

Liberty, Equality, Fraternity   Liberty, equality, and fraternity, the catchwords of the French revolution, were taken by the romantics to apply to all aspects of life. Ironically, it was outside of France that these ideals first took hold as a cultural force. It is in Germany and in England that we first see poets celebrating the ideals of the revolution, and it is there, too, that other signs of budding romanticism first show themselves. Germany's two greatest writers, Johann Wolfgang von Goethe (1749–1832) and Friedrich Schiller (1759–1805), spanned Neoclassicism and romanticism in their careers. Schiller's fervent belief in man's rights to dignity and freedom and his lofty hopes for universal brotherhood place him in the transition between the Enlightenment and romanticism. His poem "Ode to Joy," written on the eve of the French revolution, is a passionate statement of those beliefs and hopes that were stirring at the time. Immortalized by Beethoven in his Ninth Symphony some thirty years later, it has become one of the great statements of romanticism. The late eighteenth and early nineteenth centuries saw the flowering of German music as well as of German literature. Ludwig von Beethoven (1770–1827), like Goethe and Schiller, is a gigantic figure whose works rise above categories like classical or romantic but include elements of both. Like many of his generation, he was at first stirred by the ideals of the French revolution and by their embodiment in Napoleon, and later disillusioned. The English romantic poet William Wordsworth expressed his initial feelings about the revolution in the often quoted lines: "Bliss was it in that dawn to be alive,/But to be young was very heaven!" He, too, experienced a later disillusionment.

Individualism and the Romantic Hero   From the romantic version of revolutionary ideals—as from the writings of the transitional Rousseau—there developed a new sense of the value of the unique individual. Rousseau's confession, "If I am not better than other men, *at least* I am different!" would be unthinkable to a classicist. Schiller, who could write a hymn to the brotherhood of man, could also write a play *The Robbers* with an individualistic outlaw as hero. Men like Beethoven, and for that matter Napoleon, embodied the romantic doctrine of individual, unique, "titanic" genius. Howard Mumford Jones, in his *Revolution and Romanticism*, believes the types of romantic individ-

uals to be three: the sufferer, the rebel, and the liberated woman. Here we will look at the heroic rebel; we will see the other two in the next chapter.

The romantic rebel, feeling himself to be unique, alone, and misunderstood, attempts to take destiny into his own hands. Prometheus, the deity from Greek mythology who stole the secret of fire from the gods to bring it to man and who defied Zeus himself, was a favorite subject of romantic verse and drama. The romantics' Prometheus goes beyond their model, the Prometheus of the Greek tragedian Aeschylus. Prometheus combines two aspects of the romantic hero that may be separate and contradictory elsewhere: he is both a self-willed individual and a benefactor of mankind. Shelley's verse drama *Prometheus Unbound* is the most extended treatment of this theme; Byron's short lyric, "Prometheus," printed below, is an early model for what came to be known as the Byronic hero.

The poet George Gordon, Lord Byron, is a good example of a romantic who lived as well as wrote his romanticism. Spectacularly handsome, he was involved in many unhappy love affairs. He wandered restlessly over Europe and finally died while fighting for a liberal cause, the war of the Greeks against their oppressors, the Turks. Byron's literary heroes, particularly his Childe Harold, Manfred, and Cain, are rebellious individuals with a passionate belief in individual freedom. They are men of powerful emotions and a genius that may at times appear satanic. There is a "dark" side to the Byronic hero that we may see in some of the characters created in his wake, such as Melville's Captain Ahab. The "gothic" hero and the mad scientist, two other romantic types, may be seen as offshoots of the Byronic hero. The most famous of the latter, Victor Frankenstein, was created by Mary Godwin Shelley, a close friend of Byron and eventually Shelley's wife. She called her novel *Frankenstein, or the Modern Prometheus.*

Perhaps the most enduring romantic hero-rebel, one who goes beyond romanticism, is Goethe's Faust, in the long dramatic poem of that title. Faust's rebellion is really against human limits, or finitude. He embarks on a quest after the absolute: absolute knowledge, power, and love, and in the process puts his soul in the hands of the devil. He refuses to accept any limits on his individuality until the end of the poem, when he also becomes a benefactor of mankind.

The heroic individual took hold of the imaginations of Americans as well as Europeans. Some see the romantic hero as a kind of literary prototype for the "robber barons" of the later nineteenth century. In literature, Emerson celebrated the heroic individual; Melville and Poe stressed his darker side. The early nineteenth century was, of course, the time when American literature came into its own. A different, and perhaps more typically American romantic individualism emerged in the poetry of Walt Whitman, who celebrated his unique self in order to break down the artificial barriers that society creates between human beings. We will read two parts of his very long (fifty-two parts) *Song of Myself.*

Romantic Lyric Poetry and Revolutionary Ideals

The romantics were prolific writers in all *genres*—fiction, drama, and verse—but the movement is perhaps best remembered for its achievements in poetry. The individualistic, subjective, and emotional bent of romantic writers made the *lyric* a congenial form for them. In contrast to the Enlightenment and Neoclassical periods, the romantic was one of the great ages of lyricism. Accordingly, we have chosen most of the literary examples of our romantic themes from poetry.

WILLIAM WORDSWORTH

from *The Prelude*

RESIDENCE IN FRANCE

Oh! pleasant exercise of hope and joy!
For mighty were the auxiliars which then stood
Upon our side, we who were strong in love!
Bliss was it in that dawn to be alive,
But to be young was very heaven!—Oh! times,
In which the meagre, stale, forbidding ways
Of custom, law, and statute, took at once
The attraction of a country in romance!
When Reason seemed the most to assert her rights,
When most intent on making of herself
A prime Enchantress—to assist the work
Which then was going forward in her name!
Not favoured spots alone, but the whole earth,
The beauty wore of promise, that which sets

(As at some moment might not be unfelt
Among the bowers of paradise itself)
The budding rose above the rose full blown.
What temper at the prospect did not wake
To happiness unthought of? The inert
Were roused, and lively natures rapt away!
They who had fed their childhood upon dreams,
The playfellows of fancy, who had made
All powers of swiftness, subtilty, and strength
Their ministers,—who in lordly wise had stirred
Among the grandest objects of the sense,
And dealt with whatsoever they found there
As if they had within some lurking right
To wield it;—they, too, who, of gentle mood,
Had watched all gentle motions, and to these
Had fitted their own thoughts, schemers more mild,
And in the region of their peaceful selves;—
Now was it that both found, the meek and lofty
Did both find, helpers to their heart's desire,
And stuff at hand, plastic as they could wish;
Were called upon to exercise their skill,
Not in Utopia, subterranean fields,
Or some secreted island, Heaven knows where!
But in the very world, which is the world
Of all of us,—the place where in the end
We find our happiness, or not at all!

QUESTIONS

1. Whose viewpoint of the French revolution does Wordsworth give here?
2. What is romantic in his interpretation of the revolution?

WILLIAM BLAKE

The Little Black Boy

My mother bore me in the southern wild,
And I am black, but O! my soul is white;
White as an angel is the English child:
But I am black as if bereav'd of light.

My mother taught me underneath a tree,
And sitting down before the heat of day,
She took me on her lap and kisséd me,
And pointing to the east, began to say:

"Look on the rising sun: there God does live,
And gives his light, and gives his heat away;
And flowers and trees and beasts and men receive
Comfort in morning, joy in the noon day.

"And we are put on earth a little space,
That we may learn to bear the beams of love,
And these black bodies and this sun-burnt face
Is but a cloud, and like a shady grove.

"For when our souls have learn'd the heat to bear,
The cloud will vanish; we shall hear his voice,
Saying: 'Come out from the grove, my love & care,
And round my golden tent like lambs rejoice.' "

Thus did my mother say, and kisséd me;
And thus I say to little English boy:
When I from black and he from white cloud free,
And round the tent of God like lambs we joy,

I'll shade him from the heat till he can bear
To lean in joy upon our father's knee;
And then I'll stand and stroke his silver hair,
And be like him, and he will then love me.

COMMENTS AND QUESTIONS

1. William Blake was another English poet who was an enthusiast for the French revolution and for liberal causes. What particular social evil is he indirectly attacking here?
2. What do you think Blake meant by the line, "O! my soul is white." How do you as a (black or white) modern reader react to it?
3. How does this poem go beyond the social issue that it treats? What philosophical ideas are contained in it?

GEORGE GORDON, LORD BYRON

Prometheus

I

Titan! to whose immortal eyes
    The sufferings of mortality,
    Seen in their sad reality,
Were not as things that gods despise;
What was thy pity's recompense?
A silent suffering, and intense;
The rock, the vulture, and the chain,
All that the proud can feel of pain,
The agony they do not show,
The suffocating sense of woe,
    Which speaks but in its loneliness,
And then is jealous lest the sky
Should have a listener, nor will sigh
    Until its voice is echoless.

II

Titan! to thee the strife was given
    Between the suffering and the will,
    Which torture where they cannot kill;
And the inexorable Heaven,
And the deaf tyranny of Fate,
The ruling principle of Hate,
Which for its pleasure doth create
The things it may annihilate,
Refused thee even the boon to die:
The wretched gift eternity
Was thine—and thou hast borne it well.
All that the Thunderer wrung from thee
Was but the menace which flung back
On him the torments of thy rack;
The fate thou didst so well foresee,
But would not to appease him tell;
And in thy Silence was his Sentence,
And in his Soul a vain repentance,
And evil dread so ill dissembled,
That in his hand the lightnings trembled.

III

Thy Godlike crime was to be kind,
    To render with thy precepts less
    The sum of human wretchedness,
And strengthen Man with his own mind;
But baffled as thou wert from high,
Still in thy patient energy,
In the endurance, and repulse
    Of thine impenetrable Spirit,
Which Earth and Heaven could not convulse,
    A mighty lesson we inherit:
Thou art a symbol and a sign

To Mortals of their fate and force;
Like thee, Man is in part divine,
    A troubled stream from a pure source;
And Man in portions can foresee
His own funereal destiny;
His wretchedness, and his resistance,
And his sad unallied existence:
To which his Spirit may oppose
Itself—and equal to all woes,
    And a firm will, and a deep sense,
Which even in torture can descry
    Its own concenter'd recompense,
Triumphant where it dares defy,
And making Death a Victory.

QUESTIONS

1. Look up the myth of Prometheus if you are not familiar with it. How has Byron reinterpreted it?
2. What is the *meter* of the verse used here? How would you describe the language of the poem? How are both appropriate to the subject matter?
3. Of what is Prometheus a "symbol and a sign"? What makes him a hero? Would he be a fitting heroic symbol for our times?

GEORGE GORDON, LORD BYRON

On This Day I Complete My Thirty-Sixth Year

MISSOLONGHI,[1] JANUARY 22, 1824

'Tis time this heart should be unmoved,
    Since others it hath ceased to move:
Yet, though I cannot be beloved,
        Still let me love!

My days are in the yellow leaf;
    The flowers and fruits of love are gone;
The worm, the canker, and the grief
        Are mine alone!

The fire that on my bosom preys
    Is lone as some volcanic isle;
No torch is kindled at its blaze—
        A funeral pile.

The hope, the fear, the jealous care,
    The exalted portion of the pain
And power of love, I cannot share,
        But wear the chain.

But 'tis not *thus*—and 'tis not *here*—
    Such thoughts should shake my soul, nor *now*,
Where glory decks the hero's bier,
        Or binds his brow.

The sword, the banner, and the field,
    Glory and Greece, around me see!
The Spartan, born upon his shield,
        Was not more free.

Awake! (not Greece—she *is* awake!)
    Awake, my spirit! Think through *whom*
Thy life-blood tracks its parent lake,
        And then strike home!

Tread those reviving passions down,
    Unworthy manhood!—unto thee
Indifferent should the smile or frown
        Of beauty be.

If thou regrett'st thy youth, *why live?*
    The land of honorable death
Is here:—up to the field, and give
        Away thy breath!

Seek out—less often sought than found—
    A soldier's grave, for thee the best;
Then look around, and choose thy ground,
        And take thy rest.

QUESTIONS

1. What two typically romantic states of mind does Byron contrast in this poem?
2. How is political commitment understood as individual salvation?

---

[1] Town in Greece where Byron had gone to help the Greeks in their war for independence from Turkey. Less than three months later he died there.

WALT WHITMAN

from *Song of Myself*

1

I celebrate myself, and sing myself,
And what I assume you shall assume,
For every atom belonging to me as good belongs to you.

I loafe and invite my soul,
I lean and loafe at my ease observing a spear of summer
    grass.

My tongue, every atom of my blood, form'd from this
    soil, this air,
Born here of parents born here from parents the same,
    and their parents the same,
I, now thirty-seven years old in perfect health begin,
Hoping to cease not till death.

Creeds and schools in abeyance,
Retiring back a while sufficed at what they are, but
    never forgotten,
I harbor for good or bad, I permit to speak at every
    hazard,
Nature without check with original energy.

        .   .   .

24

Walt Whitman, a kosmos, of Manhattan the son,
Turbulent, fleshy, sensual, eating, drinking and
    breeding,
No sentimentalist, no stander above men and women
    or apart from them,
No more modest than immodest.

Unscrew the locks from the doors!
Unscrew the doors themselves from their jambs!

Whoever degrades another degrades me,
And whatever is done or said returns at last to me.

Through me the afflatus surging and surging, through
    me the current and index.

I speak the pass-word primeval, I give the sign of
    democracy,

By God! I will accept nothing which all cannot have
    their counterpart of on the same terms.

Through me many long dumb voices,
Voices of the interminable generation of prisoners and
    slaves,
Voices of the diseas'd and despairing and of thieves
    and dwarfs,
Voices of cycles of preparation and accretion,
And of the threads that connect the stars, and of
    wombs and of the father-stuff,
And of the rights of them the others are down upon,
Of the deform'd, trivial, flat, foolish, despised,
Fog in the air, beetles rolling balls of dung.

Through me forbidden voices,
Voices of sexes and lusts, voices veil'd and I remove the
    veil,
Voices indecent by me clarified and transfigur'd.

I do not press my fingers across my mouth,
I keep as delicate around the bowels as around the head
    and heart,
Copulation is no more rank to me than death is.

I believe in the flesh and the appetites,
Seeing, hearing, feeling, are miracles, and each part and
    tag of me is a miracle.

Divine am I inside and out, and I make holy whatever I
    touch or am touch'd from,
The scent of these arm-pits aroma finer than prayer,
This head more than churches, bibles, and all the
    creeds.

If I worship one thing more than another it shall be the
    spread of my own body, or any part of it,
Translucent mould of me it shall be you!
Shaded ledges and rests it shall be you!
Firm masculine colter it shall be you!
Whatever goes to the tilth of me it shall be you!
You my rich blood! your milky stream pale strippings
    of my life!
Breast that presses against other breasts it shall be you!
My brain it shall be your occult convolutions!
Root of wash'd sweet-flag! timorous pond-snipe! nest of

guarded duplicate eggs! it shall be you!
Mix'd tussled hay of head, beard, brawn, it shall be
    you!
Trickling sap of maple, fibre of manly wheat, it shall be
    you!
Sun so generous it shall be you!
Vapors lighting and shading my face it shall be you!
You sweaty brooks and dews it shall be you!
Winds whose soft-tickling genitals rub against me it
    shall be you!
Broad muscular fields, branches of live oak, loving
    lounger in my winding paths, it shall be you!
Hands I have taken, face I have kiss'd, mortal I have
    ever touch'd, it shall be you.

I dote on myself, there is that lot of me and all so
    luscious,
Each moment and whatever happens thrills me with
    joy,
I cannot tell how my ankles bend, nor whence the
    cause of my faintest wish,
Nor the cause of the friendship I emit, nor the cause of
    the friendship I take again.

That I walk up my stoop, I pause to consider if it really
    be,
A morning-glory at my window satisfies me more than
    the metaphysics of books.
To behold the day-break!
The little light fades the immense and diaphanous
    shadows,
The air tastes good to my palate.

Hefts of the moving world at innocent gambols silently
    rising, freshly exuding,
Scooting obliquely high and low.

Something I cannot see puts upward libidinous prongs,
Seas of bright juice suffuse heaven.

The earth by the sky staid with, the daily close of their
    junction,
The heav'd challenge from the east that moment over
    my head,
The mocking taunt, See then whether you shall be
    master!

COMMENTS AND QUESTIONS

1. Why and how does Whitman "celebrate" and "sing" himself? In what different connections does he view the self?
2. In what sense is this a democratic poem?
3. What "unpoetic" subject matters does Whitman treat? How might he have shocked his readers?
4. Whitman was the first American poet to make extensive use of *free verse*, that is, lines that are not predetermined by any metrical scheme. Why is free verse appropriate to this poem?
5. Can you find patterns of sound and rhythms in this verse? What is their effect?
6. What seems to be Whitman's idea of his role as a poet?

Romantic Visual Art and Revolution

We have seen how the painter David turned from Neoclassicism to portray Napoleon as a romantic hero. The revolutionary ideals of liberty, equality, and fraternity had a profound influence on developing romanticism in the visual arts as in literature. There were also inventions and advances that affected art internally. The development of photography; the scientific study of light, color, and perception; and the opening of Japan and China to the Western world all had immediate repercussions in painting, sculpture, and the graphic arts.

Architecture was challenged by the growing diversification of life and human needs. Commissions for palaces and churches were replaced by industrial, commercial, and transportation needs. Hospitals, housing, and prisons were demanded as never before. The manufacture of iron, then steel, glass, and finally concrete provided new building possibilities and problems without precedent. Both the private individual and governments experienced the stress of a burgeoning economy and rapidly increasing population. Systems of transportation, water, waste disposal, marketing, and housing taxed cities beyond their limits, and the vast slum became a familiar reality.

Not only were the artist and architect challenged by these things but also the systems of education and patronage experienced pressures that were either ab-

sorbed or ignored. In France the academy that had produced David and his pupils also produced a number of
artists who revolted against the doctrines of Davidian
classicism; they began searching for a form and content
expressive of revolutionary and romantic ideals. But it
is to Spain that we must first turn—to an artist whose
ability and imagination span the revolutionary years
from 1780 to 1826.

Goya   Francisco Goya (1746–1828) was a successful
and celebrated painter in the court of Charles IV. He
had begun his career as a designer of tapestries whose
subjects, the amusements of the court life, document
the end of an era with elegance and beauty. There was,
however, a toughness and tenacity about Goya that was
first revealed in a series of etchings, *Los Caprichos (Human Follies)*, executed in 1795–1796. Of this collection
perhaps the most famous is one of the first, *The Sleep
of Reason Produces Monsters* (Fig. 25-3). The title is a
complex one. A sleeping man dreams of horrible
winged creatures who hover about his head. Reason,
when she flees, permits the appearance of the dark, demonic undisciplined self; but a rigid and inflexible
Reason produces the monsters of revolution, too. Tech-
nically Goya draws on traditional conventions but
transforms them into an awful assemblage of shadow
and texture.

While serving as the court painter, he experienced
the horror of the French invasion of Spain with its
guerrilla warfare. Spanish royalists fought the invaders,
republicans fought the royalists, and the invaders and
the ensuing chaos reduced the populace to a terror-
filled mob. No longer reserved for armies and generals,
war decimated the entire population. There was loot-
ing, rape, pillage, and plunder. These years are recorded
in the etchings *The Disasters of War*. Probably made
from scenes he witnessed, the pictures reveal violence,
brutality, and man's monstrous inhumanity. Figure 25-
4, *I Saw This*, shows a family wrenched apart. In Figure
25-5 a man stumbles on a tumbled mass of bodies; the
sight and smell make him retch.

After the war Goya was commissioned to commemo-
rate the events of May 2 and 3, 1808, when the citi-
zenry of Madrid had attacked the soldiers of Napoleon
in the Puerta del Sol. That night and the next day citizens were rounded up and summarily shot in a gesture

25–3   Goya, "The Sleep of Reason Produces Monsters." (Courtesy Museum of Fine Arts, Boston. Bequest of William P. Babcock)

of reprisal. *The Shootings of the Third of May, 1808* is
among the most brilliant images that Goya created (Fig.
25-6). The huddled citizens, unarmed and frightened,
and the anonymous rank of surging soldiery spotlighted by a flaring lamp resemble a nightmare. The
open mouths and astonished faces, the blood and gore
are without precedent. The loosely handled paint is
rapidly brushed, while the earthy tones, cream, and
reds focus our eyes into the center foreground, where
the pose of the figure with upraised arms alludes to
Christ and an attitude of innocence. This is a court of
no resort; no pleading protects women or children.
Death is stark, awful, ignominious. The romantic revolt against tyranny is the theme, but Napoleon is the
villain rather than the hero.

Delacroix Goya's work was known in France and was not without influence. But for the French romantic painter Eugène Delacroix, considered a revolutionary by his peers and teachers, war's terrifying nature was still susceptible to the romanticizing distance of place, if not time. Delacroix's painting *The Massacres of Scios* (Fig. 25-7) recounts an event similar in nature to the murders in Madrid, but the event is presented as a scene from a poetic drama. The figures are drawn from Renaissance types: their deaths seem to be those of passive resignation. There is little immediate violence. The men are handsome and noble, the women are splendidly beautiful in old age or youth, the costumes are magnificent, and the horse is glorious. Yet Delacroix was condemned for his intensity of presentation and for the looseness of his brilliant paint. Compared to the hard coldness of David and his followers, Delacroix's work was considered a direct threat to the classicism of the academy.

In his painting *Liberty at the Barricades* (Fig. 25-8), a scene from the 1830 revolution, Delacroix uses a bare-breasted female to personify Liberty. The diagonal composition and the piled-up bodies recall Rubens and the monumental compositions of the baroque. Nevertheless, Delacroix, who painted nudes, animals, and scenes from the Bible, mythology, and the tales of Sir Walter Scott, exemplifies a romantic response to the strictures of the past. His emotion-filled canvases, brilliant in color and heavy with paint, are his attempt to make an art in response to his personal temperament and imagination.

Baudelaire, the French poet and critic, praised Delacroix for his imagination and energy, finding in his work an individual temperament given free reign to speak directly to the emotions and dreams of others. Yet Delacroix's work seems reserved and controlled when compared to the elemental passion tapped in Goya's work.

We can understand this only when we remember that Delacroix revered the art of the past, seeking to preserve it while giving it new values, whereas Goya seemed absolutely unable to incorporate his feelings and ideas in the old traditions. It is this split between reverence for the past and a passion for new ways of thinking, seeing, and feeling that characterizes the romantic period.

Revolutionary Ideals in Music, Classical and Romantic: Beethoven's Ninth Symphony

During the second half of the eighteenth century, music went through a period of calm, a phase of lightening, balancing, and simplifying; this brief and splendid era is one which music historians have labelled *classic*. It reached its height in the works of two towering geniuses: Josef Haydn and Wolfgang Amadeus Mozart. The music of Mozart forsook the intricate counterpoint and long-winded phrases of the baroque master Bach. The compositions of Haydn consistently employed distinct phrases and sections in new structures that achieved unity and balance through readily perceived contrasts of melodies and harmonies. Composers seemed to find a regularity in their musical lan-

25–7 Delacroix, "The Massacres of Scios." (Louvre, Paris/photo © ARCH. PHOT. PARIS—S.P.A.D.E.M., 1980)

25–8 Delacroix, "Liberty at the Barricades." (Louvre, Paris/photo © ARCH. PHOT. PARIS—S.P.A.D.E.M., 1980)

guage that brought a logical coherence to works both tiny and grandiose. They worked primarily with the short, articulated phrase; they strove for structural symmetry; and they contrasted the rhythmic activities of the melody and the harmony in such a way that "tune" and "harmony" became distinct entities. New instruments developed, as they always had in the past; but, more importantly, old instruments changed character so that eventually the piano would replace the harpsichord and clavichord and the violin would replace the viol. This came about because the new bourgeoisie created a market for music, calling it from the patron's chamber to the public concert hall. As *dynamics* became louder, the music became more appropriate for performance before large audiences. It was at this time that the symphony orchestra emerged as a primary musical medium upon which compositional ideas might be sounded in concert.

The intellectual stimulus of romanticism quickly made itself felt upon the composers of Europe, and by the turn of the nineteenth century, elements of a new flavor were beginning to surface in the works of the central European composers. Ludwig van Beethoven (1770–1827) was a genius who was able to master and sum up all the current musical ideas of his time and then, later in life, take that giant step of creation where new compositions foreshadow the principal musical ideas for decades to come. This man had both feet firmly planted in the fertile soil of classicism but was able to reach out with both hands to grapple with the giant problems of romanticism: the meaning of life, the values of human existence, the powers of man, and the importance of the individual.

What does romanticism in music really mean? What are the musical features that inform our ears about the interests and ideals of Beethoven and the nineteenth-century composers who followed him? To search for answers to these questions, let us look into a single masterpiece that fuses classical and romantic styles— the values of the Enlightenment and the passions of the romantic revolutionaries. Let us try to learn from Beethoven's last and most monumental symphony, his Symphony in D Minor, opus 125, a work familiarly known as the Ninth Symphony.

Like all classical symphonies, Beethoven's Ninth is divided into four movements, and they follow a traditional pattern: the first and fourth movements are energetic, moving at a lively speed; the second and third movements offer contrast, one slow and the other a dance form related to the classical dance called the minuet. This four-movement, balanced structure developed as a means to create a large-scale work (a half hour or more) capable of capturing intellectual attention for long periods of time using musical means only. In other words, the composers were seeking an answer to a compositional problem: if we exclude extramusical ideas and effects (such as a church service, a dance, a festival, and programmatic ideas), how can we keep from losing the listener's attention if we play a continuous piece of music for a very long time? Haydn, Mozart, and their mid-eighteenth century contemporaries solved the problem by designing symphonies that had distinct movements related by key, contrasted by mood, and subdivided by various formal designs that developed contrasting melodies in a variety of ways. Their large works lasted up to thirty or even forty minutes; Beethoven's Ninth lasts almost two hours! His first movement continues as long as do most complete classical symphonies. Although Beethoven's concept of form was classical, his expansion of dimensions, his breaking of boundaries, was romantic.

Classical composers had a knack for the well-turned phrase, a neat tune of four or eight measures' duration whose shape had character and individuality and was capable of expansion or development as the piece progressed. Classical melodies had musical characteristics that allowed these tunes, usually, to be categorized as antecedent-consequent phrases; that is, the first half is answered and completed by the second half. A good example of this type of theme is Mozart's opening theme from his Symphony no. 40 in G minor (K.550),

where both halves are similar but different, ascending and descending, opening and closing. In fact, Mozart's sense of balance was so certain and ingrained that the entire phrase can be seen as the antecedent of the next four-measure phrase.

This analytical game can be played even further, if we choose, for the two-to-two and four-to-four measure relationships can be carried even further by viewing the first eight measures as antecedent to the second eight measures. This is possible with Mozart and his G Minor symphony; it is not possible with the opening theme of Beethoven's Ninth.

Beethoven's "tune" is hardly a melody at all; it is a series of short *motives* laid out along a descending *arpeggiated* chord and a brief closing figure.

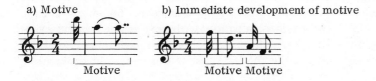

a) Motive   b) Immediate development of motive

Motive   Motive Motive

Opening musical figure (combination of motives)

Closing figure of first phrase

From small germinal ideas, Beethoven sculpts larger forms; from almost tuneless groups of notes, Beethoven creates tonal music of a relentless, soul-searching nature. Each fragment of melody is taken in turn, examined, dissected, synthesized, and reissued in a new shape within a fresh context at a later time. The rhythm of the closing fragment

becomes a driving melody for the bass instruments at one point:

and a lyrical, sweet passage for French horn at another.

In other words, even these few processes we have discussed here sound the death knell for the ease, grace, and regularity of classical music. In time the classical forms will even be replaced or set aside, but for Beethoven it was enough to fragment the old and pile smaller blocks into larger structures.

Those who already are familiar with the Ninth Symphony will say that this analysis has been deceptive thus far, for the Ninth is also called the Choral Symphony and is unlike its classical predecessors if for no other reason than that. Additionally, they might add that a chorus and vocal soloists require text and that words bring extramusical ideas immediately into play. True enough, but in the Ninth Symphony of Beethoven, the vocalists do not begin their work until the last movement. An hour of instrumental music has been performed before they sing their first note. To understand the Ninth, we must first grasp the meaning of this creation on purely musical terms, for it is a complex instrumental construction with a choral and literary element added to it. Without the chorus, it would still be a classical-romantic symphony. The chorus does not make it romantic; the notes do. Without an understanding of the first three movements, the fourth would be diminished. Beethoven binds the beginning to the end, for he takes the opening motive from the beginning of the symphony to play in the introduction to the fourth, or choral, movement; likewise he takes the melody of the scherzo, or second movement, for use in the finale's introduction. The restatement of earlier ideas in a Beethoven symphony is not merely saying the same thing twice; rather, it is a reiteration of initial ideas now seen in the new light cast from all the music that has been played since the ideas were first stated. Had the remainder of the symphony not been performed—that is, had the first three movements been omitted—the music of the opening of the last movement would be extraneous and the finale reduced to a skillfully orchestrated choral piece. Beethoven's

way made it the crowning gem of a symphonic career. The Ninth Symphony looks both ways—back to the past and forward into the future.

Since this work is indeed a choral symphony, we must look carefully at the poem, for surely a composer's preoccupation with text is the critical event that starts the compositional process for a choral setting. In Beethoven's case it was truly a preoccupation. From a letter of 1793 written by a Viennese admirer, Bartolomeus Fischenich, when the composer was only twenty-three years old, we learn that the young musician intended to set Schiller's *Freude* (Joy) poem stanza by stanza; the Ninth Symphony was completed in 1824. Obviously Beethoven was not actively working on this symphony for thirty-one years, but the Schiller poem seems to have been tucked within the composer's mind throughout the period of the Napoleonic exploits in France, a series of events that strongly molded Beethoven's philosophy. In fact, this poem gains even greater significance if the noted British composer, Ralph Vaughan Williams, is correct, for he relates:

> When I was young I was told that Schiller originally wrote his Ode to "Freedom" (*Freiheit*), not "Joy" (*Freude*), and that Beethoven knew of this when he composed the music. I have never been able to find any confirmation of this legend, but we may profitably keep it at the back of our minds when we play or sing or read, or hear this great Symphony.[1]

There is no doubt that Schiller's poem exemplifies the romantic spirit in Europe and was capable of holding special meaning for Beethoven.

Alle Menschen werden Brueder,
   Wo dein sanfter Fluegel weilt.

[1] Ralph Vaughan Williams, *Some Thoughts on Beethoven's Choral Symphony with Writings on Other Musical Subjects* (London: Oxford University Press, 1953), p. 13.

Men throughout the world are brothers,
    In the haven of thy wings.

Napoleon, until he named himself Emperor, had been a hero for Beethoven, a leader of common men against the tyranny of the rich, the oppression of the aristocracy. Beethoven did not like his indebtedness to the patronage of the rich; recognizing personal worth and artistic genius to be far superior to accident of birth, he struggled constantly throughout his life to assert his independence, his freedom. To him freedom was the greatest joy, and Schiller's poem expressed in words what he felt in his soul and was capable of translating into music. (Only the portion of the poem used by Beethoven is printed below; Louis Untermeyer is the translator.)

FRIEDRICH SCHILLER   *Hymn to Joy* ────────────────────────────────●

Baritone: O Freunde, nicht diese Toene!
    Sondern lasst uns angenehmere anstimmen, und
        freudenvollere.

Baritone: O friends, friends, not these sounds!
    Let us sing something more pleasant, more
        full of gladness. O Joy, let us praise thee!

(Baritone Solo, Quartet and Chorus)

Freude, schoener Goetterfunken,
    Tochter aus Elysium,
Wir betreten feuer-trunken,
    Himmlische, dein Heiligthum!
Deine Zauber binden wieder,
    Was die Mode streng getheilt;
Alle Menschen werden Brueder,
    Wo dein sanfter Fluegel weilt.

Joy, thou source of light immortal,
    Daughter of Elysium,
Touched with fire, to the portal
    Of thy radiant shrine we come.
Thy pure magic frees all others
    Held in Custom's rigid rings;
Men throughout the world are brothers
    In the haven of thy wings.

Wem der grosse Wurf gelungen,
    Eines Freundes Freund zu sein,
Wer ein holdes Weib errungen,
    Mische seinen Jubel ein!
Ja, wer auch nur eine Seele
    Sein nennt auf dem Erdenrund!
Und wer's nie gekonnt, der stehle
    Weinend sich aus diesem Bund!

He who knows the pride and pleasure
    Of a friendship firm and strong,
He who has a wife to treasure,
    Let him swell our mighty song.
If there is a single being
    Who can call a heart his own,
And denies it—then, unseeing,
    Let him go and weep alone.

Freude trinken alle Wesen
    An den Bruesten der Natur;
Alle Guten, alle Boesen
    Folgen ihrer Rosenspur.
Kuesse gab sie uns und Reben,
    Einen Freund, geprueft im Tod;
Wollust ward dem Wurm gegeben,
    Und der Cherub steht vor Gott.

Joy is drunk by all God's creatures
    Straight from earth's abundant breast;
Good and bad, all things are nature's,
    And with blameless joy are blessed.
Joy gives love and wine; her gladness
    Makes the universe her zone,
From the worm that feels spring's madness
    To the angel near God's throne.

(Tenor Solo and Chorus)

Froh, wie seine Sonnen fliegen	Glad, as when the suns run glorious
Durch des Himmels praecht'gen Plan,	Through the deep and dazzling skies,
Laufet, Brueder, eure Bahn,	Brothers, run with shining eyes—
Freudig, wie ein Held zum Siegen.	Heroes, happy and victorious.
Freude, schoener Gotterfunken,	Joy, thou source of light immortal,
Tochter aus Elysium,	Daughter of Elysium,
Wir betreten feuer-trunken,	Touched with fire, to the portal
Himmlische, dein Heiligthum!	Of thy radiant shrine we come.
Deine Zauber binden wieder,	Thy pure magic frees all others
Was die Mode streng getheilt;	Held in Custom's rigid rings;
Alle Menschen werden Brueder,	Men throughout the world are brothers
Wo dein sanfter Fluegel weilt.	In the haven of thy wings.

(Quartet and Chorus)

Seid umschlungen, Millionen!	Millions, myriads, rise and gather!
Diesen Kuss der ganzen Welt!	Share this universal kiss!
Brueder, ueber'm Sternenzelt	Brothers, in a heaven of bliss,
Muss ein lieber Vater wohnen.	Smiles the world's all-loving Father.
Ihr stuerzt nieder, Millionen?	Do the millions, His creation,
Ahnest du den Schoepfer, Welt?	Know Him and His works of love?
Such ihn ueber'm Sternenzelt!	Seek Him! In the heights above
Ueber Sternen muss er wohnen.	Is His starry habitation!

Beethoven's chorus, singing their heads off in a "fire-drunk" jubilation, celebrate the human spirit; they are singing a great song for all peoples, nations, and languages. And as the fervor builds and the orchestral and vocal sounds sweep you away, the listener is unlikely to notice that this great romantic outpouring is framed by Beethoven's simplest, and most classical, melody:

The simplicity of the *theme*, the clarity of its form (A–A–B–A–B–A), the unpretentious nature of its harmony and rhythm make it a song for the common man, and that it has become. The works of Beethoven live today because, in addition to their sheer beauty and historical importance, they symbolize those values that we cherish now. In the words of Romain Rolland:

> The music of Beethoven is the daughter of the same forces of imperious Nature that had just sought an outlet in the man of Rousseau's *Confessions*. Each of them is the flowering of a new season. . . . [Beethoven], too, like the eagle on his rock, goes into exile on an island lost in the expanse of the seas—more truly lost than that island in the Atlantic, for he does not hear even the waves breaking on the rocks. He is immured. And when out of the silence there rises the song of the Ego of the last ten years of his life, it is no longer the same Ego; he has renounced the empire of men; he is with his God.[2]

---

[2] Romain Rolland, *Beethoven the Creator*, trans. Ernest Newman (New York: Harper & Brothers, 1929), pp. 25ff.

26 ROMANTIC VIEWS OF WOMEN, LOVE, AND NATURE

We have seen in the last chapter how the ideals of revolution and of heroic individualism influenced the development of romantic arts and sensibility. Romantic thought and art brought forth a great many other ideals and themes, among them the medieval past, "unspoiled" primitive societies, mysticism, sentimentalism, and the supremacy of the imagination. Here we will concentrate on three related themes: the romantic woman and the romantic view of women, romantic love, and the romantic concept of nature.

In the romantic period—in life as well as in art—women undoubtedly assumed a new importance, a role more influential than in any previous cultural epoch in the West. Yet the positions assumed by women in society and the images of women in art seem, from our point of view, greatly contradictory. Let us briefly examine some of them.

The Liberated Woman

We have already mentioned the influential role played by eighteenth-century French women in the salons and other intellectual circles. Women in France and in England as well participated even more actively in revolutionary groups at the end of the century. The development of the ideas of the Enlightenment into a concern with liberty and equality in all spheres of life included a rethinking of the position of women. As if in addition to the French revolution's vindication of "the rights of man," the Englishwoman Mary Wollstonecraft published in 1792 *Vindication of the Rights of Women*. Reasoning along the lines laid out by Rousseau, Wollstonecraft asserted that the alleged inferiority or defects of women are results of the institutions of society, not of nature. "Make them free, and they will quickly become wise and virtuous...make women rational creatures and free citizens and they will quickly become good wives, and mothers; that is,—if men do not neglect the duties of husbands and fathers."

Mary Wollstonecraft, a woman of the late Enlightenment, gave birth to Mary Godwin (later the writer Mary Shelley), a true romantic, but died shortly after the birth. The early nineteenth century saw a veritable outbreak of woman writers, primarily novelists, struggling against restrictions imposed on them by family and society in order to live freely as human beings and as artists. Many of them published under male pen names. In England there were the Brontë sisters and "George Eliot," in the United States the secluded Emily Dickinson and the outspoken Margaret Fuller, in France, Germaine Necker (Madame de Staël) and "George Sand." The two Frenchwomen were particularly concerned in their novels with the nature and destinies of women. Sand was a liberated woman in her lifestyle, which included a passionate affair with the composer Chopin; but, with typical romantic contradiction, she exalts the simple, virtuous wife in many of her works. Her *Lélia* is nonetheless an apology for free love. Mme. de Staël's Corinne, in the novel by that name, is a poetic genius who suffers and dies of unrequited love. Her statement on poetic inspiration is remarkable not only for its portrayal of women, but for its typically romantic exaltation of inspired genius.

Sometimes...my impassioned excitement carries me beyond myself; teaches me to find in nature and my own heart such daring truths and forcible expressions as solitary meditation could never have engendered. My enthusiasm then seems supernatural: a spirit speaks within me far greater than my own; it often happens that I abandon the measure of verse to explain my thoughts in prose....Sometimes my lyre, by a simple national air, may complete the effect which flies from the control of words. In truth, I feel myself a poet, less when a happy choice of rhymes, of syllables, of figures, may dazzle my auditors, than when my spirit soars disdainful of all selfish baseness; when godlike deeds appear easy to me, 'tis then my verse is at its best. I am...a poet while I admire or hate, not by my personal feelings nor in my own cause, but for the sake of human dignity and the glory of the world....I cannot touch on any of the themes that affect me, without that kind of thrill which is the source of ideal beauty in the arts, of religion in the recluse, generosity in heroes and disinterestedness among men.

How far we are here from the neoclassical conception of the role of the artist and the composition of the work of art! Corinne's portrayal of herself is comparable to that of an allegorical figure, like Delacroix's *Liberty at the Barricades*.

Romantic Love and Female Types

Of course, literature and the other arts continued to be dominated by men in the romantic period, and so it is primarily woman as viewed by man that has given us the various images of woman in romantic art. These range from the idealized simple, domestic, virtuous girl and mother to the ethereal beauty, inspirer of lofty ideas, to the she-devil, temptress or *femme fatale* who seduces and ruins innocent young men. All these types may inspire romantic love, an all-consuming passion that can never be fulfilled (if it is, it usually leads to disillusionment and a new object) and often causes the hero extreme misery or even death. The romantic sufferer and the romantic lover are often one and the same, as we will see in the selection from Goethe's romantic novel *The Sorrows of Young Werther*. Werther, a lover of nature and poetry but a misfit in society, is obsessed with love for a married woman, Charlotte. Unable to find any kind of satisfaction in this world, he finally commits suicide. Young people all over Europe identified with Werther, both in their art and their lives. The novel actually provoked a rash of suicides. Romantic sufferers, pursuing an ideal, impossible love, felt themselves to be born in the wrong place at the wrong time, sensitive geniuses inevitably misunderstood by a crass society.

GOETHE

from *The Sorrows of Young Werther*

(The passage below describes the meeting of Werther with Charlotte, who is bethrothed to Albert. The entire novel—except for the end, after Werther's suicide—is written in the form of letters from Werther to his friend Wilhelm.)

I could not restrain myself—go to her I must. I have just returned, Wilhelm; and whilst I am taking supper I will write to you. What a delight it was for my soul to see her in the midst of her dear, beautiful children,— eight brothers and sisters!

But, if I proceed thus, you will be no wiser at the end of my letter than you were at the beginning. Attend, then, and I will compel myself to give you the details.

I mentioned to you the other day that I had become acquainted with S——, the district judge, and that he had invited me to go and visit him in his retirement, or rather in his little kingdom. But I neglected going, and perhaps should never have gone, if chance had not discovered to me the treasure which lay concealed in that retired spot. Some of our young people had proposed giving a ball in the country, at which I consented to be present. I offered my hand for the evening to a pretty and agreeable, but rather commonplace, sort of girl from the immediate neighborhood; and it was agreed that I should engage a carriage, and call upon Charlotte, with my partner and her aunt, to convey them to the ball. My companion informed me, as we drove along through the park to the hunting-lodge, that I should make the acquaintance of a very charming young lady. "Take care," added the aunt, "that you do not lose your heart."—"Why?" said I. "Because she is already engaged to a very worthy man," she replied, "who is gone to settle his affairs upon the death of his father, and will succeed to a very considerable inheritance."

This information possessed no interest for me. When we arrived at the gate, the sun was setting behind the tops of the mountains. The atmosphere was heavy; and the ladies expressed their fears of an approaching storm, as masses of low black clouds were gathering in the horizon. I relieved their anxieties by pretending to be weather-wise, although I myself had some apprehensions lest our pleasure should be interrupted.

I alighted; and a maid came to the door, and requested us to wait a moment for her mistress. I walked across the court to a well-built house, and, ascending the flight of steps in front, opened the door, and saw before me the most charming spectacle I had ever witnessed. Six children, from eleven to two years old, were running about the hall, and surrounding a lady of middle height, with a lovely figure, dressed in a robe of simple white, trimmed with pink ribbons. She was holding a rye loaf in her hand, and was cutting slices for the little ones all round, in proportion to their age and appetite. She performed her task in a graceful and affectionate manner; each claimant awaiting his turn with outstretched hands, and boisterously shouting his thanks. Some of them ran away at once, to enjoy their evening meal; whilst others, of a gentler disposition, retired to the courtyard to see the strangers, and to survey the carriage in which their Charlotte was to drive away. "Pray forgive me for giving you the trouble to come for me, and for keeping the ladies waiting: but dressing, and arranging some household duties before I leave, had made me forget my children's supper; and they do not like to take it from any one but me." I uttered some indifferent compliment: but my whole soul was absorbed by her air, her voice, her manner; and I had scarcely recovered myself when she ran into her room to fetch her gloves and fan. The young ones threw inquiring glances at me from a distance; whilst I approached the youngest, a most delicious little creature. He drew back; and Charlotte, entering at the very moment, said, "Louis, shake hands with your cousin." The little fellow obeyed willingly; and I could not resist giving him a hearty kiss, notwithstanding his rather dirty face. "Cousin," said I to Charlotte, as I handed her down, "do you think I deserve the happiness of being related to you?" She replied, with a ready smile, "Oh! I have such a number of cousins, that I should be sorry if you were the most undeserving of them." In taking leave, she desired her next sister, Sophy, a girl about eleven years old, to take great care of the children, and to say good-by to papa for her when he came home from his ride. She enjoined to the little ones to obey their sister Sophy as they would herself, upon which some promised that they would; but a little fair-haired girl, about six years old, looked discontented, and said, "But Sophy is not you, Charlotte; and we like you best." The two eldest boys had clambered up the carriage; and, at my request, she permitted them to accompany us a little way through the forest, upon their promising to sit very still, and hold fast.

We were hardly seated, and the ladies had scarcely exchanged compliments, making the usual remarks upon each other's dress, and upon the company they expected to meet, when Charlotte stopped the carriage, and made her brothers get down. They insisted upon kissing her hands once more; which the eldest did with all the tenderness of a youth of fifteen, but the other in a lighter and more careless manner. She desired them again to give her love to the children, and we drove off.

The aunt inquired of Charlotte whether she had finished the book she had last sent her. "No," said Charlotte; "I did not like it: you can have it again. And the one before was not much better." I was surprised, upon asking the title, to hear that it was[1]———. I found penetration and character in every thing she said: every expression seemed to brighten her features with new charms,—with new rays of genius,—which unfolded by degrees, as she felt herself understood.

"When I was younger," she observed, "I loved nothing so much as romances. Nothing could equal my delight when, on some holiday, I could settle down quietly in a corner, and enter with my whole heart and soul into the joys or sorrows of some fictitious Leonora. I do not deny that they even possess some charms for me yet. But I read so seldom, that I prefer books suited exactly to my taste. And I like those authors best whose scenes describe my own situation in life,—and the friends who are about me, whose stories touch me with interest, from resembling my own homely existence,—

which, without being absolutely paradise, is, on the whole, a source of indescribable happiness." . . .

We talked of the pleasures of dancing. "If it is a fault to love it," said Charlotte, "I am ready to confess that I prize it above all other amusements. If any thing disturbs me, I go to the piano, play an air to which I have danced, and all goes right again directly."

You, who know me, can fancy how steadfastly I gazed upon her rich dark eyes during these remarks, how my very soul gloated over her warm lips and fresh, glowing cheeks, how I became quite lost in the delightful meaning of her words, so much so, that I scarcely heard the actual expressions. In short, I alighted from the carriage like a person in a dream, and was so lost to the dim world around me, that I scarcely heard the music which resounded from the illuminated ballroom. . . .

We set off, and, at first, delighted ourselves with the usual graceful motions of the arms. With what grace, with what ease, she moved! When the waltz commenced, and the dancers whirled round each other in the giddy maze, there was some confusion, owing to the incapacity of some of the dancers. We judiciously remained still, allowing the others to weary themselves; and, when the awkward dancers had withdrawn, we joined in, and kept it up famously together with one other couple,—Andran and his partner. Never did I dance more lightly. I felt myself more than mortal, holding this loveliest of creatures in my arms, flying with her as rapidly as the wind, till I lost sight of every other object; and O Wilhelm, I vowed at that moment, that a maiden whom I loved, or for whom I felt the slightest attachment, never, never should waltz with any one else but with me, if I went to perdition for it!—you will understand this.

(*Charlotte eventually marries Albert, and Werther takes up residence near them. He sees Charlotte every day. While she is fond of him, she remains true to her husband. Werther's unrequited passion finally drives him insane.*)

Unhappy being that I am! Why do I thus deceive myself? What is to come of all this wild, aimless, endless passion? I cannot pray except to her. My imagination sees nothing but her: all surrounding objects are of no account, except as they relate to her. In this dreamy state I enjoy many happy hours, till at length I feel

---

[1] We feel obliged to suppress the passage in the letter, to prevent any one from feeling aggrieved; although no author need pay much attention to the opinion of a mere girl, or that of an unsteady young man.

compelled to tear myself away from her. Ah, Wilhelm, to what does not my heart often compel me! When I have spent several hours in her company, till I feel completely absorbed by her figure, her grace, the divine expression of her thoughts, my mind becomes gradually excited to the highest excess, my sight grows dim, my hearing confused, my breathing oppressed as if by the hand of a murderer, and my beating heart seeks to obtain relief for my aching senses. I am sometimes unconscious whether I really exist. If in such moments I find no sympathy, and Charlotte does not allow me to enjoy the melancholy consolation of bathing her hand with my tears, I feel compelled to tear myself from her, when I either wander through the country, climb some precipitous cliff, or force a path through the trackless thicket, where I am lacerated and torn by thorns and briers; and thence I find relief. Sometimes I lie stretched on the ground, overcome with fatigue and dying with thirst; sometimes, late in the night, when the moon shines above me, I recline against an aged tree in some sequestered forest, to rest my weary limbs, when, exhausted and worn, I sleep till break of day. O Wilhelm! the hermit's cell, his sackcloth, and girdle of thorns would be luxury and indulgence compared with what I suffer. Adieu! I see no end to this wretchedness except the grave.

(Werther leaves Charlotte and Albert for a while, but is driven to return. Feeling that the whole world is against him, he shoots himself with one of Albert's pistols.)

QUESTIONS

1. Describe Werther's initial perception of Charlotte. What ideal of woman does she represent?
2. Compare the passage on dancing to the ballet *Giselle*, below. Note that the waltz was at this time a new and shocking dance.
3. Analyze the last passage. What are the symptoms of romantic love? How does the sufferer find relief? Would Werther's passion really be satisfied if he married Charlotte?

Throughout American romantic fiction—the novels of James Fenimore Cooper, Hawthorne, and Melville offer some examples—one can find examples of blonde heroines who inspire the hero to noble thoughts and chaste love and brunettes who inevitably bring out his

"darker" passions. In France, the type of the fatal woman, the *femme fatale*, is exemplified in Prosper Mérimée's story *Carmen*, about a young man led to ruin by an enticing, fickle Spanish gypsy. This mythical character was developed further in the opera *Carmen* by Bizet. Romantic opera—*La Bohème* and *La Traviata* are other examples—is indeed full of free living women who inspire consuming passions. Music, many romantics were convinced, could express the passion of love better than any other art could. Words by themselves were too limited. In early nineteenth-century Germany an extraordinary cooperation between poets and composers resulted in a new art form, the *Lied* (art song), or the song cycle. One of the best known of the cycles on the theme of love is *Dichterliebe* ("The Love of a Poet") by the poet Heinrich Heine and the composer Robert Schumann. The culminating portrayal of romantic love in music is Richard Wagner's opera *Tristan und Isolde*, taking its subject from the literature that gave romantic love its prototype, the medieval romance. The music portrays the soaring passions of the lovers and the only climax possible—death.

Some of these concepts of love and women are illustrated in the poems below. The *femme fatale* and the relation between love and death figure in the English poet John Keats's "La Belle Dame sans Merci." A more sentimental (but also ironic) version of love is seen in the Heine lyrics, translated by Ernst Feise.

JOHN KEATS

La Belle Dame sans Merci[1]

A Ballad

O what can ail thee, knight-at-arms,
    Alone and palely loitering?
The sedge has withered from the lake,
    And no birds sing.

O what can ail thee, knight-at-arms,
    So haggard and so woe-begone?
The squirrel's granary is full,
    And the harvest's done.

---

[1] "The beautiful lady without pity."

I see a lily on thy brow,
  With anguish moist and fever dew,
And on thy cheeks a fading rose
  Fast withereth too.

I met a lady in the meads,[2]
  Full beautiful—a faery's child,
Her hair was long, her foot was light,
  And her eyes were wild.

I made a garland for her head,
  And bracelets too, and fragrant zone;[3]
She looked at me as she did love,
  And made sweet moan.

I set her on my pacing steed,
  And nothing else saw all day long,
For sidelong would she bend, and sing
  A faery's song.

She found me roots of relish sweet,
  And honey wild, and manna dew,
And sure in language strange she said,
  "I love thee true."

She took me to her elfin grot,
  And there she wept, and sighed full sore,
And there I shut her wild wild eyes
  With kisses four.

And there she lulléd me asleep,
  And there I dreamed—Ah! woe betide!
The latest[4] dream I ever dreamed
  On the cold hill side.

I saw pale kings and princes too,
  Pale warriors, death-pale were they all;
They cried—"La Belle Dame sans Merci
  Hath thee in thrall!"

I saw their starved lips in the gloam,
  With horrid warning gapéd wide,

And I awoke and found me here,
  On the cold hill's side.

And this is why I sojourn here,
  Alone and palely loitering,
Though the sedge has withered from the lake,
  And no birds sing.

QUESTIONS

1. Why is this a ballad?
2. In what time period does the poem seem to be set?
3. How much do we learn about the beautiful lady? Do you think she is kept deliberately vague? Why?
4. What connection does the poem establish between love and death?

HEINRICH HEINE

A Young Man Loves a Maiden

A young man loves a maiden
Whose heart for another sighed;
This other loves another
Who then becomes his bride.

The maiden takes the first man
Who happens to come her way
Just out of spite and anger;
The youth is left in dismay.

It is an old old story
And yet it's always new;
And to whomever it happens
't will break his heart in two.

QUESTIONS

1. If possible, listen to both of Heine's lyrics set to the music of Robert Schumann in his *Dichterliebe* ("Love of a Poet") song cycle.
2. Describe the tone of this poem. Does it change at the end? How is this reinforced in the music?

---

[2] Meadows.
[3] Belt.
[4] Last.

HEINRICH HEINE

You Are Just Like a Flower

You are just like a flower
So fair and chaste and dear;
Looking at you, sweet sadness
Invades my heart with fear.

I feel I should be folding
My hands upon your hair,
Praying that God may keep you
So dear and chaste and fair.

QUESTIONS

1. What different sentiments are expressed in this apparently simple lyric? How are they combined? How does the music bring them out?

The Romantic Ballet

Another romantic art form that gave great importance to women, both as artists and as mythical figures, and to romantic love was the ballet. The Neoclassical stage ballet of the eighteenth century, like the *ballet de cour* of the seventeenth, showed an equality of roles between the sexes but gave some predominance to men in the execution of showy steps. In the romantic ballet, however, the first female dancer of the company—the *prima ballerina*—upstaged everyone. Dancing on the tip of the toes, or *pointe*, and airy tulle costumes appeared at this time. Men were sometimes reduced to machines to lift the ethereal creatures in the air. The popular notion of ballet as a woman's art, as indeed in most of the best-known ballets still performed, dates from the romantic period. Romanticism in ballet as in the other arts stressed exoticism, fantasy, nature, and, of course, love; an unrealizable love for an evanescent lady or a "fatal" love for a heartless temptress.

Paris, with London a close second, was the center of romantic ballet. It was there, at the opera, that the stars—the Italians Maria Taglioni and Carlotta Grisi and the Viennese Fanny Essler—became for their admirers legendary, almost goddess-like. The poet Théophile Gautier, an admirer of the art of dance, wrote the story for the greatest romantic ballet, one which is still popular with modern audiences. His descriptive letter to Heine, whose account of a German legend inspired *Giselle*, tells the story of the ballet and describes a performance; it also gives us some idea of how ideas and feelings from "romantic" Germany succeeded in penetrating the citadel of the Enlightenment. (The translation is by Cyril W. Beaumont.)

THÉOPHILE GAUTIER

Letter to Heinrich Heine

July 5th, 1841.

My dear Heinrich Heine, when reviewing, a few weeks ago, your fine book, *De L'Allemagne*,[1] I came across a charming passage—one has only to open the book at random—the place where you speak of elves in white dresses, whose hems are always damp,[2] of nixes who display their little satin feet on the ceiling of the nuptial chamber; of snow-coloured *Wilis* who waltz pitilessly, and of all those delicious apparitions you have encountered in the Harz mountains and on the banks of the Ilse, in a mist softened by German moonlight; and I involuntarily said to myself: "Wouldn't this make a pretty ballet?" . . . Three days later, the ballet *Giselle* was accepted. At the end of the week, Adolphe Adam had improvised the music, the scenery was nearly ready, and the rehearsals were in full swing. You see, my dear Heinrich, we are not yet so incredulous and so prosaic as you think we appear. You said in a moment of ill-humour: "How could a spectre exist in Paris?[3] . . . Well, I had only to take your pale and charming phantoms by their shadowy finger-tips and present them, to ensure their receiving the most polite reception in the world. The director and public have not offered the least objection *à la Voltaire*. The *Wilis* have already received the right of citizenship in the scarcely fantastic rue Lepelletier. Some lines where you

---

[1] Heine wrote this introduction to German culture in French. It appeared in a Paris journal in 1833.
[2] In fairy tales, water spirits, no matter how disguised, can always be detected because a portion of their dress always appears to be wet.
[3] What does this say about the difference in cultural atmosphere between Germany and France?

speak of them, placed at the head of the *scenario*, have served them as passports.

Since the state of your health has prevented your being present at the first performance, I am going to attempt, if a French journalist is permitted to tell a fantastic story to a German poet, to explain to you how M. de Saint-Georges, while respecting the spirit of your legend, has made it acceptable and possible at the Opera. To allow more freedom, the action takes place in a vague country, in Silesia, in Thuringia, even in one of the Bohemian sea-ports that Shakespeare loved; it suffices for it to be on the other side of the Rhine, in some mysterious corner of Germany. Do not ask more of the geography of the ballet which cannot define the name of a town or country by means of gesture, which is its only tongue.

Hillocks weighed down with russet vines, yellowish, warmed and sweetened by the autumn sun; those beautiful vines from which hang the amber-coloured grapes which produce Rhine wine, form the background; at the summit of a grey and bare rock, so precipitous that the vine tendrils have been unable to climb it, stands, perched like an eagle's nest, one of those castles so common in Germany, with its battlemented walls, its pepper-box turrets, and its feudal weathercocks; it is the abode of Albrecht, the young Duke of Silesia. That thatched cottage to the left, cool, clean, coquettish, half-buried among the leaves, is Giselle's cottage. The hut facing it is occupied by Loys. Who is Giselle? Giselle is Carlotta Grisi, a charming girl with blue eyes, a refined and artless smile, and an alert bearing; an Italian who tries to be taken for a German, just as Fanny, the German, tried to be taken for an Andalusian from Seville. Her position is the simplest in the world; she loves Loys and she loves dancing. As for Loys, played by Petipa, there are a hundred reasons for suspecting him. Just now, a handsome esquire, adorned with gold lace, speaks to him in a low voice, standing cap in hand and maintaining a submissive and respectful attitude. What! A servant of a great house, as the esquire appears to be, fails to lord it over the humble rustic to whom he speaks! Then, Loys *is not what he appears to be* (ballet style), *but we shall see later.*

Giselle steps out of the cottage on the tip of her dainty foot. Her legs are awake already; her heart, too, sleeps no longer, for it is full morning. She has had a dream, an evil dream: a beautiful and noble lady in a gold dress, with a brilliant engagement ring on her finger, appeared to her while she slept and seemed about to be married to Loys, who himself was a great nobleman, a duke, a prince. Dreams are very strange sometimes! Loys does his best to reassure her, and Giselle, still somewhat uneasy, questions the marguerites. The little silver petals flee and scatter: "He loves me, he loves me not!" "Oh, dear! How unhappy I am, he loves me not!" Loys, who is well aware that a boy of twenty can make the daisies say whatever he chooses, repeats the test, which, this time, is favourable; and Giselle, charmed with the flowers' good augury, begins to leap about again, despite her mother, who scolds her and would rather see that agile foot turning the spinning-wheel that stands in the window, and those pretty fingers questioning marguerites busied in gathering the already over-ripe grapes or carrying a vine-dresser's basket. But Giselle scarcely listens to the advice of her mother, whom she soothes with a little caress. The mother insists: "Unhappy child! You will dance for ever, you will kill yourself, and, when you are dead, you will become a *Wili*." And the good woman, in an expressive pantomime, relates the terrible legend of the nocturnal dancers. Giselle pays no heed. What young girl of fifteen believes in a story with the moral that one should not dance? Loys and dancing, that is her conception of happiness. This, like every possible happiness, wounds unseen a jealous heart; the gamekeeper, Hilarion, is in love with Giselle, and his most ardent desire is to injure his rival, Loys. He has already been a witness of the scene where the esquire Wilfrid spoke respectfully to the peasant. He suspects some plot, staves in the window of the hut and climbs through it, hoping to find some incriminating evidence. But now trumpets resound: the Prince of Courland and his daughter Bathilde, mounted on a white hackney, wearied from hunting, come to seek a little rest and coolness in Giselle's cottage. Loys prudently steals away. Giselle, with a timid and charming grace, hastens to set out on a table shining pewter goblets, milk, and some fruit, the best and most appetising of everything in her homely larder. While the beautiful Bathilde lifts the goblet to her lips, Giselle approaches with cat-like tread, and, in a rapture of artless admiration, ventures to touch the rich, soft material of which the lady's riding costume is composed. Bathilde, enchanted by Giselle's pleasant manners, places her gold chain round her neck and wishes to take the girl with her. Giselle thanks her effusively and replies that she wants nothing more in the world but to dance and to be loved by Loys.

The Prince of Courland and Bathilde withdraw into the hut to snatch a few moments' rest. The huntsmen disperse into the wood; a call on the prince's horn will warn them when it is time to return. The vine-dressers return from the vineyards and arrange a festival of which Giselle is proclaimed the Queen and in which she takes the principal part. Joy is at its height when Hilarion appears carrying a ducal mantle, a sword, and a knightly order found in Loys's hut—all doubt is at an end. Loys is simply an imposter, a seducer who has been playing on Giselle's good faith; a duke cannot marry a humble peasant, not even in the choreographic world, in which one often sees kings marrying shepherdesses—such a marriage offers innumerable obstacles. Loys, or rather Duke Albrecht of Silesia, defends himself to the best of his ability, and declares that no great harm has been done, for Giselle will marry a duke instead of a peasant. She is pretty enough to become duchess and lady of the manor. "But you are not free, you are betrothed to another," asserts the gamekeeper; and, seizing the horn left lying on the table, he blows it like a madman. The huntsmen run up. Bathilde and the Prince of Courland come out of the cottage and are amazed to see Duke Albrecht of Silesia in such a disguise. Giselle recognises in Bathilde the beautiful lady of her dreams, she doubts her misfortune no longer; her heart swells, her head swims, her feet shake and jump; she repeats the measure she danced with her lover; but her strength is soon exhausted, she staggers, sways, seizes the fatal sword brought by Hilarion and would have fallen on its point if Albrecht had not turned it aside with the quickness born of despair. Alas, the precaution is in vain; the blow has struck home; her heart is pierced and Giselle dies, consoled at least by her lover's profound grief and Bathilde's tender pity. . . .

The second act is as nearly as possible an exact translation of the page I have taken the liberty of tearing from your book, and I hope that when you return from Cauterets, fully recovered, you will not find it too misinterpreted.

The stage represents a forest on the banks of a pool; you see tall pale trees, whose roots spring from the grass and the rushes; the water-lily spreads its broad leaves on the surface of the placid water, which the moon silvers here and there with a trail of white spangles. Reeds with their brown velvet sheaths shiver and palpitate beneath the intermittent night breeze. The flowers open languorously and exhale a giddy perfume like those broad flowers of Java which madden whoever inhales their scent. I cannot say what burning and sensuous atmosphere flows about this humid and leafy obscurity. At the foot of a willow, asleep and concealed beneath the flowers, lies poor Giselle. From the marble cross which indicates her grave is suspended, still quite fresh, the garland of vine branches with which she had been crowned at the harvest festival.

Some hunters come to find a suitable place of concealment; Hilarion frightens them by saying that it is a dangerous and sinister spot, haunted by the *Wilis*, cruel nocturnal dancers, no more forgiving than living women are to a tired waltzer. Midnight chimes in the distance; from the midst of the long grass and tufted reeds, will o' the wisps dart forth in irregular and glittering flight and make the startled hunters flee.

The reeds part and first we see a tiny twinkling star, next a chaplet of flowers, then two startled blue eyes set in an alabaster oval, and, last of all, the whole of that beautiful, slender, chaste, and graceful form known as Adèle Dumilâtre; she is the Queen of the *Wilis*. With her characteristic melancholy grace she frolics in the pale star-light, which glides over the water like a white mist, poises herself on flexible branches, leaps on the tips of the grass, like Virgil's Camilla, who walked on wheat without bending it, and, arming herself with a magic wand, she evokes the other *Wilis*, her subjects, who come forth with their moonlight veils from the tufted reeds, clusters of verdure, and calixes of flowers to take part in the dance. She announces to them that they are to admit a new *Wili* that night. Indeed, Giselle's shade, stiff and pale in its transparent shroud, suddenly leaps from the ground at Myrtha's bidding (that is the Queen's name). The shroud falls and vanishes. Giselle, still benumbed from the icy damp of the dark abode she has left, makes a few tottering steps, looking fearfully at that tomb which bears her name. The *Wilis* take hold of her and lead her to the Queen, who herself crowns her with the magic garland of asphodel and verbena. At a touch of her wand, two little wings, as restless and quivering as those of Psyche, suddenly grow from the shoulders of the youthful shade who, for that matter, had no need of them. All at once, as though she wished to make up for the time wasted in that narrow bed fashioned of six long planks and two short ones, to quote the poet of *Leonore*, she bounds and rebounds in an intoxication of liberty and joy at no longer being weighed down by that thick coverlet of heavy earth, expressed in a sublime manner by Mme. Carlotta Grisi. The sound of footsteps is heard; the *Wilis* disperse and crouch behind the trees. The noise is made by some youthful peasants returning from a festival at a neighbouring village. They provide excellent quarry. The *Wilis* come forth from their hiding-place and try to entice them into the fatal circle; fortunately, the young men pay heed to the warnings of a wiser greybeard who knows the legend of the *Wilis*, and finds it most unusual to encounter a bevy of young beings in low-necked muslin dresses with stars on their foreheads and moth-like wings on their shoulders. The *Wilis*, disappointed, pursue them eagerly; this pursuit leaves the stage unoccupied.

Enter a young man, distracted, mad with sorrow, his eyes bathed in tears; it is Loys, or Albrecht, if you prefer it, who, escaping from his guardians' observation, comes to visit the tomb of his well-beloved. Giselle cannot resist the sweet evocation of so true and profound a grief; she parts the branches and leans forward towards her kneeling lover, her charming features aglow with love. To attract his attention, she picks some flowers which she first carries to her lips and throws her kisses to him on roses. The apparition flutters coquettishly, followed by Albrecht. Like Galatea, she flies towards the reeds and willows. The transverse flight, the leaning branch, the sudden disappearance when Albrecht wishes to take her in his arms, are new and original effects which achieve complete illusion. But now the *Wilis* return. Giselle tries to hide Albrecht; she knows too well the doom that awaits him if he is encountered by the terrible nocturnal dancers. They have found another quarry. Hilarion is lost in the forest; a treacherous path brings him back to the place from which he had only just fled. The *Wilis* seize hold of him, pass him from hand to hand: when one waltzer is tired, her place is taken by another, and always the infernal dance draws nearer to the lake. Hilarion, breathless, spent, falls at the Queen's knees and begs for mercy.

But there is no mercy; the pitiless phantom strikes him with a branch of rosemary and immediately his weary legs move convulsively. He rises and makes new efforts to escape; a dancing wall bars his passage, the *Wilis* make him giddy, push him on, and, as he lets go of the cold hand of the last dancer, he stumbles and falls into the pool— Good night, Hilarion! That will teach you not to meddle in other people's love affairs! May the fish in the lake eat your eyes!

What is Hilarion but one partner for so many dancing women? Less than nothing. A *Wili*, with that wonderful woman's instinct for finding a waltzer, discovers Albrecht in his hiding-place. What good fortune, and someone who is young, handsome and light-footed! "Come, Giselle, prove your mettle, make him dance to death!" It is useless for Giselle to beg for mercy, the Queen refuses to listen; and threatens to give Albrecht to the less scrupulous *Wilis* in her band. Giselle draws her lover towards the tomb she has just left, signs to him to embrace the cross and not to leave it whatever may befall. Myrtha resorts to an infernal and feminine device. She forces Giselle, who, in her capacity of subject, must obey, to execute the most seductive and most graceful poses. At first, Giselle dances timidly and reluctantly; then she is carried away by her instinct as a woman and a *Wili*; she bounds lightly and dances with so seductive a grace, such overpowering fascination, that the imprudent Albrecht leaves the protecting cross and goes towards her with outstretched arms, his eyes burning with desire and love. The fatal madness takes hold of him, he pirouettes, bounds, follows Giselle in her most hazardous leaps; the frenzy to which he gives way reveals a secret desire to die with his mistress and to follow the beloved shade to her tomb; but four o'clock strikes, a pale streak shows on the edge of the horizon. Dawn has come and with it the sun bringing deliverance and salvation. Flee, visions of the night; vanish, pale phantoms! A celestial joy gleams in Giselle's eyes: her lover will not die, the hour has passed. The beautiful Myrtha re-enters her water-lily. The *Wilis* fade away, melt into the ground and disappear. Giselle herself is drawn towards her tomb by an invisible power. Albrecht, distracted, clasps her in his arms, carries her, and, covering her with kisses, places her upon a flowered mound; but the earth will not relinquish its prey, the ground opens, the flowers bend over.... The hunting-horn resounds; Wilfrid anxiously seeks for his master. He walks a little in front of the Prince of Courland and Bathilde. However, the flowers cover Giselle, nothing can be seen but her little transparent hand ... this too disappears, all is over!—never again will Albrecht and Giselle see each other in this world.... The young man kneels by the mound, plucks a few flowers, and clasps them to his breast, then withdraws, his head resting on the shoulder of the beautiful Bathilde, who forgives and consoles him.

There, my dear poet, that, more or less, is how M. de Saint-Georges and I have adapted your charming legend with the help of M. Coralli, who composed the *pas*, groups, and attitudes of exquisite novelty and elegance. For interpreters we chose the three graces of the opera: Mlles. Carlotta Grisi, Adèle Dumilâtre, and Forster. Carlotta danced with a perfection, lightness, boldness, and a chaste and refined seductiveness, which places her in the first rank, between Elssler and Taglioni; as for pantomime, she exceeded all expectations; not a single conventional gesture, not one false movement; she was nature and artlessness personified. True, she has Perrot the Aerial for husband and teacher. Petipa was graceful, passionate, and touching; it is a long while since a dancer has given us so much pleasure or been so well received.

M. Adam's music is superior to the usual run of ballet music; it abounds in tunes and orchestral effects; it even includes a touching attention for lovers of difficult music, a very well-produced fugue. The second act solves the musical problem of graceful fantasy and is full of melody. As for the scenery, it is by Ciceri, who is unequalled for landscapes. The sunrise which marks the conclusion is wonderfully realistic.... La Carlotta was recalled to the sound of the applause of the whole house.

So, my dear Heine, your German *Wilis* have succeeded completely at the French Opera.

COMMENTS AND QUESTIONS

1. Notice that Gautier still considers France the country of the Enlightenment, though he himself supports the romantic movement. What would Voltaire have to say about this story?

26–1 ''Carlotta Grisi in Giselle,'' from the lithograph by J. Bouvier. (Crown Copyright, Victoria and Albert Museum, London)

2. What views of woman do you find in the story and the description? What is particularly romantic about these?
3. How would the actual performance of the dance add to the interpretation of this story?
4. If you have a chance to see a modern production of this ballet, compare it with the romantic one described here.

Romantic Nature

The forest scenery of the ballet *Giselle*, the precipices over which the inconsolable, restless Werther wanders, the wintry landscape in which Keats's knight is ''palely loitering'' testify to the intimate relationship between the natural world and the inner world of feeling in romantic art. Whereas Neoclassical heroes and heroines tended to bare their emotions in palace chambers or drawing rooms and to convey them through abstract analyses or mythological allusions, the romantic seems to feel that untamed woods, waterfalls, or mountains best correspond to his states of mind. Indeed the romantic sufferer as solitary wanderer may be found pouring out his heart to rocks, clouds, flowers, or waves, sensing that they, more than other human be-ings, feel as he does and are capable of reflecting the complexities of his sensitive soul.

For the "enlightened" European or American, "na-ture" meant essentially human nature, and man's natu-ral place was certainly among his fellow beings. Human institutions might be corrupt, but they could be changed for the better. Civilization brought with it many ills, but it was still humanity's greatest achieve-ment. In the shifting from this point of view to the ro-mantic one, Rousseau is once again a pivotal figure. Just as he went beyond a doctrine of liberty to one of individuality, so he went beyond a critique of the faults of civilized society to a radical questioning of its value. Rousseau's unique individual, inevitably misun-derstood, began to cherish his solitude. In his *Reveries of a Solitary Walker*, Rousseau describes the beauty of the Swiss landscape, its mountains and lakes, and his feeling of communing with it. He also describes his joy in abandoning himself to "pure sensation" as he experi-ences the lapping of a mountain lake's waves. To be able to abandon thought and feel oneself in unison with nature: a romantic ideal is born.

Ideas like returning to nature and living a natural (that is, nonartificial, nonurban) life began in the ro-mantic period to acquire the connotations that they have today. Changes in fashion were indicative of the trend. Partly because of Rousseau, women abandoned corsets and stiffened skirts for loose, flowing, "natural" attire, while the formal, symmetrical French garden (as at Versailles) gave way to the more luxuriant, chaotic, and "natural" English garden. Hiking and mountain climbing became for the first time popular pastimes in Europe. The vine-covered cottage replaced the palace as dream house. The life of the simple peasant was prized (at least in theory) above that of the sophisticated city dweller; and feeling, or richness of sensation, above in-tellectual capacity. There was even a concern for what we could call conservation and ecology. The New Eng-lander Henry David Thoreau actually carried out a solitary back-to-nature experiment, which he described both practically and emotionally in *Walden*.

The celebration of nature in romantic art took on varying aspects, corresponding to the individualistic temperaments of the artists. Romantic artists tended to depict nature as reflecting the sensations of their own souls. For some she consoled; to others she seemed in-different. To some she was picturesque; to others fear-ful and sublime. Some romantics, weary of cold and sterile eighteenth-century deism, found their religious yearnings satisfied in their relations with the natural world. Those drawn back to a devout Christianity found God's bounty and goodness reflected in nature; those who shunned organized religion tended toward a kind of pantheism, worshiping the spirit of nature it-self. Coleridge's poetry emphasizes the mystical, up-lifting aspects of nature. A poet like Keats, on the other hand, renders through language the pure sensuous feel-ings of an autumn day or a summer night, sensations comparable to those rendered in paint by the artist Turner. In music we also find composers imitating the sounds and feelings of nature with new orchestral tex-tures. Beethoven's Pastoral Symphony (no. 6) renders a wide range of moods from the natural world: sub-lime, mysterious, joyful, humble. It even imitates a thunderstorm.

Constable   Some romantic artists were more taken with the humble, everyday aspects of nature than with its sublime or mystical ones. Two of these are the poet William Wordsworth and his compatriot, the painter John Constable. Keen observers of the world around them, both were profoundly attached to their native countryside. Constable recorded his pleasure in simple phenomena: "The sound of water escaping from mill dams, willows, old rotten planks, slimy posts, brick-work. I love such things." The statement would have been inconceivable to a Renaissance or Neoclassical artist. It reveals not only a sensitivity to the textures of ordinary objects but also (especially in the escaping wa-ter and the rotten plants) a concern with mutability, the ways in which time changes things. Constable's pursuit of a means to capture his experience of the nat-ural world led him to study clouds, rain, light, and the weather. His early pictures are not far removed from the perpetual sunlight or storm of seventeenth- and eighteenth-century pictures; but, as his ideas and abili-ties mature, we see him open the landscape to capture the broken light of moving air and clouds. Colors be-come more intense, and the surface of paint is dense and wet. His brushstrokes give trees a shimmer and clouds a sense of movement and energy. Constable painted only those things that he knew and loved. The River Stour was completely familiar to him and he took comfort and refreshment from its mossy banks, bridges, and surrounding countryside (Color Plate VII).

Wordsworth   A poem by Wordsworth, written on his return to a spot near the medieval ruins of Tintern Abbey, in many ways parallels Constable's painting. The primary theme of both works is man's relationship to nature. "Lines Composed a Few Miles above Tintern Abbey" paints a landscape in its first stanza and meditates on the poet's interaction with it in the rest of the poem. But the landscape painted by Wordsworth is not a simple one; it is superimposed, as in a double-exposure photograph. From the first lines the reader is aware that Wordsworth is *also* viewing this scene with the

26-2   Millet, "The Sower," (Courtesy Museum of Fine Arts, Boston. Gift of Quincy A. Shaw)

memory of how he viewed it five years previously. A sense of the passage of time is imposed on the place. Because of this dual perception, the poet is able to reexperience his feelings as they were five years ago. At that time he was able to enjoy the purely sensational effects of nature; now he finds that the recollection, as well as the new vision of the natural landscape, has a profound effect on his moral and intellectual being. Both of these perceptions are conveyed to the reader. Another dimension is added as the poet looks, through the person of his sister Dorothy, into the future. The sensations from nature that they experience in the present will be sublimated and perpetuated as "lovely forms" in her mind's "mansion." In Wordsworth's mention of the possibility of his own death while his sister is still alive, we experience no sense of dread, or even sadness, but a sense of life as continuity. The life and death of the individual are part of the processes of nature. Still, it is through the individual's consciousness and judgment that nature is given meaning. Wordsworth's poem, like Constable's painting, brings out the interdependence between man's life cycle and nature.

Beauty, for Wordsworth, could also be found in the simple people who inhabited his countryside. One of Wordsworth's ideals was to let his poems speak for the inarticulate, to express the poetry latent in the woodsman, the peasant, or the country girl: such a poem is his "Solitary Reaper." Here again Wordsworth emphasizes the beauty to be found in the familiar and the near at hand. The young girl reaping is a part of nature, yet her song—whether of past events or eternal emotions—gives a continuity and a temporality to the natural world that it would not otherwise have. At the end the suggestion is made that the poet will perpetuate her song into the future.

A painter who saw the same poetry in simple people at their country tasks was the Frenchman Jean François Millet. Millet portrayed the French peasantry as virtuous, humane, and monumentally enduring. In his picture *The Sower* (Fig. 26-2) the figure is huge, the gesture simple, the colors earthy and rich. Unlike the romantic hero or heroine, the romantic peasant in poem and painting is anonymous and eternal, rather than individualistic. Like Wordsworth, Millet emphasizes the harmony between the workers of the field and their natural surroundings.

WILLIAM WORDSWORTH

Lines

COMPOSED A FEW MILES ABOVE TINTERN
ABBEY ON REVISITING THE BANKS OF THE
WYE DURING A TOUR, JULY 13, 1798[1]

Five years have passed; five summers, with the
    length
Of five long winters! and again I hear
These waters, rolling from their mountain-springs
With a soft inland murmur. Once again
Do I behold these steep and lofty cliffs,
That on a wild secluded scene impress
Thoughts of more deep seclusion; and connect
The landscape with the quiet of the sky.
The day is come when I again repose
Here, under this dark sycamore, and view
These plots of cottage-ground, these orchard tufts,
Which at this season, with their unripe fruits,
Are clad in one green hue, and lose themselves
'Mid groves and copses. Once again I see
These hedge-rows, hardly hedge-rows, little lines
Of sportive wood run wild: these pastoral farms,
Green to the very door; and wreaths of smoke
Sent up, in silence, from among the trees!
With some uncertain notice, as might seem
Of vagrant dwellers in the houseless woods,
Or of some hermit's cave, where by his fire
The hermit sits alone.
               These beauteous forms,
Through a long absence, have not been to me
As is a landscape to a blind man's eye;
But oft, in lonely rooms, and 'mid the din
Of towns and cities, I have owed to them,
In hours of weariness, sensations sweet,
Felt in the blood, and felt along the heart;
And passing even into my purer mind,
With tranquil restoration—feelings too
Of unremembered pleasure: such, perhaps,
As have no slight or trivial influence
On that best portion of a good man's life,
His little, nameless, unremembered acts

---

[1] Wordsworth wrote this poem at the age of twenty-eight; he had
first visited the ruins of the medieval abbey five years earlier while
on a solitary walking tour.

Of kindness and of love. Nor less, I trust,
To them I may have owed another gift,
Of aspect more sublime; that blessèd mood,
In which the burthen of the mystery,
In which the heavy and the weary weight
Of all this unintelligible world,
Is lightened—that serene and blessèd mood,
In which the affections gently lead us on—
Until, the breath of this corporeal frame
And even the motion of our human blood
Almost suspended, we are laid asleep
In body, and become a living soul;
While with an eye made quiet by the power
Of harmony, and the deep power of joy,
We see into the life of things.
                   If this
Be but a vain belief, yet, oh! how oft—
In darkness and amid the many shapes
Of joyless daylight; when the fretful stir
Unprofitable, and the fever of the world,
Have hung upon the beatings of my heart—
How oft, in spirit, have I turned to thee,
O sylvan Wye! thou wanderer through the woods,
How often has my spirit turned to thee!

And now, with gleams of half-extinguished thought,
With many recognitions dim and faint,
And somewhat of a sad perplexity,
The picture of the mind revives again;
While here I stand, not only with the sense
Of present pleasure, but with pleasing thoughts
That in this moment there is life and food
For future years. And so I dare to hope,
Though changed, no doubt, from what I was when first
I came among these hills; when like a roe
I bounded o'er the mountains, by the sides
Of the deep rivers, and the lonely streams,
Wherever nature led: more like a man
Flying from something that he dreads than one
Who sought the thing he loved. For nature then
(The coarser pleasures of my boyish days,
And their glad animal movements all gone by)
To me was all in all—I cannot paint
What then I was. The sounding cataract
Haunted me like a passion; the tall rock,
The mountain, and the deep and gloomy wood,

Their colors and their forms, were then to me
An appetite; a feeling and a love,
That had no need of a remoter charm,
By thought supplied, nor any interest
Unborrowed from the eye. That time is past,
And all its aching joys are now no more,
And all its dizzy raptures. Not for this
Faint I, nor mourn nor murmur; other gifts
Have followed; for such loss, I would believe,
Abundant recompense. For I have learned
To look on nature, not as in the hour
Of thoughtless youth; but hearing oftentimes
The still, sad music of humanity,
Nor harsh nor grating, though of ample power
To chasten and subdue. And I have felt
A presence that disturbs me with the joy
Of elevated thoughts; a sense sublime
Of something far more deeply interfused,
Whose dwelling is the light of setting suns,
And the round ocean and the living air,
And the blue sky, and in the mind of man:
A motion and a spirit, that impels
All thinking things, all objects of all thought,
And rolls through all things. Therefore am I still
A lover of the meadows and the woods
And mountains; and of all that we behold
From this green earth; of all the mighty world
Of eye, and ear—both what they half create,
And what perceive; well pleased to recognize
In nature and the language of the sense
The anchor of my purest thoughts, the nurse,
The guide, the guardian of my heart, and soul
Of all my moral being.
               Nor perchance,
If I were not thus taught, should I the more
Suffer my genial spirits to decay:
For thou art with me here upon the banks
Of this fair river; thou my dearest Friend,[2]
My dear, dear Friend; and in thy voice I catch
The language of my former heart, and read
My former pleasures in the shooting lights
Of thy wild eyes. Oh! yet a little while
May I behold in thee what I was once,
My dear, dear Sister! and this prayer I make,

---

[2] His sister Dorothy.

Knowing that Nature never did betray
The heart that loved her; 'tis her privilege,
Through all the years of this our life, to lead
From joy to joy: for she can so inform
The mind that is within us, so impress
With quietness and beauty, and so feed
With lofty thoughts, that neither evil tongues,
Rash judgments, nor the sneers of selfish men,
Nor greetings where no kindness is, nor all
The dreary intercourse of daily life,
Shall e'er prevail against us, or disturb
Our cheerful faith that all which we behold
Is full of blessings. Therefore let the moon
Shine on thee in thy solitary walk;
And let the misty mountain-winds be free
To blow against thee: and, in after years,
When these wild ecstasies shall be matured
Into a sober pleasure; when thy mind
Shall be a mansion for all lovely forms,
Thy memory be as a dwelling-place
For all sweet sounds and harmonies; oh! then,
If solitude, or fear, or pain, or grief,
Should be thy portion, with what healing thoughts
Of tender joy wilt thou remember me,
And these my exhortations! Nor, perchance—
If I should be where I no more can hear
Thy voice, nor catch from thy wild eyes these gleams
Of past existence—wilt thou then forget
That on the banks of this delightful stream
We stood together; and that I, so long
A worshiper of Nature, hither came
Unwearied in that service; rather say
With warmer love—oh! with far deeper zeal
Of holier love. Nor wilt thou then forget,
That after many wanderings, many years
Of absence, these steep woods and lofty cliffs,
And this green pastoral landscape, were to me
More dear, both for themselves and for thy sake!

QUESTIONS

1. Find all of the places with the word *nature* in the
   poem. Does it always have the same meaning? How
   would you define Wordsworth's conception of
   nature?

2. How does the poet describe the moral effect that nature has on him?
3. With what images does he convey the differences between his present and former selves?
4. What is the role of his sister in the poem?
5. Do you find any other points of comparison with Constable? What are the different processes that a painter and a poet must go through to render a landscape?

WILLIAM WORDSWORTH

The Solitary Reaper

Behold her, single in the field,
Yon solitary Highland Lass!
Reaping and singing by herself;
Stop here, or gently pass!
Alone she cuts and binds the grain,
And sings a melancholy strain;
O listen! for the Vale profound
Is overflowing with the sound.

No Nightingale did ever chaunt
More welcome notes to weary bands
Of travellers in some shady haunt,
Among Arabian sands:
A voice so thrilling ne'er was heard
In spring-time from the Cuckoo-bird,
Breaking the silence of the seas
Among the farthest Hebrides.

Will no one tell me what she sings?—
Perhaps the plaintive numbers flow

For old, unhappy, far-off things,
And battles long ago:
Or is it some more humble lay,
Familiar matter of to-day?
Some natural sorrow, loss, or pain,
That has been, and may be again?

Whate'er the theme, the Maiden sang
As if her song could have no ending;
I saw her singing at her work,
And o'er the sickle bending;—
I listened, motionless and still;
And, as I mounted up the hill,
The music in my heart I bore,
Long after it was heard no more.

QUESTIONS

1. What is the difference in verse form between this poem and "Lines Composed a Few Miles above Tintern Abbey"? Why is this appropriate?
2. How much do we know about this girl after reading the poem? How would you describe Wordsworth's vision of her?
3. What is the significance of the song? What is the theme of the poem?
4. Would it be possible to write a poem on this subject in the late twentieth century? How would it differ from this one?
5. Judging from your experience of these poems and paintings, how does our present concept of nature resemble that of the romantics, and how does it differ?

FROM THE ENLIGHTENMENT TO ROMANTICISM: CONTINUITIES

The two great political revolutions at the end of the eighteenth century, the French and the American, not only transformed the leading philosophies of government in Western Europe but dramatically altered some basic conceptions about the nature of human beings as well. In terms of the humanities, as we have seen, these revolutions embodied the ideas of the Enlightenment while exciting the passions of romanticism.

Enlightenment Style and Ideals The primarily middle-class philosophes challenged once and for all the medieval belief that everyone had his place in a hierarchical society, a belief that still held sway in the absolutist seventeenth century. Human beings, they argued, were "naturally" equal and thus were entitled to certain natural rights. Thomas Jefferson, in a sense an American philosophe, defined these as life, liberty, and the pursuit of happiness. The writers and the artists of the Enlightenment submitted everything—social customs and institutions, religious beliefs, passions—to the cold light of reason. This produced, in clear, often satiric style, a method of exposing pretentions and fanaticism, reducing them to the dimensions of reason.

If the seventeenth century was an age for the grandiose in the arts, the eighteenth was an age for the petite and well ordered. Neoclassicism, no longer inspired by the baroque sense of splendor, became in the Enlightenment less ornate and somewhat colder and more mechanical. Eighteenth-century artists were more interested in sensuality than in love; in humble virtues more than in religious yearnings.

In our post-Freudian era we can now easily see the limitations in the Enlightenment's view of man. Human beings cannot be defined merely as atoms of reason, as many of the philosophes seemed to suppose. We also cannot share their easy optimism about progress through education and science. Yet many of the ideals first formulated in the Enlightenment are still at the basis of some of our thinking. Toleration of the beliefs of others, human equality, basic human rights, the freedom to challenge authority and to think for oneself—whatever flaws one may find in the Enlightenment's formulation of these ideals, their impact has been considerable.

Romantic Changes The romantics adapted the ideals of the Enlightenment to their own purposes. Rejecting the belief that reason is the primary human faculty, they developed a current of sentimentality already present in the eighteenth century. The transitional Jean-Jacques Rousseau makes the Enlightenment's belief in the natural goodness of human beings the basis for a romantic apology for feeling above reason and for the supremacy of the unique individual, thus laying the basis for the misunderstood romantic sufferer and the titanic romantic hero. Napoleon, the rationalistic administrator, becomes, as in David's painting, the passionate, dashing, almost superhuman general, comparable to Byron's Prometheus, the savior of mankind.

We have seen how the rationalistic goals of liberty, equality, and fraternity became passionate statements in the hands of romantic artists. Open to the entire range of human emotions, the romantics also tended to plumb the depths as well as the heights of experience. Goya, for example, who had lived through the disasters of a brutal war rather than with the theories of revolution, portrayed the demonic side of human nature while showing an intense compassion for the victims of exploitation and tyranny. The desire to portray the extremes and varieties of human passions greatly enriched the range and textures of romantic visual, literary, and musical art. The artists' need for individuality of expression also caused them to find the neat balances and rules of Neoclassical art insufficient. Beethoven expanded both classical structures and orchestration, Delacroix experimented with color and composition, and Whitman abandoned the meters and vocabulary considered suitable for poetry so that he could freely "sing himself."

Romantic Continuities Romantic exuberance for social causes, individualism, and emotionalism are still with us, especially among the young. The modern concept of the artist as a supersensitive being—more likely to be misunderstood by, and at odds with, his society than in harmony with it—was born with the romantics. The romantic concept of love and the romantic views of women have also, for good or ill, profoundly influenced our own.

We have seen that love, for the romantics, resembled an infinite yearning that could never really be satisfied by a finite human being. Romantic lovers in literature and life were doomed to desire the unattainable and to suffer—or to throw themselves into one passionate love affair after another. They viewed a stable marriage and family life either as too bourgeois and constricting or as a kind of dreamy ideal. The romantic lover might idealize the domestic and virtuous, or the mysterious and ethereal woman; the *femme fatale*, or temptress, also appears throughout romantic art. The romantic ballet, with the predominance that it gave to the ballerina, was particularly suited to this fascination with women. In the early nineteenth century women also began to explore in their own way the prevalent ideal of freedom. The notion of women's liberation begins here; we will see how it becomes more systematic in the late nineteenth century.

The modern reverence for unspoiled nature began in the romantic period. The romantics were particularly prone to see their own emotions reflected in the natural world or to look on nature as a mother, a consolation for their troubles. Many romantics shunned organized religions, finding a substitute in the worship of nature, but even orthodox Christians found that they could approach God through immersion in His works. As they idealized nature, the romantics idealized the simple life of the "natural" peasant, unspoiled by the corruptions of the modern world. For many of those peasants, however, the industrialization of Europe would mean a dramatic uprooting. It would also necessitate new responses in thought and style from the humanities.

PART SEVEN

INDUSTRIALISM
AND THE HUMANITIES:
THE MIDDLE AND
LATE NINETEENTH CENTURY

27

THE INDUSTRIAL REVOLUTION AND NEW SOCIAL THOUGHT

Already at the turn of the nineteenth century, while Wordsworth was musing on the ruins of Tintern Abbey and celebrating his solitary reaper, the face of rural England was in a state of transformation. Eighteenth-century country towns like Manchester were fast becoming makeshift cities for hundreds of thousands of poor workers who sought employment in the new factories whose belching smokestacks polluted the landscape for miles around. A few years before Wordsworth's death in 1850, engineers lay down the iron rails that were to bring the first trains across the wheat fields.

The Industrial Revolution could easily be considered the most important event in the history of the human race. In all previous societies known to man, periods of population growth were necessarily succeeded by periods of contraction caused by disease and starvation. After 1750, however, the productive capacity of the world rapidly increased to the point where population could expand unceasingly and at the same time enjoy an improved standard of living. What the so-called revolution entailed was basically the massive substitution of machines and new techniques of production for human labor. The result was that, depending on the commodity, the output of the individual worker expanded five, fifty, a hundred, and even a thousand or more times, causing accumulations of goods undreamed of earlier. That human beings in such a world continued to live in dire poverty came to appear either as the fault of a backward regional system of production or as an unjust method of distributing the rewards—or a combination of both.

The Industrial Revolution was not, of course, an event like the political revolution in France that took place within a few years' time. It exerted its effect on different areas at different times. By 1785 clearly underway in the British Isles, significant industrial development occurred on the continent only after 1815, and before 1900 it still remained limited to Western Europe, parts of North America, and Japan. Even today certain parts of the world have yet to undergo their industrial revolution.

England in the Lead   There are a number of reasons for English precedence in industrial development. By the early eighteenth century Englishmen (with the Dutch) had the highest standard of living in the world. After several centuries of applying innovative techniques, English agricultural producers were able to supply food cheaply and in abundance while still making a profit. This efficiency in agriculture also liberated a large percentage of the working population for other pursuits. English government compared with continental monarchies was inexpensive, and the low tax burden left most of the money in the pockets of those who earned it. There was consequently a good deal of money available for investment and consumption. Moreover, whereas absolutist monarchies on the continent regulated economic life closely, productive enterprise in England was relatively free; personal initiative and experimentation were encouraged. Finally, in the coming age of the machine, England was particularly

favored with its enormous deposits of a cheap fuel, coal.

The breakthrough in industrialism first came in cotton, a cloth industry that, compared with wool or silk, was very new. Because of its low cost relative to that of wool and silk, the market for cotton cloth was large, and it happened that cotton could be worked more easily by machine than by hand. By the late eighteenth century the demand for cotton cloth both in England and abroad was such that the raw material came into short supply. Eli Whitney's cotton gin remedied the major bottleneck in production of raw cotton, and the plantation economy of the American South soared from the 1790s on.

The mechanization of cotton production encouraged invention and investment in other areas of the economy. By the end of the eighteenth century the English had developed a relatively efficient steam engine, were able to mine coal and manufacture steel in impressive quantities, and were increasingly utilizing new chemical discoveries for industrial purposes. The nineteenth century in Europe was marked by the continued progress of British industry and by the desperate efforts of continental and American competitors to imitate and catch up with Britain.

Social Effects of Industrialization   The social consequences of industrialization were enormous. Within decades hundreds of thousands of workers moved into the industrial centers, overwhelming the capacity of the cities to absorb them. Shanty towns grew up on the outskirts where the new workers lived in crowded unsanitary conditions. The machines not only demanded regimentation of work but also reduced the need for skill or physical force. Especially in the cloth industry most operations involved in mechanized production could be performed by children, who were cheaper to hire than adults. By the middle 1820s a small boy working two looms could produce fifteen times more than an adult laborer working by hand.

Unable to support the family even with both mother and father working, parents were forced to send their children into the factories. Children four and five years of age worked from twelve to sixteen hours, six days a week, for pennies. Often forbidden to sit down during their hours of work, they were subject to the brutality of the overseer for the slightest infraction. In the case of babies too young to work, desperate parents, unable to pay for babysitters, resorted to "Mother's Helper" to drug the baby from early morning until late at night when they returned home. In the seething tenements of workers' quarters, twisted bodies and early death were common.

Included in the report of the "Committee on Factory Children's Labour," 1831–1832, was the following interview with a certain Samuel Coulson.

5047. At what time in the morning, in the brisk[1] time, did those girls go to the mills?

In the brisk time, for about six weeks, they have gone at 3 o'clock in the morning, and ended at 10, or nearly half past at night.

5049. What intervals were allowed for rest or refreshment during those nineteen hours of labour?

Breakfast a quarter of an hour, and dinner half an hour, and drinking a quarter of an hour.

5051. Was any of that time taken up in cleaning the machinery?

They generally had to do what they call dry down; sometimes this took the whole of the time at breakfast or drinking, and they were to get their dinner or breakfast as they could; if not, it was brought home.

5054. Had you not great difficulty in awakening your children to this excessive labour?

Yes, in the early time we had them to take up asleep and shake them, when we got them on the floor to dress them, before we could get them off to their work; but not so in the common hours.

5056. Supposing they had been a little too late, what would have been the consequence during the long hours?

They were quartered in the longest hours, the same as in the shortest time.

5057. What do you mean by quartering?

A quarter was taken off.

5058. If they had been how much too late?

Five minutes.

5059. What was the length of time they could be in bed during those long hours?

It was near 11 o'clock before we could get them into bed after getting a little victuals, and then at morning my mistress used to stop up all night, for fear that we could not get them ready for the time; sometimes we have gone to bed, and one of us generally awoke.

5060. What time did you get them up in the morning?

In general me or my mistress got up at 2 o'clock to dress them.

5061. So that they had not above four hours' sleep at this time?

No, they had not.

5062. For how long together was it?

About six weeks it held; it was only done when the throng was very much on; it was not often that.

5063. The common hours of labour were from 6 in the morning till half-past eight at night?

Yes.

5064. With the same intervals for food?

Yes, just the same.

5065. Were the children excessively fatigued by this labour?

Many times; we have cried often when we have given them the little victualling we had to give them; we had to shake them, and they have fallen to sleep with the victuals in their mouths many a time.

5066. Had any of them any accident in consequence of this labour?

Yes, my eldest daughter when she went first there; she had been about five weeks, and used to fettle the frames when they were running, and my eldest girl agreed with one of the others to fettle hers that time, that she would do her work; while she was learning more about the work, the overlooker came by and said, "Ann, what are you doing there?" she said, "I am doing it for my companion, in order that I may know more about it," he said, "Let go, drop it this minute," and the cog caught her forefinger nail, and screwed it off below the knuckle, and she was five weeks in Leeds Infirmary.

5067. Has she lost that finger?

It is cut off at the second joint.

5068. Were her wages paid during that time?

As soon as the accident happened the wages were totally stopped; indeed, I did not know which way to get her cured, and I do not know how it would have been cured but for the Infirmary.

5069. Were the wages stopped at the half-day?

She was stopped a quarter of a day; it was done about four o'clock.

5072. Did this excessive term of labour occasion much cruelty also?

Yes, with being so very much fatigued the strap was very frequently used.

5073. Have any of your children been strapped?

Yes, every one.

---

[1] Busy.

Despite the terrible conditions of life suggested in reports like this, many historians maintain that, on the whole, conditions of the laboring poor in England improved with the Industrial Revolution. Many of the poor preferred the urban slums to those in the rural districts where their misery was compounded by chronic underemployment and hunger.

Liberalism

Indeed, while no doubt regretting the sufferings of the poor, an important group of English and continental thinkers called the liberals believed that these were minor evils compared with the greater good attained by industrialization. Espousing the Enlightenment values of liberty and equality, thinkers like Adam Smith and David Ricardo argued that there was a kind of law of human nature: if individuals were allowed to follow their own self-enlightened interest, the general good and liberty of all would best be served. The state should interfere as little as possible with the exercise of individual judgment, aside from keeping order and protecting property; the economy as well as other aspects of society should be in the control of private citizens. Wages would always tend to the subsistence level because, when workers rise above this, they have more children who devour the surplus, thus forcing the family income down again. However, in a free society, the liberals argued optimistically, individuals with initiative have the opportunity of leaving this condition and joining the ranks of the successful.

Although thinkers of this stamp violently opposed it, public opinion in the 1830s and 1840s finally forced the English government to pass legislation to remedy the worst abuses. As the continent came to industrialize, government there, too, stepped in to ameliorate the condition of workers to a degree. Some of the major proponents of this legislation belonged to a new breed of liberals. These thinkers had come to realize that, if liberty and equality were truly the goals of a society, the major threats to those principles did not come so much from the government as from private pressures. A worker's freedom was essentially limited to starving or accepting the conditions offered him by an employer. The role of government, as they began to conceive it, was that of a mediator, which through its laws would prevent the oppression of one individual by another. The ideal remained, as earlier, to foster individual freedom, but the experience of the first fifty years of industrialism had shown that, paradoxically, freedom had in certain respects to be restricted by legislation in order to maximize it for everyone. The new liberals also moved gradually to the position that the lower classes must also be given the vote. Political power was not, as for earlier liberals, a privilege achieved by the successful; rather, it was a basic right. Thus, the newer liberalism endeavored to incorporate the workers into the establishment.

From the opening decades of the nineteenth century, however, there were critics of the industrial economy who believed that the major source of its evils came from the fact of private property. As long as the principle of private property was regarded as sacred, no amount of legislation, even by a government in which workers participated, could guarantee a just society. To a varying degree these critics maintained that basic industry and essential services should be taken out of private hands and operated by the community for the common welfare. Some of these thinkers, like Charles Fourier (1772–1837) went further, devising utopian communities where each would do the work for which he or she was best suited and would receive the fruits of the collective labor according to need.

Karl Marx

Doubtless the most powerful enemy of laissez-faire capitalism, that is, unregulated free enterprise, was Karl Marx (1818–1883). Although Marx expressed his theories in philosophical and economic language, at their core is a sense of moral outrage at a system of distribution in which millions, living on the borderline of subsistence, slave so that a few thousands can wallow in luxury and indolence. Marx believed, however, that bourgeois capitalism was a necessary stage in a historical development in which justice would triumph.

Human history for Marx was characterized by a series of economic organizations, the more recent evolving out of the preceding as a result of class conflict. Slavery, the economic system of the ancient world, was brought to an end because of slave revolts. The ancient economy was replaced by a feudal one in which serfs, who were not slaves because they were tied to the land and could not be sold, worked for the benefit of the landlords. According to Marx, the continued oppression of the serf by feudal lords induced numbers of these laborers to flee. These runaways constituted the founders of the medieval merchant class. From the sixteenth century on, this merchant class, or bourgeoisie, gained increasing power until finally in England in the 1640s, in France in 1789, and in Germany in 1848, they were successful in overthrowing the feudal order and establishing themselves as the masters of the economy. The Industrial Revolution was the triumph of the new oppressors; the development of the factory brought into being a new class of oppressed, the proletariat. These were the workers, men, women and children, who possessed nothing but the labor of their bodies.

In Marx's theory, fierce competition among the capitalists—those who control the means of production and the goods—would result in the concentration of wealth into fewer and fewer hands and the swelling of the worker ranks by bourgeois who go under. At the same time the need to keep up profit margins in a situation of limited markets encourages more intensive exploitation of the workers. Whereas formerly the oppressed classes had been widely diffused, the nature of industrialism brings them together; then they gradually become aware of the injustice of the system and of their own power.

Marx firmly believed that the conflicts between classes were nearing a crisis point. A revolution of the masses against the exploiters was inevitable. When that occurred, Marx thought, the course of human history would change. Because the proletariat made up the vast majority of the people, this revolution would mark the end of class struggle and a new society would result, where all would live in harmony with one another.

Although Marx developed his theories in more elaborate form in his later writings, *The Communist Manifesto*, composed in 1848, represents his basic positions most eloquently. Written in collaboration with his friend Friedrich Engels, the work was published in the very year when Europe was swept by a revolutionary fervor that threatened to destroy most of its major monarchies. In the long run all of the revolutions failed, and in none of them did Marx's thought serve as

a platform for a significant group of revolutionaries. Marxism did not become a major ideological force until the twentieth century. (The following selections from *The Communist Manifesto* were translated by Samuel Moore.)

KARL MARX AND FRIEDRICH ENGELS
from *The Communist Manifesto*

INTRODUCTION

A spectre is haunting Europe—the spectre of Communism. All the powers of old Europe have entered into a holy alliance to exorcise this spectre: Pope and Czar, Metternich and Guizot, French Radicals and German political police.

Where is the party in opposition that has not been decried as communistic by its opponents in power? Where is the Opposition that has not hurled back the branding reproach of Communism, against the more advanced opposition parties as well as against its reactionary adversaries?

Two things result from this fact:

1. Communism is already acknowledged by all European powers to be itself a power.

2. It is high time that Communists should openly, in the face of the whole world, publish their views, their aims, their tendencies, and meet this nursery tale of the spectre of Communism with a manifesto of the party itself.

To this end, Communists of various nationalities have assembled in London, and sketched the following manifesto, to be published in the English, French, German, Italian, Flemish and Danish languages.

CHAPTER I
BOURGEOIS AND PROLETARIANS

The history of all hitherto existing society is the history of class struggles.

Freeman and slave, patrician and plebeian, lord and serf, guild-master and journeyman, in a word, oppressor and oppressed, stood in constant opposition to one another, carried on an uninterrupted, now hidden, now open fight, a fight that each time ended, either in a revolutionary reconstitution of society at large, or in the common ruin of the contending classes.

In the earlier epochs of history, we find almost everywhere a complicated arrangement of society into various orders, a manifold gradation of social rank. In ancient Rome we have patricians, knights, plebeians, slaves; in the Middle Ages, feudal lords, vassals, guild-masters, journeymen, apprentices, serfs; in almost all of these classes, again, subordinate gradations.

The modern bourgeois society that has sprouted from the ruins of feudal society has not done away with class antagonisms. It has but established new classes, new conditions of oppression, new forms of struggle in place of the old ones.

Our epoch, the epoch of the bourgeoisie, possesses, however, this distinctive feature: it has simplified the class antagonisms. Society as a whole is more and more splitting up into two great hostile camps, into two great classes directly facing each other—bourgeoisie and proletariat.

From the serfs of the Middle Ages sprang the chartered Burghers of the earliest towns. From these burgesses the first elements of the bourgeoisie were developed.

The discovery of America, the rounding of the Cape, opened up fresh ground for the rising bourgeoisie. The East-Indian and Chinese markets, the colonization of America, trade with the colonies, the increase in the means of exchange and in commodities generally, gave to commerce, to navigation, to industry, an impulse never before known, and thereby, to the revolutionary element in the tottering feudal society, a rapid development.

The feudal system of industry, in which industrial production was monopolized by closed guilds, now no longer sufficed for the growing wants of the new markets. The manufacturing system took its place. The guild-masters were pushed aside by the manufacturing middle class; division of labour between the different corporate guilds vanished in the face of division of labour in each single workshop.

Meantime the markets kept ever growing, the demand ever rising. Even manufacture no longer sufficed. Thereupon, steam and machinery revolutionized industrial production. The place of manufacture was taken by the giant, modern industry, the place of the industrial middle class by industrial millionaires, the leaders of whole industrial armies, the modern bourgeois.

Modern industry has established the world market, for which the discovery of America paved the way. This market has given an immense development to commerce, to navigation, to communication by land. This development has, in its turn, reacted on the extension of industry; and in proportion as industry, commerce, navigation, railways extended, in the same proportion the bourgeoisie developed, increased its capital, and pushed into the background every class handed down from the Middle Ages.

We see, therefore, how the modern bourgeoisie is itself the product of a long course of development, of a series of revolutions in the modes of production and of exchange.

Each step in the development of the bourgeoisie was accompanied by a corresponding political advance of that class. An oppressed class under the sway of the feudal nobility, it became an armed and self-governing association in the medieval commune; here independent urban republic (as in Italy and Germany), there taxable "third estate" of the monarchy (as in France); afterwards, in the period of manufacture proper, serving either the semi-feudal or the absolute monarchy as a counterpoise against the nobility, and, in fact, cornerstone of the great monarchies in general, the bourgeoisie has at last, since the establishment of modern industry and of the world market, conquered for itself, in the modern parliamentary State, exclusive political sway. The executive of the modern State is but a committee for managing the common affairs of the whole bourgeoisie.

The bourgeoisie, historically, has played a most revolutionary part.

The bourgeoisie, wherever it has got the upper hand, has put an end to all feudal, patriarchal, idyllic relations. It has pitilessly torn asunder the motley feudal ties that bound man to his "natural superiors," and has left no other nexus between man and man than naked self-interest, than callous "cash payment." It has drowned the most heavenly ecstasies of religious fervour, of chivalrous enthusiasm, of Philistine sentimentalism, in the icy water of egotistic calculation. It has resolved personal worth in exchange value and in place of the numberless indefeasible chartered freedoms has set up that single, unconscionable freedom—Free Trade. In one word, for exploitation veiled by religious and political illusions it has substituted naked, shameless, direct, brutal exploitation. . . .

The need of a constantly-expanding market for its products chases the bourgeoisie over the whole surface of the globe. It must get a footing everywhere, settle everywhere, establish connections everywhere.

The bourgeoisie has through its exploitation of the world market given a cosmopolitan character to production and consumption in every country. To the great chagrin of reactionaries, it has drawn from under the feet of industry the national ground on which it stood. Old established national industries have been destroyed and are still being destroyed every day. They are dislodged by new industries, whose introduction becomes a life and death question for all civilized nations, by industries that no longer work up indigenous raw material, but raw material drawn from the remotest zones; industries whose products are consumed, not only at home, but in every quarter of the globe. In place of the old wants, satisfied by the production of the country, we find new wants, requiring for their satisfaction the products of distant lands and climes. In place of the old local and national seclusion and self-sufficiency, we have exchange in every direction, universal interdependence of nations. And as in material, so also in intellectual production. The intellectual creations of individual nations become common property. National onesidedness and narrowmindedness become more and more impossible, and from the numerous national and local literatures there arises a world literature.

The bourgeoisie, by the rapid improvement of all instruments of production, by the immensely facilitated means of communication, draws all, even the most barbarian, nations into civilization. The cheap prices of its commodities are the heavy artillery with which it batters down all Chinese walls, with which it forces the barbarians' intensely obstinate hatred of foreigners to capitulate. It compels all nations, on pain of extinction, to adopt the bourgeois mode of production; it compels them to introduce what it calls civilization into their midst, i.e., to become bourgeois themselves. In one word, it creates a world after its own image. . . .

We see then: the means of production and of exchange, on whose foundation the bourgeoisie built itself up, were generated in feudal society. At a certain stage in the development of these means of production and of exchange, the conditions under which feudal society produced and exchanged, the feudal organization of agriculture and manufacturing industry, in one word, the feudal relations of property, became no longer compatible with the already developed productive forces; they hindered production instead of promoting it; they became so many fetters. They had to be burst asunder; they were burst asunder.

Into their place stepped free competition, accompanied by a social and political constitution adapted to it, and by the economical and political sway of the bourgeois class.

A similar movement is going on before our own eyes. Modern bourgeois society with its relations of production, of exchange and of property, a society that has conjured up such gigantic means of production and of exchange, is like the sorcerer who is no longer able to control the powers of the nether world whom he has called up by his spells. For many a decade past the history of industry and commerce is but the history of the revolt of modern productive forces against modern conditions of production, against the property relations that are the conditions for the existence of the bourgeoisie and of its rule. It is enough to mention the commercial crises that by their periodical return put the existence of the entire bourgeois society on its trial, each time more threateningly. In these crises a great part, not only of the existing products, but also of the previously-created productive forces, are periodically destroyed. In these crises there breaks out an epidemic that, in all earlier epochs, would have seemed an absurdity—the epidemic of over-production. Society suddenly finds itself put back into a state of momentary barbarism; it appears as if a famine, a universal war of devastation, had cut off the supply of every means of subsistence; industry and commerce seem to be destroyed. And why? Because there is too much civilization, too much means of subsistence, too much industry, too much commerce. The productive forces at the disposal of society no longer tend to promote bourgeois civilization and bourgeois property; on the contrary, they have become too powerful for these relations, by which they are fettered, and so soon as they overcome these fetters, they bring disorder into the whole of bourgeois society, endanger the existence of bourgeois property. The conditions of bourgeois society are too narrow to contain the wealth created by them. And how does the bourgeoisie get over these crises? On the one hand by enforced destruction of a mass of productive forces; on the other, by the conquest of new markets, and by the more thorough exploitation of the old ones. That is to say, by paving the way for more extensive and more destructive crises, and by diminishing the means whereby crises are prevented.

The weapons with which the bourgeoisie felled feudalism to the ground are now turned against the bourgeoisie itself.

But not only has the bourgeoisie forged the weapons that bring death to itself; it has also called into existence the men who are to wield those weapons—the modern working class—the proletarians.

In proportion as the bourgeoisie, i.e., capital, is developed, in the same proportion is the proletariat developed—the modern class of workers, who live only so long as they find work, and who find work only so long as their labour increases capital. These workmen, who must sell themselves piecemeal, are a commodity, like every other article of commerce, and are consequently exposed to all the vicissitudes of competition, to all the fluctuations of the market.

Owing to the extensive use of machinery and to division of labour, the work of the proletarians has lost all independent character, and, consequently, all charm for the workman. He becomes a mere appendage of the machine, and it is only the most simple, most monotonous, and most easily acquired knack, that is required of him. Hence, the cost of production of a workman is restricted, almost entirely, to the means of subsistence that he requires for his maintenance, and for the propagation of his race. But the price of a commodity, and therefore also of labour, is equal to its cost of production. In proportion, therefore, as the repulsiveness of the work increases, the wage decreases. Nay, more, in proportion as the use of machinery and division of labour increases, in the same proportion the burden of toil also increases, whether by prolongation of the working hours, by increase of the work exacted in a given time, or by increased speed of the machinery, etc.

Modern industry has converted the little workshop of the patriarchal master into the great factory of the industrial capitalist. Masses of labourers, crowded into the factory, are organized like soldiers. As privates of the industrial army they are placed under the command of a perfect hierarchy of officers and sergeants. Not only are they slaves of the bourgeois class, and of the bourgeois State; they are daily and hourly enslaved by the machine, by the overlooker, and, above all, by the individual bourgeois manufacturer himself. The more openly this despotism proclaims gain to be its end and aim, the more petty, the more hateful and the more embittering it is.

The less the skill and exertion of strength implied in manual labour, in other words, the more modern industry becomes developed, the more is the labour of men superseded by that of women. Differences of age and sex have no longer any distinctive social validity for the working class. All are instruments of labour, more or less expensive to use, according to their age and sex.

No sooner is the exploitation of the labourer by the manufacturer so far at an end that he receives his wages in cash, than he is set upon by the other portions of the bourgeoisie, the landlord, the shopkeeper, the pawnbroker, etc.

The former lower strata of the middle class—the small manufacturers, traders and persons living on small incomes, the handicraftsmen and peasants—all these sink gradually into the proletariat, partly because their diminutive capital does not suffice for the scale on which modern industry is carried on and is swamped in the competition with the large capitalists, partly because their specialized skill is rendered worthless by new methods of production. Thus the proletariat is recruited from all classes of the population.

But with the development of industry the proletariat not only increases in number; it becomes concentrated in greater masses, its strength grows, and it feels that strength more. The various interests and conditions of life within the ranks of the proletariat are more and more equalized, in proportion as machinery obliterates all distinctions of labour, and nearly everywhere reduces wages to the same low level. The growing competition among the bourgeois, and the resulting commercial crises, make the wages of the workers ever more fluctuating. The unceasing improvement of machinery, ever more rapidly developing, makes their livelihood more and more precarious; the collisions between individual workmen and individual bourgeois take more and more the character of collisions between two classes. Thereupon the workers begin to form combinations against the bourgeois; they club together in order to keep up the rate of wages; they themselves found permanent associations in order to make provision beforehand for these occasional revolts. Here and there the contest breaks out into riots. Now and then the workers are victorious, but only for a time. The real fruit of their battles lies, not in the immediate result, but in the ever-expanding union of the workers. This union is helped on by the improved means of communication that are created by modern industry and that place the workers of different localities in contact with one another. It was just this contact that was needed to centralize the numerous local struggles, all of the same character, into one national struggle between classes. But every class struggle is a political struggle. And that union, to attain which the Burghers of the Middle Ages, with their miserable highways, required centuries, the modern proletarians, thanks to railways, achieve in a few years.

This organization of the proletarians into a class, and consequently into a political party, is continually being upset again by the competition between the workers themselves. But it ever rises up again, stronger, firmer, mightier. It compels legislative recognition of particular interests of the workers, by taking advantage of the divisions among the bourgeoisie itself. Thus the ten-hours' bill in England was carried.

Altogether, collisions between the classes of the old society further in many ways the course of development of the proletariat. The bourgeoisie finds itself involved in a constant battle. At first with the aristocracy; later on, with those portions of the bourgeoisie itself, whose interests have become antagonistic to the progress of industry; at all times with the bourgeoisie of foreign countries. In all these battles it sees itself compelled to appeal to the proletariat, to ask for its help, and thus, to drag it into the political arena. The bourgeoisie itself, therefore, supplies the proletariat with its own elements of political and general education, in other words, it furnishes the proletariat with weapons for fighting the bourgeoisie.

Further, as we have already seen, entire sections of the ruling classes are, by the advance of industry, precipitated into the proletariat, or are at least threatened in their conditions of existence. These also supply the proletariat with fresh elements of enlightenment and progress.

Finally, in times when the class struggle nears the decisive hour, the process of dissolution going on within the ruling class, in fact within the whole range of old society, assumes such a violent, glaring character, that a small section of the ruling class cuts itself adrift, and joins the revolutionary class, the class that holds the future in its hands. Just as, therefore, at an earlier period, a section of the nobility went over to the bourgeoisie, so now a portion of the bourgeoisie goes over to the proletariat, and in particular, a portion of the bourgeois ideologists who have raised themselves to the level of comprehending theoretically the historical movement as a whole.

Of all the classes that stand face to face with the bourgeoisie today, the proletariat alone is a really revolutionary class. The other classes decay and finally disappear in the face of modern industry; the proletariat is its special and essential product.

The lower middle class, the small manufacturer, the shopkeeper, the artisan, the peasant, all these fight against the bourgeoisie, to save from extinction their existence as fractions of the middle class. They are therefore not revolutionary, but conservative. Nay, more, they are reactionary, for they try to roll back the wheel of history. If by chance they are revolutionary, they are so only in view of their impending transfer into the proletariat; they thus defend not their present, but their future interests; they desert their own standpoint to place themselves at that of the proletariat.

The "dangerous class," the social scum, that passively rotting mass thrown off by the lowest layers of old society, may, here and there, be swept into the movement by a proletarian revolution; its conditions of life, however, prepare it far more for the part of a bribed tool of reactionary intrigue.

In the conditions of the proletariat, those of old society at large are already virtually swamped. The proletarian is without property; his relation to his wife and children has no longer anything in common with the bourgeois family relations; modern industrial labour, modern subjection to capital, the same in England as in

France, in America as in Germany, has stripped him of every trace of national character. Law, morality, religion, are to him so many bourgeois prejudices, behind which lurk in ambush just as many bourgeois interests.

All the preceding classes that got the upper hand sought to fortify their already-acquired status by subjecting society at large to their conditions of appropriation. The proletarians cannot become masters of the productive forces of society except by abolishing their own previous mode of appropriation, and thereby also every other previous mode of appropriation. They have nothing of their own to secure and to fortify; their mission is to destroy all previous securities for, and insurances of, individual property.

All previous historical movements were movements of minorities, or in the interest of minorities. The proletarian movement is the self-conscious, independent movement of the immense majority, in the interest of the immense majority. The proletariat, the lowest stratum of our present society, cannot stir, cannot raise itself up, without the whole superincumbent strata of official society being sprung into the air.

Though not in substance, yet in form, the struggle of the proletariat with the bourgeoisie is at first a national struggle. The proletariat of each country must, of course, first of all settle matters with its own bourgeoisie.

In depicting the most general phases of the development of the proletariat, we traced the more or less veiled civil war, raging within existing society, up to the point where that war breaks out into open revolution, and where the violent overthrow of the bourgeoisie lays the foundation for the sway of the proletariat.

Hitherto, every form of society has been based, as we have already seen, on the antagonism of oppressing and oppressed classes. But in order to oppress a class, certain conditions must be assured to it under which it can, at least, continue its slavish existence. The serf, in the period of serfdom, raised himself to membership in the commune, just as the petty bourgeois, under the yoke of feudal absolutism, managed to develop into a bourgeois. The modern labourer, on the contrary, instead of rising with the progress of industry, sinks deeper and deeper below the conditions of existence of his own class. He becomes a pauper, and pauperism develops

more rapidly than population and wealth. And here it becomes evident that the bourgeoisie is unfit to rule because it is incompetent to assure an existence to its slave within his slavery, because it cannot help letting him sink into such a state that it has to feed him, instead of being fed by him. Society can no longer live under this bourgeoisie; in other words, its existence is no longer compatible with society.

The essential condition for the existence and for the sway of the bourgeois class is the accumulation of wealth in the hands of private individuals, the formation and augmentation of capital; the condition for capital is wage-labour. Wage-labour rests exclusively on competition between the labourers. The advance of industry, whose involuntary promoter is the bourgeoisie, replaces the isolation of the labourers, due to competition, by their revolutionary combination, due to association. The development of modern industry, therefore, cuts from under the feet of the bourgeoisie the very foundation on which it produces and appropriates products. What the bourgeoisie therefore produces, above all, are its own grave-diggers. Its fall and the victory of the proletariat are equally inevitable.

QUESTIONS

1. How does Marx explain the triumph of the bourgeois over the feudal aristocracy?
2. What is the function of the state under bourgeois rule?
3. Why is bourgeois supremacy antinationalistic?
4. What does Marx mean when he writes that the productive forces of society have become too powerful for the conditions of bourgeois property?
5. Why is the wage of a worker roughly equal to his level of subsistence?
6. In what way does the bourgeoisie produce "its own grave-diggers"?
7. In what sense are all the enemies of the bourgeois save the proletariat reactionary?
8. Why does the victory of the proletariat result in the creation of a classless society?

Marx feels that the duty of communists is to help workers become more intensely conscious of their status and to weld them into a political class. While

Marx himself favored trade unions, he urged the workers not to be content with better wages and better conditions of work. Joining the system in this way would undermine the solidarity of the movement and, while improving the lot of certain individuals, would leave the mass of proletarians in their misery. The communist was dedicated to the destruction of private property, which was the primary tool in the hands of the bourgeoisie for the subjection of the lower class. Also slated for destruction was the state, which was the political means by which the bourgeois protected their property and controlled the workers. Once bourgeois property had been eliminated and the classless society achieved, social conflict would end and there would be no need for the oppressive power of the state.

Although Marx believed that certain members of the bourgeoisie like himself could work themselves free from their class allegiances, on the whole he maintained that individual mentalities were determined by the economic class to which they belonged. Accordingly, the agencies of historical change were not for him individuals but rather classes. Nevertheless, Marx remained to the end a child of the Enlightenment. His final goal for humanity remained the attainment of personal liberty and equality. He was committed to the belief that once the forces of exploitation were annihilated, men would be rational enough to live as brothers and sisters, sharing the goods of their labor. Indeed, his faith in the power of rationality and the essential goodness of man was even greater than that of the philosophes, for he thought that men in the final stage would live in freedom and equality even without the presence of a government.

The Growth of Material Progress   Paradoxically, Marxism enjoyed its greatest success in those countries where industrialism was only getting underway and where agriculture remained the dominant occupation. This was the case in Russia in 1917 and in China in the years immediately following World War II. In Western Europe and America, however, Marx's fears were realized. In the course of the century after the publication of *The Communist Manifesto*, workers proved more concerned with immediate material gains than with ultimate goals and found that these could be accomplished with greater ease and security through trade unionism and participation in the established political system than through revolution. Although the capitalist economy suffered periodic setbacks, some of great magnitude like the Depression of the 1930s, on the whole the working population of the Western world experienced a steady increase in its standard of living. Rather than polarizing between the extremes of rich bourgeois and proletariat, industrial society witnessed an enormous expansion of the middle class. Large numbers of workers were drawn into its ranks, or at least many were led to believe they belonged there.

People rich and poor flocked to the Great Exhibition in London in 1851 at the astounding Crystal Palace, which they viewed as a marvel of engineering and a symbol of an optimistic age of technological achievement. Science created new wonders in daily life at an astounding rate. The railroad, the steamship, the telegraph and telephone, electricity, and the internal combustion engine convinced most people that scientific invention was fundamentally helpful to mankind and that continuous progress was inevitable. Workers' awareness of continuing economic inequalities and social injustices was largely overcome by a trust in future improvement and in the efficacy of political action within the system eventually to correct wrongs. Material progress, combined with scientific progress, became something of a god.

Women's Rights

While Marx was publishing his *Communist Manifesto* in 1848, a group of women met peacefully at Seneca Falls, New York, in an effort to organize the fight for woman's suffrage. In the *Manifesto*, Marx had argued that for the bourgeois, women, including the wives of the bourgeois themselves, were merely instruments of production. Women supporters of the numerous antislavery societies in Europe and America had by this time already begun a campaign to broaden the goals of these organizations to include the liberation of supposedly free women. For instance, until the 1840s women could not receive a college degree nor could they own real estate in their own name in most states of the United States. But the battle was joined!

Perhaps the most eloquent of the early writings arguing for the equality of women and against the injustice of their present status was John Stuart Mill's *The Subjection of Women* written in 1861. One of the finest, most decent spirits of his age, Mill (1806–1873) was the son of John Mill, one of the leaders of early liberalism. A disciple of his father in his youth, Mill gradually grew disillusioned with a philosophy that, while committed to the freedom and equality of men, could permit the degradation of the poor and even justify it as part of the law of nature. As a writer and later a member of Parliament, he defended the rights of individuals against the oppression of the majority but at the same time urged the government to interfere when powerful individuals inflicted injury on society as a whole by abusing those same rights. Earlier liberals for him had been too selective in their espousal of the principles of liberty and equality. Conveniently they had stopped short of ensuring such freedoms when they would interfere with their own prejudices or economic and political interests. This respect for individual personality at all levels made Mill a vigorous opponent of slavery and, in his maturity, a champion of women's rights as well.

JOHN STUART MILL

From *The Subjection of Women*

The object of this Essay is to explain as clearly as I am able the grounds of an opinion which I have held from the very earliest period when I had formed any opinions at all on social or political matters, and which, instead of being weakened or modified, has been constantly growing stronger by the progress of reflection and the experience of life. That the principle which regulates the existing social relations between the two sexes—the legal subordination of one sex to the other—is wrong in itself, and now one of the chief hindrances to human improvement; and that it ought to be replaced by a principle of perfect equality, admitting no power or privilege on the one side, nor disability on the other. . . . It is one of the characteristic prejudices of the reaction of the nineteenth century against the eighteenth, to accord to the unreasoning elements in human nature the infallibility which the eighteenth century is supposed to have ascribed to the reasoning

elements. For the apotheosis of Reason we have substituted that of Instinct; and we call everything instinct which we find in ourselves and for which we cannot trace any rational foundation. This idolatry, infinitely more degrading than the other, and the most pernicious of the false worships of the present day, of all of which it is now the main support, will probably hold its ground until it gives way before a sound psychology laying bare the real root of much that is bowed down to as the intention of Nature and the ordinance of God. As regards the present question, I am willing to accept the unfavourable conditions which the prejudice assigns to me. I consent that established custom, and the general feeling, should be deemed conclusive against me, unless that custom and feeling from age to age can be shown to have owed their existence to other causes than their soundness, and to have derived their power from the worse rather than the better parts of human nature. I am willing that judgment should go against me, unless I can show that my judge has been tampered with. The concession is not so great as it might appear; for to prove this, is by far the easiest portion of my task.

The generality of a practice is in some cases a strong presumption that it is, or at all events once was, conducive to laudable ends. This is the case, when the practice was first adopted, or afterwards kept up, as a means to such ends, and was grounded on experience of the mode in which they could be most effectually attained. If the authority of men over women, when first established, had been the result of a conscientious comparison between different modes of constituting the government of society; if, after trying various other modes of social organisation—the government of women over men, equality between the two, and such mixed and divided modes of government as might be invented—it had been decided, on the testimony of experience, that the mode in which women are wholly under the rule of men, having no share at all in public concerns, and each in private being under the legal obligation of obedience to the man with whom she has associated her destiny, was the arrangement most conducive to the happiness and well-being of both; its general adoption might then be fairly thought to be some evidence that, at the time when it was adopted, it was the best: though even then the considerations which recommended it may, like so many other primeval social facts of the greatest importance, have subsequently, in the course of ages, ceased to exist. But the state of the case is in every respect the reverse of this. In the first place, the opinion in favour of the present system, which entirely subordinates the weaker sex to the stronger, rests upon theory only; for there never has been trial made of any other: so that experience, in the sense in which it is vulgarly opposed to theory, cannot be pretended to have pronounced any verdict. And in the second place, the adoption of this system of inequality never was the result of deliberation, or forethought, or any social ideas, or any notion whatever of what conduced to the benefit of humanity or the good order of society. It arose simply from the fact that from the very earliest twilight of human society, every woman (owing to the value attached to her by men, combined with her inferiority in muscular strength) was found in a state of bondage to some man. Laws and systems of polity always begin by recognising the relations they find already existing between individuals. They convert what was a mere physical fact into a legal right, give it the sanction of society, and principally aim at the substitution of public and organised means of asserting and protecting these rights, instead of the irregular and lawless conflict of physical strength. Those who had already been compelled to obedience became in this manner legally bound to it. Slavery, from being a mere affair of force between the master and the slave, became regularised and a matter of compact among the masters, who, binding themselves to one another for common protection, guaranteed by their collective strength the private possessions of each, including his slaves. In early times, the great majority of the male sex were slaves, as well as the whole of the female. And many ages elapsed, some of them ages of high cultivation, before any thinker was bold enough to question the rightfulness, and the absolute social necessity, either of the one slavery or of the other. By degrees such thinkers did arise; and (the general progress of society assisting) the slavery of the male sex has, in all the countries of Christian Europe at least (though, in one of them, only within the last few years) been at length abolished, and that of the female sex has been gradually changed into a milder form of dependence. But this dependence, as it exists at present, is not an original institution, taking a fresh start from consider-ations of justice and social expediency—it is the primitive state of slavery lasting on, through successive mitigations and modifications occasioned by the same causes which have softened the general manners, and brought all human relations more under the control of justice and the influence of humanity. It has not lost the taint of its brutal origin. No presumption in its favour, therefore, can be drawn from the fact of its existence. The only such presumption which it could be supposed to have, must be grounded on its having lasted till now, when so many other things which came down from the same odious source have been done away with. And this, indeed, is what makes it strange to ordinary ears, to hear it asserted that the inequality of rights between men and women has no other source than the law of the strongest. . . .

If people are mostly so little aware how completely, during the greater part of the duration of our species, the law of force was the avowed rule of general conduct, any other being only a special and exceptional consequence of peculiar ties—and from how very recent a date it is that the affairs of society in general have been even pretended to be regulated according to any moral law; as little do people remember or consider, how institutions and customs which never had any ground but the law of force, last on into ages and states of general opinion which never would have permitted their first establishment. Less than forty years ago, Englishmen might still by law hold human beings in bondage as saleable property: within the present century they might kidnap them and carry them off, and work them literally to death. This absolutely extreme case of the law of force, condemned by those who can tolerate almost every other form of arbitrary power, and which, of all others presents features the most revolting to the feelings of all who look at it from an impartial position, was the law of civilised and Christian England within the memory of persons now living: and in one half of Anglo-Saxon America three or four years ago, not only did slavery exist, but the slave-trade, and the breeding of slaves expressly for it, was a general practice between slave-states. Yet not only was there a greater strength of sentiment against it, but, in England at least, a less amount either of feeling or of interest in favour of it, than of any other of the customary abuses of force: for its motive was the love of gain, unmixed and undisguised; and those who profited by it were a very small numerical fraction of the country, while the natural feeling of all who were not personally interested in it, was unmitigated abhorrence. So extreme an instance makes it almost superfluous to refer to any other: but consider the long duration of absolute monarchy. In England at present it is the almost universal conviction that military despotism is a case of the law of force, having no other origin or justification. Yet in all the great nations of Europe except England it either still exists, or has only just ceased to exist, and has even now a strong party favourable to it in all ranks of the people, especially among persons of station and consequence. Such is the power of an established system, even when far from universal; when not only in almost every period of history there have been great and well-known examples of the contrary system, but these have almost invariably been afforded by the most illustrious and most prosperous communities. In this case, too, the possessor of the undue power, the person directly interested in it, is only one person, while those who are subject to it and suffer from it are literally all the rest. The yoke is naturally and necessarily humiliating to all persons, except the one who is on the throne, together with, at most, the one who expects to succeed to it. How different are these cases from that of the power of men over women! I am not now prejudging the question of its justifiableness. I am showing how vastly more permanent it could not but be, even if not justifiable, than these other dominations which have nevertheless lasted down to our own time. Whatever gratification of pride there is in the possession of power, and whatever personal interest in its exercise, is in this case not confined to a limited class, but common to the whole male sex. Instead of being, to most of its supporters, a thing desirable chiefly in the abstract, or, like the political ends usually contended for by factions, of little private importance to any but the leaders; it comes home to the person and hearth of every male head of a family, and of everyone who looks forward to being so. The clodhopper exercises, or is to exercise, his share of the power equally with the highest nobleman. And the case is that in which the desire of power is the strongest: for everyone who desires power, desires it most over those who are nearest to him, with whom his life is passed, with whom he has most concerns in common, and in whom any independence of his authority is oftenest likely to interfere with his individual preferences. If, in the other cases specified, powers manifestly grounded only on force, and having so much less to support them, are so slowly and with so much difficulty got rid of, much more must it be so with this, even if it rests on no better foundation than those. We must consider, too, that the possessors of the power have facilities in this case, greater than in any other, to prevent any uprising against it. Every one of the subjects lives under the very eye, and almost, it may be said, in the hands, of one of the masters—in closer intimacy with him than with any of her fellow-subjects; with no means of combining against him, no power of even locally overmastering him, and, on the other hand, with the strongest motives for seeking his favour and avoiding to give him offence. In struggles for political emancipation, everybody knows how often its champions are bought off by bribes, or daunted by terrors. In the case of women, each individual of the subject-class is in a chronic state of bribery and intimidation combined. In setting up the standard of resistance, a large number of the leaders, and still more of the followers, must make an almost complete sacrifice of the pleasures or the alleviations of their own individual lot. If ever any system of privilege and enforced subjection had its yoke tightly riveted on the necks of those who are kept down by it, this has. I have not yet shown that it is a wrong system: but everyone who is capable of thinking on the subject must see that even if it is, it was certain to outlast all other forms of unjust authority. And when some of the grossest of the other forms still exist in many civilised countries, and have only recently been got rid of in others, it would be strange if that which is so much the deepest rooted had yet been perceptibly shaken anywhere. There is more reason to wonder that the protests and testimonies against it should have been so numerous and so weighty as they are.

Some will object, that a comparison cannot fairly be made between the government of the male sex and the forms of unjust power which I have adduced in illustration of it, since these are arbitrary, and the effect of mere usurpation, while it on the contrary is natural. But was there ever any domination which did not appear natural to those who possessed it? There was a time when the division of mankind into two classes, a small one of masters and a numerous one of slaves, appeared, even to the most cultivated minds, to be natural, and the only natural, condition of the human race. No less an intellect, and one which contributed no less to the progress of human thought, than Aristotle, held this opinion without doubt or misgiving; and rested it on the same premises on which the same assertion in regard to the dominion of men over women is usually based, namely that there are different natures among mankind, free natures, and slave natures; that the Greeks were of a free nature, the barbarian races of Thracians and Asiatics of a slave nature. But why need I go back to Aristotle? Did not the slave-owners of the Southern United States maintain the same doctrine, with all the fanaticism with which men cling to the theories that justify their passions and legitimate their personal interests? Did they not call heaven and earth to witness that the dominion of the white man over the black is natural, that the black race is by nature incapable of freedom, and marked out for slavery? some even going so far as to say that the freedom of manual labourers is an unnatural order of things anywhere. Again, the theorists of absolute monarchy have always affirmed it to be the only natural form of government; issuing from the patriarchal, which was the primitive and spontaneous form of society, framed on the model of the paternal, which is anterior to society itself, and, as they contend, the most natural authority of all. . . .

But, it will be said, the rule of men over women differs from all these others in not being a rule of force: it is accepted voluntarily; women make no complaint, and are consenting parties to it. In the first place, a great number of women do not accept it. Ever since there have been women able to make their sentiments known by their writings (the only mode of publicity which society permits to them), an increasing number of them have recorded protests against their present social condition: and recently many thousands of them, headed by the most eminent women known to the public, have petitioned Parliament for their admission to the Parliamentary Suffrage. The claim of women to be educated as solidly, and in the same branches of knowledge, as men, is urged with growing intensity, and with a great prospect of success; while the demand for their admission into professions and occupations

hitherto closed against them, becomes every year more urgent. Though there are not in this country, as there are in the United States, periodical conventions and an organised party to agitate for the Rights of Women, there is a numerous and active society organised and managed by women, for the more limited object of obtaining the political franchise. Nor is it only in our own country and in America that women are beginning to protest, more or less collectively, against the disabilities under which they labour. France, and Italy, and Switzerland, and Russia now afford examples of the same thing. How many more women there are who silently cherish similar aspirations, no one can possibly know; but there are abundant tokens how many *would* cherish them, were they not so strenuously taught to repress them as contrary to the proprieties of their sex. It must be remembered, also, that no enslaved class ever asked for complete liberty at once. . . .

All causes, social and natural, combine to make it unlikely that women should be collectively rebellious to the power of men. They are so far in a position different from all other subject classes, that their masters require something more from them than actual service. Men do not want solely the obedience of women, they want their sentiments. All men, except the most brutish, desire to have, in the woman most nearly connected with them, not a forced slave but a willing one, not a slave merely, but a favourite. They have therefore put everything in practice to enslave their minds. The masters of all other slaves rely, for maintaining obedience, on fear; either fear of themselves, or religious fears. The masters of women wanted more than simple obedience, and they turned the whole force of education to effect their purpose. All women are brought up from the very earliest years in the belief that their ideal of character is the very opposite to that of men; not self-will, and government by self-control, but submission, and yielding to the control of others. All the moralities tell them that it is the duty of women, and all the current sentimentalities that it is their nature, to live for others; to make complete abnegation of themselves, and to have no life but in their affections. And by their affections are meant the only ones they are allowed to have—those to the men with whom they are connected, or to the children who constitute an additional and indefeasible tie between them and a man.

When we put together three things—first, the natural attraction between opposite sexes; secondly, the wife's entire dependence on the husband, every privilege or pleasure she has being either his gift, or depending entirely on his will; and lastly, that the principal object of human pursuit, consideration, and all objects of social ambition, can in general be sought or obtained by her only through him, it would be a miracle if the object of being attractive to men had not become the polar star of feminine education and formation of character. And, this great means of influence over the minds of women having been acquired, an instinct of selfishness made men avail themselves of it to the utmost as a means of holding women in subjection, by representing to them meekness, submissiveness, and resignation of all individual will into the hands of a man, as an essential part of sexual attractiveness. Can it be doubted that any of the other yokes which mankind have succeeded in breaking, would have subsisted till now if the same means had existed, and had been so sedulously used, to bow down their minds to it? If it had been made the object of the life of every young plebeian to find personal favour in the eyes of some patrician, of every young serf with some seigneur; if domestication with him, and a share of his personal affections, had been held out as the prize which they all should look out for, the most gifted and aspiring being able to reckon on the most desirable prizes; and if, when this prize had been obtained, they had been shut out by a wall of brass from all interests not centring in him, all feelings and desires but those which he shared or inculcated; would not serfs and seigneurs, plebeians and patricians, have been as broadly distinguished at this day as men and women are? and would not all but a thinker here and there, have believed the distinction to be a fundamental and unalterable fact in human nature?

The preceding considerations are amply sufficient to show that custom, however universal it may be, affords in this case no presumption, and ought not to create any prejudice, in favour of the arrangements which place women in social and political subjection to men. But I may go farther, and maintain that the course of history, and the tendencies of progressive human society, afford not only no presumption in favour of this system of inequality of rights, but a strong one against it; and that, so far as the whole course of human improvement up to the time, the whole stream of modern tendencies, warrants any inference on the subject, it is, that this relic of the past is discordant with the future, and must necessarily disappear.

For, what is the peculiar character of the modern world—the difference which chiefly distinguishes modern institutions, modern social ideas, modern life itself, from those of times long past? It is, that human beings are no longer born to their place in life, and chained down by an inexorable bond to the place they are born to, but are free to employ their faculties, and such favourable chances as offer, to achieve the lot which may appear to them most desirable. Human society of old was constituted on a very different principle. All were born to a fixed social position, and were mostly kept in it by law, or interdicted from any means by which they could emerge from it. As some men are born white and others black, so some were born slaves and others freemen and citizens; some were born patricians, others plebeians; some were born feudal nobles, others commoners and *roturiers*. A slave or serf could never make himself free, nor, except by the will of his master, become so. . . .

In modern Europe, and most in those parts of it which have participated most largely in all other modern improvements, diametrically opposite doctrines now prevail. Law and government do not undertake to prescribe by whom any social or industrial operation shall or shall not be conducted, or what modes of conducting them shall be lawful. These things are left to the unfettered choice of individuals. Even the laws which required that workmen should serve an apprenticeship, have in this country been repealed: there being ample assurance that in all cases in which an apprenticeship is necessary, its necessity will suffice to enforce it. The old theory was, that the least possible should be left to the choice of the individual agent; that all he had to do should, as far as practicable, be laid down for him by superior wisdom. Left to himself he was sure to go wrong. The modern conviction, the fruit of a thousand years of experience, is, that things in which the individual is the person directly interested, never go right but as they are left to his own discretion; and that any regulation of them by authority, except to protect the rights of others, is sure to be mischievous. . . .

If this general principle of social and economical science is not true; if individuals, with such help as they can derive from the opinion of those who know them, are not better judges than the law and the government, of their own capacities and vocation; the world cannot too soon abandon this principle, and return to the old system of regulations and disabilities. But if the principle is true, we ought to act as if we believed it, and not to ordain that to be born a girl instead of a boy, any more than to be born black instead of white, or a commoner instead of a nobleman, shall decide the person's position through all life—shall interdict people from all the more elevated social positions, and from all, except a few, respectable occupations. . . .

At present, in the more improved countries, the disabilities of women are the only case, save one, in which laws and institutions take persons at their birth, and ordain that they shall never in all their lives be allowed to compete for certain things. The one exception is that of royalty. Persons still are born to the throne; no one, not of the reigning family, can ever occupy it, and no one even of that family can, by any means but the course of hereditary succession, attain it. All other dignities and social advantages are open to the whole male sex: many indeed are only attainable by wealth, but wealth may be striven for by anyone, and is actually obtained by many men of the very humblest origin. The difficulties, to the majority, are indeed insuperable without the aid of fortunate accidents; but no male human being is under any legal ban: neither law nor opinion superadd artificial obstacles to the natural ones. . . .

Neither does it avail anything to say that the *nature* of the two sexes adapts them to their present functions and position, and renders these appropriate to them. Standing on the ground of common sense and the constitution of the human mind, I deny that anyone knows, or can know, the nature of the two sexes, as long as they have only been seen in their present relation to one another. If men had ever been found in society without women, or women without men, or if there had been a society of men and women in which the women were not under the control of the men, something might have been positively known about the mental and moral differences which may be inherent in the nature of each. What is now called the nature of women is an eminently artificial thing—the result of forced repression in some directions, unnatural stimulation in others. It may be asserted without scruple, that no other class of dependents have had

their character so entirely distorted from its natural proportions by their relation with their masters; for, if conquered and slave races have been, in some respects, more forcibly repressed, whatever in them has not been crushed down by an iron heel has generally been let alone, and if left with any liberty of development, it has developed itself according to its own laws; but in the case of women, a hot-house and stove cultivation has always been carried on of some of the capabilities of their nature, for the benefit and pleasure of their masters. Then, because certain products of the general vital force sprout luxuriantly and reach a great development in this heated atmosphere and under this active nurture and watering, while other shoots from the same root, which are left outside in the wintry air, with ice purposely heaped all round them, have a stunted growth, and some are burnt off with fire and disappear; men, with that inability to recognise their own work which distinguishes the unanalytic mind, indolently believe that the tree grows of itself in the way they have made it grow, and that it would die if one half of it were not kept in a vapour bath and the other half in the snow. . . .

Hence, in regard to that most difficult question, what are the natural differences between the two sexes—a subject on which it is impossible in the present state of society to obtain complete and correct knowledge—while almost everybody dogmatises upon it, almost all neglect and make light of the only means by which any partial insight can be obtained into it. This is, an analytic study of the most important department of psychology, the laws of the influence of circumstances on character. For, however great and apparently ineradicable the moral and intellectual differences between men and women might be, the evidence of there being natural differences could only be negative. Those only could be inferred to be natural which could not possibly be artificial—the residuum, after deducting every characteristic of either sex which can admit of being explained from education or external circumstances. The profoundest knowledge of the laws of the formation of character is indispensable to entitle anyone to affirm even that there is any difference, much more what the difference is, between the two sexes considered as moral and rational beings; and since no one, as yet, has that knowledge (for there is hardly any subject which, in proportion to its importance, has been so little studied), no one is thus far entitled to any positive opinion on the subject. Conjectures are all that can at present be made; conjectures more or less probable, according as more or less authorised by such knowledge as we yet have of the laws of psychology, as applied to the formation of character. . . . We may safely assert that the knowledge which men can acquire of women, even as they have been and are, without reference to what they might be, is wretchedly imperfect and superficial, and always will be so, until women themselves have told all that they have to tell.

And this time has not come; nor will it come otherwise than gradually. It is but of yesterday that women have either been qualified by literary accomplishments, or permitted by society, to tell anything to the general public. As yet very few of them dare tell anything, which men, on whom their literary success depends, are unwilling to hear. Let us remember in what manner, up to a very recent time, the expression, even by a male author, of uncustomary opinions, or what are deemed eccentric feelings, usually was, and in some degree still is, received; and we may form some faint conception under what impediments a woman, who is brought up to think custom and opinion her sovereign rule, attempts to express in books anything drawn from the depths of her own nature. The greatest woman who has left writings behind her sufficient to give her an eminent rank in the literature of her country, thought it necessary to prefix as a motto to her boldest work, "Un homme peut braver l'opinion; une femme doit s'y soumettre." [1] The greater part of what women write about women is mere sycophancy to men. In the case of unmarried women, much of it seems only intended to increase their chance of a husband. Many, both married and unmarried, overstep the mark, and inculcate a servility beyond what is desired or relished by any man, except the very vulgarest. But this is not so often the case as, even at a quite late period, it still was. Literary women are becoming more free-spoken, and more willing to express their real sentiments. Unfortunately, in this country especially, they are themselves such artificial products, that their sentiments are compounded of a small element of individual observation and consciousness, and a very large one of acquired associations. This will be less and less the case, but it will remain true to a great extent, as long as social institutions do not admit the same free development of originality in women which is possible to men. When that time comes, and not before, we shall see, and not merely hear, as much as it is necessary to know of the nature of women, and the adaptation of other things to it. . . .

One thing we may be certain of—that what is contrary to women's nature to do, they never will be made to do by simply giving their nature free play. The anxiety of mankind to interfere in behalf of nature, for fear lest nature should not succeed in effecting its purpose, is an altogether unnecessary solicitude. What women by nature cannot do, it is quite superfluous to forbid them from doing. What they can do, but not so well as the men who are their competitors, competition suffices to exclude them from; since nobody asks for protective duties and bounties in favour of women; it is only asked that the present bounties and protective duties in favour of men should be recalled. If women have a greater natural inclination for some things than for others, there is no need of laws or social inculcation to make the majority of them do the former in preference to the latter. Whatever women's services are most wanted for, the free play of competition will hold out the strongest inducements to them to undertake. And, as the words imply, they are most wanted for the things for which they are most fit; by the apportionment of which to them, the collective faculties of the two sexes can be applied on the whole with the greatest sum of valuable result.

The general opinion of men is supposed to be, that the natural vocation of a woman is that of a wife and mother. I say, is supposed to be, because, judging from acts—from the whole of the present constitution of society—one might infer that their opinion was the direct contrary. They might be supposed to think that the alleged natural vocation of women was of all things the most repugnant to their nature; insomuch that if they are free to do anything else—if any other means of living or occupation of their time and faculties, is open, which has any chance of appearing desirable to them—there will not be enough of them who will be willing to accept the condition said to be natural to them. If this is the real opinion of men in general, it would be well that it should be spoken out. I should like to hear somebody openly enunciating the doctrine

---

[1] Title-page of Mme de Staël's *Delphine.* "A man can go against public opinion; a woman must submit herself to it."

(it is already implied in much that is written on the subject)—"It is necessary to society that women should marry and produce children. They will not do so unless they are compelled. Therefore it is necessary to compel them." The merits of the case would then be clearly defined. It would be exactly that of the slaveholders of South Carolina and Louisiana. "It is necessary that cotton and sugar should be grown. White men cannot produce them. Negroes will not, for any wages which we choose to give. *Ergo* they must be compelled." An illustration still closer to the point is that of impressment. Sailors must absolutely be had to defend the country. It often happens that they will not voluntarily enlist. Therefore there must be the power of forcing them. How often has this logic been used! and, but for one flaw in it, without doubt it would have been successful up to this day. But it is open to the retort— First pay the sailors the honest value of their labour. When you have made it as well worth their while to serve you, as to work for other employers, you will have no more difficulty than others have in obtaining their services. To this there is no logical answer except "I will not": and as people are now not only ashamed, but are not desirous, to rob the labourer of his hire, impressment is no longer advocated. Those who attempt to force women into marriage by closing all other doors against them, lay themselves open to a similar retort. If they mean what they say, their opinion must evidently be, that men do not render the married condition so desirable to women, as to induce them to accept it for its own recommendations. It is not a sign of one's thinking the boon one offers very attractive, when one allows only Hobson's choice, "that or none." And here, I believe, is the clue to the feelings of those men, who have a real antipathy to the equal freedom of women. I believe they are afraid, not lest women should be unwilling to marry, for I do not think that anyone in reality has that apprehension; but lest they should insist that marriage should be on equal conditions; lest all women of spirit and capacity should prefer doing almost anything else, not in their own eyes degrading, rather than marry, when marrying is giving themselves a master, and a master too of all their earthly possessions. And truly, if this consequence were necessarily incident to marriage, I think that the apprehension would be very well founded. I agree in thinking it probable that few women, capable of anything else, would,

unless under an irresistible *entraînement*, rendering them for the time insensible to anything but itself, choose such a lot, when any other means were open to them of filling a conventionally honourable place in life: and if men are determined that the law of marriage shall be a law of despotism, they are quite right, in point of mere policy, in leaving to women only Hobson's choice. But, in that case, all that has been done in the modern world to relax the chain on the minds of women, has been a mistake. They never should have been allowed to receive a literary education. Women who read, much more women who write, are, in the existing constitution of things, a contradiction and a disturbing element: and it was wrong to bring women up with any acquirements but those of an odalisque, or of a domestic servant.

QUESTIONS

1. List the arguments that Mill says have been made in favor of the subjection of women and explain how he answers each of these.
2. What ideas of liberalism are reflected in this passage?
3. What comparisons does Mill make between the condition of women and slavery? How valid are these parallels in your opinion?
4. How do Mill's analyses of, and remedies for, an oppressed class differ from those of Marx?
5. How relevant are the injustices that Mill points out and the solutions that he offers to the condition of present-day women? What would Mill think of affirmative action programs?

The struggle begun by Mill's generation for equal rights for women was to last for many years. In the crucial matter of suffrage, for instance, women were not to have the vote in Canada until 1917, in the United States and England until 1920 and 1928 respectively; in France they were denied this basic right until after World War II. This chronology follows by fifty to a hundred years the granting of voting rights to all males in the various countries of Western Europe and America. Even after voting rights were won, however, large areas remained where women experienced discrimination. The decade of the 1970s showed a new determination to eliminate these inequalities wherever feasible.

28

ART AND LITERATURE IN THE INDUSTRIAL WORLD: REALISM

Artists, as well as social thinkers, were forced to come to terms with the industrialization of society. The conventions and enthusiasms that had permitted an artist to create the gentle *Experiment with a Vacuum Pump* (Fig. 23-4) were no longer appropriate in an age in which scientific progress had produced the vast, dehumanizing factories of Leeds and Birmingham. Nor did the idealizing and exotic tendencies of romanticism deal adequately with the problems of the mid-nineteenth century. Industrialism and its social consequences necessitated profound changes in *all* the arts, but our examples will be drawn from painting and architecture.

Architecture

Nineteenth-century architects were hesitant in their attempts to create a new architectural language for their age. In 1847 Professor Donaldson, speaking at a meeting of the Architectural Association (an important English architectural school) said, "The great question is, are we to have an architecture of our period, a distinct, individual, palpable style of the 19th century?" Romanticism had produced a series of revivals: Gothic, Romanesque, Renaissance. It is difficult for us to imagine the controversies that raged as to which style was the most correct or appropriate for particular needs. By mid-century, the architect tended to elect forms based on associations with the functions of the building, hence, Gothic for churches and Italian Renaissance for banks and businesses. Yet the new functions, needs, and materials of architecture posed new problems and demanded new solutions, which were more frequently offered by engineers and builders than by architects. An example of such a new problem and a new solution is the Crystal Palace, created for the Great Exhibition of 1851 in London (Fig. 28-1).

A call for designs for the main exhibition hall, one-third of a mile long, produced a variety of solutions that would take too long to build, were too costly and would be impossible to light. However, Joseph Paxton, gardener of the earl of Chatworth, proposed a modular glass box made of cast and wrought iron framing and glass. All the parts could be prefabricated, shipped by rail, and erected on the site in Hyde Park. On July 16, 1850, an agreement was signed between the commissioners of the exhibition, the engineers, and the glass manufacturers. The completed hall was handed over on January 31, 1851, ready for the installation of exhibits. Lighted naturally, cooled by giant louvered windows that could be opened mechanically, the Crystal Palace was truly a marvel (though John Ruskin, the English architectural critic, refused to call it architecture). Today we see it as a modern solution to a difficulty without reliance on the visual or technical formulas of traditional architecture.

Similar requirements—limited land, money, and time; the need for adequate space and light—were the conditions that created the tall office building in Chicago in the last decades of the nineteenth century. Tall

28–1 Crystal Palace. (Illustrated London News, Sept. 6, 1851)

28–2   Above left. William Lebaron Jenny, Chicago Home Insurance Building. (Chicago Architectural Photographing Company)

28–3   Above right. Burnham & Root, Reliance Building, Chicago. (Chicago Architectural Photographing Company)

buildings had become possible with the invention of the elevator, fireproofing, and the perfection of iron and steel framing. Yet many architects tended to clothe these stacks of floors in Greek, Gothic, or Renaissance details (Fig. 28-2). It was as if they could not decide what a tall building should look like. Should it express height, the cells of the floors? Should it resemble a column with shaft, base, and capital? After the fire of 1871 destroyed the heart of commercial Chicago, the archi-

tects of that city were faced with problems demanding innovation. The Reliance Building (Fig. 28-3) is the culmination of a number of ideas. Built in the summer of 1891, it is a self-supporting metal cage with glass infill. It was simple to erect and maintain. The walls were great expanses of glass, some fixed, some movable panels, providing light and ventilation for the offices lining each side of its central corridor. Visually, the building is a very clear expression of its function, which is to be tall, slablike, economical, and useful. There are no classical orders, no pointed arches. Chicagoans pointed with pride to the development of the "Commercial Style," but some critics felt that its simple expression of function through form was too commercial, too expedient. It would not be until after World War I that the hold of tradition would be completely broken.

Painting: Realism

In architecture, as in any art, it is never enough to solve a problem. Building forms have a profound effect on the quality of life; painting and sculpture reflect, comment on, and affect the future of the arts and of man. In mid-century what seemed most real and most important was progress and economic expansion. In painting the consequences of industrialism made the problems perceived by Delacroix, Goya, and Constable seem more acute. Again and again the artist found himself asking, what should he paint, for whom, and how? Some painters found that industrialism itself provided fascinating subject matter. The English painter William Turner interpreted the technology that had revolutionized transportation in *Rain, Steam and Speed, The Great Western Railway* (Color Plate VIII). Painted in 1845, it was, according to Turner, a literal account of an event that he had witnessed during a storm while riding on a train. The public, however, could not readily accept the modern, "unartistic" subject matter or the technique of applying thin layers of paint resembling "tinted steam."

Courbet   In fact, Turner's particular artistic vision was ahead of its time, close to that of the impressionists two generations later. The style that succeeded in dominating painting in the third quarter of the nineteenth century was realism. In an 1855 manifesto, Gustave Courbet, the pioneer in the movement, stated his principal aims as a realist to be "to translate the customs, the ideas, the appearances of my epoch." The artist was to paint what he saw. For Courbet, this meant depicting the ugly as well as the beautiful. In his view the lower classes were more important than the upper social groups because it was on their labor that modern life was founded. Born in the French countryside, Courbet was the personification of the swaggering, tough but independent socialist. In rendering the harsh reality of his peasant subjects, Courbet depicted life in the country in a way far removed from romantic idealization of it. Courbet was a realist primarily because of his sub-

ject matter and his attitudes, but he was not concerned with rendering the details and textures of every object. For this reason he usually painted in his studio, only doing sketches out-of-doors. More traditional painters criticized his strong colors and his heavily layered paint, which he sometimes applied with a palette knife, a most unconventional process. The total effect of his work, however, was shocking only to those who preferred older styles of painting.

Ford Madox Brown   In England the painter Ford Madox Brown (1821–1893), like Courbet, chose subjects that had philosophical or social relevance for the day. His paintings were filled with the minutiae of life. Brown, like Constable, worked out-of-doors, drawing his subjects from nature in an attempt to create an intensified illusion of reality. His large painting, *Work*, 1862–1865 (Fig. 28-4) shows a sharp contrast between busy laborers and elegant passers-by. To the right, watching the scene is the English philosopher Carlyle, who wrote about the dignity of labor. Beside Carlyle is Frederick D. Maurice, who helped to found the Working Men's College, an institution dedicated to combating social ills and raising working men's status through education. *Work* is certainly more than a picture of Hampstead on a sunny day.

Compare this painting with *The Stonebreakers*, painted in 1849 by Courbet (Fig. 28-5). Begin by deciding what you consider "realism." Does it have to do with the subject matter or the way in which the subject is presented? How does the stonebreaker differ from the workers in *Work*? Which is more anonymous? Which portrays workers more authentically? Which picture rouses a greater response? Why? Does Courbet's focus on two figures intensify or detract from the scene? Do you think the two pictures have a moral? What is that moral? Are location, time of day, and condition of the weather as important as they were to Constable?

Photography   While both artists in their way claimed to be realists, neither Courbet nor Ford Madox Brown could compete with the ability of the camera to give an account of the thing seen. Invented in the first decades of the nineteenth century (the earliest surviving photograph dates ca. 1826), by the 1850s it seemed that the camera could capture more detail and infor-

28–4 Above. Ford Madox Brown, "Work."
(Courtesy of the City of Manchester
Art Galleries)

28–5 Right. Gustave Courbet, "The
Stonebreakers." (Staatliche
Kunstsammlungen, Dresden,
Gemäldegalerie Neue Meister; Deutsche
Fotothek Dresden)

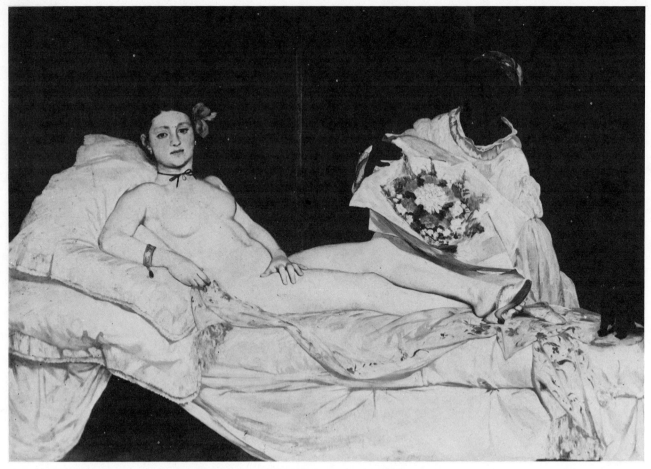

28-6   Edouard Manet, "Olympia," (Louvre, Paris/© ARCH. PHOT. PARIS—S.P.A.D.E.M., 1980)

mation than the eye could see or the hand record. If realism was to be defined by painterly conventions that rendered everything as it was seen, then painting was in danger of being replaced. Partly as a response to this growing challenge from the "realism" of the camera, but also influenced to an extent by the kind of images photography produced, a new movement in painting evolved, taking the name impressionism. In its effort to infuse subject matter with new meaning and value by the creation of painterly conventions more appropriate and relevant to modern life, impressionism was an outgrowth of realism itself.

Manet: Realism to Impressionism In the development of impressionism Edouard Manet played the role of a transitional figure. Born into the Parisian upper-middle class, thirteen years younger than Courbet,

Manet was not a conscious rebel like the latter; but the two painters shared an interest in choosing their subjects from the life that was familiar to them. Manet set out to create a personal style for recording the public and private pursuits of his milieu. Influenced by what photography had shown him, he set his subjects in a strong, harsh light that tended to flatten them against their background, even as a photograph eliminates much three-dimensionality. Unlike the photograph, which does not discriminate among objects, however, Manet concentrated on the firm contours of his subjects. He utilized sharp contrasts of light and dark to create a strong sense of three-dimensionality, unlike the surface modeling or tonal adjustments of earlier pictures.

Manet's painting *Olympia* (Fig. 28-6), exhibited in the Salon of the Refused in 1863 (a countershow to the government-sanctioned Salon), typifies his emerging style. The ideas of a reclining nude is a very old one in art, but this one is different. Who is this woman? What is her profession? Is Manet being critical or patronizing? Why or why not? Paris was shocked by this rather pert lady who engaged the viewer with her direct, quizzical look. It is certain that she is no Venus; she is too present and familiar. The flat white of the sheets and the creamy flat paint that delineates her body end in harsh dark edges and folds. The black servant and black cat seem to emphasize the black/white impact of the picture. The bouquet of flowers, brilliant slashes of painting, recalls the sensation of flowers seen in passing. The elimination of detail, the surface textures, the harsh contrasts, together with Olympia's direct, unselfconscious gaze, create the sensation of a scene glimpsed for an instant, but captured, arrested permanently.

These early paintings, which recall photography's impact and the remembrance of things past (Venus, for instance), reveal Manet's hesitancy in creating his personal style. More and more, however, he was able to compose freely, reducing gesture and pose to that which was most telling, most relevatory for a particular moment or personality. His later pictures were also coloristically richer. This later concern with color was in part due to the influence of young painters who were, properly speaking, members of the impressionist group. Manet in turn played an important role in influencing them to paint contemporary life in an appropriate way. Yet whereas Manet's subjects were almost always human beings, viewed with detachment, objectivity, and minimal setting, the impressionists' major interest was in landscape.

Impressionism: An Outgrowth of Realism

Claude Monet, August Renoir, and Camille Pissarro were the chief creators of impressionism. Painting landscapes out-of-doors, these men became committed to recording the illusive effects of sunlight on objects. They had some knowledge of the sciences of color and optics; but when we study their paintings made between 1860 and 1880, we observe that their search for a painterly language unfolds experimentally and unevenly. Consider your own experience of a landscape. The color is vivid; details attract your eyes as they

shift, adjusting to the brightness, concentrating, shifting, focusing. Even as this occurs, the scene itself is changing, for clouds, sun, air, and people move and transform what you are seeing even as you see it. If you pause only for a moment, the light/dark contrasts give you the needed information of the location of things; but if you stay to observe, you become aware of the vibrant, changing color and light.

To translate this experience onto the canvas, the painters first realized that they must eliminate black, brown, and gray from their palettes. Natural light is the product of the *hues* of the spectrum: red, orange, yellow, green, blue, and purple. Like Constable, the impressionists realized that a local color, like green grass, could be made more intense by painting it not as a flat green but as a mottled combination of green and its components, blue and yellow. Moreover, they began to take into account not only the colors of objects themselves but also the fact that objects take on the colors of objects adjacent to them, reflecting some of that color back into the air. Next they realized that shadows are not simply black, brown, or gray but rather the contrasting color of light on the object. Realizing then that all objects, light, and air are reflected, refracted waves of color that the eye perceives and joins into patterns and volumes, they considered it appropriate that the brushstroke should also be fragmented and short, in commas, dots, and dashes. In addition, this kind of brushstroke gave the pictures a sense of immediacy and tension suggesting a rapid, feverish execution.

Landscapes, seascapes (Color Plate IX), and people on boats and in gardens celebrate the apparent conquest of the momentary that is also a real experience. Monet's *Impression: Sunrise*, painted in 1873, gave the movement its name and was exhibited at the first impressionist exhibition of 1874 (Fig. 28-7). Like Courbet and Manet, these painters met with a hostile reception: their works were "crude and unfinished." Today we see the pictures made by Monet and his colleagues in the 1870s and 1880s as monuments to the splendor of the natural world. As the impressionists continued their experiments, each of their styles changed in different ways.

Monet remained most true to impressionism's ideal of recording the fleeting transformations of sunlight on objects. Resorting to numerous canvases, each to record

28–7   Claude Monet, "Impression: Sunrise." (Musée Marmottan/© S.P.A.D.E.M., 1980/photo Routhier, Studio Lourmell 77, Paris)

a different hour of the day, Monet's almost scientific obsession caused him to concentrate on a few subjects, year after year. A series of huge paintings intitled *Waterlilies*, for example, contains his impressions of a pond at different times of day. Compare a canvas of waterlilies (Fig. 28-8) with *Impression: Sunrise*. Where are Monet's references to the visual world? How are the objects of his interest defined? Does time of day make a difference in your perception of the two works? Compare the brushstrokes and the surfaces. In which painting do you sense more clearly the presence of the artist? Why? Are the pond and lilies really important? It would seem that the waterlilies become known to us now only as a concept; they are our link with reality that succumbs to Monet's intensely personal way of seeing and organizing experience.

Waterlilies represents an extremity of the artistic movement that started with realism. What began as an attempt to paint the world "as it is" has become a recording of a subjective view of the world. This approach to art will produce new, more complex, and elaborate languages with which to apprehend and render experience.

Realism in Literature

Writers in the industrial world, like artists, felt the need to portray as exactly as possible real life around them. As Courbet called for realism in painting, the French critic Duranty urged writers to strive for "the exact, complete, and sincere reproduction of the social milieu in which we live." Writers who considered themselves realists reacted against the fantastic, exotic, and ideal elements in romanticism, although in many of the greatest nineteenth-century works of literature, realism and romanticism coexist. If romanticism produced great *lyrics*, realism, as might be expected, produced great *novels*, for the novel, of all literary genres, is most capable of representing the varied dimensions of a society and its characters. If the middle to late nineteenth century was the great age of the realistic novel, there are still many writers who practice this art today. Although realism has been severely questioned in the twentieth century, it has not entirely died out. Realistic novels are still popular in the United States; and in the Soviet Union, China, and other communist countries, "socialist realism" is still the only officially accepted style for novelists.

One reason for the success of realism as a literary style in the nineteenth century was the increase in literacy among people in the middle and lower classes and the diffusion of journalism. Many novels were published in serial form in the cheap and easily accessible newspapers and journals. The new reading public was not interested in kings, gods, or ideal types; they preferred to read about people like themselves in surroundings like their own.

Realism could be considered a literary school only in France, where it had its fervent proponents and its detractors, its practitioners and its critics. The greatest re-

28–8   Claude Monet, "Waterlilies," sunrise section. (Cliché des Musées Nationaux, Paris/© S.P.A.D.E.M., 1980)

alistic novelists there were Stendhal and Balzac. The latter, in his series of novels entitled *The Human Comedy* (obviously in contrast to *The Divine Comedy*) attempted a complete portrayal of French nineteenth-century society, creating memorable characters in the process. In England, Charles Dickens, George Eliot, and William Thackeray are examples of realistic novelists. Realism in the United States began later than in Europe, but it had a considerable impact on American fiction that continues to the present day. Henry James studied the French realists for his own benefit; William Dean Howells wrote against "romantic lies" in literature in favor of realism, which portrays "men and women as they actually are, actuated by the motives and the passions in the measure we all know." Stephen Crane, who portrayed the harsher aspects of the Civil War, was another great American realist.

What are the basic characteristics of realism? As Howells' statement indicates, a belief in the possibility of realism implies a belief in an objective reality. Realism can be both material and psychological. It uses words to depict the way that things look and feel and the way that people act. Very often, the things influence or represent the people. The realist believes in "realistically" motivated characters who do not act in unexpected ways. Wishing to exclude nothing, realistic writers pay much attention to detail, especially the more sordid or shocking aspects of human life. Although nineteenth-century realists claimed to be objective in their portrayal of actual life, many of them reveal in their writings their profound convictions on contemporary social issues. The impact of industrialism on cities and on human life, particularly the wretched condition of the urban poor, was a particularly apt subject for socially concerned realists.

Dickens   Charles Dickens (1812–1870), a great literary success through his serial novels widely diffused in journals, was one of the most vivid portrayers of the new cities, the characters of all social strata within them, and the alienating effects of industrial capitalism. Because of his improbable plots and grotesque, almost monstrous characters, he cannot be called a consistently realistic novelist; still, he does to a great extent reproduce the material, social, and psychological environment of his time. This selection from *The Old Curiosity Shop* describes the arrival of the novel's heroine, little Nell, and her grandfather in the English mill town of Birmingham.

CHARLES DICKENS

from *The Old Curiosity Shop*

In all their journeying, they had never longed so ardently, they had never so pined and wearied, for the freedom of pure air and open country, as now. No, not even on that memorable morning, when, deserting their old home, they abandoned themselves to the mercies of a strange world, and left all the dumb and senseless things they had known and loved, behind—not even then, had they so yearned for the fresh solitudes of wood, hillside, and field, as now; when the noise and dirt and vapour of the great manufacturing town, reeking with lean misery and hungry wretchedness, hemmed them in on every side, and seemed to shut out hope, and render escape impossible.

"Two days and nights!" thought the child. "He said two days and nights we should have to spend among such scenes as these. Oh! if we live to reach the country once again, if we get clear of these dreadful places, though it is only to lie down and die, with what a grateful heart I shall thank God for so much mercy!"

With thoughts like this, and with some vague design of travelling to a great distance among streams and mountains, where only very poor and simple people lived, and where they might maintain themselves by very humble helping work in farms, free from such terrors as that from which they fled—the child, with no resource but the poor man's gift, and no encouragement but that which flowed from her own heart, and its sense of the truth and right of what she did, nerved herself to this last journey and boldly pursued her task.

"We shall be very slow to-day, dear," she said, as they toiled painfully through the streets; "my feet are sore, and I have pains in all my limbs from the wet of yesterday. I saw that he looked at us and thought of that, when he said how long we should be upon the road."

"It was a dreary way he told us of," returned her grandfather, piteously. "Is there no other road? Will you not let me go some other way than this?"

"Places lie beyond these," said the child, firmly, "where we may live in peace, and be tempted to do no harm. We will take the road that promises to have that end, and we would not turn out of it, if it were a hundred times worse than our fears lead us to expect. We would not, dear, would we?"

"No," replied the old man, wavering in his voice, no less than in his manner. "No. Let us go on. I am ready. I am quite ready, Nell."

The child walked with more difficulty than she had led her companion to expect, for the pains that racked her joints were of no common severity, and every exertion increased them. But they wrung from her no complaint, or look of suffering; and, though the two travellers proceeded very slowly, they did proceed; and clearing the town in course of time, began to feel that they were fairly on their way.

A long suburb of red brick houses,—some with patches of garden ground, where coal-dust and factory smoke darkened the shrinking leaves, and coarse rank flowers; and where the struggling vegetation sickened and sank under the hot breath of kiln and furnace, making them by its presence seem yet more blighting and unwholesome than in the town itself,—a long, flat, straggling suburb passed, they came by slow degrees upon a cheerless region, where not a blade of grass was seen to grow; where not a bud put forth its promise in the spring; where nothing green could live but on the surface of the stagnant pools, which here and there lay idly sweltering by the black roadside.

Advancing more and more into the shadow of this mournful place, its dark depressing influence stole upon their spirits, and filled them with a dismal gloom. On every side, and as far as the eye could see into the heavy distance, tall chimneys, crowding on each other, and presenting that endless repetition of the same dull, ugly form, which is the horror of oppressive dreams, poured out their plague of smoke, obscured the light, and made foul the melancholy air. On mounds of ashes by the wayside, sheltered only by a few rough boards, or rotten pent-house roofs, strange engines spun and writhed like tortured creatures; clanking their iron chains, shrieking in their rapid whirl from time to time as though in torment unendurable, and making the ground tremble with their agonies. Dismantled houses here and there appeared, tottering to the earth, propped up by fragments of others that had fallen down, unroofed, windowless, blackened, desolate, but yet inhabited. Men, women, children, wan in their looks and ragged in attire, tended the engines, fed their tributary fires, begged upon the road, or scowled half-naked from the doorless houses. Then came more of the wrathful monsters, whose like they almost seemed to be in their wildness and their untamed air, screeching and turning round and round again; and still, before, behind, and to the right and left, was the same interminable perspective of brick towers, never ceasing in their black vomit, blasting all things living or inanimate, shutting out the face of day, and closing in on all these horrors with a dense dark cloud.

But night-time in this dreadful spot!—night, when the smoke was changed to fire; when every chimney spirted up its flame; and places, that had been dark vaults all day, now shone red-hot, with figures moving to and fro within their blazing jaws, and calling to one another with hoarse cries—night, when the noise of every strange machine was aggravated by the darkness; when the people near them looked wilder and more savage; when bands of unemployed labourers paraded in the roads, or clustered by torchlight round their leaders, who told them in stern language of their wrongs, and urged them on to frightful cries and threats; when maddened men, armed with sword and firebrand, spurning the tears and prayers of women who would restrain them, rushed forth on errands of terror and destruction, to work no ruin half so surely as their own—night, when carts came rumbling by, filled with rude coffins (for contagious disease and death had been busy with the living crops); when orphans cried, and distracted women shrieked and followed in their wake—night, when some called for bread, and some for drink to drown their cares; and some with tears, and some with staggering feet, and some with bloodshot eyes, went brooding home—night, which, unlike the night that Heaven sends on earth, brought with it no peace, nor quiet, nor signs of blessed sleep—who shall tell the terrors of the night to that young wandering child!

And yet she lay down, with nothing between her and the sky; and, with no fear for herself, for she was past it now, put up a prayer for the poor old man. So very weak and spent she felt, so very calm and unresisting, that she had no thought of any wants of her own, but prayed that God would raise up some friend for *him*. She tried to recall the way they had come, and to look in the direction where the fire by which they had slept last night was burning. She had forgotten to ask the name of the poor man, their friend, and when she had remembered him in her prayers, it seemed ungrateful not to turn one look towards the spot where he was watching.

A penny loaf was all they had had that day. It was very little, but even hunger was forgotten in the strange tranquillity that crept over her senses. She lay down very gently, and, with a quiet smile upon her face, fell into a slumber. It was not like sleep—and yet it must have been, or why those pleasant dreams of the little scholar all night long!

Morning came. Much weaker, diminished powers even of sight and hearing, and yet the child made no complaint—perhaps would have made none, even if she had not that inducement to be silent, travelling by her side. She felt a hopelessness of their ever being extricated together from that forlorn place, a dull conviction that she was very ill, perhaps dying; but no fear or anxiety.

A loathing of food, that she was not conscious of until they expended their last penny in the purchase of another loaf, prevented her partaking even of this poor repast. Her grandfather ate greedily, which she was glad to see.

Their way lay through the same scenes as yesterday, with no variety or improvement. There was the same thick air, difficult to breathe; the same blighted ground, the same hopeless prospect, the same misery and distress. Objects appeared more dim, the noise less, the path more rugged and uneven, for sometimes she stumbled, and became roused, as it were, in the effort to prevent herself from falling. Poor child! the cause was in her tottering feet.

Towards the afternoon, her grandfather complained bitterly of hunger. She approached one of the wretched hovels by the wayside, and knocked with her hand upon the door.

"What would you have here?" said a gaunt miserable man, opening it.

"Charity. A morsel of bread."

"Do you see that?" returned the man hoarsely, point-ing to a kind of bundle on the ground. "That's a dead child. I and five hundred other men were thrown out of work three months ago. That is my third dead child, and last. Do you think I have charity to bestow, or a morsel of bread to spare?"

The child recoiled from the door, and it closed upon her. Impelled by strong necessity, she knocked at another: a neighbouring one, which, yielding to the slight pressure of her hand, flew open.

It seemed that a couple of poor families lived in this hovel, for two women, each among children of her own, occupied different portions of the room. In the centre stood a grave gentleman in black who appeared to have just entered, and who held by the arm a boy.

"Here, woman," he said, "here's your deaf and dumb son. You may thank me for restoring him to you. He was brought before me this morning, charged with theft; and with any other boy it would have gone hard, I assure you. But as I had compassion on his infirmi-ties, and thought he might have learnt no better, I have managed to bring him back to you. Take more care of him for the future."

"And won't you give me back *my* son!" said the other woman, hastily rising and confronting him. "Won't you give me back *my* son, sir, who was trans-ported for the same offence!"

"Was *he* deaf and dumb, woman?" asked the gentle-man sternly.

"Was he not, sir?"

"You know he was not."

"He was," cried the woman. "He was deaf, dumb, and blind, to all that was good and right, from his cradle. Her boy may have learnt no better! where did mine learn better? where could he? who was there to teach him better, or where was it to be learnt?"

"Peace, woman," said the gentleman, "your boy was in possession of all his senses."

"He was," cried the mother; "and he was the more easy to be led astray because he had them. If you save this boy because he may not know right from wrong, why did you not save mine who was never taught the difference? You gentlemen have as good a right to pun-ish her boy, that God has kept in ignorance of sound and speech, as you have to punish mine, that you kept in ignorance yourselves. How many of the girls and boys—ah, men and women too—that are brought before you and you don't pity, are deaf and dumb in their minds, and go wrong in that state, and are punished in that state, body and soul, while you gentlemen are quarrelling among yourselves whether they ought to learn this or that?—Be a just man, sir, and give me back my son."

"You are desperate," said the gentleman, taking out his snuff-box, "and I am sorry for you."

"I *am* desperate," returned the woman, "and you have made me so. Give me back my son, to work for these helpless children. Be a just man, sir, and for God's sake, as you have had mercy upon this boy, give me back my son!"

The child had seen and heard enough to know that this was not a place at which to ask for alms. She led the old man softly from the door, and they pursued their journey.

QUESTIONS

1. What contrast does Dickens make between the city and the country in this passage? What are the techniques that produce this contrast?
2. Is Dickens' description an entirely objective one? What subjective elements do you find in it?
3. What relationship is established between the industrial environment and the people who inhabit it? How?
4. How would you describe the social philosophy implicit in this passage?
5. Compare this passage with Courbet's paintings. Can realistic art ever be an exact reproduction of reality? Why or why not? What conventions do realistic artists use?

Since no excerpts can possibly convey the world created by any of the great nineteenth-century realistic novels, the student is urged to read at least one in its entirety. The passage from *The Old Curiosity Shop* does exemplify a characteristic of realism that was to become more and more important toward the end of the nineteenth century: the determination of human character by the material and social environment. As this belief evolved into a so-called scientific credo, the movement known as *naturalism* replaced realism. The naturalists, more interested in the new theories of Charles Darwin on human evolution than on Courbet's ideas on the reproduction of reality, tried to establish cause-and-effect laws in their novels. Certain conditions in the environment, they demonstrated, will produce certain traits in human beings. The foremost practitioner of naturalism in France was Émile Zola; he found an avid follower in the American Theodore Dreiser. As late as 1940, the black American writer Richard Wright produced a great naturalistic novel, *Native Son*, which demonstrates how a young black man becomes a criminal through the influence of the racist society in which he lives.

29

DEVELOPMENTS IN THE LATE NINETEENTH CENTURY: BEYOND REALISM

The years corresponding to the reign of Queen Victoria in England (1837–1901) produced a number of radical changes in the ways that people in the West viewed themselves and their environment. As industrialism became a fact of life, prevailing attitudes became more and more materialistic. Marx had taught human beings to see themselves as controlled by economic forces, although they could help to shape these forces for the cause of social justice. Some liberal thinkers envisaged a future time when the steady progress of capitalistic industry would create a society in which everyone would be surrounded by mechanical conveniences and physical comfort. Living in a world where every year seemed to witness dramatic technical achievements, the middle-class European or American (if he did not accept the predictions of Marx) had every reason to feel smug about himself and his society.

EUROPE in 1871

ICELAND

ARCTIC OCEAN

LAPLAND

WHITE
SEA   • Archangel

NORWAY AND SWEDEN
NORWAY

FINLAND

L. Ladoga

SHETLAND I.
(Britain)

SWEDEN

Helsingfors

St. Petersburg

• Stockholm

SCOTLAND

NORTH SEA

• Riga

Orenburg

• Moscow

RUSSIAN EMPIRE

IRELAND   • Belfast

GREAT BRITAIN   **DENMARK**   Copenhagen

BALTIC SEA

Dublin • • Liverpool

Danzig

• Vilna

HELIGOLAND
(Britain)   Hamburg

EAST
PRUSSIA

Don R.

Ural R.

ENGLAND

Bremen • Berlin

Elbe R.   *Oder R.*   *Vistula R.*   • Warsaw

Kiev •

Volga R.

London •   **NETHERLANDS**
Amsterdam

GERMAN EMPIRE

• Astrakhan

English Channel   Brussels•
BELGIUM   • Cologne

Dresden

POLAND

Dnieper R.

Rostov •

Reims • LUX. *Rhine R.*
• Paris   Metz • Strasbourg

Prague
AUSTRIA

Dniester R.

*CASPIAN
SEA*

Seine R.   *Loire R.*
• Tours

Munich •   Vienna •   Budapest

Pruth R.   *BESSARABIA*

• Odessa

*Sea of
Azov*

FRANCE   SWITZERLAND

AUSTRIA - HUNGARY

CRIMEA

CAUCASIA

• Baku

Bordeaux •   Lyons •   Milan •

HUNGARY

RUMANIA
(Autonomous)   DOBRUJA   *BLACK SEA*

• Sevastapol

Bilbao •

*ATLANTIC
OCEAN*

Rhône R.   Turin • *Po R.* Venice •

CROATIA-
SLOVENIA

BOSNIA   SERBIA
HERZE-   *(Aut.)*
GOVINA

Danube R.

• Sinope

• Tabriz

PORTUGAL

Ebro R.   Marseilles •

ADRIATIC SEA

BULGARIA

Constantinople

Lisbon •   Madrid •

Tagus R.

CORSICA
(France)

ITALY   Rome •

MONTENEGRO
(Independent)

MACEDONIA

OTTOMAN   EMPIRE

Tigris R.

SPAIN   Barcelona •

BALEARIC I.
(Spain)   *SARDINIA*

Naples •

ALBANIA

*AEGEAN
SEA*

• Smyrna

Euphrates R.

MESOPOTAMIA

PERSIA

• Seville

*IONIAN I.
(Gr.)*   Athens •

• Baghdad

Tangier • • Gibraltar

• Fez

SICILY

GREECE
(Independent)

Dardanelles

SYRIA

MOROCCO

ALGERIA
(France)   Tunis •

TUNISIA

MALTA (Britain)

MEDITERRANEAN SEA   *CRETE (Turkish)*

*CYPRUS
(Britain)*

ARABIA

Algiers •

Charles Darwin   In the pure, as opposed to the applied, sciences, more fundamental changes were taking place. Among the most important of these were the evolutionary theories put forth by Charles Darwin (1809–1882). Darwin, who published his *Origin of Species* in 1859 and *The Descent of Man* in 1871, showed through his scientific observations of the "lower" animals that man was an integral part of their world. By evolution he meant that species are mutable: that each class of living organisms has developed through a series of gradual changes from a different one that preceded it. Species developed through mutations in inherited characteristics. Those inheriting the most useful characteristics—for fighting, food gathering, or mating—survived; the others died out. Thus life was basically a struggle for existence. The "survival of the fittest" was brought about through "natural selection." Man was one of those species that had evolved from the primate family and had managed to survive.

The protest against Darwin and his theories, which lasted well into the twentieth century, was very great indeed. Fundamentalist religious groups denounced him for proposing a theory of creation contrary to the one in Genesis; other moralists and religious authorities claimed that he had turned man into a monkey and undermined the foundations of human dignity, morality, and religion. The most upsetting concept in Darwin's theory of evolution was its concept of life as a scene of struggle and survival, of "nature red in tooth and claw." Nature could no longer be seen as the harmonious work of the Supreme Being or the motherly source of consolation for wounded emotions. Constant flux, change, relativity of existence, and the elimination of the weak were in the natural order of things.

Herbert Spencer Nonscientific Darwin enthusiasts did not hesitate to apply his theories to human society. Herbert Spencer (1820–1903) proclaimed a doctrine of agnosticism (the impossibility of knowing the existence of God with certainty) and what came to be known as "social Darwinism." Spencer argued that society, like the natural world, was governed by the principle of evolution. There, too, the fittest survived and the weak went under. Social evolution was headed toward the increased freedom of the individual, and governments had no business interfering in the "natural" economic processes or protecting the weak and unfit. In stressing the freedom of individual struggle in the economic process, Spencer seemed to give a scientific confirmation to the doctrines of early liberalism. His ideas had a particularly great influence in the United States, where the individualistic capitalism that led to the "robber barons" was booming. Thus the nineteenth-century bourgeois managed to assimilate even the radical theories of evolution into their materialistic, self-satisfied view of the world.

Yet other philosophers, particularly artists, raised their voices loudly against this view of man and society. The highly influential German, Friedrich Nietzsche (1844–1900), a poetic more than a systematic philosopher, adapted evolutionary theories to purposes quite different from Spencer's. He denounced his bourgeois contemporaries for their hypocrisy, their stale morality, and their rationalism. He also saw human nature in terms of evolution toward freedom and elimination of weakness, but the freedom that interested him was spiritual and intellectual rather than economic and material. Rather than being satisfied with Western culture as he found it, he attacked not only its present state but also what we have seen to be its roots: the Greco-Roman and Judeo-Christian traditions. The Greek emphasis on reason as exemplified by Socrates worked against the healthy vitality of the instincts, according to Nietzsche. He did admire an aspect of Greek culture that, he felt, modern times had neglected—the irrational or "Dionysian" strain represented by ancient tragedy. Nietzsche advocated a revolt against the limits of reason and reasonableness and a return to greater sources of personal and cultural power in the irrational and in myth. The moral values of Jews and Christians he found to be the expressions of weaklings or of "slaves." Christian ideas such as "pity," "turning the other cheek," or "sin" were for Nietzsche notions designed to keep people in their place instead of allowing free individuals to realize themselves to their full potential.

Nietzsche's thought, interpreted in various ways, has been influential on a variety of modern doctrines. Following his profound doubts about Western culture, some thinkers turned to the Orient or to Africa in an effort to find new sources of vitality for their own times. Others, following an opposite line of thought, derived racist ideas from Nietzsche, seeing in his theory of human evolution toward the free, noble "superman" a justification for beliefs in the superiority of the white or Aryan race. The Nazis interpreted Nietzsche in this way. The "God is dead" movement has its source in Nietzsche's own words. Nietzsche's thought has been deeply influential on the philosophical school of existentialism, both in its Christian and atheistic forms.

FRIEDRICH NIETZSCHE

Quotations

The Christian religion grew upon a soil of such utter falsification, where the deepest instincts of the ruling factions were opposed to nature and natural values to such an extent, that Christianity became a death struggle against reality which has never been surpassed. *The Antichrist*

Nothing is more pathological in our pathological modernity than this disease of Christian pity. *Ibid.*

What is good? All that elevates the feeling of power, the will to power, the power itself in man. *Ibid.*

What is bad? All that proceeds from weakness. *Ibid.*

Life is an instinct of growth, for survival, for the accumulation of forces, for power. *Ibid.*

Morality is the best of all devices for leading mankind by the nose. *Ibid.*

Woman was God's second mistake. *Ibid.*

I call Christianity the one great curse, the one intrinsic depravity, ... the one immortal blemish on the human race. *Ibid.*

Life itself is *Will to Power;* self-preservation is only one of the indirect and most frequent results thereof. *Beyond Good and Evil*

The noble soul has reverence for itself. *Ibid.*

The Christian faith from the beginning, is sacrifice: the sacrifice of all freedom, all pride, all self-confidence of spirit; it is at the same time subjection, self-derision, and self-mutilation. *Ibid.*

There are no eternal facts, as there are no absolute truths. *Human, All Too Human*

I teach you the Superman. Man is something that is to be surpassed. What have you done to surpass him? *Thus Spake Zarathustra*

All the gods are dead; so we now want the superman to live. *Ibid.*

God is dead! God remains dead! And we have killed Him! *Ibid.*

He who must be a creator in good and evil—verily, he must first be a destroyer, and break values into pieces. *Ibid.*

The man who has won his freedom ... tramples ruthlessly upon that contemptible kind of comfort which tea-grocers, Christians, cows, women, Englishmen and other democrats worship in their dreams. *Ibid.*

The world is beautiful, but has a disease called Man. *The Will to Power*

The Christian resolve to find the world evil and ugly has made the world evil and ugly. *Ibid.*

Beyond Realism: Dostoevsky

Another radical critique of materialistic and rationalistic Western society came from the Russian writer Fyodor Dostoevsky (1821–1881). Dostoevsky, who was to have a major impact on Western literature and thought in the twentieth century, considered himself as a Russian outside the traditions of Western Europe and thus able to view them more critically. He envisioned a major role for Russia in the destiny of the West. History has proved him right in a way that he would not have approved.

Dostoevsky began his intellectual career as a socialist, associating with one of many groups of young Russians interested in the new doctrines from Europe. For this, the tsarist regime arrested him, sending him off to imprisonment in Siberia. He was at first sentenced to death, but the sentence was commuted at the last minute. During his stay in the Siberian prison, an experience that he recounted later in *The House of the Dead*, Dostoevsky underwent a reconversion to a mystical, Russian Orthodox Christianity. He also gained insight from observing the various criminals and political prisoners around him. In his later novels Dostoevsky portrayed characters in the extremes of moral degradation on the one hand and spiritual illumination on the other. The achievement of salvation through doubt, suffering, and even crime became one of his major themes. Like Nietzsche, Dostoevsky praised the extremes of human existence and deplored the safe, smug middle road; but, unlike Nietzsche, he believed that mankind could be saved through faith in Christ.

The much acclaimed Crystal Palace became in Dostoevsky's first major work, *Notes from the Underground* (1864), a symbol of the utopia of those who believe in the doctrines of progress through science and materialism. The kind of happiness represented by Crystal Palace could, according to Dostoevsky, be achieved only through the loss of human freedom. Freedom, not political or economic but spiritual freedom of choice, is for Dostoevsky man's precious possession. Man should be free to follow his irrational yearnings, his caprice, in order to develop his spiritual nature fully. Man in Dostoevsky's view is not naturally good, as the optimists of both the eighteenth and the nineteenth centuries believed, but fallen and yet free to choose faith in Christ. Such a choice made for reasons of certainty or stability would be, however, a false one. The choice for Christ should be made irrationally, or suprarationally, through faith, taking upon oneself the burden of humanity since "everybody is guilty for all and before all." Dostoevsky came to believe that only the Russian people and the Russian church had preserved Christianity in its pure form, and he prophesied a messianic role for Russia. The West, whether materialistic or socialistic or Catholic, was for him in complete decay. Roman Catholicism he viewed as a kind of herd religion, an attempt to force belief and conformity through authority.

Dostoevsky develops these themes in his four great novels, *Crime and Punishment* (1866), *The Idiot* (1868), *The Possessed* (1871), and *The Brothers Karamazov* (1880). There his ideas are given flesh and blood through the complexity and fullness of his tortured, extremist characters and the settings in which they play out their destinies. In his ability to create living characters, Dostoevsky is in the tradition of the great European realists and indeed one of the masters of realism; yet his belief in human freedom puts him in direct opposition to the naturalists, who portrayed man as conditioned by social and material conditions. His supreme interest in the exploration of the human soul makes Dostoevsky break through the bounds of a style limited to everyday life and "realistic" character motivation. Influenced by Dickens, he developed aspects of the grotesque already present in the English novelist's works. For Dostoevsky, reality, in art as in life, extended beyond realism. In a letter of 1869 he wrote, "I have my own view of art, and that which the majority call fantastic and exceptional is for me the very essence of reality."

It is perhaps not too surprising, then, that at the heart of *The Brothers Karamazov*, in many ways a realistic novel about nineteenth-century Russia, lies a fantastic story recounting the return of Christ to the earth during the *Inquisition* in sixteenth-century Spain. The story is told by one of the Karamazov brothers, Ivan, to his younger brother Alyosha. Ivan, with whom Dostoevsky shows great sympathy, is an atheist, or at least one who cannot accept the revelations of Christianity

though he struggles with them desperately. Alyosha, in contrast, is a novice in a monastery and a pure-souled believer. Before telling the story that he calls "The Grand Inquisitor," Ivan makes two pronouncements, both of which have been widely quoted and commented on by twentieth-century thinkers. In the first, Ivan reasons that if God and the immortality of the individual soul do not exist, "everything is permitted." Without such a foundation, there can be no universal morality, and man is free to create his own. In the second, Ivan finds the existence of human suffering a just cause for revolt against God. If God can permit innocent children to be tortured to death, Ivan asks, how can he be just? What Ivan cannot accept is the world as he finds it, the world that God has made. Ivan demands justice on his own terms.

The Grand Inquisitor in Ivan's story represents the established Church, the Roman Church, but also what Ivan would consider an authentic view of most human beings as weak, slavish, and needing authority. In the Inquisitor's view, Christ neither loved nor understood men because He believed them capable of freely chosen faith without the assurances of material comfort and proof. The arguments of the Grand Inquisitor are strong ones; they have caused many readers to believe that Dostoevsky, in spite of his professed intentions, was really on his side. What is at stake here are two fundamentally different conceptions of human nature and of religion that Dostoevsky has set against each other with exquisite balance. Each reader will choose for him or herself which view is the more convincing or the truer. The selection is taken from Constance Garnett's translation of *The Brothers Karamazov*.

FEODOR DOSTOEVSKY

The Grand Inquisitor

"Even this must have a preface—that is, a literary preface," laughed Ivan, "and I am a poor hand at making one. You see, my action takes place in the sixteenth century, and at that time, as you probably learnt at school, it was customary in poetry to bring down heavenly powers on earth. Not to speak of Dante, in France, clerks, as well as the monks in the monasteries, used to give regular performances in which the Madonna, the saints, the angels, Christ, and God Himself were brought on the stage. In those days it was done in all simplicity. In Victor Hugo's 'Notre Dame de Paris' an edifying and gratuitous spectacle was provided for the people in the Hotel de Ville of Paris in the reign of Louis XI. in honour of the birth of the dauphin. It was called *Le bon jugement de la très sainte et gracieuse Vierge Marie*, and she appears herself on the stage and pronounces her *bon jugement*. Similar plays, chiefly from the Old Testament, were occasionally performed in Moscow too, up to the times of Peter the Great. But besides plays there were all sorts of legends and ballads scattered about the world, in which the saints and angels and all the powers of Heaven took part when required. In our monasteries the monks busied themselves in translating, copying, and even composing such poems—and even under the Tatars. There is, for instance, one such poem (of course, from the Greek), 'The Wanderings of Our Lady through Hell,' with descriptions as bold as Dante's. Our Lady visits Hell, and the Archangel Michael leads her through the torments. She sees the sinners and their punishment. There she sees among others one noteworthy set of sinners in a burning lake; some of them sink to the bottom of the lake so that they can't swim out, and 'these God forgets'—an expression of extraordinary depth and force. And so Our Lady, shocked and weeping, falls before the throne of God and begs for mercy for all in Hell—for all she has seen there, and indiscriminately. Her conversation with God is immensely interesting. She beseeches Him, she will not desist, and when God points to the hands and feet of her Son, nailed to the Cross, and asks, 'How can I forgive His tormentors?' she bids all the saints, all the martyrs, all the angels and archangels to fall down with her and pray for mercy on all without distinction. It ends by her winning from God a respite of suffering every year from Good Friday till Trinity day, and the sinners at once raise a cry of thankfulness from Hell, chanting, 'Thou art just, O Lord, in this judgment.' Well, my poem would have been of that kind if it had appeared at that time. He comes on the scene in my poem, but He says nothing, only appears and passes on. Fifteen centuries have passed since He promised to come in His glory, fifteen centuries since His prophet wrote, 'Behold, I come

quickly'; 'Of that day and that hour knoweth no man, neither the Son, but the Father,' as He Himself predicted on earth. But humanity awaits him with the same faith and with the same love. Oh, with greater faith, for it is fifteen centuries since man has ceased to see signs from Heaven.

> *No signs from Heaven come to-day*
> *To add to what the heart doth say.*

There was nothing left but faith in what the heart doth say. It is true there were many miracles in those days. There were saints who performed miraculous cures; some holy people, according to their biographies, were visited by the Queen of Heaven herself. But the devil did not slumber, and doubts were already arising among men of the truth of these miracles. And just then there appeared in the north of Germany a terrible new heresy. 'A huge star like to a torch' (that is, to a church) 'fell on the sources of the waters and they became bitter.' These heretics began blasphemously denying miracles. But those who remained faithful were all the more ardent in their faith. The tears of humanity rose up to Him as before, awaiting His coming, loved Him, hoped for Him, yearned to suffer and die for Him as before. And so many ages mankind had prayed with faith and fervour, 'O Lord our God, hasten Thy coming,' so many ages called upon Him, that in His infinite mercy He deigned to come down to His servants. Before that day He had come down, He had visited some holy men, martyrs and hermits, as is written in their 'Lives.' Among us, Tyutchev, with absolute faith in the truth of his words, bore witness that

> *Bearing the Cross, in slavish dress*
> *Weary and worn, the Heavenly King*
> *Our mother, Russia, came to bless,*
> *And through our land went wandering.*

And that certainly was so, I assure you.

"And behold, He deigned to appear for a moment to the people, to the tortured, suffering people, sunk in iniquity, but loving Him like children. My story is laid in Spain, in Seville, in the most terrible time of the Inquisition, when fires were lighted every day to the glory of God, and 'in the splendid *auto da fé* the wicked heretics were burnt.' Oh, of course, this was not the coming in which He will appear according to His promise at the end of time in all His heavenly glory, and which will be sudden 'as lightning flashing from east to west.' No, He visited His children only for a moment, and there where the flames were crackling round the heretics. In His infinite mercy He came once more among men in that human shape in which He walked among men for three years fifteen centuries ago. He came down to the 'hot pavement' of the southern town in which on the day before almost a hundred heretics had, *ad majorem gloriam Dei*, been burnt by the cardinal, the Grand Inquisitor, in a magnificent *auto da fé*, in the presence of the king, the court, the knights, the cardinals, the most charming ladies of the court, and the whole population of Seville.

"He came softly, unobserved, and yet, strange to say, every one recognised Him. That might be one of the best passages in the poem. I mean, why they recognised Him. The people are irresistibly drawn to Him, they surround Him, they flock about Him, follow Him. He moves silently in their midst with a gentle smile of infinite compassion. The sun of love burns in His heart, light and power shine from His eyes, and their radiance, shed on the people, stirs their hearts with responsive love. He holds out His hands to them, blesses them, and a healing virtue comes from contact with Him, even with His garments. An old man in the crowd, blind from childhood, cries out, 'O Lord, heal me and I shall see Thee!' and, as it were, scales fall from his eyes and the blind man sees Him. The crowd weeps and kisses the earth under His feet. Children throw flowers before Him, sing, and cry hosannah. 'It is He—it is He!' all repeat. 'It must be He, it can be no one but Him!' He stops at the steps of the Seville cathedral at the moment when the weeping mourners are bringing in a little open white coffin. In it lies a child of seven, the only daughter of a prominent citizen. The dead child lies hidden in flowers. 'He will raise your child,' the crowd shouts to the weeping mother. The priest, coming to meet the coffin, looks perplexed, and frowns, but the mother of the dead child throws herself at His feet with a wail. 'If it is Thou, raise my child!' she cries, holding out her hands to Him. The procession halts, the coffin is laid on the steps at His feet. He looks with compassion, and His lips once more softly pronounce, 'Maiden, arise!' and the maiden arises. The little girl sits up in the coffin and looks round, smiling with wide-open wondering eyes, holding a bunch of white roses they had put in her hand.

"There are cries, sobs, confusion among the people, and at that moment the cardinal himself, the Grand Inquisitor, passes by the cathedral. He is an old man, almost ninety, tall and erect, with a withered face and sunken eyes, in which there is still a gleam of light. He is not dressed in his gorgeous cardinal's robes, as he was the day before, when he was burning the enemies of the Roman Church—at that moment he was wearing his coarse, old, monk's cassock. At a distance behind him come his gloomy assistants and slaves and the 'holy guard.' He stops at the sight of the crowd and watches it from a distance. He sees everything; he sees them set the coffin down at His feet, sees the child rise up, and his face darkens. He knits his thick grey brows and his eyes gleam with a sinister fire. He holds out his finger and bids the guards take Him. And such is his power, so completely are the people cowed into submission and trembling obedience to him, that the crowd immediately make way for the guards, and in the midst of deathlike silence they lay hands on Him and lead Him away. The crowd instantly bows down to the earth, like one man, before the old inquisitor. He blesses the people in silence and passes on. The guards lead their prisoner to the close, gloomy vaulted prison in the ancient palace of the Holy Inquisition and shut Him in it. The day passes and is followed by the dark, burning 'breathless' night of Seville. The air is 'fragrant with laurel and lemon.' In the pitch darkness the iron door of the prison is suddenly opened and the Grand Inquisitor himself comes in with a light in his hand. He is alone; the door is closed at once behind him. He stands in the doorway and for a minute or two gazes into His face. At last he goes up slowly, sets the light on the table and speaks.

" 'Is it Thou? Thou?' but receiving no answer, he adds at once, 'Don't answer, be silent. What canst Thou say, indeed? I know too well what Thou wouldst say. And Thou hast no right to add anything to what Thou hadst said of old. Why, then, art Thou come to hinder us? For Thou hast come to hinder us, and Thou knowest that. But dost Thou know what will be to-morrow? I know not who Thou art and care not to know whether it is Thou or only a semblance of Him, but to-morrow I shall condemn Thee and burn Thee at the stake as the worst of heretics. And the very people who have to-day kissed Thy feet, to-morrow at the faintest sign from me will rush to heap up the embers of Thy fire. Knowest Thou that? Yes, maybe Thou knowest it,' he added with thoughtful penetration, never for a moment taking his eyes off the Prisoner."

"I don't quite understand, Ivan. What does it mean?" Alyosha, who had been listening in silence, said with a smile. "Is it simply a wild fantasy, or a mistake on the part of the old man—some impossible *qui pro quo*?"

"Take it as the last," said Ivan, laughing, "if you are so corrupted by modern realism and can't stand anything fantastic. If you like it to be a case of mistaken identity, let it be so. It is true," he went on, laughing, "the old man was ninety, and he might well be crazy over his set idea. He might have been struck by the appearance of the Prisoner. It might, in fact, be simply his ravings, the delusion of an old man of ninety, over-excited by the *auto da fé* of a hundred heretics the day before. But does it matter to us after all whether it was a mistake of identity or a wild fantasy? All that matters is that the old man should speak out, should speak openly of what he has thought in silence for ninety years."

"And the Prisoner too is silent? Does He look at him and not say a word?"

"That's inevitable in any case," Ivan laughed again. "The old man has told Him He hasn't the right to add anything to what He has said of old. One may say it is the most fundamental feature of Roman Catholicism, in my opinion at least. 'All has been given by Thee to the Pope,' they say, 'and all, therefore, is still in the Pope's hands, and there is no need for Thee to come now at all. Thou must not meddle for the time, at least.' That's how they speak and write too—the Jesuits, at any rate. I have read it myself in the works of their theologians. 'Hast Thou the right to reveal to us one of the mysteries of that world from which Thou hast come?' my old man asks Him, and answers the question for Him. 'No, Thou hast not; that Thou mayest not add to what has been said of old, and mayest not take from men the freedom which Thou didst exalt when Thou wast on earth. Whatsoever Thou revealest anew will encroach on men's freedom of faith; for it will be manifest as a miracle, and the freedom of their faith was dearer to Thee than anything in those days fifteen hundred years ago. Didst Thou not

often say then, "I will make you free"? But now Thou has seen these "free" men,' the old man adds suddenly, with a pensive smile. 'Yes, we've paid dearly for it,' he goes on, looking sternly at Him, 'but at last we have completed that work in Thy name. For fifteen centuries we have been wrestling with Thy freedom, but now it is ended and over for good. Dost Thou not believe that it's over for good? Thou lookest meekly at me and deignest not even to be wroth with me. But let me tell Thee that now, to-day, people are more persuaded than ever that they have perfect freedom, yet they have brought their freedom to us and laid it humbly at our feet. But that has been our doing. Was this what Thou didst? Was this Thy freedom?' "

"I don't understand again," Alyosha broke in. "Is he ironical, is he jesting?"

"Not a bit of it! He claims it as a merit for himself and his Church that at last they have vanquished freedom and have done so to make men happy. 'For now' (he is speaking of the Inquisition, of course) 'for the first time it has become possible to think of the happiness of men. Man was created a rebel; and how can rebels be happy? Thou wast warned,' he says to Him. 'Thou hast had no lack of admonitions and warnings, but Thou didst not listen to those warnings; Thou didst reject the only way by which men might be made happy. But, fortunately, departing Thou didst hand on the work to us. Thou has promised, Thou hast established by Thy word, Thou has given to us the right to bind and to unbind, and now, of course, Thou canst not think of taking it away. Why, then, hast Thou come to hinder us?' "

"And what's the meaning of 'no lack of admonitions and warnings'?" asked Alyosha.

"Why, that's the chief part of what the old man must say."

" 'The wise and dread Spirit, the spirit of self-destruction and nonexistence,' the old man goes on, 'the great spirit talked with Thee in the wilderness, and we are told in the books that he "tempted" Thee. Is that so? And could anything truer be said than what he revealed to Thee in three questions and what Thou didst reject, and what in the books is called "the temptation"? And yet if there has ever been on earth a real stupendous miracle, it took place on that day, on the day of the three temptations. The statement of those three questions was itself the miracle. If it were possible to imagine simply for the sake of argument that those three questions of the dread spirit had perished utterly from the books, and that we had to restore them and to invent them anew, and to do so had gathered together all the wise men of the earth—rulers, chief priests, learned men, philosophers, poets—and had set them the task to invent three questions, such as would not only fit the occasion, but express in three words, three human phrases, the whole future history of the world and of humanity—dost Thou believe that all the wisdom of the earth united could have invented anything in depth and force equal to the three questions which were actually put to Thee then by the wise and mighty spirit in the wilderness? From those questions alone, from the miracle of their statement, we can see that we have here to do not with the fleeting human intelligence, but with the absolute and eternal. For in those three questions the whole subsequent history of mankind is, as it were, brought together into one whole, and foretold, and in them are united all the unsolved historical contradictions of human nature. At the time it could not be so clear, since the future was unknown; but now that fifteen hundred years have passed, we see that everything in those three questions was so justly divined and foretold, and has been so truly fulfilled, that nothing can be added to them or taken from them.

" 'Judge Thyself who was right—Thou or he who questioned Thee then? Remember the first question; its meaning, in other words, was this: "Thou wouldst go into the world, and art going with empty hands, with some promise of freedom which men in their simplicity and their natural unruliness cannot even understand, which they fear and dread—for nothing has ever been more insupportable for a man and a human society than freedom. But seest Thou these stones in this parched and barren wilderness? Turn them into bread, and mankind will run after Thee like a flock of sheep, grateful and obedient, though for ever trembling, lest Thou withdraw Thy hand and deny them Thy bread." But Thou wouldst not deprive man of freedom and didst reject the offer, thinking, what is that freedom worth, if obedience is bought with bread? Thou didst reply that man lives not by bread alone. But dost Thou know that for the sake of that earthly bread the spirit of the earth will rise up against Thee and will strive

with Thee and overcome Thee, and all will follow him, crying, "Who can compare with this beast? He has given us fire from heaven!" Dost Thou know that the ages will pass, and humanity will proclaim by the lips of their sages that there is no crime, and therefore no sin; there is only hunger? "Feed men, and then ask of them virtue!" that's what they'll write on the banner, which they will raise against Thee, and with which they will destroy Thy temple. Where Thy temple stood will rise a new building; the terrible tower of Babel will be built again, and though, like the one of old, it will not be finished, yet Thou mightest have prevented that new tower and have cut short the sufferings of men for a thousand years; for they will come back to us after a thousand years of agony with their tower. They will seek us again, hidden underground in the catacombs, for we shall be again persecuted and tortured. They will find us and cry to us, "Feed us, for those who have promised us fire from heaven haven't given it!" And then we shall finish building their tower, for he finishes the building who feeds them. And we alone shall feed them in Thy name, declaring falsely that it is in Thy name. Oh, never, never can they feed themselves without us! No science will give them bread so long as they remain free. In the end they will lay their freedom at our feet, and say to us, "Make us your slaves, but feed us." They will understand themselves, at last, that freedom and bread enough for all are inconceivable together, for never, never will they be able to share between them! They will be convinced, too, that they can never be free, for they are weak, vicious, worthless and rebellious. Thou didst promise them the bread of Heaven, but, I repeat again, can it compare with earthly bread in the eyes of the weak, ever sinful and ignoble race of man? And if for the sake of the bread of Heaven thousands and tens of thousands shall follow Thee, what is to become of the millions and tens of thousands of millions of creatures who will not have the strength to forego the earthly bread for the sake of the heavenly? Or dost Thou care only for the tens of thousands of the great and strong, while the millions, numerous as the sands of the sea, who are weak but love Thee, must exist only for the sake of the great and strong? No, we care for the weak too. They are sinful and rebellious, but in the end they too will become obedient. They will marvel at us and look on us as gods, because we are ready to endure the freedom which they have found so dreadful and to rule over them—so awful it will seem to them to be free. But we shall tell them that we are Thy servants and rule them in Thy name. We shall deceive them again, for we will not let Thee come to us again. That deception will be our suffering, for we shall be forced to lie.

" 'This is the significance of the first question in the wilderness, and this is what Thou hast rejected for the sake of that freedom which Thou hast exalted above everything. Yet in this question lies hid the great secret of this world. Choosing "bread," Thou wouldst have satisfied the universal and everlasting craving of humanity—to find some one to worship. So long as man remains free he strives for nothing so incessantly and so painfully as to find some one to worship. But man seeks to worship what is established beyond dispute, so that all men would agree at once to worship it. For these pitiful creatures are concerned not only to find what one or the other can worship, but to find something that all would believe in and worship; what is essential is that all may be *together* in it. This craving for *community* of worship is the chief misery of every man individually and of all humanity from the beginning of time. For the sake of common worship they've slain each other with the sword. They have set up gods and challenged one another, "Put away your gods and come and worship ours, or we will kill you and your gods!" And so it will be to the end of the world, even when gods disappear from the earth; they will fall down before idols just the same. Thou didst know, Thou couldst not but have known, this fundamental secret of human nature, but Thou didst reject the one infallible banner which was offered Thee to make all men bow down to Thee alone—the banner of earthly bread; and Thou hast rejected it for the sake of freedom and the bread of Heaven. Behold what Thou didst further. And all again in the name of freedom! I tell Thee that man is tormented by no greater anxiety than to find some one quickly to whom he can hand over that gift of freedom with which the ill-fated creature is born. But only one who can appease their conscience can take over their freedom. In bread there was offered Thee an invincible banner; give bread, and man will worship Thee, for nothing is more certain than bread. But if some one else gains possession of his con-

science—oh! then he will cast away Thy bread and follow after him who has ensnared his conscience. In that Thou wast right. For the secret of man's being is not only to live but to have something to live for. Without a stable conception of the object of life, man would not consent to go on living, and would rather destroy himself than remain on earth, though he had bread in abundance. That is true. But what happened? Instead of taking men's freedom from them, Thou didst make it greater than ever! Didst Thou forget that man prefers peace, and even death, to freedom of choice in the knowledge of good and evil? Nothing is more seductive for man than his freedom of conscience, but nothing is a greater cause of suffering. And behold, instead of giving a firm foundation for setting the conscience of man at rest for ever, Thou didst choose all that is exceptional, vague and enigmatic; Thou didst choose what was utterly beyond the strength of men, acting as though Thou didst not love them at all—Thou who didst come to give Thy life for them! Instead of taking possession of men's freedom, Thou didst increase it, and burdened the spiritual kingdom of mankind with its sufferings for ever. Thou didst desire man's free love, that he should follow Thee freely, enticed and taken captive by Thee. In place of the rigid ancient law, man must hereafter with free heart decide for himself what is good and what is evil, having only Thy image before him as his guide. But didst Thou not know he would at last reject even Thy image and Thy truth, if he is weighed down with the fearful burden of free choice? They will cry aloud at last that the truth is not in Thee, for they could not have been left in greater confusion and suffering than Thou hast caused, laying upon them so many cares and unanswerable problems.

" 'So that, in truth, Thou didst Thyself lay the foundation for the destruction of Thy kingdom, and no one is more to blame for it. Yet what was offered Thee? There are three powers, three powers alone, able to conquer and to hold captive for ever the conscience of these impotent rebels for their happiness—those forces are miracle, mystery and authority. Thou hast rejected all three and hast set the example for doing so. When the wise and dread spirit set Thee on the pinnacle of the temple and said to Thee, "If Thou wouldst know whether Thou art the Son of God then cast Thyself down, for it is written: the angels shall hold him up lest he fall and bruise himself, and Thou shalt know then whether Thou art the Son of God and shalt prove then how great is Thy faith in Thy Father." But Thou didst refuse and wouldst not cast Thyself down. Oh! of course, Thou didst proudly and well like God; but the weak, unruly race of men, are they gods? Oh, Thou didst know then that in taking one step, in making one movement to cast Thyself down, Thou wouldst be tempting God and have lost all Thy faith in Him, and wouldst have been dashed to pieces against that earth which Thou didst come to save. And the wise spirit that tempted Thee would have rejoiced. But I ask again, are there many like Thee? And couldst Thou believe for one moment that men, too, could face such a temptation? Is the nature of men such, that they can reject miracle, and at the great moments of their life, the moments of their deepest, most agonising spiritual difficulties, cling only to the free verdict of the heart? Oh, Thou didst know that Thy deed would be recorded in books, would be handed down to remote times and the utmost ends of the earth, and Thou didst hope that man, following Thee, would cling to God and not ask for a miracle. But Thou didst not know that when man rejects miracle he rejects God too; for man seeks not so much God as the miraculous. And as man cannot bear to be without the miraculous, he will create new miracles of his own for himself, and will worship deeds of sorcery and witchcraft, though he might be a hundred times over a rebel, heretic and infidel. Thou didst not come down from the Cross when they shouted to Thee, mocking and reviling Thee, "Come down from the cross and we will believe that Thou art He." Thou didst not come down, for again Thou wouldst not enslave man by a miracle, and didst crave faith given freely, not based on miracle. Thou didst crave for free love and not the base raptures of the slave before the might that has overawed him for ever. But Thou didst think too highly of men therein, for they are slaves, of course, though rebellious by nature. Look round and judge; fifteen centuries have passed, look upon them. Whom hast Thou raised up to Thyself? I swear, man is weaker and baser by nature than Thou hast believed him! Can he, can he do what Thou didst? By showing him so much respect, Thou didst, as it were, cease to feel for him, for Thou didst ask far too much from him—Thou who hast loved him more than Thyself!

Respecting him less, Thou wouldst have asked less of him. That would have been more like love, for his burden would have been lighter. He is weak and vile. What though he is everywhere now rebelling against our power, and proud of his rebellion? It is the pride of a child and a schoolboy. They are little children rioting and barring out the teacher at school. But their childish delight will end; it will cost them dear. They will cast down temples and drench the earth with blood. But they will see at last, the foolish children, that, though they are rebels, they are impotent rebels, unable to keep up their own rebellion. Bathed in their foolish tears, they will recognise at last that He who created them rebels must have meant to mock at them. They will say this in despair, and their utterance will be a blasphemy which will make them more unhappy still, for man's nature cannot bear blasphemy, and in the end always avenges it on itself. And so unrest, confusion and unhappiness—that is the present lot of man after Thou didst bear so much for their freedom! Thy great prophet tells in vision and in image, that he saw all those who took part in the first resurrection and that there were of each tribe twelve thousand. But if there were so many of them, they must have been not men but gods. They had borne Thy cross, they had endured scores of years in the barren, hungry wilderness, living upon locusts and roots—and Thou mayest indeed point with pride at those children of freedom, of free love, of free and splendid sacrifice for Thy name. But remember that they were only some thousands; and what of the rest? And how are the other weak ones to blame, because they could not endure what the strong have endured? How is the weak soul to blame that it is unable to receive such terrible gifts? Canst Thou have simply come to the elect and for the elect? But if so, it is a mystery and we cannot understand it. And if it is a mystery, we too have a right to preach a mystery, and to teach them that it's not the free judgment of their hearts, not love that matters, but a mystery which they must follow blindly, even against their conscience. So we have done. We have corrected Thy work and have founded it upon *miracle*, *mystery* and *authority*. And men rejoiced that they were again led like sheep, and that the terrible gift that had brought them such suffering, was, at last, lifted from their hearts. Were we right teaching them this? Speak! Did we not love mankind, so meekly acknowledging their feebleness, lovingly lightening their burden, and permitting their weak nature even sin with our sanction? Why hast Thou come now to hinder us? And why dost Thou look silently and searchingly at me with Thy mild eyes? Be angry. I don't want Thy love, for I love Thee not. And what use is it for me to hide anything from Thee? Don't I know to Whom I am speaking? All that I can say is known to Thee already. And is it for me to conceal from Thee our mystery? Perhaps it is Thy will to hear it from my lips. Listen, then. We are not working with Thee, but with *him*—that is our mystery. It's long—eight centuries—since we have been on *his* side and not on Thine. Just eight centuries ago, we took from him what Thou didst reject with scorn, that last gift he offered Thee, showing Thee all the kingdoms of the earth. We took from him Rome and the sword of Caesar, and proclaimed ourselves sole rulers of the earth, though hitherto we have not been able to complete our work. But whose fault is that? Oh, the work is only beginning, but it has begun. It has long to await completion and the earth has yet much to suffer, but we shall triumph and shall be Caesar's, and then we shall plan the universal happiness of man. But Thou mightest have taken even then the sword of Caesar. Why didst Thou reject that last gift? Hadst Thou accepted that last counsel of the mighty spirit, Thou wouldst have accomplished all that man seeks on earth—that is, some one to worship, some one to keep his conscience, and some means of uniting all in one unanimous and harmonious ant-heap, for the craving for universal unity is the third and last anguish of men. Mankind as a whole has always striven to organise a universal state. There have been many great nations with great histories, but the more highly they were developed the more unhappy they were, for they felt more acutely than other people the craving for worldwide union. The great conquerors, Timours and Ghenghis-Khans, whirled like hurricanes over the face of the earth striving to subdue its people, and they too were but the unconscious expression of the same craving for universal unity. Hadst Thou taken the world and Caesar's purple, Thou wouldst have founded the universal state and have given universal peace. For who can rule men if not he who holds their conscience and their bread in his hands. We have taken the sword of Caesar, and in taking it, of course, have rejected Thee and followed *him*. Oh, ages are yet to come of the confusion of free thought, of their science and cannibalism. For having begun to build their tower of Babel without us, they will end, of course, with cannibalism. But then the beast will crawl to us and lick our feet and spatter them with tears of blood. And we shall sit upon the beast and raise the cup, and on it will be written, "Mystery." But then, and only then, the reign of peace and happiness will come for men. Thou art proud of Thine elect, but Thou hast only the elect, while we give rest to all. And besides, how many of those elect, those mighty ones who could become elect, have grown weary waiting for Thee, and have transferred and will transfer the powers of their spirit and the warmth of their heart to the other camp, and end by raising their *free* banner against Thee. Thou didst Thyself lift up that banner. But with us all will be happy and will no more rebel nor destroy one another as under Thy freedom. Oh, we shall persuade them that they will only become free when they renounce their freedom to us and submit to us. And shall we be right or shall we be lying? They will be convinced that we are right, for they will remember the horrors of slavery and confusion to which Thy freedom brought them. Freedom, free thought and science, will lead them into such straits and will bring them face to face with such marvels and insoluble mysteries, that some of them, the fierce and rebellious, will destroy themselves, others, rebellious but weak, will destroy one another, while the rest, weak and unhappy, will crawl fawning to our feet and whine to us: "Yes, you were right, you alone possess His mystery, and we come back to you, save us from ourselves!"

" 'Receiving bread from us, they will see clearly that we take the bread made by their hands from them, to give it to them, without any miracle. They will see that we do not change the stones to bread, but in truth they will be more thankful for taking it from our hands than for the bread itself! For they will remember only too well that in old days, without our help, even the bread they made turned to stones in their hands, while since they have come back to us, the very stones have turned to bread in their hands. Too, too well they know the value of complete submission! And until men know that, they will be unhappy. Who is most to blame for their not knowing it, speak? Who scattered the flock and sent it astray on unknown paths? But the flock will come together again and will submit once more, and then it will be once for all. Then we shall give them the quiet humble happiness of weak creatures such as they are by nature. Oh, we shall persuade them at last not to be proud, for Thou didst lift them up and thereby taught them to be proud. We shall show them that they are weak, that they are only pitiful children, but that childlike happiness is the sweetest of all. They will become timid and will look to us and huddle close to us in fear, as chicks to the hen. They will marvel at us and will be awe-stricken before us, and will be proud at our being so powerful and clever, that we have been able to subdue such a turbulent flock of thousands of millions. They will tremble impotently before our wrath, their minds will grow fearful, they will be quick to shed tears like women and children, but they will be just as ready at a sign from us to pass to laughter and rejoicing, to happy mirth and childish song. Yes, we shall set them to work, but in their leisure hours we shall make their life like a child's game, with children's songs and innocent dance. Oh, we shall allow them even sin, they are weak and helpless, and they will love us like children because we allow them to sin. We shall tell them that every sin will be expiated, if it is done with our permission, that we allow them to sin because we love them, and the punishment for these sins we take upon ourselves. And we shall take it upon ourselves, and they will adore us as their saviour who have taken on themselves their sins before God. And they will have no secrets from us. We shall allow or forbid them to live with their wives and mistresses, to have or not to have children—according to whether they have been obedient or disobedient—and they will submit to us gladly and cheerfully. The most painful secrets of their conscience, all, all they will bring to us, and we shall have an answer for all. And they will be glad to believe our answer, for it will save them from the great anxiety and terrible agony they endure at present in making a free decision for themselves. And all will be happy, all the millions of creatures except the hundred thousand who rule over them. For only we, we who guard the mystery, shall be unhappy. There will be thousands of millions of happy babes, and a hundred thousand sufferers who have taken upon themselves the curse of the knowledge of good and evil. Peacefully they will die, peacefully they will expire in Thy name, and beyond the grave they will find nothing but death. But we shall keep the secret, and for their happiness we shall allure them with the reward of heaven and eternity. Though if there were anything in the other world, it certainly would not be for such as they. It is prophesied that Thou wilt come again in victory, Thou wilt come with Thy chosen, the proud and strong, but we will say that they have only saved themselves, but we have saved all. We are told that the harlot who sits upon the beast, and holds in her hands the *mystery*, shall be put to shame, that the weak will rise up again, and will rend her royal purple and will strip naked her loathsome body. But then I will stand up and point out to Thee the thousand millions of happy children who have known no sin. And we who have taken their sins upon us for their happiness will stand up before Thee and say: "Judge us if Thou canst and darest." Know that I fear Thee not. Know that I too have been in the wilderness, I too have lived on roots and locusts, I too prized the freedom with which Thou hast blessed men, and I too was striving to stand among Thy elect, among the strong and powerful, thirsting "to make up the number." But I awakened and would not serve madness. I turned back and joined the ranks of those *who have corrected Thy work*. I left the proud and went back to the humble, for the happiness of the humble. What I say to Thee will come to pass, and our dominion will be built up. I repeat, to-morrow Thou shalt see that obedient flock who at a sign from me will hasten to heap up the hot cinders about the pile on which I shall burn Thee for coming to hinder us. For if any one has ever deserved our fires, it is Thou. To-morrow I shall burn Thee. Dixi.' "

Ivan stopped. He was carried away as he talked and spoke with excitement; when he had finished, he suddenly smiled.

Alyosha had listened in silence; towards the end he was greatly moved and seemed several times on the point of interrupting, but restrained himself. Now his words came with a rush.

"But . . . that's absurd!" he cried, flushing. "Your poem is in praise of Jesus, not in blame of Him—as you meant it to be. And who will believe you about freedom? Is that the way to understand it? That's not the idea of it in the Orthodox Church...That's Rome, and not even the whole of Rome, it's false—those are the worst of the Catholics, the Inquisitors, the Jesuits!...And there could not be such a fantastic creature as your Inquisitor. What are these sins of mankind they take on themselves? Who are these keepers of the mystery who have taken some curse upon themselves for the happiness of mankind? When have they been seen? We know the Jesuits, they are spoken ill of, but surely they are not what you describe? They are not that at all, not at all.... They are simply the Romish army for the earthly sovereignty of the world in the future, with the Pontiff of Rome for Emperor...that's their ideal, but there's no sort of mystery or lofty melancholy about it.... It's simple lust of power, of filthy earthly gain, of domination—something like a universal serfdom with them as masters—that's all they stand for. They don't even believe in God perhaps. Your suffering inquisitor is a mere fantasy."

"Stay, stay," laughed Ivan, "how hot you are! A fantasy you say, let it be so! Of course it's a fantasy. But allow me to say: do you really think that the Roman Catholic movement of the last centuries is actually nothing but the lust of power, of filthy earthly gain? Is that Father Païssy's teaching?"

"No, no, on the contrary, Father Païssy did once say something rather the same as you ... but of course it's not the same, not a bit the same," Alyosha hastily corrected himself.

"A precious admission, in spite of your 'not a bit the same.' I ask you why your Jesuits and Inquisitors have united simply for vile material gain? Why can there not be among them one martyr oppressed by great sorrow and loving humanity? You see, only suppose that there was one such man among all those who desire nothing but filthy material gain—if there's only one like my old inquisitor, who had himself eaten roots in the desert and made frenzied efforts to subdue his flesh to make himself free and perfect. But yet all his life he loved humanity, and suddenly his eyes were opened, and he saw that it is no great moral blessedness to attain perfection and freedom, if at the same time one gains the conviction that millions of God's creatures have been created as a mockery, that they will never be capable of using their freedom, that these poor rebels can never turn into giants to complete the tower, that it was not for such geese that the great idealist dreamt his dream

of harmony. Seeing all that he turned back and joined—the clever people. Surely that could have happened?"

"Joined whom, what clever people?" cried Alyosha, completely carried away. "They have no such great cleverness and no mysteries and secrets.... Perhaps nothing but Atheism, that's all their secret. Your inquisitor does not believe in God, that's his secret!"

"What if it is so! At last you have guessed it. It's perfectly true that that's the whole secret, but isn't that suffering, at least for a man like that, who has wasted his whole life in the desert and yet could not shake off his incurable love of humanity? In his old age he reached the clear conviction that nothing but the advice of the great dread spirit could build up any tolerable sort of life for the feeble, unruly 'incomplete, empirical creatures created in jest.' And so, convinced of this, he sees that he must follow the counsel of the wise spirit, the dread spirit of death and destruction, and therefore accept lying and deception, and lead men consciously to death and destruction, and yet deceive them all the way so that they may not notice where they are being led, that the poor blind creatures may at least on the way think themselves happy. And note, the deception is in the name of Him in Whose ideal the old man had so fervently believed all his life long. Is not that tragic? And if only one such stood at the head of the whole army 'filled with the lust of power only for the sake of filthy gain'—would not one such be enough to make a tragedy? More than that, one such standing at the head is enough to create the actual leading idea of the Roman Church with all its armies and Jesuits, its highest idea. I tell you frankly that I firmly believe that there has always been such a man among those who stood at the head of the movement. Who knows, there may have been some such even among the Roman Popes. Who knows, perhaps the spirit of that accursed old man who loves mankind so obstinately in his own way, is to be found even now in a whole multitude of such old men, existing not by chance but by agreement, as a secret league formed long ago for the guarding of the mystery, to guard it from the weak and the unhappy, so as to make them happy. No doubt it is so, and so it must be indeed. I fancy that even among the Masons there's something of the same mystery at the bottom, and that's why the Catholics so detest the Masons as their rivals breaking up the unity of the idea, while it is so essential that there should be one flock and one shepherd. . . . But from the way I defend my idea I might be an author impatient of your criticism. Enough of it."

"You are perhaps a Mason yourself!" broke suddenly from Alyosha. "You don't believe in God," he added, speaking this time very sorrowfully. He fancied besides that his brother was looking at him ironically. "How does your poem end?" he asked, suddenly looking down. "Or was it the end?"

"I meant to end it like this. When the Inquisitor ceased speaking he waited some time for his Prisoner to answer him. His silence weighed down upon him. He saw that the Prisoner had listened intently all the time, looking gently in his face and evidently not wishing to reply. The old man longed for Him to say something, however bitter and terrible. But He suddenly approached the old man in silence and softly kissed him on his bloodless aged lips. That was all his answer. The old man shuddered. His lips moved. He went to the door, opened it, and said to Him: 'Go, and come no more. . . . Come not at all, never, never!' And he let Him out into the dark alleys of the town. The Prisoner went away."

"And the old man?"

"The kiss glows in his heart, but the old man adheres to his idea."

"And you with him, you too?" cried Alyosha, mournfully.

Ivan laughed.

"Why, it's all nonsense, Alyosha. It's only a senseless poem of a senseless student, who could never write two lines of verse. Why do you take it so seriously? Surely you don't suppose I am going straight off to the Jesuits, to join the men who are correcting His work? Good Lord, it's no business of mine. I told you, all I want is to live on to thirty, and then . . . dash the cup to the ground!"

"But the little sticky leaves, and the precious tombs, and the blue sky, and the woman you love! How will you live, how will you love them?" Alyosha cried sorrowfully. "With such a hell in your heart and your head, how can you? No, that's just what you are going away for, to join them . . . if not, you will kill yourself, you can't endure it!"

"There is a strength to endure everything," Ivan said with a cold smile.

"What strength?"

"The strength of the Karamazovs—the strength of the Karamazov baseness."

"To sink into debauchery, to stifle your soul with corruption, yes?"

"Possibly even that . . . only perhaps till I am thirty I shall escape it, and then."

"How will you escape it? By what will you escape it? That's impossible with your ideas."

"In the Karamazov way, again."

" 'Everything is lawful,' you mean? Everything is lawful, is that it?"

Ivan scowled, and all at once turned strangely pale.

"Ah, you've caught up yesterday's phrase, which so offended Miüsov—and which Dmitri pounced upon so naïvely and paraphrased!" he smiled queerly. "Yes, if you like, 'everything is lawful' since the word has been said. I won't deny it. And Mitya's version isn't bad."

Alyosha looked at him in silence.

"I thought that going away from here I have you at least," Ivan said suddenly, with unexpected feeling; "but now I see that there is no place for me even in your heart, my dear hermit. The formula, 'all is lawful,' I won't renounce—will you renounce me for that, yes?"

Alyosha got up, went to him and softly kissed him on the lips.

"That's plagiarism," cried Ivan, highly delighted. "You stole that from my poem. Thank you though. Get up, Alyosha, it's time we were going, both of us."

QUESTIONS

1. Reconstruct, as precisely as you can, the line of argument followed by the Grand Inquisitor. How does he arrive at the conclusions that Christ has caused human beings to suffer, that He is indifferent and unconcerned toward the masses of people, and that He is a heretic?
2. Describe the Grand Inquisitor's concept of human nature. Why does he believe that human beings fear freedom?
3. Does Christ answer the arguments of the Grand Inquisitor? If so, in what way? How does His view of human nature differ?
4. Whose side is the author on, in your opinion?
5. Which view of human nature seems truer to you? Which one has history borne out?

Antirealism: The Religion of Art

The need to go beyond realism—which we have seen exemplified by impressionism in painting and Dostoevsky in the novel—became by the end of the century a break with realism. From about 1870 onward, a growing segment of artists, along with poets and musicians, tended to think that the function of art was *not* to represent, or even to interpret, the everyday, normal world, but rather to create its own world and its own meaning. Traditional religion, most believed, was outmoded; its images were no longer valid for modern people. The philosophies of materialism—whether Marxist or liberal—failed to satisfy spiritual and aesthetic needs. Left to fill the vacuum was art—not art for or about something else, but art for its own sake. Thus art became a kind of new religion. The movement began in France with painters usually grouped together under the rubric "postimpressionist," with writers who came to be known as Symbolists, and with musicians, such as Claude Debussy and Maurice Ravel, who were associated with them. This end-of-the-century trend was followed in England by aesthetes or "dandies" such as Oscar Wilde and Aubrey Beardsley. Germany, Italy, and Spain produced their own Symbolist, and later decadent school. In the United States, where realism had taken a strong hold, Symbolism, and the view of art as religion, did not have any appreciable effect until the early twentieth century. Here we will attempt to view the trend briefly through a few French paintings and poems.

Van Gogh   The Dutchman Vincent Van Gogh (1853–1890) came at first to Paris to make his painting career. Oppressed by the inhumanity and materialism of city life, however, he moved to Arles in southern France. As a response to the pain and suffering that man brought into the world, Van Gogh wished to paint pictures that would be comforting and uplifting. He presents aspects of nature such as the sun, a flower, or a plowed field in a way that does not emphasize their photographic reality, but intensifies our experience of them through the use of strong, pure colors and a vigorous brushstroke. Compare Van Gogh's *Sower* (Fig. 29-1)

29–1   Van Gogh, "The Sower." (Collection National Museum Vincent Van Gogh, Amsterdam)

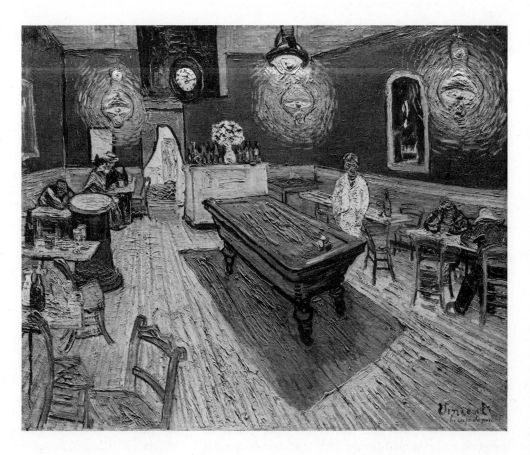

29–2 Van Gogh, "The Night Café." (Yale University Art Gallery. Bequest of Stephen Carlton Clark, B.A. 1903)

with that of Millet (Fig. 26-2). Pay particular attention to the differences created by tone and texture. What is the role of the bare tree? What does the sun stand for? How does it relate to the sower?

Van Gogh's *The Night Café* (Fig. 29-2) is obviously neither a realistic nor an impressionistic rendering of an apparently familiar subject: a café with a billiard table, chairs and smaller tables arranged around the walls, a bar, a host. But what of this place? The space seems empty and somehow threatening; the lamps have strangely glowing halos, and the patrons are anonymous bodies. Van Gogh, unlike the impressionist painters who were primarily interested in rendering account of the surface appearance of things, wished to penetrate beneath the surface. Writing of this painting, Van Gogh said, "I have tried to express humanity's terrible passions by using red and green." This basic color

scheme produces intense contrasts perceptible in the black and white reproduction, and heightens the emotions that seem to emanate from the scene. What are those emotions; what do they convey; how? What is man's plight as Van Gogh describes it here?

Though Van Gogh believed strongly in the redemptive power of art, he remained, unlike most end-of-the-century artists, a convinced Christian. His was a deep and tortured nature, not unlike that of Dostoevsky's characters. At the end of his life he went mad. The fine line between genius and madness was never more evident than in this period.

Gauguin Paul Gauguin (1848–1903) avoided both religious torments and rampant materialism by leaving the West for Tahiti, where he found a natural, instinctive culture free from inhibitions and greed. The faraway Pacific island also provided him with an unfamiliar subject matter that forces the viewer to concentrate on the experience of the picture rather than on the familiar narrative or object. In a letter to a friend he explains *The Spirit of the Dead Watching* (Fig. 29-3).

PAUL GAUGUIN

Manao Tupapau (The Spirit of the Dead Watching) 1892

From the manuscript "Cahier pour Aline," Tahiti, 1893

A young Tahitian girl is lying on her stomach, showing part of her frightened face. She rests on a bed covered by a blue *pareu* and a light chrome yellow sheet. A violet purple background, sown with flowers glowing like electric sparks; a strange figure sits beside the bed.

Captured by a form, a movement, I paint them with no other preoccupation than to execute a nude figure. As it is, it is a slightly indecent study of a nude, and yet I wish to make of it a chaste picture and imbue it with the spirit of the native, its character and tradition.

The *pareu* being intimately connected with the life of a Tahitian, I use it as a bedspread. The bark cloth sheet must be yellow, because in this color it arouses something unexpected for the spectator, and because it suggests lamplight. This, however, prevents me from making an actual effect of a lamp. I need a background of terror; purple is clearly indicated. And now the musical part of the picture is laid out.

What can a young native girl be doing completely nude on a bed, and in this somewhat difficult position? Preparing herself for making love? That is certainly in character, but it is indecent, and I do not wish it to be so. Sleeping? The amorous activity would then be over, and that is still indecent. I see here only fear. What kind of fear? Certainly not the fear of Susanna surprised by the elders. That kind of fear does not exist in Oceania.

The *tupapau* (Spirit of the Dead) is clearly indicated. For the natives it is a constant dread. A lamp is always lighted at night. No one ever goes out on the paths on a moonless night without a lantern, and even then they travel in groups.

Once I have found my *tupapau* I devote my atten-

tion completely to it and make it the motif of my picture. The nude sinks to a secondary level.

What can a spirit mean to a Tahitian? She knows neither the theatre nor the reading of novels, and when she thinks of a dead person she thinks necessarily of someone she has already seen. My spirit can only be an ordinary little woman. Her hand is outstretched as if to seize a prey.

My decorative sense leads me to strew the background with flowers. These flowers are the phosphorescent flowers of the *tupapau*; they are the sign that the spirit nears you. Tahitian beliefs.

The title *Manao tupapau* has two meanings, either the girl thinks of the spirit, or the spirit thinks of her.

To sum up: The musical part: undulating horizontal lines; harmonies of orange and blue, united by the yellows and purples (their derivatives) lit by greenish sparks. The literary part: the spirit of a living person linked to the spirit of the dead. Night and Day.

This genesis is written for those who must always know the *why* and the *wherefore*.

Otherwise it is simply a study of an Oceanian nude.

This letter reveals Gauguin's active search for an abstract pictorial language that can communicate with the viewer. While we cannot decipher all the meanings of his painting, *Whence Come We? Who Are We? Where Are We Going?* (Fig. 29-4), the juxtaposition of rich blues, golds, lavenders, and purples creates a sense of melancholy languidness. The juxtaposition of youth and old age, lovers and strangers combines and harmonizes in a mysterious landscape. The plaintive cry of the title registers clearly.

Though Van Gogh and Gauguin did not share identical aims, their concern with the value of line, color, and form to express a personal view of human truths demonstrates a common understanding of the power of the purely formal, abstract elements of art. This philosophy helps us to understand the rationale that will permit the painter to eliminate the familiar visual world from the canvas altogether.

Cézanne   Among the postimpressionists was another man of great genius, Paul Cézanne, who was older than the other two but whose work matured in the same years. His goal was to formulate a painterly lan-

29–3 Right. Gauguin, "The Spirit of the Dead Watching." (Albright-Knox Art Gallery, Buffalo, New York. A. Conger Goodyear Collection, 1965)

29–4 Below. Gauguin, "Whence Come We? Who Are We? Where Are We Going?" (Courtesy Museum of Fine Arts, Boston, Arthur Tompkins Residuary Fund)

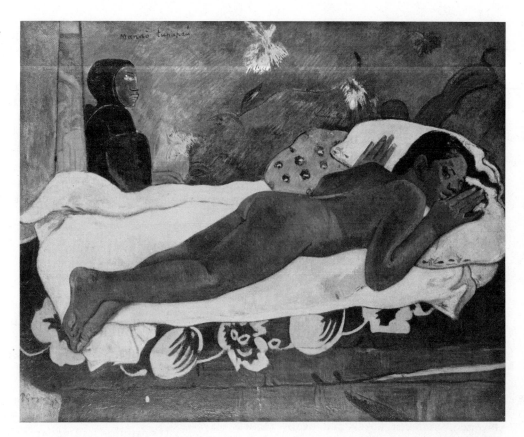

guage that would give an account of nature. He distrusted the implicit subjectivism and emotionalism of Van Gogh and Gauguin, and he felt that impressionism created ephemeral works. He wanted to make art universal and independent, timeless, and free of subjectivity and emotionalism. Cézanne's accomplishments were to be a major source for the art of our century. We will consider him in the next chapter.

The Symbolist Movement in Literature
Symbolism in literature shows much of the same tendency to radical distortion of the world (as ordinarily or "realistically" perceived) for expressive purposes. As the name suggests, the Symbolists viewed the elements of the external world as signs pointing toward inner, more occult realities. A *symbol* differs from an *allegory* in that the latter is an object or creature from the tangible world intended to stand for an invisible reality (for example, a rose = the Virgin Mary), whereas the former may *suggest* any number of thoughts, feelings, or associations. The Symbolist writer does not interpret but leaves that up to the reader. Naturally, such a focus on the inner, subjective world rather than on the outer, social world was more conducive to poetry than to other literary forms. There are, however, strangely introverted Symbolist novels and nearly plotless plays. The best of the latter, *Pelléas and Mélisande* by the Belgian Maurice Maeterlinck, was set to music by Claude Debussy and produced as an opera. The extreme subtlety and suggestiveness of Debussy's sounds lend themselves to the Symbolist aesthetic.

Symbolism in literature begins with four great French poets: Charles Baudelaire, Paul Verlaine, Arthur Rimbaud, and Stéphane Mallarmé. These poets had in common a disdain for the bourgeois and their idols of science and progress, and a belief in redemption through art or beauty. Otherwise they were quite different. Baudelaire led a dissolute life; Rimbaud, a child genius, abandoned poetry at the age of twenty and went off to Africa. Verlaine lived as a bohemian but, after breaking off a violent love affair with Rimbaud, returned to his wife and to Christianity. Mallarmé, outwardly a conventional teacher of English and a family man, lived most intensely in his inner world. He was perhaps the most consistent devotee of the religion of art. The Supreme Being of the Christians he called,

"This old and malicious plumage, overthrown, fortunately, God." Yet he had his own mystic experience: "for more than a month I have been on the purest glaciers of Aesthetics . . . after finding *Nothingness* I have found *Beauty*." Each production of a poem was for Mallarmé an enactment of the struggle to create beauty out of nothingness.

A poem by each of these poets is printed below. Since the musical and suggestive effects of language itself are so important to Symbolist poetry, we have kept the poems in the original French, with literal translations by Henri Peyre and Mary Ann Witt (*Autumn Song*).

CHARLES BAUDELAIRE

Correspondances

La nature est un temple où de vivants piliers
Laissent parfois sortir de confuses paroles;
L'homme y passe à travers des forêts de symboles
Qui l'observent avec des regards familiers.

Comme de longs échos qui de loin se confondent
Dans une ténébreuse et profonde unité,
Vaste comme la nuit et comme la clarté,
Les parfums, les couleurs et les sons se répondent.

Il est des parfums frais comme des chairs d'enfants,
Doux comme les hautbois, verts comme les prairies,
—Et d'autres, corrompus, riches et triomphants,

Ayant l'expansion des choses infinies,
Comme l'ambre, le musc, le benjoin et l'encens,
Qui chantent les transports de l'esprit et des sens.

Correspondences

Nature is a temple where living columns
Sometimes murmur indistinct words (allow confused
        words to escape);
There man passes through forests of symbols
That watch him with familiar glances.

Like prolonged echoes that mingle in the distance,
In a shadowy and profound unity,

Vast as night and as the light of day,
Perfumes, colors, and sounds respond to (answer to)
    one another.

There are perfumes, fresh as the flesh of children,
Sweet as oboe music, green as meadows,
—Others [are] corrupt, rich, and triumphant,

Having the expansion of things infinite,
Like amber, musk, benzoin, and frankincense,
Which sing the raptures of spirit and of sense.

QUESTIONS

1. What does the word "symbols" mean here?
2. How is the theme of *synaesthesia* (the relationships between the five senses) treated in this poem?
3. How does Baudelaire give the impression that all things are related through analogy? How can the poet perceive this better than the scientist can?

PAUL VERLAINE

Chanson d'Automne

Les sanglots longs
Des violons
    De l'automne
Blessent mon coeur
D'une langueur
    Monotone.

Tout suffoquant
Et blême quand
    Sonne l'heure,
Je me souviens
Des jours anciens
    Et je pleure;

Et je m'en vais
Au vent mauvais
    Qui m'emporte,
De çà, de là,
Pareil à la
    Feuille morte.

Autumn Song

The long sighs of autumn violins
Wound my heart with monotonous langour.

Stifled and pale, when the hour rings
I remember the old days, and I cry;

And I go off with the cold wind which carries me
Here and there like a dead leaf.

QUESTIONS

1. Listen to someone read this poem in the original. Even if you do not know French, you will be able to hear which sounds dominate. What emotion or sensation do these sounds suggest? Would you call the effect a musical one?
2. To what extent can a poem like this one be rendered in a translation?

ARTHUR RIMBAUD

Mystique

    Sur la pente du talus, les anges tournent leurs robes de laine dans les herbages d'acier et d'émeraude.
    Des prés de flammes bondissent jusqu'au sommet du mamelon. A gauche le terreau de l'arête est piétiné par tous les homicides et toutes les batailles, et tous les bruits désastreux filent leur courbe. Derrière l'arête de droite, la ligne des orients, des progrès.
    Et, tandis que la bande, en haut du tableau, est formée de la rumeur tournante et bondissante des conques des mers et des nuits humaines,
    La douceur fleurie des étoiles, et du ciel, et du reste descend en face du talus, comme un panier,—contre notre face, et fait l'abîme fleurant et bleu là-dessous.

Mystical

    On the slope of the hillock, angels whirl their woolen robes, in the grasses of steel and emerald.
    Meadows of flame leap up to the top of the mound. On the left, the earth mold of the ridge is trampled

upon by all murders and all battles, and all the disastrous noises race along their own curve. Behind the crest on the right, the line of orients, of progress.

And, while the strip at the top of the picture is made of the whirling and leaping murmur of conch shells from the seas and of human nights,

The flowery softness of the stars, of the sky and of all else comes down opposite the bank, like a basket—close to our faces, and makes the abyss flowering and blue below.

QUESTIONS

1. Why is this prose selection called a poem? What makes a poem in prose?
2. Can a reader understand this selection logically? If not, to what in us does the poem appeal?
3. To which paintings would you compare this poem? Why?
4. In what sense should "mystical" (*mystique*) be understood here?

STÉPHANE MALLARMÉ
Le Tombeau d'Edgar Poe

Tel qu'en Lui-même enfin l'éternité le change,
Le Poète suscite avec un glaive nu
Son siècle épouvanté de n'avoir pas connu
Que la mort triomphait dans cette voix étrange!

Eux, comme un vil sursaut d'hydre oyant jadis l'ange
Donner un sens plus pur aux mots de la tribu
Proclamèrent très haut le sortilège bu
Dans le flot sans honneur de quelque noir mélange.

Du sol et de la nue hostiles, ô grief!
Si notre idée avec ne sculpte un bas-relief
Dont la tombe de Poe éblouissante s'orne

Calme bloc ici-bas chu d'un désastre obscur
Que ce granit du moins montre à jamais sa borne
Aux noirs vols du Blasphème épars dans le futur.

The Tomb of Edgar Poe

Such as into Himself at last eternity changes him
The Poet rouses with a bare sword
His age aghast at not having known
That death was triumphing in this strange voice.

They like a hydra's vile start (a serpent's hideous
   twisting) on hearing, once (before), the angel
Giving a purer meaning to the words of the tribe
Proclaimed aloud the spell imbibed
In the honorless flood of some black brew.

Out of soil and cloud, hostile, O grief!
If our idea fails to carve a bas-relief
With which Poe's dazzling tomb is to be adorned,

Calm block fallen down here from some dim disaster,
Let this granite at least forever show (set) a limit
To the black flights of Blasphemy scattered in the
   future.

COMMENTS AND QUESTIONS

1. Baudelaire and Mallarmé both developed something of a cult for the writings of the American Edgar Allan Poe, which they both translated. They saw Poe as a poetic genius misunderstood in the crass society in which he lived. How is Mallarmé's view of Poe rendered in this poem?
2. What does Mallarmé mean by saying that Poe, and by extension all poets, give "a purer meaning to the words of the tribe?"
3. What does Poe's tomb symbolize?

INDUSTRIALISM
AND THE HUMANITIES: CONTINUITIES

The effects of industrialism on our modern world have been almost incalculable. In addition to restructuring the economic and social fabric of Western society, the so-called Industrial Revolution contributed significantly to the ways in which human beings perceive themselves and their world.

Social, Political, and Scientific Thought Much of the social and political thought of the nineteenth century takes the new conditions into account by extending the egalitarian ideas of the Enlightenment into the economic sphere. Early liberal stress on individual initiative in the market place was clearly an outgrowth of Enlightenment principles, but the cost of laissez-faire capitalism in human suffering was for many too high. Among the various socialist thinkers, Karl Marx, whose theories have produced societies that might astound him, understood best the economic, social, and human consequences of industrialism.

Whereas most nineteenth-century socialist thought approached the problems of society from a collective viewpoint—seeing man not so much as an individual but as a member of a group or class—the new liberalism from the middle decades of the century endeavored to foster social and economic justice while preserving an individualistic perspective. Its call for selective government intervention in the market place was based on the belief that such regulation would enhance the liberty of all while preventing the tyranny of the few. These newer liberals also urged extension of the suffrage to members of the lower classes in the furtherance of Enlightenment goals. John Stuart Mill maintained that this goal necessitated recognition of the rights of women as well as of men. Present-day women's liberation movements owe much to Mill's arguments.

In any event, the pragmatic philosophy of the newer liberals, together with the preference of the lower classes for immediate economic gains, prevented the social revolution predicted by Marx and other radical thinkers. The overall tendency in Western industrial societies by the end of the century was toward the amelioration of the living conditions of the lower classes and the rapid increase in the number of middle-class families.

Scientific and technological developments also contributed to changes in human perceptions. The evolutionary theories of Charles Darwin profoundly upset traditional religious and humanistic notions of man's unique position in creation. The notion of life as evolutionary, together with the increasing standard of living, generally tended to support belief in inevitable progress and to encourage an overriding interest in the material aspects of life.

Realism in the Arts Artists responded to these conditions in various ways. While romanticism remained the dominant trend in music until the very end of the nineteenth century, the style called realism came to dominate painting and literature after 1850. Realistic artists felt that the times called for a representation of the world as it really was, in its sordidness and filth as well as in its beauty. Stressing the effects of the environment on individual characters, the realists often were harshly critical of the social and psychological consequences of industrialism. The invention and development of photography seemed in many ways to replace what the realists were trying to accomplish. The impressionist painters, who rendered the external world not photographically but with the aid of experiments on the nature of light, responded to this challenge.

Architects tended either to escape from the modern world by building in revival styles like Greek classical or Gothic, or to respond enthusiastically to the new technological possibilities. Unlike the often critical realistic painting and fiction, buildings like the Crystal Palace in London and the early skyscrapers in Chicago are testimonies to a dynamic capitalistic society, proud of itself and its accomplishments.

Antirealism and the Religion of Art In the last decades of the nineteenth century many artists and thinkers reacted against both the assurance that life could be portrayed as it seemed, "realistically," and the widespread contemporary self-satisfaction with material progress. Although still in the realist tradition, Dostoevsky maintained that reality was to be found more in the human soul than in the external environment. Nietzsche, who accepted Dostoevsky's emphasis on the irrational and spiritual but not his religious beliefs, insisted on the moral and intellectual weakness of Judaism and Christianity and proclaimed: "God is dead!" As a solution to the problems of man without God, he advocated the free development of all human potentialities in the individual "superman."

Numbers of nineteenth-century poets, musicians, and painters, declaring the supremacy of aesthetic values above all others, endeavored to make art a kind of religion. Rimbaud and Mallarmé had mystical experiences during artistic creation; even a Christian like Van Gogh believed in the power of art to redeem the human spirit. The Symbolist poets and the post-impressionist artists veered sharply from the tenets of realism. The function of art was not to reproduce the crass material world but to create its own purer and indeed truer world. These artists imposed their personal, symbolic world on nature more extensively than did the romantics. Since that time, the gulf between reality as perceived by the artist and reality as perceived by the person on the street has grown wider, as has the gulf between artist and public.

PART EIGHT

DISCONTINUITIES: THE EARLY TWENTIETH CENTURY

30

A CULTURE IN SELF-DOUBT

In 1900, continuity snapped . . .

HENRY ADAMS

On or about December, 1910, human nature changed.

VIRGINIA WOOLF

Developments in Science and Politics

The study of the humanities makes it evident that change—in forms, styles, ideas, outlooks, and especially in the apprehension of the nature of reality—is inevitable. The values and the truths of one generation cannot be those of the generation that succeeds it; the children must grow away from or revolt against the parents. We have seen that in certain periods change in the humanities comes about gradually, while in others it seems to erupt violently. No culture in the history of the world, however, has experienced either the extent or the intensity of change as that which the West has seen in our own century. Changes in Western culture have had profound repercussions on the rest of the world, and the rest of the world has in turn challenged the West's claim to leadership.

As the quotations heading this chapter indicate, it seemed to artists and thinkers in the early 1900s that the twentieth century had broken in a new and radical way with previous tradition. A radical break in the arts became evident with a series of new styles which can all be loosely grouped under the name *modernism*. We will look at some examples of this trend shortly; first let us examine briefly some of the intellectual and social developments that contributed toward making this period one of discontinuity.

Scientific Developments   In the pure sciences, a series of astounding new discoveries altered the scientific picture of the natural world as radically as had Newtonian physics in the seventeenth century and Darwinian biology in the nineteenth. Among the more important was Max Planck's discovery at the turn of the century that atoms emit energy not with continuity but in separate units. A few years later Albert Einstein (1879–1955) initially expounded his theory of relativity: that space, time, and motion are not absolute (as Newtonian physics had assumed), but rather that all are relative to the observer's position. The Newtonian conceptions appeared inapplicable to the atom or the universe where movement was measured at the speed of light.

There are, however, two essential differences between this scientific revolution and the two previous ones. First, whereas the intelligent layman could read Newton and Darwin and gain a fairly good understanding of their theories, it was and is impossible for someone without scientific training to have more than a superficial understanding of the discoveries of Planck and Einstein. Secondly, whereas Newton offered a rational picture of the world and evolution stressed progressive continuity between one species and another, the new physics seemed to postulate a world without continuity or absolutes, a world in which nothing was certain. Even without a scientific knowledge of physics, twentieth-century human beings are well aware that a world composed of subatomic particles, a world in which matter and energy, space and time, interpenetrate, a world in which scientific laws are given names like "relativity" (Einstein) or "uncertainty" (Werner Hei-

senberg), is a world in which nothing is as it appears to be to the human senses.

In the social sciences, too, certainties of the past gave way to uncertainties or relativities. Developments in anthropology emphasized the relativity of cultural values. The new science of psychology (launched in the 1870s) showed, first through the work of the Russian Ivan Pavlov, that human beings could be conditioned by their environment to elicit certain responses, thus that they did not act primarily from reason and conscious decision. Foremost in upsetting traditional notions about human nature was the work of Sigmund Freud (1856–1939). Freud's theories that our actions and behavior are rooted in our unconscious, rather than our conscious mind, seemed to many more pessimistic grounds for existence than Darwin's proclamations about our ancestry. We will examine Freud's work later in more detail.

What the early twentieth century witnessed was what Nietzsche had prophesied: a radical questioning of the Greco-Roman and Judeo-Christian roots of our culture. Reason and authority, humanism and faith, the pillars of these cultures, were undermined as never before. The great minds who contributed most to this upheaval, Einstein and Freud (we could add the earlier Marx), were Jewish and steeped in humanistic culture.

Colonialism   At the same time that Western culture appeared to be casting doubts on itself, the Western powers, particularly England and France, expanded colonization in Africa, Asia, and America. The years after 1880 witnessed an increasingly bitter competition between European powers to establish their flags over as many colonies in the world as possible.

The effect of this late colonialism was devastating for the life of those areas occupied. True, the Europeans brought with them some of the benefits of communication, transportation, and scientific advancement, but the cost in terms of the social and cultural life of Asiatic and African people was tremendous. This rapid change—the disintegration of a traditional society—is graphically chronicled by the Nigerian writer Chinua Achebe in his *Things Fall Apart*. The influence, however, was not all one-way. Especially in the visual arts in the decades before World War I, western Europeans, questioning their own culture, proved receptive to the civilization of the colonized peoples.

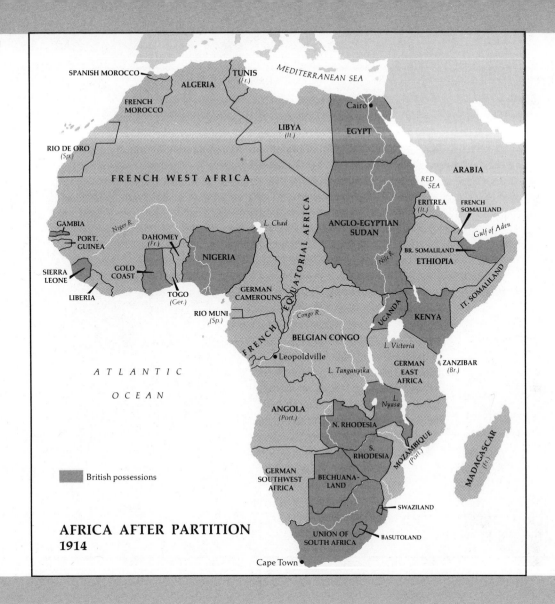

AFRICA AFTER PARTITION 1914

Map labels:

SPANISH MOROCCO · TUNIS (Fr.) · MEDITERRANEAN SEA · ALGERIA · FRENCH MOROCCO · LIBYA (It.) · Cairo · EGYPT · RIO DE ORO (Sp.) · FRENCH WEST AFRICA · ARABIA · RED SEA · ERITREA (It.) · FRENCH SOMALILAND · ANGLO-EGYPTIAN SUDAN · Niger R. · L. Chad · GAMBIA · PORT. GUINEA · DAHOMEY (Fr.) · NIGERIA · BR. SOMALILAND · ETHIOPIA · Gulf of Aden · Nile R. · SIERRA LEONE · GOLD COAST · TOGO (Ger.) · GERMAN CAMEROUNS · IT. SOMALILAND · LIBERIA · RIO MUNI (Sp.) · FRENCH EQUATORIAL AFRICA · UGANDA · KENYA · Congo R. · BELGIAN CONGO · L. Victoria · ZANZIBAR (Br.) · ATLANTIC OCEAN · Leopoldville · L. Tanganyika · GERMAN EAST AFRICA · L. Nyasa · ANGOLA (Port.) · N. RHODESIA · MOZAMBIQUE (Port.) · MADAGASCAR (Fr.) · GERMAN SOUTHWEST AFRICA · S. RHODESIA · BECHUANA-LAND · SWAZILAND · UNION OF SOUTH AFRICA · BASUTOLAND · Cape Town

British possessions

World War I By the first decade of the twentieth century, after all the desirable opportunities for colonial expansion were realized, the focus of international competition came back to the European continent itself. World War I started in 1914 in an almost careless mood with plumes and full-dress parades; but within the first year it became a war fought in muddy trenches with interminable days and nights of waiting alternating with sudden attacks, sometimes costing thousands of lives for a few square yards of ground gained. The growth of industrialism had made possible an exquisite technology of destruction: the tank, the machine gun, the airplane, and poison gas. At the outset the Central Powers—Germany, Austria-Hungary, and Turkey—opposed the Allies: Great Britain, France, and Russia. Italy joined the latter three in 1915. The loss of Russia in 1917 because of a civil war was balanced by the entrance of the United States on the Allied side.

With the Allied victory late in 1918, Europeans on both sides became almost immediately aware that the

Territory lost by:
Germany
Austria-Hungary
Bulgaria
Russia

TERRITORIAL CHANGES IN EUROPE
After World War I

war, if anything, had aggravated long-standing problems. The losses in men, land, and property were enormous, and it was difficult to say that anything had been gained. The settlement at Versailles made republics of Germany and Austria and brought into existence a whole welter of new states out of the wreckage of the Austro-Hungarian and Turkish empires. But all these new governments were unstable. The war had created a cooperative spirit between workers and bosses, but, with the war over, the social tensions severely increased. Capitalists nervously eyed developments in

Russia, where a communist state came into being infused with missionary zeal. Would the workers in the capitalist countries heed the call for revolt?

"Decline of the West" Europe in the early 1920s was worn out and discouraged. Symptomatic of the weariness and sense of decline was the work of Otto Spengler (1880–1936) with its ominous title, *The Decline of the West*. For Spengler, Western culture was in old age, its ruling classes were timid and not so much governing as administrating. Without faith and self-discipline the forces of anarchy would grow in the society and, unless strong leaders arose, it would continue its path of decline.

Sigmund Freud

The most influential thinker to examine these conflicts in Western civilization was Sigmund Freud. As a psychologist rather than historian, Freud was primarily interested in the conflicts between individuals and their society. Freud's philosophy is represented here with a selection from his culminating work on this theme, *Civilization and Its Discontents*. In order to assess his considerable impact on modern culture, however, it is also necessary to know something of the development of his ideas before that work. We will attempt to summarize this development briefly.

Depth Psychology

A Viennese neurologist, Freud left his first vocation to develop what came to be called "depth psychology." This depth psychology claimed to furnish a key to the exploration of the unconscious mind and, through this, a renewed knowledge of the conscious mind, with wider application to the understanding of literature, art, religion, and culture. The first dynamic psychiatry had been, in the main, the systematization of observations made on hypnotized patients. With Freud's method of free association, a new approach was introduced. The patient, relaxed on a couch, was told the basic rule: to tell whatever came to his mind, no matter how futile, absurd, embarrassing, or even offensive it seemed.

Three Parts of Mind

Much of Freud's understanding of the human individual rests on his contention that mental life is produced by the interaction of three psychic agencies: the ego, the id, and the super-ego. The *ego* was defined as "the coordinated organization of mental processes in a person." The *id* was not very different from what Freud had originally described as the unconscious, the seat of both the repressed material and the drives, to which had been added the unconscious fantasies and unconscious feelings, notably guilt feelings. The *super-ego* is the watchful, judging, punishing agency in the individual, the source of social and religious feelings in mankind.

The main aspects of depth psychology were Freud's dream theory and his theory of parapraxes, or faulty behavior. These theories were elaborated simultaneously and presented in two of his best-known books, *The Interpretation of Dreams* in 1900 and *The Psychopathology of Everyday Life* in 1904.

Dreams

Freud's theory of dreams has been told so often that it has become common knowledge. Among the many trivial events of the day, the dream chooses the one that shows some relationship to a childhood memory; and, as Freud puts it, the dream stands with one foot in the present and one foot in childhood. Thus one is led from the latent content still farther back to a childhood memory expressing an unfulfilled wish of that remote time. Here Freud introduced the notion he had found in his self-analysis and in his patients, the *Oedipus complex*: the little boy, wanting to possess his mother, wishes to get rid of his father; but he is frightened of this threatening rival and of castration as a punishment for his incestuous feelings toward the mother. Such is, Freud says, the terrible secret that every man keeps in the recesses of his heart, repressed and forgotten, and which appears in a veiled form in a dream every night. Freud named this complex from the Greek myth on which Sophocles built his tragedy. A great reader in the humanities, Freud was aware that profound psychological truths had been expressed in literature and art before being formulated scientifically.

The dream, for Freud, is essentially a fulfillment of a repressed, unacceptable sexual wish. When controls of consciousness are relaxed, waking acts, too, can reveal repressed wishes or desires. Such acts include forgetting proper names, slips of the tongue and speech blunders, mistakes in reading and writing, acts of physical clumsiness, and intellectual errors.

Pleasure Principle and Instincts

Also important in Freud's thinking are his theories of the pleasure principle and of the instincts, *Thanatos* and *Eros*, as discussed in his *Beyond the Pleasure Prin-*

ciple (1920). The pleasure principle may be understood as man's constant attempt to achieve pleasure and to avoid pain. As for his dualistic theory of instincts, Freud contended that Eros included the sexual instincts, most of the egoistic or self-preservative impulses, and those drives and forces that enhanced and unified life. Thanatos, on the other hand, included the tendency to self-punishment in the individual as well as those impulses that denied life and disrupted civilized existence. Thus Freud hypothesized that perhaps there was some innate tendency in the psychobiological make-up of man that overrides the pleasure principle. Or, expressed another way, since the aim of the instincts (according to Freud's older definition) was to diminish tension and since this was also his definition of pleasure, the ultimate pleasure was not life or Eros, but Thanatos, stasis or death. There is no doubt that the experience of World War I influenced Freud's concept of the "death wish."

Freud on Religion, Culture, and Literature

Soon after he had conceived his psychoanalytic theory, Freud expanded his reflection upon the fields of religion, sociology, cultural history, art, and literature. In 1907 he compared obsessive compulsive symptoms of neurotics with religious rituals and creeds, concluding that religion was a universal obsessional neurosis and that obsession was an individualized religion. Twenty years later, in *The Future of an Illusion*, Freud defined religion as an illusion inspired by infantile belief in the omnipotence of thought, a universal neurosis, a kind of narcotic that hampers the free exercise of intelligence, something that man will have to give up. With *Totem and Taboo* Freud undertook to retrace the origin, not only of religion but of human culture as well, trying to find a link between the individual Oedipus complex and the prehistory of mankind.

Whereas Freud found religion harmful, he deemed art and literature beneficial to man. *The Interpretation of Dreams* contains two major ideas that have an impact on art and the criticism of art: the conception of the unconscious and the theory of the pleasure principle. Freud sees the work of art as the expression of a wish and the artist as a neurotic. Like the neurotic, the artist yearns for honor, power, wealth, fame, and the love of women; however, he does not have the necessary means toward achieving these goals. Therefore, he turns his back on reality, transferring his interests to the expression of his wishes in fantasy as creation. Art thus becomes, in Freud's view, something like a public dream, an occasion to contemplate the unconscious. "Dostoevsky and Parricide," "Leonardo da Vinci," and "The Moses of Michelangelo" are only three of the many works by Freud that reveal this psychoanalytical approach to the work of art.

Civilization and Its Discontents   In his essay of 1930, *Civilization and Its Discontents*, Freud applies psychoanalytical methods to the study of civilization. He begins by asking the question: why do so many people blame the fact of human unhappiness on civilization and technical progress? Would we in fact be better off in a "free" primitive state? Freud analyzes the clash between individual instincts, creative and destructive, and the restrictive forces of overripe Western civilization. He nevertheless argues that all societies, even the most primitive, impose restrictions and taboos and that human cultures in fact develop through the sublimation of instinctual drives. *Eros*, as a drive for individual happiness may clash with social necessities, but it also takes the form of the urge which causes human beings to seek to bind together, first in families and then in larger social groups. The other basic instinct, *Thanatos*, both in the form of an individual "death wish" and as aggression toward others, constantly threatens the destruction of both self and society. Freud concludes, pessimistically, that civilization of necessity had to channel and restrain man's instinctual strivings if both man and civilization were to survive. Unlike Marx and the tradition of Western radicalism emerging from the Enlightenment, Freud saw no possibility for a radically different future for the majority of mankind. His philosophic outlook is often thought of as a secular variant of the doctrine of original sin or as a modern version of the tragic vision.

The selection here (translated from the German by James Strachey) represents the last four paragraphs of the essay. It begins by discussing the possibility of making an analogy between an individual psyche and the psyche of an entire civilization. Freud maintains that civilizations, like individuals, have super-egos, and that in fact the characteristics of the super-ego may sometimes be seen better in a culture than in an individual.

SIGMUND FREUD
from *Civilization and Its Discontents*

The cultural super-ego has developed its ideals and set up its demands. Among the latter, those which deal with the relations of human beings to one another are comprised under the heading of *ethics*. People have at all times set the greatest value on ethics, as though they expected that it in particular would produce especially important results. And it does in fact deal with a subject which can easily be recognized as the sorest spot in every civilization. Ethics is thus to be regarded as a therapeutic attempt—as an endeavour to achieve, by means of a command of the super-ego, something which has so far not been achieved by means of any other cultural activities. As we already know, the problem before us is how to get rid of the greatest hindrance to civilization—namely, the constitutional inclination of human beings to be aggressive towards one another; and for that very reason we are especially interested in what is probably the most recent of the cultural commands of the super-ego, the commandment to love one's neighbour as oneself. In our research into, and therapy of, a neurosis, we are led to make two reproaches against the super-ego of the individual. In the severity of its commands and prohibitions it troubles itself too little about the happiness of the ego, in that it takes insufficient account of the resistances against obeying them—of the instinctual strength of the id [in the first place], and of the difficulties presented by the real external environment [in the second]. Consequently we are very often obliged, for therapeutic purposes, to oppose the super-ego, and we endeavour to lower its demands. Exactly the same objections can be made against the ethical demands of the cultural super-ego. It, too, does not trouble itself enough about the facts of the mental constitution of human beings. It issues a command and does not ask whether it is possible for people to obey it. On the contrary, it assumes that a man's ego is psychologically capable of anything that is required of it, that his ego has unlimited mastery over his id. This is a mistake; and even in what are known

as normal people the id cannot be controlled beyond certain limits. If more is demanded of a man, a revolt will be produced in him or a neurosis, or he will be made unhappy. The commandment, 'Love thy neighbour as thyself', is the strongest defence against human aggressiveness and an excellent example of the unpsychological proceedings of the cultural super-ego. The commandment is impossible to fulfil; such an enormous inflation of love can only lower its value, not get rid of the difficulty. Civilization pays no attention to all this; it merely admonishes us that the harder it is to obey the precept the more meritorious it is to do so. But anyone who follows such a precept in present-day civilization only puts himself at a disadvantage *vis-à-vis* the person who disregards it. What a potent obstacle to civilization aggressiveness must be, if the defence against it can cause as much unhappiness as aggressiveness itself! 'Natural' ethics, as it is called, has nothing to offer here except the narcissistic satisfaction of being able to think oneself better than others. At this point the ethics based on religion introduces its promises of a better after-life. But so long as virtue is not rewarded here on earth, ethics will, I fancy, preach in vain. I too think it quite certain that a real change in the relations of human beings to possessions would be of more help in this direction than any ethical commands; but the recognition of this fact among socialists has been obscured and made useless for practical purposes by a fresh idealistic misconception of human nature.

I believe the line of thought which seeks to trace in the phenomena of cultural development the part played by a super-ego promises still further discoveries. I hasten to come to a close. But there is one question which I can hardly evade. If the development of civilization has such a far-reaching similarity to the development of the individual and if it employs the same methods, may we not be justified in reaching the diagnosis that, under the influence of cultural urges, some civilizations, or some epochs of civilization—possibly the whole of mankind—have become 'neurotic'? An analytic dissection of such neuroses might lead to therapeutic recommendations which could lay claim to great practical interest. I would not say that an attempt of this kind to carry psycho-analysis over to the cultural community was absurd or doomed to be fruitless. But we should have to be very cautious and not forget that, after all, we are only dealing with analogies and that it is dangerous, not only with men but also with concepts, to tear them from the sphere in which they have originated and been evolved. Moreover, the diagnosis of communal neuroses is faced with a special difficulty. In an individual neurosis we take as our starting-point the contrast that distinguishes the patient from his environment, which is assumed to be 'normal'. For a group all of whose members are affected by one and the same disorder no such background could exist; it would have to be found elsewhere. And as regards the therapeutic application of our knowledge, what would be the use of the most correct analysis of social neuroses, since no one possesses authority to impose such a therapy upon the group? But in spite of all these difficulties, we may expect that one day someone will venture to embark upon a pathology of cultural communities.

For a wide variety of reasons, it is very far from my intention to express an opinion upon the value of human civilization. I have endeavoured to guard myself against the enthusiastic prejudice which holds that our civilization is the most precious thing that we possess or could acquire and that its path will necessarily lead to heights of unimagined perfection. I can at least listen without indignation to the critic who is of the opinion that when one surveys the aims of cultural endeavour and the means it employs, one is bound to come to the conclusion that the whole effort is not worth the trouble, and that the outcome of it can only be a state of affairs which the individual will be unable to tolerate. My impartiality is made all the easier to me by my knowing very little about all these things. One thing only do I know for certain and that is that man's judgements of value follow directly his wishes for happiness—that, accordingly, they are an attempt to support his illusions with arguments. I should find it very understandable if someone were to point out the obligatory nature of the course of human civilization and were to say, for instance, that the tendencies to a restriction of sexual life or to the institution of a humanitarian ideal at the expense of natural selection were developmental trends which cannot be averted or turned aside and to which it is best for us to yield as though they were necessities of nature. I know, too, the

objection that can be made against this, to the effect that in the history of mankind, trends such as these, which were considered unsurmountable, have often been thrown aside and replaced by other trends. Thus I have not the courage to rise up before my fellow-men as a prophet, and I bow to their reproach that I can offer them no consolation: for at bottom that is what they are all demanding—the wildest revolutionaries no less passionately than the most virtuous believers.

The fateful question for the human species seems to me to be whether and to what extent their cultural development will succeed in mastering the disturbance of their communal life by the human instinct of aggression and self-destruction. It may be that in this respect precisely the present time deserves a special interest. Men have gained control over the forces of nature to such an extent that with their help they would have no difficulty in exterminating one another to the last man. They know this, and hence comes a large part of their current unrest, their unhappiness and their mood of anxiety. And now it is to be expected that the other of the two 'Heavenly Powers,' eternal Eros, will make an effort to assert himself in the struggle with his equally immortal adversary. But who can foresee with what success and with what result? [1]

QUESTIONS

1. Why, according to Freud, is the precept "Love thy neighbor as thyself" contrary to human happiness?
2. How does civilization impose this principle as a code of conduct?
3. What does Freud mean when he says that civilizations are "neurotic"?
4. What problems are involved in applying psychoanalytic methods to the analysis of a society?
5. How do the drives Freud calls *eros* and *thanatos* function in civilization?
6. To what extent would you argue that technological Western civilization has furthered or hampered human happiness?

---

[1] [The final sentence was added in 1931—when the menace of Hitler was already beginning to be apparent.]

31

THE MODERNIST MOVEMENT: PAINTING, SCULPTURE, AND ARCHITECTURE

In the years between 1900 and 1930 there developed a lifestyle that was self-consciously modern. The theories of Freud, often misinterpreted, led to a desire to be "liberated" from the restraints and taboos of proper Victorian society and to greater sexual freedom. Women, having finally gained the vote in England and America, began to demand greater freedoms and more of a place in society for themselves. Young women shocked their elders by wearing their hair and their skirts short and dancing modern dances like the Charleston. Blacks in America, while suffering from Jim Crow laws in the South and limited employment possibilities in the North, nevertheless made substantial contributions to the art and culture of the new age. The most substantial of these was jazz, a totally new art form that we will discuss as music in the next chapter. The modernist age can as well be called the jazz age, for jazz seemed to express the fast, frantic, free way of life that culminated in the Roaring Twenties. Automobiles, airplanes, radio, and technology that made possible the development of another new art form—the motion picture—all contributed to the impression that life was speeding up and changing at an incredible rate and that modern values and styles had to replace old-fashioned ones.

As is often the case, the changes in lifestyle were preceded by changes in the arts. Artists, too, became self-consciously modern, aware that art had to keep pace with, or advance, a rapidly changing society. In addition to jazz, another important new art form, modern dance, was an American creation, but the cradle of modernism in the early twentieth century was really Paris. There young painters, sculptors, writers, musicians, and dancers flocked from all over the world to exchange ideas and to participate in the creation of the new. Many Americans, white and black, fled what they considered to be the culturally backward, repressive atmosphere of the United States to give free rein to their creativity in Paris.

This period of intense modernist activity in Paris, beginning shortly before World War I, is described by Roger Shattuck as "the banquet years." The French accomplishments of the late nineteenth century seemed to offer developing artists a feast on which to nourish themselves. Visual, musical, literary, and theatrical artists were conscious of the interrelationships among their arts as never before. During the first three decades of the twentieth century, there developed an astounding number of literary-artistic-musical schools, all with "-isms" attached to them. Their histories have been made, and we will only mention a few of them here. What we will attempt to grasp through the rich variety of expressions is just what it meant (and means) to be "modern."

Modernist Painting 1900–1930

In the early years of this century two important trends can be distinguished. The first is the continuing transformation of the *figurative* tradition in which the human body and the objects of habitual visual experience form the basis of art. The second is the complete rejection of the visual world for an attempt to communicate through the pure plastic possibilities of the formal elements of painting, sculpture, and graphics. Two prominent figures are associated with the first: a Frenchman, Henri Matisse, and a Spaniard, Pablo Picasso. A Russian, Wassily Kandinsky, and a Dutchman, Piet Mondrian, are representative of the second. We will consider representative works from these trends and look briefly at their influence in the United States. We will then turn to two important modernist developments after World War I: Dada and surrealism.

Matisse Henri Matisse emerged as an important artist in an exhibition of his work and that of some colleagues in 1905. Called *Les Fauves* (wild beasts) because of the large areas of strong, simplified colors, slashing brushstrokes, and thick paint that characterized their work, these artists were all clearly inspired by impressionism, Gauguin, and Van Gogh. Matisse's portrait of his wife, *The Green Stripe* (Color Plate X), makes use of areas of strong, contrasting colors to create a sense of space and light instead of traditional shading and shadow. Matisse's ability to suggest weight, volume, and space through color juxtaposition was further enhanced by his command of the possibilities of line and contour. In 1905–1906, when Matisse painted *The Joy of Life* (Fig. 31-1), the heavy brushstrokes of his earlier work gave way to flowing contours and colors, spaciously arranged on a light ground. Compared to the canvases of Van Gogh and Gauguin, this work is empty of brooding and is filled with an almost musical lyricism and optimism. This painting truly affirms life and joy, resonating with exploding vigor and sensuality that we will witness in the music and ballet of Stravinsky's *Rite of Spring*.

Picasso Matisse's joyful visions of life were not shared by Pablo Picasso. In his early works, done in Paris around the turn of the century, Picasso used as subjects clowns, acrobats, peasants, and the dregs of Parisian night life that had also been used by Manet, Degas, and Toulouse-Lautrec. Filled with melancholy and a brooding sense of alienation, they remain nineteenth-century pictures in spite of Picasso's unconventional use of color, distortion, and space (Fig. 31-2).

Among Matisse's most important predecessors had been Gauguin. Picasso however, turned to the works of Paul Cézanne, finding in them another way to see and

31–1 Left. Matisse, "The Joy of Life." (Photograph Copyright 1980 by The Barnes Foundation)

31–2 Below. Picasso, "Family of Saltimbanques." (National Gallery of Art, Washington, D.C., Chester Dale Collection)

experience the world and to realize that experience in a painterly language. Let us look at one of Cézanne's paintings to try to understand what Picasso might have seen in them.

Cézanne   Cézanne liked to paint several versions of the same subject, such as Mont Sainte-Victoire in southern France. The version reproduced here (Color Plate XI) shows his technique of using bright, intense colors, applied in varying thicknesses, sometimes even reduced to transparency. Cézanne has alluded to the natural experience of the out-of-doors, but there is none of the transient quality of an impressionist picture. Each object—trees, housetops, road, bridge, mountain, sky—exists in space, separated by air and distance from us and from each other. Each object has weight and volume; but there is no consistent single point *perspective*, no consistent shadow pattern. Objects in the middle and background do not diminish in clarity as they do in traditional painting. Rather, the painted surface is made up of blocks of color; when the color changes, our eyes see that change as a change in direction toward or away from us. We follow the changes from a smoother foreground into a more complex middle and background. The overlapping colored blocks also establish the perception of behind and beside, which the mind tells us are sensations of distance and space, volume and weight. We can identify objects, but Cézanne does not attempt to emulate the texture of objects. Rather, he paints a characteristic contour, color, and mass, drawing on all our knowledge of, and associations with, that object. Mont Sainte-Victoire is a particular mountain made of rugged, substantial, colored blocks that suggest the concepts of height, weight, mass, and, therefore, mountain. The pine tree that spreads over the foreground surface, enveloping the mountain and sky, is not only that tree but every experience of the graceful, linear, light-filtering pine, whose branches and needles flatten against the sky and through which the sky literally shines. The same process has been applied to all objects; they are particular and universal. It is Cézanne's experience of the world, but it is made up of the experiences of seeing that may be everyone's.

Cézanne, Picasso saw, had wanted to paint nature and to portray the essential integrity of each object, yet he also wished to integrate each object into the framework that gives it meaning. The forest recedes when we concentrate on one tree, but we *know* that the other trees are there, acting with it to give it meaning. As our focus changes, the importance of one object is transferred to another object; it is this process of seeing that Cézanne has recorded, presenting an experience parallel to that in nature. Rather than creating the illusion of a window on the world, he wanted the canvas and paint to be present in their own right while acting as *abstract* equivalents for the seen world. This sounds difficult and as a painterly ideal it is; but as a convention it resembles those used by medieval or Renaissance artists to portray their world. What makes Cézanne's approach different is that he does not want to represent a medieval world of profound religious mystery or a Renaissance world of idealized and ordered harmonies, but the personal experience of seeing, in which to see is to know, because we come to know by focusing our attention from object to object. Cézanne makes us aware of the processes whereby we see and in this way achieves a universality different from that of Van Gogh, Gauguin, or Matisse.

African Art   Another artistic phenomenon that had a major impact on Picasso and his friends was the art of Africa and the South Pacific. Acquaintance with a completely different formal tradition is usually a very liberating experience to artists. It was so in the nineteenth century when Europeans became acquainted with Japanese prints. When Gauguin and others brought objects to Paris from Africa or the Pacific, interest was stimulated in what had heretofore been considered curiosities brought as memorabilia by colonists, travelers, or ethnographers. This so-called "primitive art" represented, as we saw in the chapter on African art in Volume I, completely different formal traditions. For example, in this mask (Fig. 31-3) the African artist has abstracted from reality those elements that are most important for the meaning and purpose of the mask. These have been exaggerated and combined into a strong, harmonious whole by the purely formal elements of the medium: plane, surface, texture, and shape. The existence of this tradition affirmed the belief of many artists that objects of art could speak in their own right, independent of the need to copy the

31–3   African Dan mask. (Copyright F. Willett, Glasgow)

felt. These *fetishes*, which have not been uninfluential in modern art, are all related to the religious passion, which is the source of the purest art.

The interest of these fetishes lies essentially in their plastic form, even though they are sometimes made of precious materials. This form is always powerful, very far removed from our conceptions and yet capable of nourishing the inspiration of artists.

It is not a question of competing with the models of classical antiquity, but of renewing subjects and forms by bringing artistic observation back to the first principles of great art.

In fact, the Greeks learned much more from the African sculptors than has been noted up to now. If it is true that Egypt exerted an appreciable influence on the very human art of Hellas (Greece), one would have to be very unfamiliar with the art of the Egyptians and of the Negro fetishes to deny that the latter provides the key to the hieraticism and the forms characteristic of Egyptian art.

The enthusiasm of today's painters and collectors for the art of fetishes is an enthusiasm for the basic principles of our arts; their taste is renewed through contact with these works. In fact, certain masterpieces of Negro sculpture can compete perfectly well with beautiful works of European sculpture of the greatest periods. I remember an African head in M. Jacques Doucet's collection that can stand up perfectly against some fine pieces of Romanesque sculpture. In any case, no one today would dream of denying these evident truths, except ignorant people who do not want to take the trouble to look at things closely.

familiar aspects of the visible world. At first these artists, including Picasso, copied the new forms and shapes, studying them and including them directly in their work. But very rapidly each artist adopted this influence to his particular uses, making the objects almost unrecognizable. Naturally, the majority of the European public did not receive either the African art or the work of artists inspired by it with enthusiasm. An apologist for both, the French poet and art critic Guillaume Apollinaire, argued persuasively for an understanding of African art. The piece that follows (translated by Susan Sulieman) was written in 1918.

> Curiosity has found a new field of exploration in the sculptures of Africa and Oceania.
>
> This new branch of curiosity, although born in France, has to this day found more commentators abroad. Since it originated in France, however, we have every reason to believe that it is here that its influence is being most deeply

Influence of Cézanne and African Art on Picasso   The combined influences of Cézanne and African art help us to better understand *Les Demoiselles d'Avignon*, an unfinished picture that Picasso showed his friends in 1907 (Fig. 31-4). What do we see? A large canvas is filled with female bodies. It is difficult to tell if they are seated, standing, or leaning because the space in which we would expect them to exist has been shattered. Look at the figure on the far left. Does she stand behind, beside, in front of, or in the drapery? Does it bother you that you cannot tell? Look at the center figure. Is she standing or lying down? Why is it confusing? Where are her legs? Can you explain the position of her arms? Which figure seems to be rushing into the space? How can you tell? Which figures seem to have had their faces transformed by masks? Does the seated figure in the lower left face you or sit with her

back to you? How does Picasso achieve a three-dimensional effect in the faces of the three figures center and left? How have the bodies been transformed? What does the picture mean? Does it matter if you cannot tell? Why or why not?

Interpretation of this picture is difficult because it is no longer a picture with subject matter that tells a story. What is happening may be clarified by remembering how Picasso and his friends looked at African masks and sculptures. They did not know the meaning or purpose of either, but in spite of that, they could recognize human and animal forms and patterns and colors that rendered an account of everyday objects. Initially, this sense of recognition was important just because it told these Western artists that, indeed, there

was more than one way to experience and give form to the world. Just as the medieval or Renaissance artist created conventions to capture experience and transmit knowledge, African artists had created their conventions. Western artists' experience of African art tended to reinforce the new (and very un-African) belief that line, color, and texture, when properly ordered in a work of art, have the power to create a personal response independent of religious or literary meaning. The problem became one of defining and understanding the limits of the power of the formal elements of art. African art, in particular, with its purposeful distortions of space, scale, and location, provided a major impetus for these artists.

Determined to free the picture from its dependence

on old formulas, Picasso and his friend Georges Braque worked together over a period of about four years. Like Cézanne they considered the act of seeing to be one in which, first, we perceive what we focus on; second, what we perceive is determined by the length of time that we focus; third, we perceive by manipulating objects within our frame of reference; and fourth, we perceive by filling in information based on what we already know. For the two painters the flat canvas became an imaginary grid of space on which fragments of the perceived world were arranged. Like the map maker who distills the elaborate, complex, three-dimensional world into an *abstraction* of lines and colors that convey information, the two painters distilled simple, everyday, familiar objects. They eliminated bright colors from their canvases because color itself can be emotionally powerful and evocative. They eliminated the traditional three-dimensional space invented in the Renaissance, and with it all references to fore-, mid-, and background. Objects or fragments of objects could now be placed anywhere in the shallow space. The artist could show us backs and sides of things, arranged at will on the canvas. A face is rendered in profile and full-face; we may see the side of the head and the back of the shoulder. References to specific objects are limited or reduced to familiar aspects.

Cubism   Examine the picture *Man with a Violin* (Fig. 31-5). What parts of the man do you see? What features of the violin? How does the painter suggest space, light, and the volume and weight of the man's body? Of the violin? Picasso, instead of creating a picture to be perceived in the most habitual, traditional mode gives us a construction, an arrangement of shapes, colors, textures, spaces, and weights that invites us to participate in the process of seeing and knowing. We are not invited completely to "find" the man and his violin but to learn how little we must know in order to see and understand. Moreover, we become more and more familiar with the purely formal qualities of the painting like *balance*, *harmony*, *contrast* of color, *texture*, and *form* that make up the experience of looking at pictures—an experience that can be enjoyable not because the picture is of "something" but because it "is." These paintings were named "cubist" by a hos-

31–5   Picasso, "Man with a Violin." (Philadelphia Museum of Art: Louise and Walter Arensberg Collection)

tile critic who pointed to their most conspicuous aspect—the small facets or planes that intersect and appear somewhat cubelike.

Collages   Neither Picasso nor Braque was content to continue in this style. They began to try other ideas such as adding materials like sand, pasted paper, or rope to the canvas to create the first *collages* (in French, "pasting," "gluing") (Fig. 31-6). The inclusion of "real" materials in their pictures increased the potential for humor and irony. For example, a head cut out of newspaper is made to stand for a three-dimensional volume, while the lettering on the paper is intrinsically flat. It is a game in which what you see may not necessarily be what you think you see; but, above all, what you see is a *made* object that is important in

31–6   Georges Braque, "Musical Forms, 1918." (Philadelphia Museum of Art: Louise and Walter Arensberg Collection)

its own right and not because it is a copy of the familiar, habitual visual world.

The rational and orderly methodology of early cubism and the simplicity of the early collages were tested by the addition of color and the simplification of the *grid*. To what extent did pictures presenting more recognizable forms still maintain their identity as painted, made things? Picasso's *Three Musicians* (Fig. 31-7) is derived from the broken space and complicated overlapping, superimposed views of *Man with a Violin*. The vivid, simple colors, along with the intersecting forms of the musicians and their instruments, create a rhythmic movement that seems to echo the syncopations of jazz. It is clear that for Picasso, as for Matisse, every accomplishment is to be weighed and used only if it enhances the power of communication between the object and the viewer.

31–7   Picasso, "Three Musicians." 1921 (summer). (Collection, The Museum of Modern Art, New York. Mrs. Simon Guggenheim Fund)

Nonobjective and Expressionist Painting

The belief in the ability of an object to act as a means of communication is nowhere more vividly tested than in the work of the painters Wassily Kandinsky and Piet Mondrian. Here we meet canvases that are completely free of any reference to the habitual, familiar objects and activities of our experience. We are left alone with arrangements of line and color that are, in Kandinsky's words, "a new world," capable of speaking to our conscious as well as our unconscious mind, if we will but permit it, asking not that it be a picture of something but that it just be.

Kandinsky Kandinsky became a painter when he saw one of Monet's *Haystacks* at an exhibition in Moscow. He tells us that he could not distinguish the subject. All that he saw was a veil of shimmering color, producing an emotional sensation like that produced when listening to great music. Stunned by this experience, Kandinsky traveled all over Europe, painting and absorbing the work of Gauguin, Van Gogh, Monet, and others. Settling in Munich, a place intellectually stimulating like Paris, Kandinsky began to experiment, seeking a method of painting that accomplished his aims. An incident recounted in his *Reminiscences* helps us to understand his concept of the idea of the nonobjective painting:

> It was the hour approaching dusk. I returned home with my paint box after making a study, still dreaming and wrapped into the work completed, when suddenly I saw an indescribably beautiful picture, imbibed by an inner glow. First I hesitated, then I quickly approached this mysterious picture, on which I saw nothing but shapes and colors, and the contents of which I could not understand. I immediately found the key to the puzzle; it was a picture painted by me, leaning against the wall, standing on its side. The next day, when there was daylight, I tried to get yesterday's impression of the painting. However, I only succeeded half-ways; on its side too, I constantly recognized the objects and the fine finish of dusk was lacking. I now knew fully well, that the object harms my paintings.
>
> A frightening abyss, a responsible load of all kinds of questions confronted me. And the most important: What should replace the missing object? . . .
>
> Only after many years of patient working, strenuous thinking, numerous careful attempts, constantly develop-

ing ability to purely and non-objectively feel artistic forms, to concentrate deeper and deeper into this endless depth, I arrived at the artistic forms, with which I am now working and which, I hope will develop much further.

The process was a long and arduous one. We already know that *line, color,* and *shape* can create sensations of space, movement, weight, and volume. But what of color disassociated from an object? Red, for example, will almost always conjure up images of fire, fire truck, stoplight, or car. Try to imagine a response to "winter"; a response not made of words or images of snow and ice, but of pure shapes, lines, and colors. The process is indeed an arduous one.

Writing as he worked, Kandinsky tried to explain his ideas, particularly in *On the Spiritual in Art*, published in 1912. In this treatise Kandinsky affirms his belief in the power of art to speak to the intellect and intuition of people without benefit of the habitual, familiar objects of the material world. He also advances a philosophical basis for this belief and suggests its social implications. Western man, he felt, had become desensitized by the materialism of his society.

Only by freeing painting from the material could the painter respond to the unconscious, the spiritual, and the immaterial longings of man. Moreover, a response freed from the material world would create a more universally understood language. He warned that his work was only a beginning and that future painters would be able to play on color harmonies as musicians play on the harmonies of the scales. Kandinsky's nonobjective pictures seem to build on Einstein's theories of the relativity of time and space, which were developing at this time. Indeed, Kandinsky embraces the buzzing, booming confusion of Einstein's universe in which all matter is energy. *Painting: Winter*, 1914 (Fig. 31-8) appears as an eruption of the energy of the universe. Slashing lines of color race and run, as if to leap from the space of the canvas. Rich in possibilities for fantasy, dream, and daydream, Kandinsky's pictures offered future artists an example of a language of color, line, texture, and shape unfiltered by the material world.

Expressionism In Munich, Kandinsky formed a group of artists called the Blue Rider. Members of this group and other German artists, writers, and musicians centered in Dresden and Berlin came to be known as

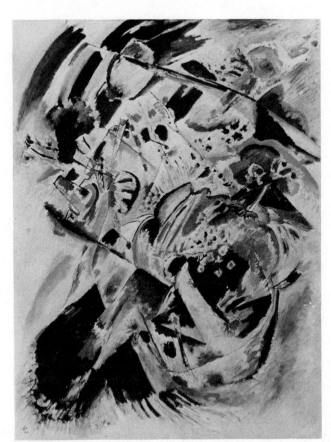

31–8   Kandinsky, "Painting No. 201 [Winter], 1914." (The Solomon R. Guggenheim Museum, New York/Photo by Robert E. Mates)

Mondrian and Purism   At the opposite pole from expressionism, another group of artists, centered primarily in Holland, celebrated the spirit of progress and man's rational and orderly faculties. The group called De Stilj were dedicated to "the devaluation of tradition, . . . the exposure of the whole swindle of lyricism and sentiment." In their work they stressed the need for abstraction and simplification, for clarity, certainty, and order. One of them, Piet Mondrian, who began as a traditional painter, visited Paris, learned from the cubists, and returned to Holland. He began to remove all references to the familiar visual world from his canvases, concentrating on the "pure" reality of the formal plastic elements of art, which he began to confine to a linear black grid imposed on a white ground. He inserted color, usually red, yellow, or blue (the three primaries) to create contrasts that were resolved in harmo-

31–9   Ernst Kirchner, "Street, Berlin." (Collection, The Museum of Modern Art, New York)

expressionists. Expressionism drew on the powerful emotional quality of Van Gogh and on the bold color and line of Gauguin and Matisse. It is essentially, as the name implies, an art of self-expression or subjectivity. Influenced by Freud, expressionist artists (and the writers and musicians associated with them) wished to express the deep, hidden drives of human beings rather than surface "reality." They sensed, along with Marxists, the alienation of the individual in modern society and the dehumanizing effects of bourgeois capitalism. They were dissatisfied with the materialism and complacency of German society and often criticized it harshly in their works. Ernst Kirchner's painting *Street, Berlin* (1913) is a good example of an expressionist work (Fig. 31-9). What is going on in the picture? What is the artist's attitude toward the way of life portrayed here? How does he express that attitude?

31–10 John Sloan, "Sunday, Women Drying Their Hair." (Addison Gallery of American Art, Phillips Academy, Andover, Massachusetts)

nious balance (Color Plate XII). Compare your experience of this work with *Painting: Winter* by Kandinsky. One is fantastic, the other orderly; both grow out of the manipulation of the essential elements of painting.

Modernism in America

The art scene in the United States was very different. Many artists were hostile to the new art of Paris, Munich, and Berlin. The painters who comprised the "ashcan school" remained loyal to an essentially realist aesthetic, basing their work on that of a nineteenth-century American realist, Thomas Eakins. Their art had developed from that of Eakins but was more reportorial and concerned with the life and times of the city. (It was this subject matter that gave them their name.) John Sloan, one of the most representative painters of this group, took his subject matter from the daily activ-

ities of the ordinary, the poor, the immigrant (Fig. 31-10). The painters in this group were not convinced that European art could make a contribution to the development of a uniquely American art.

But in fairness it must be said that painters in this group helped to give modern art its first important, large exhibition in this country. Arranged by an association of American artists, the Armory Show of February 1914, staged at the Armory of the Infantry in New York City, exhibited the work of Cézanne, Van Gogh, Gauguin, Matisse, Kandinsky, Picasso, and Duchamp, among others. The public was generally shocked and offended, but many American artists were stimulated by, and attracted to, these works, for there already existed a strong stream of innovation. Moreover, these young artists had already found a rallying point and place in the figure of Alfred Stieglitz, a photographer who had studied in Berlin and returned to this country. Stieglitz opened a gallery at 291 Fifth Avenue, where he exhibited the most advanced work from abroad and attracted artists and critics interested in it.

Georgia O'Keeffe   One of the group, Georgia O'Keeffe, who married Stieglitz, is still an active painter. In some early works she tried to eliminate objects but found that unsatisfying. Her truly great paintings began when she concentrated on one object, making it the sole inhabitant of the picture space (Fig. 31-11). In her clear, painstaking account of the magnified

31-11   Georgia O'Keeffe, "Jack-in-the-Pulpit #5." (Malcolm Varon, New York)

flower, we find a rich ground for symbolic associations. The crisp, smooth painterly surface, however, presents the object with a cold objectivity that contrasts with our resonating fantasies. This tension between the unavoidable presence of the object and the opportunity for free fantasy seems characteristic of American life: it is a contrast like that between our great dependence on the machine and our fear of its dehumanizing possibilities.

Dada and Surrealism

In 1915 a number of young people from all over Europe converged in Zurich, Switzerland, to create a movement that sought the fantastic and absurd in art, literature, and music. The movement was called Dada, a term whose origin is obscure. The most frequently quoted version is that a French-German dictionary opened at random produced the word *dada*, which means a child's hobby horse or rocking horse. The point is, of course, that life itself is random and uncontrolled: art should reflect the randomness and pessimism that is bred by the recognition of man's inability to control his life. The movement in Zurich was most concerned with poetry and music, producing events that combined the two in a nonsensical manner. Ridiculing the materialism of the middle classes and the optimism of the scientifically oriented progressives, the movement seemed at first merely a destructive one that challenged not only the traditional values of art but also the most recent. Nevertheless, there was a deep seriousness about these people that encouraged the artist to look again at the irrational, the subjective, the unconstructed side of man's psyche as it responded to life in this century.

In painting, the artist who exemplifies Dada is Marcel Duchamp. Duchamp (one of three brothers all of whom were deeply involved in new movements in Paris) had already created a masterpiece in his painting *Nude Descending a Staircase, No. 2, 1912* (Fig. 31-12). For us today, familiar with time-lapse photography, films, and the multiple images of advertising, the painting is a remarkably expressive rendering of a figure walking down the stairs. Duchamp, however was not satisfied with painting; he felt that it was a limited process, doomed to end. By attempting a startling vari-

31–12   Marcel Duchamp, "Nude Descending a Staircase, No. 2."
(Philadelphia Museum of Art: Louise and Walter
Arensberg Collection)

submitted it with the name *Fountain*. It was not shown in the exhibition. These "ready-mades," as Duchamp called them, were offensive to many, but others saw them as the realization and affirmation of the control of the machine and machine-made products in life. In 1915 Duchamp emigrated to New York, where he associated with the group at Stieglitz's 291. There he began a work that came to be considered exemplary of surrealism, the movement in art that emerged from Dada after World War I.

The chief spokesman for the new movement, André Breton, was a writer whose experiences in World War I convinced him of the unlimited depth of the human pysche. Impressed by the ideas of Freud, he identified the unconscious mind as the source for a new synthesis of the sometimes unpleasant concrete world with the world of rich associations created in dream and fantasy. The goal was to free individual creativity

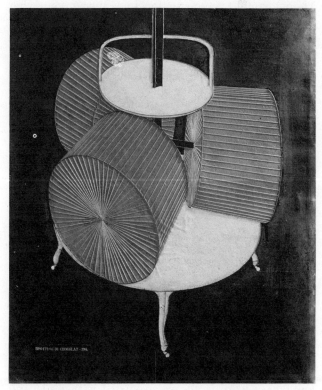

31–13   Marcel Duchamp, "Chocolate Grinder, No. 2."
(Philadelphia Museum of Art: Louise and Walter
Arensberg Collection)

ety of approaches, he called into the question all the processes of art. Sometimes he would reduce his subject matter to the components of a fantastic machine; at other times he rendered objects with a scientific accuracy that gave them a superreal and fantastic quality (Fig. 31-13). Then, denying the hand of the artist altogether, he simply chose everyday objects, designating them "art" by the application of his signature. For the Armory Show he had signed a urinal, "R Mutt," and

to respond positively to the conflict between the rational and the irrational, producing a heightened awareness of the vitality of life and the mind that would ameliorate its apparent emptiness. Techniques for achieving this synthesis included collage, automatic drawing, and photographic montage of images. Generally the results were a dreamlike or hallucinatory juxtaposition of images and objects that stimulated personal free association and intense emotional responses.

In this context Marcel Duchamp's work *The Large Glass, The Bride Stripped Bare by Her Bachelors, Even* (Fig. 31-14), became a seminal surrealist work. Duchamp had worked on the idea for years, accumulating images that he transferred to a sheet of plate glass where dust, allowed to collect, had been glued in place. Other random elements, the frame, and finally the cracks in the glass itself became part of the work. According to Breton's interpretation, these images reflect the mechanization of persons and of the sexual act. Though such a representation may appear somewhat repulsive, if not inhumane, the artist intended to play on the contrasts of man to machine, the conflict of man with machine, and the perpetual conflicts between the sexes. In so doing, he intended to enlarge our awareness of the unconscious associations that may accompany our lives.

Other artists in various media learned from surrealist techniques how to contradict our familiar and habitual perception of reality. Surrealism has been a source of inspiration not only in painting, sculpture, the graphic arts, and poetry but also in the production of motion pictures.

Modernism in Sculpture: 1900–1930

Sculpture, like painting and graphics, responded to the same ideas and impulses that had transformed art after 1900. Just as we can distinguish those artists who continue interest in the human form as a means of communication, so we can identify artists who work only in forms, shapes, and colors freed from Renaissance and baroque conventions. Similarly, we can identify cubist sculptors, expressionist sculptors, and sculptors whose work is always associated with Dada and surrealism. We will consider work by two artists, Constantin Brancusi and Jacques Lipchitz.

31–14   Marcel Duchamp, "The Bride Stripped Bare by Her Bachelors, Even" (The Large Glass). (Philadelphia Museum of Art: Bequest of Katherine S. Dreier)

Brancusi was a Rumanian whose work really parallels that of the cubists rather than being directly influenced by it. He was trained in the academic manner; but, after arriving in Paris in 1904, he turned more and more toward the evocation of forms by reducing them to bare essentials. A splendid craftsman with tremendous empathy for the textures and characteristics of a given material, he described his efforts as a search for the universally expressive essence of forms. *Bird in Space* (Fig. 31-15), made in 1928, can be interpreted as the reduction of a bird's wing, its soaring power, its light gracefulness. The beautifully polished surface of the chrome form calls out to our tactile senses, and it is possible to imagine the cool purity of the shape that a caress would produce.

The work of Jacques Lipchitz forms a strong contrast with much of that of Brancusi. Much more directly influenced by the cubist painters, he made low reliefs in stone that can be directly compared to paintings and collages by Braque and Picasso. A free-standing piece like *Figure* (made between 1926 and 1930) is strongly suggestive of the totemic power of African figures; but the juxtaposition of side with frontal views, which occurs when one moves around the figure in space, is based on the orderly perception of the interrelationship of parts—a characteristic of cubism (Fig. 31-16). Lip-

chitz modeled figures like these in clay or plasticine for bronze casting; the complex surface, which is rough and extremely tactile, is retained in the casting process. Compare this work with Brancusi's *Bird in Space.* Does *Figure* bear any relationship to other sculpture that has been considered? Why or why not? Does the interpenetration of shapes and spaces bear any relationship to painting that we have seen? Is it possible to imagine such relationships in architecture?

Modernism in Architecture: 1900–1930

While it may seem that Americans had much to learn from Europe in the visual arts, they also had much to contribute. This is nowhere more apparent

31–15 Near right. Brancusi, "Bird in Space." (Philadelphia Museum of Art: Louise and Walter Arensberg Collection)

31–16 Far right. Lipchitz, "Figure." (Collection, The Museum of Modern Art, New York. Van Gogh Purchase Fund)

31–17 Frank Lloyd Wright, Robie House, Chicago. (Hedrich Blessing, Chicago)

than in architecture and in a particular genius, Frank Lloyd Wright.

Frank Lloyd Wright Wright worked in Chicago with Louis Sullivan, an architect who had made great contributions to the development of the Chicago School. Wright left Sullivan's office in 1893 to work where he lived, in a suburb of Chicago, Oak Park. He had been greatly challenged by Sullivan, but his particular interest in these early years was the single-family dwelling. The typical, two-story wood frame house of the late nineteenth century was, to Wright, a disaster. It was cramped, ugly, dark, and dank. It wasted space, had no relationship to its site, ignored innovations in mechanical systems, and separated man from the land that was his aboriginal home. Wright asked fundamental questions about architecture, beginning with the abstract idea of dwelling, of shelter. He asked what features, forms, and shapes would place man in an harmonious relationship to the earth, giving him the comfort and warmth of the aboriginal cave. He asked what materials should be used, how, and in what forms. He asked questions about the family: how does it function as a small community, and how can the dwelling provide essential privacy for each member within the context of the family? Moreover, he asked

how use might be made of growing technology and machine-tooled elements to make the house more livable, comfortable, and responsive, as well as less time-consuming, in terms of its upkeep, to free the family for more personal leisure and growth. The approximately thirty houses that grew up on the prairie of Oak Park were the answers to these questions.

Economical to build, dependent on the direct and simple use of wood, glass, brick, and stucco, the Oak Park houses were made for owners who were neither eccentric nor particularly rich. The plans of the houses frequently grew outward from a central core of hearth and services—plumbing, electricity, and heat. Bedrooms were confined to one area, kitchen and servants to another wing; the family-oriented activities were grouped in integrated spaces around the hearth. Overhanging eaves sheltered the long windows and glass doors that opened onto patio, terrace, or balcony. Low walls of stone, brick, or shrubbery separated the houses from the intrusions of the street. The owners loved their homes. Wright's solutions were among the most innovative that this country had seen.

The Robie house in Chicago is a mature expression of Wright's ideas (Figs. 31-17, 31-18). Study the plan. Why does Wright focus the house around the hearth and fireplace? What is the effect of the deep, overhanging eaves, the long continuous lines produced by the roofs and the porches? Where does he use glass? Why does he partially conceal the house from the neighborhood streets? Does the combination of brick and concrete seem a good one? Why not simply use one or the other? The house in the "prairie style," as it came to be known, produced tremendous response in the Europeans who visited Wright in Chicago. His work became exemplary of the possibilities for an architecture that was not "in the styles."

Wright's emphasis on the orderly and rational, coupled with a deep, intuitive feeling for the nature of man and his suitable dwelling, produced a marriage of ideas that struck strong chords in European thought. His emphasis on the use of machined materials—glass, brick, veneers, and, in the Robie house, steel members for the far-reaching eaves—seemed to combine the best of two worlds: technology and the machine, man and his imagination. But, while some of Wright's contributions were influential in Europe, many of his ideas seemed

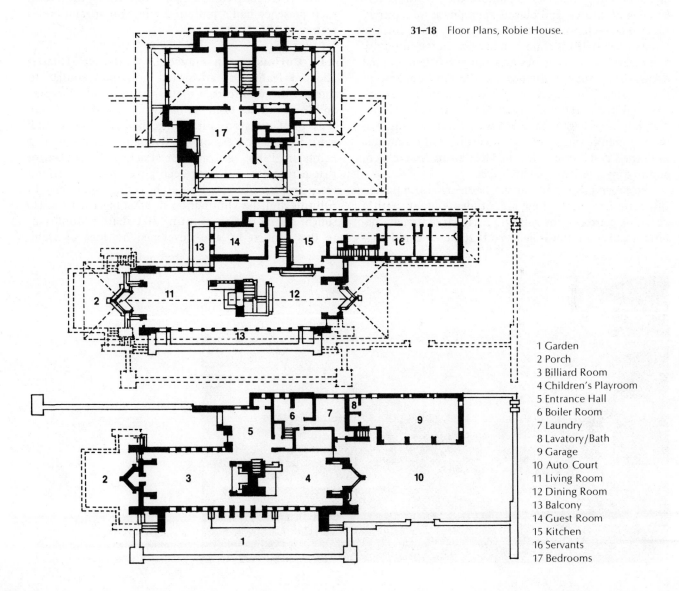

31–18 Floor Plans, Robie House.

1 Garden
2 Porch
3 Billiard Room
4 Children's Playroom
5 Entrance Hall
6 Boiler Room
7 Laundry
8 Lavatory/Bath
9 Garage
10 Auto Court
11 Living Room
12 Dining Room
13 Balcony
14 Guest Room
15 Kitchen
16 Servants
17 Bedrooms

too romantic to the architects and theorists of the school known as the Bauhaus.

The Bauhaus Founded at Weimar in 1919, then moved to Dessau, Germany, the Bauhaus became the most influential center for architects who shunned the past and wanted to create a rational, functional architecture for the twentieth century. These people wanted to use new materials in a direct way, taking advantage of the machine and machine production not only to create buildings but also to produce the furniture, textiles, light fixtures, and objects appropriate for a purely functional, scientific age. The physical plant for the school (Fig. 31-19) is almost factorylike in its simplicity and directness. In fact, factories and purely commercial design had much influence on the development of these forms. The classroom block is a steel framework enclosed in a curtain of glass. The wall, with which human buildings began, has given way to a thin, light, permeable membrane carrying no weight. It also reminds us of the Crystal Palace, for the ideas created there were admired by the Bauhaus architect.

The program of study at the Bauhaus also reflected the optimism of the new age. Students began with a year-long course in the general principles of design, materials, and color. It was believed that if they could mas-

ter the principles of design, in various media, then they could use that knowledge to solve any problem. The analogy, of course, is with the scientific method. After learning principles, students applied them by working in the shops of the Bauhaus, learning the various aspects of total design from the ground up, as it were. They could then specialize. The Bauhaus attracted the most advanced thinkers, artists, and designers. Kandinsky taught there, as did Paul Klee, Josef Albers, Walter Gropius, Marcel Breuer, and Miës van der Rohe. After the latter four emigrated to America in the 1930s, their presence had a profound effect on art and architecture in this country.

Le Corbusier In France Le Corbusier (Charles Édouard Jeanneret) advocated principles similar to those of the architects at the Bauhaus, for like Gropius and Miës van der Rohe he had worked with Peter Behrens, the German architect who had laid the groundwork for the success of the Bauhaus. Beginning as a painter in Paris, Le Corbusier attacked the cubism of that period (ca. 1918) as decorative. With his friend Ozenfant, he advocated an architectural simplicity in painting and the elimination of all subject matter. He sought a kind of pure painting, like that of Mondrian; in this context he also developed his idea of archi-

31-19 Walter Gropius, The Bauhaus, 1925–26. Dessau, Germany. (Photograph, Courtesy The Museum of Modern Art, New York)

31–20 Right. Le Corbusier, Villa Savoye, Poissy-sur-Seine, France, 1929–31. (Photograph, Courtesy The Museum of Modern Art, New York)

31–21 Below. Le Corbusier, Villa Savoye. (a) Plan of Ground Floor showing driveway and garage between the columns (pilotis), service areas, and guest quarters. (b) Plan of Second Floor with main living quarters and roof terrace.

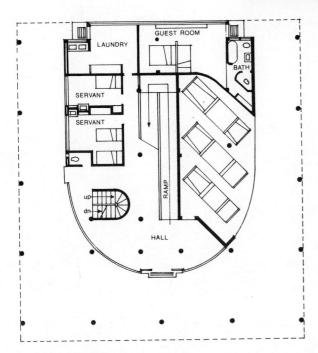

GROUND FLOOR

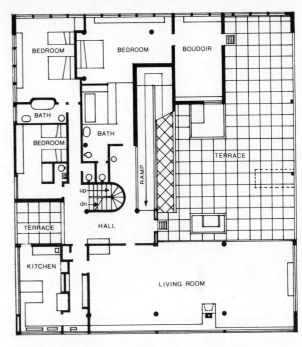

SECOND FLOOR

tecture, characterized in this period by a minimalist approach to design. At the same time he coined the phrase that a house should be a "machine for living in." In the years between 1918 and 1930 Le Corbusier pursued the problem of the house. Using reinforced concrete, which is light, strong, and malleable, he combined it with pillars to make the wall independent, free to respond to the open plan, much in the same way that Wright had done. Like Wright, he was concerned with the interpenetration of spaces, but he was more inclined to separate the house from its site, turning the house inward on itself. Compare the Villa Savoye at Poissy (Figs. 31-20, 31-21), 1929–1930, with the Robie house. Notice the difference created by materials. Which house seems more in sympathy with its site? Which house seems the more "rational" and "functional"? Which would you prefer and why?

From Cézanne and Wright to Picasso and Le Corbusier, we have covered the ground of the watershed period of this century in art. We have actually touched down only in a very few places. More is omitted than included. We have tried to outline the predicament of the artist in these years, torn between rational optimism and irrational pessimism; between the desire for an orderly and pure art and architecture and the desire to speak to the anxiety that was given its most awful expression in World War I itself, where the fruits of science produced the gas mask, shell-shock, and the romance of the airplane. On the one hand, all seems pure and promising; on the other, all life seems destined only for suffering and death. The American artist faced the years between the wars in either a self-imposed isolation or a struggle with the implications of European work. When the surrealists arrived in this country in the late 1930s and 1940s, they found a rich and complex milieu in which their ideas, and those of cubism, purism, and expressionism would fuse to produce a great American school that was also truly international.

32

THE MODERNIST MOVEMENT: LITERATURE

Closely allied with the various modernist movements in the visual arts, literary artists in the opening decades of the twentieth century showed many of the same formal and thematic concerns. Modernism, however, was not simply a movement limited to that era. In literature, as in painting, it became a new way of apprehending the world through art. Every serious artist of the twentieth century has felt the necessity either to react against modernism or to build on its innovations. Even though our present age is considered "postmodern," many of our greatest writers are still composing in a modernist vein.

A Literature of Exiles Most of the great modernist writers lived, at one time or another, in Paris. Besides the native French writers associated with the Dada, surrealist, and other artistic-literary modernist movements, there were German expressionists, Italian futurists, and other Europeans. Paris was also the cradle for a dynamic new African literature written in French by intellectuals from the French African colonies, some of whom were involved with the surrealist movement. It is no exaggeration to say that Paris in the early twentieth century was a fermenting center of British and American letters. James Joyce (1882–1941), the Irish novelist and poet who became one of the greatest and most original stylists in the English language, found as his first publisher an American in Paris—the farsighted Sylvia Beach. American expatriates such as Gertrude Stein, Ezra Pound, F. Scott Fitzgerald, and Ernest Hemingway also gathered at Miss Beach's bookstore. Gertrude Stein (1874–1946) was a close associate and supporter of Picasso and other modern painters, who were highly influential on her style. Stein coined the phrase "the lost generation" to describe these Americans who had fled their country for Europe. Common among them was the feeling that a crass, philistine American public was incapable of understanding or sustaining them and that they needed to turn elsewhere for intellectual and aesthetic nourishment.

The rift between artist and public, first sensed by the romantics and intensified by the Symbolists was, for the modernists, a fact of life. It is not surprising that a literature of expatriates, a literature responsible to no one, is a literature characterized by a sense of exile and by an extreme subjectivity. The lack of contact with a public, except for a small coterie, gives the writer great freedom to experiment but also encourages esotericism. Even the modernist writers who did not join the expatriates in Paris experienced some sort of exile. The American T. S. Eliot (1888–1965) did live briefly in Paris but emigrated to England. Those who were not in physical exile often experienced an inner exile. Franz Kafka (1883–1924), the greatest modernist writer in German, was a Jew who lived in the ghetto of the Czechoslovakian city of Prague under the Austro-Hungarian empire. The gap between artist and public, a frequent theme in modernist literature, is exemplified in our Kafka story, translated by Willa and Edwin Muir. Coupled with this, however, was a belief in the saving power of art itself, a continuation of the late-nineteenth century's adherence to the religion of art.

In a declining, empty civilization, art appeared as a refuge, a form of salvation.

Exploration of the Unconscious Other pervasive concerns of modernist writers seemed to necessitate changes in, or experiments with, form. Influenced by Freud, the surrealists attempted to render the raw state of the unconscious in words by abandoning normal syntax and logic and speaking in images. The most important experiments in rendering psychological states, however, were done by novelists. Marcel Proust, Virginia Woolf, and James Joyce, though very different as artists, shared the belief that the reality worth exploring was an inner, mental one rather than the external one of the realists. The unconscious or semiconscious part of the mind, as Freud showed, functions outside the logical order and time frame established by reason. It works rather by association, by summoning images that merge past, present, and future. To convey this state, these novelists used the device of the "interior monologue" or "stream of consciousness." Joyce, the most radical, completely abandoned rules of grammar and syntax, even inventing new words. The effect is similar to the abandonment of perspective and the juxtaposition of planes and of images in modernist painting.

Other modernist innovators work in what seems at first to be an opposite technique. Kafka, for one, writes in an apparently logical order, in clear sentences, and pays close attention to external details. Only after reading for a while do we realize that we are in a grotesque world where our ordinary values and logic do not apply, a world conveying the nightmarish quality of everyday life. Like the expressionist painters, Kafka presents to the reader distorted, shocking images, often expressive of man's fundamental isolation in society and in the cosmos.

Visual Aspects of Literature Rendering startling, concrete images as opposed to vague, loose, "romantic" sentiments became a preoccupation of many poets as well as painters. Ezra Pound (1885–1972), founder of the imagist school in Anglo-American poetry, studied Chinese poetry as well as medieval French and Italian poets in a search for "visual" poetry on which to model his own work. Gertrude Stein, by a kind of word painting, attempted to do in literature what the cubists, especially Picasso, were doing in painting. The American poet E. E. Cummings (1894–1962), who signed his name e e cummings, was a painter as well as a poet. He broke up the traditional typographical appearance of the poem on the page while experimenting with sound effects that this break-up could enhance. Cummings, like most modernists, is sharply critical of the society around him, yet his view of life is refreshingly affirmative, at times conventionally lyrical.

Theme of Spiritual Emptiness   A certain world-weariness invades much of modernist writing. The devastations of World War I seemed to confirm already present philosophical assumptions about the futility and fragility of man's existence. With traditional religion and other sustaining myths dead, the individual was often left only with questions. Politics, to most moderns, did not offer a substitute for religion; even love, or any form of real communication between individuals, seemed to many extremely problematic in the modern world. One of the best chroniclers of this state of emotional vacuum is T. S. Eliot. Eliot's most ambitious poem on this theme, "The Waste Land," portrays the spiritual desolation of a modern city, London, through references to ancient literature and oriental mythology. His earlier "Love Song of J. Alfred Prufrock," printed here, portrays a typically "modern" man, unable to make decisions, to act, or even to feel. Prufrock is an overcivilized human being in an overcivilized society, representative, before Freud's book, of "civilization and its discontents." The irony with which Eliot depicts his character has become a stable feature of much twentieth-century literature.

Eliot eventually solved his personal problems with meaninglessness and emptiness by converting to the Anglican church and becoming a loyal British subject. For many, however, the spiritual anguish at the core of modernism has remained a central fact of twentieth-century existence. The words of the great Irish poet W. B. Yeats (although not intended as such) seem to sum up this state: "Things fall apart, the centre cannot hold. . . ."

GERTRUDE STEIN

Picasso

One whom some were certainly following was one who was completely charming. One whom some were certainly following was one who was charming. One whom some were following was one who was completely charming. One whom some were following was one who was certainly completely charming.

Some were certainly following and were certain that the one they were then following was one working and was one bringing out of himself then something. Some were certainly following and were certain that the one they were then following was one bringing out of himself then something that was coming to be a heavy thing, a solid thing and a complete thing.

One whom some were certainly following was one working and certainly was one bringing something out of himself then and was one who had been all his living had been one having something coming out of him.

Something had been coming out of him, certainly it had been coming out of him, certainly it was something, certainly it had been coming out of him and it had meaning, a clear meaning.

One whom some were certainly following and some were certainly following him, one whom some were certainly following was one certainly working.

One whom some were certainly following was one having something coming out of him something having meaning and this one was certainly working then.

This one was working and something was coming then, something was coming out of this one then. This one was one and always there was something coming out of this one and always there had been something coming out of this one. This one had never been one not having something coming out of this one. This one was one having something coming out of this one. This one had been one whom some were following. This one was one whom some were following. This one was being one whom some were following. This one was one who was working.

This one was one who was working. This one was one being one having something being coming out of him. This one was one going on having something come out of him. This one was one going on working.

This one was one whom some were following. This one was one who was working.

This one always had something being coming out of this one. This one was working. This one always had been working. This one was always having something that was coming out of this one that was a solid thing, a charming thing, a lovely thing, a perplexing thing, a disconcerting thing, a simple thing, a clear thing, a complicated thing, an interesting thing, a disturbing thing, a repellent thing, a very pretty thing. This one was one certainly being one having something coming out of him. This one was one whom some were following. This one was one who was working.

This one was one who was working and certainly this one was needing to be working so as to be one being working. This one was one having something coming out of him. This one would be one all his living having something coming out of him. This one was working and then this one was working and this one was needing to be working, not to be one having something coming out of him something having meaning, but wa sneeding to be working so as to be one working.

This one was certainly working and working was something this one was certain this one would be doing and this one was doing that thing, this one was working. This one was not one completely working. This one was not ever completely working. This one certainly was not completely working.

This one was one having always something being coming out of him, something having completely a real meaning. This one was one whom some were following. This one was one who was working. This one was one who was working and he was one needing this thing needing to be working so as to be one having some way of being one having some way of working. This one was one who was working. This one was one having something come out of him something having meaning. This one was one always having something come out of him and this thing the thing coming out of him always had real meaning. This one was one who was working. This one was one who was almost always working. This one was not one completely working. This one was one not ever completely working. This one was not one working to have anything come out of him. He always did have something having meaning that did come out of him. He always did have some-

thing come out of him. He was working, he was not ever completely working. He did have some following. They were always following him. Some were certainly following him. He was one who was working. He was one having something coming out of him something having meaning. He was not ever completely working.

QUESTIONS

1. How do these short, overlapped sentences create a word portrait of Picasso?
2. What basic differences do you find between this description and realistic description?
3. Which technique in painting would you compare to this literary technique? How?
4. Is this technique effective in your opinion? Why or why not? What does it convey about Picasso's art?

This next selection is taken from the final pages of James Joyce's novel, *Ulysses*, written in 1922. Although it is a long book, the time span in *Ulysses* is only one day in Dublin. Because of the interior monologue technique, however, the novel can actually span all of the time within the characters' memory. In addition, the day in Dublin loosely parallels the events in Homer's *Odyssey* (hence the title), thus opening up a mythic dimension. The central character of the book is Leopold Bloom; the selection here is part of a half-dreaming monologue of Bloom's wife, Molly. Molly's erotic fantasies and Joyce's use of "dirty" words caused *Ulysses* to be banned in the United States until 1933. Molly has been unfaithful to her husband, but in these final pages she recalls their early love together and ends the novel with a life-affirming "Yes!"

JAMES JOYCE

from *Ulysses*

. . . a quarter after what an unearthly hour I suppose theyre just getting up in China now combing out their pigtails for the day well soon have the nuns ringing the angelus theyve nobody coming in to spoil their sleep except an odd priest or two for his night office the alarmclock next door at cockshout clattering the brains out of itself let me see if I can doze off 1 2 3 4 5 what kind of flowers are those they invented like the stars the wallpaper in Lombard Street was much nicer the apron he gave me was like that something only I only wore it twice better lower this lamp and try again so as I can get up early Ill go to Lambes there beside Findlaters and get them to send us some flowers to put about the place in case he brings him home tomorrow today I mean no no Fridays an unlucky day first I want to do the place up someway the dust grows in it I think while Im asleep then we can have music and cigarettes I can accompany him first I must clean the keys of the piano with milk whatll I wear shall I wear a white rose or those fairy cakes in Liptons I love the smell of a rich big shop at 7½d. a lb or the other ones with the cherries in them and the pinky sugar 11d. a couple of lbs of course a nice plant for the middle of the table Id get that cheaper in wait wheres this I saw them not long ago I love flowers Id love to have the whole place swimming in roses God of heaven theres nothing like nature the wild mountains then the sea and the waves rushing then the beautiful country with fields of oats and all kinds of things and all the fine cattle going about that would do your heart good to see rivers and lakes and flowers all sorts of shapes and smells and colours springing up even out of the ditches primroses and violets nature it is as for them saying theres no God I wouldnt give a snap of my two fingers for all their learning why dont they go and create something I often asked him atheists or whatever they call themselves go and wash the cobbles off themselves first then go howling for the priest and they dying and why why because theyre afraid of hell on account of their bad conscience ah yes I know them well who was the first person in the universe before there was anybody that made it all who ah that they dont know neither do I so there you are they might as well try to stop the sun from rising tomorrow the sun shines for you he said the day we were lying among the rhododendrons on Howth head in the grey tweed suit and his straw hat the day I got him to propose to me yes first [I gave him the bit of seedcake out of my mouth and it was leapyear like now yes 16 years ago my God after that long kiss I near lost my breath yes he said I was a flower of the mountain yes so we are flowers all a womans body yes that was one true thing he said in his life and the sun shines for you today yes that was why I liked him because I saw he understood or felt what a woman is and I knew I could always get

round him and I gave him all the pleasure I could leading him on till he asked me to say yes] and I wouldnt answer first only looked out over the sea and the sky I was thinking of so many things he didn't know of Mulvey and Mr Stanhope and Hester and father and old captain Groves and the sailors playing all birds fly and I say stoop and washing up dishes they called it on the pier and the sentry in front of the governors house with the thing round his white helmet poor devil half roasted and the Spanish girls laughing in their shawls and their tall combs and the auctions in the morning the Greeks and the jews and the Arabs and the devil knows who else from all the ends of Europe and Duke street and the fowl market all clucking outside Larby Sharons and the poor donkeys slipping half asleep and the vague fellows in the cloaks asleep in the shade on the steps and the big wheels of the carts of the bulls and the old castle thousands of years old yes and those handsome Moors all in white and turbans like kings asking you to sit down in their little bit of a shop and Ronda with the old windows of the posadas glancing eyes a lattice hid for her lover to kiss the iron and the wineshops half open at night and the castanets and the night we missed the boat at Algeciras the watchman going about serene with his lamp and O that awful deepdown torrent O and the sea the sea crimson sometimes like fire and the glorious sunsets and the figtrees in the Alameda gardens yes and all the queer little streets and pink and blue and yellow houses and the rosegardens and the jessamine and geraniums and cactuses and Gibraltar as a girl where I was a Flower of the mountain yes when I put the rose in my hair like the Andalusian girls used or shall I wear a red yes and how he kissed me under the Moorish wall and I thought well as well him as another and then I asked him with my eyes to ask again yes and then he asked me would I yes to say yes my mountain flower and first I put my arms around him yes and drew him down to me so he could feel my breasts all perfume yes and his heart was going like mad and yes I said yes I will Yes.

QUESTIONS

1. How long does it take you, as a reader, to "get in" to this text and discover what is going on? How do you react to it initially?

2. Does Joyce's technique effectively represent a state of semiconsciousness? Why or why not?
3. Show from the text how time is "flattened out" here; that is, how past, present, and future are superimposed. In what sense is this representation of psychic reality more "real" than a realistic text?
4. Trace the *motif* of the flower in this text. How does it function?

FRANZ KAFKA

A Hunger Artist

During these last decades the interest in professional fasting has markedly diminished. It used to pay very well to stage such great performances under one's own management, but today that is quite impossible. We live in a different world now. At one time the whole town took a lively interest in the hunger artist; from day to day of his fast the excitement mounted; everybody wanted to see him at least once a day; there were people who bought season tickets for the last few days and sat from morning till night in front of his small barred cage; even in the nighttime there were visiting hours, when the whole effect was heightened by torch flares; on fine days the cage was set out in the open air, and then it was the children's special treat to see the hunger artist; for their elders he was often just a joke that happened to be in fashion, but the children stood open-mouthed, holding each other's hands for greater security, marveling at him as he sat there pallid in black tights, with his ribs sticking out so prominently, not even on a seat but down among straw on the ground, sometimes giving a courteous nod, answering questions with a constrained smile, or perhaps stretching an arm through the bars so that one might feel how thin it was, and then again withdrawing deep into himself, paying no attention to anyone or anything, not even to the all-important striking of the clock that was the only piece of furniture in his cage, but merely staring into vacancy with half-shut eyes, now and then taking a sip from a tiny glass of water to moisten his lips.

Besides casual onlookers there were also relays of permanent watchers selected by the public, usually butchers, strangely enough, and it was their task to watch the hunger artist day and night, three of them at a time, in case he should have some secret recourse to nourishment. This was nothing but a formality, instituted to reassure the masses, for the initiates knew well enough that during his fast the artist would never in any circumstances, not even under forcible compulsion, swallow the smallest morsel of food; the honor of his profession forbade it. Not every watcher, of course, was capable of understanding this, there were often groups of night watchers who were very lax in carrying out their duties and deliberately huddled together in a retired corner to play cards with great absorption, obviously intending to give the hunger artist the chance of a little refreshment, which they supposed he could draw from some private hoard. Nothing annoyed the artist more than such watchers; they made him miserable; they made his fast seem unendurable; sometimes he mastered his feebleness sufficiently to sing during their watch for as long as he could keep going, to show them how unjust their suspicions were. But that was of little use; they only wondered at his cleverness in being able to fill his mouth even while singing. Much more to his taste were the watchers who sat close up to the bars, who were not content with the dim night lighting of the hall but focused him in the full glare of the electric pocket torch given them by the impresario. The harsh light did not trouble him at all, in any case he could never sleep properly, and he could always drowse a little, whatever the light, at any hour, even when the hall was thronged with noisy onlookers. He was quite happy at the prospect of spending a sleepless night with such watchers; he was ready to exchange jokes with them, to tell them stories out of his nomadic life, anything at all to keep them awake and demonstrate to them again that he had no eatables in his cage and that he was fasting as not one of them could fast. But his happiest moment was when the morning came and an enormous breakfast was brought them, at his expense, on which they flung themselves with the keen appetite of healthy men after a weary night of wakefulness. Of course there were people who argued that this breakfast was an unfair attempt to bribe the watchers, but that was going rather too far, and when they were invited to take on a night's vigil without a breakfast, merely for the sake of the cause, they made themselves scarce, although they stuck stubbornly to their suspicions.

Such suspicions, anyhow, were a necessary accompaniment to the profession of fasting. No one could possibly watch the hunger artist continuously, day and night, and so no one could produce first-hand evidence that the fast had really been rigorous and continuous; only the artist himself could know that, he was therefore bound to be the sole completely satisfied spectator of his own fast. Yet for other reasons he was never satisfied; it was not perhaps mere fasting that had brought him to such skeleton thinness that many people had regretfully to keep away from his exhibitions, because the sight of him was too much for them, perhaps it was dissatisfaction with himself that had worn him down. For he alone knew, what no other initiate knew, how easy it was to fast. It was the easiest thing in the world. He made no secret of this, yet people did not believe him, at the best they set him down as modest, most of them, however, thought he was out for publicity or else was some kind of cheat who found it easy to fast because he had discovered a way of making it easy, and then had the impudence to admit the fact, more or less. He had to put up with all that, and in the course of time had got used to it, but his inner dissatisfaction always rankled, and never yet, after any term of fasting—this must be granted to his credit—had he left the cage of his own free will. The longest period of fasting was fixed by his impresario at forty days, beyond that term he was not allowed to go, not even in great cities, and there was good reason for it, too. Experience had proved that for about forty days the interest of the public could be stimulated by a steadily increasing pressure of advertisement, but after that the town began to lose interest, sympathetic support began notably to fall off; there were of course local variations as between one town and another or one country and another, but as a general rule forty days marked the limit. So on the fortieth day the flower-bedecked cage was opened, enthusiastic spectators filled the hall, a military band played, two doctors entered the cage to measure the results of the fast, which were announced through a megaphone, and finally two young ladies appeared, blissful at having been selected for the honor, to help the hunger artist down the few steps leading to a small table on which was spread a carefully chosen invalid repast. And at this very moment the artist always turned stubborn. True, he would entrust his bony arms to the outstretched helping hands of the ladies bending over him,

but stand up he would not. Why stop fasting at this particular moment, after forty days of it? He had held out for a long time, an illimitably long time; why stop now, when he was in his best fasting form, or rather, not yet quite in his best fasting form? Why should he be cheated of the fame he would get for fasting longer, for being not only the record hunger artist of all time, which presumably he was already, but for beating his own record by a performance beyond human imagination, since he felt that there were no limits to his capacity for fasting? His public pretended to admire him so much, why should it have so little patience with him; if he could endure fasting longer, why shouldn't the public endure it? Besides, he was tired, he was comfortable sitting in the straw, and now he was supposed to lift himself to his full height and go down to a meal the very thought of which gave him a nausea that only the presence of the ladies kept him from betraying, and even that with an effort. And he looked up into the eyes of the ladies who were apparently so friendly and in reality so cruel, and shook his head, which felt too heavy on its strengthless neck. But then there happened yet again what always happened. The impresario came forward, without a word—for the band made speech impossible—lifted his arms in the air above the artist, as if inviting Heaven to look down upon its creature here in the straw, this suffering martyr, which indeed he was, although in quite another sense; grasped him round the emaciated waist, with exaggerated caution, so that the frail condition he was in might be appreciated; and committed him to the care of the blenching ladies, not without secretly giving him a shaking so that his legs and body tottered and swayed. The artist now submitted completely; his head lolled on his breast as if it had landed there by chance; his body was hollowed out; his legs in a spasm of self-preservation clung close to each other at the knees, yet scraped on the ground as if it were not really solid ground, as if they were only trying to find solid ground; and the whole weight of his body, a featherweight after all, relapsed onto one of the ladies, who, looking round for help and panting a little—this post of honor was not at all what she had expected it to be—first stretched her neck as far as she could to keep her face at least free from contact with the artist, then finding this impossible, and her more fortunate companion not coming to her aid but merely holding extended on her own trembling hand the little bunch of knucklebones that was the artist's, to the great delight of the spectators burst into tears and had to be replaced by an attendant who had long been stationed in readiness. Then came the food, a little of which the impresario managed to get between the artist's lips, while he sat in a kind of half-fainting trance, to the accompaniment of cheerful patter designed to distract the public's attention from the artist's condition; after that, a toast was drunk to the public, supposedly prompted by a whisper from the artist in the impresario's ear; the band confirmed it with a mighty flourish, the spectators melted away, and no one had any cause to be dissatisfied with the proceedings, no one except the hunger artist himself, he only, as always.

So he lived for many years, with small regular intervals of recuperation, in visible glory, honored by the world, yet in spite of that troubled in spirit, and all the more troubled because no one would take his trouble seriously. What comfort could he possibly need? What more could he possibly wish for? And if some good-natured person, feeling sorry for him, tried to console him by pointing out that his melancholy was probably caused by fasting, it could happen, especially when he had been fasting for some time, that he reacted with an outburst of fury and to the general alarm began to shake the bars of his cage like a wild animal. Yet the impresario had a way of punishing these outbreaks which he rather enjoyed putting into operation. He would apologize publicly for the artist's behavior, which was only to be excused, he admitted, because of the irritability caused by fasting; a condition hardly to be understood by well-fed people; then by natural transition he went on to mention the artist's equally incomprehensible boast that he could fast for much longer than he was doing; he praised the high ambition, the good will, the great self-denial undoubtedly implicit in such a statement; and then quite simply countered it by bringing out photographs, which were also on sale to the public, showing the artist on the fortieth day of a fast lying in bed almost dead from exhaustion. This perversion of the truth, familiar to the artist though it was, always unnerved him afresh and proved too much for him. What was a consequence of

the premature ending of his fast was here presented as the cause of it! To fight against this lack of understanding, against a whole world of non-understanding, was impossible. Time and again in good faith he stood by the bars listening to the impresario, but as soon as the photographs appeared he always let go and sank with a groan back on to his straw, and the reassured public could once more come close and gaze at him.

A few years later when the witnesses of such scenes called them to mind, they often failed to understand themselves at all. For meanwhile the aforementioned change in public interest had set in; it seemed to happen almost overnight; there may have been profound causes for it, but who was going to bother about that; at any rate the pampered hunger artist suddenly found himself deserted one fine day by the amusement seekers, who went streaming past him to other more favored attractions. For the last time the impresario hurried him over half Europe to discover whether the old interest might still survive here and there; all in vain; everywhere, as if by secret agreement, a positive revulsion from professional fasting was in evidence. Of course it could not really have sprung up so suddenly as all that, and many premonitory symptoms which had not been sufficiently remarked or suppressed during the rush and glitter of success now came retrospectively to mind, but it was now too late to take any countermeasures. Fasting would surely come into fashion again at some future date, yet that was no comfort for those living in the present. What, then, was the hunger artist to do? He had been applauded by thousands in his time and could hardly come down to showing himself in a street booth at village fairs, and as for adopting another profession, he was not only too old for that but too fanatically devoted to fasting. So he took leave of the impresario, his partner in an unparalleled career, and hired himself to a large circus; in order to spare his own feelings he avoided reading the conditions of his contract.

A large circus with its enormous traffic in replacing and recruiting men, animals and apparatus can always find a use for people at any time, even for a hunger artist, provided of course that he does not ask too much, and in this particular case anyhow it was not only the artist who was taken on but his famous and long-known name as well, indeed considering the peculiar nature of his performance, which was not impaired by advancing age, it could not be objected that here was an artist past his prime, no longer at the height of his professional skill, seeking a refuge in some quiet corner of a circus, on the contrary, the hunger artist averred that he could fast as well as ever, which was entirely credible, he even alleged that if he were allowed to fast as he liked, and this was at once promised him without more ado, he could astound the world by establishing a record never yet achieved, a statement which certainly provoked a smile among the other professionals, since it left out of account the change in public opinion, which the hunger artist in his zeal conveniently forgot.

He had not, however, actually lost his sense of the real situation and took it as a matter of course that he and his cage should be stationed, not in the middle of the ring as a main attraction, but outside, near the animal cages, on a site that was after all easily accessible. Large and gaily painted placards made a frame for the cage and announced what was to be seen inside it. When the public came thronging out in the intervals to see the animals, they could hardly avoid passing the hunger artist's cage and stopping there for a moment, perhaps they might even have stayed longer had not those pressing behind them in the narrow gangway, who did not understand why they should be held up on their way towards the excitements of the menagerie, made it impossible for anyone to stand gazing quietly for any length of time. And that was the reason why the hunger artist, who had of course been looking forward to these visiting hours as the main achievement of his life, began instead to shrink from them. At first he could hardly wait for the intervals; it was exhilarating to watch the crowds come streaming his way, until only too soon—not even the most obstinate self-deception, clung to almost consciously, could hold out against the fact—the conviction was borne in upon him that these people, most of them, to judge from their actions, again and again, without exception, were all on their way to the menagerie. And the first sight of them from the distance remained the best. For when they reached his cage he was at once deafened by the storm of shouting and abuse that arose from the two contending factions, which renewed themselves continuously, of those who wanted to stop and stare at him—he soon began to dislike them more than the others—not out of real interest but only out of obstinate self-assertiveness, and those who wanted to go straight on to the animals. When the first great rush was past, the stragglers came along, and these, whom nothing could have prevented from stopping to look at him as long as they had breath, raced past with long strides, hardly even glancing at him, in their haste to get to the menagerie in time. And all too rarely did it happen that he had a stroke of luck, when some father of a family fetched up before him with his children, pointed a finger at the hunger artist and explained at length what the phenomenon meant, telling stories of earlier years when he himself had watched similar but much more thrilling performances, and the children, still rather uncomprehending, since neither inside nor outside school had they been sufficiently prepared for this lesson—what did they care about fasting?—yet showed by the brightness of their intent eyes that new and better times might be coming. Perhaps, said the hunger artist to himself many a time, things would be a little better if his cage were set not quite so near the menagerie. That made it too easy for people to make their choice, to say nothing of what he suffered from the stench of the menagerie, the animals' restlessness by night, the carrying past of raw lumps of flesh for the beasts of prey, the roaring at feeding times, which depressed him continually. But he did not dare to lodge a complaint with the management; after all, he had the animals to thank for the troops of people who passed his cage, among whom there might always be one here and there to take an interest in him, and who could tell where they might seclude him if he called attention to his existence and thereby to the fact that, strictly speaking, he was only an impediment on the way to the menagerie.

A small impediment, to be sure, one that grew steadily less. People grew familiar with the strange idea that they could be expected, in times like these, to take an interest in a hunger artist, and with this familiarity the verdict went out against him. He might fast as much as he could, and he did so; but nothing could save him now, people passed him by. Just try to explain to anyone the art of fasting! Anyone who has no feeling for it cannot be made to understand it. The fine placards grew dirty and illegible, they were torn down; the little notice board telling the number of fast days achieved, which at first was changed carefully every day, had long stayed at the same figure, for after the first few weeks even this small task seemed pointless to the staff; and so the artist simply fasted on and on, as he had once dreamed of doing, and it was no trouble to him, just as he had always foretold, but no one counted the days, no one, not even the artist himself, knew what records he was already breaking, and his heart grew heavy. And when once in a time some leisurely passer-by stopped, made merry over the old figure on the board and spoke of swindling, that was in its way the stupidest lie ever invented by indifference and in-born malice, since it was not the hunger artist who was cheating, he was working honestly, but the world was cheating him of his reward.

Many more days went by, however, and that too came to an end. An overseer's eye fell on the cage one day and he asked the attendants why this perfectly good cage should be left standing there unused with dirty straw inside it; nobody knew, until one man, helped out by the notice board, remembered about the hunger artist. They poked into the straw with sticks and found him in it. "Are you still fasting?" asked the overseer, "when on earth do you mean to stop?" "For-give me, everybody," whispered the hunger artist; only the overseer, who had his ear to the bars, understood him. "Of course," said the overseer, and tapped his forehead with a finger to let the attendants know what state the man was in, "we forgive you." "I always wanted you to admire my fasting," said the hunger art-ist. "We do admire it," said the overseer, affably. "But you shouldn't admire it," said the hunger artist. "Well then we don't admire it," said the overseer, "but why shouldn't we admire it?" "Because I have to fast, I can't help it," said the hunger artist. "What a fellow you are," said the overseer, "and why can't you help it?" "Because," said the hunger artist, lifting his head a little and speaking, with his lips pursed, as if for a kiss, right into the overseer's ear, so that no syllable might be lost, "because I couldn't find the food I liked. If I had found it, believe me, I should have made no fuss and stuffed myself like you or anyone else." These were his last words, but in his dimming eyes remained the firm though no longer proud persuasion that he was still continuing to fast.

"Well, clear this out now!" said the overseer, and they buried the hunger artist, straw and all. Into the cage they put a young panther. Even the most insensi-tive felt it refreshing to see this wild creature leaping around the cage that had so long been dreary. The pan-ther was all right. The food he liked was brought him without hesitation by the attendants; he seemed not even to miss his freedom; his noble body, furnished al-most to the bursting point with all that it needed, seemed to carry freedom around with it too; some-where in his jaws it seemed to lurk; and the joy of life streamed with such ardent passion from his throat that for the onlookers it was not easy to stand the shock of it. But they braced themselves, crowded round the cage, and did not want ever to move away.

COMMENTS AND QUESTIONS

1. Kafka's style is in some ways a realistic one. In what sense is this story realistic and in what sense is it not?
2. Is the image of the hunger artist "expressionistic"? If so, what emotions or ideas does it express? Can you compare the portrayal of the hunger artist to the lonely man in Van Gogh's *Night Café* or the people in Kirchner's *Street*?
3. The hunger artist has been seen as an expression of the alienation of the artist in society or the isolation of the spiritual man from the sensual man. Support or criticize these interpretations.
4. How do you interpret the dying artist's revelation that he could never find the food that pleased him?

EZRA POUND

The Rest

O helpless few in my country,
O remnant enslaved!

Artists broken against her,
A-stray, lost in the villages,
Mistrusted, spoken-against,

Lovers of beauty, starved,
Thwarted with systems,
Helpless against the control;

You who can not wear yourselves out
By persisting to successes,
You who can only speak,
Who can not steel yourselves into reiteration;

You of the finer sense,
Broken against false knowledge,
You who can know at first hand,
Hated, shut in, mistrusted:

Take thought:
I have weathered the storm,
I have beaten out my exile.

EZRA POUND

The River-Merchant's Wife: a Letter

(after Li Po)

While my hair was still cut straight across my forehead
I played about the front gate, pulling flowers.
You came by on bamboo stilts, playing horse,
You walked about my seat, playing with blue plums.
And we went on living in the village of Chokan:
Two small people, without dislike or suspicion.

At fourteen I married My Lord you.
I never laughed, being bashful.
Lowering my head, I looked at the wall.
Called to, a thousand times, I never looked back.

At fifteen I stopped scowling,
I desired my dust to be mingled with yours
For ever and for ever and for ever.
Why should I climb the look out'

At sixteen you departed,
You went into far Ku-to-yen, by the river of swirling
    eddies,
And you have been gone five months.
The monkeys make sorrowful noise overhead.

You dragged your feet when you went out.
By the gate now, the moss is grown, the different
    mosses,
Too deep to clear them away!

The leaves fall early this autumn, in wind.
The paired butterflies are already yellow with August
Over the grass in the West garden;
They hurt me. I grow older.
If you are coming down through the narrows of the
    river Kiang,
Please let me know beforehand,
And I will come out to meet you
    As far as Cho-fu-Sa.

EZRA POUND

In a Station of the Metro[1]

The apparition of these faces in the crowd;
Petals on a wet, black bough.

QUESTIONS

1. How does Pound view the situation of the artist in America in "The Rest"?
2. What does Pound mean by "false knowledge"? What would be "true knowledge" for him?
3. Is this an effective poem or merely a position statement?
4. Do you find "In a Station of the Metro" effective as poetry? Can you compare the technique used to a technique in modern painting?
5. How does "The River-Merchant's Wife" render visual images in poetry?

---

[1] Of this poem Pound writes in *Gaudier-Brzeska: A Memoir* (1916): "Three years ago in Paris I got out of a 'metro' train at La Concorde, and saw suddenly a beautiful face, and then another and another, and then a beautiful child's face, and then another beautiful woman, and I tried all that day to find words for what this had meant to me, and I could not find any words that seemed to me worthy, or as lovely as that sudden emotion. And that evening . . . I was still trying and I found, suddenly, the expression. I do not mean that I found words, but there came an equation . . . not in speech, but in little splotches of colour. . . . The 'one-image poem' is a form of super-position, that is to say, it is one idea set on top of another. I found it useful in getting out of the impasse in which I had been left by my metro emotion. I wrote a thirty-line poem, and destroyed it. . . . Six months later I made a poem half that length; a year later I made the following *hokku*-like sentence."

E. E. CUMMINGS

[*(ponder,darling,these busted statues]*

(ponder,darling,these busted statues
of yon motheaten forum be aware
notice what hath remained
—the stone cringes
clinging to the stone,how obsolete

lips utter their extant smile . . . .
remark

a few deleted of texture
or meaning monuments and dolls

resist Them Greediest Paws of careful
time all of which is extremely
unimportant)whereas Life

matters if or

when the your- and my-
idle vertical worthless
self unite in a peculiarly
momentary

partnership(to instigate
constructive
                    Horizontal
business . . . . even so,let us make haste
—consider well this ruined aqueduct

lady,
which used to lead something into somewhere)

E. E. CUMMINGS

[*i sing of Olaf glad and big]*

i sing of Olaf glad and big
whose warmest heart recoiled at war:
a conscientious object-or

his wellbelovéd colonel(trig[1]
westpointer most succinctly bred)
took erring Olaf soon in hand;
but—though an host of overjoyed
noncoms(first knocking on the head
him)do through icy waters roll
that helplessness which others stroke
with brushes recently employed
anent this muddy toiletbowl,
while kindred intellects evoke
allegiance per blunt instruments—
Olaf(being to all intents
a corpse and wanting any rag
upon what God unto him gave)
responds,without getting annoyed
"I will not kiss your f.ing flag"

straightway the silver bird[2] looked grave
(departing hurriedly to shave)

but—though all kinds of officers
(a yearning nation's blueeyed pride)
their passive prey did kick and curse
until for wear their clarion
voices and boots were much the worse,
and egged the firstclassprivates on
his rectum wickedly to tease
by means of skilfully applied
bayonets roasted hot with heat—
Olaf(upon what were once knees)
does almost ceaselessly repeat
"there is some s. I will not eat"

our president,being of which
assertions duly notified
threw the yellowsonofabitch
into a dungeon,where he died

Christ(of His mercy infinite)
i pray to see;and Olaf,too

---

[1] Neat and tidy.
[2] An army colonel's insignia.

preponderatingly because
unless statistics lie he was
more brave than me:more blond than you.

E. E. CUMMINGS

[space being(don't forget to remember)Curved]

Space being(don't forget to remember)Curved
(and that reminds me who said o yes Frost
Something there is which isn't fond of walls)

an electromagnetic(now I've lost
the)Einstein expanded Newton's law preserved
conTinuum(but we read that beFore)

of Course life being just a Reflex you
know since Everything is Relative or

to sum it All Up god being Dead(not to

mention inTerred)
                    LONG LIVE that Upwardlooking
Serene Illustrious and Beatific
Lord of Creation,MAN:
                        at a least crooking
of Whose compassionate digit,earth's most terrific

quadruped swoons into billiardBalls!

QUESTIONS

1. Compare "ponder, darling..." with John Donne's poem "The Flea" in Chapter 20. How has Cummings used both tradition and the modernist aesthetic in his poem?
2. Does "Olaf" succeed as an antiwar poem? How? Note the mixture of *tones* in the poem. What different ones can you find?
3. What implications does Cummings draw from Einstein's law of relativity? How does he express them poetically?

T. S. ELIOT

The Love Song of J. Alfred Prufrock

> S'io credessi che mia risposta fosse
> a persona che mai tornasse al mondo,
> questa fiamma staria senza più scosse.
> Ma per ciò che giammai di questo fondo
> non tornò vivo alcun, s'i'odo il vero,
> senza tema d'infamia ti rispondo.[1]

Let us go then, you and I,[2]
When the evening is spread out against the sky
Like a patient etherised upon a table;
Let us go, through certain half-deserted streets,
The muttering retreats
Of restless nights in one-night cheap hotels
And sawdust restaurants with oyster-shells:
Streets that follow like a tedious argument
Of insidious intent
To lead you to an overwhelming question . . .
Oh, do not ask, "What is it?"
Let us go and make our visit.

In the room the women come and go
Talking of Michelangelo.

The yellow fog that rubs its back upon the window-
            panes,
The yellow smoke that rubs its muzzle on the window-
            panes,
Licked its tongue into the corners of the evening,
Lingered upon the pools that stand in drains,
Let fall upon its back the soot that falls from chimneys,
Slipped by the terrace, made a sudden leap,
And seeing that it was a soft October night,
Curled once about the house, and fell asleep.

And indeed there will be time
For the yellow smoke that slides along the street
Rubbing its back upon the window-panes;

---

[1] Epigraph from Dante's *Inferno*, Canto 27, "If I thought that my answer was to someone who would ever return to the world, this flame would shake no more. But since no one has ever returned alive from this place (hell), if I hear rightly, without fear of infamy I will answer you."
[2] Prufrock and a companion are going to make a visit to a woman.

There will be time, there will be time
To prepare a face to meet the faces that you meet;
There will be time to murder and create,
And time for all the works and days of hands
That lift and drop a question on your plate;
Time for you and time for me,
And time yet for a hundred indecisions,
And for a hundred visions and revisions,
Before the taking of a toast and tea.

In the room the women come and go
Talking of Michelangelo.

And indeed there will be time
To wonder, "Do I dare?" and, "Do I dare?"
Time to turn back and descend the stair,
With a bald spot in the middle of my hair—
(They will say: "How his hair is growing thin!")
My morning coat, my collar mounting firmly to the
    chin,
My necktie rich and modest, but asserted by a simple
    pin—
(They will say: "But how his arms and legs are thin!")
Do I dare
Disturb the universe?
In a minute there is time
For decisions and revisions which a minute will
    reverse.

For I have known them all already, known them all—
Have known the evenings, mornings, afternoons,
I have measured out my life with coffee spoons;
I know the voices dying with a dying fall
Beneath the music from a farther room.
    So how should I presume?

And I have known the eyes already, known them all—
The eyes that fix you in a formulated phrase,
And when I am formulated, sprawling on a pin,
When I am pinned and wriggling on the wall,
Then how should I begin
To spit out all the butt-ends of my days and ways?
    And how should I presume?

And I have known the arms already, known them all—
Arms that are braceleted and white and bare

(But in the lamplight, downed with light brown hair!)
Is it perfume from a dress
That makes me so digress?
Arms that lie along a table, or wrap about a shawl.
    And should I then presume?
    And how should I begin?

                .   .   .   .   .   .

Shall I say, I have gone at dusk through narrow streets
And watched the smoke that rises from the pipes
Of lonely men in shirt-sleeves, leaning out of
        windows? . . .

I should have been a pair of ragged claws
Scuttling across the floors of silent seas.

                .   .   .   .   .   .

And the afternoon, the evening, sleeps so peacefully!
Smoothed by long fingers,
Asleep . . . tired . . . or it malingers,
Stretched on the floor, here beside you and me.
Should I, after tea and cakes and ices,
Have the strength to force the moment to its crisis?
But though I have wept and fasted, wept and prayed,
Though I have seen my head (grown slightly bald)
        brought in upon a platter,[3]
I am no prophet—and here's no great matter;
I have seen the moment of my greatness flicker,
And I have seen the eternal Footman hold my coat, and
        snicker,
And in short, I was afraid.

And would it have been worth it, after all,[4]
After the cups, the marmalade, the tea,
Among the porcelain, among some talk of you and me,
Would it have been worth while,
To have bitten off the matter with a smile,
To have squeezed the universe into a ball
To roll it toward some overwhelming question,
To say: "I am Lazarus, come from the dead,
Come back to tell you all, I shall tell you all"—
If one,[5] settling a pillow by her head,

---

[3] Refers to the head of John the Baptist, brought to Queen Herodias.
[4] The use of the past tense here suggests that the moment for Prufrock to speak has passed.
[5] Prufrock's woman friend.

Should say: "That is not what I meant at all.
That is not it, at all."

And would it have been worth it, after all,
Would it have been worth while,
After the sunsets and the dooryards and the sprinkled
    streets,
After the novels, after the teacups, after the skirts that
    trail along the floor—
And this, and so much more?—
It is impossible to say just what I mean!
But as if a magic lantern threw the nerves in patterns
    on a screen:
Would it have been worth while
If one, settling a pillow or throwing off a shawl,
And turning toward the window, should say:
    "That is not it at all,
    That is not what I meant, at all."

.   .   .   .   .   .

No! I am not Prince Hamlet, nor was meant to be;
Am an attendant lord, one that will do
To swell a progress,[6] start a scene or two,
Advise the prince; no doubt, an easy tool,
Deferential, glad to be of use,
Politic, cautious, and meticulous;
Full of high sentence, but a bit obtuse;
At times, indeed, almost ridiculous—
Almost, at times, the Fool.

I grow old . . . I grow old . . .
I shall wear the bottoms of my trousers rolled.[7]

Shall I part my hair behind? Do I dare to eat a peach?
I shall wear white flannel trousers, and walk upon the
    beach.
I have heard the mermaids singing, each to each.

I do not think that they will sing to me.

I have seen them riding seaward on the waves
Combing the white hair of the waves blown back
When the wind blows the water white and black.

---

[6] A royal journey.
[7] The latest fashion.

We have lingered in the chambers of the sea
By sea-girls wreathed with seaweed red and brown
Till human voices wake us, and we drown.

QUESTIONS

1. This poem presents itself as a *narrative*, but the action that occurs is very slight. Tell what it is.
2. Describe the character of Prufrock. What images does Eliot use to tell us about him?
3. Does Prufrock's problem seem to you a particularly modern one? Why?

The next two poems were originally written in French by black African writers who were associated with the surrealist movement in Paris. The first is by Léopold Senghor, who became president of Senegal in 1960. He was the founding father of *négritude*, a black consciousness movement among African intellectuals. These poems, both originally in French, illustrate the fusion of surrealism with a specifically African aesthetic. (The translation of Senghor is by John Reed and Clive Wake; that of Damas is by Norman R. Shapiro.)

LÉOPOLD SÉDAR SENGHOR

Prayer to Masks

Masks! Masks!
Black mask, red mask, you white-and-black masks
Masks of the four points from which the Spirit blows
In silence I salute you!
Nor you the least, Lion-headed Ancestor
You guard this place forbidden to all laughter of
    women, to all smiles that fade
You distil this air of eternity in which I breathe the air
    of my Fathers.
Masks of unmasked faces, stripped of the marks of
    illness and the lines of age
You who have fashioned this portrait, this my face
    bent over the altar of white paper
In your own image, hear me!
The Africa of the empires is dying, see, the agony of a
    pitiful princess
And Europe too where we are joined by the navel.

Fix your unchanging eyes upon your children, who are
    given orders
Who give away their lives like the poor their last
    clothes.
Let us report present at the rebirth of the World
Like the yeast which white flour needs.
For who would teach rhythm to a dead world of
    machines and guns?
Who would give the cry of joy to wake the dead and
    the bereaved at dawn?
Say, who would give back the memory of life to the
    man whose hopes are smashed?
They call us men of coffee cotton oil
They call us men of death.
We are the men of the dance, whose feet draw new
    strength pounding the hardened earth.

LÉON DAMAS

They came that night

They came that night when the
tom
    tom
        rolled from
                rhythm
                    to
                      rhythm
                          the frenzy
of eyes
the frenzy of hands
the frenzy
of statue feet

SINCE THEN
how many of ME ME ME
have died
since they came that night when the
tom
    tom
        rolled from
                rhythm
                    to
                      rhythm
                          the frenzy
of eyes
the frenzy
of hands
the frenzy
of statue feet

QUESTIONS

1. What different associations and meanings does the mask have in Senghor's poem?
2. What contrast does Senghor make between African and European civilization? What future role does he see for Africa?
3. Describe the rhythm in Senghor's poem. What is its function?
4. What happens in "They Came That Night"?
5. Note how, in surrealist fashion, this poem expresses a subjective apprehension of reality by using detached, objective images. What do the images do in the poem?

33

THE MODERNIST MOVEMENT: MUSIC, DANCE, AND FILM

Stravinsky, the Russian Ballet, and *The Rite of Spring*

Igor Stravinsky, a Russian-born musician whose musical education and taste led him to Paris during the early years of this present century, was part of the artistic revolution that sets the music, art, and literature of the twentieth century apart from all that went before. His musical roots were planted in, and flourished amid, the fertile harmonic gardens of the nineteenth century; but his branches sought light among the complex ideas of the abstract painters, modern dancers, and revolutionary men and women of letters who worked in Europe during the first two decades of our century. Stravinsky became a part, some might say even a causal factor, of a revolution in classical music.

Stravinsky worked closely with a fellow Russian, Sergei Diaghilev, a theatrical impresario who had brought Russian ballet, opera, and painting exhibits to Paris in 1909. The Russian innovations in all these arts, but particularly in ballet, were to have an invigorating effect on Western Europe. In the mid-nineteenth century the world center of ballet had moved from Paris to Saint Petersburg; ballet in the West had become to a great extent reduced to pretty dancing girls executing mechanical movements. The imperial ballet in Russia, however, underwent a "classic revival" that produced the great ballets to the music of Tchaikovsky: *Sleeping Beauty, Swan Lake,* and *Nutcracker.* A young choreographer, Mikhail Fokine, revolted against the somewhat rigid, conventionalized vocabulary of this style of ballet. In a manifesto written in 1904, Fokine called for a greater unity of composition in ballet, more integration with the other arts, and gestures "built on the laws of natural expressiveness" to enable dance to "regain its spiritual forms and qualities." Fokine, whose ideas influenced Diaghilev, became the first choreographer for his Russian Ballet troupe. Fokine's training also produced the troupe's greatest male dancer, Vaslav Nijinsky. The extraordinary innovations of the Diaghilev ballets in Paris sprang from the combined talents of composers such as Stravinsky; dancers and *choreographers;* artists who designed the sets (Picasso among them); and, later on, writers such as Jean Cocteau, all under the masterful direction of Diaghilev.

In Volume I of this text we described in the chapter on the African festival that the unification of dance with the other arts, for the purpose of expressing the basic values or spiritual needs of a community, is typical of African artistic expression. European artists, seeking new ways to combine the arts through dance, were in a sense trying to recover a means of expression that they felt had been lost in their own society. Their search may be viewed as belonging to the "discontents" with "civilization" in the early twentieth century. It was in fact often combined with what is called primitivism, or an attempt to find fresh artistic sources in cultures less intellectualized and less specialized. Painters and sculptors, as we have seen, turned to the arts of Africa and Polynesia. But Stravinsky, with the other Russians in Paris, looked for inspiration to his native land, where folkloric traditions were still rich and "civilization" only recent. Both the primitivist dream and the desire to re-create the unity of the arts were instru-

mental in the conception of Stravinsky's great musical composition *Le Sacre du Printemps (The Rite of Spring)* and its ballet.

Stravinsky himself has described the sources of his inspiration. He remembered the "violent Russian spring" that seemed to begin suddenly and to set the whole earth cracking as the most exciting yearly event of his childhood. The memory of this natural event was no doubt linked to a vision that he had while in the midst of completing *The Firebird,* another ballet score.

> I saw in imagination a solemn pagan rite: sage elders, seated in a circle, watched a young girl dance herself to death. They were sacrificing her to propitiate the god of spring. Such was the theme of the *Sacre du Printemps.* I must confess that this vision made a deep impression on me, and I at once described it to my friend, Nicholas Roerich, he being a painter who had specialized in pagan subjects. He welcomed my inspiration with enthusiasm, and became my collaborator in this creation. In Paris I told Diaghileff [Diaghilev] about it, and he was at once carried away by the idea.[1]

Diaghilev chose the revolutionary Nijinsky to do the choreography; Roerich did the sets, and the entire new production was presented to the Parisian public at the opening of the Théâtre des Champs-Elysées in the spring of 1913.

The subject matter of *The Rite of Spring,* if Russian in inspiration, is in fact universal. In searching for the cultural roots of this piece, we might consider that the prehistoric origins of all modern men hide pagan and barbaric customs that we would now find repulsive and dreadful. Stravinsky's *Rite* is no figment of the imagination. The ritual of human sacrifice to appease angry gods seems to reappear in every mythology, and factual evidence proving the existence of terrifying practices by humans of more recent vintage only serve to remind us that Abraham's intended sacrifice of his son Isaac or the jungle headhunter's devouring of enemies are not entirely fairy tales of another time, place, and people. In early Greece it would appear that the Dionysian festival helped ensure a bountiful harvest in the succeed-

---

[1] Igor Stravinsky, *An Autobiography* (New York: Simon and Schuster, 1936), reprinted (New York: M. & J. Steuer, 1958), p. 31.

Plate IX Monet, "The Bridge at Argenteuil." (München, Neue Pinakothek/photo: Kunst-Dias Blauel)

Plate X   Matisse, "Portrait of Mme
Matisse" (The Green Stripe). (The Royal
Museum of Fine Arts, J. Rump
Collection, Copenhagen/©
S.P.A.D.E.M., 1980)

Plate XII   Mondrian, "Composition
with Red, Blue and Yellow," 1921.
(Collection Haags Gemeentemuseum,
The Hague)

Plate XIII "Wall of Dignity," Detroit, Michigan. (J. Edward Bailey III, Detroit)

Plate XV Andy Warhol, "Campbell's Soup," 1965. Oil, silk screened on canvas. (Collection: The Museum of Modern Art, New York. Philip Johnson Fund)

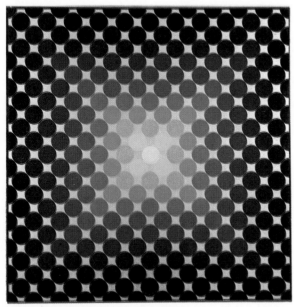

Plate XIV - Victor Vasarely, "CTA-104-E," 1965. Synthetic polymer and metallic paint on cardboard. (Collection: The Museum of Modern Art, New York. Given in memory of G. David Thompson by his New York friends)

ing season by sacrificing the festival king. With the growth of civilization, real sacrifice is replaced by ritual or symbolic sacrifice, but the need to communicate and propitiate one's god or gods seems to remain in some form a part of human nature. It is the desire of man to communicate with elemental forces that challenged Stravinsky's creativity, bringing forth one of the most remarkable musical compositions of the twentieth century.

The scenario, or story line, deals with the veneration of spring by primitive peoples, a process viewed as a mystical rebirth of the earth. The decay of vegetation during the winter was considered to be a weakening of nature's fertility, and the rejuvenation of nature called for a sacrifice in spring, *le sacre du printemps*. A female is chosen, and she pays homage for her people with her life. To show this on the stage, Stravinsky set his music in parts, each section with a self-explanatory title:

Adoration of the Earth
Dance of the Adolescents
Dance of Seduction
Rounds of Spring
Games of the Rival Communities
Procession of the Sage
Consecration of the Earth
Dance of the Earth
  (End of Part I)
Introduction
Mysterious Circles of the Adolescents
Glorification of the Chosen One
Evocation of the Ancestors
Ritual of the Ancestors
Sacrificial Dance of the Chosen One

The Music The music of Stravinsky composed to set these ritual dances had, and still has, a shocking effect on its audiences. Peculiar chords assault the ears. Not only were the combinations of notes unfamiliar to all but to the most avant-garde listeners of the day; they did not progress through familiar chord patterns that concert patrons had come to expect in music for the ballet. The music was loud, so loud; and it seemed to repeat discord after discord in irregular and jagged rhythms. Worst of all, there were no lovely, singable melodies that a music-loving Frenchman could whistle

or hum as he left the theater. In fact, the first audience found this music so distasteful upon hearing it that they literally started a riot. Jean Cocteau describes it thus:

> The public played the role that it had to play. It laughed, spat, hissed, imitated animal cries. They might have eventually tired themselves of that if it had not been for the crowd of esthetes and a few musicians, who, carried by excess of zeal, insulted and even pushed the public of the boxes (the very wealthy in the box seats). The riot degenerated into a fight. Standing in her box, her diadem askew, the old Countess de Pourtales brandished her fan and shouted all red in the face: "It is the first time in sixty years that anyone has dared to make a fool of me!"

What was happening in music in 1913 that could cause such a hostile reaction in Paris? Basically, all the musical values of the past were being questioned and replaced with new, experimental ideas. Stravinsky was not alone in working toward a new tonal idiom, although his solutions differed from those of his important contemporaries—Claude Debussy, Erik Satie, Alexander Scriabin, Arnold Schoenberg, and Anton Webern. But where music to this time had been building on the past—adding to and depending upon tradition—the new music of these composers, Stravinsky included, negated the validity of the past and imposed a new order upon the sounds of music. *Harmony*, in the traditional sense of the word, was discarded; so were the notions of *melody* and *rhythm* that prevailed at the time. New orchestral effects were pried out of the instruments, and new types of heroes, or antiheroes, were sought for the songs and scenarios of the rebellious avant-garde composers.

Stravinsky opens his work with a bassoon solo that is "too high." Traditional composers would never have spotlighted a bassoon in that register because, they thought, it sounds strange. Stravinsky needed a primeval sound, and he found it in the bassoon. He also needed a new harmonic sound, which he found by pitting two chords against each other at the same time, an F-flat chord and an E-flat chord (an E^{b7}).

Needing something to replace *harmonic progression*,

he chose to discard progression and substitute repetition. He would take one dissonant cluster of notes, hammering them over and over until he felt that a change was called for aesthetically. Then another cluster of notes would follow; but the choice of pitches for the second set was determined not by the old laws of harmony and chordal resolution, but by the laws of Stravinsky's ear. Like the painter, Picasso, Stravinsky had all the training and technique necessary to create masterpieces in the old style. His was not the frenetic searching of an ignorant musician but the conscious decision of a master. The values of the twentieth century were not the same as those that held sway a few short years before. And the change in values demanded the changes that took place in artistic expression.

Of all the innovative changes that Stravinsky demonstrated in his new composition of 1913, nothing captured the hearts of practicing musicians more emphatically than his use of rhythm. In *The Rite of Spring* we hear irregular series of pulses, changing *meters*, groupings of five and seven where multiples of two and three had been the norm. The effect is a sense of discontinuity and terror: a new style is introduced into twentieth-century music. The rhythm is similar to that of jazz in its energy and very different from the fluctuating pulse-beat of the late romantic composers.

At once both regular and irregular, at once both orderly and chaotic, *The Rite of Spring* communicates in the music basic conflicts between the barbaric and the civilized, the controlled and the ecstatic, the conflict of *id* and *super-ego*. The people of Paris were shocked with what they heard in 1913, but today this work must be called tame in comparison with those of our contemporaries. And as a commentary on how brazen we have become since Stravinsky crashed his orchestra about the ears of his public, we should note that in 1940 Walt Disney used *The Rite of Spring* as background music for a full-length cartoon, *Fantasia*, in which mesozoic monsters fight and die amid the primordial slime and volcanic dust.

But once one has overcome the effects of the novelty of the sounds themselves, one discovers that order and design are present. Reason prevails, and the artistic laws of unity and variety are still operative. The orchestration is a unifying factor; so is the dance and the story line. Rhythmic elements from earlier sections reappear at later times, sometimes transformed or disguised and sometimes not. The types of melodic units that Stravinsky employs are similar and seem to fit within a discernible style. Contrast is apparent and seems to be used judiciously. Slow sections are interspersed among the fast; heavy orchestration is balanced with solo performance and light accompaniment; chordal writing is matched with linear composition.

For all its newness *The Rite of Spring* does not abandon *tonality*, the basic feature of the harmonic language of the nineteenth century. However, Stravinsky is called upon to use different means to establish a feeling of tonal center for our ears; for, if he cannot use standard chord progressions, cadences, and tonal melodies, what can he employ to lend tonal stability to his composition? Repetition. By repeating a chordal sound over and over, the lowest-sounding pitches assume the functions of chordal roots. They spell out the "key" of the moment. He reinforces this by choosing clusters of tones that can be grouped into familiar chords, sounds that a layman's ear can organize rather quickly. Nor does Stravinsky actually abandon melody. He simply uses lines of notes that do not fit easily into our common practice major-minor tonal system; he chooses intervals that are hard to sing; he sometimes calls upon instruments to play them in manners that are difficult and therefore sound strained; and he does not develop them in the way that a nineteenth-century romantic composer might. Still we can analyze the piece and discern the most important "tunes" or motives of the various sections.

So what are the features that one needs to study before a comprehension of the work is possible? Strangely enough, the answer is probably "none." Stravinsky's *Rite* is music of our time: once the scenario has been digested, the sounds are accepted naturally. We all have the experience of today's television, movie, and radio music to help us, and the common sounds of today are not so different from what was novel in 1914. Stravinsky helped bridge our musical experience to the past or, more properly, connect the past with the music of the present. *The Rite of Spring* is perhaps the single most important composition of the twentieth century for its impact on all the music that followed.

The Ballet   What kind of dance could be created to accompany this music of tones and rhythms unrecognizable to the public of 1913? Certainly the movements on stage were as shocking to the public as the sounds. In *101 Stories of the Great Ballets* George Balanchine, Diaghilev's last choreographer (who later became director of the New York City Ballet), describes the action of the dance and its relationship with the music. The thematic link between dance and death in this ballet recalls that in *Giselle*.

GEORGE BALANCHINE AND FRANCIS MASON

The Rite of Spring

First Tableau—Adoration of the Earth   A musical prelude recalls man's first relations with the world about him. The curtain rises. In a wasteland scene dominated by great masses of stone, young girls and boys sit in separate groups. They do not move, they wait and watch, as if expecting some sign from the stone shafts they revere. The girls rise, as if drawn by the abundance of nature to which the music calls their attention. A wise man stands among the dancers; the girls rush around and around him. Now he moves toward the sacred mound of the enclosure. The girls follow and bow before him. The opening phrase of the ballet—the quiet, plaintive cry of man against all-powerful nature—is repeated.

The strings sound strong, persistent chords that rouse the young men. To the virile beat of the music, they begin to dance, their movements accelerating at its demand, their feet stamping, stamping the earth. The girls join in the dance, the music becomes joyous, and the adolescents abandon themselves to the swift, exuberant rhythms of the orchestra.

This music changes sharply. A new, penetrating melody shrieks warningly and disturbs the young people. The happiness of the boys and girls shifts abruptly to fierce savagery. They split into different groups; the boys face the girls and move toward them. The boys seem bent on attack, but at the last minute they hesitate; they move back and forth in an almost helpless effort, ignorant of their own true intent. The rhythmic crescendos give place to the soft trilling of flutes. Now the boys break their formation, and each carries a girl away.

Four boys remain on the scene. They choose four girls, lift them up on their backs, and dance slowly, bending low under the weight of their burdens in imi-

tation of the plodding chords of the music. This "Round Dance of Spring" gradually increases in volume, and all the adolescents participate. All the dancers step back as the trilling flutes repeat their love call.

Drums herald the beginning of a contest between two rival tribes. Groups of men from each tribe engage in vigorous games. In the midst of their activity, the wise man, represented in the orchestra by a portentous melody on the tuba, tries to interrupt the games. The stronger theme of the games at first drowns out the wise man's theme, then recedes. The men turn to the wise man. There is a brief, taut silence, then all the men fall to the ground and worship the earth.

The drum rolls loudly, and all rise to dance, as if they had felt the pulse of the earth and been renewed by its power. The dance grows frenzied in its intensity. The curtain falls.

Second Tableau—The Sacrifice   Night is about to fall as this second scene begins; the setting sun has turned the sky scarlet. The girls sit near the wise man at a fire. One of these girls must be chosen by the others to make the sacrifice to the earth: this girl must dance herself to death. The music is calm; the figures on stage are quiet and they are unafraid. The girls regret what they have to do, but they are resigned to it with a kind of physical tiredness that the music reflects. They do not feel that they are victimized by Nature, but rather that they must obey what they believe to be its rules.

Soon the girls rise and move in the patterns of the "Dance of the Mysterious Circles." Their movements are trancelike, as if they themselves were not to make their dreadful decision. Their inspiration arrives, and they rush to the periphery of the scene; the chosen one stands alone in the center of the stage.

Now begins the dance that glorifies the victim. The chosen one remains motionless as the girls and men of the tribe whirl around her. All are transfixed at her power. They invoke the spirit of their ancestors, terrified anew by the force of Nature. Marking the relentless, sharp rhythms of the music with their feet, their dance reaches an ultimate expression of uncontrolled glory in sacrifice.

All the tribe members retire to watch the chosen one. The orchestra sounds strong, militant chords, trumpets blare harshly, cutting the air. The dance of the chosen one begins. The brutal savagery of the demanding music compels her to imitate it. Brief moments of comparative quiet, which seem at first to be periods of rest and release, are in reality more deadly because of the thrashing force that follows them. The girl is now wholly a part of the music, part of the earth. Hypnotized by her movements, the tribe joins in the violent dance. The chosen one begins to lose her strength, but—forced on by the convulsive violence of the music—is endowed with a new, superhuman compulsion. When it seems that Nature can demand no more, the girl is pushed into a fresh frenzy. Then she falls. She is dead.

The men of the tribe catch her up in their arms and hold her high over their heads before the sacred mound. The people of the tribe rush around her, holding up their arms. At the last slapping crescendo of the music, they fall to the earth.

(Dame Marie Rambert, who had been Nijinsky's choreographic assistant, describes the nature of his choreography and the audience reaction.)

"Nijinsky again first of all established the basic position: feet very turned in, knees slightly bent, arms held in reverse of the classical position, a primitive, prehistoric posture. The steps were very simple: walking smoothly or stamping, jumps mostly off both feet, landing heavily. There was only one a little more complicated, the dance for the maidens in the first scene. It was mostly done in groups, and each group has its own precise rhythm to follow. In the dance (if one can call it that) of the Wisest Elder, he walked two steps against every three steps of the ensemble. In the second scene the dance of the sacrifice of the Chosen Virgin was powerful and deeply moving. I watched Nijinsky again and again teaching it to Maria Piltz. Her reproduction was very pale by comparison with his ecstatic performance, which was the greatest tragic dance I have ever seen.

"The first night of that ballet was the most astonishing event . . . at the first sounds of the music, shouts and hissing started in the audience, and it was very difficult for us on the stage to hear the music, the more so as part of the audience began to applaud in an attempt to drown the hissing. We all desperately tried to keep time without being able to hear the rhythm clearly. In

the wings Nijinsky counted the bars to guide us. Pierre Monteux conducted undeterred, Diaghilev having told him to continue to play at all costs.

"But after the interlude things became even worse, and during the sacrificial dance real pandemonium broke out. That scene began with Maria Piltz, the Chosen Virgin, standing on the spot trembling for many bars, her folded hands under her right cheek, her feet turned in, a truly prehistoric and beautiful pose. But to the audience of the time it appeared ugly and comical.

"A shout went up in the gallery:

"*'Un docteur!'*

"Somebody else shouted louder:

"*'Un dentiste!'*

"Then someone else screamed:

"*'Deux dentistes!'*

"And so it went on. One elegant lady leaned out of her box and slapped a man who was clapping. But the performance went on to the end.

"And yet now there is no doubt that, musically and choreographically, a masterpiece had been created that night. The only ballet that could compare with it in power was Bronislava Nijinska's *Les Noces*, created in 1923. She, like her brother, produced a truly epic ballet—so far unexcelled anywhere."

Nijinsky's sister Nijinska was in fact a better choreographer than he, though the importance of his innovations are undeniable. Stravinsky was not particularly pleased with Nijinsky's choreography for *The Rite of Spring* and the ballet has been redone many times since. Yet Nijinsky himself, a stunning dancer with great powers of characterization and capable of amazing leaps (Fig. 33-1), has become a legend in our cultural history. He and Anna Pavlova, another Russian who also danced for Diaghilev, are still for many the greatest dancers of the twentieth century. In Nijinsky as in Nietzsche, however, genius bordered on madness. For several years he was confined to an asylum in Switzerland; in 1950 he killed himself in London by leaping out of a window.

Modern Dance

While Mikhail Fokine was working to revitalize ballet in Russia, an American woman from California

33–1   Rodin, "Nijinsky." (Musée Rodin, Paris/Photo ©
Bruno Jarret)

declared, were inspired by her native California; her
first dancing masters were "wind and wave and the
winged flight of bird and bee." Since every dance she
performed was spontaneous and new, she left no school
and no choreography behind her. What she did leave
was the impression of a soul in movement (Fig. 33-2)
on those who watched her, and her re-creation of
dance as self-expression left a heritage of complete freedom to those who followed her.

The great innovators in dance in the early twentieth
century shared with modernists in the other arts a desire for freedom of expression; an experimental attitude toward the use of elements such as space, texture,

33–2   Isadora Duncan. (Harvard Theatre Collection)

named Isadora Duncan began an entirely new approach
to dance. Duncan, who made a deep impression on Fokine during a visit to Russia in 1905, wanted to free
dance entirely from the restrictions of steps, poses, and
attitudes. For her, dance meant individual spontaneity
and Dionysian contact with nature. She admired classical Greek art for its simplicity and natural forms and
believed, like the Greeks, that the human body, without artificial decoration, is the noblest form in art. Yet
she was very American in her daring defiance of tradition and reliance on individual feeling. Her dances, she

and time; and a need to return to primitive and archaic modes of expression. Some of the leaders in the modern dance movement, such as Ruth St. Denis and Louis Horst, sought to recapture both the primitive expressivity of the body and the relationship between dance and religion.

Modern dance differs from ballet in that it abandons not only the traditional steps but also *pointe* (toe-dancing) and the frothy tulle costumes. The portrayal of woman in most modern dances differs considerably from that in the romantic ballet (as we saw it in *Giselle*) or that in the Russian Neoclassical ballet. The most important innovator in this aspect as in other, more technical ones, is Martha Graham. In her major works from the 1930s through the 1950s, Graham presented woman not as ethereal and ideal, but as earthy, passionate, complex. Her choreography probes the psychic depths of her characters. She reworked classical and biblical myths for dance so that they appeared told from the woman's viewpoint; for example, she re-created the Oedipus story as the experience of Jocasta. Graham developed a technique built on the principle of contraction and release of the muscles that continues to be taught in schools of dance. The Martha Graham Company is, of course, still a major force in the American dance world.

Modern dance and ballet have remained separate art forms, but they have borrowed from each other and influenced each other extensively. Fokine, as we have noted, was influenced by Duncan. Martha Graham danced the leading role in the American premiere of *The Rite of Spring* (with new choreography by Massine) in 1930. A choreographer like Kurt Jooss in Germany composes in an idiom that is partly ballet and partly modern dance. The United States remains the world leader in modern dance and shares the honors in ballet with the Soviet Union and Britain.

Among the many exciting dance companies active today are those of Paul Taylor, Alwin Nikolais, Merce Cunningham and, most recently, Twyla Tharp. Nikolais and Cunningham have tended to create abstract dances, dances based on pure movement with little story or anecdote. Taylor and Tharp represent another trend, in a sense a departure from modernism. The tone dominating their works is that of parody; their dancers often comment on real-life situations. Tharp uses social dances from the 1920s through the 1950s as a basis for many of her movements and likes to experiment with nontraditional, nonstage environments.

Black American dance, while closely allied with the general modernist movement, has sought its own directions by exploring its African roots. We will comment on it briefly in the Afro-American Dance section in Chapter 36.

A New Modern Art Form: The Cinema

The early twentieth century saw the birth of an art form perhaps more suited than any other to express its fast-moving, rapidly changing culture. Like oral or written literature, painting, sculpture, photography, and phonograph recording, motion pictures are a cultural form of recorded memory. With the development of new technology in photography and sound recording, human beings were for the first time able to preserve not only words and images of their culture, but also its actions, sights and sounds.

Motion pictures were at first limited to short sequences such as a clown's trick or a locomotive seen head-on, rushing at the audience. But the silent movie, accompanied by captions and a live pianist, soon developed into a genuine art form. Perhaps its most memorable figure is Charlie Chaplin (Fig. 33-3), whose portrayal of the "little guy" baffled by modern civilization made him a true comic hero of the times.

The full-length motion picture that presents an entire drama is obviously analogous to the theater. The mechanics of producing a play, whether on a stage or for filming, involve the same elements: actors, script, sets, props, costumes, make-up, lighting, sound effects, director, producer, and marketing (getting the production to audiences). Recording a play on film has both advantages and disadvantages. The principal disadvantage is that the sense of immediacy is lost, and the unspoken communication between performance and audience is missing in the film.

The advantages of cinema include the ability to make a permanent and reproducible record of what happened in front of the camera and the use of *montage*, which means the ability to edit a performance.

33–3 Charlie Chaplin. (The Museum of Modern Art, New York/ Film Stills Archive)

Unlike the stage director, the film editor can remove and replace sequences in which an actor forgot his lines. He can show change in a way that is nearly impossible for a stage director.

In the American film *Citizen Kane*, directed by Orson Welles, there is a sequence introduced in the script by this note:

> The following scenes, which cover a period of nine years, are played in the same set with only changes in lighting, special effects outside the window, and wardrobe.

The scriptwriter could have noted that changes in make-up also occur; the actors seem to become older as the scenes progress. What happens is this—in each of the seven brief scenes Kane and his wife are shown in the breakfast room. The first scene presents them as newlyweds, happy, in love and just getting home after being up all night going to six parties. As the action progresses, the development of their marriage is revealed. Love turns to complacency, then to rancor and finally to resignation. The last scene is silent—they are reading different newspapers.

These scenes unfold rapidly, occupying only a few minutes of the film, but they make a point; more importantly, they could not be done as effectively on the stage because of the necessary delays for costume changing and make-up. These delays are edited out of the film.

The film maker can also move his camera. He can show close-ups of an actor, an impossibility for the stage director. He can focus attention much more easily than the stage director can, and he can take his camera out of the theater, easily moving it to many different places.

These differences between plays and films are powerful artistic tools that have been exploited effectively by the greatest film makers. Developments in technology have made it possible for cinema to change even more rapidly than the older art forms have. Modernist movements such as expressionism and surrealism had their exponents in film. Techniques such as flashback, dissolve, and close-up made it possible for avant-garde film makers to experiment with layers of time, symbolic images, or portrayal of the unconscious in ways parallel to such presentations in modernist literature and art.

MODERNISM: DISCONTINUITIES AND TRADITIONS

Western Cultural Doubt   There is no doubt that the early twentieth century marks a deep rift in the Western humanistic tradition. This was manifested most clearly by the profound doubt that thinkers, artists, and writers cast upon their culture. The Greco-Roman reliance on reason, the Judeo-Christian hope in God, and, more immediately, the nineteenth century's optimistic materialism no longer seemed valid cultural centers. The titles of two important early twentieth-century books sum up this state of affairs: Freud's *Civilization and Its Discontents* and Spengler's *The Decline of the West.*

Influence of Africa   The weariness with their own cultural roots led artists of the early twentieth century to look elsewhere for inspiration. It is at this point that the African cultural root really makes its entry into the Western humanities. European and American painters and sculptors experimenting with abstraction found that African artists, who had long been creating in this style, had much to teach them. African writers who had been educated in the Western tradition turned toward their native cultures for fresh subject matter and stylistic innovation. Dancers and choreographers saw in the African union of dance with religious rites and other forms of cultural expression an art form more meaningful than the stylized, artificial ballet. Finally, as we will see, African rhythms and tonalities entered into Western music in the form of jazz and profoundly altered its course.

Influence of Other Cultures   Africa was not the only culture to which discontented Westerners turned. Some were attracted to what they viewed as the spirituality of the orient as opposed to the materialism of the occident. Writers like Ezra Pound found the brilliant imagery in Chinese and Japanese poetry a source for experimentation. Other artists and writers turned to the arts of southeast Asia, Polynesia, or to whatever seemed primitive or at least not overcivilized. Igor Stravinsky found in the rites of his native Russia energizing sources for creating new musical sounds. Choreographers and dancers like Nijinsky and Duncan tried to express a new "primitive" wholeness in their dance. Frank Lloyd Wright looked even further away toward the aboriginal cave for a basis for his innovations in architecture.

Break-Up in the Arts   The sense of break with tradition and contact with new traditions gave the artist in this period an exhilarating sense of freedom; so did new discoveries in the sciences such as Freud's unconscious and Einstein's relativity. The name *modernism* covers a variety of experimental movements in the arts, only a few of which we have mentioned in this chapter. The breaking apart of traditional forms—of traditional ways of perceiving space, time, and reality—and the synthesizing of elements in new ways are perhaps the essential characteristics of modernism. In literature this included Joyce's abandonment of syntax, mixture of time frames, and portrayal of the unconscious; E. E. Cummings' free colloquial poetry; and Franz Kafka's stark, fantastic realism. Painting shows Picasso's experiments with abstractions of the human figure and Kandinsky's total abandonment of subject matter for the portrayal of an inner world of form and color. The music of Stravinsky demonstrates a reorganization of the elements of rhythm, harmony, and melody. The new modern art of the film is able to break apart and reorganize the closed time and space frame of the stage.

Connections with Cultural Roots   We should perhaps stress at this point that, although modernism makes a radical break with tradition, it does not make a total break. Its innovations would not be possible without a cultural tradition to react against and, in some sense, to continue. Joyce's radically experimental novel is based on one of the oldest narratives in the Greco-Roman tradition, Homer's *Odyssey*. Distortion in art for expression of the unseen was a characteristic of medieval art and part of the inheritance of the modernists. Modern poetry, modern cinema, and modern dance are incomprehensible without the prior forms of lyric, drama, and ballet. Modernism, in the form of ongoing experimentation, is very much still with us. In the middle and late twentieth century, however, we witness some other currents entering the cultural stream.

PART NINE

A PLURALITY OF CULTURES: THE MIDDLE AND LATE TWENTIETH CENTURY

34

POLITICAL UPHEAVAL AND THE RISE OF A SOCIALLY COMMITTED ART AND LITERATURE

From Between the Wars to the Nuclear Age

The years between World War I and World War II saw tremendous political and economic change in Europe and America. World War II, which in some respects can be seen as a second installment of World War I, had even more devastating results. The cultural movements emerging from these years of upheaval have shown, on the one hand, a tendency toward intensified social commitment and, on the other, a "postmodern" disillusionment and sense of alienation. Let us briefly review the social conditions from which these new cultural trends emerge.

After World War I the major European powers, France and England, set out intentionally to so cripple Germany that it could not again pose a threat to the victors. Parts of its territory were taken away, and the newly established democratic government, the Weimar Republic, was burdened with paying off an astronomical debt for reparations to its former enemies. Restrictions were placed on the size of the German army. While the fledgling government in Germany suffered peculiar handicaps, democracy there, as in the dozen new countries created out of the old Austro-Hungarian empire, also suffered from the lack of any sort of republican tradition. Most, but not all, of these governments created by the victors in the lands of the vanquished had little popular support in their own country. The weakness of these new states, therefore, made the whole political atmosphere one of instability.

The United States, unwilling to play its role as the key power in international relations, was not reluctant to assert its economic predominance. While many Europeans looked gloomily at the future of the human race, Americans exuded optimism. The magic word of the decade of the 1920s was *credit*: a generous policy of lending against future earnings led to an enormous expansion of production. The first generation of installment plan buyers in America found within its reach a range of luxuries, now considered necessities, that could be had on the promise of payment later. Because the country was the leading financial and industrial power, the economic system of other nations eventually became drawn into the same upward draft. When in 1929 panic struck Wall Street, the bubble burst and the world's economy shriveled; production statistics dropped, millions were thrown out of work, and the Great Depression of the 1930s was launched.

The Depression   The dismay was almost total. Could free enterprise and democracy survive? Almost totally independent of Western capitalism, the socialistic economy of the Soviet Union—although it had problems of its own—was insulated from the shock. In capitalistic countries millions of peasants and workers, either unemployed or threatened with unemployment, looked to communism as a way out of a depression in which they were the chief sufferers. On the other hand, large numbers of people—many members of the middle classes as well as peasants and urban workers—turned to the radical right, especially to fascism, for a solution. Partly motivated by a fear of communism, partly by an antipathy toward big business that reduced

the artisan to a laborer and threatened the shopkeeper with competition, they felt the appeal of a conservative right stressing the old values of thrift, industry, national traditions, and loyalty to the country.

Political Forces in the Thirties: Communism and Fascism   Like communism, fascism is a totalitarian political philosophy that sees the individual as having historical existence only in terms of a larger group. For the communist the larger group is the class; for the fascist it is the nation. Just as the communists declare that an individual's mentality is determined by the class to which he belongs, so the fascists claim that one's basic outlook derives from one's nationality. What we call reason, therefore, is relative to each nation. Like Rousseau's general will, the national will of the fascist is the deepest part of every member of the national group. Whereas the communists view class conflict as inevitable, the fascists see struggle between national wills as the central characteristic of human history. Indeed, national wills are defined primarily in their conflict with other nations. However, in contrast to communism, which tends to play down the importance of individual leaders in accomplishing its goals, for fascism the leader is the one who best senses the national will and, therefore, can effectively direct the people to realizing the nation's destiny.

Caught between extreme movements on the right and left, European democratic political parties were hard put to deal with enemies who would not play according to the rules. Already in the early years after World War I, Benito Mussolini in Italy had successfully used the threat of communism to destroy the government and to establish a fascist state. Now, in the early 1930s, it was Germany's turn. With six million unemployed—including their families about 40 percent of the German population was involved—Germany in 1932 was ripe for a violent change. Adolf Hitler and his National Socialist (Nazi) party utilized every trick in the election of that year to present the choice as one between communism and the forces of order. Particularly virulent were the Nazi attacks on the Jews as the authors of the Depression and the source of Germany's major ills. (This was a new element in fascism not found in Mussolini's Italy.) The result was a plurality for the Nazi party in the popular assembly, the Reichstag. Hitler was appointed chancellor, or prime minister, by the president of the Weimar Republic; within the next few years he acted to destroy any political opposition and to make Germany a fascist state. By the mid-1930s the notorious concentration camps were in operation to house political dissidents and Jews. Then Hitler embarked on his promise to the German people to undo the provisions of the Treaty of Versailles.

The Spanish Civil War   In the mid-1930s fascist Italy and Germany had an opportunity to face communist Russia in a trial war where both sides could test their weapons and the fascists their soldiers. In 1936 a combined group of high-ranking army officers, Carlist traditionalists, fascists (Falangists) and monarchists, supported by the Church hierarchy, revolted against the legally elected republican government in an effort to prevent the application of a reform program aimed primarily against the large landholders. General Francisco Franco took command of the right-wing groups, the Nationalists, at an early stage and requested the assistance of Italy and Germany in fighting the civil war. The principal ally of the republicans, or Loyalists, was the Soviet Union, but groups of sympathizers from America and Europe came as volunteers to help the cause as well. The Western democracies themselves, however, remained neutral. Fought with vicious cruelty on both sides, the war lasted almost three years. The distance of the Soviet Union from the fighting gave the Nationalists an advantage in allies. The powerful German and Italian air forces were used for merciless bombing of the cities occupied by the enemy.

By 1939, when the civil war ended with a Nationalist victory, the hope of the Allies in World War I "to make the world safe for democracy" seemed in large part frustrated. Spain became one of the seventeen European nations out of twenty-seven to fall under the rule of a dictator. The League of Nations, essentially an international debating forum, was powerless to enforce international law and agreements. Not only were Germany and Italy aggressively menacing the remaining democratic powers, but, moreover, in August of that year Germany and Russia dumbfounded the world by signing a nonaggression pact. This meant that the burden for stopping the designs of the Axis powers (the term taken by Germany and Italy for their alliance) fell on Great Britain and France, neither of whom wanted war nor was prepared for it.

World War II   World War II, beginning in September 1939, was to last for years, and hostilities were to encompass every continent of the globe. Already having gobbled up half of China, Japan joined the Axis in 1941 in the hope of being able to annex some of the colonial possessions of the Western democracies in Asia. Both Russia and the United States entered the war in 1941 on the side of Great Britain; by this time France was under German domination. In the early stages of the war the Axis powers had the initiative, but by late 1942 the Allies were slowly moving to the offensive. The Allies gradually took over the whole of North Africa from the Italians and Germans and in the spring of 1943 invaded Sicily. At the same time the Russians, despite a terrible loss of life, beat the Germans at Stalingrad, the latter's farthest point of penetration in Russia, and began pushing the Germans back toward the west. In the Pacific the Americans initiated their campaign of island hopping, defeating one Japanese garrison after the other until by early 1945 they were within three hundred miles of Japan itself. In 1944, while the Russians continued their advance all along the eastern front, the Allied armies invaded France; by the spring of 1945 Germany was invaded from both east and west. On May 8, 1945, Germany surrendered unconditionally. The dropping of the atomic bomb on two Japanese cities in August terrified the Japanese into surrendering officially on September 2, 1945.

In contrast with World War I civilians suffered more casualties than did the military. The systematic extermination of populations by the Germans and the intensive bombing of cities by both sides explain the large losses. The introduction of the atomic bomb at the very end of the war dramatically illustrated what would occur in the event of a third world war. The apprehension was only increased by the introduction of an arms race in nuclear weapons, which began with the Soviet development of its own atomic bomb in 1946.

TERRITORIAL CHANGES IN EUROPE
After World War II

Acquired by U.S.S.R.
German losses
Limit of Russian control in Europe

FINLAND

NORWAY

Oslo •

SWEDEN
• Stockholm

Helsinki •

NORTH
SEA

ESTONIAN
S.S.R.

Moscow •

LATVIAN S.S.R.

DENMARK • Copenhagen

BALTIC SEA

LITHUANIAN
S.S.R.

From Germany

U. S. S. R.

GREAT
BRITAIN

London •

NETHERLANDS

WHITE RUSSIAN
S.S.R.

Berlin •

Warsaw •

BELGIUM

• Bonn

EAST
GERMANY

POLAND

WEST
GERMANY

Prague •

• Paris

CZECHOSLOVAKIA

UKRAINIAN S.S.R.

FRANCE

Vienna •

SWITZ-
ERLAND

AUSTRIA

• Budapest

MOLDAVIAN S.S.R.

HUNGARY

RUMANIA

To
Yugoslavia

Belgrade •

• Bucharest •

BLACK SEA

ITALY

YUGOSLAVIA

To Bulgaria

• Rome

BULGARIA

• Sofia

Ankara •

ALBANIA

GREECE

TURKEY

MEDITERRANEAN SEA

The Postwar Period   After World War II the center of power moved out of Western Europe. Whereas in 1919 the United States was potentially the most powerful country in the world, after 1945 the power configuration was a bipolar one, with the United States and the Soviet Union attempting to attract the other powers into their respective spheres of influence. The dissolution of the colonial empires of the European powers, either with or without the latter's consent, produced scores of new nations and furnished a fertile field for propaganda activities on both sides.

The hope of the Allies during the war had been for an international peace-keeping institution after the war; in 1945 at San Francisco the United Nations was created for that purpose. Like the League of Nations, however, the United Nations was crippled from the start by the reluctance of nations to give up any of their sovereignty. Although it provided a means for direct communication between the world powers, the organization could not prevent the reinstitution of hostile alliance systems. The United States sought its security in a number of European and Asian alliances with democratic and right-wing governments, whereas the Soviet Union fortified its position by a tight alliance with communist satellite countries in Eastern Europe and active support for sympathetic political factions elsewhere. The communist conquest of China in 1949 seemed especially alarming to the West, and in the United States itself a fear of subversion inspired a series of investigations to ferret out spies and communist sympathizers. By the early 1950s, moreover, the United States was waging war in Korea, endeavoring to stop the spread of communism in that area. Many feared that the hostility between the two superpowers, known as the Cold War, would soon reach a point of open conflict.

Art and Social Consciousness

The economic and political upheavals taking place in Europe and America in the prewar years seemed to call for an art that, unlike aesthetically preoccupied modernism, would speak to issues of social concern. Like the realists of the nineteenth century, the artists working in the 1930s (including many modernists) wished their art to speak for the poor and oppressed, for liberty in opposition to fascism, or for other issues. In the visual arts, particularly, the problem was: in what style or form could these issues best be addressed? Realism, for some, seemed worn out; the modernist styles ill adapted to the purpose. The few examples cited here illustrate ways of dealing with this problem.

American Styles   In America in the 1930s and 1940s, artistic conflict still seemed to exist between realism and abstraction. In the years of the Great Depression, government assistance to artists helped to foster the idea of regional schools of art that reflected time and place in their particular subject matter and style. Grant Wood's painting *American Gothic* is a perfect example of the art of this movement (Fig. 34-1). His subject matter is an elderly rural couple. They are pre-

34-1   Grant Wood, "American Gothic." (Courtesy of the Art Institute of Chicago)

sented against their small, crisp, clean house and landscape. Their faces, the direct unflinching gaze, and the setting are rendered with great attention to detail. These are stalwart, upright, God-fearing Americans who represent an ideal. The regional movement also emphasized the diversity and magnitude of the American experience.

Support for artists also encouraged the development of painting that learned from Europe while creating a strongly American art not dependent on realism. Stuart Davis was among the leaders of the artists who painted what and how they chose. Davis himself had evolved his style out of the cubism of Picasso and the objects of American urban life. Choosing as subject matter cigarette packs, light bulbs, electric fans, rubber gloves, and an eggbeater, Davis subjected these ordinary banal dime-store purchases to a rigorous process of abstraction (Fig. 34-2). Using very few colors, Davis combined objects that seem caught in an energizing framework. Compare *Egg Beater No. I (Abstraction)*, 1927, with Picasso's *Man with a Violin* (Fig. 31-5) and *The Three Musicians* (Fig. 31-7). Which of the two Picassos is

more like Davis's work? Why? Is there a particular American quality to Davis's work that you do not find in Picasso's? Can you be specific?

Davis was frequently criticized for his use of "foreign" forms, but, unruffled by that, he continued to develop a way of painting and an approach to subject matter that in retrospect seems to prefigure *pop art*. But Davis was not just a painter; like Kandinsky he sought to explain the artist to society, and he defended those painters of the 1930s who were accused of being revolutionary. He personally felt that art was not a medium for propaganda of any kind, but he also defended the right of the artist to paint as he chose.

The American artist Ben Shahn did feel the need to serve social causes with his work. His series *The Passion of Sacco and Vanzetti*, 1931–1932 (Fig. 34-3) comments on a sensitive political issue. Two young immigrants, Sacco and Vanzetti, who had been born in Italy and were acknowledged leftists, were accused of committing a murder during a 1920 robbery. To the American public, still very alert to threats of Russian communism, these young men were pictured as barbarians

34–2 Stuart Davis, "Egg Beater No. I." (The Phillips Collection, Washington, D.C.)

34–3 Ben Shahn, "The Passion of Sacco and Vanzetti." From the Series of 23 Paintings. (Collection of Whitney Museum of American Art, New York: Gift of Edith & Milton Lowenthal in memory of Juliana Force)

freely. They were found guilty of murder and executed. Of Ben Shahn's series, perhaps the most poignant and pointed is the depiction of the funeral, in which the instruments of their trial—judge, prosecutor, public, and press—are either actually or symbolically present around the coffins. The harsh, sharp distortions of figures and picture plane, as well as the strong colors, suggest the anger and emotionalism that surrounded the trial. Shahn's work, in spite of its distortion, is profoundly American and in the *figurative* tradition.

The Spanish Civil War served as a rallying point for many socially committed European and American artists and intellectuals. Picasso was one who was able to use the modernist aesthetic in the service of social justice. In his painting entitled *Guernica* (Fig. 34-4) he commemorated the total destruction of a Basque village, Guernica, by saturation bombing. Because the village had given its allegiance to the republicans in the war, the terrorism of its destruction by the Nationalists was to be a lesson to other opponents. Consider *Guernica*. What elements from cubism do you discern in this painting? What elements suggest the surreal combination of the expected with the unexpected? What do you think the bull stands for? The suspended light, the broken sword, the running girl, the mother and child? Does the weeping mother remind you of anything? Compare the figure of the horse with the one that David painted for Napoleon (Fig. 25-2). What do you think the horse symbolizes? Contrast Picasso's organization of space with that of Shahn. Which seems most frightening? Compare *Guernica* with Goya's *The Shootings of the Third of May, 1808* (Fig. 25-6). How are they alike or different? It might also be useful to compare David's *Death of Marat* (Fig. 25-1) with *The Passion of Sacco and Vanzetti*. Is it possible for an artist to transform an event into a generalized, universal statement that can be easily understood? What must the artist do to accomplish this?

Picasso, in *Guernica*, did not attempt to depict the bombing of the village itself; instead, he created images that evoke the terror and destruction of war. It is the particular combination of images that induces meaning. The images also seem prophetic of the war to come and of the possibilities of total destruction unleashed by the nuclear bombs that ended the war with Japan.

within the gates of democracy. What was really on trial was their right to espouse a controversial ideology; today studies of the trial strongly suggest a travesty of justice. To many artists the young men, who barely spoke English, became martyrs to the right to think and act

34-4   Picasso, "Guernica." (On extended loan to the Museum of Modern Art, New York, from the artist's estate)

The mural was shown at the Paris Exposition, in the pavilion of the Spanish Republic, which was preempted by the Spanish fascists. Since that time it has been in the United States, at the Museum of Modern Art in New York, where it serves not only as a reminder of that war but also of war generally and of censorship and suppression—two things that spell the end of art. It is said that during the German occupation a Nazi official asked the artist "Did you do that dreadful thing?" and Picasso replied "No, you did."

Literature and Social Commitment: Between Wars

Like their fellow artists in the visual field, many writers felt that the social, economic, and political upheavals upsetting world order in the decades after World War I required a response from them in their art. The war itself furnished subject matter for numerous works of fiction, drama, and poetry. Vaunted as "the war to end all wars," it had in fact solved nothing, and the literature concerned with it is one of disillusionment. Like most serious writers who have turned to the subject of war, those who wrote on World War I stressed its senselessness, its inhumanity, and the

pointlessness of organized destruction where the individual, caught in the maelstrom of uncontrollable forces he cannot understand, loses his identity and his sense of purpose. Such is the point variously made in works like Remarque's *All Quiet on the Western Front* and Hemingway's *A Farewell to Arms*. Even when the theme is heroic valor, the individual is presented rather as victim, the unwilling actor in a mission executed without benefit of choice. This is the point made by William Faulkner in his relatively unknown but poignant *Turn About*.

Apart from books inspired by the war, however, social issues as important literary themes did not make themselves felt until the 1930s. The various schools of modernism, as we have seen, produced an introspective, artistically experimental literature demonstrating a consciousness of disintegrating values but little concern with social reality. The Great Depression of the 1930s and the impending rise of fascism, however, gave rise to a literature of social concern or social protest. A "proletarian novel" dealing with the oppressed and the downtrodden developed in the United States as well as in the Soviet Union. One of the best-known examples is John Steinbeck's *Grapes of Wrath*.

Few writers in the 1930s had the will or the ability to see the impending disaster that the growth of fascism presented to the world. André Malraux, a young writer (b. 1901) originally involved with the surrealist movement in Paris, was one of the few. He had gone to Indonesia in 1923 on an archaeological expedition; later, living in Canton and Shanghai, he saw the Chinese revolutionaries in action. Out of this experience he wrote a fictionalized account of the abortive communist uprising in Shanghai in 1927. *La Condition humaine (Man's Fate)* provides a study of conspiracy and conspirators, of idealism and betrayal, of the assertion of individual purpose against all odds. The vision that emerges is essentially a tragic one. Like the Greek tragic heroes, Malraux's heroes struggle to assert their will against overwhelming forces; the fate of man is interpreted as a series of crucifixions. It is by and large a pessimistic view of the human experience, but not entirely: through their hopeless struggle, the participants gain not only a despairing sense of loneliness but also a sense of fraternity that unites and supports them in the face of failure.

Written in 1933, Malraux's book became the bible of a generation, a source of inspiration to men and women facing the purposelessness of a world that seemed to have taken leave of its senses. The message was not escape, but commitment: humans could not ignore historical circumstance. To place Malraux's work in the proper perspective, one must remember that 1933 was also the year of Hitler's accession to power. It was also a crucial year for Spain.

Writers and the Spanish Civil War We have seen how the Spanish Civil War—the clash of the democratic left and, later, the communists with the ultraright—was in a sense a prelude to World War II. Falange Española, which adopted many of the mannerisms and oratory of Nazism, was founded in 1933. This group joined other rightist factions in 1936 in the attempt to overthrow the legally constituted Popular Front government of Spain by means of a coup d'état led by career army men. Unarmed and disorganized, the Spanish people decided to oppose it. As a result, the military rebellion failed to achieve its original objectives and led to the protracted civil war. It was this that gave the struggle its poignancy. "It was a political problem," wrote Max Aub in 1960, "but it was above all a moral problem.... It was not a revolution, as is Fidel Castro's today. We did not take up arms to overthrow a government but to uphold it.... Thence the passion that the assault on the Republic unchained and the fact that the problem continues unresolved."

Solving the problem, whatever its past or present implications, was and is the concern of Spaniards. But the moral passion to which the writer refers had an immediate international effect; within days, writers in many nations responded. Overwhelmingly they sided with the Republic, though a few took up the rebel Nationalist cause. It was, however, the Spanish Republic that spawned a literature of social commitment of both Marxist and democratic inspiration.

This literature is "political" not in a partisan sense but on the assumption that freedom is inseparably linked to the play of political forces affecting human destiny. The Spanish war, as a prelude to World War II, served to bring sharply into focus the social and economic problems afflicting the Western world at a time when thinking people were having grave doubts not only about the prevailing socioeconomic systems but also about the very future of the values of Western civilization. Such concern was manifest in these words of Albert Einstein: "The only thing in view of the circumstances surrounding our epoch that can keep the hope of better times alive within us is the heroic struggle of the Spanish people for freedom and human dignity."

Literature of social protest was not new to Western tradition: one needs only to remember the novels of Charles Dickens or the work of the naturalist writers at the turn of the century. But the economic crises of the 1920s, bringing with them a frightening disintegration of social structures coupled to the threat posed by the rise of fascism and communism, made the adoption of a political stand unavoidable. No longer could the writer, any more than the peasant or the urban worker, stand on the sidelines, leaving politics to the politicians. Politics had become everybody's business: the effective writer had to be aware that it was inseparable from intellectual activity. The writer was involved, whether he realized it or not, in the common struggle against the forces of tyranny and oppression. There was no choice; there was no escape.

Thus, Hemingway would not write a second *Farewell to Arms*, but *For Whom the Bell Tolls*, in which the message of inescapability was clearly underscored.

Malraux's contribution was *L'Espoir (Man's Hope)*, the theme of which was clearly related to that of his earlier book, *Man's Fate*. Again, the writer saw clearly a new crucifixion, this time in Spain. Hope, however, lay in the fact that, in Spain, a whole people had risen, however irrationally and with little chance of ultimate military victory, to assert their will to freedom against the onrush of tyranny and oppression. The battlefields of Spain provided the concrete rallying point where, as Archibald MacLeish put it, "we writers who contend for freedom are ourselves, whether we wish it or not, engaged."

Whatever can be said of foreign writers applied, obviously with greater compulsion, to Spanish writers and intellectuals. As was the case with their colleagues abroad, most of them, even those who had been clearly apolitical, took sides, putting their pen at the service of the Republic. The brilliant group who had come to prominence in the late 1920s found common cause with the people and welcomed the support of their foreign counterparts. The tragic death of the most distinguished of them, Federico García Lorca, shot by the Nationalists in August 1936, provided additional proof of the inseparability of the military uprising and the death of the mind. The survivors, with rare exceptions, chose exile at the end of the war rather than lend tacit approval to the victors by their continued presence in Spain.

Max Aub   Some were beginning their career as writers when the war broke out. Max Aub, born in Paris in 1903, was one of these. His father, a German facing internment at the outbreak of World War I, took his family to Spain where, in Valencia, he made his life as a salesman. Young Max followed the same trade after finishing school. Those early years of travel through the length and breadth of Spain gave him intimate knowledge of people, places, and mores—solid training for his writing. He also traveled abroad, joined literary circles in Paris and other places. His early works, between 1929 and 1936, reflect the modernist and, at times, surrealist trends that characterized literature at the time. Historical events, however, turned him to a different kind of writing.

As we have seen, the Spanish war was one of the important milestones in the career of André Malraux, one

of Aub's lifelong friends. It was decisive for Aub. After its end, he suffered internment in French concentration camps, both in France and in Algeria. All the time he wrote, hiding the crumpled pages of his manuscripts from the camp authorities who sternly forbade such activities. In 1942, he managed to escape and, after many misadventures, found his way from Casablanca to Mexico, where he rejoined his family and the thousands of other exiles who had been granted asylum. Many years later, having by then acquired Mexican nationality, he was ironically awarded the Legion of Honor by the French as a distinguished Mexican writer.

The events to which the story of "El Cojo" refers center on the fall of Málaga, a coastal city of southern Spain, in February 1937. The town was taken by an Italian expeditionary force, led by General Roatta, that had landed in Spain in support of General Franco's Nationalists, and the story was written shortly after the event. The theme of the story is the awakening of social and political consciousness in an unsophisticated, ignorant peasant, a typical representative of the Andalusian landless proletariat. El Cojo is one of the faceless millions, as faceless as all the other peasants whose real names we never learn; to each other and to us they are merely "Frenchy," "the Gabber," "Splayfoot," "Tio Merengue," and so on. Following a brief sketch of El Cojo's early life leading to his becoming a sharecropper, the story deals with the awakening in this ignorant, defeated man of a new dignity that brings with it also a sense of fraternity and a consciousness of social responsibility. The translation is by Alan Gonzalez.

MAX AUB

El Cojo[1]

You could still make out the sea from the last bend. The foothills split into gray and dun gullies and flattened out in the distance, making way for green and

---

[1] Literally, the Gimp. Nicknames have been translated when English offered an adequate equivalent (Splayfoot, the Gabber). When translation was inadequate, the original was preferred: such was the case with La Motrilera (the woman from Motril) or Tio Merengue (Old Meringue). *El Cojo* is used for the protagonist because the repeated use of "gimp" throughout the story would give a facetious, pejorative connotation absent in the original.

blue fallow fields with occasional yellow patches. Looking up, the hills were bare, as if the crust had been hewn in successive terraces, devoid of grass or flowers; only the vines, in offset rows, like crosses in a warriors' burial ground. Partition walls, covered by brambles and cacti, squared off in geometric patterns following the folds in the land.

The road snaked down towards Motril and the dust settled on everything. Honeysuckle, thistles, and a variety of other weeds took on a vague lunar air. Further off, the reeds put on a brave, if futile, struggle. Live greenery seemed stone laden; the whiteness was dirt, but what was lost in freshness was gained in time: the landscape appeared eternally durable. Successive layers of dust collected on the finest twigs: closely observed, it looked like finest snow, a sunny snow, or rather, grayish flour ground by hooves and by wheels, broadcast in the wind. Comet-like, motorcars grew a tail of dust; by its size, a knowledgeable sheepherder could guess at horsepower and speed.

From that vantage point, one could always see a procession of carts towards Málaga or, in the opposite direction, towards Almería. Two, three or four animals pulled them, usually mules; every cart had its grayish canvas, same color as the road, the driver asleep, unless he had need to relieve himself or to socialize and roll a cigarette. Axles squeaked; the stones rose on the road as obstacles. Drivers are not singing men: that is for plowmen; the land was a paradise for cicadas, that is to say, for silence. You could not sweat: dust stopped the pores; the skin changed from sallow to gray; the hair, from brown to white. You could hold the air between your fingers, it was that hot and heavy. If you traveled to Motril, you could nose the sea; on the way back, you could not realize that there was no horizon; the sky was enough.

On that bend, to the left as you look to Málaga, begins a footpath about a sixth of a mile, climbing steeply. It dies at the door of a hut, shack or bare dwelling, in the strict sense of the word. Its inhabitants were "La Motrilera," her husband, "El Cojo de Vera," and their daughter, Rafaela Pérez Montalbán, their only offspring after ten easy deliveries. So easy and fast had they been that four of them had come under the green fronds of the olive trees. Far from other human habitation, they had been unencumbered by any assistance. The timing was always off. The man worked far away and she would go, heavy with child, to bring him his lunch under the midday sun crossing the craggy slopes. Tripping over furrows and rocks, she'd arrive, dirty from the sweat of labor and of her determination to hold back the new life until she got home; the man would blaspheme and curse, and cut the umbilical cord with his jack-knife, washing it in the wine that the woman had brought for his lunch. The blood would flow, spilling now without pain; she swaddled the child in her shawl. He would then cart her back on his shoulders unless, depending on the place, a neighbor's presence allowed the use of an improvised stretcher. Once she'd had to return on foot, when he was limping badly. "They're all the same," he would comment to the godfather. "Never right in their predictions." Once she got sick and had a twenty-day fever. It eventually went away and the child miraculously lived. It was the last one. Under stress, the mother would despair, her eyes blinded by the tears that would fall directly on her clothes, missing her sunken cheeks.

Her skin was sallow, and she dressed in black. Her belly had grown steadily with the years and she had fallen into the habit of crossing her hands at waist level, resting them on the shelf-like corpulence.

They were both quiet people, ignorant of anything beyond the limits of the land on which they worked. They worked for the master, as was expected. They were looked on as strangers; they had come from somewhere and had stayed there, far from the village, out of touch. They simply lived, and no one gave a damn for them.

He was small, shriveled and more taciturn than she. He seemed to hold something against his voice. El Cojo de Vera had been a good singer; he had never had a great voice but he'd had a knack for putting across the *fandanguillos* of his region in his deep, thick voice, with the natural grace and feeling adequate to the bitter lament of the Almería mining chants. That had been his first occupation: miner, in the red hills running from Huercal to Baza. The dust that he had then breathed had undermined his voice later, when he made a living as a *cantaor*,[2] in Málaga. El Cojo de Vera

___
[2] A singer of *cante jondo* (deepsong), traditional in Andalusian folk music.

had known his day of glory; he had known many nights of revel lasting through the dawn. But not for long, as his voice weakened. First, his clients had thinned out; then, they were less distinguished; instead of folding money, they paid in coin; his services were no longer required in classy parties, at inns and cafés; instead, he had long waits at the back doors of brothels, engaging in long conversations with blind guitarists to while away the hours. The women were dark, sad, dirty and honest. Among the noise and laughter of the revel, you could hear from time to time, with mechanical insistence: "Don't get any ideas; I'm a decent woman." The "Baby," who had a reputation for heartlessness, hardly ever came down as she was kept busy by her customers, petty clerics and store clerks. Dawn would put a tawdry end to the proceedings. With the first light of day they would drink coffee at a nearby square, where the morning breeze brought in the scent of jasmine. Then they'd go off to sleep: the blind musicians would walk away, one behind the other, a walking stick in their right hand, guitars tucked under their left arms. No one knows how low El Cojo might have sunk, because one night in June a group of euphoric revelers took him, to amuse themselves, to Motril and left him there, as a prank.

As he walked around the town, which he did not know, his path crossed with Rafaela's and, being not unattractive, he did not have to insist much to have the young girl take notice. He stayed on. "What brought you here?" the girl would ask. "Horse trading," he would answer, which seemed to satisfy her. He continued to make a living as best he could. There was always some place to sleep.

One night, when he was selling his services to out-of-towners, he was recognized by one of the prominent landowners, Don Manuel Hinojosa.

"Where's that great voice of yours?"

"That's a thing of the past, Don Manuel."

"What are your plans?"

The *cantaor* shrugged his shoulders. Don Manuel was always generous in his cups. In a quiet spell, while his friends were upstairs, El Cojo was saying something about the girl, and the gentleman suddenly shot out:

"Want a job?"

We shall never know what quirk of his inebriated soul thus tapped the flow of his philanthropy. That very morning he had refused to lease the land with its ramshackle house to several peasants to whom he owed some electoral favors. Now, unexpectedly, in a fit of vague and warm optimism, it pleased him to turn that erstwhile witness of his dissolute past into the laborer of his lands. A gratuitous favor not, however, without strings.

"So long as you keep a few bottles and a guitar handy, in case we think of coming by . . ."

"The girl, does she come with the house?" asked El Cojo, sternly.

"No, man; you know me . . ."

True enough. The gentleman had a big circle of friends, he usually picked up the tab but his station in life demanded that he keep clear of certain contacts which he, apparently, judged not in keeping with his class. This air of superiority, as mediator in the revelries of others and arbiter of their pleasures, paying for their wine and even sometimes their women, caused him to be continually surrounded by a court of jesters who did not balk at the most demeaning adulation. He did not look on this circle of followers as men.

"She's a decent girl," El Cojo added with some shame.

The master burst out laughing. He was still hiccuping and belching when the mob of sycophants came down.

So El Cojo and La Motrilera took possession of the place after the wedding. Work was hard, especially for him, who had forgotten the feel of a tool-handle and had never seen a plough. The wages, two-bits a day. He never complained but he turned sullen and his face grew somber, as did hers, who, as a loyal mate, grew to resemble him with time. Up to nine male and one female births was the hard tally of her labor. Of the nine, none survived: the youngest died when he was five, run over by a car which disappeared without a trace. The burials were the hardest work of all those years.

Far off to the right was Nerja. The pure deep blue of the water seemed to stain the sky. Over there was the Miel river. It was an abrupt coast, without the white trimming of foam: the sea lay still. Cliffs and rocks could look at their clean pediments lending their polychrome hues to the water. Boats, with their lateen sails, cut the water here and there: small boats, small fish, small life, poverty, under the monochrome sky. Terrifying sameness, dryness; only the geraniums break the monotony, thriving by the grace of God. Claypots sit on andirons, and women, crooked backs bent over, fan the coals. Cooked greens, gazpacho and too much bread. Day after day and year after year. Sugar canes shiver in the breeze, whining. If you look up, to the right, olives and esparto grass. Higher up, the sierra, between blue and purple. Below, a pervading dun, colorless gray, washed out green. Ahead you can sense Málaga, the hum of a forgotten life. Life weighs down on you, like the sun; it numbs. Work, sweat; sit on the rocks when they cast no shadow to await, under the nearest olive or by a merciful crag, the arrival of lunch, twin brother to yesterday's. No more does she remember the name of El Cojo than he hers. They hardly ever talk now; their eyes have turned small; what's there to look at? They live on in their own darkness. The Virgin of Sorrows presides over everything with her tender love.

Once in a while El Cojo looks at the girl. How has she grown? How have all those years gone by? Time is measured in vine stumps, olive trees, and reeds. The measure of humans escapes him and baffles him. Her small breasts, which must be soft, bobble. The father cuts a piece of bread off the coarse loaf with his jackknife and looks vaguely towards the low-lying village. Have eighteen years gone by? There is no answer. He looks at the furrow he has just cut. Will the master let him plant tomatoes? He has already refused, but El Cojo will insist and, if he is again refused, he will plant them anyway: the master never comes. He chews his meager ration with his white teeth. "I can't pay unless I plant tomatoes and the master frowns on it." "That's all right," he tells me, "for people who have just one miserable acre and have to get from it everything they need. I'm not in that class." Some crows fly by, cawing. "I'll have to go to Cerro Gordo..."

Some vague story about a splintered hub brought a John Doe to the door, a cart driver from Vélez-Málaga, a jabbering, lighthearted man. His very gabble lent him a certain charm. From then on, he would break his run every ten or fifteen days for a few hours rest at the shack. The lass took a fancy to him and he to her; nature took its course. The parents approved (assenting with a grunt and a shrug of the shoulders) and married them. She had been anxious to try what "it" was like. It

was around Christmas, 1935. The girl left with her husband to live in Vélez-Málaga. The parents stayed behind, awaiting death. They would be buried in the paupers' pit at Nerja; it was far away—he had not been there for a long time—but, it'd be only once! The coming of the Republic caused hardly a ripple, though he heard about it; Asturias[3] had caused more comment from the son-in-law and from Alfredo, The Whiting, the muleteer who brought them the few things they needed. They dubbed him Whiting because sometimes, as chance would have it, he'd bring fish to sell to his customers. You could find everything in his wagon: clay pots, candles, sausage, toothpicks, bananas, fine-tooth combs, writing and decorative paper, soap and colored ribbons, saffron, pails, towels, hairpins, toiletries, brooches and mirrors, sewing kits and anything that had been ordered the previous week. El Cojo did not go along with all that stuff about the Republic and the revolution. That was not for him. There was an order to things. If that was the way they had been made, they should stay like that and there was no need to go looking for trouble. That was for loafers. He'd done his living, and he knew it. Let each go about his business and let well alone. The rich are the rich. We all know they are a bunch of fools. After twenty-five years, El Cojo still had the same concept of the world as when he lived in the promiscuity of the Málaga brothels. He could not imagine the world any other way. Deep down, he harbored a resentment against his mining comrades, whom he blamed for having ruined his voice, making all that powdery red dust that got into everything. The mother turned a deaf ear, wrapped up in her pregnancies and black clothing.

One morning, some day in August 1936, some men he hardly knew came from the village, shouldering shotguns.

"Salud."

"Hi."

"The Committee has assigned this land to you, from the fence over there to the ravine. Beyond that it will be Antonio's, the Woodman. You've been lucky; some people wanted to leave you out of the collective." And:

---

[3] Rising of the miners of Asturias, in the north of Spain, bloodily repressed by African troops and Foreign Legion.

"You'll have to come down and talk to the Committee." Then they left.

El Cojo shrugged his shoulders and continued leading his life as before, as if nothing had happened. One morning he bumped into Splayfoot.

"What are you doing here? This is my land."

El Cojo looked at him with contempt.

"Has Don Manuel sold it to you?"

"We'll see," said the man, and turned his back on him. They called him Splayfoot from the way he walked.

They took him the next morning between two shotguns slung across two backs. The barrels glinted in the sun. They walked down to the village, a good mile and a half. One of them on the right, said: "Frenchy's field looks good." The other assented, silently.

El Cojo was not thinking of anything in particular. He kept walking, realizing that his limbs welcomed the hike. "So what if they kill me. I haven't much left to live anyway. I've done more than my share of getting up, dressing, eating, working, sleeping. We've all got to go some day. Yeah, Frenchy's field was always good to look at. I don't care if I never see it again. In any case, they're not going to kill me." A pebble got into his shoe; he bent his leg and got it out. The others waited some feet ahead.

" 'Tio Merengue' should keep this a bit tidier," said The Gabber, the one on the right.

They soon came to the village. The Count's house was in a small plaza with six acacias circled by brick borders. It was a mansion graced by a handsome gate and two iron grilles that took up the whole side of the square. A triangular shadow falling on the ground seemed to point the way. The Committee sat in the entrance hall, amid walls lined with somber flagstones. A cooling breeze ran through it. On the floor, sat a plump pitcher, like a curled-up cat. There was a short wait. In the sudden change of temperature, the cooler air gave to the sweating bodies the feel of a frosted mantle.

"Hello, Cojo," said one of the men sitting around the table. "Sit down."

El Cojo did as he was told. He recognized, vaguely, the five men in the Committee; three wore T-shirts; the others were in shirt sleeves.

"They say you do not want the land you have been assigned."

El Cojo shrugged.

"Why?"

There was a silence and the biggest of them put in, scornfully:

"He's afraid of the Guardia Civil." [4]

Another said:

"He's been a scab all his life."

And El Cojo:

"That's not true."

The one in the center cut this off:

"You are a working man; you have tilled that land; you have a right to it, do you understand?"

El Cojo grunted. The fat man cut in:

"I am glad to tell you face to face, Cojo, like I said it some days ago at the Union hall. You are an ugly character and what we have to do with you is to make sure you do no harm."

"I haven't meddled with anyone."

The President spoke:

"That's just it; for not meddling, for putting up with everything, for being a coward: that's why the world is in the fix it is. If we were all like you, masters would always be masters." Self-importantly, he added: "Ownership is stealing."

"I know that," replied El Cojo; "I'm not that stupid."

"Your ex-master, Don" stressing the appellative "Manuel Hinojosa has joined the rebels; we have distributed his lands, to work them for the good of the community."

By now, El Cojo could not understand anything. He felt like a drunk, with an unbearable weight on his forehead.

"And because we want every working man to share in the benefits of the reform, we have decided to give you your piece of land, forgetting that you have never wanted to have anything to do with us. At least, you have not been against us."

There was a pause. The President stood up:

"Do you or do you not accept your land?"

El Cojo bent down to pick up a toothpick he had dropped; then he stood up and said:

"I accept."

To which the President replied:

"On your way, then."

---

[4] Paramilitary police force, charged with law enforcement in nonurban areas.

There was a heated discussion after he left:

"There'll always be time," said the fat one, sententiously.

El Cojo started for home, walking, hands behind his back, in a familiar attitude unusual for peasants and which had contributed to giving him the reputation for weirdness which he enjoyed, his eyes turned down, staring at the dust and the stones. "The land is mine; they give it to me." He stopped a moment. "They give it to me because I have worked it, without having to account to anyone. Sure; if I had not been there the land would just lie there, rotting. It's the work that's mine. Not the land; only what it gives." He stopped again. "But if I had not worked the land, they'd send me away and put someone else in my place. Then, of course, the land would belong to the other." He walked on, with a lighter step. "I could let it lie fallow, if I wanted." He laughed. "Without buying it, without inheriting." It surprised him to find he was thinking of his wife. "I'll plant tomatoes. Don Manuel always opposed it. He said it would spoil the grapevines. He was stubborn! Yeah, tomatoes." He stumbled on a stone and removed it from the path.

It was a bit cooler. The wind came gustily from the sea, kicking up dust. "It's still too hot for the time of year. Wonder what day it is. I can't remember, but it is an important date. From today I'm a landowner." That word jarred, made him uncomfortable. He would rather forget it but it pressed on his mind insistently, like the pebble in his shoe. He would work harder. That was it, and he could do it. He'd start tomorrow. No; that very afternoon as soon as he got there. He walked faster. "They had told him . . . or hadn't that been mentioned? Didn't Miguel tell him that now he would be working for everyone?" He couldn't remember; all that talk in the hallway had left a blank. One thing only remained: he had accepted the land. But he understood that working for himself he was also working for all. Had he heard that somewhere? He could not understand it entirely, but he felt that was good and it put him at ease. He stood to look at the view; he had never done it before; he would never have thought to look at land he did not have to till. He was discovering the land; it looked beautiful in its unending travail. Some men in the distance hurt it as they tended it. He felt like running to get home sooner. He chided himself: "Enough foolishness," and he thought of some-thing that had never crossed his mind: "If I were only twenty years younger . . ." There was a strange feeling in the air. He had a sudden craving for a smoke but he held back not to waste time. Before he realized it, he had reached the footpath leading to his shack.

The woman said nothing when she saw him. She looked at him and he averted his eyes. He saw—he had discovered so many things of late—that he had lost the habit of talk and that it was difficult, just like that, to give her the news. He froze in the middle of the room.

"What did they want with you?" she asked.

"Nothing," he replied.

He almost said: "They have given us the land." She, who was bending over something, stood still, expecting further words. But El Cojo remained silent and she straightened up slowly.

"Ah," she said. And they spoke no more.

He walked to the door and stood in it, motionless, staring out for a long time. There was dampness in the corners of his eyes. The budding tears, unfamiliar with their role, just stayed there, drying in the cold air of the dying fall. The woman dragged a chair up and sat in the threshold. El Cojo thought of the men he had always ignored, anarchists, socialists, who now had given him land. A great love for them welled up inside him now. He could not disguise that his gratefulness was not disinterested, but he understood that, in spite of everything, that feeling was pure. He felt remorse for certain jokes, his contemptuousness. "Had I but known! How could I know? Who would have said? There was no one to explain it . . ." It was the woman who broke the silence, his and hers:

"What if the others came . . ."

He did not reply. They would not come and, if they came, no one was going to take his land away from him. It was his, he felt its life-giving sap rising from the soles of his feet. His, as his hands were his, or his chest: far more a part of him than his own daughter.

"Let them come," he said, and he sat on the ground.

As he crossed his hands over his knees he remembered his craving a cigarette as he walked up from the village and how he had forgotten all about it as other thoughts assailed him. Calmly, he took out his Ubrique[5] pouch, shapeless by now, frayed—he had

---

[5] Small town known for its fine leather industry.

bought it from the peddler ten or twelve years back—
and deliberately started rolling a cigarette, tenderly
coaxing the weed on the paper between the thumbs
and guided by the index fingers; then pressed the edge
of the paper slowly, after wetting it with a sideways
movement of the head, left to right. He put it in the left
corner of the mouth, lit the tinder at the first spark. He
leaned back on the wall, inhaled deeply: the paper
burned, the tobacco caught on, his mouth swallowed
the smoke. It was his first mouthful as a man, the first
cigarette he smoked with the full realization that he
was alive. Softly, in his husky voice he began to sing
deeply. A thousand noises from the earth responded: it
was the silence of the night.

The days go by. El Cojo's thoughts ramble, as he sits
on the terraced hillside, against a wild olive tree smoking flimsy cigarettes, misshapen like his fingers. The
sun filters between the pods of nopal growing on the
edge of the next terrace.

"The vine shoots that I planted three years ago and
have grown so well . . . those belong to me much more
than the others. There's no argument, since Don
Manuel did not even know. He would not see me, two
years ago, when I went to tell him." He breaks off a tendril, puts it in his mouth and chews, savoring its acid
taste. Then he lowers his hand to the ground and feels
the dirt: it is hard dirt, difficult to break, dry, "a bit like
me," he thinks, and is overtaken by the thought of a
rich, lush land, teeming with sprouting wheat, gravid
with fruitfulness, bursting full. He strokes it, crumbles
it in his hand, rubs it as he would the hind quarter of a
lustrous horse. He feels the comfort of the tree at his
back, protecting him. He longs to go get lost in unknown paths and open ranges, but the thought suffices.
A thicket of brush grows sheltered by the retention
wall. He touches it with his foot and tries to bend the
stalks. The earth seems to flood everything—grass, tree,
stones; he feels it rise into him also: "It's up to my
waist now, my heart, I'll go mad when it reaches my
head."

Everything turns velvet at sundown. El Cojo walks
back, hoe slung over his shoulder. He comes across
Splayfoot: "Hi." "Hi." Ten yards off, he turns and asks:

"Say; where can I get a shotgun?"

"Ask the Committee."

He went.

"What do you want?"

"A weapon."

"What for?"

"Just in case . . ."

"There aren't enough for the war."

"Too bad."

And he went back to his land.

One morning, his daughter turned up, with an eight-
month belly.

"Where's your husband?"

"In Jaén, driving with the battalion . . ."

"You O.K.?"

"Sure."

"That's good."

The mother gets busy:

"They say they're coming."

"Yes, moors and Italians."

"Where are they?" asks the father.

"By Antequera."

"That's some way off still," says he. "They won't get
here."

"I don't see why not," says the mother.

The father looks at her, silent, but almost says: "Because the land is mine."

Mother and daughter spend the day on the slope
where the road has been cut asking every living person
that comes by. Motorcars come and go. Soon, more are
traveling east than west. The days go by . . . .

"Aren't you cold?" the mother asks from time to
time.

"Don't worry, mother."

They hardly know what they are waiting for. There
comes a donkey now, a woman with a child riding it.
Behind, with a stick, a peasant with an old homespun
cape, black in its day but weathered green. As they go
by, the women call:

"Where are you from?"

"Estepona."

"Are they coming?"

"So we've heard, and they burn everything."

Soon they get lost in the distance. Way below, El
Cojo will not leave his vineyard. The road is coming
alive, like a stream. Bit by bit the flow has grown. First,
in groups; now, like a parade. As the numbers grow,
more and more join them. You can be indifferent to a
demonstration, but not to an army. Next morning, El

Cojo went to the road and stood there a long time watching the caravan. They came in islands or in archipelagos, grouped behind a barrow, or a pack animal. Soon it got to look like a river. Men, women and children of all ages and in assorted clothing, in such numbers and disarray, they became an amorphous mass. The only thing you noticed was their deadened faces. Browns, grays, greens vanished against the fatigue, the fear, the sleep reflected on the folds of their cheeks; even the children looked old. Shouts, noise, words, curses, all merged in the pandemonium of the gigantic living mass, dragging on. El Cojo looked on in bafflement, unable to make a decision, cursing the evil spirits that had brought the world to such a pass. The older men carried the children; women bent under impossible loads, their tanned faces creased by recent anguish, eyes reddened by the dust, disheveled, panic-ridden. Some children attempted to play with the gravel by the roadside, only to be defeated by their own present and future exhaustion. The dull clamor would cease suddenly, giving way to a terrifying silence. Even the squeak of wheels was dampened. Pack animals would sink their heads then as if the collars were made of lead. The dirt on the copper studs of the blinders betrayed the long time wasted in the flight. Men pushed vehicles in that last climb; hand barrows rested. As they reached the brow, women readjusted their load and looked back. Babies demanded their milk, the wails of one waking the other. A woman, intent on carrying a bundle under one arm and her child astride on her waist, held by the left, gave up one hundred yards beyond. She sat on the bundle, crossed her hands over the black skirt, let pass six hundred feet of that somber chain welded by fear and by the weight it packed, got up and started walking again, dragging the bawling child: "I'm tired; I'm tired." A few cars began to show; two panting trucks surged up in low gear; as they topped the crest they declutched and engaged high: the silent interval between gears was like a farewell to the sea. Now and then you could see bandages on some wounded, the red and black of the F.A.I.[6] Terror turned to death, the rows of people into throngs. El Cojo went to the house and said to the women:

"You have to leave."
"What about you?"
"I'll stay."

They did not resist, and, with a bundle of clothes, joined the throng. They were impelled by something that forbade protest, fleeing by instinct, because they guessed at the approaching catastrophe; it was an unnatural force, a mass under which they would perish, an earthquake that one should avoid at all costs even if the attempt cost them their life. "My father, who lived in Ronda . . ." "They shot him, just like that." "They leave nothing standing." "And they came and they robbed . . ." You heard people retelling events; no comments, save for an odd "God help us" that came, angrily, out of some toothless old woman's lips. Motorcars opened a swath among the sea of people by the loud blaring of their horns; the crowd parted with rancor. Nobody ran, but shouted angrily back. The vehicles ran into thick human clusters that braked their progress. One tried to push through and the discord ended in shooting. People converged thickly on the car. A man, standing on the running board, a rifle slung across his back, pistol in hand, was shouting: "Comrades . . ." Unbraked, the car rolled back and sank softly into the embankment. The man cursed and joined the walking mob. The dead driver slumped over the wheel.

Beyond the bend the multitude felt safer, as they lost sight of the sea. They slowed down. You could see groups of people lying by the roadside. El Cojo remained standing, observing the awesome parade. Some people from the village went by and spoke to him:

"Coming?"
"No."
"They're practically here."
"If you gave me the land there's a reason. I'm staying."

They misread his thoughts, but one said: "Leave him alone," and went on.

The throng was thinning out. El Cojo decided to return home. The temperature was ideal. The land fell from terrace to terrace to the salt ponds, cloaked in a translucent dimness. He found three militiamen near his shack.

"Hello, salud."

They heard a plane engine; it must have been flying

---

[6] Federación Anarquista Ibérica, the anarchist party.

low but they could not see it. A score of men lying behind the low retaining wall raised their heads. Now the plane could be seen over the sea. Its right engine was on fire. It tried to stabilize, but fell to the water. Simultaneously, two flights of eight aircraft nosedived towards the spot, strafing the victim. Then they flew on to Málaga. Firing was heard in the distance.

"If we had a few more . . . we'd hold them here."

"Against their wishes?"

"Don't talk nonsense. Blázquez assured me that a detachment had left Jaén day before yesterday, and that three thousand men have arrived in Guadix from Lorca. Some had already left from Almería."

"I don't think . . ."

"Shut up!"

The speaker seemed to enjoy a certain ascendancy over the others. He asked El Cojo:

"Have you got water?"

Then, in a different tone:

"It's for the machine gun."

El Cojo said he had and then, unbelievingly, he heard himself add:

"If you have a rifle, I'm a pretty good shot."

"How can you tell?"

"I've done my stint."

"What party d'you belong to?"

"No party."

"Union?"

"C.N.T." [7]

"Since when?"

"A few months."

He said it without shame. One of the militiamen was from the village, and he cut in:

"He's an ornery cuss, a lackey of the former landowner here. I wouldn't trust him with a rifle, except looking up the barrel. He might shoot us from the back. I wouldn't trust him."

The other man asked:

"Whose is the land now?"

"His."

"Which land?"

"This one."

---

[7] Confederación Nacional de Trabajo, the labor federation of the anarchists.

"Give him a rifle." Then to El Cojo: "You come here, next to me."

He deployed the men along the terraces looking down on the road and went to place the machine gun a hundred yards higher up. He sent a message to another detachment that, as he said, covered their right flank.

"You, on the plowed fields, keep as low as you can. What's the distance from here to the road?"

"Roughly a mile."

"Set your sights on fifteen, then."

As he saw El Cojo was having trouble, he set them for him. They waited. The road was now empty: only an upturned truck, an upended wheelbarrow, its wheel still turning in the air. Artillery shells began falling to the right. There was the scent of thyme. El Cojo was startled; he noticed that his muscles shivered, and could do nothing to stop it. But he was not frightened. The howitzer shots came with regularity. He started to count between shots, to see how long they took. He got all confused. He tried to sink further in the dirt. Seen that close, even the tiniest cracks held astonishing things; the grass turned into jungle; some dandelion plants nearby looked like fantastic monsters. The olive tree to his left, suddenly immense, protected him. That left a concrete impression. He fired three times at something that moved in the distance and shot off the bud of a daisy. He was discovering two new worlds: he thought of peace and felt the ground with his patting hand. He unbolted the rifle and reloaded faster and more efficiently than before. His comrade to the left looked at him and laughed:

"Feel good?"

"Great."

A few stray bullets broke some twigs high in the tree. The machine gun to the right started barking. Far off, a second one joined in.

"They won't get beyond the bend," said his comrade.

Miles behind them, on the road, the exodus went on. Rafaela and her mother formed part of the amorphous mob.

The only vertical lines on the plain were the telegraph posts. At the cry of "There they come," the crowd dispersed. Only their objects remained on the highway, and a wailing baby. A flight of pursuit planes flew over, hugging the ground, strafing as they went.

You could see the pilots, so low were they. There were few wounded, but much crying; some dead animals were thrown into the ditch. The march resumed, under the terror. A woman died for no reason. Some able-bodied men ran, heedless of others. Motorcars caused irrational hate. Rafaela was getting up with difficulty. Her anguished mother looked at her:

"Does it hurt?" she asked.

Rafaela had stuck a handkerchief in her mouth and did not reply. "They're coming back!" Rafaela, in her pain, could not heed the warning of an old man, who yelled:

"Lie down; lie down!"

Holding on to the telegraph pole, open-legged, she felt the tearing of her entrails.

"Lie down, daughter, lie down!" whined her mother, on the ground. Rafaela, standing, biting the rag in her mouth, was giving birth. She felt as if her body was hacked in two. The swift, terrifying din of planes, machine guns, a few short feet above her. It must be a great acrobatic game for them. Rafaela felt only her labor. She got five bullets in the back and had no time to know. She was conscious only of losing her grip on the log and everything turned soft and easy. She said "Jesus!" and fell, dead before her body touched the ground.

The planes had gone. There were prostrated bodies whining; others, still and noiseless. Far off, a crazed child ran across the field. A mile below, the dark flowing mass began to move again. Ambulances tried to move against it. On their sides you could read: "The Swedish people to the Spanish people." They found the dead mother and heard the sobbing of the newborn. They cut the umbilical cord.

"Is it alive?"

"It is."

Someone who limped up, a bullet in his foot, said:

"I knew her. Her name is Rafaela. Rafaela Pérez Montalbán. I am the court clerk. She wanted a girl."

Someone said: "She got her wish."

"And she wanted to call her Hope."

"Why not?" somebody else put in.

.   .   .

El Cojo pressed himself further into the dirt, feeling his waist and his stomach and his thighs resting against it, his left elbow nestling in the red earth. He aimed his rifle between two brownish rocks, no higher than his head, serving as embrasure. The rifle sat firmly on his shoulder as he took careful aim. The recoil of each shot dug into his shoulder and through his body rebounded on the ground. He felt the land was grateful. He felt safe, protected, invulnerable. Each bullet carried a message to its target: "Take that. Take it and learn." The afternoon wore on. The bursts of the machine guns continued. His comrade said:

"You stay there."

The shooting was thinning out. El Cojo looked for a word and could not find it: he was defending his own, his sweat, the vines he had planted, and was defending it directly, like a man. El Cojo had never known that word, nor had he thought that it could ever denote possession. He was happy.

QUESTIONS

1. Comment on the devices that the writer uses to convey the notion of a new dawn for El Cojo.
2. Explain as fully as you can the implications for El Cojo's thinking of his wife as he walked back from the meeting with the Committee.
3. What are the full implications of El Cojo's ignoring the words of the men who first came to tell him of the new distribution of land?
4. Do you find credible the awakening of social consciousness in a man as old as the hero of this story? Why or why not? Comment not only on the events told by the writer but also on the stylistic devices used for the purpose.
5. What are the implications for El Cojo's future at the end of the story? Do you find this ending satisfactory?
6. Compare the broader or symbolic significance of the Spanish Civil War as portrayed in *Guernica* and in "El Cojo."

35

POSTWAR ABSURDITY AND ALIENATION

World War II and its aftermath left the humanities in a situation of crisis. The attempted genocide of the Jews, the large-scale death camps, and finally the use of the atomic bomb raised terrifying questions about the extreme possibilities of man's inhumanity to man. The role of the humanities as a humanizing force, the ideal of traditional humanism, had to be put seriously in doubt. Were there not S.S. men who listened to their Bach or read their Goethe after a day's work at the gas chambers? The possibility of instant extermination through nuclear war continues to make many of the traditional forms and values seem obsolete.

Sartre and Existentialism   One response to this crisis situation was the growing popularity of the philosophy of *existentialism* during the years immediately after the war. As a philosophy, existentialism had actually been developed much earlier, through the influence of Nietzsche, and the work of Martin Heidegger and Karl Jaspers in Germany. It was, however, the French intellectual Jean-Paul Sartre (born 1905) who did most to bring existentialism into the arts and into a lifestyle. Sartre's seminal philosophical work, *Being and Nothingness* (1943), was born not only of his readings in German philosophy but through his experiences in the war years as well. As a soldier and a participant in the Resistance, Sartre witnessed destruction and torture. It seemed, in those days, that every human being was constantly being put to the test in an extreme situation.

At the heart of Sartrean existentialism is a sense of limitless and therefore anxiety-producing human freedom. Life for each human being is a series of situations requiring choices and acts; the acts that one chooses determine what one *is*. According to Sartre, man is not given *being*, but only *existence*. There is no God; there are no absolute standards of morality or of truth. Each person must forge his own morality, his own truth, must indeed create his own being out of his existence. First, however, people must be aware of the dreadful state of freedom that is their true state of existence. Something like a Nietzschean "re-valuation of all values" is needed, but there is no superman to give guidance, only the individual. Sartre's words "life begins on the other side of despair" express the necessity for recognition of one's freedom. His "man is the sum of his acts" indicates that one's self is to be created through the use of this freedom.

Sartre found philosophy too limiting a vehicle with which to express the fundamental concerns of human beings. In a novel, *Nausea*, written before the war, he had already treated the theme of the absurdity (or, as he called it, the "contingency") of life and the outmoded hollowness of moralities such as traditional humanism. In the war years he turned to the theater, better adapted to illustrate his theory that each situation in human life is like a trap. One works one's way out of the trap by exercising one's freedom, making a choice, and acting on it. Certainly the situation in which France found itself, under occupation by the Nazis, had its influence on this kind of theater. And when in Sartre's adaptation of the Greek myth of Orestes, *The Flies*, Orestes revolts against the gods and proclaims, "I am my liberty!" the French audience applauded the

play's relevance. It took the Nazi censors a while to catch on.

Camus   The war and postwar literature of existentialism must include not only the fiction and theater of Sartre but also that of Albert Camus who, nonetheless, refused to call himself an existentialist. In his novel *The Stranger*, written on the eve of the war and published in 1942, Camus expresses his concept of the "absurd": the fundamental meaninglessness of human life and traditional beliefs. Yet Camus, whose native land was North Africa rather than Europe, retains a belief in the regenerative value of nature—sea and sun—that is absent from Sartre's work. His immediate postwar novel, *The Plague*, is about the effects of an imaginary plague on the Algerian city of Oran, but it is often read as an allegory of the German occupation of Paris. Camus, like Sartre, portrays human beings making choices in the face of an extreme situation. But Camus' values are finally closer to those of traditional humanism than Sartre's are. His heroes choose, in the face of death, in the face of absurdity, simply to do what they can, to help each other, to fight the plague. Friendship and love are in the end more important than political commitment. The revolt against the absurd becomes a way of reaffirming one's humanity. *The Plague* and Camus' philosophical work *The Rebel* precipitated a break between the two men who had become intellectual leaders in Western culture. The reasons were complex, but basically Sartre was critical of what he felt was Camus' compromise with humanism and liberalism. Sartre himself has moved toward a radically Marxist position and has modified considerably his view of human beings as totally free. Camus, who died in an "absurd" automobile accident in 1960, had retained his faith in the individual rebel, shunning all forms of totalitarian belief-systems.

Influences of Existentialism   Existentialism as a lifestyle in Europe and America in the postwar years produced a group of young people who rebelled against the traditional values of their parents and sought to assert their freedom in a meaningless world. In France they gathered in cafés for discussions with Sartre and his friends or to hear the "existentialist" songs of Juliette Greco. In the United States, a bit later, they hit the road or "dropped out," running away from what they perceived to be meaningless and false in American life. "Beatniks" and "hippies" were, indirectly at least, influenced by popularized existentialism. Two writers who adapted the existentialist ethic to the American scene are Jack Kerouac and Norman Mailer.

The French existentialists' consciousness of the absurdity of human life was balanced by the pressing need for social and political commitment. Sartrean man exercised his freedom in choosing to resist Nazi control. Anguish and despair could, in some limited way at least, end in triumph. In the years following the war, however, such extreme situations, or clear opportunities for commitment, did not often present themselves. One could, of course, commit oneself to a Marxist revolution, but the rise of Stalin in the Soviet Union made that solution seem much less attractive. The terrible knowledge of the concentration camps and the nuclear bomb made life seem precarious and individual human efforts vain. The sense of despair, gloom, and absurdity in existentialism seemed more relevant than its more heroic side.

The Theater of the Absurd   The 1950s and 60s gave rise to a literary movement in Europe and the United States, manifest particularly in the theater, which a well-known critic baptized "the absurd." Centered in Paris, the "absurdist" playwrights were on the whole foreigners who wrote in French, such as the Irishman Samuel Beckett, the Roumanian Eugène Ionesco and the Spaniard Fernando Arrabal. The English writer Harold Pinter and the American Edward Albee have also been grouped among the practitioners of the theater of the absurd. In a sense these playwrights develop the existentialist philosophy of the absurd into a literary *form*. Their theatrical world is one in which traditional elements like plot and character are almost abandoned, and language is freed from its everyday, logical restraints. Their experimentation grows out of modernism, but they lack on the whole both the modernist belief in the redemptive value of art and the existentialist assurance that man can create his own meaning in a meaningless world.

Arrabal   Fernando Arrabal, whose work shows many of the "absurdist" tendencies, began his career alone and independent of any school or movement. Born in Spain at the beginning of the civil war, he grew up in the repressive atmosphere of the Franco dictatorship. By his early twenties, when he moved to France, he had already written several plays, including the one here, although he knew very little about the work of other "absurdist" writers. The institutions which supported the Franco dictatorship—the army, the police and the Church—appear in a grotesque form in all of Arrabal's plays. His characters, those who are not allied with the forces of repression, are childlike, spontaneous people, alienated from but often crushed by society. Arrabal's plays often present tragic situations with a comic treatment. Theater, for him, should be seen more in its ancient function as a ceremony than as a realistic portrayal of life. Totally opposed to the classical aesthetic of unity of tone and *verisimilitude*, Arrabal is closer to the baroque in his claim that a theatrical performance can and should mix tragedy with farce and sublime poetry with sordid vulgarity.

Picnic on the Battlefield, Arrabal's most often performed play, is clearly centered on the theme of the total absurdity of war. The situation, and particularly the ending, are potentially tragic, but Arrabal's puppet-like characters and their preposterous actions make the effect on the spectator a comic one. Written in 1952, the play was perhaps directly inspired by the Korean war, but its impact extends to the phenomenon of war in general. To appreciate the distance between a literature of the thirties and forties exhorting social commitment and a postwar literature of alienation and absurdity, one need only compare El Cojo, who gives meaning to his life by joining in battle with his comrades, with the two soldiers Zapo and Zépo in the following play. The translation is by Barbara Wright.

FERNANDO ARRABAL

Picnic on the Battlefield

CHARACTERS

ZAPO, *a soldier*
MONSIEUR TÉPAN, *the soldier's father*
MADAME TÉPAN, *the soldier's mother*
ZÉPO, *an enemy soldier*
FIRST CORPSMAN
SECOND CORPSMAN

THE SCENE.   *A battlefield. Barbed wire stretches from one end of the stage to the other, with sandbags piled against it.*

Battle is in full swing. We hear bombs bursting, rifle shots and machine-gun fire.
Alone on stage, hidden flat on his belly among the sandbags, ZAPO *is very frightened.*
The fighting stops. Silence.
From a knitting-bag, ZAPO *takes out a ball of wool, knitting needles, and starts knitting a sweater that is already quite well along. The field telephone beside him suddenly rings.*

ZAPO   Hello . . . hello . . . yes, sir, Captain. . . . Yes, this is the sentry in Section 47. . . . Nothing new, Captain. . . . Excuse me, Captain, when are we going to start fighting again? . . . and what am I supposed to do with the grenades? Should I send them on up front or to the rear? . . . Don't get annoyed, I didn't say that to upset you. . . . And, Captain, I'm really feeling pretty lonesome. Couldn't you send me a companion out here? . . . Even the goat. (*Evidently the Captain gives him a good dressing down.*) Yes sir, Captain, yes sir! (ZAPO *hangs up. We hear him grumbling to himself. Silence.*)

(*Enter* MONSIEUR *and* MADAME TÉPAN, *carrying baskets as though they are off on a picnic. Their son, who is sitting with his back turned, does not see them arriving.*)

M. TÉPAN (*ceremoniously*)   My boy, get up and kiss your mother on the forehead.

(*Taken by surprise,* ZAPO *gets up and, with a great deal of respect, gives his mother a kiss on the forehead. He is about to speak, but his father beats him to it.*)

Now give *me* a kiss.
ZAPO   My dear sweet parents, how did you ever dare come all the way out to a dangerous spot like this? You must leave here right away.
M. TÉPAN   Are you trying to tell your father what war and danger are all about? For me, all this is only a game. How many times do you think I've jumped off the subway while it was still moving?
MME TÉPAN   We thought you were probably bored, so we came to pay you a little visit. After all, this war business must get pretty tiresome.
ZAPO   It all depends.
M. TÉPAN   I know perfectly well what goes on. In the beginning it's all new and exciting. You enjoy the killing and throwing grenades and wearing a helmet; it's quite the thing, but you end up bored as hell. In my day, you'd have really seen something. Wars were a lot livelier, much more colorful. And then best of all, there were horses, lots of horses. It was real pleasure: If the Captain said "Attack!" before you could shake a stick we were all assembled on horseback in our red uniforms. That was something to see. And then we'd go galloping forward, sword in hand, and suddenly find ourselves hard against the enemy. And they'd be at their finest too, with their horses—there were always loads and loads of beautifully round-bottomed horses and their polished boots, and their green uniforms.
MME TÉPAN   No, the enemy uniform wasn't green. It was blue. I remember perfectly well it was blue.
M. TÉPAN   And I say it was green.
MME TÉPAN   When I was little I went out on the balcony any number of times to watch the battle, and I'd say to the little boy next door, "I'll bet you a gumdrop the Blues win." And the Blues were our enemies.
M. TÉPAN   All right, so you win.
MME TÉPAN   I always loved battles. When I was little, I always said that when I grew up I wanted to be a Colonel in the Dragoons. But Mama didn't want me to. You know what a stickler she is.
M. TÉPAN   Your mother's a real nincompoop.
ZAPO   Forgive me, but you've got to leave. You can't go walking into a war when you're not a soldier.
M. TÉPAN   I don't give a damn. We're here to have a picnic with you in the country and spend a nice Sunday.
MME TÉPAN   I even made a lovely meal. Sausage, hard-boiled eggs, I know how much you like them! Ham sandwiches, red wine, some salad and some little cakes.
ZAPO   O.K., we'll do whatever you say. But if the Captain comes along he'll throw a fit. Plus the fact that he doesn't go for the idea of visiting the battlefront. He keeps telling us: "War calls for discipline and grenades, but no visits."
M. TÉPAN   Don't you worry about it, I'll have a few words with your Captain.
ZAPO   And what if we have to start fighting again?
M. TÉPAN   You think that scares me, I've seen worse. Now if it was only cavalry battles! Times have changed, that's something you don't understand. (*A pause.*) We came on motorcycle. Nobody said anything.
ZAPO   They probably thought you were arbitrators.

M. TÉPAN We did have some trouble getting through, though. With all those jeeps and tanks.

MME TÉPAN And the very minute we arrived, you remember that bottleneck because of the cannon?

M. TÉPAN During wartime, you've got to be prepared for anything. Everybody knows that.

MME TÉPAN Well now, we're ready to start eating.

M. TÉPAN Right you are, I could eat a horse. It's the smell of gunpowder that does it.

MME TÉPAN We'll eat sitting down on the blanket.

ZAPO All right to eat with my rifle?

MME TÉPAN Let your rifle alone. It's bad manners to bring your rifle to the table. (A pause.) Why, child, you're filthy as a little pig. How did you manage to get in such a mess? Let's see your hands.

ZAPO (Ashamed, he shows them.) I had to crawl along the ground during maneuvers.

MME TÉPAN How about your ears?

ZAPO I washed them this morning.

MME TÉPAN That should do then. Now how about your teeth? (He shows them.) Very good. Now who's going to give his little boy a great big kiss for brushing his teeth so nicely? (To her husband.) Well, give your son a kiss for brushing his teeth so nicely. (M. TÉPAN gives his son a kiss.) Because, you know, one thing I just won't allow is not washing, and blaming it on the war.

ZAPO Yes, Mama.

(They eat.)

M. TÉPAN Well, my boy, have you been keeping up a good shooting score?

ZAPO When?

M. TÉPAN Why, the last few days.

ZAPO Where?

M. TÉPAN Right here and now. After all, you are fighting a war.

ZAPO No, no great shakes. I haven't kept up a very good score. Practically no bull's-eyes.

M. TÉPAN Well, what have you been scoring best with in your shooting, enemy horses or soldiers?

ZAPO No, no horses. There aren't any horses any more.

M. TÉPAN Well, soldiers then?

ZAPO Could be.

M. TÉPAN Could be? Aren't you sure?

ZAPO It's just that I . . . I fire without taking aim (a

pause) and when I fire I say an *Our Father* for the guy I shot.

M. TÉPAN You've got to show more courage. Like your father.

MME TÉPAN I'm going to put a record on the phonograph. (She puts on a record: a Spanish pasodoble. Sitting on the ground, they all three listen.)

M. TÉPAN Now that's real music. Yes, ma'am. I tell you. *Olé!*

(As the music continues, an enemy soldier, ZÉPO, enters. He is dressed like ZAPO. Only the color of his uniform is different. ZÉPO wears green; ZAPO wears gray. Standing unseen behind the family, his mouth agape, ZÉPO listens to the music. The record comes to an end. ZAPO, getting up, spots ZÉPO. Both raise their hands in the air, while M. and MME TÉPAN look at them startled.)

M. TÉPAN What's going on?

(ZAPO seems about to act, but hesitates. Then, very decisively, he points his rifle at ZÉPO.)

ZAPO Hands up!

(ZÉPO, more terrified than ever, raises his hands still higher. ZAPO doesn't know what to do. All of a sudden, he hurriedly runs toward ZÉPO and taps him gently on the shoulder, saying)

ZAPO You're it! (Pleased as punch, to his father.) There you are! A prisoner!

M. TÉPAN That's fine. Now what are you going to do with him?

ZAPO I don't know. But could be they'll make me a corporal.

M. TÉPAN In the meantime, tie him up.

ZAPO Tie him up? What for?

M. TÉPAN That's what you do with prisoners, you tie 'em up!

ZAPO How?

M. TÉPAN By his hands.

MME TÉPAN Oh yes, you've definitely got to tie his hands. That's the way I've always seen it done.

ZAPO All right. (To the prisoner.) Please put your hands together.

ZÉPO Don't do it too hard.

ZAPO Oh, no.

ZÉPO Ouch! You're hurting me.

M. TÉPAN Come on now, don't mistreat your prisoner.

MME TÉPAN   Is that the way I brought you up? Haven't I told you over and over again that you've got to be considerate of your fellow man?

ZAPO   I didn't do it on purpose. (*To* ZÉPO.) Does it hurt the way it is now?

ZÉPO   No, like this it doesn't hurt.

M. TÉPAN   Speak right up and tell him if it does. Just pretend we're not here.

ZÉPO   This way it's O.K.

M. TÉPAN   Now his feet.

ZAPO   His feet too? How long does this go on?

M. TÉPAN   Didn't they teach you the rules?

ZAPO   Sure.

M. TÉPAN   Well?

ZAPO (*to* ZÉPO, *very politely*)   Would you kindly be good enough to please sit down on the ground?

ZÉPO   All right, but don't hurt me.

MME TÉPAN   See! Now he's taking a dislike to you.

ZAPO   No. No he's not. I'm not hurting you, am I?

ZÉPO   No, this is fine.

ZAPO (*out of nowhere*)   Papa, suppose you took a snapshot with the prisoner down there on the ground and me standing with my foot on his stomach?

M. TÉPAN   Say, yes! That'll look classy.

ZÉPO   Oh, no you don't. Not that!

MME TÉPAN   Let him. Don't be so stubborn.

ZÉPO   No. I said no and mean no.

MME TÉPAN   Just a little old snip of a snapshot. What difference could that possibly make to you? Then we could put it in the dining room right next to the Lifesaving Certificate my husband got thirteen years ago.

ZÉPO   No, you'll never talk me into it.

ZAPO   But why should you refuse?

ZÉPO   I've got a fiancée. And if she ever sees the snapshot, she'll say I don't know how to fight a war.

ZAPO   No, all you have to do is tell her it isn't you at all, it's a panther.

MME TÉPAN   C'mon, say yes.

ZÉPO   All right, but I'm only doing it to please you.

ZAPO   Stretch all the way out.

(ZÉPO *stretches all the way out.* ZAPO *puts one foot on his stomach and grabs his rifle with a military air.*)

MME TÉPAN   Throw your chest out more.

ZAPO   Like this?

MME TÉPAN   Yes, that's it. Don't breathe.

M. TÉPAN   Make like a hero.

ZAPO   How do you mean a hero, like this?

M. TÉPAN   It's a cinch. Make like the butcher when he was telling us what a lady-killer he is.

ZAPO   Like so?

M. TÉPAN   Yes, that's it.

MME TÉPAN   Just be sure your chest is puffed way out, and don't breathe.

ZÉPO   Are you about finished?

M. TÉPAN   Have a little patience. One . . . two . . . three.

ZAPO   I hope I'll come out all right.

MME TÉPAN   Oh yes, you looked very military.

M. TÉPAN   You were fine.

MME TÉPAN   That makes me want to have my picture taken, too.

M. TÉPAN   Now there's a good idea.

ZAPO   All right. I'll take it if you want me to.

MME TÉPAN   Give me your helmet so I'll look like a soldier.

ZÉPO   I don't want any more pictures. Even one was too much.

ZAPO   Don't feel that way. Come right down to it, what difference could it make?

ZÉPO   That's my final say.

M. TÉPAN (*to his wife*)   Don't push him. Prisoners are always very touchy. If we keep it up, he'll get mad and spoil all our fun.

ZAPO   Well now, what are we going to do with him?

MME TÉPAN   We could ask him to eat with us. What do you think?

M. TÉPAN   I don't see any reason why not.

ZAPO (*to* ZÉPO)   All right then, how'd you like to eat with us?

ZÉPO   Uh . . .

M. TÉPAN   We brought along a nice bottle of wine.

ZÉPO   Well, in that case O.K.

MME TÉPAN   Make yourself right at home. Don't be afraid to ask for things.

ZÉPO   Fine.

M. TÉPAN   Well now, how about you, have you been keeping up a good shooting score?

ZÉPO   When?

M. TÉPAN   Why, the last few days.

ZÉPO   Where?

M. TÉPAN   Right here and now. After all, you *are* fighting a war.

ZÉPO   No, no great shakes. I haven't kept up a very good score. Practically no bull's-eyes.

M. TÉPAN   Well, what have you been scoring best with in your shooting, enemy horses or soldiers?

ZÉPO   No, no horses. There aren't any horses any more.

M. TÉPAN   Well, soldiers then?

ZÉPO   Could be.

M. TÉPAN   Could be? Aren't you sure?

ZÉPO   It's just that I . . . I fire without taking aim *(a pause)* and when I fire I say a *Hail Mary* for the guy I shot.

ZAPO   A *Hail Mary?* I'd have thought you'd say an *Our Father.*

M. TÉPAN   Come, my boy, you have to be courageous.

ZÉPO   No. Always a *Hail Mary. (A pause.)* It's shorter.

MME TÉPAN *(to ZÉPO)*   If you like, we can untie you.

ZÉPO   No, leave me this way. It doesn't matter.

M. TÉPAN   You're not going to start putting on airs with us? If you want us to untie you, just say the word.

MME TÉPAN   Please feel free.

ZÉPO   Well, if you really mean it, untie my feet. But it's just to please you people.

M. TÉPAN   Zapo, untie him.

(ZAPO unties him.)

MME TÉPAN   Well now, feel better?

ZÉPO   Sure do. But listen, maybe I'm causing you too much trouble.

M. TÉPAN   Not at all. Make yourself right at home. And if you want us to undo your hands, just say so.

ZÉPO   No, not my hands, too. I don't want to overdo it.

M. TÉPAN   Not at all, my boy, not at all. I tell you, you don't disturb us one bit.

ZÉPO   All right, go ahead and untie my hands then. But just while we eat, huh? I don't want you to think when you give me an inch I'm going to take a mile.

M. TÉPAN   Untie his hands, sonny.

MME TÉPAN   Well, since our honorable prisoner is so nice, we're going to have a lovely day here in the country.

ZÉPO   Don't call me "honorable" prisoner. Just say

"prisoner" plain and simple.

MME TÉPAN   You're sure that won't make you feel bad?

ZÉPO   No, not at all.

M. TÉPAN   Well, you're certainly unpretentious, anyway.

(Sound of airplanes.)

ZAPO   Airplanes. They're going to bomb us for sure.

(ZAPO and ZÉPO dive for the sandbags and hide.)

ZAPO *(to his parents)*   Run for cover! The bombs are going to land right on you.

*(The sound of the planes drowns out everything. Immediately bombs start falling. Shells explode nearby. Deafening racket. ZAPO and ZÉPO are crouching among the sandbags. M. TÉPAN goes on calmly talking to his wife, who answers him with equal calm. Because of the bombardment we cannot hear their conversation.
MME TÉPAN heads for one of the picnic baskets, from which she takes an umbrella. She opens it. The TÉPANS take shelter under the umbrella as though it were raining. Standing there, they shift from one foot to the other, in rhythm, all the while discussing personal matters. The bombardment continues. At last, the airplanes take off. Silence.
M. TÉPAN stretches one arm out from under the umbrella to make certain there is no longer anything coming down from the sky.)*

M. TÉPAN   You can close your umbrella now.

(MME TÉPAN closes it. Together they go over to their son and prod him on the behind a couple of times with the umbrella.)

M. TÉPAN   All right, come on out. The bombing's over.

(ZAPO and ZÉPO come out of their hiding place.)

ZAPO   They didn't get you?

M. TÉPAN   You don't expect anything to happen to your father, do you? *(Proudly.)* Little bombs like that? Don't make me laugh.

(From the left, a pair of Red Cross CORPSMEN enter, carrying a stretcher.)

FIRST CORPSMAN   Any bodies?

ZAPO   No, none here.

FIRST CORPSMAN   You're sure you took a good look?

ZAPO   Absolutely.

FIRST CORPSMAN   And there's not one single body?

ZAPO   Didn't I just say so?

FIRST CORPSMAN   Not even someone wounded?

ZAPO   Not even.

SECOND CORPSMAN   Well, we're really up the creek! (*To* ZAPO, *persuasively.*) Take a good look all around here, see if you don't turn up a stiff someplace.

FIRST CORPSMAN   Don't press the issue. They told you once and for all there aren't any.

SECOND CORPSMAN   What a lousy deal!

ZAPO   I'm really very sorry. I swear I didn't plan it that way.

SECOND CORPSMAN   That's what they all say. That there aren't any corpses, and that they didn't plan it that way.

FIRST CORPSMAN   So let the man alone!

M. TÉPAN (*obligingly*)   If we can help you at all, we'd be delighted to. At your service.

SECOND CORPSMAN   Well, I don't know. If we keep on like this, I really don't know what the Captain's going to say to us.

M. TÉPAN   What seems to be the trouble?

SECOND CORPSMAN   Just that the others are all getting sore wrists carrying out the dead and wounded, while we still haven't come up with anything? And it's not because we haven't been looking.

M. TÉPAN   I see. That really is a bore. (*To* ZAPO.) You're quite sure there are no corpses?

ZAPO   Obviously, Papa.

M. TÉPAN   You looked under the sandbags?

ZAPO   Yes, Papa.

M. TÉPAN (*angrily*)   Why don't you come right out and say you don't want to have any part in helping these good gentlemen?

FIRST CORPSMAN   Don't jump on him like that. Leave him alone. We'll just hope we have better luck in some other trench where maybe everybody'll be dead.

M. TÉPAN   I'd be delighted for you.

MME TÉPAN   So would I. Nothing pleases me more than to see people who take their work seriously.

M. TÉPAN (*indignantly, to anyone within hearing*)   Well, isn't anyone going to do anything for these gentlemen?

ZAPO   If it was up to me, it'd be good as done.

ZÉPO   Same here.

M. TÉPAN   Look here now, isn't one of you at least wounded?

ZAPO (*ashamed*)   No, not me.

M. TÉPAN (*to* ZÉPO)   What about you?

ZÉPO (*ashamed*)   Me either. I never was lucky.

MME TÉPAN (*delighted*)   I just remembered! This morning, while I was peeling onions, I cut my finger. How's that?

M. TÉPAN   Why of course! (*Really in the swing of things.*) They'll put you on the stretcher and carry you right off!

FIRST CORPSMAN   Sorry, it's no good. Women don't count.

M. TÉPAN   Well, that didn't get us anywhere.

FIRST CORPSMAN   It doesn't matter.

SECOND CORPSMAN   Maybe we can get our fill in the other trenches. (*They start to go off.*)

M. TÉPAN   Don't you worry, if we find a corpse we'll hang onto it for you. There's not a chance we'd give it to anybody but you.

SECOND CORPSMAN   Thank you very much, sir.

M. TÉPAN   It's nothing, my boy. It's the very least I could do.

(*The* CORPSMEN *make their goodbyes. All four of the others reply in kind. The* CORPSMEN *exit.*)

MME TÉPAN   That's what's so pleasant about spending Sunday out in the battlefield. You always run into such nice folks. (*A pause.*) Come to think of it, why is it you're enemies?

ZÉPO   I don't know. I'm not too well educated.

MME TÉPAN   I mean is it from birth, or did you become enemies after?

ZÉPO   I don't know. I don't know a thing about it.

M. TÉPAN   Well then, how did you come to go to war?

ZÉPO   One day I was home fixing my mother's iron and a man came by and said to me: "Are you Zépo?" ... "Yes." ... "Good, you've got to go to war." So I asked him, "What war?" And he said to me: "Don't you read the newspapers? You are a hick!" So I told him yes I did, but not all that war stuff ...

ZAPO   That's just what happened to me; exactly what happened to me.

M. TÉPAN   Sure, they came after you, too.

MME TÉPAN   No, it's not the same. You weren't fixing

the iron that day, you were repairing the car.

M. TÉPAN   I was talking about the rest of it. (*To* ZÉPO.) Go on. Then what happened?

ZÉPO   Well, then I told him that I had a fiancée, and if I didn't take her to the movies on Sunday, she wouldn't know what to do with herself. He said that that didn't matter.

ZAPO   Same as me. Exactly the same as me.

ZÉPO   Well, then my father came down and he said I couldn't go to war because I didn't have a horse.

ZAPO   Like my father said.

ZÉPO   The man said they didn't use horses any more, and I asked him if I could take along my fiancée. He said no. Then I asked him could I take along my aunt to make me custard every Thursday. I like custard.

MME TÉPAN   (*realizing that she has forgotten something*)   Oh! The custard!

ZÉPO   Again he said no.

ZAPO   The way he did to me.

ZÉPO   And ever since then, here I am, nearly always all alone in the trench here.

MME TÉPAN   As long as you're so much alike, and both so bored, I think you and your honorable prisoner might play together this afternoon.

ZAPO   Oh no, Mama! I'm too scared. He's an enemy.

M. TÉPAN   Oh come on now, don't be scared.

ZAPO   If you knew what the general told us about the enemy.

MME TÉPAN   What did he tell you?

ZAPO   He said the enemy soldiers are very mean. When they take prisoners, they put pebbles in their socks so it hurts when they walk.

MME TÉPAN   How horrible! What savages!

M. TÉPAN   (*indignantly, to* ZÉPO)   Aren't you ashamed to be part of an army of criminals?

ZÉPO   I didn't do anything. I'm not mad at anybody.

MME TÉPAN   He's trying to put one over on us, acting like a little saint.

M. TÉPAN   We should never have untied him. Probably all we have to do is have our backs turned for him to go putting pebbles in our socks.

ZÉPO   Don't be so mean to me.

M. TÉPAN   How do you expect us to be? I'm shocked. I know just what I'm going to do. I'm going to find the Captain and ask him to let me go into battle.

ZAPO   He won't let you. You're too old.

M. TÉPAN   Well then I'll go buy a horse and a saber and I'll go to war on my own.

ZÉPO   Please, madame, don't treat me like this. Besides, I was just going to tell you, *our* general said the same thing about you people.

MME TÉPAN   How could he dare tell such a lie?

ZAPO   The very same thing, honest?

ZÉPO   Yes, the very same thing.

M. TÉPAN   Maybe it's the same one who talked to both of you.

MME TÉPAN   Well, if it is the same general, the least he could do is use a different speech. Imagine telling everybody the same thing.

M. TÉPAN   (*to* ZÉPO, *changing his tone*)   Can I fill your glass again?

MME TÉPAN   I hope you enjoyed our little lunch.

M. TÉPAN   It was better than Sunday, anyway.

ZÉPO   What happened then?

M. TÉPAN   Well, we went out to the country and laid all our chow out on the blanket. While we had our backs turned, a cow came along and ate the whole lunch, including the napkins.

ZÉPO   What a glutton, that cow!

M. TÉPAN   Yes, but then to get even, we ate the cow.

(*They laugh.*)

ZAPO (*to* ZÉPO)   I bet they weren't hungry after that.

M. TÉPAN   To your health!

(*They all drink.*)

MME TÉPAN (*to* ZÉPO)   Tell me something, what do you do for amusement in the trenches?

ZÉPO   Just to pass the time and keep myself amused, I take odds and ends of rags and make little flowers out of them. See, I get bored a lot.

MME TÉPAN   And what do you do with these rag flowers?

ZÉPO   At first I used to send them to my fiancée, but one day she told me that the cellar and the greenhouse were already filled with them, that she didn't know what to do with them any more, and would I mind sending her something else for a change?

MME TÉPAN   And what did you do?

ZÉPO   I tried learning something else, but I couldn't do

it. So, to pass the time, I just go on making my rag flowers.

MME TÉPAN   And then do you throw them away?

ZÉPO   No, now I've found a way to make use of them: I furnish one flower for each of my buddies who dies. That way, I know that even if I make a whole lot, there'll never be enough.

M. TÉPAN   You found a good way out.

ZÉPO (timidly)   Yes.

ZAPO   Well, you know what I do so's not to get bored is knit.

MME TÉPAN   But tell me, do all the soldiers get bored the way you two do?

ZÉPO   That depends on what they do for relaxation.

ZAPO   Same thing over on our side.

M. TÉPAN   Well then, let's stop the war.

ZÉPO   But how?

M. TÉPAN   Very easy. You tell your buddies that the enemy doesn't want to fight, and you tell the same thing to your comrades. And everybody goes home.

ZAPO   Terrific.

MME TÉPAN   That way you can finish fixing the iron.

ZAPO   How come nobody ever thought of that before?

MME TÉPAN   It takes your father to come up with ideas like that. Don't forget he's a Normal School graduate, and a philatelist, too.

ZÉPO   But what will all the field-marshals and the corporals do?

M. TÉPAN   We'll give 'em guitars and castanets to keep 'em quiet.

ZÉPO   Excellent idea.

M. TÉPAN   See how easy it is? It's all settled.

ZÉPO   We'll wow 'em.

ZAPO   Boy, will my buddies be glad!

MME TÉPAN   What do you say we celebrate and put on that pasodoble we were listening to before?

ZÉPO   Wonderful!

ZAPO   Yes, put on the record, Mama.

(MME TÉPAN puts on the record. She winds the phonograph and waits. Not a sound is heard.)

M. TÉPAN   You can't hear anything.

MME TÉPAN (going to the phonograph)   Oh! . . . I made a boo-boo! Instead of putting on a record, I put on a beret.

(She puts the record on. A lively pasodoble is heard. ZAPO dances with ZÉPO; MME TÉPAN with her husband.
The field telephone rings. None of the group hears it. They go on dancing in a lively manner.
The phone rings again. The dancing continues. Battle breaks out once more with a great din of bombs, rifle fire, and the crackle of machine-guns. Having noticed nothing, the two couples keep on dancing gaily.
A sudden machine-gun blast mows them all down. They fall to the ground, stone dead. One bullet seems to have nicked the phonograph: the music keeps repeating the same strain over and over, like a record with a scratch in it. We hear this repeated strain for the remainder of the play.
From the left, the two CORPSMEN enter, carrying the empty stretcher.)

FAST CURTAIN

QUESTIONS

1. Describe the characters in the play. How developed are they? To what extent are you as reader/spectator involved with them?
2. How are the similarities between Zapo and Zépo brought out? What is the effect of this?
3. How does Mr. Tépan's "idea" come about?
4. Is the comic tone maintained throughout or does the play ever become serious?
5. What is your opinion of the ending?
6. Does "theater of the absurd" seem an apt description of this play? Why or why not?

36 CONTEMPORARY AMERICAN CULTURE

Aspects of the Contemporary Climate

Though we have in a way learned to live with the possibility of nuclear war, the end of life as we know it does not seem to be right around the corner. The arms race, slowed down somewhat by SALT talks, continues, but the two superpowers no longer divide the world between them like a plaything. In spite of everything, we have become more conscious that we share the same small planet in space and need to accommodate ourselves to it.

Sense of Space Technology's rapid leaps in the course of the twentieth century have at least superficially improved our communications with each other. We can "let our fingers do the walking" to Moscow or Cairo; we can be there ourselves within hours. We can watch a parade in Peking via satellite. An unprecedented and still not fully assimilated event was our viewing of actual fighting in the Vietnam war in the comfort of our living rooms. The space program, perhaps especially those first photographs of the planet earth taken from the moon, has also made us more conscious of our small world. Buckminster Fuller, American architect, scientist, humanist, and visionary has expressed this new awareness in his concept of "spaceship earth."

> You are all astronauts [Fuller is addressing his students], for you live aboard a very little spaceship, illogically called "Earth." I say illogically because of the relative biologically photosynthesized and chemically composted "top soil"—i.e., the very complex variety of fine particle aggregates generally identified as the substance *earth*.
>
> Once in a while we launch a little spaceship at a velocity of fifteen thousand miles an hour from our bigger, sixty-thousand miles per hour speeding spherical Spaceship Earth which is only 8,000 miles in diameter. We launch our little ships from our bigger Spaceship Earth at only one quarter the speed of our own sun-orbiting travel. Our 8,000 miles diameter may seem big to the only-one-thousandth-of-a-mile-high *you* or *me* but our spaceship's size is negligible in respect to the macro distances of the sky. The nearest space "gas station" (or energy station) from which we get our energy to regenerate life aboard our spherical spaceship is the Sun which is flying in formation with us at 92 million miles distance. As our Spaceship Earth flies formation in annual circles around the Sun it rotates 365 times per orbit and thereby exposes all of its surface to the Sun's radiation thus permitting optimum impoundment of this prime life supporting energy. Our next nearest energy supply skyship "Star" maintains space flight position with us at 100 thousand times greater distance than the Sun as we all together fly formation through the vast reaches of the ever transforming Galactic Nebula.

Our Planet   Our advances into space can or should make us more aware of the inadequate job that we are doing in maintaining our own spaceship. In the late twentieth century, as opposed to all other historical periods, there are no new frontiers on earth but only an immense clean-up job to be done. Much of the clean-up is quite literal: we are finally beginning to understand the damage done by human beings to the environment that we all share, and we are searching desperately for ways to arrest our pollution machines. We know, too (although we do not seem to be acting effectively on that knowledge), that resources on this spaceship are limited. The problem of energy conservation, a watchword of the 1970s, seems as yet to have no solution in our highly industrialized civilization.

Another aspect of the "clean-up" involves finding a method for equitably distributing the resources that we do have. There is no doubt that all of earth's people could be adequately fed, yet a sizable proportion continues to subsist in starvation conditions, while a much smaller proportion keeps economies going with its affluent, avid consumerism. Unlike the Middle Ages, the age of absolutism, or the age of industrial capitalism, our era has no philosophical justification for such hierarchies. Indeed, nearly everyone at least pays lip service to the ideals of the Enlightenment and to the slogans of the French Revolution: Liberty, Equality, Fraternity (some would add to the latter, Sisterhood). Yet no major society on earth seems to have been able to modernize these ideals and bring them into proper balance. In the United States we are still wrestling with a form of the nineteenth-century liberal dilemma of reconciling claims of individual freedom with those of justice.

The Third World   The shift in balance of power on earth since the Cold War era has forced the affluent, industrial nations of the world to come to terms with the developing nations. The People's Republic of China has for some years now been in active competition with the Soviet Union for command of the international communist movement. Defeat in Vietnam made the United States aware that it could no longer act as policeman of the world. Oil has made the Arab nations one of the most important economic forces on earth. New, independent nations in Africa and developing countries in Asia and Latin America no longer accept unquestioningly the lead of either superpower. These nations are a force to be reckoned with in the United Nations forum, for the Third World easily outnumbers the populations of the United States, the Soviet Union, and their close allies. The "decline of the West" prophesied by Spengler may in some sense be at hand. Certainly, the cultural leadership that the West has exercised at least since the Renaissance may be about ready to change hands.

Liberation Movements As the Third World is liberating itself from the West, we witness, on a smaller scale, movements and demands for various forms of liberation within our own society. The most long-standing and perhaps most representative of these is the black liberation movement. It can be dated back to slave revolts and the Civil War, but it has become an established, if diversified, force primarily in the last half of this century. Black Americans and their supporters of other races have exercised pressure to bring about profound changes in our society. They continue to act both as a voice of conscience and as a group with political power in the continued struggle for equality. More important for our purposes here, Afro-American culture continues to expand and to make important contributions to the world. Throughout the twentieth century and most notably in recent years, Afro-American thinkers, artists, writers, musicians, dancers, and others have been struggling with the question of how much of their cultural identity is African and how much is Western. This tension itself has no doubt contributed to the dynamic, original quality of much black art—jazz is the most obvious example. Because of the importance of this theme and its link with the African cultural root, we will give black America a separate and lengthier treatment in our brief presentation of the contemporary American cultural scene.

Other ethnic groups demanding social and economic justice and a "liberated" cultural identity include Native Americans, Chicanos (or Spanish-speaking Americans), and oriental Americans. All of these can in one way or another identify with the larger context of the Third World's rise to power. Across ethnic and class lines, formerly oppressed groups of people such as gays and women are demanding equal rights and equal access to power. The gay liberation movement, in any organized sense, is recent, but we have seen that a call for the equality of women has been present in Western culture at least since the eighteenth century. After the acquisition of the vote in the 1920s, the women's movement lay dormant for a while, but the late 1960s saw it rise up as a many-faceted social, political, and cultural force. From the 1950s, books like *The Second Sex*, by the French existentialist writer Simone de Beauvoir, and *The Feminine Mystique*, by the American Betty Friedan, furnished a theoretical basis for the new goals that new women were setting for themselves. All women in the movement now demand nothing less than full equality with men, but (as is the case with other liberation groups) their definitions of equality and ideas on the means for achieving it vary. Some want equality and freedom for women within the framework of democratic-capitalistic society. Others claim that only a revolution in the social system can bring about equal justice for women, along with other oppressed groups.

With all this, we should perhaps mention the obvious fact that European or Euro-American males still dominate most of the world's economic, political, scientific, and cultural resources. In contrast to their Victorian grandfathers, however, the most farsighted of these no longer believe in their God-given right to do so. The self-doubts with which Western culture has been plagued since the early twentieth century have deepened, but the anxiety that accompanied the doubt has perhaps lessened. It is now common knowledge that the "center" no longer holds. Rather than a guiding belief or style holding our culture together, what we now have is a coexisting plurality of beliefs and styles.

The Arts Nowhere is this plurality more evident than in the current state of the arts. In the 1960s the slogan "do your own thing" became the only rule for many artists as well as for individual creators of lifestyle. Even earlier, as we will see, the American school of "action painting" had liberated the visual artist from almost every conceivable aesthetic code. It is now extremely difficult to identify a dominant trend in any of the arts. Mixed media, the crossing of traditional disciplinary lines, and the use of new developments in electronics encourage a vast amount of experimentation. Although rapid changes and diverse coexisting styles make evaluation difficult, such pluralism can be taken as reassuring evidence that even in our specialized, technological age, the humanities are alive and healthy.

The Culture of Afro-America: A Return to the African Root

In our brief look at the state of the humanities in contemporary America, we will focus on the cultural

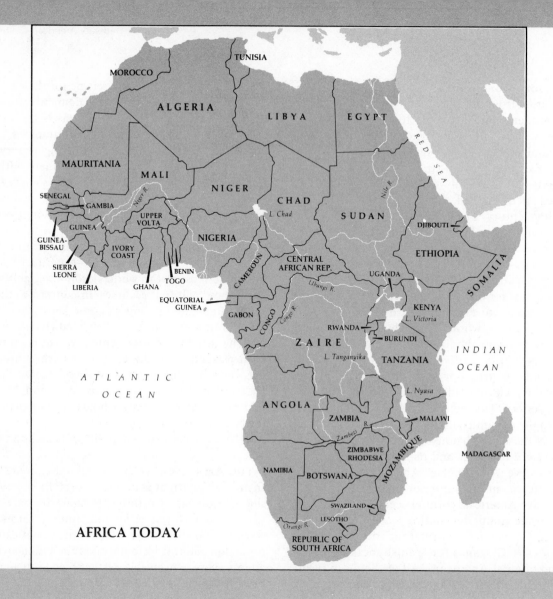

AFRICA TODAY

scene among blacks. This is not to say that the styles in which blacks create are necessarily distinct from the styles in which other Americans create; on the contrary, we can find nearly all of the cultural plurality of Western art represented by black artists. Yet there is no doubt that the black writer, painter, or musician does have unique concerns about expressing the thoughts, feelings, and needs of black people. In doing so, he or she needs to look back toward the place of origin while still working within an essentially Western tradition. In this sense Afro-American culture perhaps best demonstrates the modern amalgam of our three cultural

roots. In order to understand the contemporary manifestations of black consciousness, one must first know something of its beginnings in the early twentieth century.

The "New Negro" Between World War I and the Great Depression, the Afro-American developed a new awareness of himself and of his relationship to America. As the shift in leadership changed from the accommodationist policy of Booker T. Washington to the radical protest of W.E.B. DuBois, the Afro-American became racially conscious and self-assertive, proclaimed himself to be a human being, and demanded respect. This new man or woman could no longer view himself or herself as the shuffling darky or minstrel clown. Instead, the "New Negroes" sought recognition as complete human beings and were, if necessary, prepared to die for it.

Although the radical consciousness of the "New Negro" took its origin in the prewar years, it is generally agreed by most Afro-American historians that World War I was an important factor in the development of the Afro-American's sense of racial consciousness and racial pride. Economic opportunities produced by the war brought blacks to Northern cities in great numbers. The war dislodged blacks not only from the South but also from other countries throughout the world, as blacks from the French and British West Indies and Africa all gathered in Northern cities, New York in particular. But while many blacks developed their racial consciousness in New York and articulated it there, others from Martinique, Haiti, and Senegal delivered radical racial manifestoes from Paris and London. The result was that Pan-Africanism, the quest for black unity throughout the world, became a dominant attitude and ideology.

In addition to making Afro-Americans conscious of the international dimension of their racial struggle, the war stimulated their eagerness to produce racial peace and equality in the United States. If they could march and fight alongside white Americans to make the world "safe for democracy," then the same, they reasoned, could be done for racial harmony in America. It was, in part, the Afro-American's determined quest for racial equality and America's insistence upon racial segregation that produced the "bloody summer" of 1919, when race riots erupted in more than twenty-five cities throughout the nation. It was in reaction to this outburst of violence that Claude McKay wrote his now well-known poem "If We Must Die":

CLAUDE McKAY

If We Must Die

If we must die, let it not be like hogs
Hunted and penned in an inglorious spot,
While round us bark the mad and hungry dogs,
Making their mock at our accursed lot.

If we must die, O let us nobly die,
So that our precious blood may not be shed
In vain; then even the monsters we defy
Shall be constrained to honor us though dead!
O kinsmen! we must meet the common foe!
Though far outnumbered let us show us brave,
And for their thousand blows deal one deathblow!
What though before us lies the open grave?
Like men we'll face the murderous, cowardly pack,
Pressed to the wall, dying but fighting back!

The inability to produce rapid racial equality caused many blacks to become disillusioned with life in America altogether. One such person, Marcus Aurelius Garvey, from the West Indian island of Jamaica, attempted to alleviate this problem by initiating a "back to Africa" movement. Although shunned by the bourgeoisie and laughed at by the intellectuals for his antics, Garvey was an important influence on the image that the Afro-American shaped for himself after World War I. He is reported to have had a following anywhere between half a million and six million. The black masses thus apparently loved him.

The essence of Garvey's "back to Africa" message was that black was superior to white and that the destiny of Afro-Americans lay in Africa, not America. Garvey's efforts, however, were not confined to getting blacks back to Africa, a place Garvey himself was never to see. He also attempted to produce Afro-American pride and self-help through a program of black capitalistic enterprise that anticipated the work and ideas of Elijah Muhammad and his Nation of Islam. The Universal African Legion, Black Cross Nurses, the Universal African Motor Corps, the Black Eagle Flying Corps, and the Black Star Line represent only a few of his efforts. Although these programs and organizations were largely a failure, Garvey was most instrumental in strengthening the Afro-American's sense of racial pride and in encouraging him to think about his heritage, roots, or racial past.

The Harlem Renaissance The Harlem Renaissance, a florescence of creative activity in art, music, poetry, drama, and fiction, was a logical extension of the Afro-American's new racial, cultural, and political thinking. The movement started around 1919, reached its peak in the years 1925 to 1928, and tapered off in

1932. As an artistic, cultural, and social journey of self-discovery, it was an important time for all Afro-Americans. As Alain Locke, one of the movement's cultural mentors, expressed it in 1925:

> The pulse of the Negro world has begun to beat in Harlem. . . . Our greatest rehabilitation may possibly come through such channels, but for the present, more immediate hope rests in the revaluation by white and black alike of the Negro in terms of his artistic endowments and cultural contributions, not only in his folk-art, music especially, which has always found appreciation, but in larger, though humbler and less acknowledged ways. . . . A second crop of the Negro's gifts promises still more largely. He now becomes a conscious contributor and lays aside the status of a beneficiary and ward for that of a collaborator and participant in American civilization. The great social gain in this is the releasing of our talented group from the arid fields of controversy and debate to the productive fields of creative expression.

Locke, who often compared the Afro-American's cultural reawakening to the national movements of folk expression that were taking place in Ireland, Czechoslovakia, Yugoslavia, India, China, Egypt, Russia, Palestine, and Mexico, later edited an anthology called *The New Negro*. Designed specifically to register the inner life of the Afro-American and to document him culturally and socially, *The New Negro* reflected the idealism and optimism of most American progressive reformers, black and white. For Locke, DuBois, James Weldon Johnson, Charles S. Johnson, Carl Van Vechten, and other Harlem Renaissance leaders and participants, the creative expressions of Afro-Americans were viewed as a means toward racial peace and as adequate proof of their ability to participate in American life.

Although such hopes were not immediately realized, the Harlem Renaissance did witness an unprecedented amount of interracial activities and cooperation. By 1920 the "coon" shows had given way to the talented performances of such black actors and musicians as Josephine Baker, Charles Gilpin, Paul Robeson, Frank Wilson, Noble Sissle, and Eubie Blake. In both Europe and America interest in the New Negro was focused around jazz, African art, and the cult of the primitive. The Afro-American was in vogue, as his lifestyle had become a fad. As a result, he was often unrealistically depicted, as in Carl Van Vechten's influential novel *Nigger Heaven*, as a carefree, spontaneous, sexually uninhibited noble savage. On the other hand, Eugene O'Neill's *The Emperor Jones*, Paul Green's *Abraham's Bosom*, and DuBose and Dorothy Heyward's *Porgy* all marked a new step in the white author's attempt to offer a serious treatment of the black man on the American stage.

Black writers themselves explored the injustice of prejudice, the need for interracial peace, and the basic human worth of the black race, treating such themes as passing for white; miscegenation; the tragic mulatto; and the blacks' search for self-assertion. All were explored with a candor that the younger generation of writers felt had been lacking in the literature of the past.

Langston Hughes   Of the many writers who began to flourish in Harlem during the 1930s, Langston Hughes was undoubtedly the most famous. "The Weary Blues," which epitomizes "jazz" or "blues" poetry, displays most of the qualities that dominated Hughes' poetry throughout his career: it is loose in form, songful, and idiomatic in vocabulary.

LANGSTON HUGHES

The Weary Blues

Droning a drowsy syncopated tune,
Rocking back and forth to a mellow croon,
   I heard a Negro play.
Down on Lenox Avenue the other night
By the pale dull pallor of an old gas light
   He did a lazy sway. . . .
   He did a lazy sway. . . .
To the tune o' those Weary Blues.
With his ebony hands on each ivory key
He made that poor piano moan with melody.
   O Blues!
Swaying to and fro on his rickety stool
He played that sad raggy tune like a musical fool.
   Sweet Blues!
Coming from a black man's soul.
   O Blues!
In a deep song voice with a melancholy tone
I heard that Negro sing, that old piano moan—
   "Ain't got nobody in all this world,

Ain't got nobody but ma self.
I's gwine to quit ma frownin'
And put ma troubles on de shelf."
Thump, thump, thump, went his foot on the floor.
He played a few chords then he sang some more—
"I got de Weary Blues
And I can't be satisfied.
Got de Weary Blues
And can't be satisfied—
I ain't happy no mo'
And I wish that I had died."
And far into the night he crooned that tune.
The stars went out and so did the moon.
The singer stopped playing and went to bed.
While the Weary Blues echoed through his head
He slept like a rock or a man that's dead.

The few lines beginning with "Thump" best illustrate Hughes' jazz rhythms. Poetry for Hughes was a distillation, in rhythm, of what he took to be the distinct black medley of life, and few could match his ability to capture, in language, the moods and emotions of the common black.

Two basic impulses sustaining Hughes' drive to write about the common black folk were his genuine love for his race and his attachment to his town, Harlem. Long before the notion of *négritude* was formulated by Césaire and Senghor, Hughes had defined it through his poetry and prose. The Simple stories (with the folk commentator, Jessie B. Simple) and "The Negro Speaks of Rrvers" are proof of this observation. The latter, in particular, makes clear Hughes' recognition of the unity between all blacks and the vital spark of African life and culture.

LANGSTON HUGHES

The Negro Speaks of Rivers

I've known rivers!
I've known rivers ancient as the world and older than
the flow of human blood in human veins.
My soul has grown deep like the rivers.

I bathed in the Euphrates when dawns were young,
I built my hut near the Congo and it lulled me to sleep,

I looked upon the Nile and raised the pyramids above
it.

I heard the singing of the Mississippi when Abe
Lincoln went down to New Orleans,
And I've seen its muddy bosom turn all golden in the
sunset.

I've known rivers:
Ancient, dusky rivers,
My soul has grown deep like the rivers.

Assessments of the accomplishments of the Harlem Renaissance differ markedly. Most historians and literary critics agree, however, that its major significance lies in its contribution to the Afro-American's consciousness of his blackness and his black heritage, his search for black values, and his quest for a new beginning in America.

The prose selection that follows, from the novel *Cain* by Jean Toomer, demonstrates an adaptation of modernist techniques to evoke the black experience. The poems by Countee Cullen and Sterling A. Brown represent very different styles, one literary, one in folk idiom. Sterling A. Brown is, in fact, a highly educated man (an English professor) who, like Langston Hughes, listens carefully to black dialects and uses them in his poetry.

JEAN TOOMER

Karintha

Her skin is like dusk on the eastern horizon,
O cant you see it, O cant you see it,
Her skin is like dusk on the eastern horizon
. . . When the sun goes down.

Men always wanted her, this Karintha, even as a child, Karintha carrying beauty, perfect as dusk when the sun goes down. Old men rode her hobby-horse upon their knees. Young men danced with her at frolics when they should have been dancing with their grown-up girls. God grant us youth, secretly prayed the old men. The young fellows counted the time to pass before she would be old enough to mate with them. This interest of the male, who wishes to ripen a growing thing too soon, could mean no good to her.

Karintha, at twelve, was a wild flash that told the other folks just what it was to live. At sunset, where there was no wind, and the pine-smoke from over by the sawmill hugged the earth, and you couldnt see more than a few feet in front, her sudden darting past you was a bit of vivid color, like a black bird that flashes in light. With the other children one could hear, some distance off, their feet flopping in the two-inch dust. Karintha's running was a whir. It had the sound of the red dust that sometimes makes a spiral in the road. At dusk, during the hush just after the saw-mill had closed down, and before any of the women had started their supper-getting-ready songs, her voice, high-pitched, shrill, would put one's ears to itching. But no one ever thought to make her stop because of it. She stoned the cows, and beat her dog, and fought the other children. . . . Even the preacher, who caught her at mis-chief, told himself that she was as innocently lovely as a November cotton flower. Already, rumors were out about her. Homes in Georgia are most often built on the two-room plan. In one, you cook and eat, in the other you sleep, and there love goes on. Karintha had seen or heard, perhaps she had felt her parents loving. One could but imitate one's parents, for to follow them was the way of God. She played "home" with a small boy who was not afraid to do her bidding. That started the whole thing. Old men could no longer ride her hobby-horse upon their knees. But young men counted faster.

> Her skin is like dusk,
> O cant you see it,
> Her skin is like dusk,
> When the sun goes down.

Karintha is a woman. She who carries beauty, perfect as dusk when the sun goes down. She has been married many times. Old men remind her that a few years back they rode her hobby-horse upon their knees. Karintha smiles, and indulges them when she is in the mood for it. She has contempt for them. Karintha is a woman. Young men run stills to make her money. Young men go to the big cities and run on the road. Young men go away to college. They all want to bring her money. These are the young men who thought that all they had to do was to count time. But Karintha is a woman, and she has had a child. A child fell out of her womb onto a bed of pine-needles in the forest. Pine-needles are smooth and sweet. They are elastic to the feet of rabbits . . . A sawmill was nearby. Its pyramidal sawdust pile smouldered. It is a year before one completely burns. Meanwhile, the smoke curls up and hangs in odd wraiths about the trees, curls up, and spreads itself out over the valley . . . Weeks after Karintha returned home the smoke was so heavy you tasted it in water. Some one made a song:

> Smoke is on the hills. Rise up.
> Smoke is on the hills, O rise
> And take my soul to Jesus.

Karintha is a woman. Men do not know that the soul of her was a growing thing ripened too soon. They will bring their money; they will die not having found it out . . . Karintha at twenty, carrying beauty, perfect as dusk when the sun goes down. Karintha . . .

> Her skin is like dusk on the eastern horizon,
> O cant you see it, O cant you see it,
> Her skin is like dusk on the eastern horizon
> . . . When the sun goes down.

> Goes down . . .

QUESTIONS

1. Through what specific linguistic effects does Too-mer create this portrait of a black woman?
2. Compare the techniques used in this word portrait with those in the texts by Stein and Joyce.

STERLING A. BROWN

Long Gone

I laks yo' kin' of lovin',
    Ain't never caught you wrong,
But it jes' ain' nachal
    Fo' to stay here long;

It jes' ain' nachal
    Fo' a railroad man,
With a itch fo' travelin'
    He caint understan'. . . .

I looks at de rails,
   An' I looks at de ties,
An' I hears an ole freight
   Puffin' up de rise,

An' at nights on my pallet,
   When all is still,
I listens fo' de empties
   Bumpin' up de hill;

When I oughta be quiet,
   I is got a itch
Fo' to hear de whistle blow
   Fo' de crossin' or de switch,

An' I knows de time's a-nearin'
   When I got to ride,
Though it's homelike and happy
   At yo' side.

You is done all you could do
   To make me stay;
'Taint no fault of yours I've leavin'—
   I'se jes dataway.

I is got to see some people
   I ain't never seen,
Gotta highball thu some country
   Whah I never been.

I don't know which way I'm travelin'—
   Far or near,
All I knows fo' certain is
   I cain't stay here.

Ain't no call at all, sweet woman,
   Fo' to carry on—
Jes' my name and jes' my habit
   To be Long Gone. . . .

QUESTIONS

1. Do you find this imitation of a dialect an effective vehicle for poetry? Why or why not?
2. Does Brown succeed in creating a character in this poem? How would you describe him?

COUNTEE CULLEN

Yet Do I Marvel

I doubt not God is good, well-meaning, kind,
And did He stoop to quibble could tell why
The little buried mole continues blind,
Why flesh that mirrors Him must some day die,
Make plain the reason tortured Tantalus[1]
Is baited by the fickle fruit, declare
If merely brute caprice dooms Sisyphus
To struggle up a never-ending stair.
Inscrutable His ways are, and immune
To catechism by a mind too strewn
With petty cares to slightly understand
What awful brain compels His awful hand.
Yet do I marvel at this curious thing:
To make a poet black, and bid him sing!

QUESTIONS

1. What is the form of this poem?
2. How would you characterize the language and tone?
3. In what sense, if any, can this be called black poetry?

Protest Fiction and the Blues Tradition: James Baldwin

The Great Depression effectively ended the Harlem Renaissance and brought serious economic hardships to the entire nation. Breadlines, starving sharecroppers, and dispossessed families constituted only a few of the resulting disasters. Such sights were viewed by many as part of a larger picture of capitalism's exploitation of the masses and thus became the rallying point for black nationalist street orators and Marxist activists. As we noted in the section "Literature and Social Commitment" in Chapter 34, it also set the stage for an Ameri-

[1] Tantalus and Sisyphus are two figures from classical mythology. Both were condemned to an afterlife of punishment. Tantalus suffered eternal thirst but could *almost* reach a bunch of grapes (hence our word *tantalize*). Sisyphus was condemned to push a heavy rock up a hill, then to watch it roll back down and have to start over again.

can school of protest and "proletarian" fiction. One of the major works of this school was Richard Wright's *Native Son*.

Wright's long novel was clearly propagandistic. It argued for a humane, socialist society in which such crimes as the murder that his central character, Bigger Thomas, committed could not conceivably take place. Wright does everything within his artistic power to convince his reader that Bigger's actions, values, attitudes, and fate are all determined by his place in American society. His immediate environment is depicted as being bleak and empty, while the elegant white world around the corner is cruelly indifferent to his needs. Bigger's situation has produced in him that psychological disposition so prominent in Afro-American folk music and, as we have seen, so acutely depicted in the poetry of Langston Hughes, known as the blues. As Ralph Ellison fittingly defines it, the blues is an autobiographical chronicle of personal suffering and catastrophe expressed lyrically. Like Wright's earlier *Black Boy*, *Native Son* is filled with blues-tempered echoes of fights, deaths, disappointments, and other physical and spiritual pains that lead to protest, rebellion, and/or resignation.

The elements of protest, rebellion, and resignation constitute the essence of the blues motif in Ralph Ellison's masterpiece, *The Invisible Man*. As the novel opens, the reader discovers that the hero, Invisible Man, has been isolated for some time in his secret underground room playing a Louis Armstrong record, the refrain of which runs: "What did I do/To be so black/And blue?" It is a refrain that implicitly follows each major episode of the novel as the hero is constantly dehumanized in his efforts to play out the roles that whites have assigned him. And, just as the last verse of a blues is frequently the same as the first, *The Invisible Man* ends as it had begun, with the hero once again in his underground room.

Another author who combines protest and music is James Baldwin. Like Ellison, Baldwin maintains that music contains the most comprehensive rendering of the complexities of the Afro-American experience. Yet for Baldwin, music clearly represents something far more than the presence of human pain, suffering, and disappointment. That extra meaning constitutes the central theme of Baldwin's short story "Sonny's Blues."

JAMES BALDWIN

Sonny's Blues

I read about it in the paper, in the subway, on my way to work. I read it, and I couldn't believe it, and I read it again. Then perhaps I just stared at it, at the newsprint spelling out his name, spelling out the story. I stared at it in the swinging lights of the subway car, and in the faces and bodies of the people, and in my own face, trapped in the darkness which roared outside.

It was not to be believed and I kept telling myself that as I walked from the subway station to the high school. And at the same time I couldn't doubt it. I was scared, scared for Sonny. He became real to me again. A great block of ice got settled in my belly and kept melting there slowly all day long, while I taught my classes algebra. It was a special kind of ice. It kept melting, sending trickles of ice water all up and down my veins, but it never got less. Sometimes it hardened and seemed to expand until I felt my guts were going to come spilling out or that I was going to choke or scream. This would always be at a moment when I was remembering some specific thing Sonny had once said or done.

When he was about as old as the boys in my classes his face had been bright and open, there was a lot of copper in it; and he'd had wonderfully direct brown eyes, and great gentleness and privacy. I wondered what he looked like now. He had been picked up, the evening before, in a raid on an apartment downtown, for peddling and using heroin.

I couldn't believe it: but what I mean by that is that I couldn't find any room for it anywhere inside me. I had kept it outside me for a long time. I hadn't wanted to know. I had had suspicions, but I didn't name them, I kept putting them away. I told myself that Sonny was wild, but he wasn't crazy. And he'd always been a good boy, he hadn't ever turned hard or evil or disrespectful, the way kids can, so quick, so quick, especially in Harlem. I didn't want to believe that I'd ever see my brother going down, coming to nothing, all that light in his face gone out, in the condition I'd already seen so many others. Yet it had happened and here I was, talking about algebra to a lot of boys who might, every one of them for all I knew, be popping off needles every time they went to the head. Maybe it did more for them than algebra could.

I was sure that the first time Sonny had ever had horse, he couldn't have been much older than these boys were now. These boys, now, were living as we'd been living then, they were growing up with a rush and their heads bumped abruptly against the low ceiling of their actual possibilities. They were filled with rage. All they really knew were two darknesses, the darkness of their lives, which was now closing in on them, and the darkness of the movies, which had blinded them to that other darkness, and in which they now, vindictively, dreamed, at once more together than they were at any other time, and more alone.

When the last bell rang, the last class ended, I let out my breath. It seemed I'd been holding it for all that time. My clothes were wet—I may have looked as though I'd been sitting in a steam bath, all dressed up, all afternoon. I sat alone in the classroom a long time. I listened to the boys outside, downstairs, shouting and cursing and laughing. Their laughter struck me for perhaps the first time. It was not the joyous laughter which—God knows why—one associates with children. It was mocking and insular, its intent was to denigrate. It was disenchanted, and in this, also, lay the authority of their curses. Perhaps I was listening to them because I was thinking about my brother and in them I heard my brother. And myself.

One boy was whistling a tune, at once very complicated and very simple, it seemed to be pouring out of him as though he were a bird, and it sounded very cool and moving through all that harsh, bright air, only just holding its own through all those other sounds.

I stood up and walked over to the window and looked down into the courtyard. It was the beginning of the spring and the sap was rising in the boys. A teacher passed through them every now and again, quickly, as though he or she couldn't wait to get out of that courtyard, to get those boys out of their sight and off their minds. I started collecting my stuff. I thought I'd better get home and talk to Isabel.

The courtyard was almost deserted by the time I got downstairs. I saw this boy standing in the shadow of a doorway, looking just like Sonny. I almost called his name. Then I saw that it wasn't Sonny, but somebody we used to know, a boy from around our block. He'd been Sonny's friend. He'd never been mine, having been too young for me, and, anyway, I'd never liked him. And now, even though he was a grown-up man, he still hung around that block, still spent hours on the street corner, was always high and raggy. I used to run into him from time to time and he'd often work around to asking me for a quarter or fifty cents. He always had some real good excuse, too, and I always gave it to him, I don't know why.

But now, abruptly, I hated him. I couldn't stand the way he looked at me, partly like a dog, partly like a cunning child. I wanted to ask him what the hell he was doing in the school courtyard.

He sort of shuffled over to me, and he said, "I see you got the papers. So you already know about it."

"You mean about Sonny? Yes, I already know about it. How come they didn't get you?"

He grinned. It made him repulsive and it also brought to mind what he'd looked like as a kid. "I wasn't there. I stay away from them people."

"Good for you." I offered him a cigarette and I watched him through the smoke. "You come all the way down here just to tell me about Sonny?"

"That's right." He was sort of shaking his head and his eyes looked strange, as though they were about to cross. The bright sun deadened his damp dark brown skin and it made his eyes look yellow and showed up the dirt in his conked hair. He smelled funky. I moved a little away from him and I said, "Well, thanks. But I already know about it and I got to get home."

"I'll walk you a little ways," he said. We started walking. There were a couple of kids still loitering in the courtyard and one of them said good night to me and looked strangely at the boy beside me.

"What're you going to do?" he asked me. "I mean, about Sonny?"

"Look. I haven't seen Sonny for over a year, I'm not sure I'm going to do anything. Anyway, what the hell *can* I do?"

"That's right," he said quickly, "ain't nothing you can do. Can't much help old Sonny no more, I guess."

It was what I was thinking and so it seemed to me he had no right to say it.

"I'm surprised at Sonny, though," he went on—he had a funny way of talking, he looked straight ahead as though he were talking to himself—"I thought Sonny was a smart boy, I thought he was too smart to get hung."

"I guess he thought so too," I said sharply, "and that's how he got hung. And how about you? You're pretty goddamn smart, I bet."

Then he looked directly at me, just for a minute. "I ain't smart," he said. "If I was smart, I'd have reached for a pistol a long time ago."

"Look. Don't tell *me* your sad story, if it was up to me, I'd give you one." Then I felt guilty—guilty, probably, for never having supposed that the poor bastard *had* a story of his own, much less a sad one, and I asked, quickly, "What's going to happen to him now?"

He didn't answer this. He was off by himself some place. "Funny thing," he said, and from his tone we might have been discussing the quickest way to get to Brooklyn, "when I saw the papers this morning, the first thing I asked myself was if I had anything to do with it. I felt sort of responsible."

I began to listen more carefully. The subway station was on the corner, just before us, and I stopped. He stopped, too. We were in front of a bar and he ducked slightly, peering in, but whoever he was looking for didn't seem to be there. The juke box was blasting away with something black and bouncy and I half watched the barmaid as she danced her way from the juke box to her place behind the bar. And I watched her face as she laughingly responded to something someone said to her, still keeping time to the music. When she smiled one saw the little girl, one sensed the doomed, still-struggling woman beneath the battered face of the semi-whore.

"I never *give* Sonny nothing," the boy said finally, "but a long time ago I come to school high and Sonny asked me how it felt." He paused, I couldn't bear to watch him, I watched the barmaid, and I listened to the music which seemed to be causing the pavement to shake. "I told him it felt great." The music stopped, the barmaid paused and watched the juke box until the music began again. "It did."

All this was carrying me some place I didn't want to go. I certainly didn't want to know how it felt. It filled everything, the people, the houses, the music, the dark, quicksilver barmaid, with menace; and this menace was their reality.

"What's going to happen to him now?" I asked again.

"They'll send him away some place and they'll try to cure him." He shook his head. "Maybe he'll even think he's kicked the habit. Then they'll let him loose"—he gestured, throwing his cigarette into the gutter. "That's all."

"What do you mean, that's *all?*"

But I knew what he meant.

"I *mean*, that's *all*." He turned his head and looked at me, pulling down the corners of his mouth. "Don't you know what I mean?" he asked softly.

"How the hell *would* I know what you mean?" I almost whispered it, I don't know why.

"That's right," he said to the air, "how would *he* know what I mean?" He turned toward me again, patient and calm, and yet I somehow felt him shaking, shaking as though he were going to fall apart. I felt that ice in my guts again, the dread I'd felt all afternoon; and again I watched the barmaid, moving about the bar, washing glasses, and singing. "Listen. They'll let him out and then it'll just start all over again. That's what I mean."

"You mean—they'll let him out. And then he'll just start working his way back in again. You mean he'll never kick the habit. Is that what you mean?"

"That's right," he said, cheerfully. "*You* see what I mean."

"Tell me," I said at last, "why does he want to die? He must want to die, he's killing himself, why does he want to die?"

He looked at me in surprise. He licked his lips. "He don't want to die. He wants to live. Don't nobody want to die, ever."

Then I wanted to ask him—too many things. He could not have answered, or if he had, I could not have borne the answers. I started walking. "Well, I guess it's none of my business."

"It's going to be rough on old Sonny," he said. We reached the subway station. "This is your station?" he asked. I nodded. I took one step down. "Damn!" he said, suddenly. I looked up at him. He grinned again. "Damn if I didn't leave all my money home. You ain't got a dollar on you, have you? Just for a couple of days, is all."

All at once something inside gave and threatened to come pouring out of me. I didn't hate him any more. I felt that in another moment I'd start crying like a child.

"Sure," I said. "Don't sweat." I looked in my wallet and didn't have a dollar, I only had a five. "Here," I said. "That hold you?"

He didn't look at it—he didn't want to look at it. A terrible, closed look came over his face, as though he were keeping the number on the bill a secret from him and me. "Thanks," he said, and now he was dying to see me go. "Don't worry about Sonny. Maybe I'll write him or something."

"Sure," I said. "You do that. So long."

"Be seeing you," he said. I went on down the steps.

And I didn't write Sonny or send him anything for a long time. When I finally did, it was just after my little girl died, he wrote me back a letter which made me feel like a bastard.

Here's what he said:

DEAR BROTHER,

You don't know how much I needed to hear from you. I wanted to write you many a time but I dug how much I must have hurt you and so I didn't write. But now I feel like a man who's been trying to climb up out of some deep, real deep and funky hole and just saw the sun up there, outside. I got to get outside.

I can't tell you much about how I got here. I mean I don't know how to tell you. I guess I was afraid of something or I was trying to escape from something and you know I have never been very strong in the head (smile). I'm glad Mama and Daddy are dead and can't see what's happened to their son and I swear if I'd known what I was doing I would never have hurt you so, you and a lot of other fine people who were nice to me and who believed in me.

I don't want you to think it had anything to do with me being a musician. It's more than that. Or maybe less than that. I can't get anything straight in my head down here and I try not to think about what's going to happen to me when I get outside again. Sometime I think I'm going to flip and *never* get outside and sometime I think I'll come straight back. I tell you one thing, though, I'd rather blow my brains out than go through this again. But that's what they all say, so they tell me. If I tell you when I'm coming to New York and if you could meet me, I sure would appreciate it. Give my love to Isabel and the kids and I was sorry to hear about little Gracie. I wish I could be like Mama and say the Lord's will be done, but I don't know it seems to me that trouble is the one thing that never does

get stopped and I don't know what good it does to blame it on the Lord. But maybe it does some good if you believe it.

Your brother,
SONNY

Then I kept in constant touch with him and I sent him whatever I could and I went to meet him when he came back to New York. When I saw him many things I thought I had forgotten came flooding back to me. This was because I had begun, finally, to wonder about Sonny, about the life that Sonny lived inside. This life, whatever it was, had made him older and thinner and it had deepened the distant stillness in which he had always moved. He looked very unlike my baby brother. Yet, when he smiled, when we shook hands, the baby brother I'd never known looked out from the depths of his private life, like an animal waiting to be coaxed into the light.

"How you been keeping?" he asked me.

"All right. And you?"

"Just fine." He was smiling all over his face. "It's good to see you again."

"It's good to see you."

The seven years' difference in our ages lay between us like a chasm: I wondered if these years would ever operate between us as a bridge. I was remembering, and it made it hard to catch my breath, that I had been there when he was born; and I had heard the first words he had ever spoken. When he started to walk, he walked from our mother straight to me. I caught him just before he fell when he took the first steps he ever took in this world.

"How's Isabel?"

"Just fine. She's dying to see you."

"And the boys?"

"They're fine, too. They're anxious to see their uncle."

"Oh, come on. You know they don't remember me."

"Are you kidding? Of course they remember you."

He grinned again. We got into a taxi. We had a lot to say to each other, far too much to know how to begin.

As the taxi began to move, I asked, "You still want to go to India?"

He laughed. "You still remember that. Hell, no. This place is Indian enough for me."

"It used to belong to them," I said.

And he laughed again. "They damn sure knew what they were doing when they got rid of it."

Years ago, when he was around fourteen, he'd been all hipped on the idea of going to India. He read books about people sitting on rocks, naked, in all kinds of weather, but mostly bad, naturally, and walking barefoot through hot coals and arriving at wisdom. I used to say that it sounded to me as though they were getting away from wisdom as fast as they could. I think he sort of looked down on me for that.

"Do you mind," he asked, "if we have the driver drive alongside the park? On the west side—I haven't seen the city in so long."

"Of course not," I said. I was afraid that I might sound as though I were humoring him, but I hoped he wouldn't take it that way.

So we drove along, between the green of the park and the stony, lifeless elegance of hotels and apartment buildings, toward the vivid, killing streets of our childhood. These streets hadn't changed, though housing projects jutted up out of them now like rocks in the middle of a boiling sea. Most of the houses in which we had grown up had vanished, as had the stores from which we had stolen, the basements in which we had first tried sex, the rooftops from which we had hurled tin cans and bricks. But houses exactly like the houses of our past yet dominated the landscape, boys exactly like the boys we once had been found themselves smothering in these houses, came down into the streets for light and air and found themselves encircled by disaster. Some escaped the trap, most didn't. Those who got out always left something of themselves behind, as some animals amputate a leg and leave it in the trap. It might be said, perhaps, that I had escaped, after all, I was a school teacher; or that Sonny had, he hadn't lived in Harlem for years. Yet, as the cab moved uptown through streets which seemed, with a rush, to darken with dark people, and as I covertly studied Sonny's face, it came to me that what we both were seeking through our separate cab windows was that part of ourselves which had been left behind. It's always at the hour of trouble and confrontation that the missing member aches.

We hit 110th Street and started rolling up Lenox Avenue. And I'd known this avenue all my life, but it seemed to me again, as it had seemed on the day I'd first heard about Sonny's trouble, filled with a hidden menace which was its very breath of life.

"We almost there," said Sonny.

"Almost." We were both too nervous to say anything more.

We live in a housing project. It hasn't been up long. A few days after it was up it seemed uninhabitably new, now, of course, it's already run-down. It looks like a parody of the good, clean, faceless life—God knows the people who live in it do their best to make it a parody. The beat-looking grass lying around isn't enough to make their lives green, the hedges will never hold out the streets, and they know it. The big windows fool no one, they aren't big enough to make space out of no space. They don't bother with the windows, they watch the TV screen instead. The playground is most popular with the children who don't play at jacks, or skip rope, or roller skate, or swing, and they can be found in it after dark. We moved in partly because it's not too far from where I teach, and partly for the kids; but it's really just like the houses in which Sonny and I grew up. The same things happen, they'll have the same things to remember. The moment Sonny and I started into the house I had the feeling that I was simply bringing him back into the danger he had almost died trying to escape.

Sonny has never been talkative. So I don't know why I was sure he'd be dying to talk to me when supper was over the first night. Everything went fine, the oldest boy remembered him, and the youngest boy liked him, and Sonny had remembered to bring something for each of them; and Isabel, who is really much nicer than I am, more open and giving, had gone to a lot of trouble about dinner and was genuinely glad to see him. And she's always been able to tease Sonny in a way that I haven't. It was nice to see her face so vivid again and to hear her laugh and watch her make Sonny laugh. She wasn't, or, anyway, she didn't seem to be, at all uneasy or embarrassed. She chatted as though there were no subject which had to be avoided and she got Sonny past his first, faint stiffness. And thank God she was there, for I was filled with that icy dread again. Everything I did seemed awkward to me, and everything I said sounded freighted with hidden meaning. I was trying to remember everything I'd heard about dope addiction and I couldn't help watching Sonny for signs. I wasn't doing it out of malice. I was trying to find out something about my brother. I was dying to hear him tell me he was safe.

"Safe!" my father grunted, whenever Mama suggested trying to move to a neighborhood which might be safer for children. "Safe, hell! Ain't no place safe for kids, nor nobody."

He always went on like this, but he wasn't, ever, really as bad as he sounded, not even on weekends, when he got drunk. As a matter of fact, he was always on the lookout for "something a little better," but he died before he found it. He died suddenly, during a drunken weekend in the middle of the war, when Sonny was fifteen. He and Sonny hadn't ever got on too well. And this was partly because Sonny was the apple of his father's eye. It was because he loved Sonny so much and was frightened for him, that he was always fighting with him. It doesn't do any good to fight with Sonny. Sonny just moves back, inside himself, where he can't be reached. But the principal reason that they never hit it off is that they were so much alike. Daddy was big and rough and loud-talking, just the opposite of Sonny, but they both had—that same privacy.

Mama tried to tell me something about this, just after Daddy died. I was home on leave from the army.

This was the last time I ever saw my mother alive. Just the same, this picture gets all mixed up in my mind with pictures I had of her when she was younger. The way I always see her is the way she used to be on a Sunday afternoon, say, when the old folks were talking after the big Sunday dinner. I always see her wearing pale blue. She'd be sitting on the sofa. And my father would be sitting in the easy chair, not far from her. And the living room would be full of church folks and relatives. There they sit, in chairs all around the living room, and the night is creeping up outside, but nobody knows it yet. You can see the darkness growing against the window-panes and you hear the street noises every now and again, or maybe the jangling beat of a tambourine from one of the churches close by, but it's real quiet in the room. For a moment nobody's talking, but every face looks darkening, like the sky outside. And my mother rocks a little from the waist, and my father's eyes are closed. Everyone is looking at something a child can't see. For a minute they've forgotten the children. Maybe a kid is lying on the rug half asleep. Maybe somebody's got a kid on his lap and is absent-mindedly stroking the kid's head. Maybe there's a kid, quiet and big-eyed, curled up in a big chair in the corner. The silence, the darkness coming, and the darkness in the faces frightens the child obscurely. He hopes that the hand which strokes his forehead will never stop—will never die. He hopes that there will never come a time when the old folks won't be sitting around the living room, talking about where they've come from, and what they've seen, and what's happened to them and their kinfolk.

But something deep and watchful in the child knows that this is bound to end, is already ending. In a moment someone will get up and turn on the light. Then the old folks will remember the children and they won't talk any more that day. And when light fills the room, the child is filled with darkness. He knows that every time this happens he's moved just a little closer to that darkness outside. The darkness outside is what the old folks have been talking about. It's what they've come from. It's what they endure. The child knows that they won't talk any more because if he knows too much about what's happened to *them*, he'll know too much too soon, about what's going to happen to *him*.

The last time I talked to my mother, I remember I was restless. I wanted to get out and see Isabel. We weren't married then and we had a lot to straighten out between us.

There Mama sat, in black, by the window. She was humming an old church song, *Lord, you brought me from a long ways off.* Sonny was out somewhere. Mama kept watching the streets.

"I don't know," she said, "if I'll ever see you again, after you go off from here. But I hope you'll remember the things I tried to teach you."

"Don't talk like that," I said, and smiled. "You'll be here a long time yet."

She smiled, too, but she said nothing. She was quiet for a long time. And I said, "Mama, don't you worry about nothing. I'll be writing all the time, and you be getting the checks. . . ."

"I want to talk to you about your brother," she said, suddenly. "If anything happens to me he ain't going to have nobody to look out for him."

"Mama," I said, "ain't nothing going to happen to

you *or* Sonny. Sonny's all right. He's a good boy and he's got good sense.''

''It ain't a question of his being a good boy,'' Mama said, ''nor of his having good sense. It ain't only the bad ones, nor yet the dumb ones that gets sucked under.'' She stopped, looking at me. ''Your Daddy once had a brother,'' she said, and she smiled in a way that made me feel she was in pain. ''You didn't never know that, did you?''

''No,'' I said, ''I never knew that,'' and I watched her face.

''Oh, yes,'' she said, ''your Daddy had a brother.'' She looked out of the window again. ''I know you never saw your Daddy cry. But *I* did—many a time, through all these years.''

I asked her, ''What happened to his brother? How come nobody's ever talked about him?''

This was the first time I ever saw my mother look old.

''His brother got killed,'' she said, ''when he was just a little younger than you are now. I knew him. He was a fine boy. He was maybe a little full of the devil, but he didn't mean nobody no harm.''

Then she stopped and the room was silent, exactly as it had sometimes been on those Sunday afternoons. Mama kept looking out into the streets.

''He used to have a job in the mill,'' she said, ''and, like all young folks, he just liked to perform on Saturday nights. Saturday nights, him and your father would drift around to different places, go to dances and things like that, or just sit around with people they knew, and your father's brother would sing, he had a fine voice, and play along with himself on his guitar. Well, this particular Saturday night, him and your father was coming home from some place, and they were both a little drunk and there was a moon that night, it was bright like day. Your father's brother was feeling kind of good, and he was whistling to himself, and he had his guitar slung over his shoulder. They was coming down a hill and beneath them was a road that turned off from the highway. Well, your father's brother, being always kind of frisky, decided to run down this hill, and he did, with that guitar banging and clanging behind him, and he ran across the road, and he was making water behind a tree. And your father was sort of amused at him and he was still coming down the hill,

kind of slow. Then he heard a car motor and that same minute his brother stepped from behind the tree, into the road, in the moonlight. And he started to cross the road. And your father started to run down the hill, he says he don't know why. This car was full of white men. They was all drunk, and when they seen your father's brother they let out a great whoop and holler and they aimed the car straight at him. They was having fun, they just wanted to scare him, the way they do sometimes, you know. But they was drunk. And I guess the boy, being drunk, too, and scared, kind of lost his head. By the time he jumped it was too late. Your father says he heard his brother scream when the car rolled over him, and he heard the wood of that guitar when it give, and he heard them strings go flying, and he heard them white men shouting, and the car kept on a-going and it ain't stopped till this day. And, time your father got down the hill, his brother weren't nothing but blood and pulp.''

Tears were gleaming on my mother's face. There wasn't anything I could say.

''He never mentioned it,'' she said, ''because I never let him mention it before you children. Your Daddy was like a crazy man that night and for many a night thereafter. He says he never in his life seen anything as dark as that road after the lights of that car had gone away. Weren't nothing, weren't nobody on that road, just your Daddy and his brother and that busted guitar. Oh, yes. Your Daddy never did really get right again. Till the day he died he weren't sure but that every white man he saw was the man that killed his brother.''

She stopped and took out her handkerchief and dried her eyes and looked at me.

''I ain't telling you all this,'' she said, ''to make you scared or bitter or to make you hate nobody. I'm telling you this because you got a brother. And the world ain't changed.''

I guess I didn't want to believe this. I guess she saw this in my face. She turned away from me, toward the window again, searching those streets.

''But I praise my Redeemer,'' she said at last, ''that He called your Daddy home before me. I ain't saying it to throw no flowers at myself, but, I declare, it keeps me from feeling too cast down to know I helped your father get safely through this world. Your father always acted like he was the roughest, strongest man on earth.

And everybody took him to be like that. But if he hadn't had *me* there—to see his tears!"

She was crying again. Still, I couldn't move. I said, "Lord, Lord, Mama, I didn't know it was like that."

"Oh, honey," she said, "there's a lot that you don't know. But you are going to find it out." She stood up from the window and came over to me. "You got to hold on to your brother," she said, "and don't let him fall, no matter what it looks like is happening to him and no matter how evil you gets with him. You going to be evil with him many a time. But don't you forget what I told you, you hear?"

"I won't forget," I said. "Don't you worry, I won't forget. I won't let nothing happen to Sonny."

My mother smiled as though she were amused at something she saw in my face. Then, "You may not be able to stop nothing from happening. But you got to let him know you's *there.*"

Two days later I was married, and then I was gone. And I had a lot of things on my mind and I pretty well forgot my promise to Mama until I got shipped home on a special furlough for her funeral.

And, after the funeral, with just Sonny and me alone in the empty kitchen, I tried to find out something about him.

"What do you want to do?" I asked him.

"I'm going to me a musician," he said.

For he had graduated, in the time I had been away, from dancing to the juke box to finding out who was playing what, and what they were doing with it, and he had bought himself a set of drums.

"You mean, you want to be a drummer?" I somehow had the feeling that being a drummer might be all right for other people but not for my brother Sonny.

"I don't think," he said, looking at me very gravely, "that I'll ever be a good drummer. But I think I can play a piano."

I frowned. I'd never played the role of the older brother quite so seriously before, had scarcely ever, in fact, *asked* Sonny a damn thing. I sensed myself in the presence of something I didn't really know how to handle, didn't understand. So I made my frown a little deeper as I asked: "What kind of musician do you want to be?"

He grinned. "How many kinds do you think there are?"

"Be *serious,*" I said.

He laughed, throwing his head back, and then looked at me. "I *am* serious."

"Well, then, for Christ's sake, stop kidding around and answer a serious question. I mean, do you want to be a concert pianist, you want to play classical music and all that, or—or what?" Long before I finished he was laughing again. "For Christ's *sake,* Sonny!"

He sobered, but with difficulty. "I'm sorry. But you sound so—*scared!*" and he was off again.

"Well, you may think it's funny now, baby, but it's not going to be so funny when you have to make your living at it, let me tell you *that.*" I was furious because I knew he was laughing at me and I didn't know why.

"No," he said, very sober now, and afraid, perhaps, that he'd hurt me, "I don't want to be a classical pianist. That isn't what interests me. I mean"—he paused, looking hard at me, as though his eyes would help me to understand, and then gestured helplessly, as though perhaps his hand would help—"I mean, I'll have a lot of studying to do, and I'll have to study *everything,* but I mean, I want to play *with*—jazz musicians." He stopped. "I want to play jazz," he said.

Well, the word had never before sounded as heavy, as real, as it sounded that afternoon in Sonny's mouth. I just looked at him and I was probably frowning a real frown by this time. I simply couldn't see why on earth he'd want to spend his time hanging around night clubs, clowning around on bandstands, while people pushed each other around a dance floor. It seemed—beneath him, somehow. I had never thought about it before, had never been forced to, but I suppose I had always put jazz musicians in a class with what Daddy called "good-time people."

"Are you *serious?*"

"Hell, *yes,* I'm serious."

He looked more helpless than ever, and annoyed, and deeply hurt.

I suggested, helpfully: "You mean—like Louis Armstrong?"

His face closed as though I'd struck him. "No. I'm not talking about none of that old-time, down home crap."

"Well, look, Sonny, I'm sorry, don't get mad. I just

don't altogether get it, that's all. Name somebody—you know, a jazz musician you admire."

"Bird."

"Who?"

"Bird! Charlie Parker! Don't they teach you nothing in the goddamn army?"

I lit a cigarette. I was surprised and then a little amused to discover that I was trembling. "I've been out of touch," I said. "You'll have to be patient with me. Now. Who's this Parker character?"

"He's just one of the greatest jazz musicians alive," said Sonny, sullenly, his hands in his pockets, his back to me. "Maybe *the* greatest," he added, bitterly, "that's probably why *you* never heard of him."

"All right," I said, "I'm ignorant. I'm sorry. I'll go out and buy all the cat's records right away, all right?"

"It don't," said Sonny, with dignity, "make any difference to me. I don't care what you listen to. Don't do me no favors."

I was beginning to realize that I'd never seen him so upset before. With another part of my mind I was thinking that this would probably turn out to be one of those things kids go through and that I shouldn't make it seem important by pushing it too hard. Still, I didn't think it would do any harm to ask: "Doesn't all this take a lot of time? Can you make a living at it?"

He turned back to me and half leaned, half sat, on the kitchen table. "Everything takes time," he said, "and—well, yes, sure, I can make a living at it. But what I don't seem to be able to make you understand is that it's the only thing I want to do."

"Well Sonny," I said, gently, "you know people can't always do exactly what they *want* to do—"

"*No*, I don't know that," said Sonny, surprising me. "I think people *ought* to do what they want to do, what else are they alive for?"

"You getting to be a big boy," I said desperately, "it's time you started thinking about your future."

"I'm thinking about my future," said Sonny, grimly. "I think about it all the time."

I gave up. I decided, if he didn't change his mind, that we could always talk about it later. "In the meantime," I said, "you got to finish school." We had already decided that he'd have to move in with Isabel and her folks. I knew this wasn't the ideal arrangement because Isabel's folks are inclined to be dicty and they

hadn't especially wanted Isabel to marry me. But I didn't know what else to do. "And we have to get you fixed up at Isabel's."

There was a long silence. He moved from the kitchen table to the window. "That's a terrible idea. You know it yourself."

"Do you have a *better* idea?"

He just walked up and down the kitchen for a minute. He was as tall as I was. He had started to shave. I suddenly had the feeling that I didn't know him at all.

He stopped at the kitchen table and picked up my cigarettes. Looking at me with a kind of mocking, amused defiance, he put one between his lips. "You mind?"

"You smoking already?"

He lit the cigarette and nodded, watching me through the smoke. "I just wanted to see if I'd have the courage to smoke in front of you." He grinned and blew a great cloud of smoke to the ceiling. "It was easy." He looked at my face. "Come on, now. I bet you was smoking at my age, tell the truth."

I didn't say anything but the truth was on my face, and he laughed. But now there was something very strained in his laugh. "Sure. And I bet that ain't all you was doing."

He was frightening me a little. "Cut the crap," I said. "We already decided that you was going to go and live at Isabel's. Now what's got into you all of a sudden?"

"*You* decided it," he pointed out. "*I* didn't decide nothing." He stopped in front of me, leaning against the stove, arms loosely folded. "Look, brother. I don't want to stay in Harlem no more, I really don't." He was very earnest. He looked at me, then over toward the kitchen window. There was something in his eyes I'd never seen before, some thoughtfulness, some worry all his own. He rubbed the muscle of one arm. "It's time I was getting out of here."

"Where do you want to go, Sonny?"

"I want to join the army. Or the navy, I don't care. If I say I'm old enough they'll believe me."

Then I got mad. It was because I was so scared. "You must be crazy. You goddamn fool, what the hell do you want to go and join the *army* for?"

"I just told you. To get out of Harlem."

"Sonny, you haven't even finished *school*. And if you really want to be a musician, how do you expect to study if you're in the *army?*"

He looked at me, trapped, and in anguish. "There's ways. I might be able to work out some kind of deal. Anyway, I'll have the G.I. Bill when I come out."

"*If* you come out." We stared at each other. "Sonny, please. Be reasonable. I know the setup is far from perfect. But we got to do the best we can."

"I ain't learning nothing in school," he said. "Even when I go." He turned away from me and opened the window and threw his cigarette out into the narrow alley. I watched his back. "At least, I ain't learning nothing you'd want me to learn." He slammed the window so hard I thought the glass would fly out, and turned back to me. "And I'm sick of the stink of these garbage cans!"

"Sonny," I said, "I know how you feel. But if you don't finish school now, you're going to be sorry later that you didn't." I grabbed him by the shoulders. "And you only got another year. It ain't so bad. And I'll come back and I swear I'll help you do *whatever* you want to do. Just try to put up with it till I come back. Will you please do that? For me?"

He didn't answer and he wouldn't look at me.

"Sonny. You hear me?"

He pulled away. "I hear you. But you never hear anything *I* say."

I didn't know what to say to that. He looked out of the window and then back at me. "OK," he said, and sighed. "I'll try."

Then I said, trying to cheer him up a little, "They got a piano at Isabel's. You can practice on it."

And as a matter of fact, it did cheer him up for a minute. "That's right," he said to himself. "I forgot that." His face relaxed a little. But the worry, the thoughtfulness, played on it still, the way shadows play on a face which is staring into the fire.

But I thought I'd never hear the end of that piano. At first, Isabel would write me, saying how nice it was that Sonny was so serious about his music and how, as soon as he came in from school, or wherever he had been when he was supposed to be at school, he went straight to that piano and stayed there until suppertime. And, after supper, he went back to that piano and stayed there until everybody went to bed. He was at the piano all day Saturday and all day Sunday. Then he bought a record player and started playing records. He'd play one record over and over again, all day long sometimes, and he'd improvise along with it on the piano. Or he'd play one section of the record, one chord, one change, one progression, then he'd do it on the piano. Then back to the record. Then back to the piano.

Well, I really don't know how they stood it. Isabel finally confessed that it wasn't like living with a person at all, it was like living with sound. And the sound didn't make any sense to her, didn't make any sense to any of them—naturally. They began, in a way, to be afflicted by this presence that was living in their home. It was as though Sonny were some sort of god, or monster. He moved in an atmosphere which wasn't like theirs at all. They fed him and he ate, he washed himself, he walked in and out of their door; he certainly wasn't nasty or unpleasant or rude, Sonny isn't any of those things; but it was as though he were all wrapped up in some cloud, some fire, some vision all his own; and there wasn't any way to reach him.

At the same time, he wasn't really a man yet, he was still a child, and they had to watch out for him in all kinds of ways. They certainly couldn't throw him out. Neither did they dare to make a great scene about that piano because even they dimly sensed, as I sensed, from so many thousands of miles away, that Sonny was at that piano playing for his life.

But he hadn't been going to school. One day a letter came from the school board and Isabel's mother got it—there had, apparently, been other letters but Sonny had torn them up. This day, when Sonny came in, Isabel's mother showed him the letter and asked where he'd been spending his time. And she finally got it out of him that he'd been down in Greenwich Village, with musicians and other characters, in a white girl's apartment. And this scared her and she started to scream at him and what came up, once she began—though she denies it to this day—was what sacrifices they were making to give Sonny a decent home and how little he appreciated it.

Sonny didn't play the piano that day. By evening, Isabel's mother had calmed down but then there was the old man to deal with, and Isabel herself. Isabel says she did her best to be calm but she broke down and started crying. She says she just watched Sonny's face. She could tell, by watching him, what was happening with him. And what was happening was that they penetrated his cloud, they had reached him. Even if their fingers had been a thousand times more gentle than human fingers ever are, he could hardly help feeling that they had stripped him naked and were spitting on that nakedness. For he also had to see that his presence, that music, which was life or death to him, had been torture for them and that they had endured it, not at all for his sake, but only for mine. And Sonny couldn't take that. He can take it a little better today than he could then but he's still not very good at it and, frankly, I don't know anybody who is.

The silence of the next few days must have been louder than the sound of all the music ever played since time began. One morning, before she went to work, Isabel was in his room for something and she suddenly realized that all of his records were gone. And she knew for certain that he was gone. And he was. He went as far as the navy would carry him. He finally sent me a postcard from some place in Greece and that was the first I knew that Sonny was still alive. I didn't see him any more until we were both back in New York and the war had long been over.

He was a man by then, of course, but I wasn't willing to see it. He came by the house from time to time, but we fought almost every time we met. I didn't like the way he carried himself, loose and dreamlike all the time, and I didn't like his friends, and his music seemed to be merely an excuse for the life he led. It sounded just that weird and disordered.

Then we had a fight, a pretty awful fight, and I didn't see him for months. By and by I looked him up, where he was living, in a furnished room in the Village, and I tried to make it up. But there were lots of other people in the room and Sonny just lay on his bed, and he wouldn't come downstairs with me, and he treated these other people as though they were his family and I weren't. So I got mad and then he got mad, and then I told him that he might just as well be dead as live the way he was living. Then he stood up and he told me not to worry about him any more in life, that he *was* dead as far as I was concerned. Then he pushed me to the door and the other people looked on as though nothing were happening, and he slammed the door behind me. I stood in the hallway, staring at the door. I heard somebody laugh in the room and then the tears

came to my eyes. I started down the steps, whistling to keep from crying, I kept whistling to myself, *You going to need me, baby, one of these cold, rainy days.*

I read about Sonny's trouble in the spring. Little Grace died in the fall. She was a beautiful little girl. But she only lived a little over two years. She died of polio and she suffered. She had a slight fever for a couple of days, but it didn't seem like anything and we just kept her in bed. And we would certainly have called the doctor, but the fever dropped, she seemed to be all right. So we thought it had just been a cold. Then, one day, she was up, playing, Isabel was in the kitchen fixing lunch for the two boys when they'd come in from school, and she heard Grace fall down in the living room. When you have a lot of children you don't always start running when one of them falls, unless they start screaming or something. And, this time, Grace was quiet. Yet, Isabel says that when she heard that *thump* and then that silence, something happened in her to make her afraid. And she ran to the living room and there was little Grace on the floor, all twisted up and the reason she hadn't screamed was that she couldn't get her breath. And when she did scream, it was the worst sound, Isabel says, that she'd ever heard in all her life, and she still hears it sometimes in her dreams. Isabel will sometimes wake me up with a low, moaning, strangled sound and I have to be quick to awaken her and hold her to me and where Isabel is weeping against me seems a mortal wound.

I think I may have written Sonny the very day that little Grace was buried. I was sitting in the living room in the dark, by myself, and I suddenly thought of Sonny. My trouble made his real.

One Saturday afternoon, when Sonny had been living with us, or, anyway, been in our house, for nearly two weeks, I found myself wandering aimlessly about the living room, drinking from a can of beer, and trying to work up the courage to search Sonny's room. He was out, he was usually out whenever I was home, and Isabel had taken the children to see their grandparents. Suddenly I was standing still in front of the living room window, watching Seventh Avenue. The idea of searching Sonny's room made me still. I scarcely dared to admit to myself what I'd be searching for. I didn't know what I'd do if I found it. Or if I didn't.

On the sidewalk across from me, near the entrance to a barbecue joint, some people were holding an old-fashioned revival meeting. The barbecue cook, wearing a dirty white apron, his conked hair reddish and metallic in the pale sun, and a cigarette between his lips, stood in the doorway, watching them. Kids and older people paused in their errands and stood there, along with some older men and a couple of very tough-looking women who watched everything that happened on the avenue, as though they owned it, or were maybe owned by it. Well, they were watching this, too. The revival was being carried on by three sisters in black, and a brother. All they had were their voices and their Bibles and a tambourine. The brother was testifying and while he testified two of the sisters stood together, seeming to say, Amen, and the third sister walked around with the tambourine outstretched and a couple of people dropped coins into it. Then the brother's testimony ended and the sister who had been taking up the collection dumped the coins into her palm and transferred them to the pocket of her long black robe. Then she raised both hands, striking the tambourine against the air, and then against one hand, and she started to sing. And the two other sisters and the brother joined in.

It was strange, suddenly, to watch, though I had been seeing these street meetings all my life. So, of course, had everybody else down there. Yet, they paused and watched and listened and I stood still at the window. *"Tis the old ship of Zion,"* they sang, and the sister with the tambourine kept a steady, jangling beat, *"It has rescued many a thousand!"* Not a soul under the sound of their voices was hearing this song for the first time, not one of them had been rescued. Nor had they seen much in the way of rescue work being done around them. Neither did they especially believe in the holiness of the three sisters and the brother, they knew too much about them, knew where they lived, and how. The woman with the tambourine, whose voice dominated the air, whose face was bright with joy, was divided by very little from the woman who stood watching her, a cigarette between her heavy, chapped lips, her hair a cuckoo's nest, her face scarred and swollen from many beatings, and her black eyes glittering like coal. Perhaps they both knew this, which was why, when, as rarely, they addressed each other, they addressed each other as Sister. As the singing filled the air the watching, listening faces underwent a change, the eyes focusing on something within; the music seemed to soothe a poison out of them; and time seemed, nearly, to fall away from the sullen, belligerent, battered faces, as though they were fleeing back to their first condition, while dreaming of their last. The barbecue cook half shook his head and smiled, and dropped his cigarette and disappeared into his joint. A man fumbled in his pockets for change and stood holding it in his hand impatiently, as though he had just remembered a pressing appointment further up the avenue. He looked furious. Then I saw Sonny, standing on the edge of the crowd. He was carrying a wide, flat notebook with a green cover, and it made him look, from where I was standing, almost like a schoolboy. The coppery sun brought out the copper in his skin, he was very faintly smiling, standing very still. Then the singing stopped, the tambourine turned into a collection plate again. The furious man dropped in his coins and vanished, so did a couple of the women, and Sonny dropped some change in the plate, looking directly at the woman with a little smile. He started across the avenue, toward the house. He has a slow, loping walk, something like the way Harlem hipsters walk, only he's imposed on this his own halfbeat. I had never really noticed it before.

I stayed at the window, both relieved and apprehensive. As Sonny disappeared from my sight, they began singing again. And they were still singing when his key turned in the lock.

"Hey," he said.

"Hey, yourself. You want some beer?"

"No. Well, maybe." But he came up the window and stood beside me, looking out. "What a warm voice," he said.

They were singing *If I could only hear my mother pray again!*

"Yes," I said, "and she can sure beat that tambourine."

"But what a terrible song," he said, and laughed. He dropped his notebook on the sofa and disappeared into the kitchen. "Where's Isabel and the kids?"

"I think they went to see their grandparents. You hungry?"

"No." He came back into the living room with his can of beer. "You want to come some place with me tonight?"

I sensed, I don't know how, that I couldn't possibly say No. "Sure. Where?"

He sat down on the sofa and picked up his notebook and started leafing through it. "I'm going to sit in with some fellows in a joint in the Village."

"You mean, you're going to play, tonight?"

"That's right." He took a swallow of his beer and moved back to the window. He gave me a sidelong look. "If you can stand it."

"I'll try," I said.

He smiled to himself and we both watched as the meeting across the way broke up. The three sisters and the brother, heads bowed, were singing *God be with you till we meet again*. The faces around them were very quiet. Then the song ended. The small crowd dispersed. We watched the three women and the lone man walk slowly up the avenue.

"When she was singing before," said Sonny, abruptly, "her voice reminded me for a minute of what heroin feels like sometimes—when it's in your veins. It makes you feel sort of warm and cool at the same time. And distant. And—and sure." He sipped his beer, very deliberately not looking at me. I watched his face. "It makes you feel—in control. Sometimes you've got to have that feeling."

"Do you?" I sat down slowly in the easy chair.

"Sometimes." He went to the sofa and picked up his notebook again. "Some people do."

"In order," I asked, "to play?" And my voice was very ugly, full of contempt and anger.

"Well"—he looked at me with great, troubled eyes, as though, in fact, he hoped his eyes would tell me things he could never otherwise say—"they *think* so. And *if* they think so—!"

"And what do *you* think?" I asked.

He sat on the sofa and put his can of beer on the floor. "I don't know," he said, and I couldn't be sure if he were answering my question or pursuing his thoughts. His face didn't tell me. "It's not so much to *play*. It's to *stand* it, to be able to make it at all. On any level." He frowned and smiled: "In order to keep from shaking to pieces."

"But these friends of yours," I said, "they seem to shake themselves to pieces pretty goddamn fast."

"Maybe." He played with the notebook. And something told me that I should curb my tongue, that Sonny was doing his best to talk, that I should listen. "But of course you only know the ones that've gone to pieces. Some don't—or at least they haven't *yet* and that's just about all *any* of us can say." He paused. "And then there are some who just live, really, in hell, and they know it and they see what's happening and they go right on. I don't know." He sighed, dropped the notebook, folded his arms. "Some guys, you can tell from the way they play, they on something *all* the time. And you can see that, well, it makes something real for them. But of course," he picked up his beer from the floor and sipped it and put the can down again, "they *want* to, too, you've got to see that. Even some of them that say they don't—*some*, not all."

"And what about you?" I asked—I couldn't help it. "What about you? Do *you* want to?"

He stood up and walked to the window and remained silent for a long time. Then he sighed. "Me," he said. Then: "While I was downstairs before, on my way here, listening to that woman sing, it struck me all of a sudden how much suffering she must have had to go through—to sing like that. It's *repulsive* to think you have to suffer that much."

I said: "But there's no way not to suffer—is there, Sonny?"

"I believe not," he said, and smiled, "but that's never stopped anyone from trying." He looked at me. "Has it?" I realized, with this mocking look, that there stood between us, forever, beyond the power of time or forgiveness, the fact that I had held silence—so long!—when he had needed human speech to help him. He turned back to the window. "No, there's no way not to suffer. But you try all kinds of ways to keep from drowning in it, to keep on top of it, and to make it seem—well, like *you*. Like you did something, all right, and now you're suffering for it. You know?" I said nothing. "Well you know," he said, impatiently, "why *do* people suffer? Maybe it's better to do something to give it a reason, *any* reason."

"But we just agreed," I said, "that there's no way not to suffer. Isn't it better, then, just to—take it?"

"But nobody just takes it," Sonny cried, "that's what I'm telling you! *Everybody* tries not to. You're just hung up on the *way* some people try—it's not *your* way!"

The hair on my face began to itch, my face felt wet. "That's not true," I said, "that's not true. I don't give a damn what other people do, I don't even care how they suffer. I just care how *you* suffer." And he looked at me. "Please believe me," I said, "I don't want to see you—die—trying not to suffer."

"I won't," he said, flatly, "die trying not to suffer. At least, not any faster than anybody else."

"But there's no need," I said, trying to laugh, "is there? in killing yourself."

I wanted to say more, but I couldn't. I wanted to talk about will power and how life could be—well, beautiful. I wanted to say that it was all within; but was it? or, rather, wasn't that exactly the trouble? And I wanted to promise that I would never fail him again. But it would all have sounded—empty words and lies.

So I made the promise to myself and prayed that I would keep it.

"It's terrible sometimes, inside," he said, "that's what's the trouble. You walk these streets, black and funky and cold, and there's not really a living ass to talk to, and there's nothing shaking, and there's no way of getting it out—that storm inside. You can't talk it and you can't make love with it, and when you finally try to get with it and play it, you realize *nobody's* listening. So *you've* got to listen. You got to find a way to listen."

And then he walked away from the window and sat on the sofa again, as though all the wind had suddenly been knocked out of him. "Sometimes you'll do *anything* to play, even cut your mother's throat." He laughed and looked at me. "Or your brother's." Then he sobered. "Or your own." Then: "Don't worry. I'm all right now and I think I'll *be* all right. But I can't forget—where I've been. I don't mean just the physical place I've been, I mean where I've *been*. And *what* I've been."

"What have you been, Sonny?" I asked.

He smiled—but sat sideways on the sofa, his elbow resting on the back, his fingers playing with his mouth and chin, not looking at me. "I've been something I didn't recognize, didn't know I could be. Didn't know anybody could be." He stopped, looking inward, looking helplessly young, looking old. "I'm not talking about it now because I feel *guilty* or anything like that—maybe it would be better if I did, I don't know. Anyway, I can't really talk about it. Not to you, not to

anybody," and now he turned and faced me. "Sometimes, you know, and it was actually when I was most *out* of the world, I felt that I was in it, and that I was *with* it, really, and I could play or I didn't really have to *play*, it just came out of me, it was there. And I don't know how I played, thinking about it now, but I know I did awful things, those times, sometimes, to people. Or it wasn't that I *did* anything to them—it was that they weren't real." He picked up the beer can; it was empty; he rolled it between his palms: "And other times—well, I needed a fix, I needed to find a place to lean, I needed to clear a space to *listen*—and I couldn't find it, and I—went crazy, I did terrible things to *me*, I was terrible *for* me." He began pressing the beer can between his hands, I watched the metal begin to give. It glittered, as he played with it, like a knife, and I was afraid he would cut himself, but I said nothing. "Oh well. I can never tell you. I was all by myself at the bottom of something, stinking and sweating and crying and shaking, and I smelled it, you know? *my* stink, and I thought I'd die if I couldn't get away from it and yet, all the same, I knew that everything I was doing was just locking me in with it. And I didn't know," he paused, still flattening the beer can, "I didn't know, I still *don't* know, something kept telling me that maybe it was good to smell your own stink, but I didn't think that *that* was what I'd been trying to do—and—who can stand it?" and he abruptly dropped the ruined beer can, looking at me with a small, still smile, and then rose, walking to the window as though it were the lodestone rock. I watched his face, he watched the avenue. "I couldn't tell you when Mama died—but the reason I wanted to leave Harlem so bad was to get away from drugs. And then, when I ran away, that's what I was running from—really. When I came back, nothing had changed, *I* hadn't changed, I was just—older." And he stopped, drumming with his fingers on the window-pane. The sun had vanished, soon darkness would fall. I watched his face. "It can come again," he said, almost as though speaking to himself. Then he turned to me. "It can come again," he repeated. "I just want you to know that."

"All right," I said, at last. "So it can come again. All right."

He smiled, but the smile was sorrowful. "I had to try to tell you," he said.

"Yes," I said. "I understand that."

"You're my brother," he said, looking straight at me, and not smiling at all.

"Yes," I repeated, "yes. I understand that."

He turned back to the window, looking out. "All that hatred down there," he said, "all that hatred and misery and love. It's a wonder it doesn't blow the avenue apart."

We went to the only night club on a short, dark street, downtown. We squeezed through the narrow, chattering, jam-packed bar to the entrance of the big room, where the bandstand was. And we stood there for a moment, for the lights were very dim in this room and we couldn't see. Then, "Hello, boy," said a voice and an enormous black man, much older than Sonny or myself, erupted out of all that atmospheric lighting and put an arm around Sonny's shoulder. "I been sitting right here," he said, "waiting for you."

He had a big voice, too, and heads in the darkness turned toward us.

Sonny grinned and pulled a little away, and said, "Creole, this is my brother. I told you about him."

Creole shook my hand. "I'm glad to meet you, son," he said, and it was clear that he was glad to meet me *there*, for Sonny's sake. And he smiled, "You got a real musician in *your* family," and he took his arm from Sonny's shoulder and slapped him, lightly, affectionately, with the back of his hand.

"Well. Now I've heard it all," said a voice behind us. This was another musician, and a friend of Sonny's, a coal-black, cheerful-looking man, built close to the ground. He immediately began confiding to me, at the top of his lungs, the most terrible things about Sonny, his teeth gleaming like a lighthouse and his laugh coming up out of him like the beginning of an earthquake. And it turned out that everyone at the bar knew Sonny, or almost everyone; some were musicians, working there, or nearby, or not working, some were simply hangers-on, and some were there to hear Sonny play. I was introduced to all of them and they were all very polite to me. Yet, it was clear that, for them, I was only Sonny's brother. Here, I was in Sonny's world. Or, rather: his kingdom. Here, it was not even a question that his veins bore royal blood.

They were going to play soon and Creole installed me, by myself, at a table in a dark corner. Then I watched them, Creole, and the little black man, and Sonny, and the others, while they horsed around, standing just below the bandstand. The light from the bandstand spilled just a little short of them and, watching them laughing and gesturing and moving about, I had the feeling that they, nevertheless, were being most careful not to step into that circle of light too suddenly: that if they moved into the light too suddenly, without thinking, they would perish in flame. Then, while I watched, one of them, the small, black man, moved into the light and crossed the bandstand and started fooling around with his drums. Then—being funny and being, also, extremely ceremonious—Creole took Sonny by the arm and led him to the piano. A woman's voice called Sonny's name and a few hands started clapping. And Sonny, also being funny and being ceremonious, and so touched, I think, that he could have cried, but neither hiding it nor showing it, riding it like a man, grinned, and put both hands to his heart and bowed from the waist.

Creole then went to the bass fiddle and a lean, very bright-skinned brown man jumped up on the bandstand and picked up his horn. So there they were, and the atmosphere on the bandstand and in the room began to change and tighten. Someone stepped up to the microphone and announced them. Then there were all kinds of murmurs. Some people at the bar shushed others. The waitress ran around, frantically getting in the last orders, guys and chicks got closer to each other, and the lights on the bandstand, on the quartet, turned to a kind of indigo. Then they all looked different there. Creole looked about him for the last time, as though he were making certain that all his chickens were in the coop, and then he—jumped and struck the fiddle. And there they were.

All I know about music is that not many people ever really hear it. And even then, on the rare occasions when something opens within, and the music enters, what we mainly hear, or hear corroborated, are personal private, vanishing evocations. But the man who creates the music is hearing something else, is dealing with the roar rising from the void and imposing order on it as it hits the air. What is evoked in him, then, is of another order, more terrible because it has no words, and triumphant, too, for that same reason. And his triumph, when he triumphs, is ours. I just watched

Sonny's face. His face was troubled, he was working hard, but he wasn't with it. And I had the feeling that, in a way, everyone on the bandstand was waiting for him, both waiting for him and pushing him along. But as I began to watch Creole, I realized that it was Creole who held them all back. He had them on a short rein. Up there, keeping the beat with his whole body, wailing on the fiddle, with his eyes half closed, he was listening to everything, but he was listening to Sonny. He was having a dialogue with Sonny. He wanted Sonny to leave the shore line and strike out for the deep water. He was Sonny's witness that deep water and drowning were not the same thing—he had been there, and he knew. And he wanted Sonny to know. He was waiting for Sonny to do the things on the keys which would let Creole know that Sonny was in the water.

And, while Creole listened, Sonny moved, deep within, exactly like someone in torment. I had never before thought of how awful the relationship must be between the musician and his instrument. He has to fill it, this instrument, with the breath of life, his own. He has to make it do what he wants it to do. And a piano is just a piano. It's made out of so much wood and wires and little hammers and big ones, and ivory. While there's only so much you can do with it, the only way to find this out is to try and make it do everything.

And Sonny hadn't been near a piano for over a year. And he wasn't on much better terms with his life, not the life that stretched before him now. He and the piano stammered, started one way, got scared, stopped; started another way, panicked, marked time, started again; then seemed to have found a direction, panicked again, got stuck. And the face I saw on Sonny I'd never seen before. Everything had been burned out of it, and, at the same time, things usually hidden were being burned in, by the fire and fury of the battle which was occurring in him up there.

Yet, watching Creole's face as they neared the end of the first set, I had the feeling that something had happened, something I hadn't heard. Then they finished, there was scattered applause, and then, without an instant's warning, Creole started into something else, it was almost sardonic, it was *Am I Blue*. And, as though he commanded, Sonny began to play. Something began to happen. And Creole let out the reins. The dry, low,

black man said something awful on the drums, Creole answered, and the drums talked back. Then the horn insisted, sweet and high, slightly detached perhaps, and Creole listened, commenting now and then, dry, and driving, beautiful and calm and old. Then they all came together again, and Sonny was part of the family again. I could tell this from his face. He seemed to have found, right there beneath his fingers, a damn brand-new piano. It seemed that he couldn't get over it. Then, for awhile, just being happy with Sonny, they seemed to be agreeing with him that brand-new pianos certainly were a gas.

Then Creole stepped forward to remind them that what they were playing was the blues. He hit something in all of them, he hit something in me, myself, and the music tightened and deepened, apprehension began to beat the air. Creole began to tell us what the blues were all about. They were not about anything very new. He and his boys up there were keeping it new, at the risk of ruin, destruction, madness, and death, in order to find new ways to make us listen. For, while the tale of how we suffer, and how we are delighted, and how we may triumph is never new, it always must be heard. There isn't any other tale to tell, it's the only light we've got in all this darkness.

And this tale, according to that face, that body, those strong hands on those strings, has another aspect in every country, and a new depth in every generation. Listen, Creole seemed to be saying, listen. Now these are Sonny's blues. He made the little black man on the drums know it, and the bright, brown man on the horn. Creole wasn't trying any longer to get Sonny in the water. He was wishing him Godspeed. Then he stepped back, very slowly, filling the air with the immense suggestion that Sonny speak for himself.

Then they all gathered around Sonny and Sonny played. Every now and again one of them seemed to say, Amen. Sonny's fingers filled the air with life, his life. But that life contained so many others. And Sonny went all the way back, he really began with the spare, flat statement of the opening phrase of the song. Then he began to make it his. It was very beautiful because it wasn't hurried and it was no longer a lament. I seemed to hear with what burning he had made it his, with what burning we had yet to make it ours, how we could cease lamenting. Freedom lurked around us and I understood, at last, that he could help us to be free if we would listen, that he would never be free until we did. Yet, there was no battle in his face now. I heard what he had gone through, and would continue to go through until he came to rest in earth. He had made it his: that long line, of which we knew only Mama and Daddy. And he was giving it back, as everything must be given back, so that, passing through death, it can live forever. I saw my mother's face again, and felt, for the first time, how the stones of the road she had walked on must have bruised her feet. I saw the moonlit road where my father's brother died. And it brought something else back to me, and carried me past it, I saw my little girl again and felt Isabel's tears again, and I felt my own tears begin to rise. And I was yet aware that this was only a moment, that the world waited outside, as hungry as a tiger, and that trouble stretched above us, longer than the sky.

Then it was over. Creole and Sonny let out their breath, both soaking wet, and grinning. There was a lot of applause and some of it was real. In the dark, the girl came by and I asked her to take drinks to the bandstand. There was a long pause, while they talked up there in the indigo light and after awhile I saw the girl put a Scotch and milk on top of the piano for Sonny. He didn't seem to notice it, but just before they started playing again, he sipped from it and looked toward me, and nodded. Then he put it back on top of the piano. For me, then, as they began to play again, it glowed and shook above my brother's head like the very cup of trembling.

QUESTIONS

1. What relationship does Baldwin see between art and religion?
2. What views of life and its meaning are in conflict in this story? Which one, if any, appears to triumph?
3. What does the "privacy" of Sonny's character come from, and what are its results?
4. Interpret the following passage and relate it to the theme of the story: "For, while the tale of how we suffer, and how we are delighted, and how we may triumph is never new, it always must be heard."

NÉGRITUDE and Its Impact on America The Harlem Renaissance and the protest literature that followed were both influential in the development of what has come to be known as *négritude*. The founders of the movement, Léopold Sédar Senghor, Aimé Césaire, and Léon Damas, all acknowledged that, between 1930 and 1940, African and West Indian students living in Paris read with great admiration the works of such Afro-American writers as Claude McKay, Countee Cullen, James Weldon Johnson, Alain Locke, Jean Toomer, Sterling A. Brown, and Langston Hughes.

First coined and popularized by Aimé Césaire in his poem *Cahier d'un retour au pays natal (Notes on a Return to the Native Land)*, *négritude* may be viewed as an effort to revaluate Africa within a non-Western framework; it represents an effort toward self-definition and self-appraisal. Emphasis is placed on the nonmaterial or intangible elements that distinguish the African's approach to reality from the Westerner's and determine his daily behavior. African traditional beliefs, their survival in America, the African's "sense of the divine," and his acute ability to perceive the supernatural within the natural because of his closeness to nature are all given a great deal of attention in order to create and define a Pan-African cultural universe.

Although a certain political awareness was an explicit part of the *négritude* movement, which placed it in close relationship with African nationalism and Pan-Africanism, *négritude* remained essentially a cultural and intellectual movement. Senghor, the movement's major theoretician and most well known poet, whose work we saw represented in Chapter 32, defines *négritude* as "the sum total of African values." He speaks of a special spiritual endowment of the African, of a "Negro soul," which is shared by blacks of African descent throughout the world. One such endowment, for Senghor, is "intuitive reason" as opposed to the Greek conception of logical reason. According to Senghor, logical reason involves a *confrontation* of subject and object, a confrontation that takes in merely the surface of things. Intuitive knowledge, on the other hand, involves a kind of *participation* and *communion* in which subject and object unite to become one. It is, then, in terms of "participation" and "communion" that Senghor defines the African's approach to the world. This different kind of epistemology (different way of experiencing the world) is said to govern the entire sensibility of the African, a sensibility that is basically emotive. In Senghor's own words, "Emotion is African, as Reason is Hellenic."

Although it was quite popular among French-speaking black intellectuals, many English-speaking black African writers and Afro-Americans looked upon the movement with skepticism and suspicion. English-speaking writers—Ezekiel Mphalele, Wole Soyinka, and James Ngugi, to mention only a few—criticized the movement largely because of its romanticization of Africa and its implications for artistic freedom. Their ultimate desire was to create freely and be judged by universal standards of art. As for Afro-Americans, many of them, James Baldwin and Ralph Ellison in particular, thought that the Afro-American's "Americanness" should be given due attention. In a book titled *Shadow and Acts*, Ralph Ellison states the following:

> The American Negro people is North American in origin and has evolved under specifically American conditions: climatic, nutritional, historical, political and social. It takes its character from the experience of American slavery and the struggle for, and the achievement of, emancipation; . . . and from living in a highly industrialized and highly mobile society possessing a relatively high standard of living and an explicitly stated equalitarian concept of freedom. Its spiritual outlook is basically Protestant, its system of kinship is Western, its time and historical sense are American (United States), and its secular values are those professed, ideally at least, by all of the people of the United States.
>
> Culturally this people represents one of the many subcultures which make up that great amalgam of European and native American cultures which is the culture of the United States. This "American Negro Culture" is expressed in a body of folklore, in the musical forms of the spiritual, the blues and jazz; an idiomatic version of American speech (especially in the Southern United States): a cuisine, a body of dance forms and even a dramaturgy, which is generally unrecognized as such because still tied to the more folkish Negro churches.

Despite these and other criticisms, *négritude* received a great deal of attention, becoming a very prominent ideological, political, and cultural force. It was highly influential on black intellectuals of the 1960s, who tended to stress the African, more than the Western, aspects of the black experience.

The Black Aesthetic

Afro-American literary critics and historians often point to the continuity of the psychological, ideological, and literary line between *négritude* and the black aesthetic movement of the 1960s and 1970s. Viewed from one ideological perspective, the black aesthetic is a polemic against the dominant values and ideals of Western civilization. Franz Fanon, Malcolm X, Ron Karenga, Leroi Jones, and other black nationalists were instrumental in convincing many Afro-Americans that in the time of revolutionary struggles, traditional Western ideals are irrelevant and, therefore, need to be abolished. As a result, one of the central missions of the black aesthetic became what the literary critic Addison Gayle, Jr., called the de-Americanization of black people.

This de-Americanization of black people, along with the hostility and protest literature that often accompanied it, constituted only one phase of the movement's development. Its members soon came to the conclusion that protest literature and other modes of speaking to an unsympathetic American society were all futile. Consequently, they began to address themselves to other blacks by investing their work with the distinctive styles, rhythms, and colors of the ghetto as found, for instance, in the music of Aretha Franklin, Otis Redding, Nina Simone, and James Brown. Thus, as an artistic style, the black aesthetic may be viewed as an attempt to develop an idiom, symbolism, imagery, mythology, and iconology that reflect the uniqueness of the Afro-American experience. The following list of seven Black Aesthetic categories offered by Don L. Lee is a good example of this effort:

1. polyrhythmic, uneven, short, and explosive lines
2. intensity; depth, yet simplicity; spirituality, yet flexibility
3. irony; humor; signifying
4. sarcasm—a new comedy
5. direction; positive movement; teaching, nation building
6. subject matter—concrete; reflects a collective and personal lifestyle
7. music: the unique use of vowels and consonants with the developed rap demands that the poetry be read, and read out loud.

Implicit in these categories is the notion that the rules of grammatical form may be suspended and that poetry needs to be taken away from the academic level and written according to the realities of the black masses— to express their joys, sorrows, and concerns. Hence, for literary themes, the black aesthetic writers make use of a number of folk heroes and historical figures as subjects: Stagolee, Shine, Brer' Rabbit, Signifying Monkey, Malcolm X, Garvey, Muhammed, and others. The following poems reveal most of the thematic and stylistic elements associated with the black aesthetic. Discuss and analyze them according to the seven Black Aesthetic categories offered by Don L. Lee.

CAROLYN RODGERS

It Is Deep

> (don't never forget the bridge
> that you crossed over on)

Having tried to use the
witch cord
that erases the stretch of
thirty-three blocks
and tuning in the voice which
    woodenly stated that the
talk box was "disconnected"

My mother, religiously girdled in
her god, slipped on some love, and
laid on my bell like a truck,
blew through my door warm wind from the south
concern making her gruff and tight-lipped
    and scared
that her "baby" was starving,
she having learned, that disconnection results from
    non-payment of bill (s)
recognize the poster of the
grand le-roi (al) cat on the wall
has never even seen the book of
Black poems that I have written
thinks that I am under the influence of
    communists
when I talk about Black as anything
other than something ugly to kill before it grows

in any impression she would not be
considered "relevant" or Black

yet, there she was, standing in my room
not loudly condemning that day and
not remembering that I grew hearing her
curse the factory where she "cut uh slave"
and the cheap j-boss wouldn't allow a union,
not remembering that I heard the tears when
they told her a high school diploma was not enough,
and here now, not able to understand, what she had
been forced to deny, still—
she pushed into my kitchen so
she could open my refrigerator to see
what I had to eat, and pressed fifty
bills in my hand saying "pay the talk bill and buy
some food; you got folks who care about you . . . ."

My mother, religious-negro, proud of
having waded through a storm, is very obviously
a sturdy Black bridge that I
crossed over, on.

HAKI R. MADHUBUTI (DON L. LEE)

But He Was Cool

or: he even stopped for green lights

super-cool
ultrablack
a tan/purple
had a beautiful shade.

he had a double-natural
that wd put the sisters to shame.
his dashikis were tailor made
& his beads were imported sea shells
    (from some blk/country i never heard of)
he was triple-hip.

his tikis were hand carved
out of ivory
& came express from the motherland.

he would greet u in swahili
& say good-by in yoruba.

wooooooooooooo-jim he bes so cool & ill tel li gent
    cool-cool is so cool he was un-cooled
      by other niggers' cool
    cool-cool ultracool was bop-cool/ice
      box cool so cool cool cool
    his wine didn't have to be cooled, him
      was air conditioned cool
    cool-cool/real cool made me cool—
      now ain't that cool
    cool-cool so cool him nick-named
      refrigerator.

cool-cool so cool
he didn't know,
after detroit, newark, chicago &c.,
we had to hip
    cool-cool/super-cool/real cool
  that
to be black
is
to be
very-hot.

AMIRI BARAKA (LEROI JONES)

Leadbelly Gives an Autograph

Pat your foot
and turn
   the corner. Nat Turner, dying wood
of the church. Our lot
is vacant. Bring the twisted myth
of speech. The boards brown and falling
away. The metal bannisters cheap
and rattly. Clean new Sundays. We thought
it possible to enter
the way of the strongest.

But it is rite that the world's ills
erupt as our own. Right that we take
our own specific look into the shapely
blood of the heart.
      Looking thru trees
the wicker statues blowing softly against
the dusk.
Looking thru dusk

thru dark-
ness. A clearing of stars
and half-soft mud.

The possibilities of music. First
that it does exist. And that we do,
in that scripture of rhythms. The earth,
I mean the soil, as melody. The fit you need,
the throes. To pick it up and cut
away what does not singularly express.

Need.
Motive.
The delay of language.

A strength to be handled by giants.

The possibilities of statement. I am saying, now,
what my father could not remember
to say. What my grandfather
was killed
for believing.
    Pay me off, savages.
    Build me an equitable human assertion.

One that looks like a jungle, or one that looks like the
   cities
of the West. But I provide the stock. The beasts
and myths.
    The City's Rise!
     (And what is history, then? An old deaf
      lady
      burned to death
      in South Carolina.)

NIKKI GIOVANNI

Adulthood

for Claudia

I usta wonder who i'd be

when i was a little girl in indianapolis
sitting on doctors porches with post-dawn pre-debs
(wondering would my aunt drag me to church sunday)
i was meaningless

and i wondered if life
would give me a chance to mean

i found a new life in the withdrawal from all things
not like my image

when i was a teen-ager i usta sit
on front steps conversing
the gym teachers son with embryonic eyes
about the essential essence of the universe
(and other bullshit stuff)
recognizing the basic powerlessness of me

but then i went to college where i learned
that just because everything i was was unreal
i could be real and not just real through withdrawal
into emotional crosshairs or colored bourgeoisie
    intellectual pretensions
but from involvement with things approaching reality
i could possibly have a life

so catatonic emotions and time wasting sex games
were replaced with functioning commitments to logic
    and
necessity and the gray area was slowly darkened into
a black thing
for a while progress was being made along with a
    certain degree
of happiness cause i wrote a book and found a love
and organized a theatre and even gave some lectures on
Black history
and began to believe all good people could get
together and win without bloodshed
then
hammarskjold was killed
and lumumba was killed
and diem was killed
and kennedy was killed
and malcolm was killed
and evers was killed
and schwerner, chaney and goodman were killed
and liuzzo was killed
and stokely fled the country
and le roi was arrested
and rap was arrested
and pollard, thompson and cooper were killed

and king was killed
and kennedy was killed
and i sometimes wonder why i didn't become a
    debutante
sitting on porches, going to church all the time,
    wondering
is my eye make-up on straight
or a withdrawn discoursing on the stars and moon
instead of a for real Black person who must now feel
and inflict
pain

Afro-American Art

The art of Afro-America has been a varied conglomeration of many interests, schools of thought, and modes of expression. The works of early Afro-American artists such as Edward M. Bannister, Edmonia Lewis (the first black female sculptor), R. S. Duncanson, and Henry O. Tanner were for the most part academic in treatment, cosmopolitan in theme, and lacking in race consciousness. These artists viewed themselves primarily as artists and only incidentally as black. As a result of this attitude, they were considered pretentious by both blacks and whites, since the fine arts were generally associated with security, leisure, wealth, and "high culture."

Picasso and the other artists who discovered African art in Paris helped to stimulate interest in it in the United States. While some black artists in America rejected identification with African art, as they did with Africa itself, others spoke of the need to develop an Afro-American art idiom based on African forms. Thus the decades of the 1920s and 1930s witnessed racially conscious Afro-American artists who dealt with many of the themes that were articulated in the New Negro movement: the celebration of the beauty of black people, the illumination of the history of the Afro-American experience, and the search for identity and roots.

One of the most significant artists to emerge from the Harlem Renaissance was Aaron Douglas. With his use of highly stylized figures in geometric settings, Douglas is rightly regarded as the pioneer of African style among Afro-American painters. Two of his well-known murals in the Countee Cullen Branch of the

New York Public Library are reproduced here (Figs. 36-1, 36-2). The murals, entitled *Aspects of Negro Life,* depict the cultural and historical background of Afro-Americans. What cultural or historical element can you identify?

It was in sculpture, however, that a consciously African Afro-American style was most clearly expressed. The works of Richmond Barthé and Sargent Johnson offer the best examples of such sculpture. Sargent Johnson's bust *Chester* (Fig. 36-3) and Barthé's *African Dancer* (Fig. 36-4) are both particularly striking for their African qualities. Using your knowledge from the section on African art in Volume I, what African qualities can you identify?

36–1, 36–2   Aaron Douglas, "Aspects of Negro Life." (New York Public Library)

36-3   Left. Sargent Johnson, "Chester." (San Francisco Museum of Modern Art, Albert M. Bender Collection)

36-4   Below. Richmond Barthé, "African Dancer," (Collection of the Whitney Museum of American Art, New York)

In the decades of the 1960s and 1970s, Afro-American life became a dominant theme for a large number of artists. Like the poets and novelists of the black aesthetic, these artists sought to unite art with the struggle for racial dignity and equality and with the daily life of the black masses. To accomplish this, paintings were displayed on tenement and playground walls, in schools and recreational centers, in storefront galleries, and on corner lots. These paintings tend to be clearly ideological, the forms are simple and bold, and primary colors are used to achieve the desired psychological impact. Black Power murals, designed to teach the young about Afro-American heroes, became a major theme. One of the most popular of these murals is *The Wall of Dignity* (Color Plate XIII), located in Detroit on the side of a building fronting a vacant lot. The mural is painted in three horizontal panels: the top describes the history of black people from ancient Egypt to the kingdom of Benin; the center is dedicated to contemporary heroes; and the lower panel presents a group of angry black faces that glare accusingly.

In these two decades there were numerous other Afro-American artists who chose to communicate the Afro-American experience through the accepted aesthetic standards of modern art: pop art, op art, minimal art, kinetic art, and conceptual art. A few examples are shown in Figures 36-5, 36-6, and 36-7. Carefully analyze them for their thematic and stylistic features. Do any of them have racial overtones? If so, identify the artistic or structural elements that make them so.

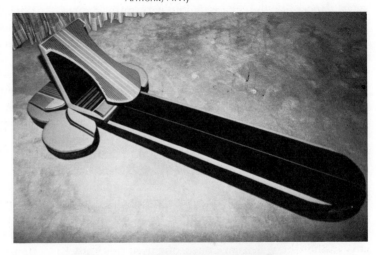

36-6 Daniel Larue Johnson, "Homage to René d'Harnancourt." (Collection of Joy and I. J. Seligsohn, Armonk, N.Y.)

36-5 David C. Driskell, "Reflection and Dream." (Mr. and Mrs. Dick E. Miller)

36-7 Joe Overstreet, "Justice, Faith, Hope and Peace." (Collection of the artist)

Afro-American Dance

The Harlem Renaissance was a spur to the creation of a black aesthetic in dance as it was in the other arts. The black dancer and choreographer could draw on a rich folkloric tradition in black America itself, on European and white American innovations in ballet and modern dance, and on his or her own observations and knowledge of African (as well as Caribbean) dance. The talents that have made use of these elements have created a truly unique idiom in dance.

There is no doubt that American blacks managed to preserve an African style of dance. This developed into social dances like the cake walk and performing dances like the tap dance. Blacks performed in the minstrel shows touring the United States from the 1840s to the beginning of World War I. In spite of the often negative way in which whites took "minstrels," these shows helped to establish blacks as entertainers and influenced the development of the American musical comedy.

The two dancers who did most to establish black dance as an art form were Katherine Dunham and Pearl Primus, both active in the 1930s and 1940s. Pearl Primus, who studied with Martha Graham, established herself as a serious concert dancer although she also performed in night clubs. Becoming interested in African dance, she went to Africa to do research, particularly in the (then) Belgian Congo. She used this knowledge, as well as Afro-American themes, in her choreography. One of her most moving compositions is "The Negro Speaks of Rivers," based on the Langston Hughes poem.

Black dance companies today continue to adapt African and Afro-American styles and themes to modern dance. Alvin Ailey is an exciting, lyrical choreographer and his company one of the best and most successful on the New York scene (Fig. 36-8). His works such as *Revelations*, set to spirituals, and *Roots of the Blues*, interpret the Afro-American musical experience in dance. *Cry*, which features the stunning dancer Judith Jamison, is a tribute to black women. The company doing most to bring African dance to the American stage is the young one of Chuck Davis. Davis, who has studied in Africa, presents authentic African dances and his own compositions based on African movements.

Jazz and Contemporary Music: Miles Davis

From the early years of jazz to the present day, there has been little doubt that this art form, along with blues, spirituals, ragtime, and other types of music in which American blacks have played leading roles, had an ancestry that clearly reached back to the cultural traditions of the natives of West Africa. It is true that jazz is not African but American, for its essence is an amalgamation of African, European, and American traditions forged in the social milieu of the late nineteenth-century United States; but essential ingredients, too numerous and complex to fully explain here, were transported to this continent by black slaves and transformed into something now called Afro-American in the acculturation process that connected slave community with ghetto and then neighborhood. By the years just following World War II, we discover that jazz has become a leading American popular music as well as an elitist music for the jazz community and an ethnic music for black society in general. In the 1940s, one could observe several styles of jazz in performance with their practitioners and followers: Dixieland with Louis Armstrong, Bunk Johnson, and Kid Ory; swing with Duke Ellington, Benny Goodman, Count Basie, and Woody Herman; and bebop with Charlie Parker, Dizzy Gillespie, and Tadd Dameron. America and American music was about to undergo some major upheavals and transformations during the 1950s and 1960s, the years of Martin Luther King, Jr., Peace Walks, integrated schools, Malcolm X, and the Black Power movement; the career of one leading jazz musician spans this era. The changes in his music and his public image reflect the changes in American society that were taking place for Americans of all races and socioeconomic backgrounds. In many ways jazz trumpeter Miles Davis is, and was, as much a social leader as he is a musical artist of the first rank, and his struggles with both music and society tell us much about ourselves and our country.

Born in the Midwest in 1926, Miles Davis traveled to New York City and played trumpet in his first professional recording session shortly before his nineteenth birthday. He had received encouragement from two jazz leaders of the period, saxophonist Charlie Parker and trumpeter Dizzy Gillespie; but he was obviously young, inexperienced, and somewhat overwhelmed by

36–8 "Revelations," Mari Kajiwara, Melvin Jones, Judith Jamison. (Alvin Ailey American Dance Theater/ Photo Fred Fehl)

the musical company that he was keeping. The then current style was "bebop," a music noted for its difficulty and complexity. Miles's first recorded performances sound shy, nervous, and tense, qualities that certainly must have reflected his own real image at that time: a young, sensitive black from the sticks trying to make it in the Big Apple. He had in common with most of black America an element of suppressed and repressed potential, and he was struggling with society to become a part of the successful establishment. His lifestyle, his music, and even his physical image as reflected in photographs of him from his early professional years project a sense of serious dedication, of striving for acceptance, and of openness. Before he reached his twenty-fifth birthday, his talent allowed him to create, along with a few other modern jazzmen of the period, a new substyle of jazz named "cool." By 1950 he had achieved success, rising to preeminence among jazz trumpeters before the decade was out. Throughout the 1950s he worked with every leading jazz musician and sold countless thousands of long-playing jazz albums. His melodies, known for their lyricism, and his characteristic mellow sound were both

qualities that made his music a favorite with Americans from all walks of life as well as with professional musicians of jazz. Even though a new form of avant-garde jazz, called free jazz, or "The New Thing," sprang up in the early 1960s, the recorded music of Miles Davis through 1965 reflected, to a large degree, the older values of American society in general—popular songs and jazz tunes of a more standard format: "Autumn Leaves," "My Funny Valentine," "Walkin'" (blues), "So What!" (modal piece in popular song form), and others. Then, an important musical change took place in this man's music. "Bitches Brew," which we will study here, illustrates not only the change in Davis's evolution but also some important trends in recent American music.

Beginning in 1966 we find works on Davis's recordings that indicate a new and profound awareness of the artist's spiritual and cultural ties to an African ancestry: "Freedom Jazz Dance," "Footprints," "Ginger Bread Boy," "Limbo," "The Sorcerer," "Prince of Darkness," and "Nefertiti." (The titles are listed in the chronological order of their recording.) We might speculate about the meanings of some of these titles in relation to social thought of this period, for, as Charles Hamm writes:

> The '60s became the age of the underground. Underground films.... Underground political activity.... Underground publications.... Underground religious movements and underground education....
>
> The '60s was . . . the age of permissiveness.... It was a time of the Free Speech Movement, of draft card burning, of nudity on stage and screen, of Women's Lib and Gay Lib, of Black Power, of long hair, of the miniskirt and the see-through blouse, of the virtual disappearance of censorship of movies, stage productions, books, and magazines, of topless and bottomless dancers and waitresses, of SDS and Young Americans for Freedom, of Hippies and Yippies, of marijuana and LSD, of wiretapping, mass arrests, mace, and assassination. The breakdown of faith in American institutions and the suspicion that the state, church, schools, and family were failing to guide people to meaningful lives persuaded more and more persons—not all of them young—to, in the classic phrase of the 1960s, "do their own thing."

Miles Davis was one of those not so young persons who reevaluated his own life and declared, along with the literary followers of the black aesthetic, "Black is beautiful." The "Freedom Jazz Dance" can be seen as an expression of the American blacks' new feeling of power and importance; "Footprints" as a philosophical query into the aftereffects of Ralph Ellison's *Invisible Man* (does he cast a shadow and does he leave footprints?); "Prince of Darkness" as a statement that black is not the color of hell but that of the royal tribes of Africa; and "Nefertiti" as a symbol representing Egypt and Africa as the source of life and civilization.

One might suspect from these facts that Miles Davis totally rejected the rest of American society in the 1960s for a return to African roots, but this is not the case. The genius of the man allowed him to synthesize both experiences into new forms of artistic expression that are greater from the combination than they could have been alone. And this we can observe clearly in a masterpiece recorded in New York City in 1969, "Bitches Brew," a record album (Columbia Records, Stereo GP 26) that proclaims in the visual art of its slip cover, in the titles of the compositions, and in the music itself the beauty and unity of the Afro-American heritage. On the cover we see an African couple embracing on the ocean beach and peering across the waters to a distant storm; dark and light skinned African

hands and faces intertwining in an attitude of balance and equality; and sculpturesque African women in traditional garb displaying pride, modesty, and beauty.

The music displays a fusion of jazz, rock, and avantgarde classical influence; it also fuses a group of white and black musicians into a cohesive artistic whole. The links to jazz are apparent in the use of rhythm section, *improvisation*, jazz *inflection* and *timbre*; the ties to rock 'n' roll appear in the use of electric guitar and bass and in the application of rock rhythmic patterns; the debt to African music is realized in the hand drumming of Lenny White and the percussion ensemble concept of "Pharaoh's Dance"; and the bond with advanced contemporary composition is heard in the sculptured electronic sounds of the electric pianos, the sonorities of the bass clarinet, and the extended forms of the individual works.

"Pharaoh's Dance" is a composition by Joe Zawinul, one of the pianists and a musician deriving much inspiration from the irregular folk rhythms of Eastern Europe. His interest in rhythm and his knowledge and feel for electronic sounds led him to call for an aggregate of sounds that portray a feeling for dance, for an exotic past circumstance, and for an African persistence of beat below a nebulous cloud of melodic and harmonic sound. The first impression of the introduction is one of *atonality*, but it is quickly set aside by the repetition of bass sounds and patterns that give a sense of a stable *tonal* center. The trumpet improvisations, in addition to fitting properly with the rest of the music, also portray the majesty of the concept of "Pharaoh." The men improvise together as jazz artists have since the beginning of the idiom, but they play no three-minute song forms; instead they spontaneously create long musical units that are bound together and unified by recurring melodic snippets, by persistent and repetitious rhythmic patterns, and by the instrumentation itself. "Pharaoh's Dance" is African in inspiration, Afro-American in performance and creation, and universal in expression. Near the end, to signal the halt to both listener and performer (and dancer), the bass repeats a single note over and over, creating a *coda* that reaffirms the *tonality*, the formal direction, and, in a sense, the beginning.

Whereas Zawinul's piece moves in an insistent recurring rhythm, Davis's work, "Bitches Brew," is plastic, malleable, and difficult to divide cleanly into units.

The sounds are intentionally distorted by electronic means, and one distinctly notices the trumpet, with more or less reverberation and echo. But clarity is not the only valid artistic concept possible in music, and this "Brew" blends contrasting sections and ideas smoothly by fusing the edges. Where traditional jazz dealt with well-shaped melodic units (often singable) and well-ordered *harmonic progressions*, this jazz employs melodic and harmonic impressions that are recognizable, even if only vaguely. The importance of the soloist is lessened as the total blend of the entire ensemble is attenuated. Instrumental virtuosity, in the old sense of the word, holds little value here, where fast notes and slow notes vie equally for the listener's attention. The production of the music becomes a communal action, and this is very much an African characteristic. The blend of ancient and modern, traditional and experimental, into an artistic unit is a signal accomplishment of this work.

The remaining four sections provide added contrast and some relief from the intensity of the album as a whole. "Spanish Key" brings the vitality of rock rhythms to the forefront; "John McLaughlin" reminds the ear of Miles Davis's earlier movement, "Bitches Brew"; "Miles Runs the Voodoo Down" uses a rhythmic *ostinato* and layers of varying percussion activity to create an African mood that is eventually penetrated by virtuosic solo flights on Wayne Shorter's soprano saxophone; and "Sanctuary" restores calm to a very active musical venture. For ninety-four minutes, the listener is called upon to attend the musical outcries of a master jazz musician searching to find a real identity in his music. Surrounded by creative younger men, Miles Davis attempted a synthesis in this creation that both spoke to the age and was part of the rebellion, too. It led other jazz musicians to question their values and sent many of these very musicians on musical and spiritual quests of their own. "Bitches Brew" is a classic, a classic of jazz of the 1960s.

Other Trends in American Visual Arts

Some of the trends in recent American art have been represented by the black artists in the last section. To see these and others from another perspective, let us look at some major recent trends in the United States, undoubtedly now the world leader in the arts.

Abstract Expressionism Abstract expressionism, or action painting, emerged as the most visible and coherent school of American painting in the years immediately after World War II. In retrospect, the painters whose work is covered by the term seem to be a most heterogeneous group of individuals: nevertheless, it is possible to discern enough similarities to explain the name. Consider this canvas by Jackson Pollock (Fig. 36-9). First, it is a very large painting, wall-sized in fact. Second, it reminds us of a work by Kandinsky in that it has no identifiable subject matter except the formal one that is the product of the combination of shapes, forms, and colors on the surface. It seems to be derived in part from the cubist notion, also supported by Kandinsky, that a painting is good because it *is*, not because it represents something. But we also know from Kandinsky, the cubists, and the surrealists (as well as from Van Gogh and Gauguin) that lines, colors, and shapes are capable of communicating directly with the viewer, through the unconscious and the intuitive. By appealing to these facilities rather than the rational, intellectualizing ones, the artist involves the spectator in a dialogue with the pure elements of the painting.

We also know, particularly from Kandinsky, how very difficult it is to create a picture outside of the habitual and familiar, so we might ask how Pollock has created such seemingly random patterns on the canvas. Pollock created his paintings by dripping, pouring, and splashing paint on a canvas laid out on the floor. It was his belief that in this uninhibited way of working, he surrendered control of his rational processes; the work produced would be a reflection of interior, personal drives and motivations. He also believed that in this way his paintings would speak directly to the unconscious, therefore allowing the viewer to apprehend a shared universality existing beyond the habitual and familiar. In this painting we seem to have the unification of a number of ideas that had already emerged in the early twentieth century. The large scale of this work, however, gives it unrelieved energy and an overwhelming appeal to the emotional and subjective, capable of creating an environment that is one with the viewer.

Not all the painters who were a part of the abstract expressionism school made paintings that had no recognizable objects. But all the painters involved gave primacy to the unconscious and to the physical act, the

36–9   Jackson Pollock, "Blue Poles, 1952." (Australian National Gallery, Canberra)

gesture of making the work. The two aims are, in a way, almost mutually exclusive. If the painter is to be uninhibited and have his gestures as free from conscious motivation as possible, then from the moment that the first bit of paint is laid down, the painter becomes involved in an emotionally charged situation.

You can demonstrate this for yourself. Take a piece of paper. Put down a random line. Now you must decide, will the first line determine the placement of the second, or will you attempt to let the second line be as random as the first? Once two lines are down you are forced, almost unconsciously, to make some kind of decision about the placement of a third line, or form. Imagine how complicated this would become if you were working not only with a black line but with colored lines. The factors that are unconsciously forcing you into a decision-making situation are first, the sheet of paper, which acts as a kind of frame; second, there is your natural orientation to the world: top, bottom, left, right, front, back, beside, behind. Then there is an unconscious need to make the arrangement "look right," to produce a sense of balance and rhythm, order and

harmony. Whether these needs are inborn or the product of culture does not matter in this instance. What is clear is the need to make "sense" of the thing; to find a personal structure and to impose it on the experience. Thus, on the one hand, the struggle is for a decisive subjective statement; on the other, it is a struggle with the powerful forces generated by the familiar knowledge of seeing, knowing, and experiencing both the painterly world and the habitual world.

It is this ambiguity between ends and means that makes abstract expressionist paintings so strong, enduring, and powerful. Drawn into the dialogue that the painter carries on with his canvas and paint, the viewer experiences the emotionally charged event of which the canvas is a record. At the same time it was this ambiguity that made this kind of painting a difficult act to sustain. Like Monet, who sought more and more transient effects in the landscape, these painters were forced to greater and greater personal and emotional extremes to sustain creative energy; otherwise, their gestures ran the risk of becoming hollow and repetitive. According to one abstract expressionist painter, the need for simplicity, clarity, order, and objectivity becomes overwhelming in the face of spending so much emotional energy.

In this light the emergence of a number of different kinds of painting in the early 1960s is understandable. First were the color field painters; then op art that celebrates the inherent complexity of vision (Color Plate XIV); then pop art that celebrates the popular imagery of films, advertising, and merchandising (Color Plate XV). These have been joined in the late 1960s and early 1970s by photorealism, naturalism, and conceptual art. One is inclined to throw up one's hands and say, so what?

Such a reaction is not, however, possible when we remember that the visual arts reflect, and respond to, the condition of people. In this enormous diversity there is the search for a constituency. Historically the patrons of art and architecture have been the establishment: city-state, empire, church, monarch, aristocracy. With the growth of population, the bureaucratization of governmental process, the greater distribution of wealth, the proliferation of political allegiances made possible by the democratization of the West, the artist and architect have no longer been bound by the establishment. In fact, it could be said that it has been hard to identify the establishment, though it could be argued that now there are various establishments: art dealers; museums; universities; local, state, and federal governments; and private corporations, to name a few. In a society that values clearly quantifiable success and demands clearly objective scientific data to support a hypothesis, the question of whether or not art is necessary remains open.

Architecture Architects, today, are as hard-pressed as are painters; they have certainly not been put in control of the built environment; moreover, many question whether or not theirs is an appropriate job. Yet it is also true that never has there been such production in art and architecture; never before have the images and ideas of the artist and architect reached so far into our lives. Films, advertising, furniture, fabrics, product design, books, cars, machines of all kinds, every aspect of our lives is in some way touched by the accomplishments of the artists and architects who broke new ground or renewed the old with their at-tempts to find a language capable of communicating with this century. In every town or city there is at least one simple, glass-enclosed, steel-framed office block or tower. There is also at least one building whose framework is made of concrete reinforced with steel. These two kinds of buildings are products of the technology of the age and the corresponding formal possibilities suggested to architects by that technology and by human needs.

In the years immediately following World War II, the United States seemed to take the lead in propagating the architecture of the Bauhaus, brought from Germany by Gropius and Miës van der Rohe, who immigrated to this country. The pure rectangular glass curtain became associated with the creation of a particular image, whether for corporation or campus. The Seagram Building (Fig. 36-10), designed by Miës in association with Philip Johnson, on New York's Park Avenue, is built of bronze anodized steel and dark glass.

36–10 Miës van der Rohe, Seagram Building, New York. (© Ezra Stoller, Esto)

36–11 Le Corbusier, Carpenter Center, Cambridge, Massachusetts. (Harvard University News Office)

Isolated on its plaza and outfitted with sumptuous interiors of beautiful wood veneers, bronze and marble, it appeared the culmination of the idea of the tall office building. Nevertheless, the continued proliferation of this type of building has met with as much concern as praise. The consistency of the glass-curtain wall building has had the effect of making the cityscape repetitive and boring, making every city look like every other. Moreover, the application of this basic idea to such diverse uses as apartment buildings, office towers, hospitals, and college campuses has seemed to deny the avowed aim of the Bauhaus architects to produce a responsive, functional, pragmatic architecture that responds to human needs. In fact, Le Corbusier had moved away from the pure geometry of his early work to use concrete and steel-reinforced concrete as a malleable sculptural medium (Fig. 36-11). Some architects in this country responded to his ideas, while others have sought greater diversity by technological innovation. Eero Saarinen worked in a variety of forms and materials, attempting to give symbolic expression and

36–12   Eero Saarinen, Dulles Airport. (© Dandelet)

imagery to building. The Dulles Airport is one example of a varied use of the reinforced concrete pier and glass-curtain wall (Fig. 36-12). His success or failure rests on a personal experience of the building and a personal attitude toward what is appropriate in architecture.

At the same time the architect himself has become more and more aware of the need for his expertise in shaping the environment and less and less secure about his ability to do so. Utopian city-planning schemes, developed in the first thirty years of this century, were applied to areas of war-devastated Europe, and to American cities with growing need for housing. Some of these schemes were successful, while others turned into just another kind of slum. It has become clear to some architects and theorists that more than "good design" is needed. Design has to find a way to take account of the extremely different needs of different groups of people.

Moreover, architects and planners must know much more about politics and pressure groups, the financial and social determinants of the successful functioning of a housing project or hospital. Some schools of design include social scientists, psychologists, anthropologists, and demographers on their faculties. The outcome is not predictable, but the premise is somewhat hopeful. Frank Lloyd Wright's dream of a different house for each different individual's needs and ideas remains desirable, but it is more and more remote.

Is it possible, then, to make any generalizations about the nature and role of the visual arts and architecture in our society—to find any evidence of their roles as capable of reflecting the humanist values that have dominated our study? This may be accomplished by defining several trends that seem to be prevalent in the visual arts and architecture in the past thirty years.

In the visual arts there has been a concern with the media of painting, sculpture, and the graphic arts. At times this interest has manifested itself in complex and rich personal expression. At other times media have been used purely, objectively, to create images of simple freshness and visual complexity. Moreover, new media —the mixture of various media—have tended to blur the lines between painting, sculpture, the graphic arts, and photography.

As artists have been concerned with media, so they have been concerned with the public. There has been a continual dialogue concerning the role of the artist in society and his obligations to that society. Some painters have been accused of willful isolationism, obscurantism, and obfuscation in the name of art. Others have returned to naturalism and realism as a means to free painting and sculpture from personal, subjective experiences. Still others have developed and maintained a highly personal style that has not responded to the various new movements in art.

A concern with media and with meaning has also been reflected in a growing tendency in the visual arts to consider the environment—the total experience—as one susceptible to art, in ways that recall the complex architectural, sculptural, and painterly arrangements of the seventeenth century. In our century, however, the aim has been not to create a religious experience but to engage the viewer in an active relationship with the situation. The earthworks that the sculptor Michael Heizer constructed in southern Nevada (Fig. 36-13), the curtain that Christo hung in Rifle Gorge, Colorado (Fig. 36-14), the beams of Corten steel that Richard Serra has planted in the earth do not make fun of art except in an ironic way, while calling attention to the natural environment and attempting to make a kind of peace with the environment through imaginative uses of technology. Moreover, these environmental works free the artist from the museum, a place considered by many to be the present perpetrator of elitism and isolationism.

In architecture we may discern some parallels with the visual arts; but, because its object is to produce utilitarian objects, other forces have an influence on its development. On the one hand, there are those architects who subscribe to the production of purely beautiful, monumental, and precious design, believing that architecture should be inspiring and that reflecting function is a secondary concern. On the other hand, some architects have turned to urban planning, urban studies, urban design, the politics of public policy, and so on, to help ensure a more responsive, place-determined, and visually rich architecture. Still other architects have

36–13 Michael Heizer, "Double Negative," 1969–70. Size 1500 x 50 x 30 feet; 240,000 tons of rhyolite and sandstone displaced. Virgin River Mesa, Nevada. (Collection: Virginia Dwan. Photo courtesy Xavier Fourcade, Inc., New York)

36–14 Christo, "Valley Curtain," 1970–72. Width: 1250–1368 feet. Height: 185–365 feet. 200,000 square feet of nylon polyamide; 110,000 pounds of steel cable; 800 tons of concrete. Grand Hogback, Rifle, Colorado. (Photo by Harry Shunk)

taken the position that architecture is a language independent of, and unable to be completely determined by, function. To this end, these architects study the formal characteristics of architecture, attempting by their manipulation to create fresh solutions and forms. Still others urge a study of the past and an imaginative use of past forms to give richer meaning to contemporary design.

In short, there are no easy answers to the role of art. The writers who have termed ours a postmodern age suggest that humanism as we have known it since the Renaissance is at an end. Faced with the awesome rela-

tivity of all knowledge and truth, we are confronted with an unknowable world, equipped with an obsolete body of information and values. Like the humanists of the Renaissance, we can see our past but we seem to have no real connections with it. But, as the study of the humanities shows, the past is necessary even if it acts as a force against which persons rebel. Without the past we have nothing on which to build our experience. Today architecture and the visual arts seem to be, more than ever, experience-centered; it is out of experience, not as spectators but as participants, that we build new awareness and new knowledge.

Literary Directions

The Challenge of the Media   As is the case with "art," the whole notion of "literature" is undergoing a serious questioning. As the development of the printing press once caused the book, or the printed word, to replace the spoken word as a primary means of both communication and literary enjoyment, so the audio-visual forms of film, radio, and television have to a great extent usurped the province of the written word. A critic like Marshall McLuhan believes that the electronic media, particularly television, will make our culture similar to the oral one of a tribal village, but on a global scale. Gradually we will lose our linear, analytical habits developed through eye-reading in favor of instantaneous communication through images. On a more mundane level, it is obvious that watching TV has become a more widespread national pastime than reading fiction or poetry, going to the theater, or even going to the movies. Television dramas and shows fill many of the needs for realism and escapism that were satisfied by novels in the nineteenth century and by vaudeville and the weekly movie in the early twentieth. A certain kind of literature has always spoken to people's needs to identify with people who have problems like their own, or to escape from them into worlds of glamour and adventure.

In spite of a somewhat frightening decline in functional literacy in this country, however, the book trade continues to flourish as never before; it seems evident that the printed word is not at all ready to die out. Literature and, to some extent, film have been put in a position analogous to that of painting at the time when photography was becoming popular. The artist who used canvas and paint had to discover ways of creating not possible to explore with the camera. The artist using words must discover what he or she can create that cannot be created by the TV studio director.

Postmodern Writing   We have seen that modernist writers responded early in the century to the challenge to portray a reality other than the superficial, apparent one and that they did so by manipulating language in new ways. The literature called postmodern continues to respond to this challenge, but without the modernist's faith in language. The "literature of si-lence" is an antiliterature, one that constantly questions the possibility of telling a tale, singing a song, saying *anything*. In so doing, it causes us to meditate on the function of language as a means of human communication. Its most famous practitioner is Samuel Beckett; in South America it is represented by J. L. Borges and in North America by Donald Barthelme, Ishmael Reed, and Ronald Sukenick.

Critics in the late twentieth century are constantly prophesying the death of traditional forms such as the novel or tragedy. Certainly these forms are all undergoing revision. We encounter antinovels, such as those by John Barth, books with antiheroes that parody all the conventions of novel making and hero identification, antiplays inviting the viewer to participate rather than sweeping him into illusion, and even, as in films by Robert Altman, anticinema. One traditional genre very much alive, however, is criticism. It can indeed be argued that ours is an age of criticism. Theoretical writings on literature and culture abound. Critics have become creative, crossing into the domain of "pure" literature.

Postmodern literature of all sorts quite often disregards traditional definitions of genre or boundaries between the arts. "Street theater" does away with the stage, while the poetry of Allen Ginsberg and his followers takes poetry out of books, mingling it with music, religious or drug-induced ecstasy, and stage antics. The "new journalists" mix a kind of subjective poetry with straight reporting. Norman Mailer has abandoned the writing of fiction for this kind of journalism. Lyric poetry, on the other hand, while it has become through the influence of Robert Lowell increasingly "confessional" or personal, does not hesitate to comment on political and social events.

Naturally, not all writers follow these trends. The novel that remains largely within the tradition of realism is far from dead. One of its best representatives is the Nobel prize winner Saul Bellow, an astute observer of American culture. Another genre that flourishes, in both novel and film, is science fiction.

The brief selections that follow do not pretend in any way to represent contemporary American literature, but the authors are two of its better practitioners. Kurt Vonnegut, especially popular among young people since the 1960s, has mixed science fiction with antinovel; and he comments on the American scene with both irony and affection. The essay printed here is a kind of exercise in new journalism in which Vonnegut comments on the space race, America, and the planet earth. Adrienne Rich writes poetry in the "confessional" mode, but her poems demonstrate an epigraph that she uses from George Eliot: "There is no private life which is not determined by a wider public life." This is, of course, true of the contemporary poets in the Afro-American section as well. Like Carolyn Rodgers and Nikki Giovanni, Rich is very much concerned with relating the particular experience of contemporary American women.

KURT VONNEGUT, JR.

Excelsior! We're Going to the Moon! Excelsior!

My brother Bernard saw a spaceship go up one time from Cape Kennedy, and he told me: "You know, if you're right *there,* the whole thing almost seems worth it." It was *almost* a billion-dollar thrill, he said—the noise in particular.

Noise.

"Some fireworks!" he said. "The earth moved!" We are so old that we have both had extensive personal experiences with fireworks. We used to buy them from mail-order houses and stores—ladyfingers, aerial salutes, cherry bombs, nigger-chasers.

Nigger-chasers.

What my brother said about the noise at Cape Kennedy triggered this childhood response in me: "Wow!" I said. "I sure want to hear that noise."

I never have heard it, though, except from a television loudspeaker about the size of a silver dollar. I went so far as to wangle a NASA invitation to a launch, then couldn't go. But the invitation got me on a mailing list for free materials which celebrate Americans and space. The best free thing so far is a book of heavenly color photographs called *Exploring Space with a Camera.* It is on my space reference shelf next to *The Look-It-Up Book of the Stars and Planets,* by Patricia Lauber (Random House).

Look-it-up.

Miss Lauber writes for children. Here is the sort of thing she says to them:

We are flying through space. Our craft is the earth, which orbits the sun at a speed of 67,000 miles an hour. As it orbits the sun, it spins on its axis. The sun is a star.

If I were drunk, I might cry about all that. Obviously, all Earthlings are my beloved fellow astronauts.

Beloved.

James E. Webb is less fraternal. He has nations on his mind: Some win, some lose. He says this in his foreword to *Exploring Space with a Camera:*

Down through the course of history, the mastery of a new environment, or of a major new technology, or of the combination of the two as we now see in space, has had profound effects on the future of nations; on their relative strength and security; on their relations with one another; on their internal economic, social, and political affairs; and on the concepts of reality held by their people.

Their people.

He gives no examples. So I think of Germany in the First World War, learning how to fight under water. I think of Germany's amazing rockets in World War Two. I think of everybody's everything in World War Three. I think of armor and chariots and gunpowder in olden times—of floating gun platforms which gave one nation and then another one mastery of the surface of the sea.

I think of the Spaniards' mastery of the New World, with several million other Earthlings already here, with at least two other Earthling civilizations already here. I think of their masterful torture of Indians—to make the Indians tell where they had hidden gold.

Gold.

I think of white America's mastery of the South by the imaginative use of kidnapped Africans. I think of DDT.

Most of the true tales of masterfulness in new environments with new technologies have been cruel or greedy, it seems to me. The concepts of reality held by the masterful people have customarily been stupid or solipsistic in retrospect. Nobody has been remarkably secure, the masters have often ceased to be masters quickly. There have been tremendous messes to be cleaned up, ravaged landscapes dotted by shattered Earthlings and their machines.

Stupid.

We have spent something like $33 billion on space so far. We should have spent it on cleaning up our filthy colonies here on earth. There is no urgency whatsoever about getting somewhere in space, much as Arthur C. Clarke wants to discover the source of the terrific radio signals coming from Jupiter. It isn't as though we aren't already going somewhere in space. Every passing hour brings the whole solar system 43,000 miles closer to Globular Cluster M13 in Hercules.

Globular Cluster M13.

Brilliant space enthusiasts like Arthur C. Clarke are treasures, of course, to the thousands of persons in the enormously profitable spaceship trade. He speaks more enchantingly than they do. His art and their commercial interests coincide. "The discovery that Jupiter is quite warm and has precisely the type of atmosphere in which life is believed to have arisen on Earth may be the prelude to the most significant biological findings of this century," he wrote recently in *Playboy*.

Playboy.

Somewhere cash registers ring.

Other innocent space boomers are scientists like Dr. Harold C. Urey and Dr. Harold Masursky and so on, men who are passionately curious to know if the craters on the moon were caused by impact or volcanic action—or both or what. They would love to know right away, if possible, and knowing *is* possible now, at fantastic expense. The money has been gathered by tax collectors, and the money has frequently been taken from American Earthlings who are poor as Job's turkey, to coin a phrase.

Job.

If all goes right with the first landing on the moon, all the Jobs in America, and all the happy people, too, will have chipped in lavishly to buy fifty pounds of rock and dust from the moon. They will also have helped an old fraternity brother of mine, who is an important man in the space program. He drives a Jaguar XKE.

XKE.

We were D.U.s together at Cornell.

D.U.s.

My fraternity brother is glowingly proud of the space program, and rightly so. (He is also proud of the fraternity, which is maybe something else again.) He is an engineer, and one night here we drank a lot of stingers, and he rhapsodized about the precision in the manufacture and launching of the "birds." And I found myself thinking of Harry Houdini, who made his living escaping from straitjackets and bank vaults and sealed chests under water.

Water.

The stingers encouraged me to suppose that Houdini, if he had had $33 billion, would have hired the best scientific minds of his time, would have had them build him a big rocket and a sort of pressure cooker in which he might ride. And he would have had them fire him at the moon.

Why would Houdini have done that? Because, even on a limited budget, he was perhaps the greatest showman of all time. He thrilled people in a way that thrills them the most: He put his life on the line. He was basically an engineer—who saved his own life again and again with strength, courage, tools, and engineering.

It is the Houdini aspects of the space program which reward most Earthlings—the dumb ones, the dropouts, the elevator operators and stenographers and so on. They are too dense ever to care about the causes of craters on the moon. Tell them about the radio signals coming from Jupiter, and they forget again right away. What they like are shows where people get killed.

Killed.

And they get them, too.

About the dumb Earthlings versus the smart Earthlings: I have known a fair number of scientists over the years, and I noticed that they were often as bored by each other's work as dumb people would be. I was a public-relations man for a while at the Research Laboratory of the General Electric Company, and I was several times privileged to see one scientist rush into the laboratory of another, ecstatic over a new piece of information. In effect, he was barking, "Eureka! Eureka! Eureka!"

Eureka.

And the scientist who had to listen to all that barking obviously couldn't wait for the visitor to shut up and go away.

I used to talk to G.E. scientists sometimes about exciting stuff I had read in *Scientific American*. I was reading it regularly in those days. I thought it was part of my job—to keep up. If the article I was discussing wasn't related to my listener's field, he would doze. I might as well have been speaking Babylonian.

So it is my guess that even our most brilliant scientists are fairly bored by the space program, unless they are directly concerned with the moon and all that. To them, too, it must look like very expensive show biz.

Eureka.

My brother is partly dependent upon the Navy for funds with which to investigate cloud physics. He was talking recently to a similarly mendicant scientist about the billions invested in space. The colleague said this, wryly: "For *that* kind of money, the least they can do is discover God."

Discover God.

You dig fifty pounds of moon rock, and what do you get? Another day older, and deeper in debt. St. Peter, don't you call me, 'cause I can't go. I owe my soul to de company sto'.

De company sto'.

Earth is such a pretty blue and pink and white pearl in the pictures NASA sent me. It looks so *clean*. You can't see all the hungry, angry Earthlings down there—and the smoke and the sewage and trash and sophisticated weaponry. I flew over Appalachia the other day—at about 500 miles an hour and five miles up. Life is said to be horrible down there in many places, but it looked like the Garden of Eden to me. I was a rich guy, way up in the sky, munching dry-roasted peanuts and sipping gin.

Eden.

"The Earth is our cradle, which we are about to leave," says Arthur C. Clarke. "And the Solar System will be our kindergarten." Most of us will never leave this cradle, of course, unless death turns out to be a form of astronautics.

There is always gin.

Gin.

I remember the apes in the great Cinerama motion picture *2001*. I remember their bloodshot eyes and their

fears at night, how they learned to use tools to smash in each other's skulls. And I suppose we're not much past that on the scale of evolution, even though we now have Cinerama. The same night I saw *2001*, Dr. Nathan Pusey, president of Harvard, called the Cambridge police to his campus, and they smashed some skulls.

Cinerama.

I wonder if we really have to go out into the rest of the solar system to find kindergarten. Isn't it just barely possible that we could build one here?

Nope.

I am now reading the book *In Defense of Nature*, by the poet-naturalist John Hay (Atlantic-Little, Brown). He describes an old clammer in Maine, who will never leave the cradle:

> While satellites take pictures of the earth from 25,000 miles up as it revolves through space, covered by swirling clouds, the old man sits down on a rock to rest. While laboratory minds, aided by computers, project their casual methodology into the future, he may be dreaming of the past. While science moves toward harnessing the methods of the sun through nuclear fusion and attaining unlimited energy for mankind, he stands, legs apart, head and shoulders down, intently and thoroughly digging away with his clam fork, working over the ground section by section.

Poor ape.

Good science-fiction writers of the present are not necessarily as eager as Arthur C. Clarke to found kindergartens on Jupiter, to leave the poor Maine ape and his clam rake far behind. Isaac Asimov, who is a great man, perceives three stages so far in the development of American science fiction, says we are in stage three now:

1. Adventure dominant.
2. Technology dominant.
3. Sociology dominant.

I can hope that this is a prophetic outline of Earthling history, too. I interpret "sociology" broadly—as a respectful, objective concern for the cradle natures of Earthlings on Earth.

Stage three.

In the course of an ordinary day where *I* live (Cape

Cod), I never meet anyone who has the exploration of space on his mind. On a day when there has been a particularly dangerous launch, people will sometimes mention it when they meet in the post office. Otherwise, they will comment on the weather. Whatever they say in the post office is really just another way of saying "Hello."

"Hello."

If a spaceship has been aloft for some time, and has splashed down safely, my neighbors may say something like, "Thank God." They are grateful that the short-haired white athletes who went up in the pressure cooker were not killed.

Interestingly, relief is expressed if a Russian cosmonaut comes home safely, too. It would seem wrong to my neighbors if the name of a defunct Communistic spaceman were mixed into the general body count in Vietnam, were mingled willy-nilly with the encouraging news of so-and-so many Communists killed that day.

Body count.

"One sacred memory from childhood is perhaps the best education," said Feodor Dostoevski. I believe that, and I hope that many Earthling children will respond to the first human footprint on the moon as a sacred thing. We need sacred things. The footprint could mean, if we let it, that Earthlings have done an unbelievably difficult and beautiful thing which the Creator, for Its own reasons, wanted Earthlings to do.

Footprint.

But that footprint will be profaned in America at once by advertising. Many profit-making corporations will congratulate themselves and their products in its name. It will come to represent, even to children, one more schlock merchandising scheme.

Merchandising scheme.

And it may be a better footprint, actually, than that. It might really be sacred. "Step by step," the old proverb says, "one goes a long way." Maybe the Creator really does want us to travel a lot more than we have traveled so far. And maybe It really does want our nervous systems to become fancier all the time. Excelsior.

Excelsior.

I prefer to think not, though, for this simple-minded reason: Earthlings who have felt that the Creator clearly wanted this or that have almost always been pig-headed and cruel. You bet.

A young American male Earthling stopped by my house the other day to talk some about a book of mine he'd read. He was the son of a Boston man who had died an alcoholic vagrant. He was on his way to Israel to find what he could find, though he wasn't a Jew. He said that his generation was the first generation to believe that it had no future. I had heard that sort of thing before.

No future.

"How can you say that," I asked him, "with the American space program going so well?"

He replied that the space program had no future, either, if the planet supporting it was being killed. That very day the papers had announced that two old Liberty ships were to be sunk in the Atlantic with tons and tons of nerve gas on board. Lake Superior, the only clean Great Lake left, was being used as a sewer for taconite waste by plants in Duluth. The amount of carbon dioxide in the atmosphere had increased by 15 percent since the start of the Industrial Revolution, he said, and further increases would turn the planet into a vast greenhouse in which we would roast. The anti-ballistic missile system, he said, which would surely be built, would, in cooperation with enemy systems, and through the integrated miracles of radar, satellites, and computers, turn the planet into one glorious hair-trigger bomb.

Bomb.

"If you really *believe* these terrible things about your planet," I said, "how can you keep on living?"

"Day by day," he said. "I travel. I read." He had no girl with him, no Eve.

No Eve.

I asked him what he was reading, and he took a book out of his rucksack. It was *Music of the Spheres*, by Guy Murchie (Houghton Mifflin, 1961). I already knew the book some. I had lifted a comment Murchie made about time for a book of my own:

I sometimes wonder whether humanity has missed the real point in raising the issue of mortality and immortality—in other words, whether mortality itself may be a finite illusion, being actually immortality and, even though constructed of just a few "years," that those few years are all the time there really is, so that, in fact, they can never cease.

I asked my visitor to show me a passage he had found to admire in the book. This was it:

Is there nothing then but illusory space-time between us and Kingdom Come? Naturally, I cannot reach out and touch it with my hand, but I can imagine it some way with my mind and feel its potentiality in my heart. And I can see beauty and order there—and most especially the elements of music. I can hear, in a real sense, the music of the spheres.

QUESTIONS

1. What uses has Vonnegut made of Buckminster Fuller's image of earth as a spaceship? (See the beginning of this chapter.)
2. What is the effect of Vonnegut's repetition of words and phrases?
3. How would you describe the *tone* of this essay? Is there more than one?
4. What does "Excelsior" signify?
5. What is, finally, Vonnegut's attitude toward the space program? Do you agree?

ADRIENNE RICH

Trying to Talk with a Man

Out in this desert we are testing bombs,

that's why we came here.

Sometimes I feel an underground river
forcing its way between deformed cliffs
an acute angle of understanding

moving itself like a locus of the sun
into this condemned scenery.

What we've had to give up to get here—
whole LP collections, films we starred in
playing in the neighborhoods, bakery windows
full of dry, chocolate-filled Jewish cookies,
the language of love-letters, of suicide notes,
afternoons on the riverbank
pretending to be children

Coming out to this desert
we meant to change the face of
driving among dull green succulents
walking at noon in the ghost town
surrounded by a silence

that sounds like the silence of the place
except that it came with us
and is familiar
and everything we were saying until now
was an effort to blot it out—
coming out here we are up against it

Out here I feel more helpless
with you than without you

You mention the danger
and list the equipment
we talk of people caring for each other
in emergencies—laceration, thirst—
but you look at me like an emergency

Your dry heat feels like power
your eyes are stars of a different magnitude
they reflect lights that spell out: EXIT
when you get up and pace the floor

talking of the danger
as if it were not ourselves
as if we were testing anything else

ADRIENNE RICH

Translations

You show me the poems of some woman
my age, or younger
translated from your language

Certain words occur: enemy, oven, sorrow
enough to let me know
she's a woman of my time

obsessed

with Love, our subject:
we've trained it like ivy to our walls
baked it like bread in our ovens
worn it like lead on our ankles
watched it through binoculars as if
it were a helicopter
bringing food to our famine
or the satellite
of a hostile power

I begin to see that woman doing things: stirring rice
ironing a skirt
typing a manuscript till dawn

trying to make a call
from a phonebooth

The phone rings unanswered
in a man's bedroom
she hears him telling someone else
Never mind. She'll get tired—
hears him telling her story to her sister

who becomes her enemy
and will in her own time
light her own way to sorrow

ignorant of the fact this way of grief
is shared, unnecessary
and political

ADRIENNE RICH

The Ninth Symphony of Beethoven Understood at Last as a Sexual Message

A man in terror of impotence
or infertility, not knowing the difference
a man trying to tell something
howling from the climacteric
music of the entirely
isolated soul
yelling at Joy from the tunnel of the ego
music without the ghost
of another person in it, music
trying to tell something the man
does not want out, would keep if he could
gagged and bound and flogged with chords of Joy
where everything is silence and the
beating of a bloody fist upon
a splintered table

QUESTIONS

1. Define the connection between the personal relationship and the bomb testing site in "Trying to Talk with a Man." How does the poet establish this relationship?
2. Define the concept of love in "Translations." What is the effect of the *similes* in the stanza beginning "with Love . . ."?
3. What is the meaning of "political" in "Translations?" Why do you think that the poem ends with this word?
4. Describe the rhythm in "The Ninth Symphony . . ." Do you see any relationship with Beethoven's music?
5. What is the "sexual message?"
6. What kind of dialogue is established here between a contemporary poet and a major monument of Western culture?

THE HUMANITIES: CONTINUITIES?

The human creations of the present day exhibit a discontinuity with tradition in appearance even more radical than did those of the early twentieth century. The great systems of the past that once served as intellectual frameworks "fell apart," as we have seen, at that time. As yet, no dominant system of belief has arisen to restore to Western culture its lost unity. Our own time is rather one of searching, of experimentation, and of multiplicity in morality and ideology as well as in the arts. The artistic freedom for which the great modernist innovators struggled has been achieved, or overachieved. Whereas the artists who made the first break with the representation of the real world shocked their public by challenging its cultural assumptions and traditions, contemporary artists confront a public that is virtually shockproof. The necessity to innovate seems constant; indeed styles, trends, and schools appear and disappear within periods of a few years. The fact that they also coexist makes the contemporary scene one characterized by a bewildering but exhilarating plurality of forms.

The explanation of this state of affairs lies not only in the evolution of the humanities themselves but also in the economic, political, and social environment in which the changes have taken place. In contrast to ancient Greece or to traditional Africa, support for arts and letters in the West has been until recently in the keeping of a well educated, relatively small class of individuals, who had both leisure and wealth to devote to such pursuits. During the past century, with the gradual redistribution of income and the rise in the standard of living of the lower classes, this cultural hegemony has gradually diminished. Mass communications, too, have increased facility and speed for distributing cultural products. In European and North American countries, almost the whole population is able to make demands on artistic creators, thereby establishing a plurality of standards for success.

Mass communication has also vastly increased our awareness of the cultures outside the one in which we live and has given us, in Marshall McLuhan's phrase, the impression of living in a "global village." This in turn has tended to make our sense of cultural relativity deeper and more pervasive than it was in the days of Montaigne or Voltaire. The shifting balance of the West's position in international politics has also had its effect here. Western culture, which has imposed its values on the rest of the planet, at least since the seventeenth century, is no longer an unquestioned leader. Economic power is bringing the Third World countries cultural power as well. Sensing a spiritual vacuum at the heart of the free and fast-moving West, many Europeans and Americans have turned to Eastern philosophical and religious traditions such as Zen Buddhism or one of the varieties of Indian yoga in hopes of finding a new center to their lives. Others study societies among American Indians or in the South Pacific in a search for fresh approaches to understanding reality.

Along with the democratization of the artist's audience and the growing internationalization of taste, there has been a demystification of the creative act itself. While continuing, or accelerating, the modernist urge for innovation and confrontation, contemporary "postmodern" artists have more or less abandoned an elitist religion of art. Contemporary poets, painters, architects, and film makers tend first of all to challenge, or to scoff at, the very notion of art as a sacred, self-enclosed world, separated from life. Popular and "high" cultures, less distinct than formerly, blend and exchange forms. We have seen, particularly in the case of Afro-America, how this healthy interchange is at least partially the result of contact with the African cultural root.

Contemporary "serious" composers learn from and incorporate pop, rock, and jazz; painters and advertisers share some of the same visual language; films and television programs speak to cultured and uncultured alike. Still, it is possible to make at least one basic distinction between the true artist and the producer of mass entertainment. The former demands from his or her public an *active* participation—an involvement of the mind, spirit, and senses—very much, as we have seen, within the humanistic spirit. The latter, in accord with many other aspects of modern life, encourages passive consumption.

Rather than luring or spellbinding their audiences with a smooth, finished product, many artists today like to show the wheels in their machines. People in the theater are constantly reminded that they are witnessing a play, an artifice, and not a window on the world. The actors may even enter into a dialogue with the audience. Visual artists, taking their work out of the museum and into the environment, emphasize both the differences between their creations and the natural world, and the dialogue that must take place between them. Architects are not afraid to expose such things as wiring and plumbing. Musicians make compositions of *sounds*, not pure music, using tape recorders and electronic synthesizers. A composer like John Cage wants his audience to be aware of the silences in his compositions and of the sounds in the environment heard during those silences.

Our acceptance of an art without bounds is closely related to the growing tendency to integrate the arts into society. The elitist quality, characteristic of Western art since the Renaissance, might in a sense be viewed as a deviation from the history of the humanities not only in other areas of the world but even in Europe itself. Our present vision of art as a form of relating to the world and to other human beings seems to echo John Donne's words, "No man is an island." Although modern Americans lack the cohesive, unitary vision of the ancient Greeks or the traditional Africans, they, too, are coming to treat the humanities as playing a vital role in the life of the community and to see the artist as making a social contribution.

Everyone is aware of the fact that our world today is characterized by increased bureaucracy and regimentation. Data banks, computers, and officials intervene constantly in daily life. This regimentation is in large part motivated by the belief that fairness to everyone requires governmental order and supervision, but it often has the effect of making individuals feel that they are being reduced to automatons. This phenomenon, certainly a threat to humanistic values from many points of view, seems, however, to have led to a widespread awareness of the need for creative expression, and for the humanities generally, in modern life. One

of the most important tasks before those dedicated to the humanities today is to help prevent the vital, creative being from being replaced by a passive, docile consumer.

The increasing importance of science and the veneration of the scientist has seemed to many people a threat to the humanities or even a confirmation that the humanities are obsolete. Yet the predominance of science should offer an opportunity to the humanities to reconstruct themselves. Our most sophisticated scientists recognize the fact that, although they can provide answers to a wide range of questions and can develop instruments for transforming the material life of mankind, they cannot offer a moral code and establish ultimate values. The humanities, if they do not offer any definite answers, still encourage the reformulation of such questions and fresh approaches to them. Naturally, if the humanities are to be relevant to contemporary problems, they must keep pace with the rapid changes in contemporary life. What is called for are forms and thoughts oriented toward the future, not a self-satisfied idealization of the past.

Yet, paradoxically, the humanist who would be future-oriented must be well versed in the past. Human beings are not islands in time as they are not islands in space—their modes of feeling and thinking, as well as their material way of life, were to a great extent shaped by what took place before their existence. It is only through awareness of cultural roots, as we have tried to emphasize throughout this book, that men and women can be equipped to understand and to shape the humanities of the future. Of course, every generation will conceive of its roots in slightly different ways and will find that certain works or periods from the past speak to it more urgently than do others. We are only beginning, for example, to understand the African contribution to our cultural heritage and to be aware of what other non-Western cultures have to contribute to our present needs. The Western humanities, with their roots in the Greco-Roman and Judeo-Christian cultures, are still present in all our forms of expression. Even if artists see Beethoven's Ninth Symphony as a sexual message or the *Mona Lisa* as a computer printout, if they work with laser beams rather than gold paint, if they decry the monuments of Western culture as bourgeois, sexist, or racist, they affirm a certain kind of continuity by the very force of their reaction. In the midst of change and diversity, we can be fairly certain that, if we manage not to destroy our planet, people centuries from now will still be reading *Oedipus*, looking at Chartres Cathedral, and listening to Beethoven. They will react to these works with their intelligence and sensibility, absorbing them as part of their individual and collective cultures. Westerners will also, with increasing frequency, make the great monuments of the African and Asian humanities part of their culture. It is possible that, if we develop an urgent sense of the planet earth as our common spaceship, we will witness the evolution of a world culture with forms of artistic communication accessible to everyone. The humanistic tradition will in some way be carried forward. What forms its future continuities will take is for the present generation to determine.

GLOSSARY

Italics are used within the definitions to indicate terms that are themselves defined elsewhere in the glossary and, in a few cases, to distinguish titles of works or foreign words.

ABA Form MUSIC: A particular organization of parts used in a musical *composition* in which there are three units, the first and third of which are the same. See *Da capo aria*.

Absolutism The theory that all political power in a society is derived from one authority, normally a monarch.

Abstract VISUAL ARTS: Not representational or *illusionistic*. Describes painting or sculpture that simplifies or distills figures from the material world into *forms*, lines, *colors*.

Affect MUSIC: The production of emotional reactions in the listener by certain musical sounds, according to a theory from the baroque period. For example, sorrow should be characterized by slow-moving music; hatred by very repulsive harmonies.

Allegory LITERATURE, VISUAL ARTS: The technique of making concrete things, animals, or persons represent abstract ideas or morals. A literary allegory usually takes the form of a *narrative* which may be read on at least two levels; for example, Dante's *Divine Comedy*. Medieval sculptures often have allegorical significance.

Anaphora (ah-na'for-ah) LITERATURE: A rhetorical figure which uses the repetition of the same word or phrase to introduce two or more clauses or lines of verse.

Antithesis LITERATURE: The balance of parallel word groups conveying opposing ideas.

Apse (aap'ss) ARCHITECTURE: A large semicircular or polygonal *niche*, *domed* or *vaulted*. In a Roman basilica the apse was placed at one or both ends or sides of the building. In a Christian church it is usually placed at the east end of the *nave* beyond the *choir*.

Arcade ARCHITECTURE: A covered walk made of *arches* on *piers* or *columns*, rather than *lintels*.

Arch ARCHITECTURE: 1. Commonly, any curved structural member that is used to span an opening. 2. Specifically, restricted to the spanning members of a curved opening that are constructed of wedge-shaped stones called *voussoirs*. Arches may be of many shapes, basically round or pointed.

Aria (ah'ree-ah) MUSIC: An elaborate *composition* for solo voice with instrumental accompaniment.

Aristocracy Form of government from Greek word meaning "rule by the few for the common good."

Arpeggiated MUSIC: Describes a rippling effect produced by playing the notes of a chord one after another instead of simultaneously. See *Chord*.

Atmospheric Perspective See *Perspective*.

Atonal MUSIC: Describes music written with an intentional disregard for a central keynote (or tonal center). This style of composition was developed after World War I by Arnold Schoenberg and his followers.

Axis VISUAL ARTS: The imaginary line that can be passed through a building or a figure, around which the principal parts revolve. See *Balance*.

Balance VISUAL ARTS: The creation of an apparent equilibrium or *harmony* between all the parts of a *composition*, be it a building, painting, or sculpture.

Balustrade ARCHITECTURE: A rail or handrail along the top edge of a roof or balcony, made up of a top horizontal rail, a bottom rail, and short *columns* between.

Baroque Term first applied to the visual arts and later to the music and literature of the 17th and 18th centuries to designate a style characterized by energy, movement, realism, and violent contrasts. The baroque style is often set in opposition to the orderly and formal "classical" style of the High Renaissance.

Cadence MUSIC: A formula or cliché that indicates a point of repose. The cadence is one of several possible melodic, rhythmic, or harmonic combinations that signal a slowing down or stopping of the forward motion.

Cantilever ARCHITECTURE: 1. A horizontally projecting member, sometimes called a bracket, used to carry the cornice or eaves of a building. 2. A beam or slab, projecting beyond the wall or supporting column, whose outward thrust or span is held down at one end only. See Robie House (Ch. 31).

Chord MUSIC: The simultaneous sounding of three or more usually harmonious tones.

Chordal MUSIC: Characterized by the employment of *chords* in a logical progression of harmonies.

Choreographer DANCE: Person responsible for the *choreography* of a dance.

Choreography DANCE: The design and arrangement of the movements of a ballet or modern dance.

Chromatic MUSIC: Describes a scale progressing by half-tones instead of the normal degrees of the scale; e.g., in C major: c-c#-d-d#-e instead of c-d-e. VISUAL ARTS: Refers to the visual spectrum of hues. See *Color*.

Classic, Classical ALL ARTS: Recognized generally to be excellent, time-tested. LITERATURE AND VISUAL ARTS: 1. From ancient Greece or Rome. 2. From "classical" (fifth century B.C.) Greece or having properties such as *harmony*, *balance*, moderation, and magnitude characteristic of art of that period. See also *Neoclassicism*. MUSIC: The musical *style* of the late 18th century. Leading composers in the classical style are Haydn, Mozart, and the early Beethoven.

Coda MUSIC: A passage of music added to the end of a piece to confirm an impression of finality.

Collage (kohl-lahzh') VISUAL ARTS: From the French, *coller*, "to glue." A technique for creating *compositions* by pasting or in some way attaching a variety of materials or objects to a flat surface or canvas.

Color VISUAL ARTS: A quality perceived in objects by the human eye that derives from the length of the light waves reflected by individual surfaces. The visible spectrum is divided into six basic hues: red, orange, yellow, green, blue, and violet. Red, yellow and blue are called the *primary colors*; the others, which result from mixing adjacent primary colors, are called *secondary colors*. White, black, and grays result from mixing these six hues and are not *chromatic*; they cannot be distinguished by hue, only by value. Value is the property of a color that distinguishes it as light or dark. Colors that are "high" in value are light colors; those that are "low" in value are dark colors. Adding white to a color will raise its value to make a *tint*; adding black to a color will lower its value to make a *shade*. Saturation is the property of a color by which its vividness or purity is distinguished. See also *Complementary Colors*, *Cool Colors*, *Warm Colors*.

Comedy LITERATURE: A drama that ends happily, intended to provoke laughter from its audience. Comedy often includes *satire* on types of characters or societies.

Complementary Colors Hues that form a neutral grey when mixed but, when juxtaposed, form a sharp contrast. The complementary of any *primary color* (red, yellow, or blue) is made by mixing the other two primaries. Example: The complementary of red is green, obtained by mixing yellow with blue.

Composition VISUAL ARTS: The arrangements of elements within the work in order to create a certain effect based on a variety of principles and conventions: e.g., *balance*, *color*, *contour*, *focal point*, proportion, scale, *symmetry*, volume. MUSIC: The putting together of elements such as *melody*, *harmony*, *rhythm*, and orchestration into a musical *form*. The term may be used similarly to denote a putting together of elements in a dance or film. LITERATURE: The act of composing an oral or written work.

Concerto (con-chair'toe) MUSIC: A composition for one or more solo instruments and an orchestra, each competing with the other on an equal basis.

Content ALL ARTS: What the *form* contains and means. Content may include subject matter and theme. The quality of a work of art is often judged by the appropriateness, or apparent inseparability, of form and content.

Continuo MUSIC: In the scores of baroque composers (Bach, Handel) the bass part, performed by the harpsichord or organ, together with a viola da gamba or cello. The continuo, during the baroque era, provided the harmonic structure of the pieces being performed.

Contour PAINTING, DRAWING: The visible edge or outline of an object, *form* or shape, used especially to suggest volume or mass by means of the distinctness, thickness, or color of the edge or line.

Contrapuntal (con-tra-pun'tal) MUSIC: In a *style* that employs *counterpoint*.

Cool Colors VISUAL ARTS: Blues, greens, and associated hues. Cool colors will appear to recede from the viewer in a picture, while *warm colors* will tend to project.

Cornice ARCHITECTURE: 1. The horizontal projection that finishes the top of a *wall*. 2. In classical architecture, the third or uppermost horizontal section of an *entablature*. See *Orders*.

Counterpoint MUSIC: Music consisting of two or more *melodies* played simultaneously. The term is practically synonymous with *polyphony*.

Da Capo Aria (dah cah'poh ahr'ee-ah) MUSIC: A particular type of *aria* that developed in the baroque period (17th and 18th centuries). It consists of two sections, the first of which is repeated after the second. The result is the *ABA form*. See *Aria*, *ABA Form*.

Deduction PHILOSOPHY: Reasoning from a general principle to a specific fact or case, or from a premise to a logical conclusion.

Democracy From the Greek word meaning "rule by the people." A form of government in which the electorate is coincident with the adult population (sometimes only the adult males) of a community.

Despotism Government by a ruler with unlimited powers.

Dialectic PHILOSOPHY: 1. Platonic—A method of logical examination of beliefs, proceeding by question and answer. 2. Hegelian and Marxian—A logical method that proceeds by the contradiction of opposites (thesis, antithesis) to their resolution in a synthesis.

Dome ARCHITECTURE: A curved or

hemispherical roof structure spanning a space and resting on a curved, circular, or polygonal base. Theoretically, a dome is an *arch* rotated 360 degrees around a central *axis*.

Dynamics MUSIC: Words or signs that indicate the varying degrees of loudness in the music. For instance, *forte* (loud), *piano* (soft, quiet), *diminuendo* (decrease volume gradually).

Ego In Freudian theory, one of the three parts of the mind. The ego is the conscious, controlling, self-directed part.

Empiricism PHILOSOPHY: The theory that knowledge is derived from observation of nature and by experiment.

Entablature ARCHITECTURE: The upper section of a classical *order* resting on the capitals of the columns and including architrave, frieze, *cornice*, and pediment.

Eros 1. In Greek mythology, son of Aphrodite and god of sexual love, called "Cupid" by the Romans. 2. For Freud, the vital, life-giving human force, originating in but not limited to sexual desire.

Ethics PHILOSOPHY: The branch of philosophy dealing with problems of good and bad, right and wrong, in human conduct.

Façade (fa-sahd') ARCHITECTURE: A face of a building.

Fetish Statue or other object believed to embody supernatural power.

Figurative VISUAL ARTS: Describes painting or sculpture in which the human body and the objects of habitual visual experience are clearly recognizable in the work.

Focal Point VISUAL ARTS: The place of major or dominant interest on which the eyes repeatedly focus in a painting, drawing, or architectural arrangement.

Foreshortening PAINTING: The method of representing objects or parts of objects as if seen from an angle so that the object seems to recede into space instead of being seen in a frontal or profile view. The technique is based on the principle of continuous diminution in size along the length

of the object or figure. See *Perspective* and *Vanishing Point*.

Form ALL ARTS: The arrangement or organization of the elements of a work of art in space (visual arts) or time (literary, musical, performing arts). A form may be conventional or imposed by tradition (the Greek temple, the sonnet, the sonata, the five-act play) or original with the artist. In the latter case, form is said to follow from, or adapt itself to, *content*.

Free Verse LITERATURE: Poetic lines with no conventional meter or rhyme.

Fresco PAINTING: The technique of making a painting on new, wet plaster. Fresco painting was particularly favored in Italy from Roman times until the eighteenth century.

Fugal MUSIC: Characteristic of the *fugue*.

Fugue (fewg) MUSIC: A *composition* based on a *theme* (known as the *subject*) that is stated at the beginning in one voice part alone and is then restated by the other voice parts in succession. The theme reappears at various places throughout the composition in one voice part or another in combination with forms of itself.

Gable ARCHITECTURE: The triangular space at the end of a building formed by the slopes of a pitched roof, extending from the *cornice* or eaves to the ridge. In classical architecture the gable is called a pediment.

Gallery ARCHITECTURE: A long, covered area, usually elevated, that acts as a passageway on the inside or exterior of a building.

Genre (john'ruh) LITERATURE: A literary type or form. Genres include *tragedy, comedy,* epic, *lyric, novel,* short story, essay.

Grid VISUAL ARTS: A pattern of vertical and horizontal lines forming squares of uniform size on a chart, map, drawing, etc.

Groin Vault See *Vault*.

Groundplan ARCHITECTURE: A drawing of a horizontal *section* of a building that shows the arrangement of the *walls*, windows, supports, and

other elements. A groundplan is used to produce blueprints.

Ground Plane PAINTING: In a picture, the surface, apparently receding into the distance, on which the figures seem to stand. It is sometimes thought of as comparable to a kind of stage space.

Harmonic Modulation MUSIC: The change of key within a composition. Modulations are accomplished by means of a *chord* (or chords) common to the old key as well as the new one.

Harmony MUSIC: The chordal structure of music familiar to most Western listeners in popular music accompanied by guitars, in Romantic orchestral music, etc.

Homophonic (hawm-o-fon'ic) Characteristic of *homophony*.

Homophony (hoh-maw'foh-nee) MUSIC: A single *melody* line supported by its accompanying *chords* and/or voice parts. See *Monophony, Polyphony, Chord,* and *Texture*.

Hue See Color.

Hyperbole (high-purr'boh-lee) LITERATURE: A figure of speech that uses obvious exaggeration.

Iamb (eye'amb) LITERATURE: A metrical "foot" consisting of one short (or unaccented) syllable and one long (or accented) syllable. Example: hĕllō.

Iambic Pentameter (eye-am'bic pentam'eh-ter) LITERATURE: The most common metrical line in English verse, consisting of five *iambs*. Example, from Shakespeare: "Shăll Ī cŏmpāre thĕe tō ă sŭmmĕr's dāy?"

Id In Freudian theory, one of the three parts of the mind. The id is the instinctive, non-controlled part.

Illusionism VISUAL ARTS: The attempt by artists to create the illusion of reality in their work. Illusionism may also be called *realism*. It is important to remember that illusionism is not the motivating intention of all works of art.

Image ALL ARTS: The representation of sense impressions to the imagination. Images are a fundamental part of the language of art. They differ from the abstract terminology of science and philosophy in that they are a means whereby complex emotional experience is communicated. Images may be tactile, auditory, olfactory, etc., but the word is ordinarily used for visual impressions.

Impasto (em-pah'stoh) PAINTING: Paint that has the consistency of thick paste, used for bright highlights or to suggest *texture*. Examples: Rembrandt and Van Gogh.

Improvisation MUSIC: The art of performing spontaneously rather than recreating written music.

Induction PHILOSOPHY: Reasoning from particular facts or cases to a general conclusion.

Inflection MUSIC: The shaping or changing of a musical passage in a way that is unique to the individual performer of the music.

Inquisition A former tribunal in the Roman Catholic Church directed at the suppression of heresy.

Irony LITERATURE: A manner of speaking by which the author says the opposite of what he means, characteristically using words of praise to imply scorn. Dramatic or tragic irony means that the audience is aware of truths which the character speaking does not understand.

Lantern ARCHITECTURE: The windowed turret or tower-like form that crowns a *dome* or roof.

Libretto (lih-bret'toe) MUSIC: The text of an opera, *oratorio*, or other dramatic musical work.

Linear Perspective See *Perspective*.

Lyric LITERATURE: A short poem characterized by personal feeling and intense emotional expression. Originally, in Greece, lyrics were accompanied by the music of a lyre. Today they may often be set to music.

Medium (pl. media) ALL ARTS: 1. The material or materials with which the artist works. Examples from VISUAL ARTS: paint, stone, wood, bronze, plaster, concrete. MUSIC: sound. LITERATURE: language. CINEMA: film. DANCE: human body. DRAMA: language, costume, lighting, actors, sound, etc. 2. Modern means

of communication (television, radio, newspapers). 3. PAINTING: A substance such as oil, egg, or water with which *pigment* is mixed.

Melodic Elaboration MUSIC: The ornamentation of *melody* by one or more of a number of possible musical devices, such as added notes, interval changes, etc.

Melody MUSIC: A succession of musical *tones*. Often the melody is known as the "tune," and is not to be confused with the other accompanying parts of a song. See *Homophony*.

Metaphor LITERATURE: A figure of speech that states or implies an analogy between two objects or between an object and a mental or emotional state. Example: "My days are in the yellow leaf;/The flowers and fruits of love are gone" (Byron) makes an analogy between the poet's life and the seasonal changes of a tree.

Metaphorical Describing statements or representations to be taken as analogy, not to be taken literally.

Meter POETRY: A regularly recurring rhythmic pattern. Meter in English is most commonly measured by accents, or stresses, and syllables. The most common metric "foot" in English is the *iamb*. The most common verse line is the *iambic pentameter* (five iambs). MUSIC: A pattern of fixed temporal units. For example, ¾ meter means one beat to a quarter note and three beats to a measure. In a musical *compositon* meter is the basic grouping of notes in time.

Modeling VISUAL ARTS: 1. The creation of a three-dimensional *form* in clay or other responsive material, such as wax, soap, soft bone, ivory, etc. 2. By analogy, in painting and drawing, the process of suggesting a three-dimensional *form* by the creation of *shade* and shadow.

Modernism Generic name given to a variety of movements in all the arts, beginning in the early 20th century. Promotes a subjective or inner view of reality and uses diverse experimental techniques.

Molding ARCHITECTURE: A member

used in construction or decoration that produces a variety in edges or contours by virtue of its curved surface.

Monophonic (mo-no-fohn'ic) Characteristic of *monophony*.

Monophony (mo-nof'o-nee) MUSIC: A simple *melody* without additional parts or accompaniment, such as the music of a flute playing alone or of a woman singing by herself. See *Homophony*, *Polyphony*, *Texture*.

Motif (moh-teef'), **Motive** (moh-teev') LITERATURE: A basic element which recurs, and may serve as a kind of foundation, in a long poem, fiction, or drama. A young woman awakened by love is the motif of many tales, such as *Sleeping Beauty*. VISUAL ARTS: An element of design repeated and developed in a painting, sculpture or building. MUSIC: A recurring melodic phrase, sometimes used as a basis for variation.

Mural PAINTING: Large painting in oil, fresco, or other *medium* made for a particular *wall*, ceiling, or similar large surface.

Narrative LITERATURE: 1. (noun) Any *form* that tells a story or recounts a sequence of events (*novel*, *tale*, essay, article, film). 2. (adj.) In story form, recounting.

Narthex ARCHITECTURE: The entrance hall or porch that stands before the *nave* of a church.

Naturalism LITERATURE, VISUAL ARTS: 1. Faithful adherence to the appearance of nature or outer reality. 2. A late nineteenth-century literary movement that developed in France but had great impact in the United States. The naturalists wished to apply scientific laws to literature and to show in particular how human beings are the creations of their environment.

Nave ARCHITECTURE: In Roman architecture, the central space of a basilica; in Christian architecture, the central longitudinal or circular space in the church, bounded by aisles.

Nave Arcade ARCHITECTURE: The open passageway or screen between the central space and the *side aisles* in a church.

Neoclassicism ALL ARTS: A movement that flourished in Europe and America in the late seventeenth and eighteenth centuries, heavily influenced by the classical style of Greece and Rome. Neoclassical art and literature is characterized by sobriety, balance, logic, and restraint. The corresponding musical style (18th century) is usually called *classical*.

Nonobjective VISUAL ARTS: Not representing objects in the material world.

Novel LITERATURE: A lengthy prose narrative, traditionally spanning a broad period of time, containing a plot and developing characters. The modern European novel took form in the eighteenth century.

Oil Painting The practice of painting by using *pigments* suspended in oil (walnut, linseed, etc.).

Oratorio MUSIC: An extended musical setting for solo voices, chorus, and orchestra, of a religious or contemplative nature. An oratorio is performed in a concert hall or church, without scenery, costumes, or physical action. One of the greatest examples is Handel's *Messiah*.

Orchestration MUSIC: Orchestration is the art of writing music for the instruments of the orchestra that will bring out desired effects of the various instruments. Indeed, it is the art of "blending" the voices of the orchestra so that a pleasing sound is the end result.

Orders ARCHITECTURE: Types of columns with *entablatures* developed in classical Greece. The orders are basically three: Doric, Ionic, and Corinthian. They determine not only the scale and therefore dimensions of a temple but also the experience generated by the building, or its *style*.

Oxymoron (ock-see-mohr'on) LITERATURE: A figure of speech that brings together two contradictory terms, such as "sweet sorrow."

Palazzo (pa-laht'so) ARCHITECTURE: Italian for palace, or large, impressive building.

Palladian ARCHITECTURE: Designating the Renaissance architectural style of Andrea Palladio.

Parapet ARCHITECTURE: In an exterior *wall*, the part entirely above the roof. The term may also describe a low wall that acts as a guard at a sudden edge or drop, as on the edge of a roof, battlement, or wall.

Parody LITERATURE: A work that exaggerates or burlesques another, serious one. Often a parody pokes fun at an author and his style. The parody may be compared to a visual caricature or cartoon.

Pathos (pay'thaws) ALL ARTS: A quality that sets off deep feeling or compassion in the spectator or reader.

Pentatonic Scale MUSIC: Five-note scale that occurs in the music of nearly all ancient cultures. It is common in West African music and is found in jazz.

Perspective VISUAL ARTS: Generally, the representation of three-dimensional objects in space on a two-dimensional surface. There are a variety of means to achieve this. The most familiar is that of "linear perspective" developed in the fifteenth century and codified by Brunelleschi, in which all parallel lines and edges of surfaces recede at the same angle and are drawn, on the picture plane, to converge at a single *vanishing point*. The process of diminution in size of objects with respect to location is very regular and precise. Other techniques, often used in combination with linear perspective, include: (a) vertical perspective—objects further from the observer are shown higher up on the picture, (b) diagonal perspective—objects are not only higher but aligned along an oblique *axis* producing the sensation of continuous recession, (c) overlapping, (d) *foreshortening*, (e) *modeling*, (f) *shadows*, and (g) atmospheric perspective, the use of conventions such as blurring of outlines, alternation of hue toward blue, and decrease of *color* saturation.

Philosophe (fee-low-soph') Eighteenth-century French intellectual and writer; not usually a systematic philosopher.

Phrase MUSIC: A natural division of the *melody*; in a manner of speaking, a musical "sentence."

Picture Plane PAINTING: The surface on which the picture is painted.

Picture Space PAINTING: The space that extends behind or beyond the picture plane; created by devices such as *linear perspective*. Picture space is usually described by foreground, middleground, and background.

Pigment PAINTING: The grains or powder that give a *medium* its *color*. Can be derived from a variety of sources: clays, stones, metals, shells, animal and vegetable matter.

Pitch MUSIC: A technical term identifying a single musical sound, taking into consideration the frequency of its fundamental vibrations. Some songs, or instruments, are pitched high and others are pitched low.

Plan See *Groundplan*.

Plane A flat surface.

Plasticity VISUAL ARTS: The quality of roundness, palpability, solidity, or three-dimensionality of a *form*.

Podium ARCHITECTURE: The high platform or base of a Roman temple or any elevated platform.

Polis (poh'liss) The ancient Greek city-state.

Polyphonic (paul-ee-fon'ick) Characteristic of *polyphony*.

Polyphony (paul-if'o-nee) MUSIC: Describes *compositions* or *improvisations* in which more than one *melody* sounds simultaneously, that is, two or more tunes at the same time. Polyphony is characterized by the combining of a number of individual melodies into a harmonizing and agreeable whole. See *Homophony*, *Monophony*, and *Texture*.

Portico ARCHITECTURE: Porch or covered walk consisting of a roof supported by columns.

Primary Colors Red, Yellow, Blue—the three primary hues of the spectrum. See *Color*.

Prose LITERATURE: Generally, may mean any kind of discourse, written or spoken, which cannot be classified as poetry. More specifically, prose refers to written expression characterized by logical, grammatical order, *style*, and even *rhythm* (but not *meter*).

Rationalism PHILOSOPHY: The theory that general principles are essentially deductive; i.e., deducible from an examination of human reason. Reason, not the senses, is the ultimate source of basic truths.

Realism LITERATURE, VISUAL ARTS: A movement which began in the mid-nineteenth century and which holds that art should be a faithful reproduction of reality and that artists should deal with contemporary people and their everyday experience.

Recitative (reh-see-tah-teev') MUSIC: A vocal style used to introduce ideas and persons in the musical *composition*, or to relate a given amount of information within a short period of time. The recitative has practically no melodic value. This device is employed extensively in Handel's *Messiah*.

Republic A form of government in which ultimate power resides in the hands of a fairly large number of people but not necessarily the entire community. This power is exercized through representatives. The word derives from Latin meaning "public thing."

Response MUSIC: A solo-chorus relationship in which the soloist alternates performance with the chorus.

Responsorial MUSIC: Describing the performance of a chant in alternation between a soloist and a chorus. (It is unlike antiphonal music, where alternating choruses sing.)

Rhythm ALL ARTS: An overall sense of systematic movement. In music, poetry, and dance this movement may be literally felt; in the visual arts it refers to the regular repetition of a *form*, conveying a sense of movement by the contrast between a form and its interval.

Ridge ARCHITECTURE: The line defined by the meeting of the two sides of a sloping roof.

Romanticism A movement in all of the arts as well as in philosophy, religion, and politics that spread throughout Europe and America in the early nineteenth century. The romantics revolted against the Neoclassical emphasis on order and reason and substituted an inclination for nature and imagination. See Chs. 25 & 26.

Satire A mode of expression that criticizes social institutions or human foibles humorously. The Romans invented the verse satire, but satire may appear in any literary *genre*, in visual art, in film, mime, and dance.

Secondary Colors See *Color*.

Section ARCHITECTURE: The drawing that represents a vertical slide through the interior or exterior of a building, showing the relation of floor to floor.

Shade PAINTING: A *color* mixed with black. Mixing a color with white produces a *tint*.

Shading VISUAL ARTS: The process of indicating by graphics or paint the change in *color* of an object when light falls on its surface revealing its three-dimensional qualities. Shading can be produced not only by a change of color, but also by the addition of black, brown, or gray, or by drawing techniques.

Shadow VISUAL ARTS: The *form* cast by an object in response to the direction of light.

Side Aisle ARCHITECTURE: The aisles on either side of, and therefore parallel to, the *nave* in a Christian church or Roman basilica.

Simile (sim'eh-lee) LITERATURE: A type of *metaphor* which makes an explicit comparison. Example: "My love is like a red, red rose."

Sonata MUSIC: An important form of instrumental music in use from the baroque era to the present. It is a *composition* usually with three or four movements, each movement adhering to a pattern of contrasting tempos. Example: Allegro, Adagio, Scherzo, Allegro.

Sonnet LITERATURE: A *lyric* poem of fourteen lines, following one of several conventions. The two main types of sonnet are the Italian (Petrarchan) which divides the poem into octave (eight lines) and sestet (six lines) and the English (Shakespearean) which divides the poem into three quatrains of four lines each and a final rhyming couplet.

Stretto MUSIC: The repetition of a *theme (subject)* that has been collapsed by diminishing the time values of the notes. As a result, the listener is literally propelled to the dramatic end or climactic conclusion of the music. Handel used this *fugal* device effectively in the last chorus of his *Messiah*.

Structure ALL ARTS: The relationship of the parts to the whole in a work of art. A structure may be mechanical (division of a play into acts, a symphony into movements) or may be more concealed and based on such things as the inter-relationships of *images, themes, motifs, colors,* shapes. In a *narrative* the structure usually refers to the arrangement of the sequence of events. In architecture structure may refer either to the actual system of building or to the relationships between the elements of the system of building.

Style ALL ARTS: Characteristics of *form* and technique that enable us to identify a particular work with a certain historical period, place, group, or individual. The *impressionist* painters in France at the end of the nineteenth century used light and *color* in a particular way: a painting in which this technique is followed has an impressionistic style. But the use of certain *forms, colors,* design and *composition* enables us to distinguish within this group the style of Renoir from that of Monet. Afro-European *rhythms* and *improvisation* distinguish a jazz style, but within that general category are many schools of jazz or even different styles of one individual, such as

Duke Ellington. Literary style is determined by choices of words, sentence *structure* and syntax *rhythm*, figurative language, rhetorical devices, etc. One may speak of an ornate, simple, formal, or colloquial style; of a period style such as *Neoclassical*, *romantic*, *realist*; or of an individual's style. Style is sometimes contrasted with *content*.

Subject ALL ARTS: What the work is about. The subject of the painting "Mont Ste Victoire" is that particular mountain; the subject of Richard Wright's *Native Son* is a young black man in Chicago. MUSIC: The *melody* used as the basis of a *contrapuntal composition* (e.g., the subject of a *fugue*).

Suite MUSIC: An important instrumental form of baroque music, consisting of a grouping of several dance-like movements, all in the same key.

Superego In Freudian theory, one of the three parts of the mind. The superego is the censuring faculty, replacing parents or other authorities.

Symbol VISUAL ARTS, LITERATURE: An *image* that suggests an idea, a spiritual or religious concept, or an emotion beyond itself. It differs from *metaphor* in that the term of comparison is not explicitly stated. Symbols may be conventional; i.e., have a culturally defined meaning such as the Christian cross or the Jewish star of David. Since the nineteenth century, symbols have tended to denote a variety or an ambiguity of meanings.

Symbolism 1. The use of symbol in any art. 2. A literary school which began in France in the late nineteenth century, characterized by the use of obscure or ambiguous *symbols*.

Symmetry VISUAL ARTS: The balance of proportions achieved by the repetition of parts on either side of a central *axis*. The two sides may be identical, in which case we can speak of bilateral symmetry.

Syncopation MUSIC: A rhythmic device characterized as a deliberate disturbance of a regularly recurring pulse. Accented offbeats or irregular *meter* changes are two means of achieving syncopation.

Tactile VISUAL ARTS, LITERATURE: Refers to the sense of touch. In the visual arts, tactile values are created by techniques and conventions that specifically stimulate the sense of touch in order to enhance suggestions of weight, volume (roundness), visual approximation, and therefore three-dimensionality. Writers may also create tactile effects, as in the description of cloth, or skin.

Tale LITERATURE: A simple *narrative*, whose subject matter may be real or imaginary, and whose purpose is primarily to entertain. Tales may also make use of "morals" to instruct.

Tempera (tehm'per-ah) PAINTING: Technique in which the *pigment* is suspended in egg, glue, or similar soluble *medium*, like water. Tempera paint dries very quickly and does not blend easily, producing a matte (flat, nonreflective) surface, because, unlike *oil paint*, it is essentially an opaque medium.

Texture VISUAL ARTS: Surface quality (rough, smooth, grainy, etc.). LITERATURE: Elements such as *imagery*, sound patterns, etc. apart from the *subject* and *structure* of the work. MUSIC: The working relationship between the *melody* line and the other accompanying parts, or the characteristic "weaving" of a musical *composition*. There are three basic musical textures: *Monophonic* (a single line), *Homophonic* (a melody supported by *chords*), and *Polyphonic* (multiple melodic lines).

Thanatos Greek word for death. For Freud, the death-wish or death-force, opposed to Eros, the life force.

Theme VISUAL ARTS: A *color* or pattern taken as a subject for repetition and modification. Example: a piece of sculpture may have a cubical theme. MUSIC: A *melody* which constitutes the basis of variation and development. Example: The "Ode to Joy" song in the last movement of Beethoven's *Ninth Symphony*. LITERATURE AND PERFORMING ARTS: An emotion or idea that receives major attention in the work. A novel or film may contain several themes, such as love, war, death. A dance may be composed on the theme of struggle, joy, etc. Theme is sometimes used in this sense for visual arts and music as well.

Thrust ARCHITECTURE: The downward and outward pressure exerted by a *vault* or *dome* on the *walls* supporting it.

Timbre (taam'bruh) MUSIC: The quality or "color" of a particular musical *tone* produced by the various instruments. For instance, the very "nasal" sound of the oboe is markedly different from the very "pure" sound of the flute.

Tint VISUAL ARTS: The *color* achieved by adding white to a hue to raise its *value*, in contrast to a *shade*, which is a hue mixed with black to lower its value.

Tonal MUSIC: Organized around a pitch center. A tonal *composition* is one in which the *pitches* of all the various *chords* and *melodies* relate well to one another. Tonal music has a recognizable beginning, middle, and end. See *Chord, Melody, Pitch*.

Tonality MUSIC: The specific *tonal* organization of a composition.

Tone ALL ARTS: The creation of a mood or an emotional state. In painting, tone may refer specifically to the prevailing effect of a *color*. Thus, a painting may be said to have a silvery, bluish, light, or dark tone as well as a wistful, melancholy, or joyful tone. The term may also refer to *value* or *shade* (see *Color*). In literature, tone usually describes the prevailing attitude of an author toward his material, audience, or both. Thus a tone may be cynical, sentimental, satirical, etc. In music, "tone color" may be used as a synonym for *timbre*. Tone in music also means a sound of definite *pitch* and duration (as distinct from noise), the true building material of music. The notes on a written page of music are merely symbols that represent the tones that actually make the music.

Tragedy LITERATURE: A serious drama that recounts the events in the life of a great person which bring him or her from fortune to misfortune. Tragedies usually meditate on the relation between human beings and their destiny. Tragedies first developed in ancient Greece; other great periods of tragedy include Elizabethan England and France under Louis XIV. The word may be used to describe a novel or story.

Transept ARCHITECTURE: The transverse portion of a church that crosses the central *axis* of the *nave* at right angles between the nave and *apse* to form a cross-shaped (cruciform) planned building.

Value See *Color.*

Vanishing Point PAINTING: The point of convergence for all lines forming an angle to the *picture plane* in pictures constructed according to the principles of linear *perspective.*

Vault ARCHITECTURE: The covering or spanning of a space employing the principle of the *arch* and using masonry, brick, plaster, or similar malleable materials. The extension of an arch infinitely in one plane creates a barrel or tunnel vault. The intersection of two barrel vaults at right angles to each other produces a cross or groin vault. Ribs are sometimes placed along the intersections of a groin vault to produce a ribbed vault.

Veneer VISUAL ARTS: A thin layer of precious or valuable material glued or otherwise attached to the surface of another, less expensive, or less beautiful material. The Romans, for example, applied thin layers of marble to the concrete and rubble fill surfaces of their buildings to produce a more splendid effect. In this century, valuable woods like walnut or mahogany are applied as veneers to the surfaces of plywood.

Verisimilitude Literally, "true-seeming." LITERATURE: A doctrine prevalent in the *Neoclassical* period, which hold that elements in a story must be so arranged that they seem to be true or that they could actually occur. VISUAL ARTS: The effect of near perfect emulation or reproduction of objects in the visual world. Not to be confused with *realism.*

Wall ARCHITECTURE: A broad, substantial upright slab that acts as an enclosing *form* capable of supporting its own weight and the weight of beams or *arches* to span and enclose space.

Warm Colors VISUAL ARTS: The hues commonly associated with warmth —yellow, red, and orange. In *compositions* the warm colors tend to advance, in contrast to the *cool colors,* which tend to recede from the viewer.

Watercolor PAINTING: Technique using water as the *medium* for very fine *pigment.* Watercolor dries very fast and can be extremely transparent.

INDEX